SEVENTH EDITION

Foundations of
Financial Management

The IRWIN Series in Finance

SEVENTH EDITION

Foundations of Financial Management

Stanley B. Block
Professor of Finance
Texas Christian University

Geoffrey A. Hirt
Chairman of the Department of Finance
DePaul University

IRWIN

Burr Ridge, Illinois
Boston, Massachusetts
Sydney, Australia

© RICHARD D. IRWIN, Inc., 1978, 1981, 1984, 1987, 1989, 1992, and 1994

Publisher: *Michael W. Junior*
Senior sponsoring editor: *James M. Keefe*
Developmental editor: *Beth Bortz*
Marketing manager: *Ron Bloecher*
Project editor: *Gladys True*
Production manager: *Bette K. Ittersagen*
Designer: *Mary Sailer*
Design coordinator: *Laurie Entringer*
Art coordinator: *Mark Malloy*
Art studio: *Carlisle Communications*
Compositor: *Beacon Graphics Corp.*
Typeface: *11/13 Times Roman*
Printer: *Von Hoffmann Press*

Library of Congress Cataloging-in-Publication Data

Block, Stanley B.
    Foundations of financial management / Stanley B. Block, Geoffrey A. Hirt.—7th ed.
        p.   cm.
    Includes bibliographical references and index.
    ISBN 0-256-13102-3   ISBN 0-256-13618-1 (Instructor's Edition)
    1. Corporations—Finance.   I. Hirt, Geoffrey A.   II. Title.
HG4026.B589   1994
658.15—dc20   93-14482

To our wives, children,
and parents

About the Authors

of Foundations of Financial Management, Seventh Edition

Stanley B. Block Professor Block teaches financial management and investments at Texas Christian University, where he received the Burlington Northern Outstanding Teaching Award. His research interests include financial futures, mergers, and high-yield bonds. He has served as President of the Southwestern Finance Association and is a Chartered Financial Analyst. Professor Block holds a Ph.D. from Louisiana State University.

Geoffrey A. Hirt Professor Hirt teaches investments and financial management at DePaul University, where he chairs the Finance Department. He is the former President of the Midwest Finance Association. Professor Hirt has held seminars for the Harris Bank and the American Association of Individual Investors. He is past editor of the Journal of Financial Education and received his Ph.D. from the University of Illinois.

Editor's Note

Over one-half million students strong—and growing. The past six editions of Block and Hirt's *Foundations of Financial Management* have been used by over a half million students. Impressed by its clear and thorough treatment of financial concepts and their applications, an increasing number of instructors have turned to *Foundations of Financial Management*. The exponential growth of the book can be attributed to one basic factor: It works! After adopting Block and Hirt, few instructors find other approaches to be as successful in teaching basic financial concepts.

The seventh edition builds on the strengths of previous editions, but it has been revised and updated to incorporate significant new developments in the financial environment. We invite you to use this edition of *Foundations of Financial Management* and let it work for you!

Preface

Opening up a textbook can seem a glum prospect for many enrolled in a foundations of financial management course. All too often, what is already perceived to be a difficult and intimidating subject is only compounded by the text you are assigned. In contrast, *Foundations of Financial Management* is committed to making finance accessible to you. In fact, many pedagogical changes were made in the sixth and seventh editions with the objective of enhancing your learning. Significant content revisions have also been made in order to maintain the high quality that the market has come to expect from *Foundations of Financial Management*. As always, in the seventh edition we remain strongly committed to presenting the concepts of finance in an enlightening and interesting manner.

Reinforcing Prerequisite Knowledge

Employers of business graduates report that the most successful analysts, planners, and executives have both facility and confidence in their financial skills. The authors of this text concur. One of the best ways to increase your facility in financial planning is to integrate your knowledge from prerequisite courses. Therefore, the text is designed to build on your knowledge from basic courses in accounting and economics. By applying tools learned in these courses, you can develop a conceptual and analytical understanding of financial management.

We realize, however, that for some of you two years have passed since you've completed your accounting courses. Therefore, we included Chapter 2, a thorough review of accounting principles, finance terminology, and financial statements.

With a working knowledge of Chapter 2, you will have a more complete understanding of financial statements and the impact of your decisions on financial statements. Furthermore, as you are about to begin your career you will be much better prepared when called upon to apply financial concepts.

Features

Functional Use of Four Colors

The seventh edition enhances the functional use of four colors to build your understanding of tables, graphs, and exhibits. For example, the financial analysis chapter (Chapter 3) uses color to make the origin of the ratios easier to follow. For easy identification, the balance sheet appears in green and the income statement appears in red. These same two colors continue to be traced through the numerical ratios, with each number appearing in the same color as the financial statement from which it was derived. This linkage helps easily identify whether the ratio is a balance sheet ratio (debt to assets), an income statement ratio (profit margin), or a mixed ratio (asset turnover).

In-Book Chapter 9 Acetates on Time Value of Money

The concept of the "time value of money" is one of the most difficult topics in any financial management book for professors to communicate to students. We think we have created a visual method for teaching future value and present value that will allow you to understand the concept simply and quickly. The seventh edition includes four-color acetates in the text that visually relate future values and present values. We hope you agree that this innovation is an advancement in financial pedagogy.

More Real World Examples

We have *expanded and revised* our use of *real world examples* in an integrated fashion throughout the book to bring finance to life. These real world examples have been listed on pages xxxiii through xxxv for your convenience. We have also included boxes highlighting real world situations. Titled, "Finance in Action," these boxes address topics such as capital budgeting at Sony and the aftereffects of leveraged buyouts.

Comprehensive International Coverage

In keeping with the rapid *internationalization* of today's capital markets, we have expanded and updated our coverage of how this development has impacted the U.S. economy and corporations. Also included is a discussion of the implications of the *European Community 92*. Although we continue to have a separate chapter on international finance, not all classes will be able to include a whole chapter on this topic. Integrating international material into a number of earlier chapters demonstrates that financial decisions are becoming more global in scope.

Other Contemporary Issues

Contemporary issues remain a strong feature of the seventh edition. They include *international cash management, Dutch Auction Preferred Stock, European Community 1992,* and the effects of the Clinton administration on financial markets. We have included updates and revisions on corporate restructuring and divestitures, leveraged buyouts, the changing nature of the investment banking and financial services industries, corporate stock repurchases, and uses of electronic funds transfer in cash management on the international level. The material on shelf registrations, floating rate, and zero-coupon debt, as well as Euro-convertible debt, has been revised.

Summary List of Equations

End-of-Chapter Material

At the end of every chapter that includes equations, we have provided a list of all equations used in that chapter. The formulas appear in red facilitating easy recognition. This summary list will help students review the mathematics of financial analysis.

List of Key Terms

Similarly, you can use the list of key terms provided at the end of each chapter to test your comprehension and retention. Page numbers are provided for each term so that you can quickly locate the term's discussion within the text. Every term listed at the end of the chapter is fully defined in the Glossary, located at the end of the book.

Discussion Questions and Problems

The material in the text is supported by a large number of questions that emphasize definitions, concepts, and the application of theory. The problems are a very important part of the text and have been written with care to be consistent with the chapter material. To encourage your identification of concepts and facilitate the instructor's assignment of problem material, each problem is labeled. There are a large number of problems, particularly in the areas of financial analysis and capital budgeting. Overall, there are approximately 250 questions and 335 problems in the edition. Over two-thirds of the problems are new, and the remainder have been rewritten to better reflect the changing corporate environment.

Comprehensive Problems

Several chapters have optional comprehensive problems that integrate and require the application of several financial concepts into one problem. Sometimes these comprehensive problems will cover several concepts from one chapter. Occasionally, a comprehensive problem at the end of the last chapter in a section (such as the Masco Oil and Gas Co. in Chapter 11) will include material from as many as four chapters.

Supplemental Material

Study Guide

An excellent student Study Guide and Workbook has been created by Dwight C. Anderson. The manual contains chapter summaries, outlines with page references, multiple choice questions with solutions provided, and problems with solutions provided.

The Wall Street Journal: Applications in Finance 1994 Edition

Free of charge to all students who purchase a copy of *Foundations of Financial Management* from IRWIN, this item has been updated and revised to include an even greater variety of situations from the world of finance. Many of the articles also provide global perspectives. With concept questions integrated throughout each article, you'll discover key finance concepts in practice. This fine item may be purchased separately.

Acknowledgments

We wish to thank those professors who have contributed directly to the preparation of the manuscript, particularly Tim Gallagher for his help in problem development and G.N. Naidu for his work in the area of international financial management.

For their valuable reviews and helpful comments, we are grateful to:

Dwight C. Anderson	Fred Ebeid	Peter R. Kensicki
Eric Anderson	Barry Farber	Tom Kewley
Charles Barngrover	Mohamed Gaber	Robert Kleiman
Brian T. Belt	Robert Gaertner	Morris Lamberson
Joseph Bentley	Jim Gahlon	Joe Lavely
William J. Bertin	Tim Gallagher	Joseph Levitsky
Debela Birru	James Gentry	John H. Lewis
Ezra Byler	Bernie J. Grablowsky	Joe Lipscomb
Rolf Christensen	Debbie Griest	John P. Listro
Allan Conway	Kidane Habteselassie	Paul Marciano
Tom Copeland	John R. Hall	Thomas Maroney
Andrea DeMaskey	Charles Higgins	Michael Matukonis
Bob Diberio	Stanley Jacobs	Wayne E. McWee

Heber Moulton	Franklin Potts	Jan R. Squires
Jerry D. Miller	Chris Prestopino	Mark Sunderman
John D. Markese	David Rankin	Robert Swanson
Joe Massa	Robert Rittenhouse	Richard Taylor
Patricia Matthews	Frederick Rommel	Mike Tuberose
Dimitrios Pachis	Robert Saemann	Donald E. Vaughn
Coleen C. Pantalone	Sandra Schickele	Gary Wells
Rosemary C. Peavler	James Scott	Lawrence Wolken
Mario Picconi	Abu Selimuddin	Don Wort
Beverly Piper	Joanne Sheridan	Ergun Yener
Harlan Platt	Fred Shipley	Lowell Young
Roger Potter	William Smith	Terry Zivney

We wish to thank Joyce Roeder for word processing all supplemental manuscripts, and Brian Hirt for technical computer assistance. A special thanks is due Andy Urganus, who double-checked the authors on all problem solutions found in the Instructor's Manual and to Joe Andrew for his special work in case development. We also express our thanks to our respective institutions for their administrative support and encouragement; to our project editor, Gladys True; editorial assistant, Andrea Smith; developmental editor, Beth Bortz; and last to our editor, Mike Junior, for his feedback, support, and enduring commitment to excellence.

Stanley B. Block
Geoffrey A. Hirt

Brief Contents

Contents

PART 3   **Working Capital Management**   *136*

---

6   **Working Capital and the Financing Decision**   *139*

Table of Real World Examples and Boxes

SEVENTH EDITION

Foundations of Financial Management

PART 1

Introduction

Chapter 1
The Goals and Functions
of Financial Management

The Goals and Functions of Financial Management

CHAPTER CONCEPTS

1 The field of finance integrates concepts from economics, accounting, and a number of other areas.

2 A central focus of finance is the relationship of risk to return.

3 The primary goal of financial managers is to maximize the wealth of the shareholders.

4 Financial managers attempt to achieve wealth maximization through daily activities such as credit and inventory management and through longer-term decisions related to raising funds.

5 Financial managers must carefully consider domestic and international business conditions in carrying out their responsibilities.

The financial manager's contribution to directing the firm's operations has become increasingly critical in the last decade. Some have referred to the era we live in as the morning after the biggest credit binge in U.S. history. In a time of unpredictable economic turns, fluctuating interest rates, inflation and disinflation, painful shortages and excesses, and extreme optimism and pessimism, the chief financial officer must maintain the financial viability of the firm. Financial markets have become international and huge amounts of capital are free to move from one country to another. The chief financial officer must manage the global affairs of the firm and be able to react quickly to changing foreign exchange rates. The board of directors and the president look to the financial division to provide a precious resource—capital—and to manage it efficiently and profitably.

The Field of Finance

The field of finance is closely related to economics and accounting, and financial managers need to understand the relationships between these fields. Economics provides a structure for decision making in such areas as risk analysis, pricing theory through supply and demand relationships, comparative return analysis, and many other important areas. Economics also provides the broad picture of the economic environment in which corporations must continually make decisions. A financial manager must understand the institutional structure of the Federal Reserve System, the commercial banking system, and the interrelationships between the various sectors of the economy. Economic variables, such as gross domestic product, industrial production, disposable income, unemployment, inflation, interest rates, and taxes (to name a few), must fit into the financial manager's decision model and be applied correctly. These terms will be presented throughout the text and integrated into the financial process.

Accounting is sometimes said to be the language of finance because it provides financial data through income statements, balance sheets, and the statement of cash flows. The financial manager must know how to interpret and use these statements in allocating the firm's financial resources to generate the best return possible in the long run. Finance links economic theory with the numbers of accounting, and all corporate managers—whether in production, sales, research, marketing, management, or long-run strategic planning—must know what it means to assess the financial performance of the firm.

Many students approaching the field of finance for the first time might wonder what career opportunities exist. For those who develop the necessary skills and training, jobs include corporate financial officer, banker, stockbroker, financial analyst, portfolio manager, investment banker, financial consultant, or personal financial planner. As the student progresses through the text, he or she will become increasingly familiar with the important role of the various participants in the financial decision-making process. A financial manager addresses such varied issues as decisions on plant location, the raising of capital, or simply how to get the highest return on x million dollars between 5 o'clock this afternoon and 8 o'clock tomorrow morning. Training in finance has served as a stepping-stone to a number of top corporate positions.

To appreciate and understand the shifting emphasis in finance as a field of study, some historical perspective is essential. We see a field that has matured with the passage of time.

Evolution of Finance as a Field of Study

At the turn of the century, finance emerged as a field separate from economics but still closely linked. The major focus of study reflected the developments of the time, namely the building of giant industrial corporations by Rockefeller, Carnegie, Du Pont, and others. A student of finance would have spent much time learning about the financial instruments that were essential to mergers and acquisitions.

In the 1930s the shock of the Depression ushered in an era of conservatism, and attention shifted to such topics as preservation of capital, maintenance of liquidity, reorganization of financially troubled corporations, and the bankruptcy process. The federal government assumed a much larger role in regulating business.

The 1940s and early 1950s offered little new in the study or practice of corporate finance. However, in the mid-50s a major shift in emphasis occurred. Until then, the study of finance had been descriptive or definitional in nature. Furthermore, the orientation had been from the viewpoint of a third party, or outsider looking in. This all changed in the mid-50s as a more analytical, decision-oriented approach began to evolve.

The first area of study to generate the newfound enthusiasm for decision-related analysis was capital budgeting, in which the financial manager was presented with analytical techniques for allocating resources among the various assets of the firm.[1] The enthusiasm spread to other decision-making areas of the firm—such as cash and inventory management, capital structure formulation, and dividend policy. The emphasis shifted from that of the outsider looking in to that of the financial manager forced to make tough day-to-day decisions affecting the performance of the firm.

Current Emphasis

From the late 1960s through today, financial management has focused on risk-return relationships and the maximization of return for a given level of risk. The awarding of the 1990 Nobel prize in economics to Professors Harry Markowitz and William Sharpe for their contributions to the financial theories of risk-return and portfolio management demonstrates the importance of these concepts. In addition, Professor Merton Miller received the Nobel prize in economics for his work in the area of **capital structure theory**, the study of the relative importance of debt and equity. These three men were the first finance professors to ever win a Nobel prize in economics, and their work has been very influential in the field of finance over the last 30 years.

During this 30-year period, corporate managers employed many strategies for dealing with risk-return trade-offs under varying economic conditions. They focused on risk, return, and capital structure, and the interrelationship

---

[1]A starting point was Joel Dean's *Capital Budgeting* (New York: Columbia University Press, 1951).

between them. Sometimes they were successful, and other times they were forced to retrench or rethink their ideas due to changes in the economy, new ideas, or new competition.

A new area of financial research that is also receiving more attention in the early 1990s is **agency theory.** This theory examines the relationship between the owners of the firm and the managers of the firm. In privately owned firms, management and the owners are usually the same people. Management operates the firm to satisfy its own goals, needs, financial requirements, and the like. As a company moves from private to public ownership, management now represents all the owners. This places management in the agency position of making decisions in the best interests of all shareholders. Because of the diversified ownership interests, conflicts between managers and shareholders can arise that impact the financial decisions of the firm. Also, because of the increased level of corporate stock repurchases, corporate restructuring, and mergers and acquisitions that took place in the 1980s, agency theory has become more important in assessing whether shareholder goals are being achieved by management in the long run.

One transformation occurring in the early 1990s that seems bound to continue is the activism of large institutional investors such as pension and mutual funds. The managers of these funds represent a large group of individual investors who by themselves would have little impact on corporate strategy. But the managers of these large institutional portfolios have become very aggressive in dealing with corporations on behalf of their shareholders, and their clout with corporate boards of directors has become very visible. The restructuring and management changes at General Motors Corp. in 1992 and of International Business Machines Corp., American Express Company, and Sears, Roebuck & Co. in 1993 were a direct result of these institutional investors effecting change by influencing the board of directors to exercise control over all facets of the company's activities. Until this time quite a few boards of directors were viewed by many as rubber stamps for management. Large investors have changed this perception.

Goals of Financial Management

One may suggest that the most important goal for financial management is to "earn the highest possible profit for the firm." Under this criterion, each decision would be evaluated on the basis of its overall contribution to the firm's earnings. While this seems to be a desirable approach, there are some serious drawbacks to profit maximization as the primary goal of the firm.

First, a change in profit may also represent a change in risk. A conservative firm that earned $1.25 per share may be a less desirable investment if its earnings per share increase to $1.50, but the risk inherent in the operation increases even more.

A second possible drawback to the goal of maximizing profit is that it fails to consider the timing of the benefits. For example, if we could choose between the following two alternatives, we might be indifferent if our emphasis were solely on maximizing earnings.

	Earnings per Share		
	Period One	Period Two	Total
Alternative A . . .	$1.50	$2.00	$3.50
Alternative B . . .	2.00	1.50	3.50

Both investments would provide $3.50 in total earnings, but Alternative B is clearly superior because the larger benefits occur earlier. We could reinvest the difference in earnings for Alternative B one period sooner.

Finally, the goal of maximizing profit suffers from the almost impossible task of accurately measuring the key variable in this case, namely, "profit." As you will observe throughout the text, there are many different economic and accounting definitions of profit, each open to its own set of interpretations. Furthermore, problems related to inflation and international currency transactions complicate the issue. Constantly improving methods of financial reporting offer some hope in this regard, but many problems remain.

A Valuation Approach

While there is no question that profits are important, the key issue is how to use them in setting a goal for the firm. The ultimate measure of performance is not what we earned but how the earnings are *valued* by the investor. In analyzing the firm, the investor will also consider the risk inherent in the firm's operation, the time pattern over which the firm's earnings increase or decrease, the quality and reliability of reported earnings, and many other factors. The financial manager, in turn, must be sensitive to all of these considerations. He or she must question the impact of each decision on the firm's overall valuation. If a decision maintains or increases the firm's overall value, it is acceptable from a financial viewpoint; otherwise, it should be rejected. This principle is demonstrated throughout the text.

Maximizing Shareholder Wealth

The broad goal of the firm can be brought into focus if we say the financial manager should attempt to *maximize the wealth of the firm's shareholders* through achieving the highest possible value for the firm. **Shareholder wealth maximization** is not a simple task, since the financial manager cannot directly control the firm's stock price, but can only act in a way that is consistent with the desires of the shareholders. Since stock prices are affected by expectations of the future as well as by the economic environment, much of what affects stock prices is beyond management's direct control. Even firms with good earnings and favorable financial trends do not always perform well in a declining stock market over the short term.

The concern is not so much with daily fluctuations in stock value as with long-term wealth maximization. This can be difficult in light of changing investor expectations. In the 1950s and 1960s, the investor emphasis was on maintaining rapid rates of earnings growth. In the 1970s and 1980s, investors became more conservative, putting a premium on lower risk and, at times, high current dividend payments.

In the 1990s, investors emphasize lean, efficient, well-capitalized companies able to compete effectively in the global environment. Investors are concerned about the long-term competitive viability of companies, and the popularity of global investing makes investors focus on the world's leading companies as standards of excellence, rather than domestic leaders.

Does modern corporate management always follow the goal of maximizing shareholder wealth as we have defined it? Under certain circumstances, management may be more interested in maintaining its own tenure and protecting "private spheres of influence" than in maximizing stockholder wealth. For example, suppose the management of a corporation receives a tender offer to merge the corporation into a second firm; while this offer might be attractive to shareholders, it might be quite unpleasant to present management. Historically, management may have been willing to maintain the status quo rather than to maximize stockholder wealth.

As mentioned earlier, this is now changing. First, in most cases "enlightened management" is aware that the only way to maintain its position over the long run is to be sensitive to shareholder concerns. Poor stock price performance relative to other companies often leads to undesirable takeovers and proxy fights for control. Second, management often has sufficient stock option incentives that motivate it to achieve market value maximization for its own benefit. Third, powerful institutional investors are making management more responsive to shareholders.

Social Responsibility and Ethical Behavior

Is our goal of shareholder wealth maximization consistent with a concern for social responsibility for the firm? In most instances the answer is yes. By adopting policies that maximize values in the market, the firm can attract capital, provide employment, and offer benefits to its community. This is the basic strength of the private enterprise system.

Nevertheless, certain socially desirable actions such as pollution control, equitable hiring practices, and fair pricing standards may at times be inconsistent with earning the highest possible profit or achieving maximum valuation in the market. For example, pollution control projects frequently offer a very low return. Does this mean firms should not exercise social responsibility in regard to pollution control? The answer is no—but certain cost-increasing activities may have to be mandatory rather than voluntary, at least initially, to ensure the burden falls equally over all business firms.

Unethical and illegal financial practices on Wall Street by corporate financial "deal makers" have made news headlines through the late 1980s and early 1990s. Insider trading has been one of the most widely publicized issues in recent years. **Insider trading** occurs when someone has information that is not available to the public and then uses this information to profit from trad-

FINANCE IN ACTION

McDonald's Corporation—Good Corporate Citizen

Given that stock market investors emphasize financial results and the maximization of shareholder value, one can wonder if it makes sense for a company to be socially responsible. Can companies be socially responsible and oriented toward shareholder wealth at the same time? The authors think so, and McDonald's thinks the two go together. For a company with thousands of restaurants throughout the country, being a good neighbor is important. Many companies are socially responsible; we highlight McDonald's as an example.

At its 1992 annual meeting, McDonald's stated, "Community involvement sets McDonald's apart, builds brand loyalty, and promotes local pride and respect. It is the heart of our commitment to exceptional customer satisfaction. The people we serve at the front counter and the people we serve in the communities—they are one and the same. People do business with people they feel good about. Many customers visit McDonald's because we are a responsible corporate citizen."

Ronald McDonald's Children's Charities has donated over $50 million to help children, and over 150 Ronald McDonald Houses in nine countries provide a place for families to stay when their children are hospitalized for serious illnesses.

Additionally McDonald's has been active in working with the Environmental Defense Fund and the government to implement effective environmental programs. In 1990 over 6,000 restaurants diverted up to 40 percent of their waste from landfills by recycling items such as corrugated cardboard. In 1990 McDonald's established McRecycle U.S.A. with the goal of using recycled materials for construction and remodeling of its restaurants. The company purchased over $200 million of recycled materials in 1991. In April 1991 McDonald's began a Waste Reduction Action Plan and states in its fourth-quarter 1992 report, "We reduced the weight of Happy Meal bags and boxes by 20 to 25 percent; redesigned the paper wrapping for Quarter Pounder sandwiches, eliminating 8 percent of its weight; and cut the weight of sundae cups by 5 percent. We also trimmed the amount of corrugated cardboard coming into our restaurants in the form of shipping containers for hot cups, coffee stirrers, and ice cream cones. In addition, we replaced the wax coatings on meat containers with innovative alternatives to maximize our recycling efforts."

The benefits come a little at a time, but you can be sure they all add up. if an investor wants wealth maximization, management that minimizes waste and notices the weight of sundae cups might do the other little things right that make a company well run and profitable.

ing in a company's publicly traded securities. This practice is illegal and protected against by the Securities and Exchange Commission (SEC). Sometimes the insider is a company manager; other times it is the company's lawyer, investment banker, or even the printer of the company's financial statement. Anyone who has knowledge before public dissemination of that information stands to benefit from either good news or bad news.

Several major Wall Street news stories involved insider trading by Ivan Boesky and Dennis Levine. Both were sentenced to jail, and Ivan Boesky was barred from trading stock and forced to return over $100 million in illegal insider trading profits. The prosecution of Boesky uncovered a large ring of insiders and led to Michael Milken, the famous junk bond deal maker for Drexel Burnham Lambert, who pleaded guilty to several counts of illegal securities activities in 1990. He received the toughest sentence ever given in a securities case.

Such activities as insider trading serve no beneficial economic or financial purpose, and it could be argued that they have a negative impact on shareholder interests. Illegal security trading destroys confidence in U.S. securities markets and makes it more difficult for managers to achieve shareholder wealth maximization.

Functions of Financial Management

Having examined the goals and objectives of financial management, let us turn our attention to the functions it must perform. It is the responsibility of financial management to allocate funds to current and fixed assets, to obtain the best mix of financing alternatives, and to develop an appropriate dividend policy within the context of the firm's objectives. These functions are performed on a day-to-day basis as well as through infrequent approaches to the capital markets to acquire new funds. The daily activities of financial management include credit management, inventory control, and the receipt and disbursement of funds. Less routine functions encompass the sale of stocks and bonds and the establishment of a capital budgeting and dividend plan.

As indicated in Figure 1–1, all these functions are carried out while balancing the profitability and risk components of the firm.

FIGURE 1–1
Functions of the financial manager

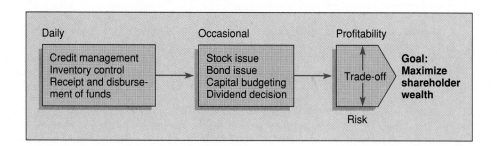

The appropriate risk-return trade-off must be determined to maximize the market value of the firm for its shareholders. The risk-return decision will influence not only the operational side of the business (capital versus labor or Product A versus Product B) but also the financing mix (stocks versus bonds versus retained earnings).

Forms of Organization

The finance function may be carried out within a number of different forms of organizations. Of primary interest are the sole proprietorship, the partnership, and the corporation.

Sole Proprietorship   The **sole proprietorship** form of organization represents single-person ownership and offers the advantages of simplicity of decision making and low organizational and operating costs. Most small businesses with 1 to 10 employees are sole proprietorships. The major drawback of the sole proprietorship is that there is unlimited liability to the owner. In settlement of the firm's debts, the owner can lose not only the capital that has been invested in the business, but also personal assets. This drawback can be serious, and the student should realize that few lenders are willing to advance funds to a small business without a personal liability commitment.

The profits or losses of a sole proprietorship are taxed as though they belong to the individual owner. Thus if a sole proprietorship makes $25,000, the owner will claim the profits in his or her tax return. (In the corporate form of organization, the corporation first pays a tax on profits, and then the owners of the corporation pay a tax on any distributed profits.) Approximately 75 percent of the 12 million business firms in this country are organized as sole proprietorships, and these produce approximately 10 percent of the total revenue and 25 percent of the total profits of the U.S. economy.

Partnership   The second form of organization is the **partnership**, which is similar to a sole proprietorship except there are two or more owners. Multiple ownership makes it possible to raise more capital and to share ownership responsibilities. Most partnerships are formed through an agreement between the participants, known as the **articles of partnership**, which specifies the ownership interest, the methods for distributing profits, and the means for withdrawing from the partnership. For taxing purposes, partnership profits or losses are allocated directly to the partners, and there is no double taxation as there is in the corporate form.

Like the sole proprietorship, the partnership arrangement carries unlimited liability for the owners. While the partnership offers the advantage of *sharing* possible losses, it presents the problem of owners with unequal wealth having to absorb losses. If three people form a partnership with a $10,000 contribution each and the business loses $100,000, one wealthy partner may have to bear a disproportionate share of the losses if the other two partners do not have sufficient personal assets.

To circumvent this shared unlimited liability feature, a special form of partnership, called a **limited partnership**, can be utilized. Under this arrangement, one or more partners are designated general partners and have unlimited liability for the debts of the firm; other partners are designated limited partners and are liable only for their initial contribution. The limited partners are normally prohibited from being active in the management of the firm. You may have heard of limited partnerships in real estate syndications in which a number of limited partners are doctors, lawyers, and CPAs and there is one general partner who is a real estate professional. Not all financial institutions will extend funds to a limited partnership.

Corporation   In terms of revenue and profits produced, the corporation is by far the most important type of economic unit. While only 17 percent of U.S. business firms are corporations, over 80 percent of sales and over 65 percent of profits can be attributed to the corporate form of organization. The **corporation** is unique—it is a legal entity unto itself. Thus the corporation may sue or be sued, engage in contracts, and acquire property. A corporation is formed through **articles of incorporation**, which specify the rights and limitations of the entity.

A corporation is owned by shareholders who enjoy the privilege of limited liability, meaning their liability exposure is generally no greater than their initial investment.[2] A corporation also has a continual life and is not dependent on any one shareholder for maintaining its legal existence.

A key feature of the corporation is the easy divisibility of the ownership interest by issuing shares of stock. While it would be nearly impossible to have more than 50 or 100 partners in most businesses, a corporation may have more than a million shareholders. A current example of a firm with over 1 million stockholders is General Motors.

The shareholders' interests are ultimately managed by the corporation's board of directors. The directors, who may include key management personnel of the firm as well as outside directors not permanently employed by it, serve in a stewardship capacity and may be liable for the mismanagement of the firm or for the misappropriation of funds. Outside directors of large public corporations may be paid more than $25,000 a year to attend meetings and share in important decisions.

Because the corporation is a separate legal entity, it reports and pays taxes on its *own* income. As previously mentioned, any remaining income that is paid to the shareholders in the form of dividends will require the payment of a second tax by the shareholders. One of the key disadvantages to the corporate form of organization is this potential double taxation of earnings.

There is, however, one way to circumvent the double taxation of a normal corporation and that is through formation of a Subchapter S corporation. With a **Subchapter S corporation**, the income is taxed as direct income to the stockholders and thus is taxed only once, as in a partnership. Nevertheless, the shareholders receive all the organizational benefits of a corporation, including limited liability. The Subchapter S designation can apply to corporations with up to 35 stockholders.[3]

While the proprietorship, traditional partnership, and various forms of limited partnerships are all important, the corporation is given primary emphasis in this text. Because of the all-pervasive impact of the corporation on our economy, and because most growing businesses eventually become corporations, the effects of most decisions in this text are considered from the corporate viewpoint.

Recent Economic Developments

Inflation and Disinflation

A number of key issues receive special attention in the text. Even though inflation was significantly reduced from double digits during the late 1970s to

---

[2]An exception to this rule is made if they buy their stock at less than par value. Then they would be liable for up to the par value.

[3]If there are more than 35 investors, a master limited partnership can be formed in which there is limited liability and single taxation of owners.

a 3 to 4 percent current range, leading economists and financial analysts now accept some degree of **inflation,** or price increases, as a way of life in the United States and throughout the world. A 3 to 4 percent inflation rate is still several times the average rate from 1925 to 1965. Inflation-induced profits of the late 1960s and 1970s are somewhat in the past, but the student should not ignore the lessons of inflated phantom profits and undervalued assets of the past few decades. The student should be equally aware of the benefits, draw-backs, and implications of **disinflation** (a slowing down of price increases). The problems and opportunities related to inflation and disinflation receive particular attention in the later discussion of financial analysis.

Reliance on Debt

A second aspect of contemporary finance is the extreme reliance financial managers have placed on the use of debt. Debt-to-assets ratios have moved from 25 percent to approximately 45 percent in the last 20 years, and the typi-cal firm's ability to pay its interest expenses has eroded. This is not a short-term, cyclical phenomenon but rather a slow, steady process that has occurred in good times as well as bad. While many firms that were formerly in finan-cial trouble have recovered miraculously (Safeway, for instance), other firms in industries such as farm equipment, steel, trucks, and oil well drilling equipment are suffering from low profitability, international competition, fal-tering domestic markets, and high debt.

Corporate Restructuring

Third, **restructuring** of the balance sheet is possibly one of the most impor-tant phenomena currently taking place in corporate America, and one result is an increase in the use of debt relative to ownership capital. Firms repurchase shares of common stock in the open market either because they do not have better investment opportunities (Exxon); because management thinks the stock is underpriced (Ford, Amoco); or because management is trying to avoid an unfriendly takeover (Phillips Petroleum, Revlon, CBS).[4] The shares may be repurchased with excess cash or through the issuance of new debt. In the 1980s Exxon bought back 46.6 million common shares worth $2.3 billion, Ford repurchased 20 million shares for $980 million, and Phillips Petroleum thwarted a takeover by T. Boone Pickens by repurchasing 81.5 million shares of stock valued at $4.1 billion.

Restructuring was not just confined to stock repurchases in the 1980s, but also included mergers and acquisitions of gigantic proportions unheard of in other decades. Firms were buying or merging with companies in similar and related industries. Rather than just seeking risk reduction through diversifica-tion, firms were acquiring greater market share, brand name products, hidden

---

[4]The corporate repurchase of shares may also be viewed as an alternative to paying a cash dividend. This topic is covered more thoroughly in Chapter 18, "Dividend Policy and Retained Earnings."

asset values, or technology—or they were simply looking for size to help them "play the game" in an international arena.

In the biggest restructuring deal yet, RJR Nabisco carried out a 1989 leveraged buyout of over $25 billion with a combination of high-yield junk bonds, preferred stock, and a small amount of equity capital. By 1991 the firm was restructuring again by selling common stock and replacing high-cost debt. Philip Morris, the consumer products company that holds such brand names as Miller beer and Marlboro cigarettes, acquired General Foods for $5.8 billion, Kraft Foods for $10.2 billion, and Jacob Suchard (a Swiss candy company) for $2.8 billion. These acquisitions made Philip Morris the largest food company in the world and opened up international marketing channels for a wide array of products.

As another example, General Motors went after technology by buying Electronic Data Systems (a computer services company, for $2.5 billion) and Hughes Aircraft (a huge defense and electronics company, for $5.8 billion). Many of these stories are covered in more detail in later chapters. Some corporations have restructured their balance sheets by selling (divesting) unprofitable or unwanted divisions over a period of time.

High Foreign and Domestic Deficits

Another economic problem facing corporations has been the foreign trade deficit and the federal deficit. The **foreign trade deficit** occurs because Americans have been buying more foreign goods than American companies have been selling to foreigners. This trade imbalance affects the U.S. economy by keeping U.S. workers less than fully employed, by U.S. companies not being able to fully utilize plant and equipment in the production process, and by making the United States a net borrower of foreign capital.

The **federal deficit** represents the difference between U.S. government revenues and expenses. The annual deficit of hundreds of billions of dollars per year was attacked by Congress with the Deficit Reduction Act of 1990, but by the 1992 presidential election, deficits had not been reduced. William Clinton won the presidential election with a call for economic renewal, new jobs, and deficit reduction. The deficit can be reduced by generating more revenue (higher taxes), spending less, or a combination of both. President Clinton promised to reduce the annual federal deficit by 50 percent by the end of his first term through a combination of cutting government spending and raising taxes. Only time will tell whether his programs will accomplish these goals.

The economy has been plagued with deficit problems for the last decade. In the midst of these foreign and federal deficit problems, the U.S. stock markets, as well as international stock markets, crashed on October 19, 1987. To put the crash of 1987 into perspective, the Great Crash of 1929 accounted for a one-day decline on the Dow Jones Industrial Average of 30 high-quality stocks of 12.9 percent while the Crash of 1987 saw common stock prices decline 22.6 percent (the Dow Jones Industrial Average fell 508 points, from the previous close of 2,246.74, to 1,738.74). This total erosion in confidence caused many companies to cancel or postpone planned sales of common stock whose proceeds would have been used for capital expansion, debt reduction, or other corporate purposes.

Nevertheless, the stock market reached new highs by summer 1990 largely because of optimism about the unification of Germany in a unified European Community and the economic benefits expected from a more capitalistic Eastern Europe, including Russia. By 1993 Europe was languishing in a recession and the United States was recovering from one, but the U.S. stock market set new records in May 1993.

One obvious thing from these worldwide events is that we live in a world where international events impact economies of all industrial countries. We live in a world where capital moves from country to country faster than ever thought possible, where computers interact in a vast international financial network, and where markets are more vulnerable to the emotions of the players than they have been in the past. The corporate financial manager has an increasing number of external impacts to consider. Future financial managers will need to have the sophistication to understand international capital flows, computerized electronic funds transfer systems, foreign currency hedging strategies, and many other factors.

Format of the Text

The material in this text is covered under six major headings. The student progresses from the development of basic analytical skills in accounting and finance to the utilization of decision-making techniques in working capital management, capital budgeting, long-term financing, and other related areas. A total length of 21 chapters should make the text appropriate for one-semester coverage.

The student is given a thorough grounding in financial theory in a highly palatable and comprehensive fashion—with careful attention to definitions, symbols, and formulas. The intent is that the student develop a thorough understanding of the basic concepts in finance.

Parts

1. Introduction   This section examines the goals and objectives of financial management. The emphasis on decision making and risk management is stressed, with an update of significant events influencing the study of finance.

2. Financial Analysis and Planning   The student first has the opportunity to review the basic principles of accounting as they relate to finance (financial statements and funds flow are emphasized). This review material, in Chapter 2, is optional—and the student may judge whether he or she needs this review before progressing through the section.

Additional material in this part includes a thorough study of ratio analysis, budget construction techniques, and development of comprehensive pro forma statements. The effect of heavy fixed commitments, in the form of either debt or plant and equipment, is examined in a discussion of leverage.

3. Working Capital Management   The techniques for managing the short-term assets of the firm and the associated liabilities are examined. The material is introduced in the context of risk-return analysis. The financial manager must constantly choose between liquid, low-return assets (perhaps marketable securities) and more profitable, less liquid assets (such as inventory). Sources of short-term financing are also considered.

4. The Capital Budgeting Process   The decision on capital outlays is among the most significant a firm will have to make. In terms of study procedure, we attempt to carefully lock down "time value of money" calculations, then proceed to the valuation of bonds and stocks, emphasizing present value techniques. The valuation chapter develops the traditional dividend valuation model and examines bond price sensitivity in response to discount rates and inflation. An appendix presents the supernormal dividend growth model, or what is sometimes called the "two-stage" dividend model. After careful grounding in valuation practice and theory, we examine the cost of capital and capital structure. The text then moves to the actual capital budgeting decision, making generous use of previously learned material and employing the concept of marginal analysis. The concluding chapter in this part covers risk-return analysis in capital budgeting, with a brief exposure to portfolio theory and a consideration of market value maximization.

5. Long-Term Financing   The student is introduced to U.S. financial markets as they relate to corporate financial management. The student considers the sources and uses of funds in the capital markets—with warrants and convertibles covered, as well as the more conventional methods of financing. The guiding role of the investment banker in the distribution of securities is also analyzed. Furthermore, the student is encouraged to think of leasing as a form of debt.

6. Expanding the Perspective of Corporate Finance   A chapter on corporate mergers considers external growth strategy and serves as an integrative tool to bring together such topics as profit management, capital budgeting, portfolio considerations, and valuation concepts. A second chapter on international financial management describes the growth of the international financial markets, the rise of multinational business, and the related effects on corporate financial management. The issues discussed in these two chapters highlight corporate diversification and risk-reduction attempts prevalent in the 1980s and continuing into the 1990s.

List of Terms

capital structure theory 7	insider trading 10
agency theory 8	sole proprietorship 12
shareholder wealth maximization 9	partnership 13
	articles of partnership 13

Discussion Questions

1. What was the first area of study to generate newfound enthusiasm for decision-related analysis in finance?
2. What is meant by the goal of maximization of shareholder wealth? Why is profit maximization, by itself, an inappropriate goal?
3. What issue does agency theory examine? Why is it important in a public corporation as opposed to a private corporation?
4. When does insider trading occur? What government agency is responsible for protecting against the unethical practice of insider trading?
5. Suggest two forms of daily functions and two forms of occasional functions that the financial manager performs.
6. Contrast the liability provisions for a sole proprietorship, a partnership, a limited partnership, and a corporation.
7. Why is the corporate form of organization best suited to a large organization?
8. What has happened to the typical debt-to-assets ratio and the interest coverage ratio of most corporations?
9. What are some ways in which corporations are restructuring their balance sheets and other related activities?
10. What is meant by the U.S. foreign trade deficit? How does the trade deficit affect the U.S. economy?

Selected References

Branch, Ben. "Corporate Objectives and Market Performance." *Financial Management* 2 (Summer 1973), pp. 22–29.

Brennen, Michael J., and Eduardo S. Schwartz. "Regulation and Corporate Investment Policy." *Journal of Finance* 37 (May 1982), pp. 289–300.

Byrd, John W., and Kent A. Hickman. "Do Outside Directors Monitor Managers? Evidence from Tender Offer Bids." *Journal of Financial Economics* 32 (October 1992), pp. 195–221.

Cornell, Bradford, and Alan C. Shipiro. "Corporate Stakeholders and Corporate Finance." *Financial Management* 16 (Spring 1987), pp. 5–14.

Davis, Keith. "Social Responsibility Is Inevitable." *California Management Review* 19 (Fall 1976), pp. 14–20.

Donaldson, Gordon. "Financial Goals: Management vs. Stockholders." *Harvard Business Review* 41 (May–June 1963), pp. 16–29.

Dowd, Ann Reilly. "CEOs Speak out on Clintonomics." *Fortune* 127 (December 14, 1992), pp. 69–74.

Furtado, Eugene P. H., and Vijay Karan. "Causes, Consequences, and Shareholder Wealth Effects of Management Turnover: A Review of the Empirical Evidence." *Financial Management* 19 (Summer 1990), pp. 60–75.

Gitman, Lawrence J., and Charles E. Maxwell. "Financial Activities of Major U.S. Firms: Survey and Analysis of Fortune's 1000." *Financial Management* 14 (Winter 1985), pp. 57–65.

Hirt, Geoffrey A. "Integrating Financial Theory and Practice with Institutional–Descriptive Finance." *Journal of Financial Education* 13 (Fall 1984), pp. 19–27.

Jensen, Michael C. "The Eclipse of the Public Corporation." *Harvard Business Review* 67 (September–October 1989), pp. 61–74.

————. "Corporate Control and the Politics of Finance." *Journal of Applied Corporate Finance* 4 (Summer 1991), pp. 13–33.

Kose, John, Larry H. P. Lang, and Jeffrey Netter. "The Voluntary Restructuring of Large Firms in Response to Performance Decline." *Journal of Finance* 47 (July 1992), pp. 891–917.

Seitz, Neil. "Shareholder Goals, Firm Goals and Firm Financing Decisions." *Financial Management* 11 (Autumn 1982), pp. 20–26.

Solomon, Ezra. *The Theory of Financial Management.* New York: Columbia University Press, 1963, pp. 15–26.

Wenner, David L., and Richard W. LeBer. "Managing for Shareholder Value—From Top to Bottom." *Harvard Business Review* 67 (November–December 1989), pp. 52–66.

Weston, J. Fred. "The Development of Finance Theory." *Financial Management* 10 (Tenth Anniversary Issue, 1981), pp. 5–22.

Financial Analysis and Planning

Chapter 2
Review of Accounting

Chapter 3
Financial Analysis

Chapter 4
Financial Forecasting

Chapter 5
Operating and Financial
Leverage

INTRODUCTION

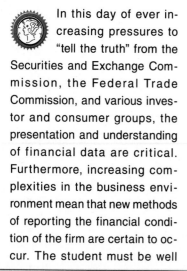 In this day of ever increasing pressures to "tell the truth" from the Securities and Exchange Commission, the Federal Trade Commission, and various investor and consumer groups, the presentation and understanding of financial data are critical. Furthermore, increasing complexities in the business environment mean that new methods of reporting the financial condition of the firm are certain to occur. The student must be well positioned to understand the old rules of the game and to appreciate new developments on the horizon. • In Chapter 2, we review some of the basic principles of accounting. The student should have a reasonable understanding of financial statements and related concepts before studying the more analytical material. Students with a strong background in accounting may choose to merely gloss over this material. • We then proceed to a study of company performance through ratio analysis in Chapter 3. The purpose of ratio analysis is to examine financial data on a relative basis. Net profit means very little unless it is compared to some other measure such as sales, total assets, or net worth in an appropriate ratio format. Net income of $100,000 offers little insight, but a ratio of net income to sales of 5 percent may suggest a great deal in comparison to past performance and other companies. • An important dimension in financial analysis is consideration of the impact of inflation and disinflation on the financial fortunes of the firm.

The authors present examples showing how changing prices may distort the normally reported income of the firm. • In Chapter 4, we shift the emphasis from "what was" to "what will be" as we go through the process of financial forecasting. To anticipate future financing requirements, the firm must determine what the income statement, balance sheet, and cash budget will look like for the planning period. In the process of financial forecasting, we are forced to make predictions about future sales, inventory levels, receivables, and other accounts, and then to combine our forecasts into a structured set of financial statements. On completion of Chapter 4, the student should have a better understanding not only of forecasting but also of all the elements that make up the financial structure of the firm. • As a last topic in Part 2, we look at management's use of leverage to magnify the results of the firm. By leverage, we mean the utilization of a high percentage of fixed assets or "fixed cost" debt in the management and operation of the firm. As indicated in Chapter 5, if we achieve a high volume of operation, our fixed costs should allow for strong profitability as our revenues go up while much of our costs remain constant. At a low level of operation, perhaps in a recession, the opposite results will take place, and our heavy fixed costs could force us into bankruptcy. We must learn how to handle this two-edged sword effectively.

Review of Accounting

CHAPTER CONCEPTS

1 The income statement measures profitability.

2 The price-earnings ratio indicates the relative evaluation of earnings.

3 The balance sheet shows assets and the financing of those assets.

4 The statement of cash flows indicates the change in the cash position of the firm.

5 Depreciation provides a tax reduction benefit.

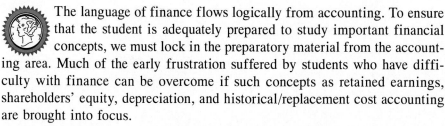 The language of finance flows logically from accounting. To ensure that the student is adequately prepared to study important financial concepts, we must lock in the preparatory material from the accounting area. Much of the early frustration suffered by students who have difficulty with finance can be overcome if such concepts as retained earnings, shareholders' equity, depreciation, and historical/replacement cost accounting are brought into focus.

In this chapter, we examine the three basic types of financial statements—the income statement, the balance sheet, and the statement of cash flows—with particular attention paid to the interrelationships among these three measurement devices. As special preparation for the financial manager, we briefly examine income tax considerations affecting financial decisions.

Income Statement

The **income statement** is the major device for measuring the profitability of a firm over a period of time. An example of the income statement for the Kramer Corporation is presented in Table 2–1.

TABLE 2–1

KRAMER CORPORATION
Income Statement
For the Year Ended December 31, 1994

1. Sales	$2,000,000
2. Cost of goods sold	1,500,000
3. Gross profits	500,000
4. Selling and administrative expense	220,000
5. Depreciation expense	50,000
6. Operating profit (EBIT)*	230,000
7. Interest expense	20,000
8. Earnings before taxes (EBT)	210,000
9. Taxes	99,500
10. Earnings after taxes (EAT)	110,500
11. Preferred stock dividends	10,500
12. Earnings available to common stockholders	$ 100,000
13. Shares outstanding	100,000
14. Earnings per share	$1.00

*Earnings before interest and taxes.

[handwritten margin notes: EAT: used as Net Income for Statement of CASH FLOWS]

[handwritten margin notes: goes on Statement of Cash Flows (3rd sect.) Financing]

First, note that the income statement covers a defined period of time, whether it be one month, three months, or a year. The statement is presented in a stair-step or progressive fashion so we can examine the profit or loss after each type of expense item is deducted.

We start with sales and deduct cost of goods sold to arrive at gross profit. The $500,000 thus represents the difference between what we bought or manufactured our goods for and the sales price. We then subtract selling and administrative expense and depreciation from gross profit to determine our profit (or loss) purely from operations of $230,000. It is possible for a company to enjoy a high gross profit margin (25–50 percent) but a relatively low operating profit because of heavy expenses incurred in marketing the product and managing the company.[1]

Having obtained operating profit (essentially a measure of how efficient management is in generating revenues and controlling expenses), we now adjust for revenues and expenses not related to operational matters. In this case we pay $20,000 in interest and arrive at earnings before taxes of $210,000. The tax payments are $99,500, leaving aftertax income of $110,500.

Return to Capital

Before proceeding further, we should note that there are three primary sources of capital—the bondholders, who received $20,000 in interest (item 7); the preferred stockholders, who receive $10,500 in dividends (item 11); and the common stockholders. After the $10,500 dividend has been paid to the preferred stockholders, there will be $100,000 in earnings available to the common stockholders (item 12). In computing **earnings per share,** we must interpret this in terms of the number of shares outstanding. As indicated in item 13, there are 100,000 shares outstanding, so the $100,000 of earnings available to the common stockholders may be translated into earnings per share of $1. Common stockholders are sensitive to the number of shares outstanding—the more shares, the lower the earnings per share. Before any new shares are issued, the financial manager must be sure they will eventually generate sufficient earnings to avoid reducing earnings per share.

The $100,000 of profit ($1 earnings per share) may be paid out to the common stockholders in the form of dividends or retained in the company for subsequent reinvestment. The reinvested funds theoretically belong to the common stockholders, who hope they will provide future earnings and dividends. In the case of the Kramer Corporation, we assume $50,000 in dividends will be paid out to the common stockholders, with the balance retained in the corporation for their benefit. A short supplement to the income statement, a statement of retained earnings (Table 2–2), usually indicates the disposition of earnings.[2]

TABLE 2–2

Statement of Retained Earnings For the Year Ended December 31, 1994	
Retained earnings, balance, January 1, 1994	$250,000
Add: Earnings available to common stockholders, 1994 . .	100,000
Deduct: Cash dividends declared in 1994	50,000
Retained earnings, balance, December 31, 1994	300,000

---

[1]Depreciation was not treated as part of cost of goods sold in this instance, but rather as a separate expense. All or part of depreciation may be treated as part of cost of goods sold, depending on the circumstances.

[2]The statement may also indicate any adjustments to previously reported income as well as any restrictions on cash dividends.

We see that a net value of $50,000 has been added to previously accumulated earnings of $250,000 to arrive at $300,000.

Price–Earnings Ratio Applied to Earnings per Share

A concept utilized throughout the text is the **price-earnings ratio.** This refers to the multiplier applied to earnings per share to determine current value of the common stock. In the case of the Kramer Corporation, earnings per share were $1. If the firm had a price-earnings ratio of 15, the market value of each share would be $15. The price-earnings ratio (or P/E ratio, as it is commonly called) is influenced by the earnings and the sales growth of the firm, the risk (or volatility in performance), the debt-equity structure of the firm, the dividend payment policy, the quality of management, and a number of other factors. Since companies have various levels of earnings per share, price-earnings ratios allow us to compare the relative market value of many companies based on $1 of earnings per share.

The P/E ratio indicates expectations about the future of a company. Firms expected to provide returns greater than those for the market in general with equal or less risk often have P/E ratios higher than the market P/E ratio. Expectations of returns and P/E ratios do change over time, as Table 2–3 illustrates.

TABLE 2–3
P/E ratios for selected U.S. companies

Corporation	Industry	Jan. 2, 1980	Jan. 2, 1983	Jan. 2, 1986	Jan. 2, 1990	Jan. 2, 1993
Apple	Computers	24	30	12	11	13
H&R Block	Taxes	9	11	16	17	27
Exxon	Oil	6	10	9	18	16
General Cinema	Movies	8	11	19	15	24
Helene Curtis	Cosmetics	4	8	11	25	20
Lockheed	Aerospace	10	9	8	6	10
McDonald's	Restaurants	9	10	16	18	20
Southwest Air	Airlines	5	20	14	15	38
Texas Utilities	Public utilities	7	6	7	8	15
Wal-Mart	Retail	13	26	28	24	39
Standard & Poor's (500 Stock Index)		7	11	14	15	22

Price-earnings ratios can be confusing. When a firm's earnings are dropping rapidly or perhaps even approaching zero, its stock price, though declining too, may not match the magnitude of falloff in earnings. This process can give the appearance of an increasing P/E ratio under adversity. This happens from time to time in the steel industry and other cyclical industries. For example, in mid-1992 Reynolds Metals was trading at a P/E ratio over 40 because of cyclically low earnings. Earnings per share had declined from $9.20 in 1989 to $1.50 in 1992. Normally the P/E ratio for the firm is under 10.

Limitations of the Income Statement

The economist defines income as the change in real worth that occurs between the beginning and the end of a specified time period. To the economist an increase in the value of a firm's land as a result of a new airport being built on adjacent property is an increase in the real worth of the firm and therefore represents income. Similarly, the elimination of a competitor might also increase the firm's real worth and therefore result in income in an economic sense. The accountant does not ordinarily employ such broad definitions. Accounting values are established primarily by actual transactions, and income that is gained or lost during a given period is a function of verifiable transactions. While the potential sales price of your property may go from $100,000 to $200,000 as a result of new developments in your area, your stockholders may perceive only a much smaller gain or loss from operations.

Also, as will be pointed out in Chapter 3, "Financial Analysis," there is some flexibility in the reporting of transactions, so similar events may result in differing measurements of income at the end of a time period. The intent of this section is not to criticize the accounting profession, for it is certainly among the best-organized, trained, and paid professions, but to alert students to imperfections already well recognized within the profession.

Balance Sheet

The **balance sheet** indicates what the firm owns and how these assets are financed in the form of liabilities or ownership interest. While the income statement purports to show the profitability of the firm, the balance sheet delineates the firm's holdings and obligations. Together, these statements are intended to answer two questions: How much did the firm make or lose, and what is a measure of its worth? A balance sheet for the Kramer Corporation is presented in Table 2–4.

Note that the balance sheet is a picture of the firm at a point in time—in this case December 31, 1994. It does not purport to represent the result of transactions for a specific month, quarter, or year, but rather is a cumulative chronicle of all transactions that have affected the corporation since its inception. In contrast, the income statement measures results only over a short, quantifiable period. Generally, balance sheet items are stated on an original cost basis rather than at present worth.

Interpretation of Balance Sheet Items

Asset accounts are listed in order of **liquidity** (convertibility to cash). The first category of *current assets* covers items that may be converted to cash within one year (or within the normal operating cycle of the firm). A few items are worthy of mention. *Marketable securities* are temporary investments of excess cash. The value shown in the account is the lower of cost or current market value. *Accounts receivable* include an allowance for bad debts (based on historical evidence) to determine their anticipated collection value. *Inventory* may be in the form of raw material, goods in process, or finished goods, while *prepaid expenses* represent future expense items that have already been paid, such as insurance premiums or rent.

Investments, unlike marketable securities, represent a longer-term commitment of funds (at least one year). They may include stocks, bonds, or investments in other corporations. Frequently, the account will contain stock in companies that the firm is acquiring.

TABLE 2–4

KRAMER CORPORATION
Statement of Financial Position (Balance Sheet)
December 31, 1994

Assets

Current assets:

Cash.		$ 40,000
Marketable securities		10,000
Accounts receivable	$ 220,000	
Less: Allowance for bad debts	20,000	200,000
Inventory.		180,000
Prepaid expenses		20,000
Total current assets		450,000
Other assets:		
Investments		50,000
Fixed assets:		
Plant and equipment, original cost	1,100,000	
Less: Accumulated depreciation	600,000	
Net plant and equipment		500,000
Total assets		$1,000,000

Liabilities and Stockholders' Equity

Current liabilities:

Accounts payable		$ 80,000
Notes payable		100,000
Accrued expenses		30,000
Total current liabilities		210,000
Long-term liabilities:		
Bonds payable, 2001		90,000
Total liabilities		300,000
Stockholders' equity:		
Preferred stock, $100 par value, 500 shares . .		50,000
Common stock, $1 par value, 100,000 shares . .		100,000
Capital paid in excess of par (common stock). .		250,000
Retained earnings		300,000
Total stockholders' equity		700,000
Total liabilities and stockholders' equity.		$1,000,000

Plant and equipment is carried at original cost minus accumulated depreciation. Accumulated depreciation is not to be confused with the depreciation expense item indicated in the income statement in Table 2–1. Accumulated depreciation is the sum of all past and present depreciation charges on currently owned assets, while depreciation expense is the current year's charge. If we subtract accumulated depreciation from the original value, the balance ($500,000) tells us how much of the original cost has not been expensed in the form of depreciation.

Total assets are financed through either liabilities or stockholders' equity. Liabilities represent financial obligations of the firm and move from current liabilities (due within one year) to longer-term obligations, such as bonds payable in 2001.

Among the short-term obligations, *accounts payable* represent amounts owed on open account to suppliers, while *notes payable* are generally short-term signed obligations to the banker or other creditors. An *accrued expense* is generated when a service has been provided or an obligation incurred and payment has not yet taken place. The firm may owe workers additional wages for services provided or the government taxes on earned income.

In the balance sheet presented in Table 2–4, we see the $1,000,000 in total assets of the Kramer Corporation was financed by $300,000 in debt and $700,000 in the form of shockholders' equity. Stockholders' equity represents the total contribution and ownership interest of preferred and common stockholders.

The *preferred stock* investment position is $50,000, based on 500 shares at $100 par. In the case of *common stock,* 100,000 shares have been issued at a total par value of $100,000, plus an extra $250,000 in *capital paid in excess of par* for a sum of $350,000. We can assume that the 100,000 shares were originally sold at $3.50 each.

100,000 shares	$1.00	Par value	$100,000
	2.50	Capital paid in excess of par . . .	250,000
	$3.50	Price per share.	$350,000

Finally, there is $300,000 in *retained earnings.* This value, previously determined in the statement of retained earnings (Table 2–2), represents the firm's cumulative earnings since inception minus dividends and any other adjustments.

Concept of Net Worth

Stockholders' equity minus the preferred stock component represents the **net worth,** or **book value,** of the firm. There is some logic to the approach. If you take everything that the firm owns and subtract the debt and preferred stock obligation,[3] the remainder belongs to the common stockholder and represents net worth. In the case of the Kramer Corporation, we show:

Total assets	$1,000,000
Total liabilities	300,000
Stockholders' equity	700,000
Preferred stock obligation.	50,000
Net worth assigned to common	$ 650,000
Common shares outstanding	100,000
Net worth, or book value, per share . . .	$6.50

The original cost per share was $3.50; the net worth, or book value, per share is $6.50; and the market value (based on a P/E ratio of 15 and earnings per share of $1) is $15. This last value is of primary concern to the financial manager and the security analyst.

_____

[3] An additional discussion of preferred stock is presented in Chapter 17, "Common and Preferred Stock Financing." Preferred stock represents neither a debt claim nor an ownership interest in the firm. It is a hybrid, or intermediate, type of security.

Limitations of the Balance Sheet

Lest we attribute too much significance to the balance sheet, we need to examine some of the underlying concepts supporting its construction. Most of the values on the balance sheet are stated on a historical or original cost basis. This may be particularly troublesome in the case of plant and equipment and inventory, which may now be worth two or three times the original cost or—from a negative viewpoint—may require many times the original cost for replacement.

The accounting profession has been grappling with this problem for decades, and the discussion becomes particularly intense each time inflation rears its ugly head. In October 1979 the Financial Accounting Standards Board (FASB) issued a ruling that required large companies to disclose inflation-adjusted accounting data in their annual reports. This information was to be disclosed in addition to the traditional historical cost data and could show up in footnotes or in a separate full-fledged financial section with detailed explanations. However, the standard is no longer in force, and the inclusion of inflation-adjusted data is no longer required in any form. If a company wishes to adjust its balance sheet or income statement data for inflation, it is purely a voluntary act.

Table 2–5 looks at large disparities between market value per share and historical book value per share for a number of publicly traded companies in 1992. Besides asset valuation, a number of other factors may explain the wide differences between per share values, such as industry outlook, growth prospects, quality of management, and risk-return expectations.

TABLE 2–5
Comparison of market value to book value per share in December 1992

Corporation	Market Value per Share	Book Value per Share	Ratio of Market Value to Book Value
Wal-Mart	62.25	7.65	8.13
Merck & Co	43.25	5.50	7.86
Biogen	39.75	8.40	4.13
Liz Claiborne	41.50	12.25	3.39
Fieldcrest Cannon	18.00	23.75	.76
Boise Cascade	21.50	31.25	.69
Travelers Corp.	25.00	42.40	.59
Acme Metals	12.00	28.20	.43
United Inns	1.75	8.70	.20

Statement of Cash Flows

In November 1987 the accounting profession designated the "statement of cash flows" as the third required financial statement, along with the balance sheet and income statement. Referred to as Financial Accounting Standards Board (FASB) 95, it replaces the old statement of changes in financial position (and the sources and uses of funds statement).

The purpose of the **statement of cash flows** is to emphasize the critical nature of cash flow to the operations of the firm. Cash flow generally represents cash or cash equivalent items that can easily be converted into cash within 90 days (such as a money market fund).

The income statement and balance sheet that we have studied thus far are normally based on the accrual method of accounting, in which revenues and expenses are recognized as they occur, rather than when cash actually changes hands. For example, a $100,000 credit sale may be made in December 1994 and shown as revenue for that year—despite the fact the cash payment will not be received until March 1995. When the actual payment is finally received under accrual accounting, no revenue is recognized (it has already been accounted for previously). The primary advantage of accrual accounting is that it allows us to match revenues and expenses in the period in which they occur in order to appropriately measure profit; but a disadvantage is that adequate attention is not directed to the actual cash flow position of the firm.

Say a firm made a $1 million profit on a transaction but will not receive the actual cash payment for two years. Or perhaps the $1 million profit is in cash, but the firm increased its asset purchases by $3 million (a new building). If you merely read the income statement, you might assume the firm is in a strong $1 million cash position; but if you go beyond the income statement to cash flow considerations, you would observe the firm is $2 million short of funds for the period.

As a last example, a firm might show a $100,000 loss on the income statement, but if there were a depreciation expense write-off of $150,000, the firm would actually have $50,000 in cash. Since depreciation is a noncash deduction, the $150,000 deduction in the income statement for depreciation can be added back to net income to determine cash flow.

The statement of cash flows addresses these issues by translating income statement and balance sheet data into cash flow information. A corporation that has $1 million in accrual-based accounting profits can determine whether it can afford to pay a cash dividend to stockholders, buy new equipment, or undertake new projects. In the low-profit and cash-tight era of the 1990s, cash flow analysis takes on a very special meaning.

Developing an Actual Statement

We shall use the information previously provided for the Kramer Corporation in this chapter to illustrate how the statement of cash flows is developed.

But first, let's identify the three primary sections of the statement of cash flows:

1. Cash flows from operating activities.
2. Cash flows from investing activities.
3. Cash flows from financing activities.

After each of these sections is completed, the results are added together to compute the net increase or decrease in cash flow for the corporation. An example of the process is shown in Figure 2–1 on page 34. Let's begin with cash flows from operating activities.

FIGURE 2–1
Illustration of concepts behind the statement of cash flows

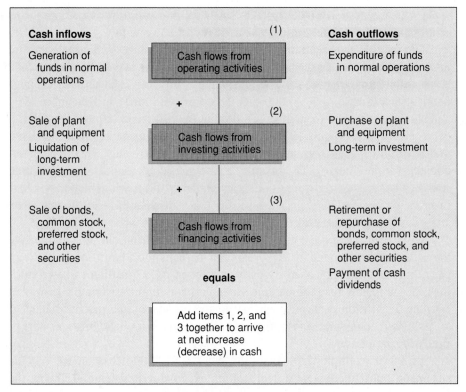

Determining Cash Flows from Operating Activities

Basically, we are going to translate *income from operations* from an accrual to a cash basis. According to FASB 95, there are two ways to accomplish this objective. First, the firm may use a *direct method,* in which every item on the income statement is adjusted from accrual accounting to cash accounting. This is a tedious process, in which all sales must be adjusted to cash sales, all purchases must be adjusted to cash purchases, and so on. A more popular method is the *indirect method,* in which net income represents the starting point and then adjustments are made to convert net income to cash flows from operations.[4] This is the method we will use. Regardless of whether the direct or indirect method is used, the same final answer will be derived.

We follow these procedures in computing **cash flows from operating activities** using the indirect method.[5]

- Start with net income. *EAT*
- Recognize that depreciation is a non-cash deduction in computing net income and should be added back to net income to *increase* the cash balance.

---

[4]The indirect method is similar to procedures used to construct the old sources and uses of funds statement.

[5]In addition to the items mentioned, we may need to recognize the *gains* or *losses* on the sale of operating and nonoperating assets. We exclude these for ease of analysis.

3A • Recognize that increases in current assets are a use of funds and *reduce* the cash balance (indirectly)—as an example, the firm spends more funds on inventory.

3B • Recognize that decreases in current assets are a source of funds and *increase* the cash balance (indirectly)—that is, the firm reduces funds tied up in inventory.

4A • Recognize that increases in current liabilities are a source of funds and increase the cash balance (indirectly)—the firm gets more funds from creditors.

4B • Recognize that decreases in current liabilities are a use of funds and *decrease* the cash balance (indirectly)—that is, the firm pays off creditors.

These steps are illustrated in Figure 2–2.

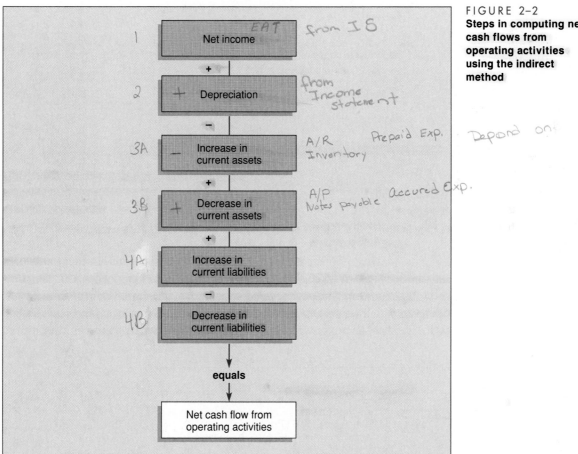

FIGURE 2–2
Steps in computing net cash flows from operating activities using the indirect method

We will follow these procedures for the Kramer Corporation, drawing primarily on material from Table 2–1 (the previously presented income statement) and from Table 2–6. (which shows balance sheet data for the most recent two years).

TABLE 2-6

KRAMER CORPORATION
Comparative Balance Sheets

	Year-End 1993	Year-End 1994
Assets		
Current assets:		
Cash	$ 30,000	$ 40,000
Marketable securities	10,000	10,000
Accounts receivable (net)	170,000	200,000
Inventory	160,000	180,000
Prepaid expenses	30,000	20,000
Total current assets	400,000	450,000
Investments (long term)	20,000	50,000
Plant and equipment	1,000,000	1,100,000
Less: Accumulated depreciation	550,000	600,000
Net plant and equipment	450,000	500,000
Total assets	$ 870,000	$1,000,000
Liabilities and Stockholders' Equity		
Current liabilities:		
Accounts payable	$ 45,000	$ 80,000
Notes payable	100,000	100,000
Accrued expenses	35,000	30,000
Total current liabilities	180,000	210,000
Long-term liabilities:		
Bonds payable, 1998	40,000	90,000
Total liabilities	220,000	300,000
Stockholders' equity:		
Preferred stock, $100 par value	50,000	50,000
Common stock, $1 par value	100,000	100,000
Capital paid in excess of par	250,000	250,000
Retained earnings	250,000	300,000
Total stockholders' equity	650,000	700,000
Total liabilities and stockholders' equity	$ 870,000	$1,000,000

Handwritten margin notes: Operating Act. 3; Investing Act.; Operating Act. 4; Financing Act.; 30,000; 20,000; (10,000); 30,000; 100,000; 35,000; (5,000); 50,000

Left margin notes: assets / yrly chg ↑ / Cash flow ↓ / yrly chg ↓ / Cash flow ↑

The analysis is presented in Table 2–7. We begin with net income (earnings after taxes) of $110,500 and add back depreciation of $50,000. We then show that increases in current assets (accounts receivable and inventory) reduce funds and decreases in current assets (prepaid expenses) increase funds. Also, we show increases in current liabilities (accounts payable) as an addition

TABLE 2–7
Cash flows from operating activities

Net income (earnings after taxes) (Table 2–1)		$110,500
Adjustments to determine cash flow from operating activities:		
Add back depreciation (Table 2–1)	50,000	
Increase in accounts receivable (Table 2–6)	(30,000)	
Increase in inventory (Table 2–6)	(20,000)	
Decrease in prepaid expenses (Table 2–6)	10,000	
Increase in accounts payable (Table 2–6)	35,000	
Decrease in accrued expenses (Table 2–6)	(5,000)	
Total adjustments		40,000
Net cash flows from operating activities		$150,500

Handwritten notes on Table 2-7: EAT; 1; 2; 3A; 3B; 4A; 4B

Left margin notes: liabilities / yrly chg ↑ / Cash flow ↑ / yrly chg ↓ / Cash flow ↓

to funds and decreases in current liabilities (accrued expenses) as a reduction of funds.

   We see in Table 2–7 that the firm generated $150,500 in cash flows from operating activities. Of some significance is that this figure is $40,000 larger than the net income figure reported to stockholders ($150,500 − $110,500). A firm with little depreciation and a massive buildup of inventory might show lower cash flow than reported net income. Once cash flows from operating activities are determined, management has a better feel for what can be allocated to investing or financing needs (such as paying cash dividends).

Determining Cash Flows from Investing Activities

DATA from Comparative Balance Sheet

Cash flows from investing activities represent the second section in the statement of cash flows. The section relates to long-term investment activities in other issuers' securities or, more importantly, in plant and equipment. Increasing investments represent a *use* of funds, and decreasing investments represent a *source* of funds.

   Examining Table 2–6 for the Kramer Corporation, we show the following information in Table 2–8.

Increase in investments (long-term securities) (Table 2–6)	($30,000)
Increase in plant and equipment (Table 2–6)	(100,000)
Net cash flows from investing activities	($130,000)

TABLE 2–8
Cash flows from investing activities

before deduction of deprec.

Determining Cash Flows from Financing Activities

Data from Comparative Balance Sheet and Income Statement Statement of Retained Earnings

In the third section of the statement of cash flows, **cash flows from financing activities,** we show the effects of financing activities on the corporation. Financing activities apply to the sale or retirement of bonds, common stock, preferred stock, and other corporate securities. Also, the payment of cash dividends is considered a financing activity. The sale of the firm's securities represents a *source* of funds, and the retirement or repurchase of such securities represents a *use* of funds. The payment of dividends also represents a *use* of funds.

   Using data from Table 2–1, Table 2–2, and Table 2–6, the financing activities of the Kramer Corporation are shown in Table 2–9.

Increase in bonds payable (Table 2–6)	$50,000
Preferred stock dividends paid (Table 2–1)	(10,500)
Common stock dividends paid (Table 2–2)	(50,000)
Net cash flows from financing activities	($10,500)

TABLE 2–9
Cash flows from financing activities

Combining the Three Sections of the Statement

We now combine the three sections of the statement on cash flows to arrive at the one overall statement that the corporation provides to security analysts and stockholders. The information is shown in Table 2–10.

TABLE 2–10

KRAMER CORPORATION
Statement of Cash Flows
For the Year Ended December 31, 1994

Cash flows from operating activities:		
Net income (earnings after taxes)		$110,500
Adjustments to determine cash flow from operating activities:		
Add back depreciation	$ 50,000	
Increase in accounts receivable	(30,000)	
Increase in inventory.	(20,000)	
Decrease in prepaid expenses	10,000	
Increase in accounts payable	35,000	
Decrease in accrued expenses.	(5,000)	
Total adjustments		40,000
Net cash flows from operating activities . . .		$150,500
Cash flows from investing activities:		
Increase in investments (long-term securities) . . .	(30,000)	
Increase in plant and equipment	(100,000)	
Net cash flows from investing activities . . .		($130,000)
Cash flows from financing activities:		
Increase in bonds payable	50,000	
Preferred stock dividends paid	(10,500)	
Common stock dividends paid	(50,000)	
Net cash flows from financing activities . . .		($10,500)
Net increase (decrease) in cash flows		$10,000

[handwritten annotation: Can account for the chg in cash on the Comparative Balance Sheet]

We see in Table 2–10 that the firm created excess funds from operating activities that were utilized heavily in investing activities and somewhat in financing activities. As a result, there is a $10,000 increase in the cash balance, and this can also be reconciled with the increase in the cash balance of $10,000 from $30,000 to $40,000, as indicated in Table 2–6.

One might also do further analysis on how the buildups in various accounts were financed. For example, if there is a substantial increase in inventory or accounts receivable, is there an associated buildup in accounts payable and short-term bank loans? If not, the firm may have to use long-term financing to carry part of the short-term needs. An even more important question might be: How are increases in long-term assets being financed? Most desirably, there should be adequate long-term financing and profits to carry these needs. If not, then short-term funds (trade credit and bank loans) may be utilized to carry long-term needs. This is a potentially high-risk situation, in that short-term sources of funds may dry up while long-term needs continue to demand funding. In problems at the back of the chapter, you will have an opportunity to further consider these points.

One of the most confusing items to finance students is whether depreciation is a source of funds to the corporation. In Table 2–7, we listed depreciation as a source of funds (cash flow). This item deserves further clarification. The reason we added back depreciation was not that depreciation was a new source of funds, but rather that we subtracted this noncash expense in arriving at net income and now have to add it back to determine the amount of actual funds on hand.

Depreciation represents an attempt to allocate the initial cost of an asset over its useful life. In essence, we attempt to match the annual expense of plant and equipment ownership against the revenues being produced. Nevertheless the charging of depreciation is purely an accounting entry and does not directly involve the movement of funds. To go from accounting flows to cash flows in Table 2–7, we restored the noncash deduction of $50,000 for depreciation that was subtracted in Table 2–1, the income statement.

Let us examine a very simple case involving depreciation in Table 2–11. Assume we purchase a machine for $500 with a five-year life and we pay for it in cash. Our depreciation schedule calls for equal annual depreciation charges of $100 per year for five years. Assume further that our firm has $1,000 in earnings before depreciation and taxes and the tax obligation is $300. Note the difference between accounting flows and cash flows for the first two years in Table 2–11.

Depreciation and Funds Flow

	Year 1	
	(A) Accounting Flows	**(B)** Cash Flows
Earnings before depreciation and taxes (EBDT) . .	$1,000	$1,000
Depreciation	100	100
Earnings before taxes (EBT)	900	900
Taxes.	300	300
Earnings after taxes (EAT)	$ 600	600
Purchase of equipment		−500
Depreciation charged without cash outlay		+100
Cash flow.		$ 200
	Year 2	
Earnings before depreciation and taxes (EBDT) . .	$1,000	$1,000
Depreciation	100	100
Earnings before taxes	900	900
Taxes.	300	300
Earnings after taxes (EAT)	$ 600	600
Depreciation charged without cash outlay		+100
Cash flow.		$ 700

TABLE 2–11
Comparison of accounting and cash flows

Since we took $500 out of cash flow originally to purchase equipment (in column B), we do not wish to take it out again. Thus we add back $100 in depreciation each year for five years to "wash out" the subtraction in the income statement.

Ernst & Young Pays $400 Million to the Government for Faulty Audits

In preparing financial statements, accounting firms must audit, or check, the operating and financial affairs of the company. While auditors do an excellent job in most cases, there are exceptions. Since investors, lenders, and government regulators depend on audited financial statements for decision making, a poorly conducted audit can result in liability for the accounting firm.

In early 1992 Ernst & Young, a highly respected accounting firm, agreed to pay the U.S. government $400 million to settle federal charges that the accounting firm inadequately audited four large savings and loans that eventually were closed at a cost of $6.6 billion to the government (and ultimately to taxpayers).

The failed institutions were Lincoln Savings and Loan of Irvine, California; Vernon Savings and Loan in Dallas; Western Savings Association in Phoenix; and Silverado Banking Savings and Loan Association of Denver. The latter institution was a particular embarrassment to then-President George Bush because his son Neil was on the institution's board of directors.

Among the faulty practices of Ernst & Young was a failure to perform adequate reviews of property appraisals used by the financial institutions to justify loans. By vastly overstating values of collateral for loans, the S&Ls made loans well in excess of the true value of the property. This eventually led to huge losses and bankruptcies for the institutions when the property could not be sold during foreclosures at values approaching the appraised values. The government then had to cover the losses.

As part of the settlement with the government, Ernst & Young also agreed to increase the training of auditors for financial institutions, present future work of audit partners to outside third parties for review, and generally increase the scrutiny of accounting decisions related to federally insured financial institutions.

Of the $400 million Ernst & Young agreed to pay, $300 million was covered by the firm's malpractice insurance. Nevertheless Ernst & Young and other major accounting firms are certain to see skyrocketing insurance premiums as a result of the $400 million settlement. It's as if the insurance industry is saying, "We pay now and you pay later."

Free Cash Flow

A term that has received increasingly greater attention in the 1990s is **free cash flow** (FCF). This is actually a by-product of the previously discussed statement of cash flows. Free cash flow is equal to:

Cash flow from operating activities

Minus: Capital expenditures (required to maintain the productive capacity of the firm)

Minus: Dividends (needed to maintain the necessary payout on common stock and to cover any preferred stock obligation).

The concept of free cash flow forces the stock analyst or banker not only to consider how much cash is generated from operating activities, but also to subtract out the necessary capital expenditures on plant and equipment to maintain normal activities. Similarly, dividend payments to shareholders must be subtracted out as these dividends must generally be paid to keep shareholders satisfied.

The balance, free cash flow, is then available for *special financial activities.* In the last decade special financing activities have often been synonymous with leveraged buyouts, in which a firm borrows money to buy its stock and take itself private, with the hope of restructuring its balance sheet and perhaps going public again in a few years at a higher price than it paid. Leveraged buyouts are discussed more fully in Chapter 15. The analyst or banker normally looks at *free cash flow* to determine whether there are sufficient excess funds to pay back the loan associated with the leveraged buyout.

Income Tax Considerations

Virtually every financial decision is influenced by federal income tax considerations. Primary examples are the lease versus purchase decision, the issuance of common stock versus debt decision, and the decision to replace an asset. While the intent of this section is not to review the rules, regulations, and nuances of the Federal Income Tax Code, we will examine how tax matters influence corporate financial decisions. The primary orientation will be toward the principles governing corporate tax decisions, though many of the same principles apply to a sole proprietorship or a partnership.

Corporate Tax Rates

Corporate federal tax rates have changed four times since 1980. Basically the rate is progressive, meaning lower levels of income (such as below $50,000 or $100,000) are taxed at lower rates. Higher levels of income are taxed at higher rates, normally in the mid-30 percent rate. In the illustrations in the text, we will use various rates to illustrate the impact on decision making. Keep in mind that corporations may also pay some state and foreign taxes, so the effective rate can get to 40 percent or higher in some instances. For corporations with low taxable income, the effective rate may only be 15 to 20 percent.

Cost of a Tax-Deductible Expense

The businessperson often states that a tax-deductible item, such as interest on business loans, travel expenditures, or salaries, costs substantially less than the amount expended, on an aftertax basis. We shall investigate how this process works. Let us examine the tax statements of two corporations—the first pays $100,000 in interest, and the second has no interest expense. An average tax rate of 40 percent is used for ease of computation.

	Corporation A	Corporation B
Earnings before interest and taxes	$400,000	$400,000
Interest	100,000	0
Earnings before taxes (taxable income) . . .	300,000	400,000
Taxes (40%)	120,000	160,000
Earnings after taxes	$180,000	$240,000
Difference in earnings after taxes—$60,000		

Although Corporation A paid out $100,000 more in interest than Corporation B, its earnings after taxes are only $60,000 less than those of

Corporation B. Thus we say the $100,000 in interest costs the firm only $60,000 in aftertax earnings. The aftertax cost of a tax-deductible expense can be computed as the actual expense times one minus the tax rate. In this case, we show $100,000 (1 − Tax rate), or $100,000 × 0.60 = $60,000. The reasoning in this instance is that the $100,000 is deducted from earnings before determining taxable income, thus saving us $40,000 in taxes and costing only $60,000 on a net basis.

Because a dividend on common stock is not tax deductible, we say it cost us 100 percent of the amount paid. From a purely corporate cash flow viewpoint, the firm would be indifferent between paying $100,000 in interest and $60,000 in dividends.

Depreciation as a Tax Shield

Although depreciation is not a new source of funds, it provides the important function of shielding part of our income from taxes. Let us examine Corporations A and B again, this time with an eye toward depreciation rather than interest. Corporation A charges off $100,000 in depreciation, while Corporation B charges off none.

	Corporation A	Corporation B
Earnings before depreciation and taxes . . .	$400,000	$400,000
Depreciation	100,000	0
Earnings before taxes	300,000	400,000
Taxes (40%)	120,000	160,000
Earnings after taxes	180,000	240,000
+ Depreciation charged without cash outlay .	100,000	0
Cash flow	$280,000	$240,000
Difference — $40,000		

We compute earnings after taxes and then add back depreciation to get cash flow. The difference between $280,000 and $240,000 indicates that Corporation A enjoys $40,000 more in cash flow. The reason is that depreciation shielded $100,000 from taxation in Corporation A and saved $40,000 in taxes, which eventually showed up in cash flow. Though depreciation is not a new source of funds, it does provide tax shield benefits that can be measured as depreciation times the tax rate, or in this case $100,000 × 0.40 = $40,000. A more comprehensive discussion of depreciation's effect on cash flow is presented in Chapter 12, as part of the long-term capital budgeting decision.

Summary

The financial manager must be thoroughly familiar with the language of accounting to administer the financial affairs of the firm. The income statement provides a measure of the firm's profitability over a specified period. Earnings per share represents residual income to the common stockholder that may be paid out in the form of dividends or reinvested to generate future profits and dividends. A limitation of the income statement is that it reports income and expense primarily on a transaction basis and thus may not recognize certain major economic events as they occur.

The balance sheet is a snapshot of the financial position of the firm at a point in time, with the stockholders' equity section purporting to represent ownership interest. Because the balance sheet is presented on a historical-cost basis, it may not necessarily reflect the true value of the firm.

The statement of cash flows, the third major statement the corporation presents to stockholders and security analysts, emphasizes the importance of cash flow data to the operations of the firm. It translates the information on the income statement and balance sheet that was prepared on an accrual accounting basis to a cash basis. From this data, the firm can better assess its ability to pay cash dividends, invest in new equipment, and so on.

Finally, we examine the corporate tax structure and the tax implications of interest, dividends, and depreciation. The aftertax cost and cash flow implications of these items are important throughout the text.

List of Terms

income statement 26	cash flows from investing
earnings per share 27	activities 37
price-earnings ratio 28	cash flows from financing
balance sheet 29	activities 37
liquidity 29	depreciation 39
net worth or book value 31	free cash flow 40
statement of cash flows 32	
cash flows from operating	
activities 34	

Discussion Questions

1. Discuss some financial variables that affect the price-earnings ratio.
2. What is the difference between book value per share of common stock and market value per share? Why does this disparity occur?
3. Explain how depreciation generates actual cash flows for the company.
4. What is the difference between accumulated depreciation and depreciation expense? How are they related?
5. How is the income statement related to the balance sheet?
6. Comment on why inflation may restrict the usefulness of the balance sheet as normally presented.
7. Explain why the statement of cash flows provides useful information that goes beyond income statement and balance sheet data.
8. What are the three primary sections of the statement of cash flows? In what section would the payment of a cash dividend be shown?
9. What is free cash flow? Why is it important to leveraged buyouts?
10. Why is interest expense said to cost the firm substantially less than the actual expense, while dividends cost it 100 percent of the outlay?

Problems

Income statement

1. Given the following information, prepare, in good form, an income statement for Goodman Software, Inc.

Selling and administrative expense	$ 50,000
Depreciation expense	80,000
Sales	400,000
Interest expense	30,000
Cost of goods sold	150,000
Taxes	18,550

Determination of profitability

2. The Kane Book Company sold 1,200 finance textbooks to State University for $60 each in 1993. These books cost Kane $42 to produce. In addition Kane spent $2,000 (selling expense) to persuade the university to buy its books. Kane borrowed $30,000 on January 1, 1993, on which it paid 10 percent interest. Both interest and principal were paid on December 31, 1993. Kane's tax rate is 30 percent. Depreciation expense for the year was $4,000.

    Did Kane make a profit in 1993? Verify with an income statement presented in good form.

Balance sheet

3. Classify the following balance sheet items as current or noncurrent:

Inventory	Retained earnings
Accounts payable	Marketable securities
Preferred stock	Accounts receivable
Prepaid expenses	Plant and equipment
Bonds payable	Accrued wages payable

Income statement

4. Arrange the following income statement items so they are in the proper order of an income statement:

Depreciation expense	Operating profit
Gross profit	Selling and administrative expense
Interest expense	Sales
Taxes	Earnings before taxes
Preferred stock dividends	Cost of goods sold
Shares outstanding	Earnings available to common
Earnings per share	stockholders
Earnings after taxes	

Cash flow

5. Identify whether each of the following items increases or decreases cash flow:

Decrease in inventory	Decrease in notes payable
Decrease in prepaid expenses	Depreciation expense
Decrease in accounts receivable	Increase in accounts payable
Decrease in inventory	Increase in investments
Dividend payment	

6. Harrison Ford Company has an operating profit of $200,000. Interest expense for the year was $10,000; preferred dividends paid were $18,750; and common dividends paid were $30,000. The tax was $61,250. The Harrison Ford Company has 20,000 shares of common stock outstanding.

   a. Calculate the earnings per share and the common dividends per share for the Harrison Ford Company.

   b. What was the increase in retained earnings for the year?

Earnings per share and retained earnings

7. Johnson Alarm Systems had $800,000 of retained earnings on December 31, 1994. The company paid dividends of $60,000 in 1994 and had retained earnings of $640,000 on December 31, 1993. How much did Johnson earn during 1994, and what would earnings per share be if 50,000 shares of common stock are outstanding?

Determination of earnings and earnings per share

8. Fill in the blank spaces with categories 1 through 7 below:

Balance sheet and income statement classification

   1. Balance sheet (BS)
   2. Income statement (IS)
   3. Current assets (CA)
   4. Fixed assets (FA)
   5. Current liabilities (CL)
   6. Long-term liabilities (LL)
   7. Stockholders' equity (SE)

Indicate Whether Item Is on Balance Sheet (BS) or Income Statement (IS)	If on Balance Sheet, Designate Which Category	Item
_____	_____	Accounts receivable
_____	_____	Retained earnings
_____	_____	Income tax expense
_____	_____	Accrued expenses
_____	_____	Cash
_____	_____	Selling and administrative expenses
_____	_____	Plant and equipment
_____	_____	Operating expenses
_____	_____	Marketable securities
_____	_____	Interest expense
_____	_____	Sales
_____	_____	Notes payable (6 months)
_____	_____	Bonds payable, maturity 2001
_____	_____	Common stock
_____	_____	Depreciation expense
_____	_____	Inventories
_____	_____	Capital in excess of par value
_____	_____	Net income (earnings after taxes)
_____	_____	Income tax payable

9. The Rogers Corporation has a gross profit of $880,000 and $360,000 in depreciation expense. The Evans Corporation has $880,000 in gross

Cash flow

profit, with $60,000 in depreciation expense. Selling and administrative expense is $120,000 for each company.

Given that the tax rate is 40 percent, compute the cash flow for both companies. Explain the difference in cash flow between the two firms.

Book value and P/E ratio

10. The Holtzman Corporation has assets of $400,000, current liabilities of $50,000, and long-term liabilities of $100,000. There is $40,000 in preferred stock outstanding; 20,000 shares of common stock have been issued.

   a. Compute book value (net worth) per share.

   b. If there is $22,000 in earnings available to common stockholders and Holtzman's stock has a P/E ratio of 15 times earnings per share, what is the current price of the stocks?

   c. What is the ratio of market value per share to book value per share?

Development of balance sheet

11. Arrange the following items in proper balance sheet presentation:

Accumulated depreciation.	$200,000
Retained earnings	110,000
Cash	5,000
Bonds payable	142,000
Accounts receivable	38,000
Plant and equipment—original cost	720,000
Accounts payable.	35,000
Allowance for bad debts	6,000
Common stock, $1 par, 150,000 shares outstanding . . .	150,000
Inventory	66,000
Preferred stock, $50 par, 1,000 shares outstanding . . .	50,000
Marketable securities.	15,000
Investments	20,000
Notes payable	83,000
Capital paid in excess of par (common stock)	88,000

Book value and market value

12. Bradley Gypsum Company has assets of $1,900,000, current liabilities of $700,000, and long-term liabilities of $580,000. There is $170,000 in preferred stock outstanding; 30,000 shares of common stock have been issued.

   a. Compute book value (net worth) per share.

   b. If there is $42,000 in earnings available to common stockholders and Bradley's stock has a P/E of 15 times earnings per share, what is the current price of the stock?

   c. What is the ratio of market value per share to book value per share?

Book value and P/E ratio

13. In problem 12, if the firm sells at two times book value per share, what will the P/E ratio be?

Construction of income statement and balance sheet

14. For December 31, 1993, the balance sheet of the Gardner Corporation is as follows:

Current Assets		**Liabilities**	
Cash.	$ 15,000	Accounts payable	$ 20,000
Accounts receivable	22,500	Notes payable	30,000
Inventory.	37,500	Bonds payable	75,000
Prepaid expenses	18,000		
Fixed Assets		**Stockholders' Equity**	
Plant and equipment		Common stock	112,500
(gross).	375,000	Paid-in capital.	37,500
Less: Accumulated		Retained earnings.	118,000
depreciation	75,000	Total liabilities and	
Net plant and assets	300,000	stockholders' equity . . .	$393,000
Total assets	$393,000		

Sales for 1994 were $330,000, with cost of goods sold being 60 percent of sales. Depreciation expense was 10 percent of plant and equipment (gross) at the beginning of the year. Interest expense for the bonds payable was 12 percent, while interest on the notes payable was 10 percent. These are based on December 31, 1993, balances. Selling and administrative expenses were $33,000, and the tax rate averaged 20 percent.

During 1994, the cash balance and prepaid expense balance were unchanged. Accounts receivable and inventory each increased by 20 percent, and accounts payable increased by 30 percent. A new machine was purchased on December 31, 1994, at a cost of $60,000. A cash dividend of $6,100 was paid to common stockholders at the end of 1994. Also notes payable increased by $10,000 and bonds payable decreased by $15,000. The common stock and paid-in capital accounts did not change.

a. Prepare an income statement for 1994.

b. Prepare a balance sheet as of December 31, 1994.

15. Prepare a statement of cash flows for the Crosby Corporation. Follow the general procedures indicated in Table 2–10.

Statement of cash flows

CROSBY CORPORATION
Income Statement
For the Year Ended December 31, 1994

Sales	$2,200,000
Cost of goods sold	1,300,000
Gross profits.	900,000
Selling and administrative expense.	420,000
Depreciation expense	150,000
Operating income	330,000
Interest expense	90,000
Earnings before taxes	240,000
Taxes	80,000
Earnings after taxes	160,000
Preferred stock dividends.	10,000
Earnings available to common stockholders	150,000
Shares outstanding.	120,000
Earnings per share.	$1.25

Statement of Retained Earnings
For the Year Ended December 31, 1994

Retained earnings, balance, January 1, 1994	$500,000
Add: Earnings available to common stockholders, 1994	150,000
Deduct: Cash dividends declared and paid in 1994	50,000
Retained earnings, balance, December 31, 1994	$600,000

Comparative Balance Sheets
For 1993 and 1994

	Year-End 1993	Year-End 1994	
Assets			
Current assets:			
Cash.	$ 70,000	$ 100,000	
Accounts receivable (net)	300,000	350,000	50,000
Inventory.	410,000	430,000	20,000
Prepaid expenses	50,000	30,000	(20,000)
Total current assets	830,000	910,000	
Investments (long-term securities)	80,000	70,000	(10,000)
Plant and equipment	2,000,000	2,400,000	400,000
Less: Accumulated depreciation	1,000,000	1,150,000	
Net plant and equipment	1,000,000	1,250,000	
Total assets	$1,910,000	$2,230,000	
Liabilities and Stockholders' Equity			
Current liabilities:			
Accounts payable	$ 250,000	$ 440,000	190,000
Notes payable	400,000	400,000	
Accrued expenses	70,000	50,000	(20,000)
Total current liabilities	720,000	890,000	
Long-term liabilities:			
Bonds payable, 2004.	70,000	120,000	50,000
Total liabilities	790,000	1,010,000	
Stockholders' equity:			
Preferred stock, $100 par value.	90,000	90,000	
Common stock, $1 par value	120,000	120,000	
Capital paid in excess of par	410,000	410,000	
Retained earnings	500,000	600,000	100,000
Total stockholders' equity	1,120,000	1,220,000	
Total liabilities and stockholders' equity.	$1,910,000	$2,230,000	

(The following questions apply to the Crosby Corporation, as presented in problem 15.)

Net income and cash flows

16. Describe the general relationship between net income and net cash flows from operating activities for the firm.

Financing of assets

17. Has the buildup in plant and equipment been financed in a satisfactory manner? Briefly discuss.

Book value

18. Compute the book value per common share for 1993 and 1994 for the Crosby Corporation.

P/E ratio

19. If the market value of a share of common stock is 2.4 times book value for 1994, what is the firm's P/E ratio for 1994?

Selected References

Bierman, Harold, Jr. "Toward a Constant Price-Earnings Ratio." *Financial Analysis Journal* 38 (September–October 1982), pp. 62–65.

Clayman, Michelle. "In Search of Excellence: The Investor's Viewpoint." *Financial Analysts Journal* 43 (May–June 1987), pp. 54–63.

Dharan, Bala G., and Briance Mascarenhas. "Determinants of Accounting Change: An Industry Analysis of Depreciation Change." *Journal of Accounting, Auditing & Finance* 7 (Winter 1992), pp. 1–21.

Haugen, Robert A., and Lemma W. Senbet. "Corporate Finance and Taxes: A Review." *Financial Management* 15 (Winter 1986), pp. 5–21.

Kroll, Yoman. "On the Differences Between Accrual Accounting Figures and Cash Flows: The Case of Working Capital." *Financial Management* 13 (Spring 1985), pp. 33–35.

Lambert, S. J., III., and Christine V. Zavgren. "The Objectives of the Statement of Financial Accounting Concepts No. 1." *Financial Executive,* May 1982, pp. 26–30.

Lee, John Y. "Making Financial and Non-Financial Data Add Up." *Journal of Accountancy* 174 (September 1992), pp. 62–66.

Norby, William C. "Accounting for Financial Analysis." *Financial Analysis Journal* 38 (July–August 1982), pp. 33–35.

Opinions and Statements of the American Institute of Certified Public Accountant (AICPA) and the Financial Accounting Standard Boards (FASB).

Prezas, Alexandros P. "Effects of Depreciation and Corporate Taxes on Asset Life Under Debt-Equity Financing." *Financial Management* 21 (Summer 1992), pp. 24–30.

CHAPTER

3

Financial Analysis

CHAPTER CONCEPTS

Trend Time

1 Ratio analysis provides a meaningful comparison of a company to its industry.

2 Ratios can be used to measure profitability, asset utilization, liquidity, and debt utilization.

3 The Du Pont system of analysis identifies the true sources of return on assets and return to stockholders.

ROA + ROE R to S

4 Trend analysis shows company performance over time.

5 Reported income must be further evaluated to identify sources of distortion.

In Chapter 2, we examined the basic assumptions of accounting and the various components that make up the financial statements of the firm. We now use this fundamental material as a springboard into financial analysis—to evaluate the financial performance of the firm.

The format for the chapter is twofold. In the first part we will use financial ratios to evaluate the relative success of the firm. Various measures such as net income to sales and current assets to current liabilities will be computed for a hypothetical company and examined in light of industry norms and past trends.

In the second part of the chapter we explore the impact of inflation and disinflation on financial operations over the last decade. The student begins to appreciate the impact of rising prices (or at times, declining prices) on the various financial ratios. The chapter concludes with a discussion of how other factors—in addition to price changes—may distort the financial statements of the firm. Terms such as *net income to sales, return on investment,* and *inventory turnover* take on much greater meaning when they are evaluated through the eyes of a financial manager who does more than merely pick out the top or bottom line of an income statement. The examples in the chapter are designed from the viewpoint of a financial manager (with only minor attention to accounting theory).

Ratio Analysis

Ratios are used in much of our daily life. We buy cars based on miles per gallon; we evaluate baseball players by earned run averages and batting averages, basketball players by field goal and foul-shooting percentages, and so on. These are all ratios constructed to judge comparative performance. Financial ratios serve a similar purpose, but you must know what is being measured to construct a ratio and to understand the significance of the resultant number.

Financial ratios are used to weigh and evaluate the operating performance of the firm. While an absolute value such as earnings of $50,000 or accounts receivable of $100,000 may appear satisfactory, its acceptability can be measured only in relation to other values. For this reason, financial managers emphasize ratio analysis.

For example, are earnings of $50,000 actually good? If we earned $50,000 on $500,000 of sales (10 percent "profit margin" ratio), that might be quite satisfactory—whereas earnings of $50,000 on $5,000,000 could be disappointing (a meager 1 percent return). After we have computed the appropriate ratio, we must compare our results to those achieved by similar firms in our industry as well as to our own performance record. Even then, this "number-crunching" process is not fully adequate, and we are forced to supplement our financial findings with an evaluation of company management, physical facilities, and numerous other factors.

For comparative purposes, a number of organizations provide industry data. For example, Dun & Bradstreet compiles data on 800 different lines of business, while Robert Morris Associates provides ratios on over 150 industry classifications. Often the most valuable industry figures come from the various trade organizations to which firms belong (for example, the National Retail Furniture Association or the National Hardware Association).

Many libraries and universities subscribe to financial services such as Standard & Poor's Industry Surveys and Corporate Reports, the Value Line Investment Survey, and Moody's Investment Service. Standard & Poor's also leases a computer data base called Compustat to banks, corporations, investment organizations, and universities. Compustat contains financial statement data on over 3,000 companies for a 20-year period. These data can be used to make countless ratios to measure corporate performance. The ratios used in this text are a sample of the major ratio categories used in business, but other classification systems can also be constructed.

Classification System

We will separate 13 significant ratios into four primary categories.

A. Profitability ratios.
    1. Profit margin.
    2. Return on assets (investment).
    3. Return on equity.
B. Asset utilization ratios.
    4. Receivable turnover.
    5. Average collection period.
    6. Inventory turnover.
    7. Fixed asset turnover.
    8. Total asset turnover.
C. Liquidity ratios.
    9. Current ratio.
    10. Quick ratio.
D. Debt utilization ratios.
    11. Debt to total assets.
    12. Times interest earned.
    13. Fixed charge coverage.

The first grouping, the **profitability ratios,** allows us to measure the ability of the firm to earn an adequate return on sales, total assets, and invested capital. Many of the problems related to profitability can be explained, in whole or in part, by the firm's ability to effectively employ its resources. Thus the next category of ratios is **asset utilization.** Under this heading, we measure the speed at which the firm is turning over accounts receivable, inventory, and longer-term assets. In other words, asset utilization ratios measure how many times per year a company sells its inventory or collects its entire accounts receivable. For long-term assets, the utilization ratio tells us how productive the fixed assets are in terms of generating sales.

In category C, the **liquidity ratios,** the primary emphasis moves to the firm's ability to pay off short-term obligations as they come due. In category D, **debt utilization ratios,** the overall debt position of the firm is evaluated in light of its asset base and earning power.

The users of financial statements will attach different degrees of importance to the four categories of ratios. To the potential investor or security analyst, the critical consideration is profitability, with secondary consideration given to such matters as liquidity and debt utilization. For the banker or trade creditor, the emphasis shifts to the firm's current ability to meet debt obligations. The bondholder, in turn, may be primarily influenced by debt to total assets—while also eyeing the profitability of the firm in terms of its ability to cover debt obligations. Of course, the experienced analyst looks at all the ratios, but with different degrees of attention.

The Analysis

Definitions alone carry little meaning in analyzing or dissecting the financial performance of a company. For this reason, we shall apply our four categories of ratios to a hypothetical firm, the Saxton Company, as presented in Table 3–1. The use of ratio analysis is rather like solving a mystery in which each clue leads to a new area of inquiry.

A. Profitability Ratios   We first look at profitability ratios. The appropriate ratio is computed for the Saxton Company and is then compared to representative industry data.

A. *Profitability Ratios—*

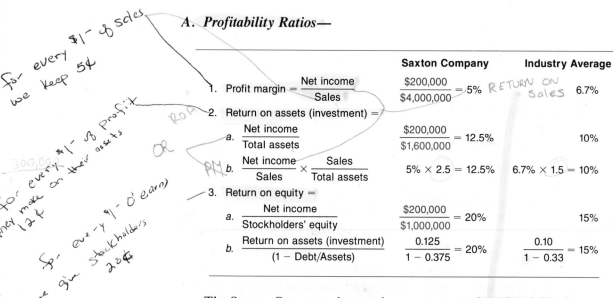

		Saxton Company	Industry Average
1. Profit margin $= \dfrac{\text{Net income}}{\text{Sales}}$		$\dfrac{\$200,000}{\$4,000,000} = 5\%$	6.7%
2. Return on assets (investment) $=$			
a.	$\dfrac{\text{Net income}}{\text{Total assets}}$	$\dfrac{\$200,000}{\$1,600,000} = 12.5\%$	10%
b.	$\dfrac{\text{Net income}}{\text{Sales}} \times \dfrac{\text{Sales}}{\text{Total assets}}$	$5\% \times 2.5 = 12.5\%$	$6.7\% \times 1.5 = 10\%$
3. Return on equity $=$			
a.	$\dfrac{\text{Net income}}{\text{Stockholders' equity}}$	$\dfrac{\$200,000}{\$1,000,000} = 20\%$	15%
b.	$\dfrac{\text{Return on assets (investment)}}{(1 - \text{Debt/Assets})}$	$\dfrac{0.125}{1 - 0.375} = 20\%$	$\dfrac{0.10}{1 - 0.33} = 15\%$

The Saxton Company shows a lower return on the sales dollar (5 percent) than the industry average of 6.7 percent. However, its return on assets (investment) of 12.5 percent exceeds the industry norm of 10 percent. There is only one possible explanation for this occurrence—a more rapid turnover of assets

TABLE 3–1
Financial statement for ratio analysis

SAXTON COMPANY
Income Statement
For the Year Ended December 31, 1994

Sales (all on credit)	$4,000,000
Cost of goods sold	3,000,000
Gross profit	1,000,000
Selling and administrative expense*	450,000
Operating profit	550,000
Interest expense	50,000
Extraordinary loss	200,000
Net income before taxes	300,000
Taxes (33%)	100,000
Net income	$ 200,000

*Includes $50,000 in lease payments. ~~is a fixed chg~~

[handwritten: *Fixed* pointing to Interest expense / Extraordinary loss]

Balance Sheet
As of December 31, 1994
Assets

Cash	$ 30,000
Marketable securities	50,000
Accounts receivable	350,000
Inventory	370,000
Total current assets	800,000
Net plant and equipment	800,000
Total assets	$1,600,000

Liabilities and Stockholders' Equity

Accounts payable	$ 50,000
Notes payable	250,000
Total current liabilities	300,000
Long-term liabilities	300,000
Total liabilities	600,000
Common stock	400,000
Retained earnings	600,000
Total liabilities and stockholders' equity . . .	$1,600,000

[handwritten: total liabilities = 600,000]
[handwritten: total stockholders equity → 1,000,000]

[handwritten right margin: Satisfactory ROA can be achieved through; high PM or rapid turnover of assets TOA]

than that generally found within the industry. This is verified in ratio *2b*, in which sales to total assets is 2.5 for the Saxton Company and only 1.5 for the industry. Thus Saxton earns less on each sales dollar, but it compensates by turning over its assets more rapidly (generating more sales per dollar of assets).

Return on total assets as described through the two components of profit margin and asset turnover is part of the **Du Pont system of analysis.**

$$\text{Return on assets (investment)} = \text{Profit margin} \times \text{Asset turnover}$$

The Du Pont company was a forerunner in stressing that satisfactory return on assets may be achieved through high profit margins or rapid turnover of assets, or a combination of both. We shall also soon observe that under the Du Pont system of analysis, the use of debt may be important. The Du Pont system causes the analyst to examine the sources of a company's profitability. Since the profit margin is an income statement ratio, a high profit margin indicates good cost control, whereas a high asset turnover ratio demonstrates efficient use of the assets on the balance sheet. Different industries have different operating and financial structures. For example, in the heavy capital goods industry the emphasis is on a high profit margin with a low asset turnover—whereas in food processing, the profit margin is low and the key to satisfactory returns on total assets is a rapid turnover of assets.

Equally important to a firm is its return on equity or ownership capital. For the Saxton Company, return on equity is 20 percent, versus an industry norm of 15 percent. Thus the owners of Saxton Company are more amply rewarded than are other shareholders in the industry. This may be the result of one or two factors: a high return on total assets or a generous utilization of debt or a combination thereof. This can be seen through Equation 3b, which represents a modified or second version of the Du Pont formula.

$$\text{Return on equity} = \frac{\text{Return on assets (investment)}}{(1 - \text{Debt/Assets})}$$

Note the numerator, return on assets, is taken from Formula 2, which represents the initial version of the Du Pont formula (Return on assets = Net income/Sales × Sales/Total assets). Return on assets is then divided by $[1 - (\text{Debt/Assets})]$ to account for the amount of debt in the capital structure. In the case of the Saxton Company, the modified version of the Du Pont formula shows:

$$\text{Return on equity} = \frac{\text{Return on assets (investment)}}{(1 - \text{Debt/Assets})}$$

$$= \frac{12.5\%}{1 - 0.375} = 20\%$$

Actually the return on assets of 12.5 percent in the numerator is higher than the industry average of 10 percent, and the ratio of debt to assets in the denominator of 37.5 percent is higher than the industry norm of 33 percent. Both the numerator and denominator contribute to a higher return on equity than the industry average (20 percent versus 15 percent). Note that if the firm had a 50 percent debt-to-assets ratio, return on equity would go up to 25 percent.[1]

$$\text{Return on equity} = \frac{\text{Return on assets (investment)}}{(1 - \text{Debt/Assets})}$$

$$= \frac{12.5\%}{1 - 0.50} = 25\%$$

This does not necessarily mean debt is a positive influence, only that it can be used to boost return on equity. The ultimate goal for the firm is to achieve maximum valuation for its securities in the marketplace, and this goal

---

[1]The return could be slightly different from 25 percent because of changing financial costs with higher debt.

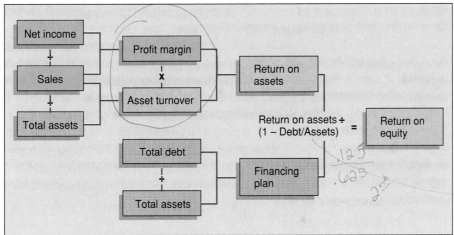

FIGURE 3–1
Du Pont analysis

may or may not be advanced by using debt to increase return on equity. Because debt represents increased risk, a lower valuation of higher earnings is possible.[2] Every situation must be evaluated individually.

The reader may wish to review Figure 3–1, which illustrates the key points in the Du Pont system of analysis.

As an example of the Du Pont analysis, Table 3–2 compares Wal-Mart and Dillard's, two well-known retailers. For 1992 Dillard's was much more profitable in terms of profit margin (4.9 percent versus 3.6 percent). However, Wal-Mart had a 23.4 percent return on equity versus 13 percent for Dillard's. Why the reversal in performance? It comes back to the Du Pont system of analysis. Wal-Mart turned over its assets 3.4 times a year versus a considerably lower 1.3 times for Dillard's. Wal-Mart was following the philosophy of its late founder, Sam Walton—give the customer a bargain in terms of low prices (and low profit margins), but move the merchandise very quickly. Wal-Mart was able to turn a low return on sales (profit margin) to a high return on assets and equity. In terms of debt ratios, the firms were similar (47.9 percent for Wal-Mart and 51.6 percent for Dillard's), so most of the *action* in this example was in asset turnover.

TABLE 3–2   **Position of Wal-Mart versus Dillard's using the Du Pont method of analysis, 1992**

	Profit margin	×	Asset turnover	=	Return on assets	÷	(1 − Debt/Assets)	=	Return on equity
Wal-Mart	3.6%	×	3.4	=	12.2%	÷	(1 − 47.9%)	=	23.4%
Dillard's	4.9%	×	1.3	=	6.4%	÷	(1 − 51.6%)	=	13.0%

Finally as a general statement in computing all the profitability ratios, the analyst must be sensitive to the age of the assets. Plant and equipment purchased 15 years ago may be carried on the books far below its replacement

---

[2]Further discussion of this point is presented in Chapter 5, "Operating and Financial Leverage," and Chapter 10, "Valuation and Rates of Return."

value in an inflationary economy. A 20 percent return on assets purchased in the 1970s may be inferior to a 15 percent return on newly purchased assets.

B. Asset Utilization Ratios   The second category of ratios relates to asset utilization, and the ratios in this category may explain why one firm can turn over its assets more rapidly than another. Notice that all of these ratios relate the balance sheet (assets) to the income statement (sales). The Saxton Company's rapid turnover of assets is explained in ratios 4, 5, and 6.

B. Asset Utilization Ratios—

how fast we collect our receivables

	Saxton Company	Industry Average
4. Receivables turnover = $\dfrac{\text{Sales (credit)}}{\text{Receivables}}$	$\dfrac{\$4,000,000}{\$350,000} = 11.4$	10 times
5. Average collection period = $\dfrac{\text{Accounts receivable}}{\text{Average daily credit sales}}$	$\dfrac{\$350,000}{\$11,111} = 32$	36 days
6. Inventory turnover = $\dfrac{\text{Sales}}{\text{Inventory}}$	$\dfrac{\$4,000,000}{\$370,000} = 10.8$	7 times
7. Fixed asset turnover = $\dfrac{\text{Sales}}{\text{Fixed assets}}$	$\dfrac{\$4,000,000}{\$800,000} = 5$	5.4 times
8. Total asset turnover = $\dfrac{\text{Sales}}{\text{Total assets}}$	$\dfrac{\$4,000,000}{\$1,600,000} = 2.5$	1.5 times

Handwritten margin notes:

Sales on credit / 360 days

$\dfrac{\text{Sales on credit}}{360} = \dfrac{4,000,000}{360} = 11,111$

Fixed assets — non-movable
Equipment
Land
Buildings
improvements

Saxton collects its receivables faster than does the industry. This is shown by receivables turnover of 11.4 times versus 10 times for the industry, and in daily terms by the average collection period of 32 days, which is 4 days faster than that of the industry norm. The average collection period suggests how long, on average, our customers' accounts stay on our books. The Saxton Company has $350,000 in accounts receivable and $4,000,000 in credit sales, which when divided by 360 days yields average daily credit sales of $11,111. We divide accounts receivable of $350,000 by average daily credit sales of $11,111 to determine how many days that credit sales are on the books (32 days).

In addition the firm turns over its inventory 10.8 times per year as contrasted with an industry average of 7 times.[3] This tells us that Saxton generates more sales per dollar of inventory than the average company in the industry does, and we can assume the firm uses very efficient inventory-ordering and cost-control methods.

---

[3]This ratio may also be computed by using "cost of goods sold" in the numerator. While this offers some theoretical advantages in terms of using cost figures in both the numerator and denominator, Dun & Bradstreet and other credit reporting agencies generally show turnover as in ratio 6.

The firm maintains a slightly lower ratio of sales to fixed assets (plant and equipment) than does the industry (5 versus 5.4). This is a relatively minor consideration in view of the rapid movement of inventory and accounts receivable. Finally, the rapid turnover of total assets is again indicated (2.5 versus 1.5).

C. Liquidity Ratios   After considering profitability and asset utilization, the analyst needs to examine the liquidity of the firm. The Saxton Company's liquidity ratios fare well in comparison with the industry. Further analysis might call for a cash budget to determine if we can meet each maturing obligation as it comes due.

C. *Liquidity Ratios—*

	Saxton Company	Industry Average
9. Current ratio =		
$\dfrac{\text{Current assets}}{\text{Current liabilities}}$	$\dfrac{\$800,000}{\$300,000} = 2.67$	2.1
10. Quick ratio =		
$\dfrac{\text{Current assets} - \text{Inventory}}{\text{Current liabilities}}$	$\dfrac{\$430,000}{\$300,000} = 1.43$	1.0

D.   Debt Utilization Ratios   The last grouping of ratios, debt utilization, allows the analyst to measure the prudence of the debt management policies of the firm.

Debt to total assets of 37.5 percent as shown in Equation 11 is slightly above the industry average of 33 percent, but well within the prudent range of 50 percent or less. One of the ways to benefit from an inflationary economy is through the use of heavy long-term debt, enabling long-standing obligations to be repaid in inflated dollars with the passage of time.

D. *Debt Utilization Ratios—*   or leverage is debt

[handwritten: Financing Plan — how much debt con to O' still have to operating profit a profit]

	Saxton Company	Industry Average
11. Debt to total assets =		
$\dfrac{\text{Total debt}}{\text{Total assets}}$	$\dfrac{\$600,000}{\$1,600,000} = 37.5\%$	33%
12. Times interest earned =		
$\dfrac{\text{Income before interest and taxes}}{\text{Interest}}$	$\dfrac{\$550,000}{\$50,000} = 11$	7 times
13. Fixed charge coverage =		
$\dfrac{\text{Income before fixed charges and taxes}}{\text{Fixed charges}}$	$\dfrac{\$600,000}{\$100,000} = 6$	5.5 times

[handwritten annotations: financing 37.5% of total assets; can O' meet interest pymts operating profit + fixed chg's; For every $1 income 11¢ goes to int. exp]

Ratios for times interest earned and fixed charge coverage show that the Saxton Company debt is being well managed compared to the debt management of other firms in the industry. Times interest earned indicates the number of times that our income before interest and taxes covers the interest obligation (11 times). The higher the ratio, the stronger is the interest-paying ability of the firm. The figure for income before interest and taxes in the ratio is the equivalent of the operating profit figure presented in Table 3–1.

Fixed charge coverage measures the firm's ability to meet all fixed obligations rather than interest payments alone, on the assumption that failure to meet any financial obligation will endanger the position of the firm. In the present case the Saxton Company has lease obligations of $50,000 as well as the $50,000 in interest expenses. Thus the total fixed charge financial obligation is $100,000. We also need to know the income before all fixed charge obligations. In this case we take income before interest and taxes (operating profit) and add back the $50,000 in lease payments.

usually leased pymts

Income before interest and taxes.	$550,000
Lease payments	50,000
Income before fixed charges and taxes. . . .	$600,000

The fixed charges are safely covered 6 times, exceeding the industry norm of 5.5 times. The various ratios are summarized in Table 3–3. The conclusions reached in comparing the Saxton Company to industry averages are generally valid, though exceptions may exist. For example, a high inventory turnover is considered "good" unless it is achieved by maintaining unusually low inventory levels, which may hurt future profitability.

TABLE 3–3 **Ratio analysis**

	Saxton Company	Industry Average	Conclusion
A. Profitability			
1. Net income to sales.	5%	6.7%	Below average
2. Net income to total assets	12.5%	10%	Above average due to high turnover
3. Net income to stockholders' equity . . .	20%	15%	Good due to ratios 2 and 10
B. Asset Utilization			
4. Receivables turnover	11.4	10	Good
5. Average collection period	32	36	Good
6. Inventory turnover	10.8	7	Good
7. Fixed asset turnover	5	5.4	Below average
8. Total asset turnover.	2.5	1.5	Good
C. Liquidity			
9. Current ratio	2.67	2.1	Good
10. Quick ratio	1.43	1.0	Good
D. Debt Utilization			
11. Debt to total assets	37.5%	33%	Slightly more debt
12. Times interest earned.	11	7	Good
13. Fixed charge coverage	6	5.5	Good

In summary, the Saxton Company more than compensates for a lower return on the sales dollar by a rapid turnover of assets, principally inventory and receivables, and a wise use of debt. The student should be able to use these 13 measures to evaluate the financial performance of any firm.

Trend Analysis

Over the course of the business cycle, sales and profitability may expand and contract, and ratio analysis for any one year may not present an accurate picture of the firm. Therefore we look at **trend analysis** of performance over a number of years. However, without industry comparisons even trend analysis may not present a complete picture. For example, in Figure 3–2 we see that the profit margin for the Saxton Company has improved, while asset turnover has declined. This by itself may look good for the profit margin and bad for asset turnover. However, when compared to industry trends, we see the firm's

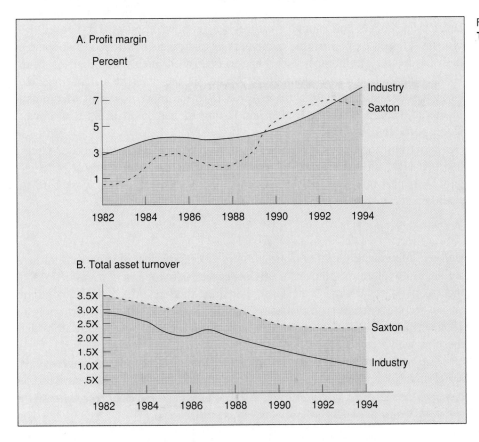

FIGURE 3–2
Trend analysis

profit margin is still below the industry average. On asset turnover, Saxton has improved in relation to the industry even though it is in a downward trend. Similar data could be generated for the other ratios.

By comparing companies in the same industry, the analyst can analyze trends over time. In looking at data in Table 3–4 on the computer industry, it

TABLE 3–4
**Trend analysis in the
computer industry**

		Apple		Compaq		IBM	
		Profit Margin	Return on Equity	Profit Margin	Return on Equity	Profit Margin	Return on Equity
	1983	7.8%	20.3%	2.3%	2.9%	13.7%	23.6%
	1984	3.9	12.7	3.9	11.8	14.3	24.8
	1985	3.2	11.1	5.3	19.9	13.1	20.5
	1986	8.1	22.2	6.9	23.4	9.3	13.9
	1987	8.2	26.0	10.9	33.4	9.7	13.7
	1988	9.8	39.9	12.0	30.5	9.8	14.7
	1989	7.7	27.3	11.1	27.2	8.4	13.6
	1990	8.5	32.8	12.0	23.2	8.7	14.1
	1991	7.1	25.4	7.0	11.8	3.2	5.7
	1992	7.0	23.2	4.5	8.0	Deficit	

is evident that Apple Computer is the star performer over time in comparison to Compaq and IBM. This is particularly evident in 1991 and 1992. Compaq's relatively poor results were caused by fierce competition in its desktop and laptop models and supply shortages for its new products. IBM faced declining sales on its mainframe computers as customers continued to downsize their hardware. The company also had to deal with intense competition from IBM-compatible personal computers. Apple, on the other hand, continued to enjoy a successful transition from Apple II to the more powerful Macintosh in the educational market. It also had strong movement with its new Power Book portable computer.

What will the trends be for these companies for the rest of decade? Compaq and IBM are taking radical moves to restructure their companies to regain their past profitability. Apple, obviously, will also have to work hard to maintain its profitable trends.

Impact of Inflation on Financial Analysis

Before, coincident with, or following the computation of financial ratios, we should explore the impact of **inflation** and other sources of distortion on the financial reporting of the firm. As illustrated in this section, inflation causes phantom sources of profit that may mislead even the most alert analyst. **Disinflation** also causes certain problems and we shall eventually consider these as well.

The major problem during inflationary times is that revenue is almost always stated in current dollars, whereas plant and equipment or inventory may have been purchased at lower price levels. Thus profit may be more a function of increasing prices than of satisfactory performance.

An Illustration

The Stein Corporation shows the accompanying income statement for 1993 (Table 3–5). At year-end the firm also has 100 units still in inventory at $1 per unit and $200 worth of plant and equipment with a 20-year life.

TABLE 3-5

STEIN CORPORATION
Net Income for 1993

Sales	$200 (100 units at $2)
Cost of goods sold.	100 (100 units at $1)
Gross profit	100
Selling and administrative expense. . . .	20 (10% of ratio)
Depreciation.	10
Operating profit	70
Taxes (40%)	28
Aftertax income	$ 42

Assume that in 1994 the number of units sold remains constant at 100. However, inflation causes a 10 percent increase in price, from $2 to $2.20. Total sales will go up to $220 as shown in Table 3–6, but with no actual increase in physical volume. Further assume the firm uses FIFO inventory pricing, so that inventory first purchased will be written off against current sales. In this case 1993 inventory will be written off against 1994 sales revenue.

TABLE 3-6

STEIN CORPORATION
Net Income for 1994

Sales	$220 (100 units at 1994 price of $2.20)
Cost of goods sold	100 (100 units at $1.00)
Gross profit	120
Selling and administrative expense	22 (10% of sales)
Depreciation	10
Operating profit	88
Taxes (40%)	35
Aftertax income	$ 53

In Table 3–6, the company appears to have increased profit by $11 simply as a result of inflation. But not reflected is the increased cost of replacing inventory and plant and equipment. Presumably, their **replacement costs** have increased in an inflationary environment.

As mentioned in Chapter 2, inflation-related information was formerly required by the FASB for large companies, but this is no longer the case. It is now purely voluntary. What are the implications of this type of inflation adjusted data? From a study of 10 chemical firms and eight drug companies, using current cost (replacement cost) data found in the financial 10K statements that these companies filed with the Securities and Exchange Commission, it was found that the changes shown in Table 3–7 occurred in their assets, income, and selected ratios.[4]

---

[4]Jeff Garnett and Geoffrey A. Hirt, "Replacement Cost Data: A Study of the Chemical and Drug Industry for Years 1976 through 1978." Replacement cost is but one form of current cost. Nevertheless, it is often used as a measure of current cost.

3

FINANCE IN ACTION

With the New Accounting Rule on Retirement Benefits, Will Companies Have to Replace People with Machines?

When the Financial Accounting Standards Board announced FASB 106 on retirement benefits, a shock ran through the financial community. The rule by the board that oversees the practices of accountants stated that companies must expense charges for retirees' medical and life insurance benefits as they are earned by employees. Previously, such benefits were deducted from income when they were actually paid. As an example, if you are 25 years old and working for a company that provides retirement benefits, the firm must recognize its future obligations to you as a current charge because you are earning the benefits now, not when you are 70 years old.

General DataComm, a communications equipment maker, has been in business for slightly over 20 years and has but six retirees from a work force of 1,700. Normally retirement charges for six people would be minimal, but now the firm must currently recognize earned retirement benefits for the full work force.

And that's only part of FASB 106. The other part says companies must set up a huge catch-up reserve for failing to take such action in the past. Companies were allowed to take this write-down fully in 1991 or 1992 or begin spreading it out over 20 years starting in 1993. General Motors decided to take a $22.2 billion onetime charge. Others are using the full 20-year period.

The two parts of FASB 106 will have the largest impact on corporate profits of any accounting pronouncement in history! The reduction to profits may reach $1 trillion over the next few years.*

Companies particularly hard hit are in labor-intensive industries such as airlines, aerospace, automobiles, chemicals, machinery, metal, and steel.

The solutions may be to continue to replace people with machinery or to reduce retirement benefits to the current work force.

*"New Medical-Benefits Accounting Rule Seen Wounding Profits, Hurting Shares," *The Wall Street Journal,* April 22, 1991, p. C1.

TABLE 3–7   **Comparison of replacement cost accounting and historical cost accounting**

	10 Chemical Companies		8 Drug Companies	
	Replacement Cost	Historical Cost	Replacement Cost	Historical Cost
Increase in assets	28.4%	—	15.4%	—
Decrease in net income before taxes.	45.8%	—	19.3%	—
Return on assets	2.8%	6.2%	8.3%	11.4%
Return on equity.	4.9%	13.5%	12.8%	19.6%
Debt-to-assets ratio	34.3%	43.8%	30.3%	35.2%
Interest coverage ratio (times interest earned).	7.1×	8.4×	15.4×	16.7×

The comparison of replacement cost and historical cost accounting methods in the table shows that replacement cost reduces income but at the same time increases assets. This increase in assets lowers the debt-to-assets ratio since debt is a monetary asset that is not revalued because it is paid back in nominal dollars. The decreased debt-to-assets ratio would indicate the financial leverage of the firm is decreased, but a look at the interest coverage ratio tells a different story. Because the interest coverage ratio measures the operating income available to cover interest expense, the declining income penalizes this ratio and the firm has decreased its ability to cover its interest cost.

Disinflation Effect

As long as prices continue to rise in an inflationary environment, profits appear to feed on themselves. The main objection is that when price increases moderate (disinflation), there will be a rude awakening for management and unsuspecting stockholders as expensive inventory is charged against softening retail prices. A 15 or 20 percent growth rate in earnings may be little more than an "inflationary illusion." Industries most sensitive to inflation-induced profits are those with cyclical products, such as lumber, copper, rubber, and food products, and also those in which inventory is a significant percentage of sales and profits.

A leveling off of prices is not necessarily bad. Even though inflation-induced corporate profits may be going down, investors may be more willing to place their funds in financial assets such as stocks and bonds. The reason for the shift may be a belief that declining inflationary pressures will no longer seriously impair the purchasing power of the dollar. Lessening inflation means the required return that investors demand on financial assets will be going down, and with this lower demanded return, future earnings or interest should receive a higher current valuation.

None of the above happens with a high degree of certainty. To the extent that investors question the permanence of disinflation (leveling off of price increases), they may not act according to the script. That is, lower rates of inflation will not necessarily produce high stock and bond prices unless the price pattern appears sustainable over a reasonable period.

Whereas financial assets such as stocks and bonds have the potential (whether realized or not) to do well during disinflation, such is not the case for tangible (real) assets. Precious metals, such as gold and silver, gems, and collectibles, that boomed in the highly inflationary environment of the late 1970s fell off sharply in the mid-1980s, as softening prices caused less perceived need to hold real assets as a hedge against inflation. The shifting back and forth by investors between financial and real assets may occur many times over a business cycle.

Other Elements of Distortion in Reported Income

The effect of changing prices is but one of a number of problems the analyst must cope with in evaluating a company. Other issues, such as the reporting of revenue, the treatment of nonrecurring items, and the tax write-off policy, cause dilemmas for the financial manager or analyst. The point may be illustrated by considering the income statements for two hypothetical companies in the same industry (Table 3–8). Both firms had identical operating performances for 1994—but Company A is very conservative in reporting its results, while Company B has attempted to maximize its reported income.

TABLE 3–8

Income Statement For the Year 1994	Conservative A	High Reported Income B
Sales.	$4,000,000	$4,200,000
Cost of goods sold	3,000,000	2,700,000
Gross profit.	1,000,000	1,500,000
Selling and administrative expense	450,000	450,000
Operating profit.	550,000	1,050,000
Interest expense	50,000	50,000
Extraordinary loss	100,000	—
Net income before taxes	400,000	1,000,000
Taxes (30%)	120,000	300,000
Net income.	280,000	700,000
Extraordinary loss (net of tax)	—	70,000
Net income transferred to retained earnings. . . .	$ 280,000	$ 630,000

If both companies had reported income of $280,000 in the prior year of 1993, Company B would be thought to be showing substantial growth in 1994 with net income of $700,000, while Company A is reporting a "flat" or no-growth year in 1994. However, we have already established that the companies have equal operating performance.

Explanation of Discrepancies

Let us examine how the inconsistencies in Table 3–8 could occur. Emphasis is given to a number of key elements on the income statement.

Sales Company B reported $200,000 more in sales, although actual volume was the same. This may be the result of different concepts of revenue recognition.

For example, certain assets may be sold on an installment basis over a long period. A conservative firm may defer recognition of the sales or revenue until each payment is received, while other firms may attempt to recognize a fully effected sale at the earliest possible date. Similarly, firms that lease assets may attempt to consider a long-term lease as the equivalent of a sale, while more conservative firms, such as IBM or Digital Equipment, only recognize as revenue each lease payment as it comes due. Although the accounting profession attempts to establish appropriate methods of financial reporting through generally accepted accounting principles, there is variation of reporting among firms.

Cost of Goods Sold   The conservative firm (Company A) may well be using **LIFO** accounting in an inflationary environment, thus charging the last-purchased, more expensive items against sales, while Company B uses **FIFO** accounting—charging off less expensive inventory against sales. The $300,000 difference in cost of goods sold may also be explained by varying treatment of research and development costs and other items.

Extraordinary Gain/Losses   Nonrecurring gains or losses may occur from the sale of corporate fixed assets, lawsuits, or similar nonrecurring events. Some analysts argue that such extraordinary events should be included in computing the current income of the firm, while others would leave them off in assessing operating performance. Unfortunately, there is inconsistency in the way nonrecurring losses are treated despite attempts by the accounting profession to ensure uniformity. The conservative Firm A has written off its $100,000 extraordinary loss against normally reported income, while Firm B carries a subtraction against net income only after the $700,000 amount has been reported. Both had similar losses of $100,000, but Firm B's is shown net of tax implications at $70,000.

Extraordinary gains and losses occur among large companies more often than you might think. In the 1980s (1983–85) Chrysler Corporation was a good example of a firm whose earnings had been affected by tax loss carry forwards from the accumulated losses of more than $3.5 billion suffered during 1978–82. Chevron had nonrecurring per-share losses of 24 cents in 1982, 50 cents in 1983, 46 cents in 1984, and 56 cents in 1986. These losses arose from its consolidation and disposition of assets when it acquired the Gulf Oil Corporation. In this age of mergers, tender offers, and buyouts, understanding the finer points of financial statements becomes even more important.

Net Income

Firm A has reported net income of $280,000, while Firm B claims $700,000 before subtraction of extraordinary losses. The $420,000 difference is attributed to different methods of financial reporting, and it should be recognized as such by the analyst. No superior performance has actually taken place. The analyst must remain ever alert in examining each item in the financial statements, rather than accepting bottom-line figures.

Blockbuster Entertainment Example

One of the classic examples of discrepancies in financial reporting was provided by Blockbuster Entertainment Corporation in 1988. Blockbuster Entertainment is the country's most popular chain distributor of videocassettes. Lee Seidler, a respected analyst for Bear Sterns and Company (stock brokerage house), actually demonstrated that the reported earnings per share of the company of $.57 in the "outstanding" year of 1988 would have been only $.07

if more appropriate accounting practices had been used. The firm not only stretched the accounting rules to the limit to report maximum revenue from store franchising fees and product sales to franchisees, but it also amortized goodwill and other costs over an unreasonably long time to bolster reported earnings. On the day the critical report by Seidler came out, Blockbuster Entertainment's stock dropped 20 percent. You might ask, "What accounting firm audited and certified such financial statements?" The answer is Arthur Andersen & Co., the world's second largest accounting firm.

Summary

The subject of financial analysis is divided into two categories: an examination of ratio analysis and a study of the shortcomings in reported financial data from the viewpoint of a financial manager. Under ratio analysis, we develop four categories of ratios: profitability, asset utilization, liquidity, and debt utilization. Each ratio for the firm should be compared to industry measures and analyzed in light of past trends. The use of ratio analysis is rather like the solving of a mystery in which each clue leads to a new area of inquiry.

One particularly important ratio technique is the Du Pont system of analysis, which identifies the factors influencing return on assets and return on stockholders' equity.

Financial analysis also calls for an awareness of the impact of inflation and disinflation on the reported income of the firm. Inflation leads to phantom profits, which are created as a result of buying goods and reselling them at inflation-induced higher prices. The process is further magnified by the use of FIFO accounting, in which older inventory items are costed against current prices. Alternate methods of financial reporting may allow firms with equal performance to report different results.

List of Terms

profitability ratios 53
asset utilization ratios 53
liquidity ratios 54
debt utilization ratios 54
Du Pont system of analysis 55
trend analysis 61

inflation 62
disinflation 62
replacement costs 63
LIFO 67
FIFO 67

Discussion Questions

1. If we divide users of ratios into short-term lenders, long-term lenders, and stockholders, which ratios would each group be *most* interested in, and for what reasons?

2. Inflation can have significant effects on income statements and balance sheets, and therefore on the calculation of ratios. Discuss the possible impact of inflation on the following ratios, and explain the direction of the impact based on your assumptions.

   a. Return on investment.

   b. Inventory turnover.

   c. Fixed asset turnover.

   d. Debt-to-assets ratio.

3. Explain how the Du Pont system of analysis breaks down return on assets. Also explain how it breaks down return on stockholders' equity.

4. What advantage does the fixed charge coverage ratio offer over simply using times interest earned?

5. Is there any validity in rule-of-thumb ratios for all corporations, for example, a current ratio of 2 to 1 or debt to assets of 50 percent?

6. Why is trend analysis helpful in analyzing ratios?

7. What effect will disinflation following a highly inflationary period have on the reported income of the firm?

8. Why might disinflation prove to be favorable to financial assets?

9. Comparisons of income can be very difficult for two companies even though they sell the same products in equal volume. Why?

Problems

1. Bass Chemical, Inc., is considering expanding into a new product line. New assets to support this expansion will cost $800,000. It is estimated that Bass can generate $2 million in annual sales, with a 5 percent profit margin. What would net income and return on assets (investment) for the year be?

   Profitability ratios

2. Fonda Pistol and Gun Shop can open a new store that will do an annual volume of $750,000. It will turn over its assets 2.5 times per year. The profit margin on sales will be 6 percent. What would net income and return on assets (investment) for the year be?

   Profitability ratios

3. Gates Appliances has a return on assets (investment) ratio of 8 percent.

   a. If the debt-to-total-assets ratio is 40 percent, what is the return on equity?

   b. If the firm had no debt, what would the return on equity ratio be?

   Profitability ratios

4. Using the Du Pont method, please evaluate the effects of the following relationships for the Butters Corporation.

   a. Butters Corporation has a profit margin of 7 percent and its return on assets (investment) is 25.2 percent. What is its assets turnover?

   Du Pont system of analysis

b. If Butters Corporation has a debt-to-total-assets ratio of 50 percent, what would the firm's return on equity be?

c. What would happen to the return on equity if the debt-to-total-assets ratio decreased to 35 percent?

Profitability ratios

5. Baker Oats had an asset turnover of 1.6 times per year.

a. If the return on total assets (investment) was 11.2 percent, what was Baker's profit margin?

b. The following year, on the same level of assets, Baker's assets turnover declined to 1.4 times and its profit margin was 8 percent. How did the return on total assets change from that of the previous year?

Du Pont system of analysis

6. Joe Jackson's Shoe Stores, Inc., has $2,000,000 in sales and turns over its assets 2.5 times per year. The firm earns 3.8 percent on each sales dollar. It has $60,000 in current liabilities and $140,000 in long-term liabilities.

a. What is its return on stockholders' equity?

b. If the asset base remains the same as computed in part *a*, but total asset turnover goes up to 3, what will be the new return on stockholders' equity? Assume the profit margin stays the same as does current and long-term liabilities.

Average collection period

7. A firm has sales of $3 million, and 10 percent of the sales are for cash. The year-end accounts receivable balance is $285,000. What is the average collection period? (Use a 360-day year.)

Average daily rates

8. Martin Electronics has accounts receivable turnover equal to 15 times. If accounts receivable are $80,000, what is the value for average daily credit sales?

Overall ratio analysis

9. The balance sheet for Stud Clothiers is given below. Sales for the year were $2,400,000, with 90 percent of sales sold on credit.

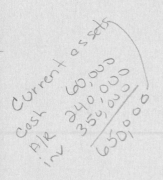

STUD CLOTHIERS
Balance Sheet 199X

Assets		Liabilities and Equity	
Cash.	$ 60,000	Accounts payable.	$ 220,000
Accounts receivable . .	240,000	Accrued taxes	30,000
Inventory.	350,000	Bonds payable	
Plant and equipment . .	410,000	(long term)	150,000
		Common stock	80,000
		Paid-in capital	200,000
		Retained earnings	380,000
		Total liabilities and	
Total assets	$1,060,000	equity	$1,060,000

Compute the following ratios:

a. Current ratio.

b. Quick ratio.

c. Debt-to-total-assets ratio.

d. Asset turnover.

e. Average collection period.

10. Neeley Office Supplies income statement is given below.   Debt utilization ratios

   a. What is the times interest earned ratio?

   b. What would be the fixed charge coverage ratio?

NEELEY OFFICE SUPPLIES	
Sales.	$200,000
Cost of goods sold	115,000
Gross profit.	85,000
Fixed charges (other than interest) . . .	25,000
Income before interest and taxes	60,000
Interest.	15,000
Income before taxes	45,000
Taxes	15,300
Income after taxes	$ 29,700

11. Using the income statement for Paste Management Company, compute the following ratios: Debt utilization and Du Pont system of analysis

   a. The interest coverage.

   b. The fixed charge coverage.

The total assets for this company equal $80,000. Set up the equation for the Du Pont system of ratio analysis and compute *c*, *d*, and *e*.

   c. Profit margin.

   d. Total asset turnover.

   e. Return on assets (investment).

PASTE MANAGEMENT COMPANY	
Sales.	$126,000
Less: Cost of goods sold	93,000
Gross profit	33,000
Less: Selling and administrative expense . . .	11,000
Less: Lease expense	4,000
Operating profit*	$ 18,000
Less: Interest expense	3,000
Earnings before taxes.	$ 15,000
Less: Taxes (30%)	4,500
Earnings after taxes	$ 10,500

*Equals income before interest and taxes

12. A firm has net income before taxes of $120,000 and interest expense of $24,000.   Debt utilization

   a. What is the times interest earned ratio?

   b. If the firm's lease payments are $40,000, what is the fixed charge coverage?

Return on assets analysis   13. In January 1984 the Status Quo Company was formed. Total assets were $500,000, of which $300,000 consisted of depreciable fixed assets. Status Quo uses straight-line depreciation, and in 1984 it estimated its fixed assets to have useful lives of 10 years. Aftertax income has been $26,000 per year each of the last 10 years. Other assets have not changed since 1984.

    a. Compute return on assets at year-end for 1984, 1986, 1989, 1991, and 1993. (Use $26,000 in the numerator for each year.)

    b. To what do you attribute the phenomenon shown in part *a?*

    c. Now assume income increased by 10 percent each year. What effect would this have on your above answers? Comment.

Trend analysis   14. Calloway Products has the following data. Industry information is also shown.

Year	Net Income	Total Assets	Industry Data on Net Income/Total Assets
1992	$360,000	$3,000,000	11%
1993	380,000	3,400,000	8
1994	380,000	3,800,000	5

Year	Debt	Total Assets	Industry Data on Debt/Total Assets
1992	$1,600,000	$3,000,000	52%
1993	1,750,000	3,400,000	40
1994	1,900,000	3,800,000	31

As an industry analyst comparing the firm to the industry, are you likely to praise or criticize the firm in terms of:

    a. Net income/total assets.

    b. Debt/total assets.

Analysis by divisions   15. The United World Corporation has three subsidiaries.

	Computers	Magazines	Cable TV
Sales	$16,000,000	$4,000,000	$8,000,000
Net income (after taxes) . . .	1,000,000	160,000	600,000
Assets.	5,000,000	2,000,000	5,000,000

    a. Which division has the lowest return on sales?

    b. Which division has the highest return on assets?

    c. Compute the return on assets for the entire corporation.

    d. If the $5,000,000 investment in the Cable TV division is sold and redeployed in the computer subsidiary at the same rate of return on assets currently achieved in the computer division, what will be the new return on assets for the entire corporation?

16. Bard Corporation shows the following income statement. The firm uses FIFO inventory accounting.

Inflation and inventory accounting effect

BARD CORPORATION
Income Statement for 1993

Sales	$200,000 (10,000 units at $20)
Cost of goods sold	100,000 (10,000 units at $10)
Gross profit	100,000
Selling and administrative expense. . . .	10,000
Depreciation	20,000
Operating profit	70,000
Taxes (30%)	21,000
Aftertax income	$ 49,000

---

a. Assume in 1994 the same 10,000 unit volume is maintained, but the sales price increases by 10 percent. Because of FIFO inventory policy, old inventory will still be charged off at $10 per unit. Also assume that selling and administrative expense will be 5 percent of sales and depreciation will be unchanged. The tax rate is 30 percent. Compute aftertax income for 1994.

b. In part a, by what percent did aftertax income increase as a result of a 10 percent increase in the sales price? Explain why this impact occurred.

c. Now assume in 1995 the volume remains constant at 10,000 units, but that the sales price decreases by 15 percent from its 1994 level. Also, because of FIFO inventory policy, cost of goods sold reflects the inflationary conditions of the prior year and is $11 per unit. Further assume that selling and administrative expense will be 5 percent of sales and depreciation will be unchanged. The tax rate is 30 percent. Compute aftertax income.

17. Construct the current assets section of the balance sheet from the following data. (Use cash as a plug figure after computing the other values.)

Using ratios to construct financial statements

Yearly sales (credit)	$720,000
Inventory turnover	6 times
Current liabilities	$105,000
Current ratio	2
Quick ratio	1
Average collection period	35 days

Current assets:
Cash	$_____
Accounts receivable	_____
Inventory	_____
Total current assets . . .	_____

Using ratios to construct
financial statements

18. The Griggs Corporation has credit sales of $1,200,000. Given the following ratios, fill in the balance sheet below.

Total assets turnover	2.4 times
Cash to total assets	2.0%
Accounts receivable turnover . . .	8.0 times
Inventory turnover	10.0 times
Current ratio	2.0 times
Debt to total assets	61.0%

GRIGGS CORPORATION
Balance Sheet 199X

Assets		Liabilities and Stockholders' Equity	
Cash.	_____	Current debt	_____
Accounts receivable	_____	Long-term debt	_____
Inventory.	_____	Total debt	_____
Total current assets . . .	_____	Equity	_____
Fixed assets	_____	Total debt and	_____
Total assets	_____	stockholders' equity . . .	_____

Using ratios to determine
account balances

19. We are given the following information for Coleman Machine Tools Corporation.

Sales (credit)	$7,200,000
Cash	300,000
Inventory	2,150,000
Current liabilities	1,400,000
Asset turnover	1.20 times
Current ratio	2.50 times
Debt-to-assets ratios . . .	40%
Receivables turnover . . .	8 times

Current assets are composed of cash, marketable securities, accounts receivable, and inventory. Calculate the following balance sheet items:

a. Accounts receivable.

b. Marketable securities.

c. Fixed assets.

d. Long-term debt.

Using ratios to construct
financial statements

20. The following data are from Sharon Stone, Inc., financial statements. The firm manufactures home decorative material. Sales (all credit) were $60 million for 1993.

Sales to total assets	3.0 times
Total debt to total assets . . .	40%
Current ratio	2.0 times
Inventory turnover	10.0 times
Average collection period . . .	18.0 days
Fixed asset turnover	7.5 times

Fill in the brief balance sheet:

Cash.	_____	Current debt	_____
Accounts receivable	_____	Long-term debt	_____
Inventory.	_____	Total debt	_____
Total current assets . . .	_____	Equity	_____
Fixed assets	_____	Total debt and	_____
Total assets	_____	stockholders' equity . . .	_____

21. Using the financial statements of the Hot Air Company, calculate the 13 basic ratios found in the chapter.

Computing all the ratios

THE HOT AIR COMPANY
Balance Sheet
December 31, 1993

Assets

Current assets:	
Cash	$ 40,000
Marketable securities	30,000
Accounts receivable (net)	120,000
Inventory	180,000
Total current assets	$370,000
Investments.	40,000
Plant and equipment	450,000
Less: Accumulated depreciation.	(100,000)
Net plant and equipment	350,000
Total assets.	$760,000

Liabilities and Stockholders' Equity

Current liabilities:	
Accounts payable.	$ 90,000
Notes payable	10,000
Accrued taxes	10,000
Total current liabilities	110,000
Long-term liabilities:	
Bonds payable	170,000
Total liabilities	280,000
Stockholders' equity	
Preferred stock, $100 par value	90,000
Common stock, $1 par value	60,000
Capital paid in excess of par	230,000
Retained earnings	100,000
Total stockholders' equity.	480,000
Total liabilities and stockholders' equity	$760,000

THE HOT AIR COMPANY
Income Statement
For the Year Ending December 31, 1993

Sales (on credit)	$2,000,000
Less: Cost of goods sold	1,300,000
Gross profit.	700,000
Less: Selling and administrative expenses . . .	400,000*
Operating profit (EBIT)	300,000
Less: Interest expense	20,000
Earnings before taxes (EBT)	280,000
Less: Taxes.	112,000
Earnings after taxes (EAT)	$ 168,000

*Includes $10,000 in lease payments.

Ratio computation and
analysis

22. Given the financial statements for Turner Corporation and Brady Corporation shown here:

    a. To which one would you, as credit manager for a supplier, approve the extension of (short-term) trade credit? Why? Compute all ratios before answering.

    b. In which one would you buy stock? Why?

TURNER CORPORATION

Current Assets			**Liabilities**	
Cash	$ 5,000		Accounts payable	$110,000
Accounts receivable.	90,000		Bonds payable—(long-term) . .	80,000
Inventory	55,000			

Long-Term Assets			**Stockholders' Equity**	
Fixed assets	$600,000		Common stock	$140,000
Less: Accumulated depreciation	(150,000)		Paid-in capital	70,000
Net fixed assets.	450,000		Retained earnings	200,000
			Total liabilities and	
Total assets.	$600,000		stockholders' equity. . . .	$600,000

Sales (on credit)	$1,500,000
Cost of goods sold	1,000,000
Gross profit	500,000
Selling and administrative expense . . .	244,500*
Less: Depreciation expense	50,000
Operating profit	205,500
Interest expense	8,000
Earnings before taxes	197,500
Tax expense (40%)	79,000
Net income	$ 118,500

*Includes $9,000 in lease payments.

---

*Turner Corporation has 75,000 shares outstanding.

BRADY CORPORATION

Current Assets			Liabilities	
Cash	$ 30,000		Accounts payable	$ 75,000
Marketable securities	7,500		Bonds payable—10%	
Accounts receivable	70,000		(long-term)	210,000
Inventory	72,500			

Long-Term Assets			Stockholders' Equity	
Fixed assets	$500,000		Common stock	$ 75,000
Less: Accumulated depreciation	(250,000)		Paid-in capital	30,000
Net fixed assets	250,000		Retained earnings	40,000
			Total liabilities and	
Total assets	$430,000		stockholders' equity	$430,000

Sales (on credit)	$1,000,000
Cost of goods sold	650,000
Gross profit	350,000
Selling and administrative expense	175,000*
Depreciation expense	69,000
Operating profit	106,000
Interest expense	21,000
Earnings before taxes	85,000
Tax expense (40%)	34,000
Net income	51,000

*Includes $6,000 in lease payments.

*Brady Corporation has 75,000 shares outstanding.

COMPREHENSIVE PROBLEM

Al Thomas has recently been approached by his brother-in-law, Robert Watson, with a proposal to buy 20 percent interest in Watson Leisure Time Sporting Goods. The sporting goods company manufactures golf clubs, baseball bats, basketball goals, and other similar items.

Watson Leisure Time Sporting Goods (trend analysis and industry comparison)

Mr. Watson is quick to point out the increase in sales over the last three years as indicated in the income statement, Exhibit 1. The annual growth rate is 20 percent. A balance sheet for a similar time period is shown in Exhibit 2, and selected industry ratios are presented in Exhibit 3. Note the industry growth rate in sales is only approximately 10 percent per year.

There was a steady real growth of 2 to 3 percent in gross domestic product during the period under study. The rate of inflation was in the 3 to 4 percent range.

The stock in the corporation has become available due to the ill health of a current stockholder, who needs cash. The issue here is not to determine the exact price for the stock, but rather whether Watson Leisure Time Sporting Goods represents an attractive investment situation. Although Mr. Thomas has a primary interest in the profitability ratios, he will take a close look at all the ratios. He has no fast and firm rules about required return on investment, but rather wishes to analyze the overall condition of the firm. The firm does not currently pay a cash dividend, and return to the investor must come from selling the stock in the future. After doing a thorough analysis (including ratios for each year and comparisons to the industry), what comments and recommendations can you offer to Mr. Thomas?

EXHIBIT 1

WATSON LEISURE TIME SPORTING GOODS
Income Statement

	199x	199y	199z
Sales (all on credit).	$1,500,000	$1,800,000	$2,160,000
Cost of goods sold	950,000	1,120,000	1,300,000
Gross profit.	550,000	680,000	860,000
Selling and administrative expense*	380,000	490,000	590,000
Operating profit.	170,000	190,000	270,000
Interest expense	30,000	40,000	85,000
Net income before taxes	140,000	150,000	185,000
Taxes	46,120	48,720	64,850
Net income.	$ 93,880	$ 101,280	$ 120,150
Shares.	40,000	40,000	46,000
Earnings per share	$2.35	$2.53	$2.61

*Includes $20,000 in lease payments for each year.

EXHIBIT 2

WATSON LEISURE TIME SPORTING GOODS
Balance Sheet

	199x	199y	199z
Assets			
Cash.	$ 20,000	$ 30,000	$ 20,000
Marketable securities.	30,000	35,000	50,000
Accounts receivable	150,000	230,000	330,000
Inventory.	250,000	285,000	325,000
Total current assets	450,000	580,000	725,000
Net plant and equipment	550,000	720,000	1,169,000
Total assets	$1,000,000	$1,300,000	$1,894,000
Liabilities and Stockholders' Equity			
Accounts payable	$ 100,000	$ 225,000	$ 200,000
Notes payable (bank).	100,000	100,000	300,000
Total current liabilities	200,000	325,000	500,000
Long-term liabilities	250,000	331,120	550,740
Total liabilities	450,000	656,120	1,050,740
Common stock ($10 par)	400,000	400,000	460,000
Capital paid in excess of par	50,000	50,000	80,000
Retained earnings	100,000	193,880	303,260
Total stockholders' equity	550,000	643,880	843,260
Total liabilities and stockholders' equity. . .	$1,000,000	$1,300,000	$1,894,000

EXHIBIT 3

Selected Industry Ratios

	199x	199y	199z
Growth in sales	—	9.98%	10.02%
Profit margin	5.75%	5.80%	5.81%
Return on assets (investment)	8.22%	8.24%	8.48%
Return on equity	13.26%	13.62%	14.16%
Receivable turnover	10×	9.5×	10.1×
Average collection period	36 days	37.9 days	35.6 days
Inventory turnover	5.71×	5.62×	5.84×
Fixed asset turnover	2.75×	2.66×	2.20×
Total asset turnover	1.43×	1.42×	1.46×
Current ratio	2.10×	2.08×	2.15×
Quick ratio	1.05×	1.02×	1.10×
Debt to total assets	38%	39.5%	40.1%
Times interest earned	5.00×	5.20×	5.26×
Fixed charge coverage	3.85×	3.95×	3.97×
Growth in EPS	—	9.7%	9.8%

COMPREHENSIVE PROBLEM

The pharmaceutical industry has been under attack by politicians for profits higher than are thought to be socially acceptable. Much of the rise in health care costs has been blamed on the pharmaceutical industry even though the total cost of drugs as a percentage of medical care is a small percentage of the total cost. While it may be true that pharmaceutical prices have risen faster than the rate of inflation, so have many other goods. Nevertheless, many Wall Street analysts feel that the profitability of pharmaceutical firms will come under increasing pressure in the future. Because of these dire predictions Lilly's stock price has fallen from a high of $87.75 in the first quarter of 1992 to a low of $45 in 1993. Its price-earnings ratio fell from 19 in 1991 to a low of 10 in 1993.

Eli Lilly and Company (trends, ratios, and Du Pont analysis)

Using the information provided on page 80, please analyze the financial health of Eli Lilly, one of the premier firms in the United States. We have provided a five-year summary of selected financial data from Eli Lilly's annual report. It includes some data from the income statement and balance sheet as well as some ratios already calculated. Note that in 1992, Eli Lilly wrote off restructuring of assets and investments in joint ventures with small biotechnology firms. This activity penalized before-tax earnings by $565.7 million. Additionally there is an accounting adjustment for "Employers' Accounting for Postretirement Benefits Other Than Pensions" (FAS 106), and "Accounting for Income Taxes" (FAS 109). These charges accounted for $118.9 million and are shown as the cumulative effect of accounting changes on page 80.

1. Analyze the five-year trends for Eli Lilly, and determine if they are positive or negative. You should concentrate on return on sales, return on total assets, and return on stockholders' equity.

Selected Financial Data (unaudited)

ELI LILLY AND COMPANY AND SUBSIDIARIES
(Dollars in millions, except per-share data)

	1992*	1991	1990	1989	1988
Operations					
Net sales	$6,167.3	$5,725.7	$5,191.6	$4,175.6	$3,607.4
Research and development expenses	924.9	766.9	702.7	605.4	511.6
Other operating costs and expenses	3,521.2	3,190.5	2,949.5	2,405.4	2,144.8
Restructuring and special charges	565.7	—	—	—	—
Other income—net	26.8	110.9	59.6	165.1	129.7
Income before taxes and changes in accounting principles	1,182.3	1,879.2	1,599.0	1,329.9	1,080.7
Income taxes	354.7	564.5	471.7	390.4	319.7
Cumulative effect of accounting changes	118.9	—	—	—	—
Net income	708.7	1,314.7	1,127.3	939.5	761.0
As a percent of sales					
Net income	11.5%	23.0%	21.7%	22.5%	21.1%
Research and development	15.0	13.4	13.5	14.5	14.2
Per-share data					
Before effect of accounting changes	$2.81	$4.50	$3.90	$3.20	$2.67
Net income	2.41	4.50	3.90	3.20	2.67
Dividends declared	2.255	2.05	1.73	1.4225	1.20
Dividends paid	2.20	2.00	1.64	1.35	1.15
Average number of shares and share equivalents (thousands)**	294,478	294,244	289,993	294,507	287,374
Financial Position					
Current assets	$3,006.0	$2,939.3	$2,501.3	$2,274.4	$2,293.7
Current liabilities	2,398.6	2,272.0	2,817.6	1,328.8	1,241.6
Working capital	607.4	667.3	(316.3)	945.6	1,052.1
Current ratio	1.3	1.3	.9	1.7	1.8
Other assets	$1,594.7	$1,576.8	$1,704.8	$1,459.0	$1,162.4
Property and equipment	4,072.1	3,782.5	2,936.7	2,114.6	1,806.6
Total assets	8,672.8	8,298.6	7,142.8	5,848.0	5,262.7
Long-term debt	582.3	395.5	277.0	269.5	387.7
Deferred income taxes	169.7	415.6	351.2	300.4	282.4
Other noncurrent liabilities	630.1	249.4	229.5	192.2	125.7
Shareholders' equity	4,892.1	4,966.1	3,467.5	3,757.1	3,225.3
Long-term debt as a percent of equity	11.9%	8.0%	8.0%	7.2%	12.0%
Supplementary Data					
Return on shareholders' equity	14.4%	31.2%	31.2%	26.9%	24.3%
Return on assets	8.3%	17.2%	17.5%	17.0%	14.8%
Number of employees	32,200	30,800	29,500	27,800	26,300
Net sales per employee (thousands)	$191.5	$185.9	$176.0	$150.2	$137.2
Net income per employee (thousands)	22.0	42.7	38.2	33.8	28.9
Capital expenditures	912.9	1,142.4	1,007.3	554.5	372.1
Depreciation and amortization	368.1	299.5	247.5	229.3	204.0
Effective tax rate	30.0%	30.0%	29.5%	29.4%	29.6%
Number of shareholders	53,900	46,000	39,300	36,000	32,200

*Reflects impact of restructuring, special charges, and accounting changes.
**Adjusted for a two-for-one stock split, effected in the form of a stock dividend in March 1989.

2. Be sure to explain how the extraordinary charges have affected the analysis.

3. What role does research and development play in this industry and what ratio can you devise to examine the significance of R&D?

4. Discuss whether the past is a good indicator of the future for Eli Lilly. How do you see the future of this company and the outlook for its P/E ratio?

5. If this problem arouses your curiosity, feel free to use any library resources available to complete your analysis.

Selected References

Altman, Edward I. "Financial Ratios, Discriminant Analysis, and the Prediction of Corporate Bankruptcy." *Journal of Finance* 23 (September 1968), pp. 586–609.

Callard, Charles G., and David C. Kleinman. "Inflation-Adjustment Accounting: Does It Matter?" *Financial Analysts Journal* 41 (May–June 1985), pp. 51–59.

Chen, Kung H., and Thomas A. Shimerda. "An Empirical Analysis of Financial Ratios." *Financial Management* 10 (Spring 1981), pp. 51–60.

D'Ambrosio, Charles A. "Truth Reality and Financial Analysis." *Financial Analysts Journal* 38 (July–August 1982), pp. 24–25.

Dwyer, Hubert J., and Richard Lynn. "Small Capitalization Companies: What Does Financial Analysis Tell Us about Them?" *Financial Review* 24 (August 1990), pp. 397–415.

Elmer, Peter J., and David M. Borowski. "An Expert System Approach to Financial Analysis: The Case of S&L Bankruptcy." *Financial Management* 17 (Autumn 1988), pp. 66–76.

Estep, Tony. "Security Analysis and Stock Selection: Turning Financial Information Into Return Forecasts." *Financial Analysts Journal* 43 (July–August 1987), pp. 34–43.

Fodor, Gary, and Edward Mazza. "Business Valuation Fundamentals for Planners." *Journal of Financial Planning* 5 (October 1992), pp. 170–79.

Froot, Kenneth A., David S. Scharfstein, and Jeremy C. Stein. "Heard on the Street: Informational Inefficiencies in a Market with Short-Term Speculation." *Journal of Finance* 47 (September 1992), pp. 1461–84.

Gandolfi, Arthur E. "Inflation, Taxation, and Interest Rates." *Journal of Finance* 37 (June 1982), pp. 797–807.

Garnett, Jeff, and Geoffrey A. Hirt. "Replacement Costs Data: A Study of the Chemical and Drug Industry for Years 1976 Through 1978." An unpublished study at Illinois State University, January 1980.

Hollingsworth, Danny P., and Walter T. Harrison, Jr. "Deducting the Cost of Intangibles." *Journal of Accounting* 174 (July 1992), pp. 85–90.

Malburg, Chris, and Steve Wagner. "Using Financial Projections." *Cash Flow* 8 (July 1987), pp. 25–37.

Modigliani, Franco, and Richard A. Cohn. "Inflation, Rational Valuation and the Market." *Financial Analysts Journal* 35 (March–April 1979), pp. 24–44.

Ramakrisnan, Ram T. S., and Jacob K. Thomas. "What Matters from the Past: Market Value, Book Value or Earnings?" *Journal of Accounting, Auditing & Finance* 7 (Fall 1992), pp. 423–64.

Siegel, Joel G. "The 'Quality of Earnings' Concept—A Survey." *Financial Analysts Journal* 38 (March–April 1982), pp. 60–68.

Financial Forecasting

1 Financial forecasting is essential to the strategic growth of the firm.

2 The three financial statements for forecasting are the pro forma income statement, the cash budget, and the pro forma balance sheet.

3 The percent-of-sales method may also be used for forecasting on a less precise basis.

4 The various methods of forecasting enable the firm to determine the amount of new funds required in advance.

5 The process of forecasting forces the firm to consider seasonal and other effects on cash flow.

The old notion of the corporate treasurer burning the midnight oil to find new avenues of financing before dawn is no longer in vogue. If there is one talent that is essential to the financial manager, it is the ability to plan ahead and to make necessary adjustments before actual events occur. We likely could construct the same set of external events for two corporations (inflation, recession, severe new competition, and so on), and one would survive, while the other would not. The outcome might be a function not only of their risk-taking desires, but also of their ability to hedge against risk with careful planning.

While we may assume that no growth or a decline in volume is the primary cause for a shortage of funds, this is not necessarily the case. A rapidly growing firm may witness a significant increase in accounts receivable, inventory, and plant and equipment that cannot be financed in the normal course of business. Assume sales go from $100,000 to $200,000 in one year for a firm that has a 5 percent profit margin on sales. At the same time, assume assets represent 50 percent of sales and go from $50,000 to $100,000 as sales double. The $10,000 of profit (5 percent × $200,000) will hardly be adequate to finance the $50,000 asset growth. The remaining $40,000 must come from suppliers, the bank, and perhaps stockholders. The student should recognize that profit alone is generally inadequate to finance significant growth and a comprehensive financing plan must be developed. Too often, the small businessperson (and sometimes the big one as well) is mystified by an increase in sales and profits but less cash in the till.

Constructing Pro Forma Statements

The most comprehensive means of financial forecasting is to develop a series of pro forma, or projected, financial statements. We will give particular attention to the **pro forma income statement,** the **cash budget,** and the **pro forma balance sheet.** Based on the projected statements, the firm is able to judge its future level of receivables, inventory, payables, and other corporate accounts as well as its anticipated profits and borrowing requirements. The financial officer can then carefully track actual events against the plan and make necessary adjustments. Furthermore, the statements are often required by bankers and other lenders as a guide for the future.

A systems approach is necessary to develop pro forma statements. We first construct a pro forma income statement based on sales projections and the production plan, then translate this material into a cash budget, and finally assimilate all previously developed material into a pro forma balance sheet. The process of developing pro forma financial statements is depicted in Figure 4–1. We will use a six-month time frame to facilitate the analysis, though the same procedures could be extended to one year or longer.

Pro Forma Income Statement

Assume the Goldman Corporation has been asked by its bank to provide pro forma financial statements for midyear 1994. The pro forma income statement will provide a projection of how much profit the firm anticipates making over

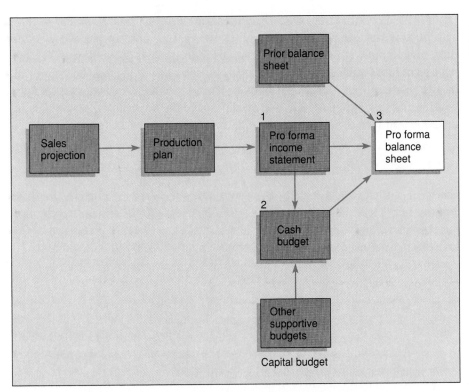

FIGURE 4–1
Development of pro forma statements

the ensuing time period. In developing the pro forma income statement, we will follow four important steps.

1. Establish a sales projection.
2. Determine a production schedule and the associated use of new material, direct labor, and overhead to arrive at gross profit.
3. Compute other expenses.
4. Determine profit by completing the actual pro forma statement.

Establish a Sales Projection

For purposes of analysis, we shall assume the Goldman Corporation has two primary products: wheels and casters. Our sales projection calls for the sale of 1,000 wheels and 2,000 casters at prices of $30 and $35, respectively. As indicated in Table 4–1, we anticipate total sales of $100,000.

Step 1:

	Wheels	Casters	
Quantity	1,000	2,000	*Projected UNIT SALE*
Sales price	$30	$35	
Sales revenue . . .	$30,000	$70,000	
Total			$100,000

TABLE 4–1
Projected wheel and caster sales (first six months, 1994)

It is assumed that the sales projections were derived from both an external and internal viewpoint. Using the former, we analyze our prospective sales in light of economic conditions affecting our industry and our company. Statistical techniques such as regression and time series analysis may be employed in the process. Internal analysis calls for surveying our own salespeople within their territories. Ideally, we would proceed along each of those paths in isolation and then assimilate the results into one meaningful projection.

Step 2A.

Determine a Production Schedule and the Gross Profit

Based on anticipated sales, we determine the necessary production plan for the six-month period. The number of units produced will depend on the beginning inventory of wheels and casters, our sales projection, and the desired level of ending inventory. Assume that on January 1, 1994, the Goldman Corporation has in stock the items shown in Table 4–2.

Figuring out – units that need to be produced

TABLE 4–2
Stock of beginning inventory   *A*

	Wheels	Casters
Quantity . . .	85	180
Cost	$16	$20
Total value . .	$1,360	$3,600
Total		$4,960

We will add the projected quantity of unit sales for the next six months to our desired ending inventory and subtract our stock of beginning inventory (in units) to determine our production requirements.

B

Units that need to be Produced (period)

Units
+ Projected sales
+ Desired ending inventory
− *Beginning* inventory
= Production requirements

In Table 4–3 we see a required production level of 1,015 wheels and 2,020 casters.

TABLE 4–3
Production requirements for six months

	Wheels	Casters
Projected unit sales (Table 4–1)	+1,000	+2,000
Desired ending inventory (assumed to represent 10% of unit sales for the time period)	+100	+200
Beginning inventory (Table 4–2)	−85	−180
Units to be produced	1,015	2,020

Step 2B.

We must now determine the cost to produce these units. In Table 4–2 we saw that the cost of units in stock was $16 for wheels and $20 for casters. However, we shall assume the price of materials, labor, and overhead going into the products is now $18 for wheels and $22 for casters, as indicated in Table 4–4.

TABLE 4-4
Unit costs

	Wheels	Casters
Materials . . .	$10	$12
Labor	5	6
Overhead . . .	3	4
Total . . .	$18	$22

The *total* cost to produce the required items for the next six months is shown in Table 4–5.

TABLE 4-5
Total production costs

	Wheels	Casters	
Units to be produced (Table 4–3) . . .	1,015	2,020	
Cost per unit (Table 4–4)	$18	$22	
Total cost	$18,270	$44,440	$62,710

Cost of Goods Sold   The main consideration in constructing a pro forma income statement is the costs specifically associated with units sold during the time period (**the cost of goods sold**). Note that in the case of wheels we anticipate sales of 1,000 units, as indicated in Table 4–1, but are producing 1,015, as indicated in Table 4–3, to increase our inventory level by 15 units. For profit measurement purposes, we will *not* charge these extra 15 units against current sales.[1] Furthermore, in determining the cost of the 1,000 units sold during the current time period, we will *not* assume that all of the items sold represent inventory manufactured in this period. We shall assume the Goldman Corporation uses FIFO (first-in, first-out) accounting and it will first allocate the cost of current sales to beginning inventory and then to goods manufactured during the period.

In Table 4–6 we look at the revenue, associated cost of goods sold, and gross profit for both products. For example, 1,000 units of wheels are to be sold at a total revenue of $30,000. Of the 1,000 units, 85 units are from beginning inventory at a $16 cost (Table 4–2) and the balance of 915 units are from current production at an $18 cost. The total cost of goods sold for wheels is

---

[1]Later in the analysis we will show the effect these extra units have on the cash budget and the balance sheet.

	Wheels	Casters	Combined
Quantity sold (Table 4–1)	1,000	2,000	3,000
Sales price.	$30	$35	
Sales revenue	$30,000	$70,000	$100,000
Cost of goods sold:			
Old inventory (Table 4–2)			
Quantity (units)	85	180	
Cost per unit	$16	$20	
Total	$ 1,360	$ 3,600	
New inventory (the remainder)			
Quantity (units)	915	1,820	
Cost per unit (Table 4–4)	$18	$22	
Total	16,470	40,040	
Total cost of goods sold . .	17,830	43,640	$ 61,470
Gross profit	$12,170	$26,360	$ 38,530

$17,830, yielding a gross profit of $12,170. The pattern is the same for casters, with sales of $70,000, cost of goods sold of $43,640, and gross profit of $26,360. The combined sales for the two products are $100,000, with cost of goods sold of $61,470 and gross profit of $38,530.

At this point, we also compute the value of ending inventory for later use in constructing financial statements. As indicated in Table 4–7, the value of ending inventory will be $6,200.

+ Beginning inventory (Table 4–2) . . .	$ 4,960
+ Total production costs (Table 4–5) . .	62,710
Total inventory available for sales . . .	67,670
− Cost of goods sold (Table 4–6)	61,470
Ending inventory	$ 6,200

Other Expense Items   Step 3

Having computed total revenue, cost of goods sold, and gross profits, we must now subtract other expense items to arrive at a net profit figure. We deduct general and administrative expenses as well as interest expenses from gross profit to arrive at earnings before taxes, then subtract taxes to determine after-tax income, and finally deduct dividends to ascertain the contribution to retained earnings. For the Goldman Corporation, we shall assume general and administrative expenses are $12,000, interest expense is $1,500, and dividends are $1,500.

Actual Pro Forma Income Statement   Step 4

Combining the gross profit in Table 4–6 with our assumptions on other expense items, we arrive at the pro forma income statement presented in

Table 4–8. We anticipate earnings after taxes of $20,024, dividends of $1,500, and an increase in retained earnings of $18,524.

TABLE 4–8

	Pro Forma Income Statement June 30, 1994	
Sales revenue		$100,000
Cost of goods sold		61,470
Gross profit		38,530
General and administrative expense . . .		12,000
Operating profit (EBIT)		26,530
Interest expense		1,500
Earnings before taxes (EBT)		25,030
Taxes (20%)*.		5,006
Earnings after taxes (EAT)		20,024
Common stock dividends.		1,500
Increase in retained earnings.		$ 18,524

*Though profit before taxes is slightly over $25,000, a convenient rate of 20 percent is applied to the full amount.

Cash Budget

As previously indicated, the generation of sales and profits does not necessarily ensure there will be adequate cash on hand to meet financial obligations as they come due. A profitable sale may generate accounts receivables in the short run but no immediate cash to meet maturing obligations. For this reason, we must translate the pro forma income statement into cash flows. In this process we divide the longer-term pro forma income statement into smaller and more precise time frames to appreciate the seasonal and monthly patterns of cash inflows and outflows. Some months may represent particularly high or low sales volume or may require dividends, taxes, or capital expenditures.

Cash Receipts

In the case of the Goldman Corporation, we break down the pro forma income statement for the first half of 1994 into a series of monthly cash budgets. In Table 4–1 we showed anticipated sales of $100,000 over this time period; we shall now assume these sales can be divided into monthly projections, as indicated in Table 4–9.

TABLE 4–9
Monthly sales pattern

January	February	March	April	May	June
$15,000	$10,000	$15,000	$25,000	$15,000	$20,000

A careful analysis of past sales and collection records indicates 20 percent of sales are collected in the month of sales and 80 percent in the following month. The cash receipt pattern related to monthly sales is shown in Table 4–10. It is assumed that sales for December 1993 were $12,000.

TABLE 4–10   **Monthly cash receipts**

	December	January	February	March	April	May	June
Sales	$12,000	$15,000	$10,000	$15,000	$25,000	$15,000	$20,000
Collections: (20% of current sales) . . . . (15,000 × .20)		$ 3,000	$ 2,000	$ 3,000	$ 5,000	$ 3,000	$ 4,000
Collections: (80% of previous month's sales). . . . . (12,000 × .80)		9,600	12,000	8,000	12,000	20,000	12,000
Total cash receipts . . .		$12,600	$14,000	$11,000	$17,000	$23,000	$16,000

(handwritten note: Proforma Balance sheet See pg 94)

The cash inflows will vary between $11,000 and $23,000, with the high point in receipts coming in May.

We now examine the monthly outflows.

Cash Payments

The primary considerations for cash payments are monthly costs associated with inventory manufactured during the period (material, labor, and overhead) and disbursements for general and administrative expenses, interest payments, taxes, and dividends. We must also consider cash payments for any new plant and equipment, an item that does not show up on our pro forma income statement.

 *(handwritten note: total production cost schedule)* Costs associated with units manufactured during the period may be taken from the data provided in Table 4–5. In Table 4–11 we simply recast these data in terms of material, labor, and overhead.

TABLE 4–11   **Component costs of manufactured goods**

	Wheels			Casters			
	Units Produced	Cost per Unit	Total Cost	Units Produced	Cost per Unit	Total Cost	Combined Cost
Materials	1,015	$10	$10,150	2,020	$12	$24,240	$34,390
Labor.	1,015	5	5,075	2,020	6	12,120	17,195
Overhead. . . .	1,015	3	3,045	2,020	4	8,080	11,125
							$62,710

We see that the total costs for components in the two products are materials, $34,390; labor, $17,195; and overhead, $11,125. We shall assume all these costs are incurred on an equal monthly basis over the six-month period. Even though the sales volume varies from month to month, we assume we are employing level monthly production to ensure maximum efficiency in the use of various productive resources. Average monthly costs for materials, labor, and overhead are as shown in Table 4–12.

TABLE 4-12
**Average monthly
manufacturing costs**

	Total Costs	Time Frame	Average Monthly Cost
Materials . . .	$34,390	6 months	$5,732
Labor	17,195	6 months	2,866
Overhead . . .	11,125	6 months	1,854

We shall pay for materials one month after the purchase has been made. Labor and overhead represent direct monthly cash outlays, as is true of interest, taxes, dividends, and assumed purchases of $8,000 in new equipment in February and $10,000 in June. We summarize all of our cash payments in Table 4–13. Past records indicate that $4,500 in materials was purchased in December.

TABLE 4-13   **Summary of all monthly cash payments**

	December	January	February	March	April	May	June
From Table 4–12:							
Monthly material purchase . . .	$4,500	$ 5,732	$ 5,732	$ 5,732	$ 5,732	$ 5,732	$ 5,732
Payment for material (prior month's purchase) . . .		$ 4,500	$ 5,732	$ 5,732	$ 5,732	$ 5,732	$ 5,732
Monthly labor cost		2,866	2,866	2,866	2,866	2,866	2,866
Monthly overhead		1,854	1,854	1,854	1,854	1,854	1,854
From Table 4–8:							
General and administrative expense ($12,000 over 6 months)		2,000	2,000	2,000	2,000	2,000	2,000
Interest expense							1,500
Taxes (two equal payments) . .				2,503			2,503
Cash dividend							1,500
Also:							
New equipment purchases . . .			8,000				10,000
Total payments.		$11,220	$20,452	$14,955	$12,452	$12,452	$27,953

Actual Budget

We are now in a position to bring together our monthly cash receipts and payments into a cash flow statement, illustrated in Table 4–14. The difference between monthly receipts and payments is net cash flow for the month.

TABLE 4-14   **Monthly cash flow**

	January	February	March	April	May	June
Total receipts (Table 4–10)	$12,600	$14,000	$11,000	$17,000	$23,000	$16,000
Total payments (Table 4–13) . . .	11,220	20,452	14,955	12,452	12,452	27,953
Net cash flow	$ 1,380	($ 6,452)	($ 3,955)	$ 4,548	$10,548	($11,953)

The primary purpose of the cash budget is to allow the firm to anticipate the need for outside funding at the end of each month. In the present case, we shall assume the Goldman Corporation wishes to have a minimum cash balance of $5,000 at all times. If it goes below this amount, the firm will borrow funds from the bank. If it goes above $5,000 and the firm has a loan outstanding, it will use the excess funds to reduce the loan. This pattern of financing is demonstrated in Table 4–15—a fully developed cash budget with borrowing and repayment provisions.

TABLE 4–15   **Cash budget with borrowing and repayment**

		January	February	March	April	May	June
1.	Net cash flow	$1,380	($6,452)	($3,955)	$ 4,548	$10,548	($11,953)
2.	Beginning cash balance.	5,000*	6,380	5,000	5,000	5,000	11,069
3.	Cumulative cash balance	6,380	(72)	1,045	9,548	15,548	(884)
4.	Monthly loan or (repayment) . . .	—	5,072	3,955	(4,548)	(4,479)	5,884
5.	Cumulative loan balance	—	5,072	9,027	4,479	—	5,884
6.	Ending cash balance	6,380	5,000	5,000	5,000	11,069	5,000

*We assume the Goldman Corporation has a beginning cash balance of $5,000 on January 1, 1994, and it desires a minimum monthly ending cash balance of $5,000.

The first line in Table 4–15 shows our net cash flow, which is added to the beginning cash balance to arrive at the cumulative cash balance. The fourth entry is the additional monthly loan or loan repayment, if any, required to maintain a minimum cash balance of $5,000. To keep track of our loan balance, the fifth entry represents cumulative loans outstanding for all months. Finally, we show the cash balance at the end of the month, which becomes the beginning cash balance for the next month.

At the end of January the firm has $6,380 in cash, but by the end of February the cumulative cash position of the firm is negative, necessitating a loan of $5,072 to maintain a $5,000 cash balance. The firm has a loan on the books until May, at which time there is an ending cash balance of $11,069. During the months of April and May the cumulative cash balance is greater than the required minimum cash balance of $5,000, so loan repayments of $4,548 and $4,479 are made to retire the loans completely in May. In June the firm is once again required to borrow $5,884 to maintain a $5,000 cash balance.

Pro Forma Balance Sheet

Now that we have developed a pro forma income statement and a cash budget, it is relatively simple to integrate all of these items into a pro forma balance sheet. Because the balance sheet represents cumulative changes in the corporation over time, we first examine the *prior* period's balance sheet and then translate these items through time to represent June 30, 1994. The last balance sheet, dated December 31, 1993, is shown in Table 4–16.

In constructing our pro forma balance sheet for June 30, 1994, some of the accounts from the old balance sheet will remain unchanged, while others will take on new values, as indicated by the pro forma income statement and cash budget. The process is depicted in Figure 4–2.

TABLE 4–16

Balance Sheet
December 31, 1993
Assets

Current assets:

Cash	$ 5,000
Marketable securities	3,200
Accounts receivable.	9,600
Inventory	4,960
Total current assets	22,760
Plant and equipment	27,740
Total assets	$50,500

Liabilities and Stockholders' Equity

Accounts payable	$ 4,500
Notes payable.	0
Long-term debt	15,000
Common stock	10,500
Retained earnings.	20,500
Total liabilities and stockholders' equity . . .	$50,500

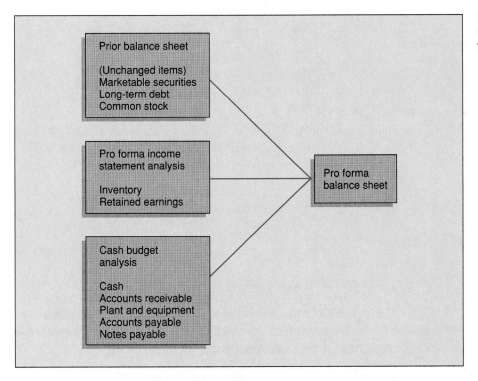

FIGURE 4–2
Development of a pro forma balance sheet

We present the new pro forma balance sheet as of June 30, 1994, in Table 4–17.

TABLE 4–17

Pro Forma Balance Sheet
June 30, 1994
Assets

Current assets:

1.	Cash.	$ 5,000
2.	Marketable securities	3,200
3.	Accounts receivable	16,000
4.	Inventory.	6,200
	Total current assets	30,400
5.	Plant and equipment	45,740
Total assets.		$76,140

Liabilities and Stockholders' Equity

6.	Accounts payable	$ 5,732
7.	Notes payable	5,884
8.	Long-term debt	15,000
9.	Common stock.	10,500
10.	Retained earnings	39,024
Total liabilities and stockholders' equity . . .		$76,140

Explanation of Pro Forma Balance Sheet

Each item in Table 4–17 can be explained on the basis of a prior calculation or assumption.

1. Cash ($5,000)—minimum cash balance as shown in Table 4–15.
2. Marketable securities ($3,200)—remains unchanged from prior period's value in Table 4–16.
3. Accounts receivable ($16,000)—based on June sales of $20,000 in Table 4–10. Twenty percent will be collected that month, while 80 percent will become accounts receivable at the end of the month.

$20,000   sales
× 80%   receivables
$16,000

4. Inventory ($6,200)—ending inventory as shown in Table 4–7.
5. Plant and equipment ($45,740).

Initial value (Table 4–16) . . .	$27,740
Purchases* (Table 4–13) . . .	18,000
Plant and equipment	$45,740

*For simplicity, depreciation is not explicitly considered.

6. Accounts payable ($5,732)—based on June purchases in Table 4–13. They will not be paid until July, and thus are accounts payable.

7. Notes payable ($5,884)—the amount we must borrow to maintain our cash balance of $5,000, as shown in Table 4–15.

8. Long-term debt ($15,000)—remains unchanged from prior period's value in Table 4–16.

9. Common stock ($10,500)—remains unchanged from prior period's value in Table 4–16.

10. Retained earnings ($39,024).

Initial value (Table 4–16)	$20,500
Transfer of pro forma income to	
retained earnings (Table 4–8) . . .	18,524
Retained earnings	$39,024

Analysis of Pro Forma Statement

In comparing the pro forma balance sheet (Table 4–17) to the prior balance sheet (Table 4–16), we note that assets are up by $25,640.

Total assets (June 30, 1994) . . .	$76,140
Total assets (Dec. 31, 1993) . . .	50,500
Increase.	$25,640

The growth must be financed by accounts payable, notes payable, and profit (as reflected by the increase in retained earnings). Though the company will enjoy a high degree of profitability, it must still look to bank financing of $5,884 to support the increase in assets. This represents the difference between the $25,640 buildup in assets, and the $1,232 increase in accounts payable as well as the $18,524 buildup in retained earnings.

Percent-of-Sales Method

An alternative to tracing cash and accounting flows to determine financial needs is to assume that accounts on the balance sheet will maintain a given percentage relationship to sales. We then indicate a change in the sales level and ascertain our related financing needs. This is known as the **percent-of-sales method.** For example, for the Howard Corporation, introduced in Table 4–18 on page 96, we show the following balance sheet accounts in dollars and their percent of sales, based on a sales volume of $200,000.

TABLE 4–18

HOWARD CORPORATION
Balance Sheet and Percent-of-Sales Table

Assets		Liabilities and Stockholders' Equity	
Cash.	$ 5,000	Accounts payable	$ 40,000
Accounts receivable	40,000	Accrued expenses	10,000
Inventory	25,000	Notes payable.	15,000
Total current assets . . .	$ 70,000	Common stock	10,000
Equipment	50,000	Retained earnings	45,000
Total assets	$120,000	Total liabilities and stockholders' equity. . .	$120,000

$200,000 sales
Percent of Sales

Cash.	2.5%	Accounts payable	20.0%
Accounts receivable	20.0	Accrued expenses	5.0
Inventory	12.5		25.0%
Total current assets . . .	35.0		
Equipment	25.0		
	60.0%		

Cash of $5,000 represents 2.5 percent of sales of $200,000; receivables of $40,000 is 20 percent of sales; and so on. No percentages are computed for notes payable, common stock, and retained earnings because they are not assumed to maintain a direct relationship with sales volume. Note that any dollar increase in sales will necessitate a 60 percent increase in assets,[2] of which 25 percent will be spontaneously or automatically financed through accounts payable and accrued expenses, leaving 35 percent to be financed by profit or additional outside sources of financing. We will assume the Howard Corporation has an aftertax return of 6 percent on the sales dollar and 50 percent of profits are paid out as dividends.[3]

If sales increase from $200,000 to $300,000, the $100,000 increase in sales will necessitate $35,000 (35 percent) in additional financing. Since we will earn 6 percent on total sales of $300,000, we will show a profit of $18,000. With a 50 percent dividend payout, $9,000 will remain for internal financing. This means $26,000 out of the $35,000 must be financed from outside sources. Our formula to determine the need for new funds is:

Required new funds—

$$(RNF) = \frac{A}{S}(\Delta S) - \frac{L}{S}(\Delta S) - PS_2(1 - D) \qquad (4-1)$$

---

[2]We are assuming equipment increases in proportion to sales. In certain cases, there may be excess capacity, and equipment (or plant and equipment) will not increase.

[3]Some may wish to add back depreciation under the percent-of-sales method. Most, however, choose the assumption that funds generated through depreciation (in the sources and uses of funds sense) must be used to replace the fixed assets to which depreciation is applied.

only include current assets [handwritten]

where

current assets [handwritten]

$\dfrac{A}{S}$ = Percentage relationship of variable assets to sales [60%]

ΔS = Change in sales [$100,000]

current [handwritten]

$\dfrac{L}{S}$ = Percentage relationship of variable liabilities to sales [25%]

liabilities [handwritten]

P = Profit margin [6%]

S_2 = New sales level [$300,000]

D = Dividend payout ratio [.50]

[handwritten right margin]
Profit margin .06 or 6%
net income / net sales = 18,000 / 30,000

Dividend Payout Ratio .5 or 50%
cash dividends / net income = 9,000 / 18,000

Plugging in the values, we show:

RNF = 60% ($100,000) − 25% ($100,000) − 6% ($300,000) (1 − 0.5)

[handwritten above equation: $\frac{A}{S}$ ΔS $\frac{L}{S}$ ΔS P ⟶ multiply ⟵ S_2 D]

    = $60,000 − $25,000 − $18,000 (0.5)

[handwritten: profit margin based on projected sales level]

    = $35,000 − $9,000

    = $26,000 required sources of new funds

Presumably the $26,000 can be financed at the bank or through some other appropriate source.

Using the percent-of-sales method is much easier than tracing through the various cash flows to arrive at the pro forma statements. Nevertheless, the output is much less meaningful and we do not get a month-to-month breakdown of the data. The percent-of-sales method is a broadbrush approach, while the development of pro forma statements is more exacting. Of course, whatever method we use, the results are only as meaningful or reliable as the assumptions about sales and production that went into the numbers.

[handwritten right margin]
Based or assumed
PM = 18,000 / 200,000 = .09 or 9%

Summary

Financial forecasting allows the financial manager to anticipate events before they occur, particularly the need for raising funds externally. An important consideration is that growth may call for additional sources of financing because profit is often inadequate to cover the net buildup in receivables, inventory, and other asset accounts.

We develop pro forma financial statements from an overall corporate systems viewpoint. The time perspective is usually six months to a year in the future. In developing a pro forma income statement, we begin by making sales projections, then we construct a production plan, and finally we consider all other expenses. From the pro forma income statement we proceed to a cash budget, in which the monthly or quarterly cash inflows and outflows related to sales, expenditures, and capital outlays are portrayed. All of this information can be assimilated into a pro forma balance sheet in which asset, liability, and stockholders' equity accounts are shown. Any shortage of funds is assumed to be financed through notes payable (bank loans).

We may take a shortcut to financial forecasting through the use of the percent-of-sales method. Under this approach selected balance sheet accounts are assumed to maintain a constant percentage relationship to sales, and thus for any given sales amount we can ascertain balance sheet values. Once again a shortage of funds is assumed to be financed through notes payable.

List of Terms

pro forma income statement 84   cost of goods sold 87
cash budget 84   percent-of-sales method 95
pro forma balance sheet 84

Discussion Questions

1. What are the basic benefits and purposes of developing pro forma statements and a cash budget?
2. Explain how the collections and purchases schedules are related to the borrowing needs of the corporation.
3. With inflation, what are the implications of using LIFO and FIFO inventory methods? How do they affect the cost of goods sold?
4. Explain the relationship between inventory turnover and purchase needs.
5. Rapid corporate growth in sales and profits can cause financing problems. Elaborate on this statement.
6. Discuss the advantage and disadvantage of level production schedules in firms with cyclical sales.
7. What conditions would help make a percent-of-sales forecast as accurate as pro forma financial statements and cash budgets?

Problems

Production requirements

1. Sales for Ross Pro's Sports Equipment are expected to be 4,800 units for the coming month. The company likes to maintain 10 percent of unit sales for each month in ending inventory. Beginning inventory is 300 units. How many units should the firm produce for the coming month?

Production requirements

2. Sam's Leather Goods has beginning inventory of 16,000 units, will sell 60,000 units for the month, and desires to reduce ending inventory to 30 percent of beginning inventory. How many units should Sam produce?

Production requirements

3. Laser Systems Inc. anticipates sales of 125,000 units for the first six months of the year. Beginning inventory is maintained at 15 percent of anticipated sales. Ending inventory will be equal to 25 percent of the

projected sales of 140,000 units for the last six months of the year. How many units should the firm produce during the first six months of the year?

4. On December 31 of last year, Barton Air Filters had in inventory 600 units of its product, which cost $28 per unit to produce. During January, the company produced 1,200 units at a cost of $32 per unit. Assuming Barton Air Filters sold 1,500 units in January, what was the cost of goods sold (assume FIFO inventory method)?

   Cost of goods sold—FIFO

5. At the end of January, Lemon Auto Parts had an inventory of 825 units, which cost $12 per unit to produce. During February the company produced 750 units at a cost of $16 per unit. If the firm sold 1,050 units in February, what was its cost of goods sold?

   Cost of goods sold—LIFO and FIFO

   a. Assume LIFO inventory accounting.

   b. Assume FIFO inventory accounting.

6. Convex Mechanical Supplies produces a product with the following costs as of July 1, 1993:

   Gross profit and ending inventory

Material	$ 6
Labor	4
Overhead . . .	2
	$12

   Beginning inventory on July 1 was 5,000 units. From July 1 to December 1, Convex produced 15,000 units. These units had a material cost of $10 per unit. The costs for labor and overhead were the same. Convex uses FIFO inventory accounting.

   Assuming Convex sold 17,000 units during the last six months of the year at $20 each, what would gross profit be? What is the value of ending inventory?

7. Assume in problem 6, Convex used LIFO inventory accounting instead of FIFO, what would gross profit be? What is the value of ending inventory?

   Gross profit and ending inventory

8. Clinton Flower Shops has forecast credit sales for the fourth quarter of the year:

   Schedule of cash receipts

September (actual)	$70,000
Fourth Quarter	
October	$60,000
November	55,000
December	80,000

   Experience has shown that 30 percent of sales are collected in the month of sale, 60 percent are collected in the following month, and 10 percent are never collected.

Prepare a schedule of cash receipts for Clinton Flower Shops covering the fourth quarter (October through December).

Schedule of cash receipts

9. Pirate Video Company has made the following sales projections for the next six months. All sales are credit sales.

March	$24,000	June	$28,000
April	30,000	July	35,000
May	18,000	August	38,000

Sales in January and February were $27,000 and $26,000, respectively.

Experience has shown that of total sales, 10 percent are uncollectible, 30 percent are collected in the month of sale, 40 percent are collected in the following month, and 20 percent are collected two months after sale.

Prepare a monthly cash receipts schedule for the firm for March through August.

Of the sales expected to be made during the six months from March through August, how much will still be uncollected at the end of August? How much of this is expected to be collected?

Schedule of cash payments

10. The Elway Corporation has forecast the following sales for the first seven months of the year.

January	$12,000	May	$12,000
February	16,000	June	20,000
March	18,000	July	22,000
April	24,000		

Monthly material purchases are set equal to 20 percent of forecasted sales for the next month. Of the total material costs, 40 percent are paid in the month of purchase and 60 percent in the following month. Labor costs will run $6,000 per month, and fixed overhead is $3,000 per month. Interest payments on the debt will be $4,500 for both March and June. Finally, Elway salespeople will receive a 3 percent commission on total sales for the first six months of the year, to be paid on June 30.

Prepare a monthly summary of cash payments for the six months from January through June. (Note: Compute prior December purchases to help get total material payments for January.)

Schedule of cash payments

11. Wright Lighting Fixtures forecasts its sales in units for the next four months as follows.

March	4,000
April	10,000
May	8,000
June	6,000

Wright maintains an ending inventory for each month in the amount of one and one half times the expected sales in the following month. The ending inventory for February (March's beginning inventory) reflects this policy. Materials cost $7 per unit and are paid in the month after production. Labor cost is $3 per unit and is paid for in the month incurred. Fixed overhead is $10,000 per month. Dividends of $14,000 are to be paid in May. Eight thousand units were produced in February.

Complete a production schedule and a summary of cash payments for March, April, and May. Remember that production in any one month is equal to sales plus desired ending inventory minus beginning inventory.

12. Dina's Dress Company has forecast its sales in units as follows:

Schedule of cash payments

January	1,000	May	1,550
February	800	June	1,800
March	900	July	1,400
April	1,400		

Dina always keeps an ending inventory equal to 120 percent of the next month's expected sales. The ending inventory for December (January's beginning inventory) is 1,200 units, which is consistent with this policy.

Materials cost $14 per unit and are paid for in the month after production. Labor cost is $7 per unit and is paid in the month the cost is incurred. Overhead costs are $8,000 per month. Interest of $10,000 is scheduled to be paid in March, and employee bonuses of $15,500 will be paid in June.

Prepare a monthly production schedule and a monthly summary of cash payments for January through June. Dina produced 800 units in December.

13. Graham Potato Company has expected sales of $6,000 in September, $10,000 in October, $16,000 in November, and $12,000 in December. Of the company's sales, 20 percent are for cash and 80 percent are on credit. Experience shows that 40 percent of accounts receivable are paid in the month after the sale, while the remaining 60 percent are paid two months after. Determine collections for November and December.

Cash budget

Also assume Graham's cash payments for November and December are $13,000 and $6,000, respectively. The beginning cash balance in November is $5,000, which is the desired minimum balance.

Prepare a cash budget with borrowing needed or repayments made for November and December. (You will need to prepare a cash receipts schedule first.)

14. Paco's Pizza Company has restaurants in five college towns. Paco wants to expand into Normal and French Lick and needs a bank loan to do this. Mr. Sousse, the banker, will finance construction if Paco

Complete cash budget

can present an acceptable three-month financial plan for January through March. Following are actual and forecasted sales figures:

Actual		Forecast		Additional information	
November	$120,000	January	$190,000	April forecast	$230,000
December	140,000	February	210,000		
		March	230,000		

Of Paco's sales, 30 percent are for cash and the remaining 70 percent are on credit. Of credit sales, 40 percent are paid in the month after sale and 60 percent are paid in the second month after the sale. Materials cost 20 percent of sales and are purchased and received each month in an amount sufficient to cover the following month's expected sales. Materials are paid for in the month after they are received. Labor expense is 50 percent of sales and is paid in the month of sales. Selling and administrative expense is 5 percent of sales and is also paid in the month of sales. Overhead is $12,000 in cash per month; depreciation expense is $25,000 per month. Taxes of $20,000 and dividends of $16,000 will be paid in March. Cash at the beginning of January is $70,000, and the minimum desired cash balance is $65,000.

For January, February, and March, prepare a schedule of monthly cash receipts, monthly cash payments, and a complete monthly cash budget with borrowings and repayments.

Complete cash budget   15. Hickman Avionics' actual sales and purchases for April and May are shown here along with forecasted sales and purchases for June through September.

	Sales	Purchases
April (actual)	$410,000	$220,000
May (actual)	400,000	210,000
June (forecast)	380,000	200,000
July (forecast)	360,000	250,000
August (forecast)	390,000	300,000
September (forecast)	420,000	220,000

The company makes 10 percent of its sales for cash and 90 percent on credit. Of the credit sales, 20 percent are collected in the month after the sale and 80 percent are collected two months after. Hickman pays for 40 percent of its purchases in the month after purchase and 60 percent two months after.

Labor expense equals 10 percent of the current month's sales. Overhead expense equals $15,000 per month. Interest payments of $40,000 are due in June and September. A cash dividend of $20,000 is scheduled to be paid in June. Tax payments of $35,000 are due in June and September. There is a scheduled capital outlay of $300,000 in September.

Hickman Avionics' ending cash balance in May is $20,000. The minimum desired cash balance is $15,000. Prepare a schedule of monthly cash receipts, monthly cash payments, and a complete monthly cash budget with borrowing and repayments for June through September. The maximum desired cash balance is $50,000. Excess cash (above $50,000) is used to buy marketable securities. Marketable securities are sold before borrowing funds in case of a cash shortfall (less than $15,000).

16. Carter Paint Company has plants in nine midwestern states. Sales for last year were $100 million, and the balance sheet at year-end is similar in percentage of sales to that of previous years (and this will continue in the future). All assets and current liabilities will vary directly with sales.

Percent-of-sales method

Balance Sheet
(in $ millions)

Assets		Liabilities and Stockholders' Equity	
Cash	$ 5	Accounts payable	$15
Accounts receivable . .	15	Accrued wages	6
Inventory	30	Accrued taxes	4
Current assets . . .	50	Current liabilities . .	25
Fixed assets	40	Notes payable	30
		Common stock	15
		Retained earnings	20
		Total liabilities and	
Total assets	$90	stockholders' equity . .	$90

Carter Paint has an aftertax profit margin of 5 percent and a dividend payout ratio of 30 percent.

If sales grow by 10 percent next year, determine how many dollars of new funds are needed to finance the expansion. (Assume Carter Paint is already using assets at full capacity and that plant must be added.)

17. Jordan Aluminum Supplies has the following financial statements, which are representative of the company's historical average.

Percent-of-sales method

Income Statement

Sales	$300,000
Expenses	247,000
Earnings before interest and taxes . . .	$ 53,000
Interest	3,000
Earnings before taxes	$ 50,000
Taxes	20,000
Earnings after taxes	$ 30,000
Dividends	$ 18,000

Balance Sheet

Assets		Liabilities and Stockholders' Equity	
Cash	$ 8,000	Accounts payable	$ 6,000
Accounts receivable. . . .	20,000	Accrued wages	2,000
Inventory	62,000	Accrued taxes	4,000
Current assets	$ 90,000	Current liabilities	$ 12,000
Fixed assets	100,000	Notes payable	10,000
		Long-term debt	20,000
		Common stock	80,000
		Retained earnings	68,000
		Total liabilities and	
Total assets	$190,000	stockholders' equity	$190,000

Jordan is expecting a 20 percent increase in sales next year, and
management is concerned about the company's need for external funds.
The increase in sales is expected to be carried out without any
expansion of fixed assets; instead it will be done through more
efficient asset utilization in the existing stores. Of liabilities, only
current liabilities vary directly with sales.

Using a percent-of-sales method, determine whether Jordan
Aluminum has external financing needs. (Hint: A profit margin and
payout ratio must be found from the income statement.)

Percent-of-sales method   18. Cambridge Prep Shops, a national clothing chain, had sales of $200
million last year. The business has a steady net profit margin of
12 percent and a dividend payout ratio of 40 percent. The balance sheet
for the end of last year is shown below.

Balance Sheet
End of Year
($ millions)

Assets		Liabilities and Stockholders' Equity	
Cash.	$ 10	Accounts payable	$ 15
Accounts receivable	15	Accrued expenses.	5
Inventory.	50	Other payables	40
Plant and equipment	75	Common stock	30
		Retained earnings.	60
		Total liabilities and	
Total assets	$150	stockholders' equity	$150

Cambridge's marketing staff tells the president that in this coming
year there will be a large increase in the demand for tweed sport coats
and various shoes. A sales increase of 15 percent is forecast for the
Prep Shop.

All balance sheet items are expected to maintain the same
percent-of-sales relationships as last year, except for common stock and
retained earnings. No change in the number of common stock shares

outstanding is scheduled, and retained earnings will change as dictated by the profits and dividend policy of the firm. (Remember the net profit margin is 12 percent.)

a. Will external financing be required for the Prep Shop during the coming year?

b. What would the need for external financing be if the net profit margin went up to 14 percent and the dividend payout ratio was increased to 70 percent? Explain.

COMPREHENSIVE PROBLEMS

The Landis Corporation had 1993 sales of $100 million. The balance sheet items that vary directly with sales and the profit margin are as follows:

Landis Corporation (external funds requirement)

	Percent
Cash	5%
Accounts receivable	15
Inventory	25
Net fixed assets	40
Accounts payable	15
Other payables	10
Profit margin after taxes	6

The dividend payout rate is 50 percent of earnings, and the balance in retained earnings at the beginning of 1994 was $33 million. Common stock and the company's long-term bonds are constant at $10 million and $5 million, respectively. Notes payable are currently $12 million.

a. How much additional external capital will be required for next year if sales increase 15 percent? (Assume the company is already operating at full capacity.)

b. What will happen to external fund requirements if Landis Corporation reduces the payout ratio, grows at a slower rate, or suffers a decline in its profit margin? Discuss each of these separately.

c. Prepare a pro forma balance sheet for 1994, assuming that any external funds being acquired will be in the form of notes payable. Disregard the information in part *b* in answering this question (that is, use the original information and part *a* in constructing your pro forma balance sheet.)

The difficult part of solving a problem of this nature is to know what to do with the information contained within a story problem. Therefore, this problem will be easier to complete if you rely on Chapter 4 for the format of all required schedules.

Adams Corporation (financial forecasting with seasonal production)

The Adams Corporation makes standard-size 2-inch fasteners, which it sells for $155 per thousand. Mr. Adams is the majority owner and manages the inventory and finances of the company. He estimates sales for the following months to be:

January	$263,500 (1,700,000 fasteners)
February . . .	$186,000 (1,200,000 fasteners)
March	$217,000 (1,400,000 fasteners)
April	$310,000 (2,000,000 fasteners)
May	$387,500 (2,500,000 fasteners)

Last year Adams Corporation's sales were $175,000 in November and $232,500 in December (1,500,000 fasteners).

Mr. Adams is preparing for a meeting with his banker to arrange the financing for the first quarter. Based on his sales forecast and the following information provided by him, your job as his new financial analyst is to prepare a monthly cash budget, a monthly and quarterly pro forma income statement, a pro forma quarterly balance sheet, and all necessary supporting schedules for the first quarter.

Past history shows the Adams Corporation collects 50 percent of its accounts receivable in the normal 30-day credit period (the month after the sale) and the other 50 percent in 60 days (two months after the sale). It pays for its materials 30 days after receipt. In general, Mr. Adams likes to keep a two-month supply of inventory in anticipation of sales. Inventory at the beginning of December was 2,600,000 units. (This was not equal to his desired two-month supply.)

The major cost of production is the purchase of raw materials in the form of steel rods, which are cut, threaded, and finished. Last year raw material costs were $52 per 1,000 fasteners, but Mr. Adams has just been notified that material costs have risen, effective January 1, to $60 per 1,000 fasteners. The Adams Corporation uses FIFO inventory accounting. Labor costs are relatively constant at $20 per thousand fasteners, since workers are paid on a piecework basis. Overhead is allocated at $10 per thousand units, and selling and administrative expense is 20 percent of sales. Labor expense and overhead are direct cash outflows paid in the month incurred, while interest and taxes are paid quarterly.

The corporation usually maintains a minimum cash balance of $25,000, and it puts its excess cash into marketable securities. The average tax rate is 40 percent, and Mr. Adams usually pays out 50 percent of net income in dividends to stockholders. Marketable securities are sold before funds are borrowed when a cash shortage is faced. Ignore the interest on any short-term borrowings. Interest on the long-term debt is paid in March, as are taxes and dividends.

As of year-end, the Adams Corporation balance sheet was as follows:

ADAMS CORPORATION
Balance Sheet
December 31, 199X
Assets

Current assets:
Cash	$ 30,000	
Accounts receivable	320,000	
Inventory	237,800	
Total current assets		$ 587,800
Fixed assets:		
Plant and equipment	1,000,000	
Less: Accumulated depreciation	200,000	800,000
Total assets		$1,387,800

Liabilities and Stockholders' Equity

Accounts payable	$ 93,600
Notes payable	0
Long-term debt, 8 percent	400,000
Common stock	504,200
Retained earnings	390,000
Total liabilities and stockholders' equity . . .	$1,387,800

Selected References

Brown, Lawrence D.; Gordon D. Richardson; and Stephen J. Schwager. "An Information Interpretation of Financial Analysts Superiority in Forecasting Earnings." *Journal of Accounting Research* 51 (Spring 1987), pp. 49–67.

Carter, J. R. "A Systematic Integration of Strategic Analysis and Cash Flow Forecasting." *Journal of Commercial Lending* 74 (April 1992), pp. 12–23.

Coulsen, N. Edward, and Russell P. Robins. "Forecast Combination in a Dynamic Setting." *Journal of Forecasting* 12 (January 1993), pp. 63–67.

Francis, Jack Clark, and Dexter T. Rowell. "A Simultaneous Equation Model of the Firm for Financial Analysis and Planning." *Financial Management* 7 (Spring 1978), pp. 29–44.

Gage, Theodore Justin. "Forecasts Get Clearer when Current Data, Not History, Is Used." *Corporate Cashflow* 9 (November 1990), pp. 7–8.

Higgins, Robert C. "How Much Growth Can a Firm Afford?" *Financial Management* 6 (Fall 1977), pp. 7–16.

Jennings, Robert. "Unsystematic Security Price Movements, Management Earnings Forecasts and Revisions in Consensus Analysts Earnings Forecasts." *Journal of Accounting Research* 51 (Spring 1987), pp. 90–110.

Maier, Steven F.; David W. Robinson; and James H. Vander Weide. "A Short-Term Disbursement Forecasting Method." *Financial Management* 10 (Spring 1981), pp. 9–19.

Stilwell, Martin C. "Prospective Reporting and Small Business Clients." *Journal of Accountancy* 161 (May 1986), pp. 68–87.

Van Der Knoop, Han S. "Control Charts to Check Yearly Predictions by Monthly Observations." *Journal of Forecasting* 11 (November 1992), pp. 629–43.

Wild, John J. "The Prediction Performance of a Structural Model of Accounting Numbers." *Journal of Accounting Research* 51 (Spring 1987), pp. 139–60.

Operating and Financial Leverage

CHAPTER CONCEPTS

1 Leverage represents the use of fixed cost items to magnify the firm's results.

2 Operating leverage indicates the extent fixed assets (plant and equipment) are utilized by the firm.

3 Financial leverage shows how much debt the firm employs in its capital structure.

4 By increasing leverage, the firm increases its profit potential, but also its risk of failure.

In the physical sciences as well as in politics, the term **leverage** has been popularized to mean the use of special force and effects to produce more than normal results from a given course of action. In business the same concept is applied, with the emphasis on the employment of fixed cost items in anticipation of magnifying returns at high levels of operation. The student should recognize that leverage is a two-edged sword—producing highly favorable results when things go well, and quite the opposite under negative conditions.

Leverage in a Business

Assume you are approached with an opportunity to start your own business. You are to manufacture and market industrial parts, such as ball bearings, wheels, and casters. You are faced with two primary decisions.

First you must determine the amount of fixed cost plant and equipment you wish to use in the production process. By installing modern, sophisticated equipment, you can virtually eliminate labor in the production of inventory. At high volume, you will do quite well, as most of your costs are fixed. At low volume, however, you could face difficulty in making your fixed payments for plant and equipment. If you decide to use expensive labor rather than machinery, you will lessen your opportunity for profit, but at the same time you will lower your exposure to risk (you can lay off part of the work force).

Second you must determine how you will finance the business. If you rely on debt financing and the business is successful, you will generate substantial profits as an owner, paying only the fixed costs of debt. Of course, if the business starts off poorly, the contractual obligations related to debt could mean bankruptcy. As an alternative, you might decide to sell equity rather than borrow, a step that will lower your own profit potential (you must share with others) but minimize your risk exposure.

In both decisions, you are making very explicit decisions about the use of leverage. To the extent that you go with a heavy commitment to fixed costs in the operation of the firm, you are employing operating leverage. To the extent that you utilize debt in the financing of the firm, you are engaging in financial leverage. We shall carefully examine each type of leverage and then show the combined effect of both.

Operating Leverage

Operating leverage reflects the extent to which fixed assets and associated fixed costs are utilized in the business. As indicated in Table 5–1, a firm's operational costs may be classified as fixed, variable, or semivariable.

TABLE 5–1
Classification of costs

Fixed	Variable	Semivariable
Rental	Raw material	Utilities
Depreciation	Factory labor	Repairs and maintenance
Executive salaries	Sales commissions	
Property taxes		

For purposes of analysis, variable and semivariable costs will be combined. In order to evaluate the implications of heavy fixed asset use, we employ the technique of break-even analysis.

Break-even Analysis

How much will changes in volume affect cost and profit? At what point does the firm break even? What is the most efficient level of fixed assets to employ in the firm? A break-even chart is presented in Figure 5–1 to answer some of these questions. The number of units produced and sold are shown along the horizontal axis, and revenue and costs are shown along the vertical axis.

Note, first of all, that our fixed costs are $60,000, regardless of volume, and that our variable costs (at $0.80 per unit) are added to fixed costs to determine total costs at any point. The total revenue line is determined by multiplying price ($2) times volume.

[handwritten] 2 × 50,000 = 100,000
[handwritten] VC .80 × 50,000 = 40,000

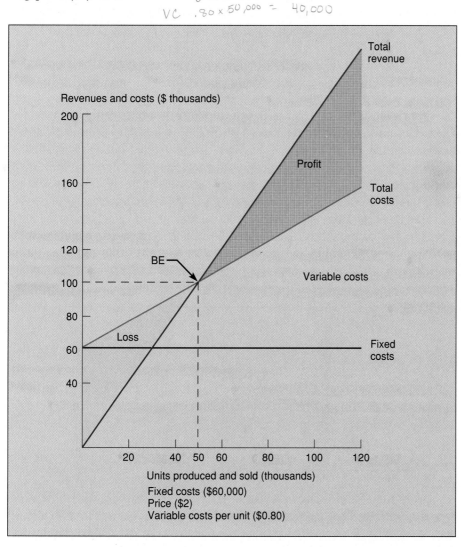

FIGURE 5–1
**Break-even chart:
Leveraged firm**

[handwritten]
FC   60,000
VC   40,000
total   100,000
costs

operating w/
high degree
of leverage

Revenues and costs ($ thousands)

Fixed costs ($60,000)
Price ($2)
Variable costs per unit ($0.80)

Units produced and sold (thousands)

Of particular interest is the break-even (BE) point at 50,000 units, where the total costs and total revenue lines intersect. The numbers are as follows:

Units = 50,000				
Total Variable Costs (TVC)	Fixed Costs (FC)	Total Costs (TC)	Total Revenue (TR)	Operating Income (loss)
(50,000 × $0.80) $40,000	$60,000	$100,000	(50,000 × $2) $100,000	0

The break-even point for the company may also be determined by use of a simple formula—in which we divide fixed costs by the contribution margin on each unit sold, with the **contribution margin** defined as price minus variable cost per unit.

$$BE = \frac{\text{Fixed costs}}{\text{Contribution margin}} = \frac{\text{Fixed costs}}{\text{Price} - \text{Variable cost per unit}} = \frac{FC}{P - VC} \quad (5-1)$$

$$\frac{\$60,000}{\$2.00 - \$0.80} = \frac{\$60,000}{\$1.20} = 50,000 \text{ units}$$

Since we are getting a $1.20 contribution toward covering fixed costs from each unit sold, minimum sales of 50,000 units will allow us to cover our fixed costs (50,000 units × $1.20 = $60,000 fixed costs). Beyond this point, we move into a highly profitable range in which each unit of sales brings a profit of $1.20 to the company. As sales increase from 50,000 to 60,000 units, operating profits increase by $12,000 as indicated in Table 5–2; as sales increase from 60,000 to 80,000 units, profits increase by another $24,000; and so on. As further indicated in Table 5–2, at low volumes such as 40,000 or 20,000 units our losses are substantial ($12,000 and $36,000 in the red).

TABLE 5-2
Volume-cost-profit analysis: Leveraged firm

Units Sold	Total Variable Costs	Fixed Costs	Total Costs	Total Revenue	Operating Income (loss)
0	0	$60,000	$ 60,000	0	$(60,000)
20,000	$16,000	60,000	76,000	$ 40,000	(36,000)
40,000	32,000	60,000	92,000	80,000	(12,000)
50,000	40,000	60,000	100,000	100,000	0
60,000	48,000	60,000	108,000	120,000	12,000
80,000	64,000	60,000	124,000	160,000	36,000
100,000	80,000	60,000	140,000	200,000	60,000

It is assumed that the firm depicted in Figure 5–1 on page 111 is operating with a high degree of leverage. The situation is analogous to that of an airline that must carry a certain number of people to break even, but beyond that point is in a very profitable range.

A More Conservative Approach

Not all firms would choose to operate at the high degree of operating leverage exhibited in Figure 5–1. Fear of not reaching the 50,000-unit break-even level may discourage some companies from heavy utilization of fixed assets. More expensive variable costs may be substituted for automated plant and equipment. Assume fixed costs for a more conservative firm can be reduced to $12,000—but variable costs will go from $0.80 to $1.60. If the same price assumption of $2 per unit is employed, the break-even level is 30,000 units.

$$BE = \frac{\text{Fixed costs}}{\text{Price} - \text{Variable cost per unit}} = \frac{FC}{P - VC} = \frac{\$12,000}{\$2 - \$1.60}$$

$$= \frac{\$12,000}{\$0.40}$$

$$= 30,000 \text{ units}$$

With fixed costs reduced from $60,000 to $12,000, the loss potential is small. Furthermore, the break-even level of operations is a comparatively low 30,000 units. Nevertheless, the use of a virtually unleveraged approach has cut into the potential profitability of the more conservative firm, as indicated in Figure 5–2 on page 114.

Even at high levels of operation, the potential profit is rather small. As indicated in Table 5–3 at a 100,000-unit volume, operating income is only $28,000—some $32,000 less than that for the "leveraged" firm previously analyzed in Table 5–2.

TABLE 5–3
Volume-cost-profit analysis: Conservative firm

Units Sold	Total Variable Costs	Fixed Costs	Total Costs	Total Revenue	Operating Income (loss)
0	0	$12,000	$ 12,000	0	$(12,000)
20,000	$32,000	12,000	44,000	$ 40,000	(4,000)
30,000	48,000	12,000	60,000	60,000	0
40,000	64,000	12,000	76,000	80,000	4,000
60,000	96,000	12,000	108,000	120,000	12,000
80,000	128,000	12,000	140,000	160,000	20,000
100,000	160,000	12,000	172,000	200,000	28,000

The Risk Factor

Whether management follows the path of the leveraged firm or of the more conservative firm depends on its perceptions about the future. If the vice-president of finance is apprehensive about economic conditions, the conservative plan may be undertaken. For a growing business, in times of relative prosperity, management might maintain a more aggressive, leveraged position. The firm's competitive position within its industry will also be a factor. Does the firm desire to merely maintain stability or to become a market leader? To a certain extent, management should tailor the use of leverage to

FIGURE 5-2
**Break-even chart:
Conservative firm**

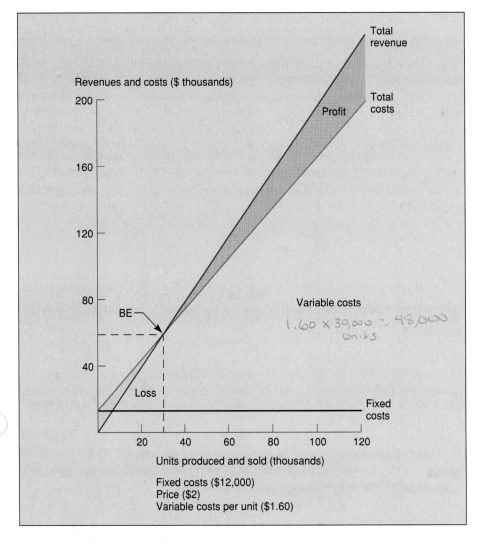

Revenues and costs ($ thousands)

Fixed costs ($12,000)
Price ($2)
Variable costs per unit ($1.60)

Units produced and sold (thousands)

meet its own risk-taking desires. Those who are risk averse (prefer less risk to more risk) should anticipate a particularly high return before contracting for heavy fixed costs. Others, less averse to risk, may be willing to leverage under more normal conditions. Simply taking risks is not a virtue—our prisons are full of risk takers. The important idea, which is stressed throughout the text, is to match an acceptable return with the desired level of risk.

Cash Break-even Analysis

Our discussion to this point has dealt with break-even analysis in terms of accounting flows rather than cash flows. For example, depreciation has been implicitly included in fixed expenses, but it represents an accounting entry rather than an explicit expenditure of funds. To the extent that we were doing break-even analysis on a strictly cash basis, depreciation would be excluded from fixed expenses. In the example of the leveraged firm in Formula 5–1 on page 112, if we eliminate $20,000 of "assumed" depreciation from fixed costs, the break-even level is reduced to 33,333 units.

$$\frac{FC}{P - VC} = \frac{(\$60,000 - \$20,000)}{\$2.00 - \$0.80} = \frac{\$40,000}{\$1.20} = 33,333 \text{ units}$$

Other adjustments could also be made for noncash items. For example, sales may initially take the form of accounts receivable rather than cash, and the same can be said for the purchase of materials and accounts payable. An actual weekly or monthly cash budget would be necessary to isolate these items.

While cash break-even analysis is helpful in analyzing the short-term outlook of the firm, particularly when it may be in trouble, most break-even analysis is conducted on the basis of accounting flows rather than strictly cash flows. Most of the assumptions throughout the chapter are based on concepts broader than pure cash flows.

Degree of Operating Leverage

Degree of operating leverage (DOL) may be defined as the percentage change in operating income that occurs as a result of a percentage change in units sold.

$$\text{DOL} = \frac{\text{Percent change in operating income}}{\text{Percent change in unit volume}} \qquad (5\text{--}2)$$

Highly leveraged firms, such as those in the auto or construction industry, are likely to enjoy a rather substantial increase in income as volume expands, while more conservative firms will participate to a lesser extent. Degree of operating leverage should be computed only over a profitable range of operations. However, the closer DOL is computed to the company break-even point, the higher the number will be due to a large percentage increase in operating income.[1]

Let us apply the formula to the leveraged and conservative firms previously discussed. Their income or losses at various levels of operation are summarized in Table 5–4.

We will now consider what happens to operating income as volume moves from 80,000 to 100,000 units.

Units	Leveraged Firm (Table 5–2)	Conservative Firm (Table 5–3)
0 . . .	$(60,000)	$(12,000)
20,000 . . .	(36,000)	(4,000)
40,000 . . .	(12,000)	4,000
60,000 . . .	12,000	12,000
80,000 . . .	36,000	20,000
100,000 . . .	60,000	28,000

TABLE 5–4
Operating income or loss

---

[1]While the value of DOL varies at each level of output, the beginning level of volume determines the DOL regardless of the location of the end point.

Leveraged Firm

$$\text{DOL} = \frac{\text{Percent change in operating income}}{\text{Percent change in unit volume}} = \frac{\dfrac{\$24,000}{\$36,000} \times 100}{\dfrac{20,000}{80,000} \times 100}$$

$$= \frac{67\%}{25\%} = 2.7$$

Conservative Firm

$$\text{DOL} = \frac{\text{Percent change in operating income}}{\text{Percent change in unit volume}} = \frac{\dfrac{\$8,000}{\$20,000} \times 100}{\dfrac{20,000}{80,000} \times 100}$$

$$= \frac{40\%}{25\%} = 1.6$$

We see the DOL is much greater for the leveraged firm, indicating at 80,000 units, a 1 percent increase in volume will produce a 2.7 percent change in operating income versus a 1.6 percent increase for the conservative firm.

The formula for degree of operating leverage may be algebraically manipulated to read:

$$\text{DOL} = \frac{Q(P - VC)}{Q(P - VC) - FC} \tag{5-3}$$

where

$$Q = \text{Quantity at which DOL is computed.}$$
$$P = \text{Price per unit.}$$
$$VC = \text{Variable costs per unit.}$$
$$FC = \text{Fixed costs.}$$

Using the newly stated formula for the first firm at $Q = 80,000$, with $P = \$2$, $VC = \$0.80$, and $FC = \$60,000$:

$$\text{DOL} = \frac{80,000(\$2.00 - \$0.80)}{80,000(\$2.00 - \$0.80) - \$60,000}$$

$$= \frac{80,000(\$1.20)}{80,000(\$1.20) - 60,000} = \frac{96,000}{96,000 - 60,000}$$

$$\text{DOL} = 2.7$$

We once again derive an answer of 2.7.[2] The same type of calculation could also be performed for the conservative firm.

Limitations of Analysis

Throughout our analysis of operating leverage, we have assumed that a constant or linear function exists for revenues and costs as volume changes. For example, we have used $2 as the hypothetical sales price at all levels of operation. In the "real world," however, we may face price weakness as we attempt to capture an increasing market, or we may face cost overruns as we move beyond an optimum-size operation. Relationships are not so fixed as we have assumed.

Nevertheless, the basic patterns we have studied are reasonably valid for most firms over an extended operating range (in our example that might be between 20,000 and 100,000 units). It is only at the extreme levels that linear assumptions break down, as indicated in Figure 5–3 on page 118.

Financial Leverage

Having discussed the effect of fixed costs on the operations of the firm (operating leverage), we now turn to the second form of leverage. **Financial leverage** reflects the amount of debt used in the capital structure of the firm. Because debt carries a fixed obligation of interest payments, we have the opportunity to greatly magnify our results at various levels of operation. You may have heard of the real estate developer who borrows 100 percent of the costs of his project and will enjoy an infinite return on his zero investment if all goes well.

It is helpful to think of *operating leverage* as primarily affecting the left-hand side of the balance sheet and *financial leverage* as affecting the right-hand side.

Balance Sheet	
Assets	**Liabilities and Net Worth**
Operating leverage	Financial leverage

---

[2]The formula for DOL may also be rewritten as:

$$DOL = \frac{Q(P - VC)}{Q(P - VC) - FC} = \frac{QP - QVC}{QP - QVC - FC}$$

We can rewrite the second terms as:

QP = S, or Sales (Quantity × Price)
QVC = TVC, or Total variable costs (Quantity × Variable costs per unit)
FC = Total fixed costs (remains the same term)

We then have:

$$DOL = \frac{S - TVC}{S - TVC - FC}, \text{ or } \frac{\$160,000 - \$64,000}{\$160,000 - \$64,000 - \$60,000} = \frac{\$96,000}{\$36,000} = 2.7$$

FIGURE 5–3
Nonlinear break-even analysis

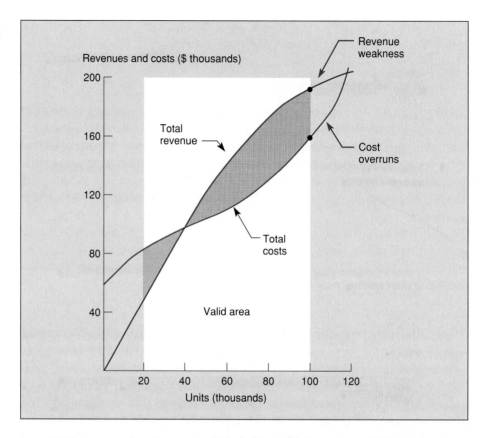

Whereas operating leverage influences the mix of plant and equipment, financial leverage determines how the operation is to be financed. It is possible for two firms to have equal operating capabilities and yet show widely different results because of the use of financial leverage.

Impact on Earnings

In studying the impact of financial leverage, we shall examine two financial plans for a firm, each employing a significantly different amount of debt in the capital structure. Financing totaling $200,000 is required to carry the assets of the firm.

	Total Assets—$200,000	
	Plan A (leveraged)	**Plan B (conservative)**
Debt (8% interest)	$150,000 ($12,000 interest)	$ 50,000 ($4,000 interest)
Common stock	50,000 (8,000 shares at $6.25)	150,000 (24,000 shares at $6.25)
Total financing	$200,000	$200,000

Under *leveraged* Plan A we will borrow $150,000 and sell 8,000 shares of stock at $6.25 to raise an additional $50,000, whereas *conservative* Plan B

TABLE 5–5
Impact of financing plan on earnings per share

	Plan A (leveraged)	Plan B (conservative)
1. EBIT (0)		
Earnings before interest and taxes (EBIT) .	0	0
− Interest (I)	$(12,000)	$(4,000)
Earnings before taxes (EBT)	(12,000)	(4,000)
− Taxes (T)*	(6,000)	(2,000)
Earnings after taxes (EAT)	$ (6,000)	$(2,000)
Shares	8,000	24,000
Earnings per share (EPS)	$(0.75)	$(0.08)
2. EBIT ($12,000)		
Earnings before interest and taxes (EBIT) .	$ 12,000	$12,000
− Interest (I)	12,000	4,000
Earnings before taxes (EBT)	0	8,000
− Taxes (T)	0	4,000
Earnings after taxes (EAT)	$ 0	$ 4,000
Shares	8,000	24,000
Earnings per share (EPS)	0	$0.17
3. EBIT ($16,000)		
Earnings before interest and taxes (EBIT) .	$ 16,000	$16,000
− Interest (I)	12,000	4,000
Earnings before taxes (EBT)	4,000	12,000
− Taxes (T)	2,000	6,000
Earnings after taxes (EAT)	$ 2,000	$ 6,000
Shares	8,000	24,000
Earnings per share (EPS)	$0.25	$0.25
4. EBIT ($36,000)		
Earnings before interest and taxes (EBIT) .	$ 36,000	$36,000
− Interest (I)	12,000	4,000
Earnings before taxes (EBT)	24,000	32,000
− Taxes (T)	12,000	16,000
Earnings after taxes (EAT)	$ 12,000	$16,000
Shares	8,000	24,000
Earnings per share (EPS)	$1.50	$0.67
5. EBIT ($60,000)		
Earnings before interest and taxes (EBIT) .	$ 60,000	$60,000
− Interest (I)	12,000	4,000
Earnings before taxes (EBT)	48,000	56,000
− Taxes (T)	24,000	28,000
Earnings after taxes (EAT)	$ 24,000	$28,000
Shares	8,000	24,000
Earnings per share (EPS)	$3.00	$1.17

*The assumption is that large losses can be written off against other income, perhaps in other years, thus providing the firm with a tax savings benefit. The tax rate is 50 percent for ease of computation.

calls for borrowing only $50,000 and acquiring an additional $150,000 in stock with 24,000 shares.

In Table 5–5, we compute earnings per share for the two plans at various levels of "earnings before interest and taxes" (EBIT). These earnings represent the operating income of the firm—before deductions have been made for financial charges or taxes. We assume EBIT levels of 0, $12,000, $16,000, $36,000, and $60,000.

The impact of the two financing plans is dramatic. Although both plans assume the same operating income, or EBIT, for comparative purposes at each

FIGURE 5–4
Financing plans and earnings per share

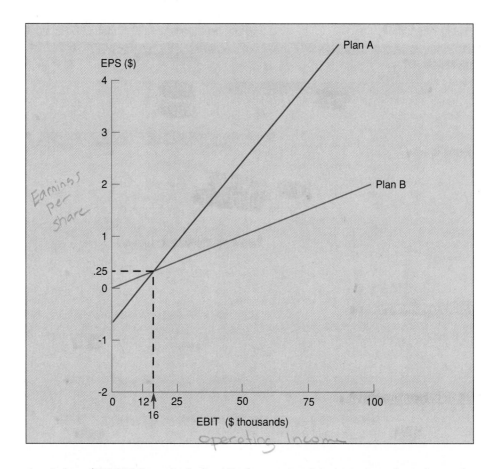

level (say $36,000 in calculation 4) the reported income per share is vastly different ($1.50 versus $0.67). It is also evident the conservative plan will produce better results at low income levels—but the leveraged plan will generate much better earnings per share as operating income, or EBIT, goes up. The firm would be indifferent between the two plans at an EBIT level of $16,000 as previously presented in Table 5–5.

In Figure 5–4, we graphically demonstrate the effect of the two financing plans on earnings per share.

With an EBIT of $16,000, we are earning *8 percent* on total assets of $200,000—precisely the percentage cost of borrowed funds to the firm. The use or nonuse of debt does not influence the answer. Beyond $16,000, Plan A, employing heavy financial leverage, really goes to work, allowing the firm to greatly expand earnings per share as a result of a change in EBIT. For example, at the EBIT level of $36,000, an 18 percent return on assets of $200,000 takes place—and financial leverage is clearly working to our benefit as earnings greatly expand.

Degree of Financial Leverage

As was true of operating leverage, degree of financial leverage measures the effect of a change in one variable on another variable. **Degree of financial**

leverage (DFL) may be defined as the percentage change in earnings (EPS) that occurs as a result of a percentage change in earnings before interest and taxes EBIT).

$$DFL = \frac{\text{Percent change in EPS}}{\text{Percent change in EBIT}} \qquad (5\text{--}4)$$

For purposes of computation, the formula for DFL may be conveniently restated as:

$$DFL = \frac{\text{EBIT}}{\text{EBIT} - \text{I}} \qquad (5\text{--}5)$$

Let's compute the degree of financial leverage for Plan A and Plan B, previously presented in Table 5–5, at an EBIT level of $36,000. Plan A calls for $12,000 of interest at all levels of financing, and Plan B requires $4,000.

Plan A (Leveraged)

$$DFL = \frac{\text{EBIT}}{\text{EBIT} - \text{I}} = \frac{\$36,000}{\$36,000 - \$12,000} = \frac{\$36,000}{\$24,000} = 1.5$$

Plan B (Conservative)

$$DFL = \frac{\text{EBIT}}{\text{EBIT} - \text{I}} = \frac{\$36,000}{\$36,000 - \$4,000} = \frac{\$36,000}{\$32,000} = 1.1$$

As expected, Plan A has a much higher degree of financial leverage. At an EBIT level of $36,000, a 1 percent increase in earnings will produce a 1.5 percent increase in earnings per share under Plan A, but only a 1.1 percent increase under Plan B. DFL may be computed for any level of operation, and it will change from point to point, but Plan A will always exceed Plan B.

Limitations to Use of Financial Leverage

The alert student may quickly observe that if debt is such a good thing, why sell any stock? (Perhaps one share to yourself.) With exclusive debt financing at an EBIT level of $36,000, we would have a degree of financial leverage factor (DFL) of 1.8.

$$DFL = \frac{\text{EBIT}}{\text{EBIT} - \text{I}} = \frac{\$36,000}{\$36,000 - \$16,000} = \frac{\$36,000}{\$20,000} = 1.8$$

(With no stock, we would borrow the full $200,000.)

$$(8\% \times \$200,000 = \$16,000 \text{ interest})$$

As stressed throughout the text, debt financing and financial leverage offer unique advantages, but only up to a point—beyond that point, debt financing may be detrimental to the firm. For example, as we expand the use of debt in our capital structure, lenders will perceive a greater financial risk for the firm. For that reason, they may raise the average interest rate to be paid and they may demand that certain restrictions be placed on the corporation. Furthermore, concerned common stockholders may drive down the price of the stock—forcing us away from the *objective of maximizing the firm's overall value* in the market. The impact of financial leverage must be carefully weighed.

This is not to say that financial leverage does not work to the benefit of the firm—it does if properly used. Further discussion of appropriate debt-equity mixes is covered in Chapter 11, "Cost of Capital." For now, we accept the virtues of financial leverage, knowing that all good things must be used in moderation. For firms in industries that offer some degree of stability, are in a positive stage of growth, and are operating in favorable economic conditions, the use of debt is recommended.

Combining Operating and Financial Leverage

If both operating and financial leverage allow us to magnify our returns, then we will get maximum leverage through their combined use in the form of **combined leverage**. We have said that operating leverage affects primarily the asset structure of the firm, while financial leverage affects the debt-equity mix. From an income statement viewpoint, operating leverage determines return from operations, while financial leverage determines how the "fruits of our labor" will be allocated to debt holders and, more importantly, to stockholders in the form of earnings per share. Table 5–6 shows the combined influence of operating and financial leverage on the income statement. The values in Table 5–6 are drawn from earlier material in the chapter (Tables 5–2 and 5–5). We assumed in both cases a high degree of operating and financial leverage. The sales volume is 80,000 units.

TABLE 5–6
Income statement

Sales (total revenue) (80,000 units @ $2) . . .	$160,000	
— Fixed costs	60,000	Operating
— Variable costs ($0.80 per unit)	64,000	leverage
Operating income	$ 36,000	
Earnings before interest and taxes	$ 36,000	
— Interest	12,000	
Earnings before taxes	24,000	Financial
— Taxes	12,000	leverage
Earnings after taxes	$ 12,000	
Shares	8,000	
Earnings per share	$1.50	

The student will observe, first, that operating leverage influences the top half of the income statement—determining operating income. The last item under operating leverage, operating income, then becomes the initial item for determining financial leverage. "Operating income" and "earnings before interest and taxes" are one and the same, representing the return to the corporation after production, marketing, and so forth—but before interest and taxes are paid. In the second half of the income statement, we then show the extent to which earnings before interest and taxes are translated into earnings per share. A graphical representation of these points is provided in Figure 5–5.

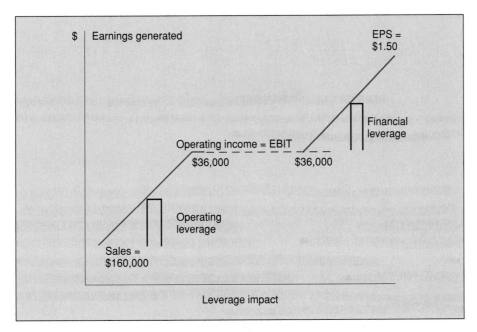

FIGURE 5–5
**Combining operating
and financial leverage**

Degree of Combined Leverage

Degree of combined leverage (DCL) uses the entire income statement and shows the impact of a change in sales or volume on bottom-line earnings per share. Degree of operating leverage and degree of financial leverage are, in effect, being combined. Table 5–7 shows what happens to profitability as the firm's sales go from $160,000 (80,000 units) to $200,000 (100,000 units).

TABLE 5–7
**Operating and
financial leverage**

	(Taken from Table 5–6)		
Sales—$2 per unit (80,000 units)	$160,000	(100,000 → units)	$200,000
– Fixed costs.	60,000		60,000
– Variable costs ($0.80 per unit)	64,000		80,000
Operating income = EBIT	36,000		60,000
– Interest.	12,000		12,000
Earnings before taxes.	24,000		48,000
– Taxes	12,000		24,000
Earnings before taxes.	$ 12,000		$ 24,000
Shares	8,000		8,000
Earnings per share	$1.50		$3.00

The formula for degree of combined leverage is stated as:

$$\text{Degree of combined leverage (DCL)} = \frac{\text{Percent change in EPS}}{\text{Percent change in sales (or volume)}} \qquad (5-6)$$

Using data from Table 5–7:

$$\frac{\text{Percent change in EPS}}{\text{Percent change in sales}} = \frac{\dfrac{\$1.50}{\$1.50} \times 100}{\dfrac{\$40,000}{\$160,000} \times 100} = \frac{100\%}{25\%} = 4$$

Every percentage point change in sales will be reflected in a 4 percent change in earnings per share at this level of operation (quite an impact).

An algebraic statement of the formula is:

$$\text{DCL} = \frac{Q(P - VC)}{Q(P - VC) - FC - I} \qquad (5-7)$$

From Table 5–7: Q (quantity) = 80,000; P (price per unit) = \$2.00; VC (variable costs per unit) = \$0.80; FC (fixed costs) = \$60,000; and I (interest) = \$12,000.

$$\text{DCL} = \frac{80,000(\$2.00 - \$0.80)}{80,000(\$2.00 - \$0.80) - \$60,000 - \$12,000}$$

$$= \frac{80,000(\$1.20)}{80,000(\$1.20) - \$72,000}$$

$$\text{DCL} = \frac{\$96,000}{\$96,000 - \$72,000} = \frac{\$96,000}{\$24,000} = 4$$

The answer is once again shown to be 4.[3]

A Word of Caution

In a sense, we are piling risk on risk as the two different forms of leverage are combined. Perhaps a firm carrying heavy operating leverage may wish to moderate its position financially, and vice versa. One thing is certain—the decision will have a major impact on the operations of the firm.

---

[3]The formula for DCL may be rewritten as:

$$\text{DCL} = \frac{Q(P - VC)}{Q(P - VC) - FC - I} = \frac{QP - QVC}{QP - QVC - FC - I}$$

We can rewrite the second terms as:

QP = S, or Sales (Quantity × Price)
QVC = TVC, or Total variable costs (Quantity × Variable cost per unit)
FC = Total fixed costs (remains the same term)
I = Interest (remains the same term)

We then have:

$$\text{DCL} = \frac{S - TVC}{S - TVC - FC - I} = \frac{\$160,000 - \$64,000}{\$160,000 - \$64,000 - \$60,000 - \$12,000} = \frac{\$96,000}{\$24,000} = 4$$

Summary

Leverage may be defined as the use of fixed cost items to magnify returns at high levels of operation. Operating leverage primarily affects fixed versus variable cost utilization in the operation of the firm. An important concept—degree of operating leverage (DOL)—measures the percentage change in operating income as a result of a percentage change in volume. The heavier the utilization of fixed cost assets, the higher DOL is likely to be.

Financial leverage reflects the extent to which debt is used in the capital structure of the firm. Substantial use of debt will place a great burden on the firm at low levels of profitability, but it will help to magnify earnings per share as volume or operating income increases. We combine operating and financial leverage to assess the impact of all types of fixed costs on the firm. There is a multiplier effect when we use the two different types of leverage.

Because leverage is a two-edged sword, management must be sure the level of risk assumed is in accord with its desires for risk and its perceptions of the future. High operating leverage may be balanced off against lower financial leverage if this is deemed desirable, and vice versa.

Review of Formulas

1. $BE = \dfrac{FC}{P - VC}$ (5–1)

   BE is break-even point
   FC is fixed costs
     P is price per unit
   VC is variable cost per unit

2. $DOL = \dfrac{Q(P - VC)}{Q(P - VC) - FC}$ (5–3)

   DOL is degree of operating leverage
     Q is quantity at which DOL is computed
     P is price per unit
   VC is variable cost per unit
   FC is fixed costs

3. $DOL = \dfrac{S - TVC}{S - TVC - FC}$ (footnote 2)

   DOL is degree of operating leverage
     S is sales (QP) at which DOL is computed
   TVC is total variable costs
     FC is fixed costs

4. $DFL = \dfrac{EBIT}{EBIT - I}$ (5–5)

   DFL is degree of financial leverage
   EBIT is earnings before interest and taxes
      I is interest

5. $DCL = \dfrac{Q(P - VC)}{Q(P - VC) - FC - I}$ (5-7)

DCL is degree of combined leverage
Q is quantity at which DCL is computed
P is price per unit
VC is variable cost per unit
FC is fixed costs
I is interest

6. $DCL = \dfrac{S - TVC}{S - TVC - FC - I}$ (footnote 3)

DCL is degree of combined leverage
S is sales (QP) at which DCL is computed
TVC is total variable costs
FC is fixed costs
I is interest

List of Terms

leverage 110
operating leverage 110
contribution margin 112
degree of operating leverage
  (DOL) 115
financial leverage 117

degree of financial leverage
  (DFL) 120
combined leverage 122
degree of combined leverage
  (DCL) 123

Discussion Questions

1. Discuss the various uses for break-even analysis.
2. What factors would cause a difference in the use of financial leverage for a utility company and an automobile company?
3. Explain how the break-even point and operating leverage are affected by the choice of manufacturing facilities (labor intensive versus capital intensive).
4. What role does depreciation play in break-even analysis based on accounting flows? Based on cash flows? What perspective is longer term in nature?
5. What does risk taking have to do with the use of operating and financial leverage?
6. Discuss the limitations of financial leverage.
7. How does the interest rate on new debt influence the use of financial leverage?
8. Explain how combined leverage brings together operating income and earnings per share.

9. Explain why operating leverage decreases as a company increases sales and shifts away from the break-even point.

10. Why does the starting level of sales determine the degree of operating leverage rather than the ending level of sales?

11. One could say financial leverage has its most important impact on earnings per share rather than net income after taxes. How would you support this statement?

12. Does being at the EPS indifference point mean you are always indifferent between two financing plans? Explain.

Problems

1. The Hazardous Toys Company produces boomerangs that sell for $8 each and have a variable cost of $7.50. Fixed costs are $15,000.
   a. Compute the break-even point in units.
   b. Find the sales (in units) needed to earn a profit of $25,000.

   Break-even analysis

2. Gibson & Sons, an appliance manufacturer, computes its break-even point strictly on the basis of cash expenditures related to fixed costs. Its total fixed costs are $1,200,000, but 25 percent of this value is represented by depreciation. Its contribution margin (price minus variable cost) for each unit sold is $2.40. How many units does the firm need to sell to reach the cash break-even point.

   Break-even analysis

3. Draw two break-even graphs—one for a conservative firm using labor-intensive production and another for a capital-intensive firm. Assuming these companies compete within the same industry and have identical sales, explain the impact of changes in sales volume on both firms' profits.

   Break-even analysis

4. The Ripken Company produces baseball gloves. The company's income statement for 1994 is as follows:

   Degree of leverage

RIPKEN COMPANY
Income Statement
For the Year Ended December 31, 1994

Sales (20,000 gloves at $60 each).	$1,200,000
Less: Variable costs (20,000 gloves at $20) . . .	400,000
Fixed costs	600,000
Earnings before interest and taxes (EBIT)	200,000
Interest expense	80,000
Earnings before taxes (EBT)	120,000
Income tax expense (30%)	36,000
Earnings after taxes (EAT)	$ 84,000

Given this income statement, compute the following:
a. Degree of operating leverage.
b. Degree of financial leverage.
c. Degree of combined leverage.

Degree of leverage

5. Freudian Slips and Gowns, Inc., income statement for 1994 is as follows:

FREUDIAN SLIPS AND GOWNS
Income Statement
For the Year Ended December 31, 1994

Sales (30,000 lessons at $25)	$750,000
Less: Variable costs (30,000 units at $7). . .	210,000
Fixed costs	270,000
Earnings before interest and taxes (EBIT) . . .	270,000
Interest expense.	170,000
Earnings before taxes (EBT).	100,000
Income tax expense (35%)	35,000
Earnings after taxes (EAT)	$ 65,000

Given this income statement, compute the following:

a. Degree of operating leverage.

b. Degree of financial leverage.

c. Degree of combined leverage.

d. Break-even point in units.

Break-even point and degree of leverage

6. University Catering sells 50-pound bags of popcorn to university dormitories for $10 a bag. The fixed costs of this operation are $80,000, while the variable costs of the popcorn are $.10 per pound.

a. What is the break-even point in bags?

b. Calculate the profit or loss on 12,000 bags and 25,000 bags.

c. What is the degree of operating leverage at 20,000 bags and 25,000 bags? Why does the degree of operating leverage change as quantity sold increases?

d. If University Catering has an annual interest payment of $10,000, calculate the degree of financial leverage at both 20,000 and 25,000 bags.

e. What is the degree of combined leverage at both sales levels?

Earnings per share and financial leverage

7. Leno's Drug Stores and Hall's Pharmaceuticals are competitors in the discount drug chain store business. The separate capital structures for Leno and Hall are presented below.

Leno		**Hall**	
Debt @ 10%.	$100,000	Debt @ 10%	$200,000
Common stock, $10 par	200,000	Common stock, $10 par. . . .	100,000
Total	$300,000	Total	$300,000
Shares.	20,000	Common shares	10,000

---

a. Compute earnings per share if earnings before interest and taxes are $20,000, $30,000, and $120,000 (assume a 30 percent tax rate).

b. Explain the relationship between earnings per share and level of EBIT.

c. If the cost of debt went up to 12 percent and all other factors remained equal, what would be the break-even level for EBIT?

8. In problem 7, compute the stock price for Hall Pharmaceuticals if it sells at 13 times earnings per share and EBIT is $80,000.

P/E ratio

9. Firms in Japan often employ both high operating and financial leverage because of the use of modern technology and close borrower-lender relationships. Assume the Susaki Company has a sales volume of 100,000 units at a price of $25 per unit; variable costs are $5 per unit and fixed costs are $1,500,000. Interest expense is $250,000. What is the degree of combined leverage for this Japanese firm?

Japanese firm and combined leverage

10. Glynn Enterprises and Monroe, Inc., both produce fluid control products. Their financial information is as follows:

Combining operating and financial leverage

Capital Structure	Glynn	Monroe
Debt @ 10%.	$1,500,000	0
Common stock, $10 per share	500,000	2,000,000
	$2,000,000	$2,000,000
Common shares.	50,000	200,000
Operating Plan		
Sales (200,000 units at $5 each).	$1,000,000	$1,000,000
Less: Variable costs.	600,000	200,000
	($3 per unit)	($1 per unit)
Fixed costs	0	400,000
Earnings before interest and taxes (EBIT)	$ 400,000	$ 400,000

a. If you combine Glynn's capital structure with Monroe's operating plan, what is the degree of combined leverage?

b. If you combine Monroe's capital structure with Glynn's operating plan, what is the degree of combined leverage?

c. Explain why you got the results you did in parts a and b.

d. In part b, if sales double, by what percent will EPS increase?

11. DeSoto Tools, Inc., is planning to expand production. The expansion will cost $300,000, which can either be financed by bonds at an interest rate of 14 percent or by selling 10,000 shares of common stock at $30 per share. The current income statement before expansion is as follows:

Expansion and leverage

DESOTO TOOLS, INC
Income Statement
199X

Sales		$1,500,000
Less: Variable costs	$450,000	
Fixed costs	550,000	1,000,000
Earnings before interest and taxes		500,000
Less: Interest expense		100,000
Earnings before taxes		400,000
Less: taxes @ 34%		136,000
Earnings after taxes		$ 264,000
Shares.		100,000
Earnings per share.		$2.64

After the expansion, sales are expected to increase by $1,000,000. Variable costs will remain 30 percent of sales, and fixed costs will increase to $800,000. The tax rate is 34 percent.

a. Calculate the degree of operating leverage, the degree of financial leverage, and the degree of combined leverage before expansion. (For the degree of operating leverage, use the formula developed in footnote 2; for the degree of combined leverage, use the formula developed in footnote 3. These instructions apply throughout this problem.)

b. Calculate the income statement for the two alternative financing plans.

c. Calculate the degree of operating leverage, the degree of financial leverage, and the degree of combined leverage, after expansion.

d. Explain which financing plan you favor and the risks involved with each plan.

Leverage analysis with actual companies

12. Using Standard & Poor's data or annual reports, compare the financial and operating leverage of Exxon, Eastman Kodak, and Southwest Airlines for the most current year. Explain the relationship between operating and financial leverage for each company and the resultant combined leverage. What accounts for the differences in leverage of these companies?

Leverage and sensitivity analysis

13. Dickinson Company has $12 million in assets. Currently half of these assets are financed with long-term debt at 10 percent and half with common stock having a par value of $8. Ms. Smith, vice-president of finance, wishes to analyze two refinancing plans, one with more debt (D) and one with more equity (E). The company earns a return on assets before interest and taxes of 10 percent. The tax rate is 45 percent.

Under Plan D, a $3 million long-term bond would be sold at an interest rate of 12 percent and 375,000 shares of stock would be purchased in the market at $8 per share and retired.

Under Plan E, 375,000 shares of stock would be sold at $8 per share and the $3,000,000 in proceeds would be used to reduce long-term debt.

a. How would each of these plans affect earnings per share? Consider the current plan and the two new plans.

b. Which plan would be most favorable if return on assets fell to 5 percent? Increased to 15 percent? Consider the current plan and the two new plans.

c. If the market price for common stock rose to $12 before the restructuring, which plan would then be most attractive? Continue to assume that $3 million in debt will be used to retire stock in Plan D and $3 million of new equity will be sold to retire debt in Plan E. Also assume for calculations in part c that return on assets is 10 percent.

Leverage and sensitivity analysis

14. Johnson Grass and Garden Centers has $20 million in assets, 75 percent financed by debt and 25 percent financed by common stock. The interest rate on the debt is 12 percent and the par value of the stock is $10 per share. President Johnson is considering two financing plans for

an expansion to $30 million in assets.

Under plan A, the debt-to-total-assets ratio will be maintained, but new debt will cost 15 percent! New stock will be sold at $10 per share. Under plan B, only new common stock at $10 per share will be issued. The tax rate is 40 percent.

a. If EBIT is 12 percent on total assets, compute earnings per share (EPS) before the expansion and under the two alternatives.

b. What is the degree of financial leverage under each of the three plans?

c. If stock could be sold at $20 per share due to increased expectations for the firm's sales and earnings, what impact would this have on earnings per share for the two expansion alternatives? Compute earnings per share for each.

d. Explain why corporate financial officers are concerned about their stock values!

15. Mr. Katz is in the widget business. He currently sells 2 million widgets a year at $4 each. His variable cost to produce the widgets is $3 per unit, and he has $1,500,000 in fixed costs. His sales-to-assets ratio is four times, and 40 percent of his assets are financed with 9 percent debt, with the balance financed by common stock at $10 per share. The tax rate is 30 percent.

Operating leverage and ratios

His brother-in-law, Mr. Doberman, says he is doing it all wrong. By reducing his price to $3.75 a widget, he could increase his volume of units sold by 40 percent. Fixed costs would remain constant, and variable costs would remain $3 per unit. His sales-to-assets ratio would be 5 times. Furthermore, he could increase his debt-to-assets ratio to 50 percent, with the balance in common stock. It is assumed that the interest rate would go up by 1 percent and the price of stock would remain constant.

a. Compute earnings per share under the Katz plan.

b. Compute earnings per share under the Doberman plan.

c. Mr. Katz's wife does not think fixed costs would remain constant under the Doberman plan but they would go up by 20 percent. If this is the case, should Mr. Katz shift to the Doberman plan, based on earnings per share?

16. Highland Cable Company is considering an expansion of its facilities. Its current income statement is as follows:

Expansion, break-even analysis, and leverage

Sales	$4,000,000
Less: Variable expense (50% of sales) . . .	2,000,000
Fixed expense	1,500,000
Earnings before interest and taxes (EBIT) . . .	500,000
Interest (10% cost)	140,000
Earnings before taxes (EBT)	360,000
Tax (30%).	108,000
Earnings after taxes (EAT)	252,000
Shares of common stock	200,000
Earnings per share	$1.26

Highland Cable Company is currently financed with 50 percent debt and 50 percent equity (common stock, par value of $10). To expand facilities, Mr. Highland estimates a need for $2 million in additional financing. His investment banker has laid out three plans for him to consider:

1. Sell $2 million of debt at 13 percent.
2. Sell $2 million of common stock at $20 per share.
3. Sell $1 million of debt at 12 percent and $1 million of common stock at $25 per share.

Variable costs are expected to stay at 50 percent of sales, while fixed expenses will increase to $1,900,000 per year. Mr. Highland is not sure how much this expansion will add to sales, but he estimates sales will rise by $1 million per year for the next five years.

Mr. Highland is interested in a thorough analysis of his expansion plans and methods of financing. He would like you to analyze the following:

a. The break-even point for operating expenses before and after expansion (in sales dollars).

b. The degree of operating leverage before and after expansion. Assume sales of $4 million before expansion and $5 million after expansion. Use the formula in footnote 2.

c. The degree of financial leverage before expansion at sales of $4 million and for all three methods of financing after expansion. Assume sales of $5 million for the second part of this question.

d. Compute EPS under all three methods of financing the expansion at $5 million in sales (first year) and $9 million in sales (last year).

e. What can we learn from the answer to part d about the advisability of the three methods of financing the expansion?

COMPREHENSIVE PROBLEM

Aspen Ski Company
(review of Chapters 2 through 5)

ASPEN SKI Company
Balance Sheet
December 31, 1993

Assets		Liabilities and Stockholders' Equity	
Cash.	$ 40,000	Accounts payable	$1,800,000
Marketable securities. . .	60,000	Accrued expenses	100,000
Accounts receivable . . .	1,000,000	Notes payable (current). . . .	600,000
Inventory.	3,000,000	Bonds (10%)	2,000,000
Gross plant and		Common stock (1.5 million	
equipment	5,000,000	shares, par value $1)	1,500,000
Less: Accumulated		Retained earnings	1,100,000
depreciation	2,000,000		
		Total liabilities and	
Total assets	$7,100,000	stockholders' equity	$7,100,000

Income Statement 1993

Sales (credit)	$6,000,000
Fixed costs*	1,800,000
Variable costs (0.60)	3,600,000
Earnings before interest and taxes	600,000
Less: Interest	200,000
Earnings before taxes	400,000
Less: Taxes @ 40%	160,000
Earnings after taxes	240,000
Dividends	43,200
Increased retained earnings	$ 196,800

*Fixed costs include (*a*) lease expense of $190,000 and
(*b*) depreciation of $400,000.

Note: Aspen Ski also has $100,000 per year in sinking fund
obligations associated with its bond issue. The sinking fund
represents an annual repayment of the principal amount of the
bond. It is not tax deductible.

Ratios

	Aspen Ski (to be filled in)	Industry
Profit margin		6.1%
Return on assets		6.5%
Return on equity		8.9%
Receivables turnover		4.9 ×
Inventory turnover		4.4 ×
Fixed asset turnover		2.1 ×
Total asset turnover		1.06 ×
Current ratio		1.4 ×
Quick ratio		1.1 ×
Debt to total assets		27%
Interest coverage		4.2 ×
Fixed charge coverage		3.0 ×

---

a. Analyze Aspen Ski Company, using ratio analysis. Compute the ratios above for Aspen and compare them to the industry data that is given. Discuss the weak points, strong points, and what you think should be done to improve the company's performance.

b. In your analysis, calculate the overall break-even point in sales dollars and the cash break-even point. Also compute the degree of operating leverage, degree of financial leverage, and degree of combined leverage.

c. Use the information in parts *a* and *b* to discuss the risk associated with this company. Given the risk, decide whether a bank should loan funds to Aspen Ski.

Aspen Ski Company is trying to plan the funds needed for 1994. The management anticipates an increase in sales of 20 percent, which can be absorbed without increasing fixed assets.

d. What would be Aspen's needs for external funds based on the current balance sheet? Compute RNF (required new funds). Notes payable (current) are not part of the liability calculation.

e. What would be the required new funds if the company brings its ratios into line with the industry average during 1994? Specifically examine receivables turnover, inventory turnover, and the profit margin. Use the new values to recompute the factors in RNF (assume liabilities stay the same).

f. Do not calculate, only comment on these questions. How would required new funds change if the company:

1. Were at full capacity?
2. Raised the dividend payout ratio?
3. Suffered a decreased growth in sales?
4. Faced an accelerated inflation rate?

Selected References

Bhide, Amar. "Why Not Leverage Your Company to the Hilt?" *Harvard Business Review* 66 (May–June 1988), pp. 92–98.

Dugan, Michael T., and Keith A. Shriver. "An Empirical Comparison of Alternative Methods for the Estimation of the Degree of Operating Leverage." *Financial Review* 27 (May 1992), pp. 309–21.

Leibowitz, Martin L., Stanley Kogelman, and Eric B. Lindenberg. "A Shortfall Approach to the Creditor's Decision: How Much Leverage Can a Firm Support?" *Financial Analysts* 46 (May–June 1990), pp. 43–52.

Levy, Haim, and Robert Brooks. "Financial Break-Even Analysis and the Value of the Firm." *Financial Management* 15 (Autumn 1986), pp. 22–26.

Lewellen, Wilbur G., and William A. Kracaw. "Inflation, Corporate Growth, and Corporate Leverage." *Financial Management* 16 (Winter 1987), pp. 29–36.

Maur, David C., and Wilbur G. Lewellen. "Debt Management Under Corporate and Personal Taxation." *Journal of Finance* 42 (December 1987), pp. 1275–92.

Miller, Merton. "Leverage." *Journal of Applied Corporate Finance* 4 (Summer 1991), pp. 6–12.

O'Brien, Thomas J., and Paul A. Vanderheiden. "Empirical Measurement of Operating Leverage for Growing Firms." *Financial Management* 16 (Summer 1987), pp. 43–53.

Prezas, Alexandros P. "Effects of Debt on the Degree of Operating and Financial Leverage." *Financial Management* 16 (Summer 1987), pp. 329–44.

Rendleman, Richard J., Jr. "The Effect of Default Risk on the Firm's Investment and Financing Decisions." *Financial Management* 7 (Spring 1978), pp. 45–53

Sarig, Oded, and James Scott. "The Puzzle of Financial Leverage Clienteles." *Journal of Finance* 40 (December 1985), pp. 1459–67.

Scott, David F., and J. D. Martin. "Industry Influence on Financial Structure." *Financial Management* 4 (Spring 1975), pp. 67–73.

————, **and Dana J. Johnson.** "Financing Policies and Practices in Large Corporations." *Financial Management* 11 (Summer 1982), pp. 51–57.

Working Capital Management

INTRODUCTION

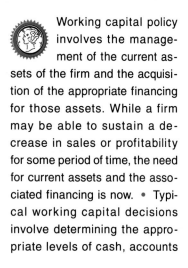

Working capital policy involves the management of the current assets of the firm and the acquisition of the appropriate financing for those assets. While a firm may be able to sustain a decrease in sales or profitability for some period of time, the need for current assets and the associated financing is now. • Typical working capital decisions involve determining the appropriate levels of cash, accounts receivable, and inventory that the firm should maintain. On the financing side, we must determine whether to carry these assets through credit extension from our supplier, short-term bank loans, or longer-term credit arrangements. The smaller firm usually has a limited number of options. • As we shall see, one of the unfortunate choices of terms in the vernacular of finance and accounting is the phrase *current asset.* The normal definition of a current asset is a short-term asset that can be converted to cash within one year or within the normal operating cycle of the firm. As a business begins to grow, some current assets become more "permanent" in nature—a minimum amount of inventory is always on hand, and, as sales on credit increase, so do accounts receivable. These so-called current assets become more and more permanent and remain on the books of the firm. All too often, firms think of current assets as being temporary, when, in fact, those that become more

permanent in nature may require longer-term financing. A mismatching of asset needs and financing can lead to bankruptcy as attested to by the unfortunate experiences of some retailers, oil equipment supply firms, farmers, and others in the last decade. • In the initial chapter on working capital, Chapter 6, we examine some of the basic conceptual items related to working capital and the financing decision, with an eye toward the various risk-return alternatives that are available to the financial manager. Some real world examples of the publishing and retail industries demonstrate the concept of cyclical sales and earnings on a quarterly basis. • In Chapter 7 we look at specific techniques for the management of cash, marketable securities, accounts receivable, and inventory. Our focus is on the use of efficient management techniques in the allocation of funds. Techniques for controlling asset levels such as just-in-time inventory management (JIT) are given special attention. • Finally, in Chapter 8, we examine the various sources of short-term financing that are available to the firm. The emphasis is on trade credit, bank financing, and the use of secured loans through the pledging of receivables or inventory as collateral. The relative costs, advantages, and disadvantages of these financing outlets are considered. Also, at the end of the chapter, we examine how the financial futures market can be used to hedge the firm's exposure to changing interest rates.

CHAPTER 6

Working Capital and the Financing Decision

CHAPTER CONCEPTS

1 Working capital management involves financing and controlling the current assets of the firm.

2 Management must distinguish between those current assets that are easily converted to cash and those that are more permanent.

3 The financing of an asset should be tied to how long the asset is likely to be on the balance sheet.

4 Long-term financing is usually more expensive than short-term financing based on the theory of the term structure of interest rates.

5 Risk as well as profitability determine the financing plan for current assets.

The rapid growth of business firms in the last two decades has challenged the ingenuity of financial managers to provide adequate financing. Rapidly expanding sales may cause intense pressure for inventory and receivables buildup—draining the cash resources of the firm. As indicated in Chapter 4, "Financial Forecasting," a large sales increase creates an expansion of current assets, especially accounts receivable and inventory. Some of the increased current assets can be financed through the firm's retained earnings, but in most cases internal funds will not provide enough financing and some external sources of funds must be found. In fact, the faster the growth in sales, the more likely it is that an increasing percentage of financing will be external to the firm. These funds could come from the sale of common stock, preferred stock, long-term bonds, short-term securities, and bank loans, or from a combination of short- and long-term sources of funds.

Working capital management involves the financing and management of the current assets of the firm. The financial executive probably devotes more time to working capital management than to any other activity. Current assets, by their very nature, are changing daily, if not hourly, and managerial decisions must be made. "How much inventory is to be carried, and how do we get the funds to pay for it?" Unlike long-term decisions, there can be no deferral of action. While long-term decisions, involving plant and equipment or market strategy, may well determine the eventual success of the firm, short-term decisions on working capital determine whether the firm gets to the long term.

In this chapter we examine the nature of asset growth, the process of matching sales and production, financial aspects of working capital management, and the factors that go into development of an optimum policy.

The Nature of Asset Growth

Any company that produces and sells a product, whether the product is consumer or manufacturer oriented, will have current assets and fixed assets. If a firm grows, those assets are likely to increase over time. The key to current asset planning is the ability of management to forecast sales accurately and then to match the production schedules with the sales forecast. Whenever actual sales are different from forecasted sales, unexpected buildups or reductions in inventory will occur that will eventually affect receivables and cash flow.

In the simplest case, all of the firm's current assets will be **self-liquidating assets** (sold at the end of a specified time period). Assume that at the start of the summer you buy 100 tires to be disposed of by September. It is your intention that all tires will be sold, receivables collected, and bills paid over this time period. In this case your working capital (current asset) needs are truly short term.

Now let us begin to expand the business. In stage two you add radios, seat covers, and batteries to your operation. Some of your inventory will again be completely liquidated, while other items will form the basic stock for your operation. To stay in business, you must maintain floor displays and multiple items for selection. Furthermore not all items will sell. As you eventually grow to more than one store, this "permanent" aggregate stock of current assets will continue to increase. Problems of inadequate financing arrangements are often the result of the businessperson's failure to realize the firm is carrying not only self-liquidating inventory, but also the anomaly of **"permanent" current assets.**

The movement from stage one to stage two growth for a typical business is depicted in Figure 6–1. In Panel A the buildup in current assets is **temporary**—while in Panel B, part of the growth in current assets is temporary and part is permanent. (Fixed assets are included in the illustrations, but they are not directly related to the present discussion.)

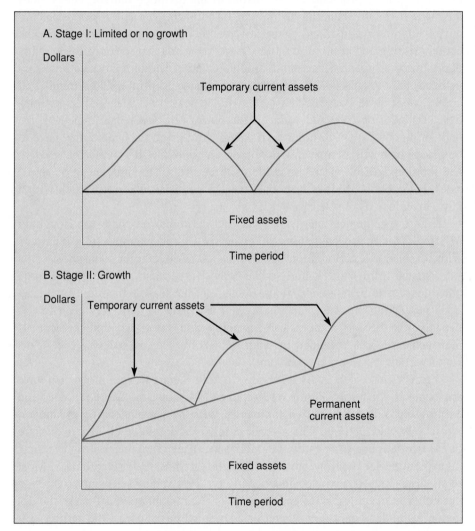

FIGURE 6–1
The nature of asset growth

A. Stage I: Limited or no growth

Dollars

Temporary current assets

Fixed assets

Time period

B. Stage II: Growth

Dollars

Temporary current assets

Permanent current assets

Fixed assets

Time period

In most firms, fixed assets grow slowly as productive capacity is increased and old equipment is replaced, but current assets fluctuate in the short run, depending on the level of production versus the level of sales. When the firm produces more than it sells, inventory rises. When sales rise faster than production, inventory declines and receivables rise.

Controlling Assets— Matching Sales and Production

As discussed in the treatment of the cash budgeting process in Chapter 4, some firms employ **level production** methods to smooth production schedules and use manpower and equipment efficiently at a lower cost. One consequence of level production is that current assets go up and down when sales and production are not equal. Other firms may try to match sales and production as closely as possible in the short run. This allows current assets to increase or decrease with the level of sales and eliminates the large seasonal bulges or sharp reductions in current assets that occur under level production.

Publishing companies are good examples of companies with seasonal sales and an inventory problem. By the nature of the textbook market, heavy sales are made in the third quarter of the year for fall semester sales. Most sales occur in July and August, and again in December for the second semester. The actual printing and binding of a book has fixed costs that make printing many copies more efficient. Since publishing companies cannot reproduce books on demand, they contract with the printing company to print a fixed number of copies, depending on expected sales over at least one year and sometimes based on sales over several years. If the books sell better than expected, the publishing company will order a second or third printing. Orders may have to be placed as much as nine months before the books will actually be needed, and reorders will be placed as much as three or four months ahead of actual sales. If the book declines in popularity, the publisher could get stuck with a large inventory of obsolete books.

Figure 6–2 depicts quarterly sales and earnings per share for Houghton Mifflin. This major publishing company is a good example of a company with seasonal sales. Houghton Mifflin has all of its earnings and most of its sales in the third quarter, and so the heavy fixed costs of publishing force other quarters to be relatively weak. Because of the seasonal nature of the textbook publishing business, lenders as well as financial managers need to understand the need for inventory financing and inventory management. If management has not planned inventory correctly, the lost sales or excess inventory could be a serious problem.

Retail firms, such as J. C. Penney Co. and Kmart Corporation, also have seasonal sales patterns. Figure 6–3 on page 144 shows the quarterly sales and earnings per share of these two companies, with the quarters ending in January, April, July, and October. These retail companies do not stock a year or more of inventory at one time as do the publishers. They are either selling products manufactured for them by others or manufactured by their subsidiaries. Most retail stores are not involved in deciding on level versus seasonal production but rather in matching sales and inventory. Their suppliers must make the decision to produce on either a level or a seasonal basis. Since the selling seasons are very much affected by the weather and holiday periods, the suppliers and retailers cannot avoid the inventory risk. The fourth quarter beginning in October and ending in December is the biggest quarter for retailers and accounts for as much as one half of their earnings. You can be sure that inventory not sold during the Christmas season will be put on sale during January.

Figure 6–3 demonstrates that over several years, each peak and trough in quarterly sales is generally higher for both companies. These seasonal peaks and troughs will also be reflected in cash, receivables, and inventory. Both

FIGURE 6–2

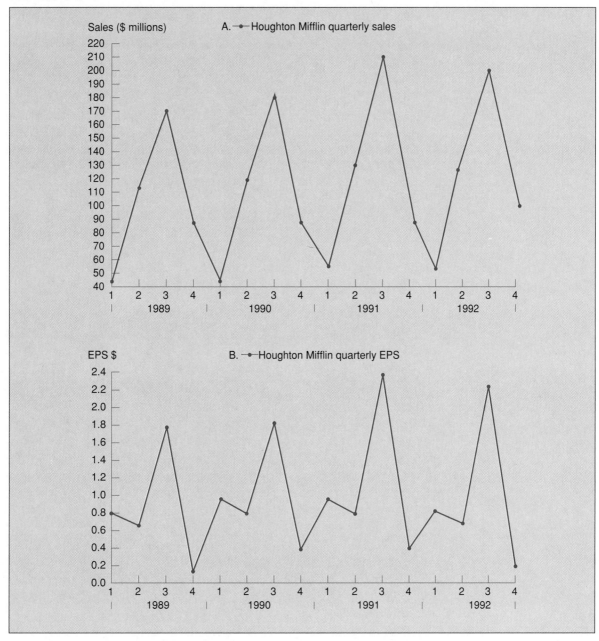

companies demonstrate the impact of leverage on earnings as discussed in Chapter 5. Notice that when J. C. Penney's sales surge, earnings per share rise by a far greater percentage (bottom of Figure 6–3 on page 144). We shall see as we go through the chapter that seasonal sales can cause asset management problems. A financial manager must be aware of these problems to avoid getting caught short of cash or unprepared to borrow when necessary.

Many retail-oriented firms have been more successful in matching sales and orders in recent years because of new, computerized inventory control systems linked to on-line point-of-sales terminals. These **point-of-sales**

FIGURE 6–3

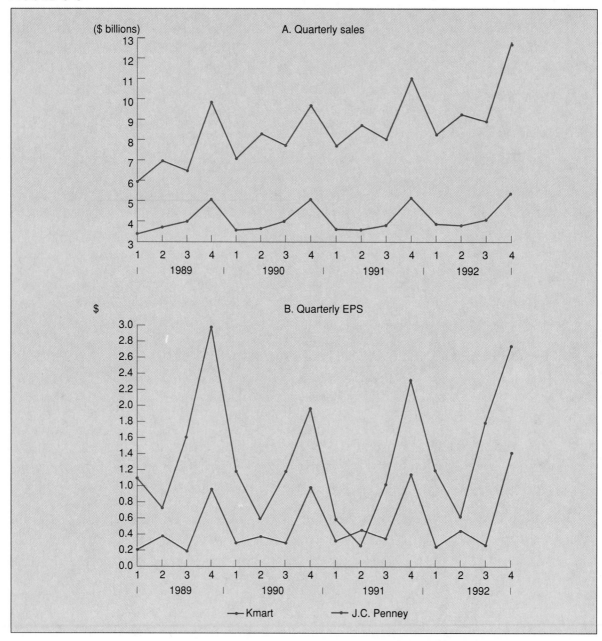

terminals either allow digital input or use of optical scanners to record the inventory code numbers and the amount of each item sold. At the end of the day, managers can examine sales and inventory levels item by item and, if need be, adjust orders or production schedules. The predictability of the market will influence the speed with which the manager reacts to this information, while the length and complexity of the production process will dictate just how fast production levels can be changed.

Temporary Assets under Level Production—An Example

To get a better understanding of how current assets fluctuate, let us use the example of the Yawakuzi Motorcycle Company, which manufactures and sells in the snowy U.S. Midwest. Not too many people will be buying motorcycles during October through March, but sales will pick up in early spring and summer and will trail off during the fall. Because of the fixed assets and the skilled labor involved in the production process, Yawakuzi decides that level production is the least expensive and the most efficient production method. The marketing department provides a sales forecast for October through September (Table 6–1).

TABLE 6-1   **Yawakuzi sales forecast (in units)**

1st Quarter		2nd Quarter		3rd Quarter		4th Quarter	
October	300	January . . .	0	April	1,000	July	2,000
November	150	February. . .	0	May	2,000	August.	1,000
December	50	March	600	June	2,000	September. . . .	500

Total sales of 9,600 units at $3,000 each = $28,800,000 in sales.

After reviewing the sales forecast, Yawakuzi decides to produce 800 motorcycles per month, or one year's production of 9,600 divided by 12. A look at Table 6–2 shows how level production and seasonal sales combine to create fluctuating inventory. Assume that October's beginning inventory is one month's production of 800 units. The ending inventory level is computed for each month and then multiplied by the production cost per unit of $2,000.

TABLE 6-2   **Yawakuzi's production schedule and inventory**

	Beginning inventory	+	Production (level production)	−	Sales	=	Ending inventory	Inventory (at cost of $2,000 per unit)
October	800		800		300		1,300	$2,600,000
November	1,300		800		150		1,950	3,900,000
December	1,950		800		50		2,700	5,400,000
January	2,700		800		0		3,500	7,000,000
February. . . .	3,500		800		0		4,300	8,600,000
March	4,300		800		600		4,500	9,000,000
April	4,500		800		1,000		4,300	8,600,000
May	4,300		800		2,000		3,100	6,200,000
June	3,100		800		2,000		1,900	3,800,000
July	1,900		800		2,000		700	1,400,000
August.	700		800		1,000		500	1,000,000
September	500		800		500		800	1,600,000

The inventory level at cost fluctuates from a high of $9 million in March, the last consecutive month in which production is greater than sales, to a low of $1 million in August, the last month in which sales are greater than production. Table 6–3 on page 146 combines a sales forecast, a cash receipts schedule,

TABLE 6–3 Sales forecast, cash receipts and payments, and cash budget

	Oct.	Nov.	Dec.	Jan.	Feb.	March	April	May	June	July	Aug.	Sept.
Sales Forecast ($ millions)												
Sales (units)	300	150	50	0	0	600	1,000	2,000	2,000	2,000	1,000	500
Sales (unit price, $3,000)	$0.9	$0.45	$0.15	$ 0	$ 0	$1.8	$3.0	$6.0	$6.0	$6.0	$3.0	$1.5
Cash Receipts Schedule ($ millions)												
50% cash	$0.45	$0.225	$0.075	$ 0	$ 0	$0.9	$1.5	$3.0	$3.0	$3.0	$1.5	$0.75
50% from prior month's sales	0.75*	0.450	0.225	0.075	0	0	0.9	1.5	3.0	3.0	3.0	1.50
Total cash receipts	$1.20	$0.675	$0.300	$0.075	0	$0.9	$2.4	$4.5	$6.0	$6.0	$4.5	$2.25

*Assumes September sales of $1.5 million.

	Oct.	Nov.	Dec.	Jan.	Feb.	March	April	May	June	July	Aug.	Sept.
Cash Payments Schedule ($ millions)												
Constant production of 800 units/month (cost, $2,000 per unit)	$1.6	$1.6	$1.6	$1.6	$1.6	$1.6	$1.6	$1.6	$1.6	$1.6	$1.6	$1.6
Overhead	0.4	0.4	0.4	0.4	0.4	0.4	0.4	0.4	0.4	0.4	0.4	0.4
Dividends and interest	—	—	—	—	—	—	—	—	—	—	1.0	—
Taxes	0.3	—	—	0.3	—	—	0.3	—	—	0.3	—	—
Total cash payments	$2.3	$2.0	$2.0	$2.3	$2.0	$2.0	$2.3	$2.0	$2.0	$2.3	$3.0	$2.0

	Oct.	Nov.	Dec.	Jan.	Feb.	March	April	May	June	July	Aug.	Sept.
Cash Budget ($ millions; required minimum balance is $0.25 million)												
Cash flow	$(1.1)	$(1.325)	$(1.7)	$(2.225)	$(2.0)	$(1.1)	$0.1	$ 2.5	$4.0	$3.7	$1.5	$0.25
Beginning cash	0.25†	0.25	0.25	0.250	0.25	0.25	0.25	0.25	0.25	0.25	1.1	2.60
Cumulative cash balance	$(0.85)	$(1.075)	$(1.45)	$(1.975)	$(1.75)	$(0.85)	$0.35	$ 2.75	$4.25	$3.95	$2.6	$2.85
Monthly loan or (repayment)	1.1	1.325	1.7	2.225	2.0	1.1	(0.1)	(2.5)	(4.0)	(2.85)	0	0
Cumulative loan	1.1	2.425	4.125	6.350	8.35	9.45	9.35	6.85	2.85	0	0	0
Ending cash balance	0.25	0.25	0.25	0.25	0.25	0.25	0.25	0.25	0.25	1.1	2.6	2.85

†Assumes cash balance of $0.25 million at the beginning of October and that this is the desired minimum cash balance.

146

a cash payments schedule, and a brief cash budget in order to examine the buildup in accounts receivable and cash.

In Table 6–3 the *sales forecast* is based on assumptions in Table 6–1. The unit volume of sales is multiplied by a sales price of $3,000 to get sales dollars in millions. Next, *cash receipts* represent 50 percent collected in cash during the month of sale and 50 percent from the prior month's sales. For example, in October this would represent $0.45 million from the current month plus $0.75 million from the prior month's sales.

Cash payments in Table 6–3 are based on an assumption of level production of 800 units per month at a cost of $2,000 per unit, or $1.6 million, plus payments for overhead, dividends, interest, and taxes.

Finally the *cash budget* in Table 6–3 represents a comparison of the cash receipts and cash payments schedules to determine cash flow. We further assume the firm desires a minimum cash balance of $0.25 million. Thus in October, a negative cash flow of $1.1 million brings the cumulative cash balance to a negative $0.85 million and $1.1 million must be borrowed to provide an ending cash balance of $0.25 million. Similar negative cash flows in subsequent months necessitate expanding the bank loan. For example, in November there is a negative cash flow of $1.325 million. This brings the cumulative cash balance to −$1.075 million, requiring additional borrowings of $1.325 million to ensure a minimum cash balance of $0.25 million. The cumulative loan through November (October and November borrowings) now adds up to $2.425 million. Our cumulative bank loan is highest in the month of March.

We now wish to ascertain our total current asset buildup as a result of level production and fluctuating sales for October through September. The analysis is presented in Table 6–4. The cash figures come directly from the last line of Table 6–3. The accounts receivable balance is based on the assumption that accounts receivable represent 50 percent of sales in a given month, as the other 50 percent is paid for in cash. Thus the accounts receivable figure in Table 6–4 represents 50 percent of the sales figure from the second numerical line in Table 6–3. Finally, the inventory figure in Table 6–4 is taken directly from the last column of Table 6–2, which presented the production schedule and inventory data.

TABLE 6–4
Total current assets, first year ($ millions)

	Cash	Accounts Receivable	Inventory	Total Current Assets
October	$0.25	$0.450	$2.6	$ 3.30
November . . .	0.25	0.225	3.9	4.375
December . . .	0.25	0.075	5.4	5.725
January	0.25	0.00	7.0	7.25
February	0.25	0.00	8.6	8.85
March	0.25	0.90	9.0	10.15
April	0.25	1.50	8.6	10.35
May	0.25	3.00	6.2	9.45
June	0.25	3.00	3.8	7.05
July	1.10	3.00	1.4	5.50
August	2.60	1.50	1.0	5.10
September . . .	2.85	0.75	1.6	5.20

Total current assets in Table 6–4 start at $3.3 million in October and rise to $10.35 million in the peak month of April. From April through August, sales are larger than production and inventory falls to its low of $1 million in August, but accounts receivables peak at $3 million in the highest sales months of May, June, and July. The cash budget in Table 6–3 on page 146 explains the cash flows and external funds borrowed to finance asset accumulation. From October to March, Yawakuzi borrows more and more money to finance the inventory buildup, but from April forward it eliminates all borrowing as inventory is liquidated and cash balances rise to complete the cycle. In October the cycle starts over again; but now the firm has accumulated cash it can use to finance next year's asset accumulation, pay a larger dividend, replace old equipment, or—if growth in sales is anticipated—invest in new equipment to increase productive capacity. Table 6–5 presents the cash budget and total current assets for the second year. Under a simplified no-growth assumption, the monthly cash flow is the same as that of the first year, but beginning cash in October is much higher from the first year's ending cash balance and this lowers the borrowing requirement and increases the ending cash balance and total current assets at year-end. Higher current assets are present despite the fact accounts receivable and inventory do not change.

Figure 6–4 is a graphic presentation of the current asset cycle. It includes the two years covered in Tables 6–4 and 6–5 assuming level production and no sales growth.

FIGURE 6–4
The nature of asset growth (Yawakuzi)

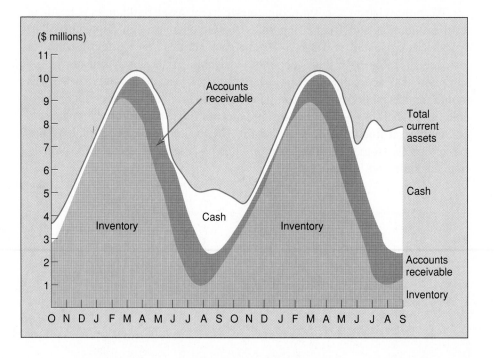

Patterns of
Financing

The financial manager's selection of external sources of funds to finance assets may be one of the firm's most important decisions. The axiom that all current assets should be financed by current liabilities (accounts payable, bank

TABLE 6–5 Cash budget and assets for second year with no growth in sales ($ millions)

	End of First Year	Second Year											
	Sept.	Oct.	Nov.	Dec.	Jan.	Feb.	March	April	May	June	July	Aug.	Sept.
Cash flow	$0.25	$(1.1)	$(1.325)	$(1.7)	$(2.225)	$(2.0)	$(1.1)	$ 0.1	$2.5	$ 4.0	$ 3.7	$1.5	$0.25
Beginning cash	2.60	2.85	1.750	0.425	0.25	0.25	0.25	0.25	0.25	0.25	0.25	3.7	5.2
Cumulative cash balance		1.75	0.425	(1.275)	(1.975)	(1.75)	(0.85)	0.35	2.75	4.25	3.95	5.2	5.45
Monthly loan or (repayment)		—	—	1.525	2.225	2.0	1.1	(0.1)	(2.5)	(4.0)	(0.25)	—	—
Cumulative loan		—	—	1.525	3.750	5.75	6.85	6.75	4.25	0.25	0	—	—
Ending cash balance	$2.85	$ 1.75	$ 0.425	$ 0.25	$ 0.25	$ 0.25	$ 0.25	$ 0.25	$ 0.25	$ 0.25	$ 3.70	$5.2	$5.45
Total Current Assets													
Ending cash balance	$2.85	$ 1.75	$ 0.425	$ 0.25	$ 0.25	$ 0.25	$ 0.25	$ 0.25	$ 0.25	$ 0.25	$ 3.70	$5.2	$5.45
Accounts receivable	0.75	0.45	0.225	0.075	0	0	0.95	1.50	3.0	3.0	3.0	1.5	0.75
Inventory	1.6	2.6	3.9	5.4	7.0	8.6	9.0	8.6	6.2	3.8	1.4	1.0	1.60
Total current assets	$5.2	$ 4.8	$ 4.55	$ 5.725	$ 7.25	$ 8.85	$10.15	$10.35	$ 9.45	$7.05	$ 8.1	$7.7	$7.80

149

loans, commercial paper, etc.) is subject to challenge when one sees the permanent buildup that can occur in current assets. In the Yawakuzi example, the buildup in inventory was substantial, at $9 million. The example had a logical conclusion in that the motorcycles were sold, cash was generated, and current assets became very liquid. What if a much smaller level of sales had occurred? Yawakuzi would be sitting on a large inventory that needed to be financed and would be generating no cash. Theoretically, the firm could be declared technically insolvent (bankrupt) if short-term sources of funds were used but were unable to be renewed when they came due. How would the interest and principal be paid without cash flow from inventory liquidation? The most appropriate financing pattern would be one in which asset buildup and length of financing terms are perfectly matched, as indicated in Figure 6–5.

FIGURE 6–5
Matching long-term and short-term needs

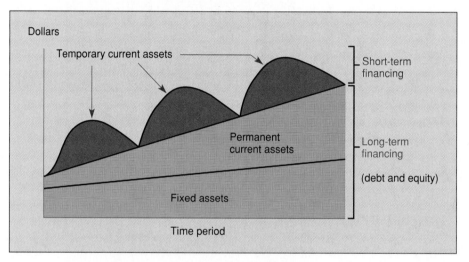

In the upper part of Figure 6–5 we see that the temporary buildup in current assets is financed by short-term funds (represented by red). More importantly, however, permanent current assets, as well as fixed assets, are financed with long-term funds (represented by green) from the sale of stock, the issuance of bonds, or retention of earnings.

Alternative Plans

Only a financial manager with unusual insight and timing could construct a financial plan for working capital that adhered perfectly to the design in Figure 6–5. The difficulty rests in precisely determining what part of current assets is temporary and what part is permanent. Even if dollar amounts could be ascertained, the exact timing of asset liquidation is a difficult matter. To compound the problem, we are never quite sure how much short-term or long-term financing is available at a given time. While the precise synchronization of temporary current assets and short-term financing depicted in Figure 6–5 may be the most desirable and logical plan, other alternatives must be considered.

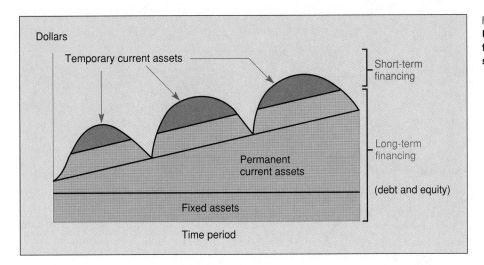

FIGURE 6-6
Using long-term financing for part of short-term needs

Long-Term Financing

To protect against the danger of not being able to provide adequate short-term financing in tight money periods, the financial manager may rely on long-term funds to cover some short-term needs. As indicated in Figure 6–6, long-term capital is now being used to finance fixed assets, permanent current assets, and part of *temporary current assets.*

By using long-term capital to cover part of short-term needs, the firm virtually assures itself of having adequate capital at all times. The firm may prefer to borrow a million dollars for 10 years—rather than attempt to borrow a million dollars at the beginning of each year for 10 years and paying it back at the end of each year.

Short-Term Financing (Opposite Approach)

This is not to say that all financial managers utilize long-term financing on a large scale. To acquire long-term funds, the firm must generally go to the capital markets with a bond or stock offering or must privately place longer-term obligations with insurance companies, wealthy individuals, and so forth. Many small businesses do not have access to such long-term capital and are forced to rely heavily on short-term bank and trade credit. In the capital shortage era of the 1980s, even some large businesses were forced to operate with short-term funds.

Furthermore, short-term financing offers some advantages over more extended financial arrangements. As a general rule, the interest rate on short-term funds is lower than that on long-term funds. We might surmise then that a firm could develop a working capital financing plan in which short-term funds are used to finance not only temporary current assets but also part of the permanent working capital needs of the firm. As depicted in Figure 6–7, bank and trade credit as well as other sources of short-term financing are now supporting part of the permanent capital asset needs of the firm.

FIGURE 6–7
Using short-term financing for part of long-term needs

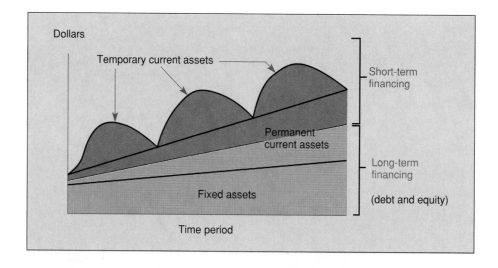

The Financing Decision

Some corporations are more flexible than others because they are not locked into a few available sources of funds. Corporations would like many financing alternatives in order to minimize their cost of funds at any point. Unfortunately, not many firms are in this enviable position through the duration of a business cycle. During an economic boom period, a shortage of low-cost alternatives exists and firms often minimize their financing costs by raising funds in advance of forecasted asset needs.

Not only does the financial manager encounter a timing problem, but he or she also needs to select the right type of financing. Even for companies having many alternative sources of funds, there may be only one or two decisions that will look good in retrospect. At the time the financing decision is made, the financial manager is never sure it is the right one. Should the financing be long term or short term, debt or equity, and so on? Figure 6–8 is a decision-tree diagram that shows many of the financing decisions. A decision is made at each point until a final financing method is reached. In most cases a corporation will use a combination of these financing methods. At all times the financial manager will balance short-term versus long-term considerations against the composition of the firm's assets and the firm's willingness to accept risk. The ratio of long-term financing to short-term financing at any point in time will be greatly influenced by the *term structure of interest rates.*

Term Structure of Interest Rates

The **term structure of interest rates** is often referred to as a yield curve. It shows the relative level of short-term and long-term interest rates at a point in time. Generally U.S. government securities are used to construct yield curves because they have many maturities and each of the securities has an equally low risk of default. Corporate securities will move in the same direction as government securities, but will have higher interest rates because of their greater financial risk. Yield curves for both corporations and government

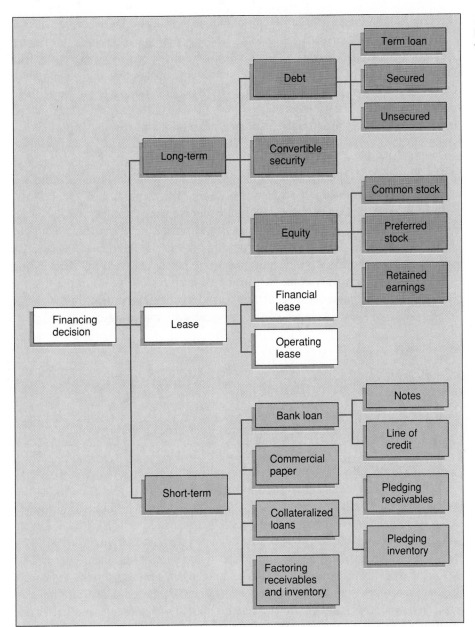

FIGURE 6–8
**Decision tree of the
financing decision**

securities change daily to reflect current competitive conditions in the money and capital markets, expected inflation, and changes in economic conditions.

Three basic theories describe the shape of the yield curve. The first theory is called the **liquidity premium theory** and states that long-term rates should be higher than short-term rates. This premium of long-term rates over short-term rates exists because short-term securities have greater liquidity and, therefore, higher rates have to be offered to potential long-term bond buyers to entice them to hold these less liquid and more price sensitive securities. The **segmentation theory** (the second theory) states that Treasury securities are divided into market segments by the various financial institutions investing in the market. Commercial banks prefer short-term securities of one year or less to match their short-term lending strategies. Savings and loans and other mortgage-oriented financial institutions prefer the intermediate length securities of between 5 and 7 years, while life insurance companies prefer long-term 20 to 30-year securities to offset the long-term nature of their commitments to policyholders. The changing needs, desires, and strategies of these investors tend to strongly influence the nature and relationship of short-term and long-term interest rates.

The third theory describing the term structure of interest rates is called the **expectations hypothesis.** This theory explains the yields on long-term securities as a function of the short-term rates. The expectations theory says long-term rates reflect the average of short-term expected rates over the time period that the long-term security is outstanding. Using a four-year example and a simple mean, we will demonstrate this theory in Table 6–6. In the left-hand panel of the table, we show the anticipated one-year rate on T-bill (Treasury bill) securities at the beginning of each of four years in the future. Treasury bills are short-term securities issued by the government. In the right-hand panel, we show averages of the one-year anticipated rates.

TABLE 6–6   **The expectations theory**

1 yr. T-bill at beginning of yr. 1 = 4%	
1 yr. T-bill at beginning of yr. 2 = 5%	2 yr. security (4% + 5%)/2 = 4.5%
1 yr. T-bill at beginning of yr. 3 = 6%	3 yr. security (4% + 5% + 6%)/3 = 5.0%
1 yr. T-bill at beginning of yr. 4 = 7%	4 yr. security (4% + 5% + 6% + 7%)/4 = 5.5%

For example the two-year security rate is the average of the expected yields of two one-year T-bills, while the rate on the four-year security is the average of all four one-year rates. In this example, the progressively higher rates for two-, three- and four-year securities represent a reflection of higher anticipated one-year rates in the future. The expectations hypothesis is especially useful in explaining the shape and movement of the yield curve. The result of the expectations hypothesis is that, when long-term rates are much higher than short-term rates, the market is saying it expects short-term rates to rise. When long-term rates are lower than short-term rates, the market is expecting short-term rates to fall. This theory is useful to financial managers in helping them set expectations for the cost of financing over time and, especially, in making choices about when to use short-term debt or long-term debt.

In fact, all three theories presented have some impact on interest rates. At times the liquidity premium or segmentation theory dominates the shape of the curve and, at other times, the expectations theory is the most important. The financial manager cannot escape making judgments about future developments, and, sometimes, knowledge of yield curve theories provides a managerial edge for more accurate judgment.

Figure 6–9 on page 156 depicts four panels of term structures (yield curves) covering various time periods. These four panels present very different pictures of interest rate cycles.

Panel A shows five yield curves in a period of falling interest rates—from August 1974 to November 1976. Each yield curve in Panel A has a different shape. The August 1974 curve is called *downward sloping,* or *inverted,* because short-term interest rates are higher than long-term rates. This shape is usually present at peak periods in economic expansions and sometimes continues into economic recessions. The September 1975 curve is called a *humped* curve, because the intermediate rates are higher than both the short- and long-term rates. The other three yield curves are all *upward sloping,* which is considered to be the normal case.

Panel B represents interest rate changes in a period of rising rates. If you start with the December 1976 yield curve and move to each successive curve, you will trace the most dramatic rise in interest rates in U.S. history, caused by record high inflation rates. In Panel C, you can see that short-term rates on U.S. Treasury bills reached historic levels in September 1981. The Federal Reserve Board maintained high interest rates during this period in an attempt to break the back of inflation even though the economy was quite weak. By 1982 Federal Reserve Board policy had reduced inflation to its lowest level since 1971 but had also created a 16-month recession that ended in November 1982. However, the recession finally caused interest rates to decline, as evidenced by the May, November, and December 1982 yield curves. Interest rates can change dramatically in a short time. Between November and December 1982, interest rates on intermediate- and long-term securities dropped as much as 2 percentage points.

A business recovery began in December 1982 and the yield curve in Panel C bottomed out in that month. Gross domestic product (GDP) grew at a rate of over 6 percent in 1983, and the economic expansion increased the demand for funds. Panel D shows the resulting rise in rates by August 1983 and March 1984. By 1985 the economy was growing at a slow rate of about 2.5 percent per year, and inflation came down to a 1.1 percent annual rate for 1986. The slow economy and low inflation rates combined to decrease the yield curve (September 1986), but by August 1987, rates were moving back up in response to increased economic growth and renewed inflationary pressures. The economy grew at a slow rate from 1987 to 1990, but rates remained high in order to attract foreign investment to finance the U.S. fiscal deficit. By November 1990 the economy was poised for a recession and rates retreated and continued to fall into October 1992. In an attempt to stimulate the economy, the Fed lowered short-term interest rates but kept long-term rates from falling. This created a steep upward sloping yield curve that, in fact, continued into 1993.

In designing working capital policy, the astute financial manager is interested not only in the term structure of interest rates but also in the relative volatility and the historical level of short-term and long-term rates. The four panels in Figure 6–9 indicate that interest rates have been on a roller coaster ride since 1974. Figure 6–10 covers a longer period but still demonstrates the large historical differences in relative volatility, with short-term rates being much more volatile than long-term rates. This volatility is what makes a short-term financing strategy so risky. On top of this volatility, most

FIGURE 6–9   **Yield curves: Yields on U.S. government securities**

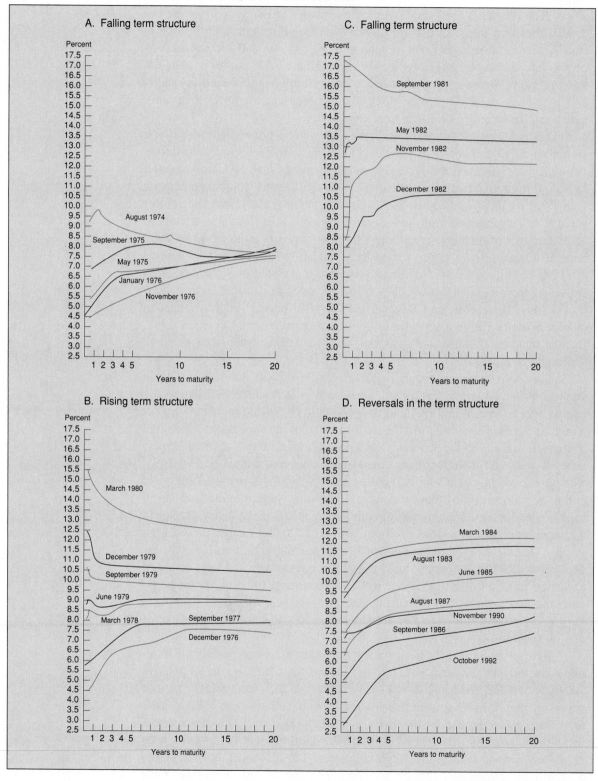

FIGURE 6-10 **Long- and short-term interest rates (annually)**

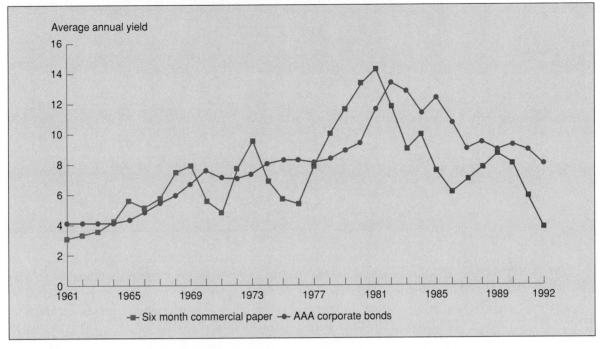

economists will admit to the great uncertainty of forecasting more than one year ahead. The record of the professionals for accurate interest rate predictions is spotty at best for periods longer than six months.

How should the financial manager respond to fluctuating interest rates and changing term structures? When interest rates are high, the financial manager generally tries to borrow short term (if funds are available). As rates decline, the chief financial officer will try to lock in the lower rates with heavy long-term borrowing. Some of these long-term funds will be used to reduce short-term debt and the rest will be available for future expansion of plant and equipment and working capital if necessary.

A Decision Process

Assume we are comparing alternative financing plans for working capital. As indicated in Table 6–7, $500,000 of working capital (current assets) must be financed for the Edwards Corporation. Under Plan A, we will finance all our current asset needs with short-term funds, while under Plan B we will finance only a relatively small portion of current assets with short-term money—relying heavily on long-term funds. In either case we will carry $100,000 of fixed assets with long-term financing commitments. As indicated in part 3 of Table 6–7, under Plan A we will finance total needs of $600,000 with $500,000 of short-term financing and $100,000 of long-term financing, whereas with Plan B we will finance $150,000 short term and $450,000 long term.

TABLE 6–7
Alternative financing plans

EDWARDS CORPORATION		
	Plan A	**Plan B**
Part 1. Current assets		
Temporary.	$250,000	$250,000
Permanent.	250,000	250,000
Total current assets	500,000	500,000
Short-term financing (6%)	500,000	150,000
Long-term financing (10%)	0	350,000
	$500,000	$500,000
Part 2. Fixed assets	$100,000	$100,000
Long-term financing (10%)	$100,000	$100,000
Part 3. Total financing (summary of parts 1 and 2)		
Short-term (6%)	$500,000	$150,000
Long-term (10%)	100,000	450,000
	$600,000	$600,000

Plan A carries the lower cost of financing, with interest of 6 percent on $500,000 of the $600,000 required. We show the impact of both plans on bottom-line earnings in Table 6–8.[1] Assuming the firm generates $200,000 in earnings before interest and taxes, Plan A will provide aftertax earnings of $80,000, while Plan B will generate only $73,000.

TABLE 6–8
Impact of financing plans on earnings

EDWARDS CORPORATION	
Plan A	
Earnings before interest and taxes	$200,000
Interest (short-term), 6% × $500,000. . . .	− 30,000
Interest (long-term), 10% × $100,000. . . .	− 10,000
Earnings before taxes	160,000
Taxes (50%)	80,000
Earnings after taxes	$ 80,000
Plan B	
Earnings before interest and taxes	$200,000
Interest (short-term), 6% × $150,000. . . .	− 9,000
Interest (long-term), 10% × $450,000 . . .	− 45,000
Earnings before taxes	146,000
Taxes (50%)	73,000
Earnings after taxes	$ 73,000

Introducing Varying Conditions

Although Plan A, employing cheaper short-term sources of financing, appears to provide $7,000 more in return, this is not always the case. During **tight**

---

[1]Common stock is eliminated from the example to simplify the analysis. If it were included, all of the basic patterns would still hold.

money periods, when capital is scarce, short-term financing may be difficult to find or may carry exorbitant rates. Furthermore, inadequate financing may mean lost sales or financial embarrassment. For these reasons, the firm may wish to evaluate Plans A and B based on differing assumptions about the economy and the money markets.

Expected Value

Past history combined with economic forecasting may indicate an 80 percent probability of normal events and a 20 percent chance of extremely tight money. Using Plan A, under normal conditions the Edwards Corporation will enjoy a $7,000 superior return over Plan B (as indicated in Table 6–8). Let us now assume that under disruptive tight money conditions, Plan A would provide a $15,000 lower return than Plan B because of high short-term interest rates. These conditions are summarized in Table 6–9, and an expected value of return is computed. The **expected value** represents the sum of the expected outcomes under the two conditions.

EDWARDS CORPORATION				
1. Normal conditions	Expected higher return under Plan A $7,000	×	Probability of normal conditions .80	= +$ 5,600 Expected outcome
2. Tight money	Expected lower return under Plan A ($15,000)	×	Probability of tight money .20	= (3,000)
Expected value of return for Plan A versus Plan B			=	+$ 2,600

TABLE 6-9
Expected returns under different economic conditions

We see that even when downside risk is considered, Plan A carries a higher expected return of $2,600. For another firm in the same industry that might suffer $50,000 lower returns during tight money conditions, Plan A becomes too dangerous to undertake, as indicated in Table 6–10. Plan A's expected return is now $4,400 less than that of Plan B.

1. Normal conditions	Expected higher return under Plan A $7,000	×	Probability of normal conditions .80	= +$ 5,600 Expected outcome
2. Tight money	Expected lower return under Plan A ($50,000)	×	Probability of tight money .20	= (10,000)
Negative expected value of return for Plan A versus Plan B			=	($4,400)

TABLE 6-10
Expected returns for high-risk firm

Shifts in Asset Structure

Thus far our attention has been directed to the risk associated with various financing plans. Risk-return analysis must also be carried to the asset side. A firm with heavy risk exposure due to short-term borrowing may compensate in part by carrying highly liquid assets. Conversely, a firm with established long-term debt commitments may choose to carry a heavier component of less liquid, highly profitable assets.

Either through desire or compelling circumstances, business firms have decreased the liquidity of their current asset holdings since the early 1960s. Let's take a look at the evidence over an extended time period. For U.S. nonfinancial corporations, cash and equivalents have decreased from 18.98 percent of current assets in 1963 to approximately 10 percent in 1993, while inventory increased from 30.44 percent of current assets in 1963 to about 38 percent in 1993. The ratio of cash and cash equivalents to current liabilities has fallen from 35.44 percent at the end of 1963 to approximately 15 percent by 1993. Clearly U.S. nonfinancial corporations are less liquid today than two decades ago.

The reasons for diminishing liquidity can be traced in part to more sophisticated, profit-oriented financial management as well as better utilization of cash balances via the computer. Less liquidity can also be traced to the long-term effect inflation has had on corporate balance sheets—forcing greater borrowing to carry more expensive assets and to decreasing profitability during recessions. The average current ratio for nonfinancial corporations is presented in Figure 6–11. After the recession in 1974–75, corporate liquidity increased to the highest level of the 1970s in 1976. Since reaching that peak, corporate liquidity has been squeezed. Generally corporations are relying more and more on short-term borrowings to carry less liquid assets—a potentially dangerous situation.

FIGURE 6–11   **Nonfinancial corporations' current ratio**

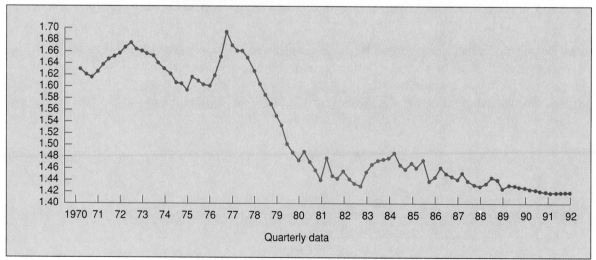

Quarterly data

Toward an Optimal Policy

As previously indicated, the firm should attempt to relate asset liquidity to financing patterns, and vice versa. In Table 6–11, a number of working capital alternatives are presented. Along the top of the table, we show asset liquidity; along the side, the type of financing arrangement. The combined impact of the two variables is shown in each of the four panels of the table.

	Asset Liquidity	
Financing Plan	**Low Liquidity**	**High Liquidity**
Short-term	1 High profit High risk	2 Moderate profit Moderate risk
Long-term	3 Moderate profit Moderate risk	4 Low profit Low risk

TABLE 6–11
Asset liquidity and financing assets

Each firm must decide how it wishes to combine asset liquidity and financing needs. The aggressive, risk-oriented firm in Panel 1 of Table 6–11 will borrow short term and maintain relatively low levels of liquidity, hoping to increase profit. It will benefit from low-cost financing and high-return assets, but it will be vulnerable to a credit crunch. The more conservative firm, following the plan in Panel 4, will utilize established long-term financing and maintain a high degree of liquidity. In Panels 2 and 3, we see more moderate positions in which the firm compensates for short-term financing with highly liquid assets (2) or balances off low liquidity with precommitted, long-term financing (3).

Each financial manager must structure his or her working capital position and the associated risk-return trade-off to meet the company's needs. For firms whose cash flow patterns are predictable, typified by the public utilities sector, a low degree of liquidity can be maintained. Immediate access to capital markets, such as that enjoyed by large, prestigious firms, also allows a greater risk-taking capability. In each case, the ultimate concern must be for maximizing the overall valuation of the firm through a judicious consideration of risk-return options.

In the next two chapters, we will examine the various methods for managing the individual components of working capital. In Chapter 7 we consider the techniques for managing cash, marketable securities, receivables, and inventory. In Chapter 8 we look at trade and bank credit and also at other sources of short-term funds.

Summary

Working capital management involves the financing and management of the current assets of the firm. A firm's ability to properly manage current assets and the associated liability obligations may determine how well it is able to survive in the short run. To the extent that part of the buildup in current assets is permanent, financial arrangements should carry longer maturities.

The financial manager must also give careful attention to the relationship of the production process to sales. Level production in a seasonal sales environment increases operating efficiency, but it also calls for more careful financial planning. The astute financial manager must also keep an eye on the general cost of borrowing, the term structure of interest rates, and the relative volatility of short- and long-term rates.

The firm has a number of risk-return decisions to consider. Though long-term financing provides a safety margin in availability of funds, its higher cost may reduce the profit potential of the firm. On the asset side, carrying highly liquid current assets assures the bill-paying capability of the firm—but detracts from profit potential. Each firm must tailor the various risk-return trade-offs to meet its own needs. The peculiarities of a firm's industry will have a major impact on the options open to management.

List of Terms

working capital
  management 140
self-liquidating assets 140
permanent current assets 141
temporary current assets 141
level production 142
point-of-sales terminals 143

term structure of interest
  rates 152
liquidity premium theory 153
segmentation theory 153
expectations hypothesis 154
tight money 158
expected value 159

Discussion Questions

1. Explain how rapidly expanding sales can drain the cash resources of the firm.

2. Discuss the relative volatility of short- and long-term interest rates.

3. What is the significance to working capital management of matching sales and production?

4. How is a cash budget used to help manage current assets?

5. "The most appropriate financing pattern would be one in which asset buildup and length of financing terms are perfectly matched." Discuss the difficulty involved in achieving this financing pattern.

6. By using long-term financing to finance part of temporary current assets, a firm may have less risk but lower returns than a firm with a normal financing plan. Explain the significance of this statement.

7. A firm that uses short-term financing methods for a portion of permanent current assets is assuming more risk but expects higher returns than a firm with a normal financing plan. Explain.

8. What does the term *structure of interest rates* indicate?

9. What are three theories for describing the shape of the term structure of interest rates (the yield curve)? Briefly describe each theory.

10. Since the early 1960s, corporate liquidity has been declining. What reasons can you give for this trend?

Problems

1. Gary's Pipe and Steel Company expects next year's sales to be $800,000 if the economy is strong, $500,000 if the economy is steady, and $350,000 if the economy is weak. Gary believes there is a 20 percent probability the economy will be strong, a 50 percent probability of a steady economy, and a 30 percent probability of a weak economy. What is the expected level of sales for next year?

Expected value

2. Tobin Supplies Company expects sales next year to be $500,000. Inventory and accounts receivable will have to be increased by $90,000 to accommodate this sales level. The company has a steady profit margin of 12 percent with a 40 percent dividend payout. How much external funding will Tobin Supplies Company have to seek? Assume there is no increase in liabilities other than that which will occur with the external financing.

External financing

3. Sauer Food Company has decided to buy a new computer system with an expected life of three years. The cost is $150,000. The company can borrow $150,000 for three years at 10 percent annual interest or for one year at 8 percent annual interest.

Short-term financing versus longer-term borrowing

   How much would Sauer Food Company save in interest over the three-year life of the computer system if the one-year loan is utilized and the loan is rolled over (reborrowed) each year at the same 8 percent rate? Compare this to the 10 percent three-year loan. What if interest rates on the 8 percent loan go up to 13 percent in year two and 18 percent in year three? What is the total interest cost now compared to the 10 percent, three-year loan?

4. Assume Stratton Health Clubs, Inc., has $3,000,000 in assets. If it goes with a low liquidity plan for the assets, it can earn a return of 20 percent, but with a high liquidity plan, the return will be 13 percent. If the firm goes with a short-term financing plan, the financing costs on the $3,000,000 will be 10 percent, and with a long-term financing plan, the financing costs on the $3,000,000 will be 12 percent. (Review Table 6–11 for parts *a*, *b*, and *c* of this problem.)

Optimal policy mix

   a. Compute the anticipated return after financing costs on the most aggressive asset-financing mix.

   b. Compute the anticipated return after financing costs on the most conservative asset-financing mix.

   c. Compute the anticipated return after financing costs on the two moderate approaches to the asset-financing mix.

   d. Would you necessarily accept the plan with the highest return after financing costs? Briefly explain.

Matching asset mix and financing plan

5. Goniff Steel has $4,200,000 in assets.

Temporary current assets . . .	$1,000,000
Permanent current assets . . .	2,000,000
Fixed assets	1,200,000
Total assets	$4,200,000

Short-term rates are 8 percent. Long-term rates are 13 percent. Earnings before interest and taxes are $996,000. The tax rate is 40 percent.

If long-term financing is perfectly matched (synchronized) with long-term asset needs, and the same is true of short-term financing, what will earnings after taxes be? For an example of perfectly matched plans, see Figure 6–5.

Impact of term structure of interest rates on financing plan

6. In problem 5, assume the term structure of interest rates becomes inverted, with short-term rates going to 12 percent and long-term rates 4 percentage points lower than short-term rates.

If all other factors in the problem do not change, what will earnings after taxes be? Why has the company benefited?

Conservative versus aggressive financing

7. Guardian, Inc., is trying to develop an asset-financing plan. The firm has $400,000 in temporary current assets and $300,000 in permanent current assets. Guardian also has $500,000 in fixed assets. Assume a tax rate of 40 percent.

   a. Construct two alternative financing plans for Guardian. One of the plans should be conservative, with 75 percent of assets financed by long-term sources, and the other should be aggressive, with only 56.25 percent of assets financed by long-term sources. The current interest rate is 15 percent on long-term funds and 10 percent on short-term financing.

   b. Given that Guardian's earnings before interest and taxes are $200,000, calculate earnings after taxes for each of your alternatives.

   c. What would happen if the short- and long-term rates were reversed?

Alternative financing plans

8. Lear, Inc., has $800,000 in current assets, $350,000 of which are considered permanent current assets. In addition, the firm has $600,000 invested in fixed assets.

   a. Lear wishes to finance all fixed assets and half of its permanent current assets with long-term financing costing 10 percent. Short-term financing currently costs 5 percent. Lear's earnings before interest and taxes are $200,000. Determine Lear's earnings after taxes under this financing plan. The tax rate is 30 percent.

   b. As an alternative, Lear might wish to finance all fixed assets and permanent current assets plus half of its temporary current assets with long-term financing. The same interest rates apply as in part a. Earnings before interest and taxes will be $200,000. What will be Lear's earnings after taxes? The tax rate is 30 percent.

   c. What are some of the risks associated with each of these alternative financing strategies?

9. Modern Tombstones has estimated monthly financing requirements for the next six months as follows:

Interest costs under
alternative plans

January	$20,000	April . . .	$10,000
February . . .	6,000	May . . .	22,000
March	8,000	June . . .	12,000

Short-term financing will be utilized for the next six months. Projected annual interest rates are:

January	9.0%	April . . .	15.0%
February	8.0%	May	12.0%
March	12.0%	June . . .	9.0%

   a. Compute total dollar interest payments for the six months. To convert an annual rate to a monthly rate, divide by 12.
   b. If long-term financing at 12 percent had been utilized throughout the six months, would the total-dollar interest payments be larger or smaller?

10. In problem 9, what long-term interest rate would represent a break-even point between using short-term financing as described in part *a* and long-term financing? Hint: Divide the interest payments in 9*a* by the amount of total funds provided for the six months and multiply by 12.

Break-even point in
interest rates

11. Sherwin Paperboard Company expects to sell 600 units in January, 700 units in February, and 1,200 units in March. January's beginning inventory is 800 units. Expected sales for the whole year are 12,000 units. Sherwin has decided on a level monthly production schedule of 1,000 units (12,000 units/12 months = 1,000 units per month). What is the expected end-of-month inventory for January, February, and March? Show the beginning inventory, production, and sales for each month to arrive at ending inventory.

Sales and inventory
buildup

$$\frac{\text{Beginning}}{\text{inventory}} + \frac{\text{Production}}{\text{(level)}} - \text{Sales} = \frac{\text{Ending}}{\text{inventory}}.$$

12. Sharpe Computer Graphics Corporation has forecasted the following monthly sales:

Level production and
related financing costs

January	$80,000	July	$ 30,000
February . . .	70,000	August	31,000
March	10,000	September . . .	40,000
April	10,000	October	70,000
May	15,000	November . . .	90,000
June	20,000	December . . .	110,000
	Total sales = $576,000		

The firm sells its graphic forms for $5 per unit, and the cost to produce the forms is $2. A level production policy is followed. Each month's production is equal to annual sales (in units) divided by 12.

Of each month's sales, 30 percent are for cash and 70 percent are on account. All accounts receivable are collected in the month after the sale is made.

a. Construct a monthly production and inventory schedule in units. Beginning inventory in January is 15,000 units. (Note: To do part a, you should work in terms of units of production and units of sales.)

b. Prepare a monthly schedule of cash receipts. Sales in the December before the planning year are $90,000. Work part b using dollars.

c. Determine a cash payments schedule for January through December. The production costs of $2 per unit are paid for in the month in which they occur. Other cash payments, besides those for production costs, are $30,000 per month.

d. Prepare a monthly cash budget for January through December. The beginning cash balance is $5,000 and that is also the minimum desired.

Level production and
related financing costs

13. Seasonal Products Corporation expects the following monthly sales:

January . . .	$20,000	May	$ 1,000	September . . .	$20,000
February . . .	15,000	June	3,000	October.	25,000
March	5,000	July	10,000	November . . .	30,000
April	3,000	August . . .	14,000	December . . .	22,000

Total sales = $168,000

Sales are 20 percent for cash in a given month, with the remainder going into accounts receivable. All 80 percent of the credit sales are collected in the month following the sale. Seasonal Products sells all of its goods for $2 each and produces them for $1 each. Seasonal Products uses level production, and average monthly production is equal to annual production divided by 12.

a. Generate a monthly production and inventory schedule in units. Beginning inventory in January is 5,000 units. (Note: To do part a, you should work in terms of units of production and units of sales.)

b. Determine a cash receipts schedule for January through December. Assume dollar sales in the prior December were $15,000. Work part b using dollars.

c. Determine a cash payments schedule for January through December. The production costs ($1 per unit produced) are paid for in the month in which they occur. Other cash payments, besides those for production costs, are $6,000 per month.

d. Construct a cash budget for January through December. The beginning cash balance is $1,000, and that is also the required minimum.

e. Determine total current assets for each month. (Note: Accounts receivable equal sales minus 20 percent of sales for a given month.)

14. Pick a day within the past week and construct a yield curve for that day. Pick a day approximately a year ago and construct a yield curve for that day. How are interest rates different? *The Wall Street Journal* and the *Federal Reserve Bulletin* should help in setting up this problem.

Constructing a simple yield curve

15. Using the expectations hypothesis theory for the term structure of interest rates, determine the expected return for securities with maturities of two, three, and four years based on the following data. Do an analysis similar to that in Table 6–6.

Expectations hypothesis and interest rates

1-year T-bill at beginning of year 1	6%
1-year T-bill at beginning of year 2	7%
1-year T-bill at beginning of year 3	9%
1-year T-bill at beginning of year 4	11%

Selected References

Acheson, Marcus W. "From Cash Management to Bank Reform." *Journal of Applied Corporate Finance* 4 (Summer 1991), pp. 105–16.

Bernstein, Leopold A., and Mostafa M. Maksy. "Again Now: How Do We Measure Cash Flow from Operations?" *Financial Analysts Journal* 41 (July–August 1985), pp. 74–77.

Fass, Greg. "Capital Allocation and Pricing Credit Risk." *Journal of Commercial Lending* 75 (September 1992), pp. 35–53.

Gentry, James A. "State of the Art of Short-Run Financial Management." *Financial Management* 17 (Summer 1988), pp. 41–57.

————, **and Darrel Greitzu.** "Short-Run Financial Management Model on Lotus 1–2–3." *Journal of Financial Education* 14 (Fall 1985), pp. 75–85.

Jones, Edward B. "Building the Bank Corporate Relationship." *Cash Flow* 8 (November 1987), pp. 64–74.

Rush, Ned C., and Daniel M. Ferguson. "EDI: Time for a Win-Win Change in Credit Terms." *Cash Flow* 8 (October 1987), pp. 30–47.

Stewart, G. Bennet, III, and David M. Glassman. "Why Restructuring Adds Value: Shedding All Too-Tempting Cash Flow." *Cash Flow* 8 (December 1987), pp. 44–47.

Viscione, Jerry A. "How Long Should You Borrow Short-Term?" *Harvard Business Review* 64 (March–April 1986), pp. 20–24.

Current Asset Management

CHAPTER CONCEPTS

1 Current asset management is an extension of concepts discussed in the previous chapter and involves the management of cash, marketable securities, accounts receivable, and inventory.

2 Cash management involves control over the receipt and payment of cash so as to minimize nonearning cash balances.

3 The management of marketable securities involves selecting between various short-term investments.

4 Accounts receivable and inventory management require credit and inventory level decisions to be made with an eye toward profitability.

5 An overriding concept is that the less liquid an asset is, the higher the required return.

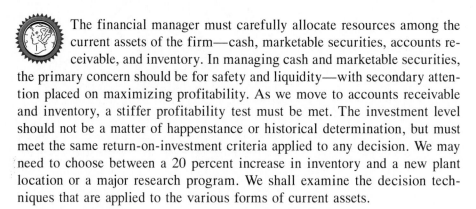

The financial manager must carefully allocate resources among the current assets of the firm—cash, marketable securities, accounts receivable, and inventory. In managing cash and marketable securities, the primary concern should be for safety and liquidity—with secondary attention placed on maximizing profitability. As we move to accounts receivable and inventory, a stiffer profitability test must be met. The investment level should not be a matter of happenstance or historical determination, but must meet the same return-on-investment criteria applied to any decision. We may need to choose between a 20 percent increase in inventory and a new plant location or a major research program. We shall examine the decision techniques that are applied to the various forms of current assets.

Cash Management

Managing cash is becoming ever more sophisticated in the global and electronic age of the 1990s as financial managers try to squeeze the last dollar of profit out of their cash management strategies. Despite whatever lifelong teachings you might have learned about the virtues of cash, the corporate financial manager actively seeks to keep this nonearning asset to a minimum. The less cash you have, generally the better off you are, but still you do not want to get caught without cash when you need it. Minimizing cash balances as well as having accurate knowledge of when cash moves into and out of the company can improve overall corporate profitability. First we discuss the reasons for holding cash and then examine the cash flow cycle for the typical firm.

Reasons for Holding Cash Balances

There are several reasons for holding cash: for transactions balances, for compensating balances for banks, and for precautionary needs. The transactions motive involves the use of cash to pay for planned corporate expenses such as supplies, payrolls, and taxes, but also can include infrequent planned acquisitions of long-term fixed assets. The second major reason for holding cash results from the practice of holding balances to compensate a bank for services provided rather than pay directly for those services.

Holding cash for precautionary motives assumes management wants cash for emergency purposes when cash inflows are less than projected. Precautionary cash balances are more likely to be important in seasonal or cyclical industries where cash inflows are more uncertain. Firms with precautionary needs usually rely on untapped lines of bank credit. For most firms the primary motive for holding cash is the transactions motive.

Cash Flow Cycle

Cash balances are largely determined by cash flowing through the company on a daily, weekly, and monthly basis as determined by the **cash flow cycle.** As discussed in Chapter 4, the cash budget is a common tool used to track cash flows and resulting cash balances. Cash flow relies on the payment pattern of customers, the speed at which suppliers and creditors process checks, and the efficiency of the banking system. The primary consideration in managing the cash flow cycle is to ensure that inflows and outflows of cash are properly synchronized for transaction purposes. In Chapter 6 we discussed the cyclical nature of asset growth and its impact on cash, receivables, and inventory, and we now expand on that by examining the cash flow process more fully.

Figure 7–1 illustrates the simple cash flow cycle where the sale of finished goods or services produce either a cash sale or accounts receivable for future collection. Eventually the accounts receivable are collected and become cash, which is used to buy or produce inventory that is then sold. Thus the cash-generating process is continuous even though the cash flow may be unpredictable and uneven.

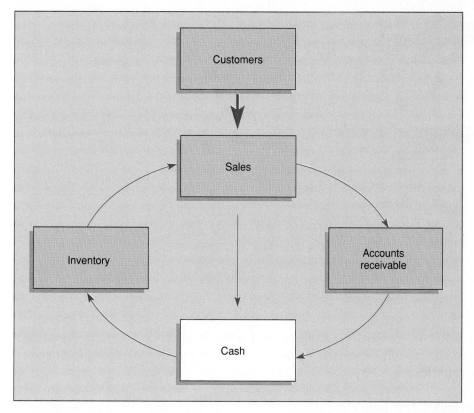

FIGURE 7–1
The cash flow cycle

Sales, receivables, and inventory form the basis for cash flow, but other activities in the firm can also affect cash inflows and outflows. The cash flow cycle presented in Figure 7–2 expands the detail and activities that influence cash. Cash inflows are driven by sales and influenced by the type of customers, their geographical location, the product being sold, and the industry. A sale can be made for cash (e.g., McDonald's) or on credit (e.g., IBM). Some industries like textbook publishing will grant credit terms of 60 days to bookstores, and others like department stores will grant customers credit for 30 days. When receivables are paid, cash balances increase and the firm uses cash to pay interest to lenders, dividends to stockholders, taxes, suppliers, and wages, and to repurchase inventory. When the firm has excess cash, it will

FIGURE 7–2
Expanded cash flow cycle

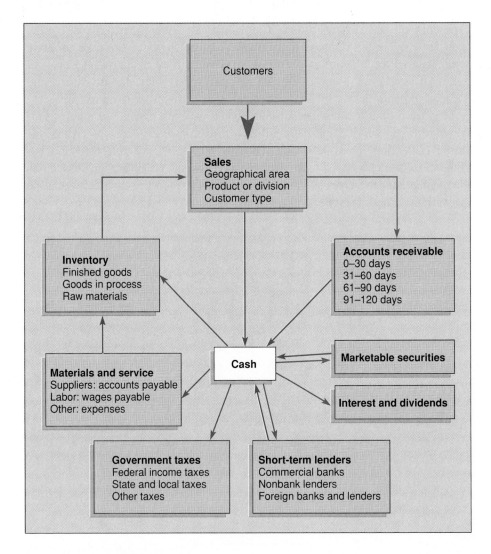

invest in marketable securities, and when it needs cash for current assets, it will usually either sell marketable securities or borrow funds from short-term lenders.

Collections and Disbursements

Managing the cash inflows and payments in Figure 7–2 is a function of many variables such as float, the mail system, use of electronic funds transfer mechanisms, lockboxes, international sales, and more. These are presented in detail in the following section.

Float

Some people are shocked to realize that even the most trusted asset on a corporation's books, *cash,* may not portray actual dollars at a given time. There are actually two cash balances of importance: the corporation's recorded amount and the amount credited to the corporation by the bank. The difference between the two is called **float**, and it arises from time delays in mailing, processing, and clearing checks through the banking system. Once a check is received in the mail and a deposit is made, the deposited funds are not available for use until the check has cleared the banking system and been credited to the corporate bank account. This works both for checks written to pay suppliers as well as checks deposited from customers. This means float can be managed to some extent through a combination of disbursement and collection strategies.

Let us examine the use of float. Our firm has deposited $1,000,000 in checks received from customers during the week and has written $900,000 in checks to suppliers. If the initial balance were $100,000, the corporate books would show $200,000. But what will the bank records show in the way of usable funds? Perhaps $800,000 of the checks from customers will have cleared their accounts at other banks and been credited to us, while only $400,000 of our checks may have completed a similar cycle. As indicated in Table 7–1, we have used "float" to provide us with $300,000 extra in available short-term funds.

TABLE 7–1
The use of float to provide funds

	Corporate Books	Bank Books (usable funds) (amounts actually cleared)
Initial amount	$ 100,000	$100,000
Deposits	+ 1,000,000	+ 800,000
Checks	− 900,000	− 400,000
Balance	+$ 200,000	+$500,000
	+$300,000 float	

Some companies actually operate with a negative cash balance on the corporate books, knowing float will carry them through at the bank. In the above example, the firm may write $1.2 million in checks on the assumption that only $800,000 will clear by the end of the week, thus leaving it with surplus funds in its bank account. The results, shown in Table 7–2, represent the phenomenon known as "playing the float." A float of $200,000 turns a negative balance on the corporation's books into a positive temporary balance on the bank's books. Float can also work against you if checks going out are being processed more quickly than checks coming in.

TABLE 7–2
Playing the float

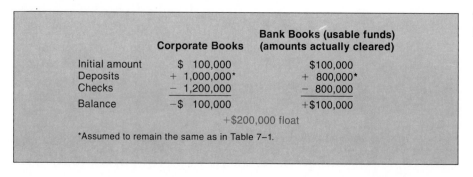

	Corporate Books	Bank Books (usable funds) (amounts actually cleared)
Initial amount	$ 100,000	$100,000
Deposits	+ 1,000,000*	+ 800,000*
Checks	− 1,200,000	− 800,000
Balance	−$ 100,000	+$100,000
	+$200,000 float	
*Assumed to remain the same as in Table 7–1.		

Improving Collections

We may expedite the collection and check-clearing process through a number of strategies.[1] A popular method is to utilize a variety of collection centers throughout our marketing area. A dress manufacturer with headquarters in Chicago may have 75 collection offices disbursed throughout the country, each performing a billing and collection-deposit function. One of the collection offices in San Francisco, using a local bank, may be able to clear a check on a San Jose bank in one day—whereas a Chicago bank would require a substantially longer time to remit and clear the check at the California bank.[2]

For those who wish to enjoy the benefits of expeditious check clearance at lower costs, a **lockbox system** may replace the network of regional collection offices. Under this plan, customers are requested to forward their checks to a post office box in their geographic region and a local bank picks up the checks. The bank can then process the local checks through the local clearinghouse for rapid collection and perhaps have the funds available for use in 24 hours or less. Whether the corporation uses a collection system or the less expensive lockbox system, excess cash balances at the local banks are remitted to the corporate headquarter bank through a daily wire transfer that makes the funds immediately available for corporate use. More will be presented on wire transfers later in the chapter.

Extending Disbursements

Perhaps you have heard of the multimillion-dollar corporation with its headquarters located in the most exclusive office space in downtown Manhattan, but with its primary check disbursement center in Fargo, North Dakota. Though the firm may engage in aggressive speedup techniques in the processing of incoming checks, a slowdown pattern more aptly describes the payment procedures.

While the preceding example represents an extreme case, the slowing of disbursements is not uncommon in cash management. It has even been given the title "extended disbursement float." Many full-service banks offer customers consulting services pointing out structural defects in the Federal Reserve and other collection systems that allow the firm to extend the payment period. While it is not the intent of this text to encourage or discourage such practices, their fairly widespread use is worthy of note.

Cost-Benefit Analysis

An efficiently maintained cash management program can be an expensive operation. The use of remote collection and disbursement centers involves addi-

---

[1]Larger banks have cash management advisory groups that can offer valuable consultation on these matters.

[2]Checks deposited with a bank are cleared through the Federal Reserve System, through a correspondent bank, or through a locally established clearinghouse system. A check is collected when it is remitted to the payer's bank and actually paid by that bank to the payee's bank.

tional costs, and banks involved in the process will require that the firm maintain adequate deposit balances or pay sufficient fees to justify the services. Though the use of a lockbox system may reduce total corporate overhead, the costs may still be substantial.

These expenses must be compared to the benefits that may accrue through the use of **cost-benefit analysis.** If a firm has an average daily remittance of $2 million and 1.5 days can be saved in the collection process by establishing a sophisticated collection network, the firm has freed $3 million for investment elsewhere. Also, through stretching the disbursement schedule by one day, perhaps another $2 million will become available for alternate uses. An example of this process is shown in Figure 7–3. If the firm is able to earn 10 percent on the $5 million that is freed up, as much as $500,000 may be expended on the administrative costs of cash management before the new costs are equal to the generated revenue.

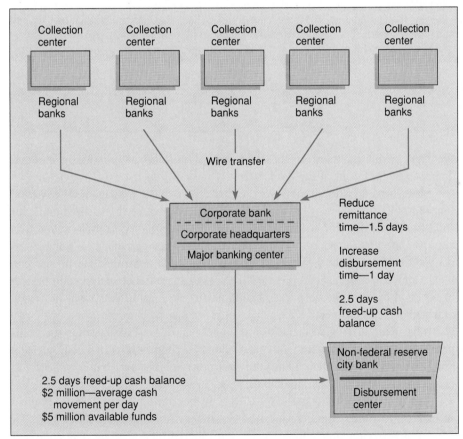

FIGURE 7–3
Cash management network

Electronic Funds Transfer

As we move into the next decade, some of the techniques of delaying payment will be reduced through the techniques of **electronic funds transfer,** a system in which funds are moved between computer terminals without the use of a "check." Through the use of terminal communication between the store and

The Role of SWIFT in International Cash Management

SWIFT is an acronym for the Society for Worldwide Interbank Financial Telecommunications, an international electronic funds transfer network. It was started by a group of banks in 1979 to offer a standardized interbank system to provide continuous automated international message processing and transmission services for financial transactions. Some of the services it provides around the clock are international payments between banks, foreign exchange, and trade finance transactions. SWIFT usage has grown at about a 15 percent annual rate over the last five years and currently has over 2,300 users representing 1,580 banks in over 70 countries. The increased use of correspondent banks using funds transfer systems has placed capacity burdens on SWIFT.

Rigid security standards are enforced and each message is encrypted (secretly coded) and every money transaction is authenticated by another code. These security measures are important to the bank members as well as SWIFT, which assumes the financial liability for the accuracy, completeness, and confidentiality of transaction instructions from and to the point of connection to member bank circuits. Each new member must meet SWIFT's rigid standards and is screened to safeguard the system's security.

In 1987 the society agreed to extend SWIFT service to selected nonbank financial institutions, and four exchanges, including the Chicago Mercantile Exchange and the International Stock Exchange in London, were added to the society as well as Morgan Stanley & Co. and 42 other broker-dealers.

the bank, your payment to the supermarket will be automatically charged against your account at the bank before you walk out the door.

Most large corporations have computerized cash management systems. For example, a firm may have 55 branch offices and 56 banks, one bank for each branch office and a lead bank in which the major corporate account is kept. At the end of each day the financial manager can check all the company's bank accounts through an on-line computer terminal. He or she can then transfer through the computer all excess cash balances from each branch or regional bank to the corporate lead bank for overnight investment in money market securities.

It has been estimated that close to 77 percent of large companies use computers to initiate money transfers, and about 70 percent now use computers to receive reports from their banks on lockbox receipts and bank balances to judge the amount of float available.

Automated clearinghouses (ACH) are becoming an important element in electronic funds transfer. An ACH transfers information between one financial institution and another and from account to account via computer tape. There are approximately 30 regional automated clearinghouses throughout the United States, claiming total membership of over 10,000 financial institutions. The biggest use of ACHs so far has been in payroll processing, as more banks are offering direct deposit options. In the future more companies will use these automated clearinghouses for transfer of payments between the company and customers, suppliers, and utilities.

International Cash Management

Multinational corporations can shift funds around from country to country much as a firm may transfer funds from regional banks to the lead bank. Just as financial institutions in the United States have become more involved in electronic funds transfer, an international payments system has also developed.

A company may prefer to hold cash balances in one currency rather than another or to take advantage of the high interest rates available in a particular country for short-term investments in marketable securities. In periods in which one country's currency is rising in value relative to other currencies, an astute financial manager will try to keep as much cash as possible in the country with the strong currency. In periods in which the dollar is rising relative to other currencies, many balances are held in U.S. bank accounts or in dollar-denominated bank accounts in foreign banks, more commonly known as Eurodollar deposits. The international money markets have been growing in scope and size, so these markets have become a much more important aspect of efficient cash management. Cash management at the international level employs the same techniques as domestic cash management, using such forecasting devices as the cash budget and daily cash reports, so that excess funds may be collected and invested until needed in Eurodollar money market securities or other appropriate investments in securities denominated by strong currencies. An in-depth coverage of international cash and asset management is presented in Chapter 21.

Marketable Securities

The firm may hold excess funds in anticipation of a cash outlay. When funds are being held for other than immediate transaction purposes, they should be converted from cash into interest-earning marketable securities.[3]

The financial manager has a virtual supermarket of securities from which to choose. Among the factors influencing that choice are yield, maturity, minimum investment required, safety, and marketability. Under normal conditions, the longer the maturity period of the security, the higher the yield, as indicated in Figure 7–4 on page 179.

The problem in "stretching out" the maturity of your investment is not that you are legally locked in (you can generally sell your security when you need funds), but that you may have to take a loss. A $5,000 Treasury note issued initially at 5.5 percent, with three years to run, may only bring $4,500 if the going interest rate climbs to 7 percent. This risk is considerably greater as the maturity date is extended. A complete discussion of the "interest rate risk" is presented in Chapter 16, "Long-Term Debt and Lease Financing."

The various forms of marketable securities and investments, emphasizing the short term, are presented in Table 7–3. The key characteristics of each

---

[3] The one possible exception to this principle is found in the practice of holding compensating balances at commercial banks — a topic for discussion in Chapter 8.

TABLE 7–3   **Types of short-term investments**

	Maturity*	Minimum Amount	Safety	Marketability	Yield March 22, 1980	Yield January 12, 1993
Federal government securities:						
Treasury bills	3 months	$10,000	Excellent	Excellent	14.76	3.06
Treasury bills	1 year	10,000	Excellent	Excellent	13.89	3.52
Treasury notes	3–5 years	5,000	Excellent	Excellent	13.86	3.55
Federal agency securities:						
Federal Home Loan Bank . . .	1–5 years	5,000	Excellent	Excellent	14.40	5.72
Federal Land Bank	1–5 years	5,000	Excellent	Excellent	14.32	5.86
Nongovernment securities:						
Certificates of deposit (large).	1 month	100,000	Good	Good	16.97	3.15
Certificates of deposit (small)	90 days	500	Good	Poor	15.90	3.20
Commercial paper.	3 months	25,000	Good	Fair	17.04	3.21
Banker's acceptances.	90 days	None	Good	Good	17.22	3.11
Eurodollar deposits	3 months	25,000	Good	Excellent	18.98	3.38
LIBOR (London Interbank Offered Rates)	3 months	100,000	Good	Excellent	—	3.38
Savings accounts	Open	None	Excellent	None[†]	5–5.5	2.50
Money market funds.	Open	500	Good	None[†]	14.50	2.90
Money market deposit accounts (financial institutions)	Open	1,000	Excellent	None[†]	—	2.70

*Several of the above securities can be purchased with maturities longer than those indicated. The above are the most commonly quoted.
[†]Though not marketable, these investments are still highly liquid in that funds may be withdrawn without penalty.

investment will be reviewed along with examples of yields at two different time periods. Yields on March 22, 1980, were extremely high because of high inflationary expectations, but they dropped over the next decade as the U.S. economy entered a period of lower inflation. By January 12, 1993, interest rates had been driven to artificially low levels in an attempt by the Federal Reserve to stimulate a languishing economy. Inflation, at 2.9 percent for 1992, had reached its second lowest level in 25 years and in the view of President Clinton, the economy needed the stimulation of low interest rates to continue its recovery. With one-year interest rates at 3.5 percent and inflation expected at 3 percent for 1993, the real return on short-term investments was at a low 0.5 percent.

Let us examine the characteristics of each security. **Treasury bills** are short-term obligations of the federal government and are a popular place to "park funds" because of a large and active market. Although these securities are originally issued with maturities of 91 days, 182 days, and one year, the investor may buy an outstanding T-bill with as little as one day remaining (perhaps two prior investors have held it for 45 days each). With the government issuing new Treasury bills weekly, a wide range of choices is always available. Treasury bills are unique in that they trade on a discount basis—

FIGURE 7-4   **An examination of yield and maturity characteristics**

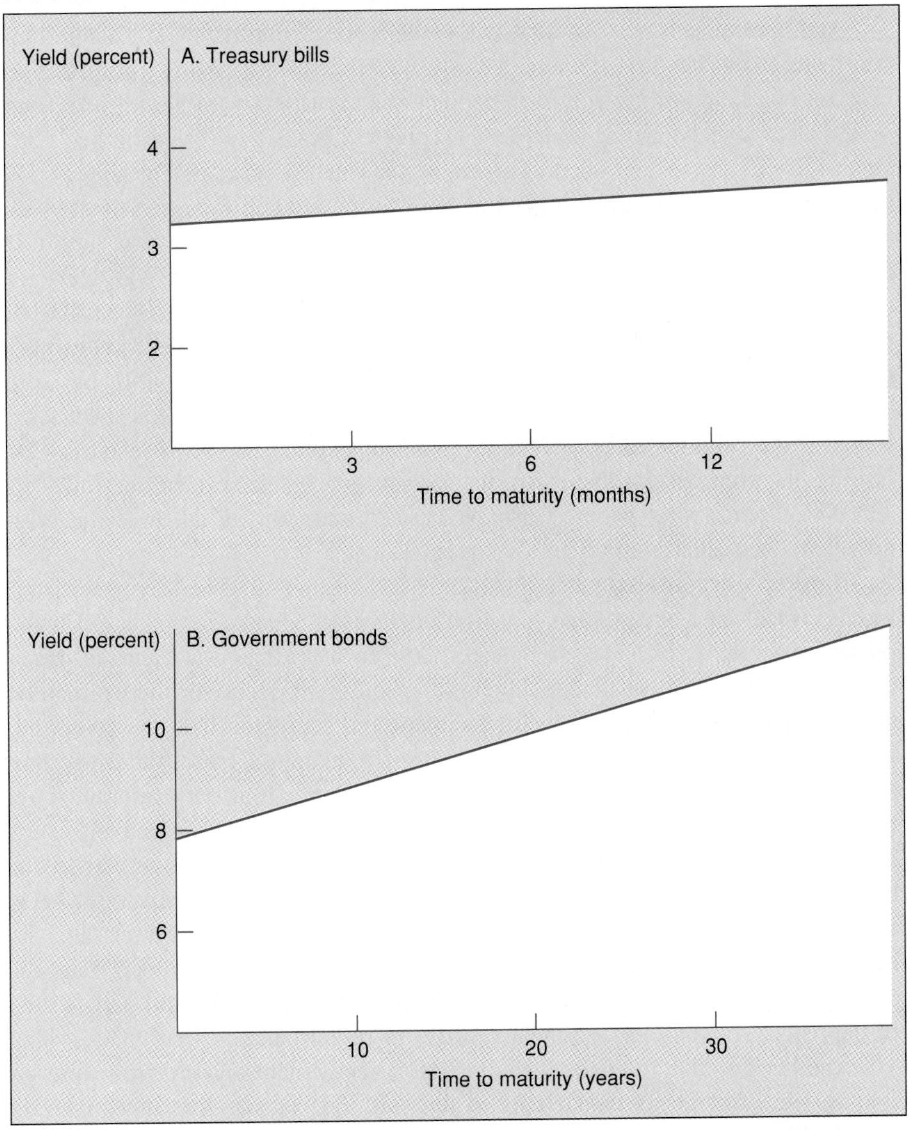

meaning the yield you receive occurs as a result of the difference between the price you pay and the maturity value.

Treasury notes are government obligations with a maturity of three to five years, and they may be purchased with short- to intermediate-term funds. **Federal agency securities** represent the offerings of such governmental organizations as the Federal Home Bank Board and the Federal Land Bank. Though lacking the direct backing of the U.S. Treasury, they are guaranteed by the issuing agency and provide all the safety that one would normally require. There is an excellent secondary market for agency securities that allows investors to sell an outstanding issue in an active and liquid market before the maturity date. Government agency issues pay slightly higher yields than direct Treasury issues.

Another outlet for investment is a **certificate of deposit (CD)**, offered by commercial banks, savings and loans, and other financial institutions. The investor places his or her funds on deposit at a specified rate over a given time period as evidenced by the certificate received. This is a two-tier market, with small CDs ($500 to $10,000) carrying lower interest rates, while larger CDs ($100,000 and more) have higher interest provisions and a degree of marketability for those who wish to turn over their CDs before maturity. The CD market became fully deregulated by the federal government in 1986. CDs are normally insured (guaranteed) by the federal government for up to $100,000.

Comparable in yield and quality to large certificates of deposit, **commercial paper** represents unsecured promissory notes issued to the public by large business corporations. When Ford Motor Credit Corporation needs short-term funds, it may choose to borrow at the bank or expand its credit resources by issuing its commercial paper to the general public in minimum units of $25,000. Commercial paper is usually held to maturity by the investor, with no active secondary market in existence.

Banker's acceptances are short-term securities that generally arise from foreign trade. The acceptance is a draft drawn on a bank for payment when presented to the bank. The difference between a draft and a check is that a company does not have to deposit funds at the bank to cover the draft until the bank has accepted the draft for payment and presented it to the company. In the case of banker's acceptances arising from foreign trade, the draft may be accepted by the bank for *future* payment of the required amount. This means the exporter who now holds the banker's acceptance may have to wait 30, 60, or 90 days to collect the money. Because there is an active market for banker's acceptances, the exporter can sell the acceptance on a discount basis to any buyer and in this way receive the money before the importer receives the goods. This provides a good investment opportunity in banker's acceptances. Banker's acceptances rank close behind Treasury bills and certificates of deposits as a vehicle for viable short-term investments.

Another popular international short-term investment arising from foreign trade is the **Eurodollar certificate of deposit.** The rate on this investment is usually higher than the rates on U.S. Treasury bills and bank certificates of deposit at large U.S. banks. Eurodollars are U.S. dollars held on deposit by foreign banks and in turn lent by those banks to anyone seeking dollars. Since the U.S. dollar is the only international currency that is also used as a domestic currency abroad, any country can use it to help pay for goods. Therefore, there is a large market for Eurodollar deposits and loans, mostly centered in the London international banking market.

London Interbank Offered Rate (LIBOR) is the rate offered for dollar deposits in the London market.[4] While this is essentially a Eurodollar deposit,

---

[4]LIBOR is not a direct security but rather a rate offered on a type of instrument.

the difference is that the deposit is centered in London rather than Paris or Frankfurt or some other part of Europe. LIBOR is often used as a base lending rate for U.S. companies that may borrow abroad at a floating interest rate of LIBOR plus a small premium. LIBOR is even being used as a base rate for some U.S. domestic loans to corporations. The use of LIBOR is discussed further in Chapter 21, "International Financial Management."

The lowest yielding investment may well be a **passbook savings account** at a bank or a savings and loan. Although rates on savings accounts are no longer prescribed by federal regulation, they are still a relatively unattractive form of investment in terms of yield.

Of particular interest to the smaller investor is the **money market fund**— a product of the tight money periods of the 1970s and early 1980s. For as little as $500 or $1,000, an investor may purchase shares in a money market fund, which in turn reinvests the proceeds in higher-yielding $100,000 bank CDs, $25,000 to $100,000 commercial paper, and other large-denomination, higher-yielding securities. The investor then receives his or her pro rata portion of the interest proceeds daily as a credit to his or her shares.

Money market funds allow the small businessperson or investor to participate directly in higher-yielding securities. All too often in the past, the small investor was forced to place funds in low-yielding savings accounts, while "smart" money was parked at higher yields in large-unit investments. Examples of money market funds are Dreyfus Liquid Assets Inc. and Fidelity Daily Income Trust. The investor can normally write checks on a money market fund.

Beginning in December 1982, money market funds got new competition when commercial banks, savings and loans, and credit unions were permitted by the regulatory agencies and Congress to offer **money market accounts** modeled after the money market funds. Due to deregulation, financial institutions are able to pay competitive market rates on money market deposit accounts. While there is not a federally prescribed minimum balance, the normal minimum is $1,000. Terms do vary from institution to institution. Generally these accounts may have only three deposits and three withdrawals per month and are not meant to be transaction accounts, but a place to keep excess cash balances. They may be used by individuals or corporations, but are more attractive to smaller firms than to larger firms (which have many more alternatives available). These accounts are insured up to $100,000 by federal agencies, which make them slightly less risky than money market funds.

Although not a short-term investment as such, most financial institutions also offer NOW accounts. NOW accounts are checking accounts that pay interest. (These accounts are not included in Table 7–3 because their primary purpose is for check writing.)

Management of Accounts Receivable

An increasing portion of the investment in corporate assets has been in accounts receivable as expanding sales, fostered at times by inflationary pressures, have placed additional burdens on firms to carry larger balances for their customers. Frequently, recessions have also stretched out the terms of payment as small customers have had to rely on suppliers for credit. Accounts receivable as a percentage of total assets have almost doubled between 1950 and the early 1990s, representing over 20 percent of total assets for the average U.S. corporation.[5]

Accounts Receivable as an Investment

As is true of other current assets, accounts receivable should be thought of as an investment. The level of accounts receivable should not be judged too high or too low based on historical standards of industry norms, but rather the test should be whether the level of return we are able to earn from this asset equals or exceeds the potential gain from other commitments. For example if we allow our customers five extra days to clear their accounts, our accounts receivable balance will increase—draining funds from marketable securities and perhaps drawing down the inventory level. We must ask whether we are optimizing our return, in light of appropriate risk and liquidity considerations.

An example of a buildup in accounts receivable is presented in Figure 7–5, with supportive financing provided through reducing lower-yielding assets and increasing lower-cost liabilities.

FIGURE 7–5
Financing growth in accounts receivable

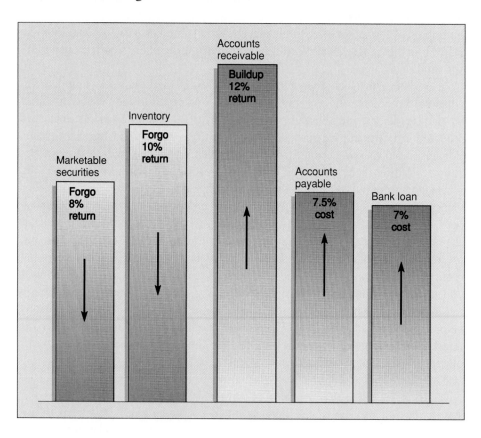

Credit Policy Administration

In considering the extension of credit, there are three primary policy variables to consider in conjunction with our profit objective.

1. Credit standards.
2. Terms of trade.
3. Collection policy.

Credit Standards The firm must determine the nature of the credit risk on the basis of prior record of payment, financial stability, current net worth, and other factors. An extensive electronic network of credit information has been developed by credit agencies throughout the country (Big Brother is watching). The most prominent source is **Dun & Bradstreet,** which publishes a *Reference Book* listing over 3 million business establishments. Information is given on the firm's line of business, net worth, and credit worthiness. This information is usually accessed through computer information networks. An example of the rating system used by Dun & Bradstreet is presented in Table 7–4.

TABLE 7–4
Dun & Bradstreet credit rating system

	Key to Ratings				
		Composite Credit Appraisal			
Estimated Financial Strength		**High**	**Good**	**Fair**	**Limited**
5A	Over $50,000,000	1	2	3	4
4A . . . . $10,000,000 to	50,000,000	1	2	3	4
3A . . . . 1,000,000 to	10,000,000	1	2	3	4
2A . . . . 750,000 to	1,000,000	1	2	3	4
1A . . . . 500,000 to	750,000	1	2	3	4
BA . . . . 300,000 to	500,000	1	2	3	4
BB . . . . 200,000 to	300,000	1	②	3	4
CB . . . . 125,000 to	200,000	1	2	3	4
CC . . . . 75,000 to	125,000	1	2	3	4
DC . . . . 50,000 to	75,000	1	2	3	4
DD . . . . 35,000 to	50,000	1	2	3	4
EE . . . . 20,000 to	35,000	1	2	3	4
FF . . . . 10,000 to	20,000	1	2	3	4
GG . . . . 5,000 to	10,000	1	2	3	4
HH . . . . Up to	5,000	1	2	3	4

A firm with a BB2 rating has estimated financial strength, based on net worth, of $200,000 to $300,000, with an overall composite credit rating of "Good." Besides the *Reference Book,* Dun & Bradstreet can also provide extensive individualized credit reports on potential customers.

Certain industries have also developed their own special credit reporting agencies, such as the Lyon Furniture Mercantile Agency and the National Credit Office (textiles). Even more important are the local credit bureaus that keep close tabs on day-to-day transactions in a given community.

Terms of Trade The stated terms of credit extension will have a strong impact on the eventual size of the accounts receivable balance. If a firm averages

$5,000 in daily credit sales and allows 30-day terms, the average accounts receivable balance will be $150,000. If customers are carried for 60 days, we must maintain $300,000 in receivables and much additional financing will be required.

In establishing credit terms the firm should also consider the use of a cash discount. Offering the terms 2/10, net 30, enables the customer to deduct 2 percent from the face amount of the bill when paying within the first 10 days, but if the discount is not taken, the customer must remit the full amount within 30 days. As later demonstrated in Chapter 8, the annualized cost of not taking a cash discount may be substantial.

Collection Policy   A third area for consideration under credit policy administration is the collection function. A number of quantitative measures may be applied to the credit department of the firm.

$$a. \text{ Average collection period} = \frac{\text{Accounts receivable}}{\text{Average daily credit sales}}$$

An increase in the **average collection period** may be the result of a predetermined plan to extend credit terms or the consequence of poor credit administration.

b. Ratio of bad debts to credit sales.

An increasing ratio may indicate too many weak accounts or an aggressive market expansion policy.

c. Aging of accounts receivables.

Aging of accounts receivable is one way of finding out if customers are paying their bills within the time prescribed in the credit terms. If there is a buildup in receivables beyond normal credit terms, cash inflows will suffer and more stringent credit terms and collection procedures may have to be implemented. An aging schedule is presented to illustrate the concept.

Age of receivables, May 31, 199X			
Month of Sales	**Age of Account (days)**	**Amounts**	**Percent of Account Due**
May	0–30	$ 60,000	60%
April	31–60	25,000	25%
March	61–90	5,000	5%
February	91–120	10,000	10%
Total receivables . . .		$100,000	100%

If the normal credit terms are 30 days, the firm is doing something wrong because 40 percent of accounts are overdue with 10 percent over 90 days outstanding.

An Actual Credit Decision

We now examine a credit decision that brings together the various elements of accounts receivable management. Assume a firm is considering selling to a group of customers that will bring $10,000 in new annual sales, of which 10 percent will be uncollectible. While this is a very high rate of nonpayment, the critical question is, What is the potential contribution to profitability?

Assume the collection cost on these accounts is 5 percent and the cost of producing and selling the product is 77 percent of the sales dollar. We are in a 40 percent tax bracket. The profit on new sales is as follows:

Additional sales	$10,000
Accounts uncollectible (10% of new sales)	1,000
Annual incremental revenue	9,000
Collection costs (5% of new sales).	500
Production and selling costs (77% of new sales) . .	7,700
Annual income before taxes	800
Taxes (40%).	320
Annual incremental income after taxes.	$ 480

Though the return on sales is only 4.8 percent ($480/$10,000), the return on invested dollars may be considerably higher. Let us assume the only new investment in this case is a buildup in accounts receivable. (Present working capital and fixed assets are sufficient to support the higher sales level.) Assume analysis of our accounts indicates a turnover ratio of 6 to 1 between sales and accounts receivable. Our new accounts receivable balance will average $1,667.

$$\frac{\text{Sales}}{\text{Turnover}} = \frac{\$10,000^6}{6} = \$1,667$$

Thus we are committing an average investment of only $1,667 to provide an aftertax return of $480, so that the yield is a very attractive 28.8 percent. If the firm had a minimum required aftertax return of 10 percent, this would clearly be an acceptable investment. We might ask next if we should consider taking on 12 percent or even 15 percent in uncollectible accounts—remaining loyal to our concept of maximizing profit and forsaking any notion about risky accounts being inherently good or bad.

In a manufacturing company, inventory is usually divided into the three basic categories: raw materials used in the product; work in progress, which reflects partially finished products; and finished goods, which are ready for sale. All

Inventory Management

---

[6] We could actually argue that our out-of-pocket commitment to sales is 82 percent (77 percent production and sales costs plus 5 percent collection costs) times $10,000, or $8,200. This would indicate an even smaller commitment to receivables.

these forms of inventory need to be financed, and their efficient management can increase a firm's profitability. The amount of inventory is not always totally controlled by company management because it is affected by sales, production, and economic conditions.

Because of its cylical sales that are highly sensitive to the U.S. economic business climate, the automobile industry is a good case study in inventory management. The automakers have often suffered from inventory buildups when sales declined because adjusting production levels required time. During the 1980s the big three (General Motors, Ford, and Chrysler) took turns implementing buyer incentive programs such as discount financing at rates well below market rates and cash rebate programs to stimulate sales. These programs cut profit margins per car but generated cash flow and reduced investment expenses associated with holding high inventories. General Motors seemed to suffer more overcapacity than the others, and its profits suffered from these tactics, while Ford had high demand for its cars and less inventory problems. Occasionally Ford didn't have a car in stock that someone wanted and it lost the sale, but for a while its profits outpaced the industry because Ford had less discounting and less below-market financing than the competition.

Because inventory is the least liquid of current assets, it should provide the highest yield to justify the investment. While the financial manager may have direct control over cash management, marketable securities, and accounts receivable, control over inventory policy is generally shared with production management and marketing. Let us examine some key factors influencing inventory management.

Level versus Seasonal Production

A manufacturing firm must determine whether a plan of level or seasonal production should be followed. Level production was discussed in Chapter 6. While level (even) production throughout the year allows for maximum efficiency in the use of manpower and machinery, it may result in unnecessarily high inventory buildups before shipment, particularly in a seasonal business. We may have 100,000 bathing suits in stock in November.

If we produce on a seasonal basis, the inventory problem is eliminated, but we will then have unused capacity during slack periods. Furthermore, as we shift to maximum operations to meet seasonal needs, we may be forced to pay overtime wages to labor and to sustain other inefficiencies as equipment is overused.

We have a classic problem in financial analysis. Are the cost savings from level production sufficient to justify the extra expenditure in carrying inventory? Let us look at a typical case.

	Production	
	Level	Seasonal
Average inventory	$100,000	$70,000
Operating costs — after tax. . . .	50,000	60,000

Though we will have to invest $30,000 more in average inventory under level production, we will save $10,000 in operating costs. This represents a 33 percent return on investment. If our required rate of return is 10 percent, this would clearly be an acceptable alternative.[7]

Inventory Policy in Inflation (and Deflation)

The price of copper went from $0.50 to $1.40 a pound and back again in the 1980s. Similar price instability has occurred in wheat, sugar, lumber, and a number of other commodities. Only the most astute inventory manager can hope to prosper in this type of environment. The problem can be partially controlled by taking moderate inventory positions (do not fully commit at one price).

Another way of protecting your inventory position would be by hedging with a futures contract to sell at a stipulated price some months from now.

Rapid price movements in inventory may also have a major impact on the reported income of the firm, a process described in Chapter 3, "Financial Analysis." A firm using FIFO (first-in, first-out) accounting may experience large inventory profits when old, less expensive inventory is written off against new high prices in the marketplace. The benefits may be transitory, as the process reverses itself when prices decline.

The Inventory Decision Model

Substantial research has been devoted to determining optimum inventory size, order quantity, usage rate, and similar considerations. An entire branch in the field of operations research is dedicated to the subject.

In developing an inventory model, we must evaluate the two basic costs associated with inventory: the carrying costs and the ordering costs. Through a careful analysis of both of these variables, we can determine the optimum order size to place to minimize costs.

Carrying Costs   **Carrying costs** include interest on funds tied up in inventory and the cost of warehouse space, insurance premiums, and material handling expenses. There is also an implicit cost associated with the dangers of obsolescence and rapid price change. The larger the order we place, the greater the average inventory we will have on hand, and the higher the carrying cost.

Ordering Costs   As a second factor, we must consider the **cost of ordering** and processing inventory into stock. If we maintain a relatively low average inventory in stock, we must order many times and total ordering cost will be high. The opposite patterns associated with the two costs are portrayed in Figure 7–6.

---

[7]The problem may be further evaluated by using the capital budgeting techniques presented in
    Chapter 12.

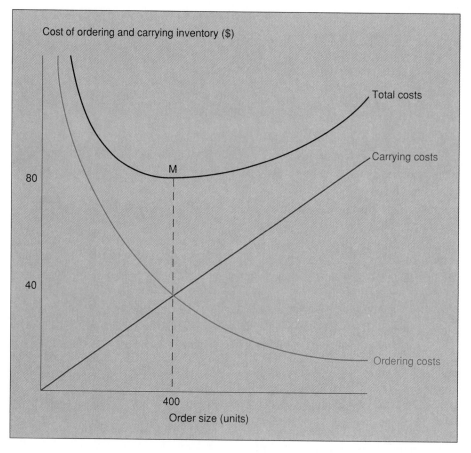

As the order size increases, carrying costs go up because we have more inventory on hand. With larger orders, of course, we will order less frequently and overall ordering costs will go down. The approximate trade-off between the two can best be judged by examining the total cost curve. At point *M*, we have appropriately played the advantages and disadvantages of the respective costs against each other. With larger orders, carrying costs will be excessive, while at a reduced order size, constant ordering will put us at an undesirably high point on the ordering cost curve.

Economic Ordering Quantity

The question becomes, How do we mathematically determine the minimum point (*M*) on the total cost curve? We may use the following formula as the first step.

$$\text{EOQ} = \sqrt{\frac{2SO}{C}} \qquad\qquad (7\text{--}1)$$

EOQ is the **economic ordering quantity,** the most advantageous amount for the firm to order each time. We will determine this value, translate it into average inventory size, and determine the minimum total cost amount (*M*). The terms in the *EOQ* formula are defined as follows:

S = Total sales in units

O = Ordering cost for each order

C = Carrying cost per unit in dollars

Let us assume we anticipate selling 2,000 units, it will cost us $8 to place each order, and the price per unit is $1, with a 20 percent carrying cost to maintain the average inventory (the carrying charge per unit is $0.20). Plugging these values into our formula, we show:

$$EOQ = \sqrt{\frac{2SO}{C}} = \sqrt{\frac{2 \times 2,000 \times \$8}{\$0.20}} = \sqrt{\frac{\$32,000}{\$0.20}} = \sqrt{160,000}$$
$$= 400 \text{ units}$$

The optimum order size is 400 units. On the assumption that we will use up inventory at a constant rate throughout the year, our average inventory on hand will be 200 units, as indicated in Figure 7–7. Average inventory equals EOQ/2.

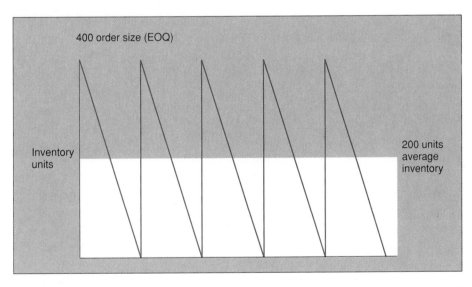

FIGURE 7-7
Inventory usage pattern

Our total costs with an order size of 400 and an average inventory size of 200 units are computed in Table 7–5.

TABLE 7-5
Total costs for inventory

1. Ordering costs = $\frac{2,000 \text{ units}}{400 \text{ order size}}$ = 5 orders

   5 orders at $8 per order = $40

2. Carrying costs = Average inventory in units × Carrying cost per unit

   200 × $0.20 = $40

3. Order cost $40
   Carrying cost   + 40
   Total cost $80

Point *M* in Figure 7–6 on page 188 can be equated to a total cost of $80 at an order size of 400 units. At no other order point can we hope to achieve lower costs. The same basic principles of total cost minimization that we have applied to inventory can be applied to other assets as well. For example, we may assume cash has a carrying cost (opportunity cost of lost interest on marketable securities as a result of being in cash) and an ordering cost (transaction costs of shifting in and out of marketable securities) and then work toward determining the optimum level of cash. In each case we are trying to minimize the overall costs and increase profit.

Safety Stock and Stock Outs

In our analysis thus far we have assumed we would use inventory at a constant rate and we would receive new inventory when the old level of inventory reached zero. To verify this point, you may wish to reexamine Figure 7–7 on page 189. We have not specifically considered the problem of being out of stock.

A stock out occurs when a firm is out of a specific inventory item and is unable to sell or deliver the product. The risk of losing sales to a competitor may cause a firm to hold a **safety stock** to reduce this risk. Although the company may use the EOQ model to determine the optimum order quantity, management cannot always assume the delivery schedules of suppliers will be constant or assure delivery of new inventory when inventory reaches zero. A safety stock will guard against late deliveries due to weather, production delays, equipment breakdowns, and the many other things that can go wrong between the placement of an order and its delivery.

A minimum safety stock will increase the cost of inventory because the carrying cost will rise. This cost should be offset by eliminating lost profits on sales due to stock outs and also by increased profits from unexpected orders that can now be filled.

In the prior example, if a safety stock of 50 units were maintained, the average inventory figure would be 250 units.

$$\text{Average inventory} = \frac{\text{EOQ}}{2} + \text{Safety stock} \qquad (7\text{–}2)$$

$$\text{Average inventory} = \frac{400}{2} + 50$$

$$= 200 + 50 = 250$$

The inventory carrying cost will now increase to $50.

$$\text{Carrying costs} = \text{Average inventory in units} \times \text{Carrying cost per unit}$$

$$= \$250 \times \$0.20 = \$50$$

The amount of safety stock that a firm carries is likely to be influenced by the predictability of inventory usage and the time period necessary to fill inventory orders. The following discussion indicates safety stock may be reduced in the future.

Just-in-Time Inventory Management

A relatively new concept in inventory management, **just-in-time inventory management (JIT)**, was designed for Toyota by the Japanese firm Shigeo Shingo and found its way to the United States. Just-in-time inventory management is part of a total production concept that often interfaces with a total quality control program. A JIT program has several basic requirements: (1) quality production that continually satisfies customer requirements; (2) close ties between suppliers, manufacturers, and customers; and (3) minimizing the level of inventory.

Usually suppliers are located near manufacturers and are able to make orders in small lot sizes because of short delivery times. One side effect has been for manufacturers to reduce their number of suppliers to assure quality as well as to ease the complexity of ordering and delivery. Computerized ordering/inventory tracking systems both on the assembly line and in the supplier's production facility are necessary for JIT to work.

Major U.S. companies such as Xerox, General Electric, Hewlett-Packard, Samsonite, Dow Chemical, Harley-Davidson, and Square D Co. have used just-in-time inventory methods, which save money in surprising ways. Perhaps one of the best examples is Buick City, a General Motors plant in Flint, Michigan. By using JIT methods, Buick City maintains very little inventory, receiving the necessary inventory just in time for production. Inventory levels range from 1 hour to a maximum of 16 hours' worth of parts.

Cost Savings from Lower Inventory   Cost savings from lower levels of inventory and reduced financing costs are expected. Square D Co.'s Control Products Business in Asheville, North Carolina, reduced its inventory by 40 percent over a three-year period. Harley-Davidson reduced its in-process and in-transit inventory by $20 million at a single plant, and General Electric trimmed inventory by 70 percent in 40 plants. In one sense the manufacturer pushes some of the cost of financing onto the supplier. If the supplier also imposes JIT on *its* suppliers, these efficiencies work their way down the supplier chain to create a leaner production system for the whole economy.

Other Benefits   There are other, not so obvious cost savings to just-in-time systems. The Buick City plant uses 70 percent less space than the standard automobile plant and therefore saves construction costs and reduces its overhead expenses for utilities and manpower. General Electric increased productivity by 35 percent in its 40 plants operating under JIT. The computerized ordering systems and electronic data interchange systems (EDI) between suppliers, production, and manufacturing reduce rekeying errors and duplication of forms for the accounting and finance functions. Xerox implemented a quality process along with JIT and reduced its supplier list to 450, which created a $15 million savings in quality control programs. JIT can reduce quality control costs as much as 60 percent, but these costs can often be overlooked by financial analysts because JIT prevents defects rather than detecting poor quality; therefore no cost savings are recognized. One last item is the elimination of waste, which is one of the side benefits of a total quality control system coupled with JIT.

It is important to realize that the just-in-time inventory system is very compatible with the concept of economic ordering quantity. The focus is to balance reduced carrying costs from maintaining less inventory with increased ordering costs. Fortunately electronic data interchange minimizes the impact of having to place orders more often.

Summary

An overriding concept in current asset management is that the less liquid an asset is, the higher the required return. In cash management the primary goal should be to keep the balances as low as possible, consistent with the notion of maintaining adequate funds for transactions purposes and compensating balances. Cash moves through the firm in a cycle as customers make payments and the firm pays its bills. We try to speed the inflow of funds and defer their outflow in managing the company's float. The increased use of electronic funds transfer systems both domestically and internationally is reducing float and making collections and disbursements more timely. Excess short-term funds may be placed in marketable securities—with a wide selection of issues, maturities, and yields from which to choose.

The management of accounts receivable calls for the determination of credit standards and the forms of credit to be offered as well as the development of an effective collection policy. There is no such thing as bad credit—only unprofitable credit extension.

Inventory is the least liquid of the current assets, so it should provide the highest yield. We recognize three different inventory types: raw materials, work-in-progress, and finished goods inventory. We manage inventory levels through models such as the economic ordering quantity (EOQ) model, which helps us determine the optimum average inventory size that minimizes the total cost of ordering and carrying inventory. The just-in-time inventory management model (JIT) focuses on the minimization of inventory through quality production techniques and close ties between manufacturers and suppliers. Both EOQ and JIT models are compatible and can work together in the management of inventory.

List of Terms

Discussion Questions

1. In the management of cash and marketable securities, why should the primary concern be for safety and liquidity rather than maximization of profit?

2. Briefly explain how a corporation may use float to its advantage.

3. Why does float exist and what effect would electronic funds transfer systems have on float?

4. How can a firm operate with a negative cash balance on its corporate books?

5. Explain the similarities and differences of lockbox systems and regional collection offices.

6. Why would a financial manager want to slow down disbursements?

7. Use *The Wall Street Journal* or some other financial publication to find the going interest rates for the list of marketable securities in Table 7–3. Which security would you choose for a short-term investment? Why?

8. Why are Treasury bills a favorite place for financial managers to invest excess cash?

9. Explain why the bad debt percentage or any other similar credit-control percentage is not the ultimate measure of success in the management of accounts receivable. What is the key consideration?

10. What are three quantitative measures that can be applied to the collection policy of the firm?

11. What does the EOQ formula tell us? What assumption is made about the usage rate for inventory?

12. Why might a firm keep a safety stock? What effect is it likely to have on carrying cost of inventory?

13. If a firm uses a just-in-time inventory system, what effect is that likely to have on the number and location of suppliers?

Problems

Cost-benefit analysis of
cash management

1. City Farm Insurance has collection centers around the country to speed up cash collections. The company also makes its disbursements from remote disbursement centers so checks written by City Farm take longer to clear the bank. Collection time has been reduced by two days and disbursement time increased by one because of these policies. Excess funds are being invested in short-term instruments yielding 12 percent per annum.

   a. If City Farm has $5 million per day in collections and $3 million per day in disbursements, how many dollars has the cash management system freed up?

   b. How much can City Farm earn per year on short-term investments made possible by the freed-up cash?

Average collection period

2. Thompson Wood Products has credit sales of $2,160,000 and accounts receivable of $288,000. Compute the value for the average collection period.

Accounts receivable
balance

3. Darla's Cosmetics has annual credit sales of $1,440,000 and an average collection period of 45 days in 1993. Assume a 360-day year.

   What is the company's average accounts receivable balance? Accounts receivable are equal to the average daily credit sales times the average collection period.

Credit policy

4. In problem 3, if accounts receivable change to $200,000 in 1994, while credit sales are $1,800,000, should we assume the firm has a more lenient credit policy?

Determination of credit
sales

5. Hubbell Electronic Wiring Company has an average collection period of 35 days. The accounts receivable balance is $105,000. What is the value of credit sales?

Economic ordering
quantity

6. Nowlin Pipe & Steel has expected sales of 72,000 pipes this year, an ordering cost of $6 per order, and carrying costs of $2.40 per pipe.

   a. What is the economic ordering quantity?

   b. How many orders will be placed during the year?

   c. What will the average inventory be?

Economic ordering
quantity

7. Howe Corporation is trying to improve its inventory control system and has installed an on-line computer at its retail stores. Howe anticipates sales of 126,000 units per year, an ordering cost of $4 per order, and carrying costs of $1.008 per unit.

   a. What is the economic ordering quantity?

   b. How many orders will be placed during the year?

   c. What will the average inventory be?

   d. What is the total cost of inventory expected to be?

Economic ordering
quantity

8. (See problem 7 for basic data.) In the second year, Howe Corporation finds it can reduce ordering costs to $1 per order but carrying costs stay the same at $1.008 per unit.

    a. Recompute *a*, *b*, *c*, and *d* in problem 7 for the second year.

    b. Now compare years one and two and explain what happened.

9. Higgins Athletic Wear has expected sales of 22,500 units a year, carrying costs of $1.50 per unit, and an ordering cost of $3 per order.

    a. What is the economic order quantity?

    b. What is average inventory? What is the total carrying cost?

    c. Assume an additional 30 units will be required as safety stock. What will the new average inventory be? What will the new total carrying cost be?

Economic ordering quantity with safety stock

10. Standard Business Forms is considering extending trade credit to some customers previously considered poor risks. Sales would increase by $100,000 if credit is extended to these new customers. Of the new accounts receivable generated, 12 percent will prove to be uncollectible. Additional collection costs will be 4 percent of sales, and production and selling costs will be 77 percent of sales. Assume a tax rate of 30 percent.

Credit policy decision

    a. Compute the incremental income after taxes.

    b. What will the firm's incremental return on sales be if these new credit customers are accepted?

    c. If the receivable turnover ratio is 5 to 1, and no other asset buildup is needed to serve the new customers, what will Standard Business Forms' incremental return on new average investment be?

11. Ron's checkbook shows a balance of $400. A recent statement from the bank (received last week) shows all checks written as of the date of the statement have been paid, except numbers 325 and 326, which were for $35 and $58, respectively. Since the statement date, checks 327, 328, and 329 have been written for $22, $45, and $17, respectively.

Determining float

    There is an 80 percent probability that checks 325 and 326 have been paid by this time. There is a 50 percent probability that checks 327, 328, and 329 have been paid.

    a. What is the total value of the five checks outstanding?

    b. What is the expected value of payments for the five checks outstanding?

    c. What is the difference between parts *a* and *b*? This represents a type of float.

12. Dimaggio Sports Equipment, Inc., is considering a switch to level production. Cost efficiencies would occur under level production and aftertax costs would decline by $35,000, but inventory would increase by $400,000. Dimaggio would have to finance the extra inventory at a cost of 10.5 percent.

Level versus seasonal production

    a. Should the company go ahead and switch to level production?

    b. How low would interest rates need to fall before level production would be feasible?

Credit policy
decision—receivables and
inventory

13. Collins Office Supplies is considering a more liberal credit policy to increase sales, but expects that 9 percent of the new accounts will be uncollectible. Collection costs are 5 percent of new sales, production and selling costs are 78 percent, and accounts receivable turnover is five times. Assume an income tax rate of 30 percent and an increase in sales of $80,000. No other asset buildup will be required to service the new accounts.

   a. What is the level of accounts receivable to support this sales expansion?

   b. What would be Collins's incremental aftertax return on investment?

   c. Should Collins liberalize credit if a 15 percent aftertax return on investment is required?

   Assume Collins also needs to increase its level of inventory to support new sales and that inventory turnover is four times.

   d. What would be the total incremental investment in accounts receivable and inventory to support a $80,000 increase in sales?

   e. Given the income determined in part *b* and the investment determined in part *d*, should Collins extend more liberal credit terms?

Credit policy decision
with changing variables

14. Curtis Toy Manufacturing Company is evaluating extending credit to a new group of customers. Although these customers will provide $240,000 in additional credit sales, 12 percent are likely to be uncollectible. The company will incur $21,000 in additional collection expenses. Production and marketing expenses represent 72 percent of sales. The company is in a 30 percent tax bracket and has a receivables turnover of six times. No other asset buildup will be required to service the new customers. The firm has a 10 percent desired return on investment.

   a. Should Curtis extend credit to these customers?

   b. Should credit be extended if 14 percent of the new sales prove uncollectible?

   c. Should credit be extended if the receivables turnover drops to 1.5 and 12 percent of the accounts are uncollectible (as was the case in part *a*)?

Continuation of
problem 14

15. Reconsider problem 14. Assume the average collection period is 120 days. All other factors are the same (including 12 percent uncollectibles). Should credit be extended?

   (Problems 16–19 are a series and should be taken in order.)

Credit policy decision
with changing variables

16. Maddox Resources has credit sales of $180,000 yearly with credit terms of net 30 days, which is also the average collection period. Maddox does not offer a discount for early payment, so its customers take the full 30 days to pay.

   Which is the average receivables balance? What is the receivables turnover?

17. If Maddox offered a 2 percent discount for payment in 10 days and every customer took advantage of the new terms, what would the new average receivables balance be? Use the full sales of $180,000 for your calculation of receivables.

18. If Maddox reduces its bank loans, which cost 12 percent, by the cash generated from reduced receivables, what will be the net gain or loss to the firm?

19. Assume the new trade terms of 2/10, net 30 will increase sales by 20 percent because the discount makes Maddox price competitive. If Maddox earns 16 percent on sales before discounts, should it offer the discount? (Consider the same variables as you did for problems 16 through 18.)

COMPREHENSIVE PROBLEM

Baily Distributing Company (receivables and inventory policy)

Bailey Distributing Company sells small appliances to hardware stores in the southern California area. Michael Bailey, the president of the company, is thinking about changing the credit policies offered by the firm to attract customers away from competitors. The current policy calls for a 1/10, net 30, and the new policy would call for a 3/10, net 50. Currently 40 percent of Bailey customers are taking the discount, and it is anticipated that this number would go up to 50 percent with the new discount policy. It is further anticipated that annual sales would increase from a level of $200,000 to $250,000 as a result of the change in the cash discount policy.

The increased sales would also affect the inventory level carried by Bailey. The average inventory carried by Bailey is based on a determination of an EOQ. Assume unit sales of small appliances will increase from 20,000 to 25,000 units. The ordering cost for each order is $100 and the carrying cost per unit is $1 (these values will not change with the discount). The average inventory is based on EOQ/2. Each unit in inventory has an average cost of $6.50.

Cost of goods sold is equal to 65 percent of net sales, general and administrative expenses are equal to 10 percent of net sales, and interest payments of 12 percent will be necessary only for the increase in the accounts receivable and inventory balances. Taxes will equal 25 percent of before-tax income.

a. Compute the accounts receivable balance before and after the change in the cash discount policy. Use the net sales (Total sales − Cash discounts) to determine the average daily sales and the accounts receivable balances.

b. Determine EOQ before and after the change in the cash discount policy. Translate this into average inventory (in units and dollars) before and after the change in the cash discount policy.

c. Complete the income statement.

	Before Policy Change	After Policy Change
Net sales (sales − cash discounts)		
Cost of goods sold		
Gross profit		
General and administrative expense		
Operating profit		
Interest on increase in accounts receivable and inventory (12%)		
Income before taxes		
Taxes		
Income after taxes		

d. Should the new cash discount policy be utilized? Briefly comment.

Selected References

Armstrong, David J. "Sharpening Inventory Management." *Harvard Business Review* 63 (November–December 1985), pp. 42–58.

Batlin, C. A., and Susan Hinko. "Lockbox Management and Value Maximization." *Financial Management* 10 (Winter 1981), pp. 39–44.

Daniels, Carol. "Timing Cash Flow: Will Finality Changes Delay Funds Availability?" *Corporate Cashflow* 11 (January 1990), pp. 40–41.

Devine, Matthew E. "Managing a Corporate Short-Term Portfolio." *Cash Management* 7 (May–June 1987), pp. 46–48.

Emery, Gary W. "Some Empirical Evidence on the Properties of Daily Cash Flows." *Financial Management* 10 (Spring 1981), pp. 21–28.

Gallinger, George W., and A. James Ifflander. "Monitoring Accounts Receivables Using Variance Analysis." *Financial Management* 16 (Winter 1987), pp. 69–76.

Gentry, James A., and Jesus M. De La Garza. "A Generalized Model for Monitoring Accounts Receivable." *Financial Management* 14 (Winter 1985), pp. 28–38.

Kamath, Ravindra R., Shahriar Khaksari, Heidi Hylton Meier, and John Winklepleck. "Management of Excess Cash: Practices and Developments." *Financial Management* 14 (Autumn 1985), pp. 70–77.

Mian, Schzad L., and Clifford W. Smith, Jr. "Accounts Receivable Management Policy: Theory and Evidence." *Journal of Finance* 47 (March 1992), pp. 169–99.

Miller, Tom W., and Bernell K. Stone. "Daily Cash Modeling and Seasonal Resolution: Alternative Models and Techniques for Using the Distribution Approach." *Journal of Financial and Quantitative Analysis* 20 (September 1985), pp. 335–51.

Pohlman, Randolph A., Emmanuel S. Santiago, and Lynn F. Markel. "Cash Flow Estimation Practices of Large Firms." *Financial Management* 17 (Summer 1988), pp. 71–79.

Purnell, King. "Credit Administration: The Key to Recovery in the Short Term and Success in the Long Term." *Journal of Commercial Lending* 75 (April 1992), pp. 52–57.

Scholl, William C. "Commercial Lenders' Guide to Cash Management." *Journal of Commercial Lending* 75 (December 1992), pp. 44–48.

Srinivasan, Venkat, and Yong H. Kim. "Designing Expert Financial Systems: A Case Study of Corporate Credit Management." *Financial Management* 17 (Autumn 1986), pp. 32–44.

Stancill, James McNeill. "When Is There Cash in Cash Flow?" *Harvard Business Review* 65 (March–April 1987), pp. 38–49.

Walleigh, Richard C. "What's Your Excuse for Not Using JIT?" *Harvard Business Review* 64 (March–April 1986), pp. 38–54.

Sources of Short-Term Financing

CHAPTER CONCEPTS

1 Trade credit from suppliers is normally the most available form of short-term financing.

2 Bank loans are usually short term in nature and should be paid off from the normal operations of the firm.

3 Commercial paper represents a short-term, un-secured promissory note issued by the firm.

4 Through borrowing in foreign markets, a firm may lower its borrowing costs.

5 By using accounts receivable and inventory as collateral for a loan, the firm may be able to borrow larger amounts.

In Chapter 8 we examine the cost and availability of the various outlets for short-term funds, with primary attention to trade credit from suppliers, bank loans, corporate promissory notes, foreign borrowing, and loans against receivables and inventory. It is sometimes said the only way to be sure a bank loan will be approved is to convince the banker that you don't really need the money. The learning objective of this chapter is the opposite—namely, to demonstrate how badly needed funds can be made available on a short-term basis from the various credit suppliers.

Trade Credit

The largest provider of short-term credit is usually at the firm's doorstep—the manufacturer or seller of goods and services. Approximately 40 percent of short-term financing is in the form of accounts payable or trade credit. Accounts payable is a **spontaneous source of funds,** growing as the business expands on a seasonal or long-term basis and contracting in a like fashion.

Payment Period

Trade credit is usually extended for 30 to 60 days. Many firms attempt to "stretch the payment period" to receive additional short-term financing. This is an acceptable form of financing as long as it is not carried to an abusive extent. Going from a 30- to a 35-day average payment period may be tolerated within the trade, while stretching payments to 65 days might alienate suppliers and cause a diminishing credit rating with Dun & Bradstreet and local credit bureaus. A major variable in determining the payment period is the possible existence of a cash discount.

Cash Discount Policy

A **cash discount** allows for a reduction in price if payment is made within a specified time period. A 2/10, net 30 cash discount means we can deduct 2 percent if we remit our funds 10 days after billing, but failing this, we must pay the full amount by the 30th day.

On a $100 billing, we could pay $98 up to the 10th day or $100 at the end of 30 days. If we fail to take the cash discount, we will get to use $98 for 20 more days at a $2 fee. The cost is a whopping 36.72 percent. Note that we first consider the interest cost and then convert this to an annual basis. The standard formula is:

$$\begin{matrix} \text{Cost of failing} \\ \text{to take a} \\ \text{cash discount} \end{matrix} = \frac{\text{Discount percent}}{100 \text{ percent} - \text{Discount percent}} \times \frac{360}{\text{Final due date} - \text{Discount period}} \qquad (8\text{--}1)$$

$$= \frac{2\%}{100\% - 2\%} \times \frac{360}{(30 - 10)}$$

$$= 2.04\% \times 18 = 36.72\%$$

Cash discount terms may vary. For example, on a 2/10, net 90 basis, it would cost us only 9.18 percent not to take the discount and to pay the full amount after 90 days.

$$\frac{2\%}{100\% - 2\%} \times \frac{360}{(90 - 10)} = 2.04\% \times 4.5 = 9.18\%$$

In each case, we must ask ourselves whether bypassing the discount and using the money for a longer period is the cheapest means of financing. In the first example, with a cost of 36.72 percent, it probably is not. We would be better off borrowing $98 for 20 days at some lesser rate. For example, at 10 percent interest we would pay 54 cents[1] in interest as opposed to $2 under the cash discount policy. With the 2/10, net 90 arrangement, the cost of missing the discount is only 9.18 percent and we may choose to let our suppliers carry us for an extra 80 days.

Net Credit Position

In Chapter 2, "Review of Accounting," we defined accounts receivable as a use of funds and accounts payable as a source of funds. The firm should closely watch the relationship between the two to determine its **net trade credit** position. Net trade credit is positive when accounts receivable are greater than accounts payable and vice versa. If a firm has average daily sales of $5,000 and collects in 30 days, the accounts receivable balance will be $150,000. If this is associated with average daily purchases of $4,000 and a 25-day average payment period, the average accounts payable balance is $100,000—indicating $50,000 more in credit extended than received. Changing this situation to an average payment period of 40 days increases the accounts payable to $160,000 ($4,000 × 40). Accounts payable now exceed accounts receivable by $10,000, thus leaving funds for other needs. Larger firms tend to be net providers of trade credit (relatively high receivables), with smaller firms in the user position (relatively high payables).

Bank Credit

Banks may provide funds for the financing of seasonal needs, product line expansion, and long-term growth. The typical banker prefers a **self-liquidating loan** in which the use of funds will ensure a built-in or automatic repayment scheme. Actually, two thirds of bank loans are short term in nature. Nevertheless, through the process of renewing old loans, many of these 90- or 180-day agreements take on the characteristics of longer-term financing.

Major changes occurring in banking today are centered on the concept of "full-service banking." The modern banker's function is much broader than merely accepting deposits, making loans, and processing checks. A banking institution may be providing trust and investment services, a credit card operation, real estate lending, data processing services, cash management services

---

[1] $\dfrac{20}{360} \times 10\% \times \$98 = 54¢.$

both domestically and internationally, pension fund management, and many other services for large and small businesses. Many of these services have been made possible through the development of the **bank holding company**—a legal entity in which one key bank owns a number of affiliate banks as well as other nonbanking subsidiaries engaged in closely related activities. For example, in 1990 the New York bank J. P. Morgan was the first bank given permission to engage in investment banking, an area of the securities markets that banks have been excluded from since the 1930s.

The banking scene today has become more international to accommodate increased world trade and the rise of international corporations. The largest banks in the world today are the Japanese banks, and international banks are expanding into the United States through bank acquisitions and branch offices. Every major city from New York to San Francisco has experienced a growth in foreign banks.

Bank deregulation has created greater competition among financial institutions, such as commercial banks, savings and loans, credit unions, brokerage houses, and new companies offering financial services. Difficult problems face the whole U.S. financial system. The collapse of the savings and loan industry, the decline in real estate values, the increased debt loads of highly leveraged companies, risky bank loans to Third World countries, and international competition will all force consolidations and major changes in the banking structure and relationships with corporations during the 1990s.

General Electric Corporation is an example of the new type of competition facing the traditional banker. General Electric's financial services group now generates over 20 percent of General Electric's earnings. The company purchased Kidder Peabody, Inc., an old-line stockbroker and investment banker (investment banking is covered in Chapter 15), and Employers Reinsurance Corporation. In addition, GE Credit has large-scale activities in leasing and asset management. It is diversifying into commercial real estate and corporate financial services and is considered one of the top 10 financial services companies in the United States. GE's large size, combined with its top credit rating, gives it an edge over less creditworthy competitors in raising low-cost funds. The "cost of funds" issue has many traditional bankers worried.

We will look at a number of terms generally associated with banking (and other types of lending activity) and consider the significance of each. Attention is directed to the prime interest rate, compensating balances, the term loan arrangement, and methods of computing interest.

Prime Rate

The **prime rate** is the rate the bank charges its most creditworthy customers, and it is scaled up proportionally to reflect the various credit classes. At certain slack loan periods in the economy, banks may actually charge top customers less than the published prime rate; however, such activities are difficult to track. The average customer can expect to pay 1 or 2 percentage points above prime, while in tight money periods a builder in a speculative construction project may pay 5 or more percentage points over prime.

FIGURE 8–1   **Pattern of prime rate movements**

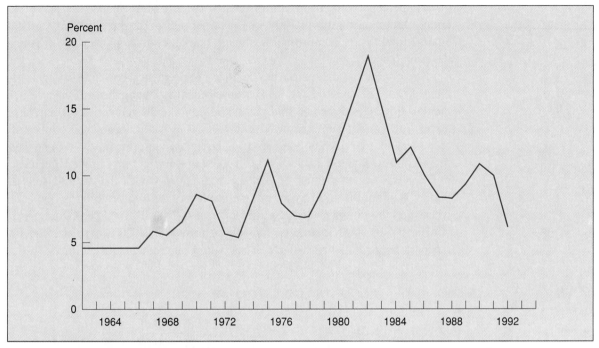

Figure 8–1 presents the annual average prime rate from 1962 through 1992. Interest rates in the 1950s and early 1960s were relatively stable, hovering between 3 percent and 5 percent. Beginning in 1965 and continuing into the present, the prime rate has become highly volatile, moving as much as 8 percentage points in a 12-month period. In the early 1980s, the prime rate went above 20 percent for several months (the annual average in 1981 reached 18.87 percent) before sharply declining. With lower inflation from 1982 to 1992, interest rates followed the same pattern and the prime rate began 1986 at 9.5 percent and fell to 7.5 percent by September 1986 before rebounding to 10 percent in 1990. With a recession in 1991, the prime rate once again began to fall, reaching 6.0 in July 1992 and staying at that level into mid 1993.

Compensating Balances

In providing loans and other services, a bank may require that *business* customers either pay a fee for the service or maintain a minimum average account balance, referred to as a **compensating balance.** In some cases both fees and compensating balances are required. According to a survey of over 100 major commercial banks in large cities, the average compensating balance these banks required to offset $100 in service fees was $23,379.[2] For a large company that generates service fees of $100,000, the equivalent compensating balance would be $23,379,000.

---

[2]Barry B. Burr, "Services Anything but Uniform," *Pensions & Investment Age,* August 10, 1987, p. CM1.

When compensating balances are required to receive a loan, the required amount is usually computed as a percentage of customer loans outstanding, or as a percentage of bank commitments toward future loans to a given account. A common ratio is 20 percent against outstanding loans or 10 percent against total future commitments, though market conditions tend to influence the percentages.

Some view the compensating balance requirement as an unusual arrangement. Where else would you walk into a business establishment, buy a shipment of goods, and then be told you could not take 20 percent of the purchase home with you? If you borrow $100,000, paying 8 percent interest on the full amount with a 20 percent compensating balance requirement, you will be paying $8,000 for the use of $80,000 in funds, or an effective rate of 10 percent.

The amount that must be borrowed to end up with the desired sum of money is simply figured by taking the needed funds and dividing by $(1 - c)$, where c is the compensating balance expressed as a decimal. For example, if you need $100,000 in funds, you must borrow $125,000 to ensure the intended amount will be available. This would be calculated as follows:

$$\text{Amount to be borrowed} = \frac{\text{Amount needed}}{(1 - c)}$$
$$= \frac{\$100,000}{(1 - 0.2)}$$
$$= \$125,000$$

A check on this calculation could be done to see if we actually end up with the use of $100,000.

$125,000	Loan
−25,000	20% compensating balance requirement
$100,000	Available funds

The intent here is not to suggest that the compensating balance requirement represents an unfair or hidden cost. If it were not for compensating balances, quoted interest rates would be higher or gratuitous services now offered by banks would carry a price tag.

Of banks responding to a *Pensions & Investment Age* survey, 27 percent of corporate clients paid a fee for cash management services while the other 73 percent eliminated the direct fee with compensating balances.[3] Fees and compensating balances varied widely among banks. As the competition heats up among the providers of financial services, corporations can be expected to selectively shop for high-quality, low-cost institutions.

---

[3]See prior footnote.

Maturity Provisions

As previously indicated, bank loans have been traditionally short term in nature (though perhaps renewable). In the last decade there has been a movement to the use of the **term loan,** in which credit is extended for one to seven years. The loan is usually repaid in monthly or quarterly installments over its life rather than in one single payment. Only superior credit applicants, as measured by working capital strength, potential profitability, and competitive position, can qualify for term loan financing. Here the banker and the business firm are said to be "climbing into bed together" because of the length of the loan.

Bankers are hesitant to fix a single interest rate to a term loan. The more common practice is to allow the interest rate to change with market conditions. Thus the interest rate on a term loan may be tied to the prime rate or LIBOR (the London Interbank Offered Rate). Often loans will be priced at a premium over one of these two rates reflecting the risk of the borrower. For example a loan may be priced at 1.5 percentage points above LIBOR and will move up and down with changes in the base rate.

Cost of Commercial Bank Financing

The effective interest rate on a loan is based on the loan amount, the dollar interest paid, the length of the loan, and the method of repayment. It is easy enough to observe that $60 interest on a $1,000 loan for one year would carry a 6 percent interest rate, but what if the same loan were for 120 days? We use the formula:

$$\text{Effective rate} = \frac{\text{Interest}}{\text{Principal}} \times \frac{\text{Days in the year (360)}}{\text{Days loan is outstanding}} \qquad (8\text{--}2)$$

$$= \frac{\$60}{\$1,000} \times \frac{360}{120} = 6\% \times 3 = 18\%$$

Since we have use of the funds for only 120 days, the effective rate is 18 percent. To highlight the impact of time, if you borrowed $20 for only 10 days and paid back $21, the effective interest rate would be 180 percent—a violation of almost every usury law.

$$\frac{\$1}{\$20} \times \frac{360}{10} = 5\% \times 36 = 180\%$$

Not only is the time dimension of a loan important, but also the way in which interest is charged. We have assumed that interest would be paid when the loan comes due. If the bank uses a **discounted loan** and deducts the interest in advance, the effective rate of interest increases. For example, a $1,000 one-year loan with $60 of interest deducted in advance represents the payment of interest on only $940, or an effective rate of 6.38 percent.

$$\text{Effective rate on} \atop \text{discounted loan} = \frac{\text{Interest}}{\text{Principal} - \text{Interest}} \times \frac{\text{Days in the year (360)}}{\text{Days loan is outstanding}} \quad (8\text{–}3)$$

$$= \frac{\$60}{\$1{,}000 - \$60} \times \frac{360}{360} = \frac{\$60}{\$940} = 6.38\%$$

Interest Costs with Compensating Balances

When a loan is made with compensating balances, the effective interest rate is the stated interest rate divided by $(1 - c)$, where c is the compensating balance expressed as a decimal. Assume that 6 percent is the stated annual rate and that a 20 percent compensating balance is required.

$$\text{Effective rate with} \atop \text{compensating balances} = \frac{\text{Interest rate}}{(1 - c)} \quad (8\text{–}4)$$

$$= \frac{6\%}{(1 - 0.2)}$$

$$= 7.5\%$$

If dollar amounts are used and the stated rate is unknown, Formula 8–5 can be used. The assumption is that we are paying $60 interest on a $1,000 loan, but are able to use only $800 of the funds. The loan is for a year.

$$\text{Effective rate} \atop \text{with} \atop \text{compensating} \atop \text{balances} = \frac{\text{Interest}}{\text{Principal} - \text{Compensating} \atop \text{balance in dollars}} \times \frac{\text{Days in the} \atop \text{year (360)}}{\text{Days loan is} \atop \text{outstanding}} \quad (8\text{–}5)$$

$$= \frac{\$60}{\$1{,}000 - \$200} \times \frac{360}{360} = \frac{\$60}{\$800} = 7.5\%$$

Only when a firm has idle cash balances that can be used to cover compensating balance requirements would the firm not use the higher effective-cost formulas (Formulas 8–4 and 8–5).

Rate on Installment Loans

The most confusing borrowing arrangement to the average bank customer or a consumer is the installment loan. An **installment loan** calls for a series of equal payments over the life of the loan. Though federal legislation prohibits a misrepresentation of interest rates on loans to customers, a loan officer or an overanxious salesperson may quote a rate on an installment loan that is approximately half the true rate.

Assume that you borrow $1,000 on a 12-month installment basis, with regular monthly payments to apply to interest and principal, and the interest requirement is $60. Though it might be suggested that the rate on the loan is 6 percent, this is clearly not the case. Though you are paying a total of $60 in interest, you do not have the use of $1,000 for one year—rather, you are paying back the $1,000 on a monthly basis, with an average outstanding loan balance for the year of approximately $500. The effective rate of interest is 11.08 percent.

$$\text{Effective rate on installment loan} = \frac{2 \times \text{Annual no. of payments} \times \text{Interest}}{(\text{Total no. of payments} + 1) \times \text{Principal}} \quad (8\text{--}6)$$

$$= \frac{2 \times 12 \times \$60}{13 \times \$1,000} = \frac{\$1,440}{\$13,000} = 11.08\%$$

Annual Percentage Rate

Because the way interest is calculated makes the effective rate different from the stated rate, Congress passed the Truth in Lending Act in 1968. This act required that the actual **annual percentage rate (APR)** be given to the borrower. The APR is really a measure of the effective rate we have presented. Congress was primarily trying to protect the unwary consumer from paying more than the stated rate without his or her knowledge. For example, the stated rate on an installment loan might be 8 percent but the APR might be 14.8 percent. It has always been assumed that businesses should be well versed in business practices and financial matters and, therefore, the Truth in Lending Act was not intended to protect business borrowers but, rather, individuals.

The annual percentage rate requires the use of the actuarial method of compounded interest when calculating the APR. This requires knowledge of the time value of money techniques presented in Chapter 9. For our purposes in this chapter, it is enough to know that the lender must calculate interest for the period on the outstanding loan balance at the beginning of the period. Any payments are first credited against interest due, and any amount left is used to reduce the principal or loan balance. Because there are so many ways to structure loan repayment schedules, no one formula is applicable for computing the APR. For example, loans do not all have 365 days—some have only 10 or 15 days or other portions of a year.

Since most consumer loans are installment types, the APR is usually based on the assumption of amortization. Amortization means an equal dollar amount is paid each period to retire principal and interest. According to the law, a loan amortization schedule is the final authority in the calculation of the APR. The amortization schedule always has an annual percentage rate that diminishes the principal to zero over the loan period. You will learn how to develop an amortization schedule in Chapter 9.

The Credit Crunch Phenomenon

In 1969–70, 1973–74, and 1979–81, the economy went through a period of extreme credit shortages in the banking sector and other financial markets. We seem to find ourselves in the midst of a tight money situation every three to five years. The anatomy of a credit crunch is as follows. The Federal Reserve tightens the growth in the money supply in its battle against inflation, causing a decrease in lendable funds and an increase in interest rates. To compound the difficulty, business requirements for funds may be increasing to carry inflation-laden inventory and receivables. A third problem is the massive withdrawal of savings deposits at banking and thrift institutions, all in search of higher returns. There simply are not enough lendable funds.

Recent history has taught us that the way *not* to deal with credit shortages is to impose artificial limits on interest rates in the form of restrictive usury laws or extreme governmental pressure. In 1969–70 the prime rate went to 8.5 percent in a tight money period—a level not high enough to bring the forces of demand and supply together, and little credit was available. In 1974 the prime rose to 12 percent, a rate truly reflecting market conditions, and funds were available. The same was true in 1980 and 1981 as the prime went to 20 percent and higher, but lendable funds were available.

By the 1990s a different type of credit crunch evolved. The financial system was suffering from bad loans made to real estate, Third World countries, and high-risk corporations. These bad loans resulted in the partial collapse of the savings and loan industry, the decline of U.S. banks and insurance companies, and an inability or unwillingness by lenders to lend money to moderate or high-risk borrowers. While interest rates did not soar as in past credit crunches, lenders became more risk-averse, allocating capital more on risk considerations related to the borrower rather than the interest rate that could be charged. After President Clinton took office, banks responded to increased loan demand fostered by an improving economy and some of the lowest interest rates in 20 years.

Financing through Commercial Paper

For large and prestigious firms, commercial paper may provide an outlet for raising funds. **Commercial paper** represents a short-term, unsecured promissory note issued to the public in minimum units of $25,000. As Figure 8–2 indicates, the total amount of commercial paper outstanding has increased dramatically, rising from $83 billion in 1978 to over $500 billion in 1991. This large increase in the commercial paper market reflects the willingness of qualified companies to borrow at the lowest rate available. The larger market that has emerged in the last five years has improved the ability of corporations to raise short-term funds.

Commercial paper falls into two categories. First, there are finance companies, such as General Motors Acceptance Corporation (GMAC), General Electric Credit, and CIT Financial Corporation, that issue paper primarily to institutional investors such as pension funds, insurance companies, and money market mutual funds. It is probably the growth of money market mutual funds that has had such a great impact on the ability of companies to sell such an increased amount of commercial paper in the market. Paper sold by financial firms such as GMAC is referred to as **finance paper,** and since it is usually sold directly to the lender by the finance company, it is also referred

FIGURE 8-2
**Total commercial paper
outstanding**

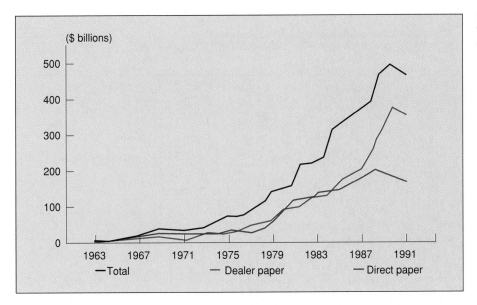

to as **direct paper.** The second type of commercial paper is sold by industrial companies, utility firms, or financial companies too small to have their own selling network. These firms use an intermediate dealer network to distribute their paper, and so this type of paper is referred to as **dealer paper.**

Traditionally commercial paper is just that. A paper certificate is issued to the lender to signify the lender's claim to be repaid. This certificate could be lost, stolen, misplaced, or damaged and, in rare cases, someone could fail to cash it in at maturity. There is a growing trend among companies that sell commercial paper directly to computerize the handling of commercial paper with what is called **book-entry transactions,** in which no actual certificate is created. All transactions simply occur on the books. The use of computer-based electronic issuing methods lowers cost and simplifies administration, as well as linking the lender or lender's bank and the issuing company. General Motors Acceptance Corporation, the largest single issuer of commercial paper, has been a heavy user of the book-entry method and currently has over 40 percent of its $31 billion commercial paper in this form. As the market becomes more accustomed to this electronic method, large users ($500 million or more) will likely find it profitable to switch from physical paper to the book-entry system, where all transfers of money are done by wiring cash between lenders and commercial paper issuers.

Advantages of Commercial Paper

The growing popularity of commercial paper can be attributed to other factors besides the rapid growth of money market mutual funds and their need to find short-term securities for investment. For example, commercial paper may be issued at below the prime interest rate. As indicated in the last column of Table 8–1 on page 212, this rate differential reached over 5 percent in the tight money markets of 1981.

TABLE 8–1
Comparison of commercial paper rate to prime rate (annual rate)*

Year	Finance Co. Paper (directly placed) 4–6 months	Other Paper (dealer-placed) 4–6 months	Average Bank Prime Rate	Prime Rate Minus Finance Paper
1971	4.89	5.11	5.50	0.61
1972	4.55	4.69	5.25	0.70
1973	7.38	8.15	8.30	0.92
1974	8.61	9.84	11.12	2.51
1975	6.16	6.32	7.86	1.70
1976	5.22	5.35	6.84	1.62
1977	5.50	5.60	6.82	1.32
1978	7.78	7.99	9.06	1.28
1979	10.25	10.91	12.67	2.42
1980	11.28	12.29	15.27	3.99
1981	13.73	14.76	18.87	5.14
1982	11.20	11.89	14.86	3.66
1983	8.69	8.89	10.79	2.10
1984	9.65	10.16	12.04	2.39
1985	7.75	8.01	9.93	2.18
1986	6.31	6.39	8.33	2.02
1987	6.37	6.85	8.21	1.84
1988	7.14	7.68	9.32	2.18
1989	8.16	8.80	10.87	2.71
1990	7.53	7.95	10.00	2.47
1991	5.60	5.85	8.46	2.86
1992	3.63	3.82	6.00	2.37

*Averages for the year.
Source: Federal Reserve bulletins, *Business Statistics*.

A second advantage of commercial paper is that no compensating balance requirements are associated with its issuance, though the firm is generally required to maintain commercial bank lines of approved credit equal to the amount of the paper outstanding (a procedure somewhat less costly than compensating balances). Finally, a number of firms enjoy the prestige associated with being able to float their commercial paper in what is considered a "snobbish market" for funds.

Limitations on the Issuance of Commercial Paper

The commercial paper market is not without its problems. When the Penn Central Railroad went bankrupt in 1970 with its $85 million in "bad" commercial paper floating around, many lenders in the market panicked and refused to roll over (renew) existing paper as it came due. The market shrank by 15 percent from May to December, and the unnerving situation almost caused Chrysler Financial Corporation to be towed away.

Although the funds provided through the issuance of commercial paper are cheaper than bank loans, they are also less predictable. Although a firm may pay a higher rate for a bank loan, it is also buying a degree of loyalty and commitment that is unavailable in the commercial paper market.

Foreign Borrowing

An increasing source of funds for U.S. firms has been the large Eurodollar market. Loans from foreign banks denominated in dollars are called **Eurodol-**

lar loans. Such loans are usually short term to intermediate term in maturity. Many multinational corporations are finding cheaper ways of borrowing in foreign markets. A new approach has been for financial managers to borrow *foreign currencies* either directly or through foreign subsidiaries at very favorable interest rates. The companies *convert* the borrowed francs or marks to dollars, which are then sent to the United States to be used by the parent company. There is, however, foreign exchange exposure risk associated with these loans. This topic is given greater coverage in Chapter 21.

As an example of an international loan, IBM arranged a seven-year loan in Swiss francs at an interest rate of 6 percent at a time when the prime rate in the United States was 19 percent. Because of the different financial practices in foreign countries, the differential is not as great as it seems, but this did save IBM several percent in borrowing costs. Similarly, a foreign subsidiary of a large U.S. drug and medical supply company borrowed from its foreign banks at rates below prevailing U.S. interest rates and then loaned the money back to its parent firm. These examples simply show that the world financial markets have become more sophisticated, and so must financial managers.

Use of Collateral in Short-Term Financing

Almost any firm would prefer to borrow on an unsecured (no-collateral) basis; but if the borrower's credit rating is too low or its need for funds too great, the lending institution will require that certain assets be pledged. A secured credit arrangement might help the borrower to obtain funds that would otherwise be unavailable.

In any loan the lender's primary concern, however, is whether the borrower's capacity to generate cash flow is sufficient to liquidate the loan as it comes due. Few lenders would make a loan strictly on the basis of collateral. Collateral is merely a stopgap device to protect the lender when all else fails. The bank or finance company is in business to collect interest, not to repossess and resell assets.

Though a number of different types of assets may be pledged, our attention will be directed to accounts receivable and inventory. All states have now adopted the Uniform Commercial Code, which standardizes and simplifies the procedures for establishing security on a loan.

Accounts Receivable Financing

Accounts receivable financing may include **pledging accounts receivable** as collateral for a loan or an outright *sale* (**factoring**) of receivables. Receivables financing is popular because it permits borrowing to be tied directly to the level of asset expansion at any point in time. As the level of accounts receivable goes up, we are able to borrow more.

A drawback is that this is a relatively expensive method of acquiring funds, so it must be carefully compared to other forms of credit. Accounts receivable represent one of the firm's most valuable short-term assets, and they should be committed only where the appropriate circumstances exist. An ill-advised accounts receivable financing plan may exclude the firm from a less expensive bank term loan. Let us investigate more closely the characteristics and the costs associated with the pledging and selling of receivables.

Pledging Accounts Receivable

The lending institution will generally stipulate which of the accounts receivable are of sufficient quality to serve as collateral for a loan. On this basis, we may borrow 60 to 80 percent of the value of the acceptable collateral. The loan percentage will depend on the financial strength of the borrowing firm and on the creditworthiness of its accounts. The lender will have full recourse against the borrower if any of the accounts go bad. The interest rate in a receivables borrowing arrangement is generally well in excess of the prime rate.

The interest is computed against the loan balance outstanding, a figure that may change quite frequently, as indicated in Table 8–2. In the illustration, interest is assumed to be 12 percent annually, or 1 percent per month. In month 1, we are able to borrow $8,000 against $10,000 in acceptable receivables and we must pay $80 in interest. Similar values are developed for succeeding months.

TABLE 8–2
Receivable loan balance

	Month 1	Month 2	Month 3	Month 4
Total accounts receivable.	$11,000	$15,100	$19,400	$16,300
Acceptable accounts receivable (to finance company).	10,000	14,000	18,000	15,000
Loan balance (80%)	8,000	11,200	14,400	12,000
Interest 12% annual — 1% per month . .	80	112	144	120

Factoring Receivables

When we factor receivables, they are sold outright to the finance company. Our customers may be instructed to remit the proceeds directly to the purchaser of the account. The factoring firm generally does not have recourse against the seller of the receivables. As a matter of practice, the finance company may do part or all of the credit analysis directly to ensure the quality of the accounts. As a potential sale is being made, the factoring firm may give immediate feedback to the seller on whether the account will be purchased.

When the factoring firm accepts an account, it may forward funds immediately to the seller, in anticipation of receiving payment 30 days later as part of the normal billing process. The factoring firm is not only absorbing risk, but also is actually advancing funds to the seller a month earlier than the seller would normally receive them.

For taking the risk, the factoring firm is generally paid on a fee or commission basis equal to 1 to 3 percent of the invoices accepted. In addition, it is paid a lending rate for advancing the funds early. If $100,000 a *month* is processed at a 1 percent commission and a 12 percent annual borrowing rate, the total effective cost will be 24 percent on an *annual* basis.

1%	Commission
<u>1%</u>	Interest for one month (12% annual/12)
2%	Total fee monthly
2%	Monthly × 12 = 24% annual rate

FINANCE IN ACTION

Georgia Pacific Sale of Receivables

In 1990 Georgia Pacific Corporation (GP), a large lumber, building products, and paper company with over $10 billion in annual sales, acquired Great Northern Nekoosa (GNN), another paper company, for $3.8 billion. Georgia Pacific increased its borrowings by $4.2 billion to fund the purchase and the acquisition of GNN's $1.7 billion of debt. To reduce debt, GP has sold several divisions and entered into the sale of $800 million of receivables.

In its 1992 Annual report to shareholders Georgia Pacific stated:

Note 7. Receivables

The Corporation has a large, diversified customer base.

The Corporation had sold fractional ownership interests in a defined pool of trade accounts receivable for $800 million as of December 31, 1992 and 1991 and $850 million as of December 31, 1990. The net cash proceeds are reported as operating cash flow in the accompanying statements of cash flows. The sold accounts receivable are reflected as a reduction of receivables in the accompanying balance sheets. Under the agreement, which expires in June 1994, the maximum amount of the purchasers'

investment is currently $800 million and is subject to change based on the level of eligible receivables and restrictions on concentrations of receivables. The full amount of the allowance for doubtful accounts has been retained because the Corporation has retained substantially the same risk of credit loss as if the receivables had not been sold. A portion of the cost of the accounts receivable sale program is based on the purchasers' level of investment and borrowing costs. Additionally, the Corporation pays fees based on its senior debt ratings. The total cost of the program, which was $35 million, $59 million, and $48 million for 1992, 1991, and 1990, respectively, is included in selling, general, and administrative expense in the accompanying statements of income.

Source: Georgia Pacific 1992 Annual Report, pp. 43–44.

While it is not made known who the purchasers of the accounts receivables are, they are most likely factors, or institutional investors. Georgia Pacific did have to pay fees to the purchasers for this arrangement, but the cost is less than might be needed to fund an $800 million loan.

If one considers that the firm selling the accounts is transferring risk as well as receiving funds early, which may allow it to take cash discounts, the rate may not be considered exorbitant. Also the firm is able to pass on much of the credit-checking cost to the factor.

Asset-Backed Public Offerings

A new wrinkle in accounts receivable financing is the sale of receivables by large firms in public offerings. While factoring has long been one way of selling receivables, public offerings of securities backed by receivables as collateral gained respectability when General Motors Acceptance Corporation made a public offering of $500 million of asset-backed securities in December 1985.

These **asset-backed securities** are nothing more than the sale of receivables. In former years companies that sold receivables were viewed as short of cash, financially shaky, or in some financial trouble. This negative perception has been diminished by new issues of receivables-backed securities by such companies as Unisys (computer receivables), Bank of America (credit card receivables), GMAC (car loan receivables), and Mack Truck (truck loan receivables).

These asset-backed public offerings have continued to be popular, and in 1990 IBM added a new wrinkle by selling a public offering of receivables due from state and municipal governments. The interest paid to the owners of these securities is not taxable by the federal government. This allows IBM to raise cash at below-market rates. This strategy may be available only to large companies having significant business with state and local government units. Investment bankers continue to develop new types of asset-backed securities, and they are optimistic that the use of all asset-backed securities will continue to grow because of the predictable cash flows they offer investors.

One of the benefits to the issuer is that they trade future cash flows for immediate cash. The asset-backed security is likely to carry a high credit rating of AA or better, even when the issuing firm may have a low credit rating. This allows the issuing firm to acquire lower cost funds than it could with a bank loan or a bond offering. While this short-term market is still relatively small by money market standards, it could provide an important avenue for corporate liquidity and short-term financing.

Several problems face the public sale of receivables. Computer systems need to be upgraded to service securities and handle the paperwork. For GMAC to offer such a large public issue, it had to change its whole data processing system to keep track of the loans for the investors in the securities. A second consideration for the buyer of these securities is the probability that the receivable will actually be paid. Even though the loss rates on loans were about one half of 1 percent in the 1980s, bad debts can be as much as 5 to 10 percent in tight money markets.[4] For example a serious recession might cause many car owners to default on their car payments to GMAC and thus leave the owners of the asset-backed security without the promised cash flows. To counteract these fears, many issuers set up a loan-loss reserve fund to partially insure against the possibility of a loss. In markets this new, only time will tell what the future growth will be.

Figure 8–3 shows an issue by Mack Trucks for $215,140,000 of TRUCS (truck receivables underlying certificates). These securities are short to intermediate term in nature.

The creation of asset-backed securities is also referred to as **securitization of assets.** Securitization of receivables has spread to Europe. For example, the annual report of Philips Group, a Dutch electronics firm, states:

> Trade receivables were sold in 1991 by means of securitization transactions with provisions for limited recourse. The receivables sold and not yet collected as of December 31, 1991, amounting to 1,490 "Dutch Guilders" ... have been deducted from the balance of trade accounts receivable.

---

[4]Ann Monroe, "Sales of Receivables by Big Firms Gain Respect in Public Offerings," *The Wall Street Journal,* December 2, 1985, p. 41.

FIGURE 8–3

This announcement is neither an offer to sell nor a solicitation of an offer to buy these securities.
The offer is made only by the Prospectus and the related Prospectus Supplement

$215,140,000

Mack Trucks Receivables Corporation

Truck Receivables Underlying Certificates
TRUCS℠ Series 1
Collateralized by Truck and Other Commercial Vehicle Receivables

$103,685,000   7.15% Class 1-A Notes Due June 15, 1988

Price 99.9925%

$111,455,000   8.05% Class 1-B Notes Due June 15, 1992

Price 100%

(Plus accrued interest at the applicable rate from June 15, 1987.)

Copies of the Prospectus and the related Prospectus Supplement may be obtained only from
the undersigned in any State where the undersigned may lawfully offer the securities.

Shearson Lehman Brothers Inc.   Lazard Frères & Co.

July 7, 1987

This securitization accomplishes the same cash flow for the company selling the receivables as a factor would, and it creates a security that is marketable in secondary markets (can be sold to other potential investors).

We may also borrow against inventory to acquire funds. The extent to which inventory financing may be employed is based on the marketability of the pledged goods, their associated price stability, and the perishability of the product. Another significant factor is the degree of physical control that can be exercised over the product by the lender. We can relate some of these factors to the stages of inventory production and the nature of lender control.

Inventory Financing

Stages of Production

Raw materials and finished goods are likely to provide the best collateral, while goods in process may qualify for only a small percentage loan. To the extent that a firm is holding such widely traded raw materials as lumber, metals, grain, cotton, and wool, a loan of 70 to 80 percent or higher is possible. The lender may have to place only a few quick phone calls to dispose of the goods at market value if the borrower fails to repay the loan. For standardized finished goods, such as tires, canned goods, and building products, the same principle would apply. Goods in process, representing altered but unfinished raw materials, may qualify for a loan of only one fourth of their value or less.

Nature of Lender Control

The methods for controlling pledged inventory go from the simple to the complex, providing ever greater assurances to the lender but progressively higher administrative costs.

Blanket Inventory Liens   The simplest method is for the lender to have a general claim against the inventory of the borrower through **blanket inventory liens.** Specific items are not identified or tagged, and there is no physical control.

Trust Receipts   A **trust receipt** is an instrument acknowledging that the borrower holds the inventory and proceeds from sales in trust for the lender. Each item is carefully marked and specified by serial number. When sold, the proceeds are transferred to the lender and the trust receipt is canceled. Also known as *floor planning,* this financing device is very popular among auto and industrial equipment dealers and in the television and home appliance industries. Although it provides tighter control than does the blanket inventory lien, it still does not give the lender direct control over inventory—only a better and more legally enforceable system of tracing the goods.

Warehousing   Under this arrangement goods are physically identified, segregated, and stored under the direction of an independent warehousing company. The firm issues a warehouse receipt to the lender, and goods can be moved only with the lender's approval.

   The goods may be stored on the premises of the warehousing firm, an arrangement known as **public warehousing,** or on the *borrower's premises*—under a **field warehousing** agreement. When field warehousing is utilized, it is still an independent warehousing company that exercises control over inventory.

Appraisal of Inventory Control Devices

While the more structured methods of inventory financing appear somewhat restrictive, they are well accepted in certain industries. For example field warehousing is popular in grain storage and food canning. Well-maintained control measures involve substantial administrative expenses, and they raise the overall costs of borrowing. The costs of inventory financing may run 15 percent or higher. However, as is true of accounts receivable financing, the extension of funds is well synchronized with the need.

Hedging to Reduce Borrowing Risk

Those who are in continual need of borrowed funds to operate their firm are exposed to the risk of interest rate changes. One way to partially reduce that risk is through interest rate hedging activities in the financial futures market. **Hedging** means to engage in a transaction that partially or fully reduces a prior risk exposure.

The **financial futures market** is set up to allow for the trading of a financial instrument at a future point in time. For example, in January 1994 one might sell a Treasury bond contract that is to be closed out in June 1994. The sales price of the June 1994 contract is established by the initial January transaction. However, a subsequent purchase of a June 1994 contract at a currently unknown price will be necessary to close out the transaction. In the futures market, you do not physically deliver the goods; you merely execute a later transaction that reverses your initial position. Thus if you initially sell a futures contract, you later buy a contract that covers your initial sale. If you initially buy a futures contract, the opposite is true and you later sell a contract that covers your initial purchase position.

In the case of selling a Treasury bond futures contract, the subsequent pattern of interest rates will determine whether it is profitable or not. If interest rates go up, Treasury bond prices will go down and you will be able to buy a subsequent contract at a lower price than the sales value you initially established. This will result in a profitable transaction. Note the following example.

Sales price, June 1994 Treasury bond contract* (sale occurs in January 1994)	$95,000
Purchase price, June 1994 Treasury bond contract (the purchase occurs in June 1994)	90,000
Profit on futures contract	$ 5,000

*Only a small percentage of the actual dollars involved must be invested to initiate the contract. This is known as margin.

The reason Treasury bond prices went down is that, as previously mentioned, interest rates and bond prices move in opposite directions, and interest rates went up. The lesson to be learned from this example is that rising interest rates can mean profits in the financial futures market if you initially sell a contract and later buy it back.

The financial manager who continually needs to borrow money and fears changes in interest rates can partially hedge his or her position by engaging in the type of futures contract described above. If interest rates do rise, the extra cost of borrowing money to actually finance the business can be offset by the profit on a futures contract. If interest rates go down, there will be a loss on the futures contract as bond prices go up, but this will be offset by the more desirable lower borrowing costs of financing the firm.

The financial futures market can be used to partially or fully hedge against almost any financial event. In addition to Treasury bonds, trades may be initiated in Treasury bills, certificates of deposits, GNMA certificates,[5] and many other instruments.[6] The trades may be executed on such exchanges

---

[5]GNMA stands for Government National Mortgage Association, also known as Ginnie Mae.

[6]For a more complete discussion of corporate hedging in the futures market, see "Commodities and Financial Futures" in Chapter 16 of Geoffrey Hirt and Stanley Block, *Fundamentals of Investment Management*, 4th ed. (Homewood, Ill.: Richard D. Irwin, 1993).

as the Chicago Board of Trade, the Chicago Mercantile Exchange, or the New York Futures Exchange.

Summary

A firm in search of short-term financing must be aware of all the institutional arrangements that are available. The easiest access is to trade credit provided by suppliers as a natural outgrowth of the buying and reselling of goods. Larger firms tend to be net providers of trade credit, while smaller firms are net users.

Bank financing is usually in the form of short-term, self-liquidating loans. A financially strong customer will be offered the prime, or lowest rate, with the rates to other accounts scaled up appropriately. The use of compensating balances tends to increase the effective yield to the bank and serves as a device to compensate the bank for the many services it provides to a commercial account.

An alternative to bank credit for the large, prestigious firm is the use of commercial paper. Though generally issued at a rate below prime, it is an impersonal means of financing that may "dry up" during difficult financing periods.

Firms are also turning to foreign sources of funds, either through the Eurodollar market (foreign dollar loans) or through borrowing foreign currency directly.

By using a secured form of financing, the firm ties its borrowing requirements directly to its asset buildup. We may pledge our accounts receivable as collateral or sell them outright, as well as borrow against inventory. Though secured-asset financing devices may be expensive, they may well fit the credit needs of the firm, particularly those of a small firm that cannot qualify for premium bank financing or the commercial paper market.

Finally the financial manager may wish to consider the use of hedging through the financial futures market. The consequences of rapid interest rate changes can be reduced through participation in the futures market.

Review of Formulas

1. Cost of failing to take a cash discount

$$\text{Cost of failing to take a cash discount} = \frac{\text{Discount percent}}{100 \text{ percent} - \text{Discount percent}} \times \frac{360}{\text{Final due date} - \text{Discount period}} \qquad (8\text{--}1)$$

2. Amount of funds to be borrowed to meet needs under compensating balances

$$\text{Amount of funds to be borrowed to meet needs under compensating balances} = \frac{\text{Amount needed}}{(1 - c)}$$

c is the compensating balance requirement expressed as a decimal.

3. $\text{Effective rate on a loan} = \dfrac{\text{Interest}}{\text{Principal}} \times \dfrac{\text{Days in the year}}{\text{Days loan is outstanding}}$ (8–2)

4. $\text{Effective rate on a } \textit{discounted} \text{ loan} = \dfrac{\text{Interest}}{\text{Principal} - \text{Interest}} \times \dfrac{\text{Days in the year (360)}}{\text{Days loan is outstanding}}$ (8–3)

5. $\text{Effective loan rate with compensating balances} = \dfrac{\text{Interest rate}}{(1 - c)}$ (8–4)

   c is the compensating balance requirement expressed as a decimal.

6. $\text{Effective loan rate with compensating balances (based on dollar values)} = \dfrac{\text{Interest}}{\text{Principal} - \text{Compensating balance in dollars}} \times \dfrac{\text{Days in the year (360)}}{\text{Days loan is outstanding}}$ (8–5)

7. $\text{Effective loan rate on an installment loan} = \dfrac{2 \times \text{Annual no. of payments} \times \text{Interest}}{(\text{Total no. of payments} + 1) \times \text{Principal}}$ (8–6)

List of Terms

spontaneous source of funds 202
cash discount 202
net trade credit 203
self-liquidating loan 203
bank holding company 204
prime rate 204
compensating balance 205
term loan 207
discounted loan 207
installment loan 208
annual percentage rate (APR) 209
commercial paper 210
finance paper 210

direct paper 211
dealer paper 211
book-entry transaction 211
Eurodollar loan 212
pledging accounts receivable 213
factoring 213
asset-backed securities 215
securitization of assets 216
blanket inventory liens 218
trust receipt 218
public warehousing 218
field warehousing 218
hedging 218
financial futures market 219

Discussion Questions

1. Under what circumstances would it be advisable to borrow money to take a cash discount?
2. Discuss the relative use of credit between large and small firms. Which group is generally in the net creditor position, and why?

3. What is the prime interest rate? How does the average bank customer fare in regard to the prime interest rate? Are companies ever allowed by banks to borrow at less than prime?

4. What advantages do compensating balances have for banks? Are the advantages to banks necessarily disadvantages to corporations?

5. A borrower is often confronted with a stated interest rate and an effective interest rate. What is the difference, and which one should the financial manager recognize as the true cost of borrowing?

6. Commercial paper may show up on corporate balance sheets as either a current asset or a current liability. Explain this statement.

7. What are the advantages of commercial paper in comparison with bank borrowing at the prime rate? What are the disadvantages?

8. Discuss the major types of collateralized short-term inventory loans.

9. What is an asset-backed public offering?

10. What is the difference between raising cash with asset-backed securities (securitization) or by using a factor?

11. What is meant by hedging in the financial futures market to offset interest rate risks?

Problems

Cash discount

1. Compute the cost of not taking the following trade discounts.
   a. 2/10, net 40.
   b. 2/15, net 30.
   c. 2/10, net 45.
   d. 3/10, net 90.

Effective rate of interest

2. Your bank will lend you $3,000 for 50 days at a cost of $45 interest. What is your effective rate of interest?

Effective rate on installment loan

3. I. M. Boring is going to borrow $5,000 for one year at 13 percent interest. What is the effective rate of interest if the loan is discounted?

Net credit position

4. Simpson Orange Juice Company normally takes 20 days to pay for its average daily credit purchases of $6,000. Its average daily sales are $7,000, and it collects its accounts in 28 days.

   a. What is its net credit position? That is, compute its accounts receivable and its accounts payable and subtract the latter from the former.

   $$\text{Accounts receivable} = \text{Average daily credit sales} \times \text{Average collection period}$$

   $$\text{Accounts payable} = \text{Average daily credit purchases} \times \text{Average payment period}$$

   b. If the firm extends its average payment period from 20 days to 35 days (and all else remains the same), what is the firm's new net credit position? Has it improved its cash flow?

5. Carey Company is borrowing $200,000 for one year at 12 percent from Second Intrastate Bank. The bank requires a 20 percent compensating balance. What is the effective rate of interest? What would the effective rate be if Carey were required to make 12 equal monthly payments to retire the loan? The principal, as used in Formula 8–6, refers to funds the firm can effectively utilize (Amount borrowed − Compensating balance).

   Compensating balances and installment loans

6. Capone Child Care Centers, Inc., plans to borrow $250,000 for one year at 10 percent from the Chicago Bank and Trust Company. There is a 20 percent compensating balance requirement. Capone keeps minimum transaction balances of $18,000 in the normal course of business. This idle cash counts toward meeting the compensating balance requirement. What is the effective rate of interest?

   Compensating balances with idle balances

7. The treasurer of Hi-Cost Supermarkets is seeking a $30,000 loan for 180 days from Midland Bank. The stated interest rate is 10 percent and there is a 15 percent compensating requirement. The treasurer always keeps a minimum of $2,500 in the firm's checking account. These funds could count toward meeting any compensating balance requirements. What is the effective rate of interest on this loan?

   Compensating balances with idle balances

8. Tucker Drilling Corp. plans to borrow $200,000. Northern National Bank will lend the money at one half percentage point over the prime rate of 8½ percent (9 percent total) and requires a compensating balance of 20 percent. Principal in this case refers to funds that the firm can effectively use in the business.

   What is the effective rate of interest? What would the effective rate be if Tucker Drilling were required to make four quarterly payments to retire the loan?

   Effective rate under different terms

9. Your company plans to borrow $5 million for 12 months, and your banker gives you a stated rate of 14 percent interest. You would like to know the effective rate of interest for the following types of loans. (Each of the following parts stands alone.)

   Effective rates under different terms

   a. Simple 14 percent interest with a 10 percent compensating balance.

   b. Discounted interest.

   c. An installment loan (12 payments).

   d. Discounted interest with a 5 percent compensating balance.

10. If you borrow $12,000 at $900 interest for one year, what is your effective interest cost for the following payment plan?

    Effective rates under different terms

    a. Annual payment.

    b. Semiannual payments.

    c. Quarterly payments.

    d. Monthly payments.

11. Vroom Motorcycle Company is borrowing $30,000 from First State Bank. The total interest charge is $9,000. The loan will be paid by making equal monthly payments for the next three years. What is the effective rate of interest on this installment loan?

    Cash discount under special circumstances

<table>
<tr><td>Bank loan to take cash discount</td><td>12. Mr. Paul Promptly is a very cautious businessman. His suppliers offer trade credit terms of 3/10, net 70. Mr. Promptly never takes the discount offered, but he pays his suppliers in 60 days rather than the 70 days allowed so he is sure the payments are never late. What is Mr. Promptly's cost of not taking the cash discount?</td></tr>
</table>

Bank loan to take cash discount

13. The Ogden Timber Company buys from its suppliers on terms of 2/10, net 35. Ogden has not been utilizing the discount offered and has been taking 50 days to pay its bills. The suppliers seem to accept this payment pattern, and Ogden's credit rating has not been hurt.

Mr. Wood, Ogden Timber Company's vice-president, has suggested the company begin to take the discount offered. Mr. Wood proposes the company borrow from its bank at a stated rate of 15 percent. The bank requires a 25 percent compensating balance on these loans. Current account balances would not be available to meet any of this compensating balance requirement. Do you agree with Mr. Wood's proposal?

Bank loan to take cash discount

14. In problem 13, if the compensating balance requirement were 10 percent instead of 25 percent, would you change your answer? Do the appropriate calculation.

Bank loan to take cash discount

15. Bosworth Petroleum needs $500,000 to take a cash discount of 2/10, net 70. A banker will loan the money for 60 days at an interest cost of $8,100.

a. What is the effective rate on the bank loan?

b. How much would it cost (in percentage terms) if Bosworth did not take the cash discount, but paid the bill in 70 days instead of 10 days?

c. Should Bosworth borrow the money to take the discount?

d. If the banker requires a 20 percent compensating balance, how much must Bosworth borrow to end up with the $500,000?

e. What would be the effective interest rate in part d if the interest charge for 60 days were $13,000? Should Bosworth borrow with the 20 percent compensating balance? (He has no funds to count against the compensating balance requirement.)

Competing terms for banks

16. Columbus Shipping Company is negotiating with two banks for a $100,000 loan. Bankcorp of Ohio requires a 20 percent compensating balance, discounts the loan, and wants to be paid back in four quarterly payments. Cleveland Bank requires a 10 percent compensating balance, does not discount the loan, but wants to be paid back in 12 monthly installments. The stated rate at both banks is 10 percent. Compensating balances and any discounts will be subtracted from the $100,000 in determining the available funds in part a.

a. Which loan should Columbus accept?

b. Recompute the effective cost of interest, assuming Columbus ordinarily maintains $20,000 at each bank in deposits that will serve as compensating balances.

c. How much did the compensating balances inflate the percentage interest costs? Does your choice of banks change if the assumption in part *b* is correct?

17. Texas Oil Supplies sells to the 12 accounts listed below.

Accounts receivable financing

Account	Receivable Balance Outstanding	Average Age of the Account over the Last Year
A	$ 50,000	35
B	80,000	25
C	120,000	47
D	10,000	15
E	250,000	35
F	60,000	51
G	40,000	18
H	180,000	60
I.	15,000	43
J	25,000	33
K	200,000	41
L	60,000	28

Hedging to offset risk

J&J Financial Corporation will lend 90 percent against account balances that have averaged 30 days or less; 80 percent for account balances between 30 and 40 days; and 70 percent for account balances between 40 and 45 days. Customers that take over 45 days to pay their bills are not considered as adequate accounts for a loan.

The current prime rate is 12 percent, and J&J Financial Corporation charges 3 percent over prime to Texas Oil Supplies as its annual loan rate.

a. Determine the maximum loan for which Texas Oil Supplies could qualify.

b. Determine how much one month's interest expense would be on the loan balance determined in part *a*.

18. The treasurer for Thornton Pipe and Steel Company wishes to use financial futures to hedge her interest rate exposure. She will sell five Treasury futures contracts at $105,000 per contract. It is July and the contracts must be closed out in December of this year. Long-term interest rates are currently 7.4 percent. If they increase to 8.5 percent, assume the value of the contracts will go down by 10 percent. Also if interest rates do increase by 1.1 percentage points, assume the firm will have additional interest expense on its business loans and other commitments of $60,800. This expense, of course, is separate from the futures contracts.

a. What will be the profit or loss on the futures contract if interest rates go to 8.5 percent?

    b. Explain why a profit or loss occurred on the futures contracts.

    c. After considering the hedging in part *a*, what is the net cost to the firm of the increased interest expense of $60,800? What percent of this increased cost did the treasurer effectively hedge away?

    d. Indicate whether there would be a profit or loss on the futures contracts if interest rates went down.

Selected References

Barr, Ann, and R. P. McWhorter. "Understanding and Strengthening Bank Credit Culture." *Journal of Commercial Lending* 74 (April 1992), pp. 6–11.

Hawkins, Gregory D. "An Analysis of Revolving Credit Agreements." *Journal of Financial Economics* 59 (March 1982), pp. 59–81.

Hirt, Geoffrey A., and Stanley B. Block. *Fundamentals of Investment Management,* 4th ed. Homewood, Ill.: Richard D. Irwin, 1993.

James, Christopher. "An Analysis of Bank Loan Indexation." *Journal of Finance* 37 (June 1982), pp. 809–25.

Kolb, Robert W., and Raymond Chiang. "Improving Performance Using Interest-Rate Futures." *Financial Management* 10 (Autumn 1981), pp. 72–79.

Monroe, Ann. "Sales of Receivables by Big Firms Gain Respect in Public Offerings." *The Wall Street Journal,* December 2, 1985, p. 41.

Nadler, Paul S. "Compensating Balances and the Prime at Twilight." *Harvard Business Review* 50 (January–February 1972), pp. 112–20.

Peterik, Paul. "Getting by Your Banker: Tips on How to Come Away with the Loan." *Cash Flow* 8 (January 1987), pp. 31–35.

Rose, Peter S. "Agency Theory and Entry Barriers in Banking." *Financial Review* 27 (August 1992), pp. 323–53.

Smith, Janet K. "Trade Credit and Information Asymmetry." *Journal of Finance* 42 (September 1987), pp. 863–72.

PART 4

The Capital Budgeting Process

Chapter 9
The Time Value of Money

Chapter 10
Valuation and Rates of
Return

Chapter 11
Cost of Capital

Chapter 12
The Capital Budgeting
Decision

Chapter 13
Risk and Capital
Budgeting

INTRODUCTION

A capital budgeting decision is one that involves the allocation of funds to projects that will have a life of at least one year and usually much longer. Examples might include development of a major new product, a plant site location, or an equipment replacement decision. Because we may be locked into our decision for 10 to 20 years and large sums of money are usually involved, the capital budgeting decision must be approached with great care. Basic capital budgeting decisions determine whether there is under- or overcapacity in a given firm or within an industry. • The capital budgeting decision is of interest not only to students of finance, but also to those who desire careers in accounting, marketing, production management, and a number of other areas. Whether the marketing manager gets a new product approved for production and distribution may be a function of how well he or she provides data into the capital budgeting process and understands the analy-sis. • Because the capital budgeting process is long term in nature, we must develop a methodology for translating future inflows and outflows to the present. Thus our first step is to consider the time value of money in Chapter 9. Our understanding of future value, present value, annuities, and yields allows us to move back and forth between the future and the present. The student may be particularly interested in the extensive summary and review material at the end of the chapter. • We then move to the topic

of valuation of sources of financing in Chapter 10. By understanding what measures investors use to determine required rates of return and current values for bonds, preferred stock, and common stock, we are also considering what the corporation must pay for these funds. The chapter on valuation thus naturally extends into the next chapter on cost of capital (financing) to the firm. As described in Chapter 11, the cost of capital represents the weighted cost of the various sources of financing to the firm and is generally a minimum standard for accepting an investment. The capital asset pricing model, an analytical approach to relating individual asset returns to market returns, is considered briefly in Chapter 11 and is also covered on an optional basis in Appendix 11A. • In Chapter 12 we bring together the concepts of time value of money and cost of capital to develop actual investment decisions. Though a number of methods of evaluating capital investments are discussed, such as the payback method and the internal rate of return method, the primary emphasis is on the net present value method. Here we discount future flows from an investment at the cost of capital to see whether they equal or exceed the required investment. • In Chapter 13 we study risk in the capital budgeting decision process. Most managers and investors are risk-averse—that is, all things being equal, they would prefer a certain predictable outcome of 10 percent, rather than a 50–50 chance of going broke or doubling their money.

The Time Value of Money

CHAPTER CONCEPTS

1 Money has a time value associated with it and therefore a dollar received today is worth more than a dollar received in the future.

2 The future value and present value of a dollar is based on the number of periods involved and the going interest rate.

3 Tables for future value and present value can be applied to any problem to ease the analysis.

4 Not only can future value and present value be computed, but other factors such as yield (rate of return) can be determined as well.

In 1624 the Indians sold Manhattan Island at the ridiculously low figure of $24. But wait, was it really ridiculous? If the Indians had merely taken the $24 and reinvested it at 6 percent annual interest up to 1994, they would have had $55 billion, an amount sufficient to repurchase much of New York City. If the Indians had been slightly more astute and had invested the $24 at 7.5 percent compounded annually, they would now have over $9 trillion—and tribal chiefs would now rival oil sheikhs and Japanese tycoons as the richest people in the world. Another popular example is that $1 received 1,994 years ago, invested at 6 percent, could now be used to purchase all the wealth in the world.

While not all examples are this dramatic, the time value of money applies to many day-to-day decisions. Understanding the effective rate on a business loan, the mortgage payment in a real estate transaction, or the true return on an investment depends on understanding the time value of money. As long as an investor can garner a positive return on idle dollars, distinctions must be made between money received today and money received in the future. The investor/lender essentially demands that a financial "rent" be paid on his or her funds as current dollars are set aside today in anticipation of higher returns in the future.

Relationship to the Capital Outlay Decision

The decision to purchase new plant and equipment or to introduce a new product in the market requires using capital allocating or capital budgeting techniques. Essentially we must determine whether future benefits are sufficiently large to justify current outlays. It is important that we develop the mathematical tools of the time value of money as the first step toward making capital allocating decisions. Let us now examine the basic terminology of "time value of money."

Future Value— Single Amount

In determining the **future value,** we measure the value of an amount that is allowed to grow at a given interest rate over a period of time. Assume an investor has $1,000 and wishes to know its worth after four years if it grows at 10 percent per year. At the end of the first year, he will have $1,000 × 1.10, or $1,100. By the end of year two, the $1,100 will have grown to $1,210 ($1,100 × 1.10). The four-year pattern is indicated below.

$$1\text{st year}\quad \$1,000 \times 1.10 = \$1,100$$
$$2\text{nd year}\quad \$1,100 \times 1.10 = \$1,210$$
$$3\text{rd year}\quad \$1,210 \times 1.10 = \$1,331$$
$$4\text{th year}\quad \$1,331 \times 1.10 = \$1,464$$

After the fourth year, the investor has accumulated $1,464. Because compounding problems often cover a long period, a more generalized formula is necessary to describe the compounding procedure. We shall let:

$$FV = \text{Future value}$$

$$PV = \text{Present value}$$

$$i = \text{Interest rate}$$

$$n = \text{Number of periods}$$

The simple formula is:

$$FV = PV(1 + i)^n$$

In this case, PV = \$1,000, i = 10 percent, n = 4, so we have:

$$FV = \$1,000(1.10)^4, \quad \text{or} \quad \$1,000 \times 1.464 = \$1,464$$

The term $(1.10)^4$ is found to equal 1.464 by multiplying 1.10 four times itself (the fourth power) or by using logarithms. An even quicker process is using an interest rate table, such as Table 9–1 for the future value of a dollar. With n = 4 and i = 10 percent, the value is also found to be 1.464.

TABLE 9–1
Future value of \$1 (FV_{IF})

Periods	1%	2%	3%	4%	6%	8%	10%
1	1.010	1.020	1.030	1.040	1.060	1.080	1.100
2	1.020	1.040	1.061	1.082	1.124	1.166	1.210
3	1.030	1.061	1.093	1.125	1.191	1.260	1.331
4	1.041	1.082	1.126	1.170	1.262	1.360	1.464
5	1.051	1.104	1.159	1.217	1.338	1.469	1.611
10	1.105	1.219	1.344	1.480	1.791	2.159	2.594
20	1.220	1.486	1.806	2.191	3.207	4.661	6.727

The table tells us the amount that \$1 would grow to if it were invested for any number of periods at a given interest rate. We multiply this factor times any other amount to determine the future value. An expanded version of Table 9–1 is presented at the back of the text in Appendix A.

In determining the future value, we will change our formula from $FV = PV(1 + i)^n$ to:

$$FV = PV \times FV_{IF} \qquad (9–1)$$

where FV_{IF} equals the **interest factor** found in the table.

If \$10,000 were invested for 10 years at 8 percent, the future value, based on Table 9–1, would be:

$$FV = PV \times FV_{IF} \quad (n = 10, i = 8\%)$$

$$FV = \$10,000 \times 2.159 = \$21,590$$

**Present Value—
Single Amount**

In recent years the sports pages have been filled with stories of athletes who receive multimillion-dollar contracts for signing with sports organizations. Perhaps you have wondered how the Lakers or Yankees can afford to pay such fantastic sums. The answer may lie in the concept of present value—a sum payable in the future is worth less today than the stated amount.

The **present value** is the exact opposite of the future value. For example, earlier we determined that the future value of $1,000 for four periods at 10 percent was $1,464. We could reverse the process to state that $1,464 received four years into the future, with a 10 percent interest or **discount rate,** is worth only $1,000 today—its present value. The relationship is depicted in Figure 9–1.

FIGURE 9–1   **Relationship of present value and future value**

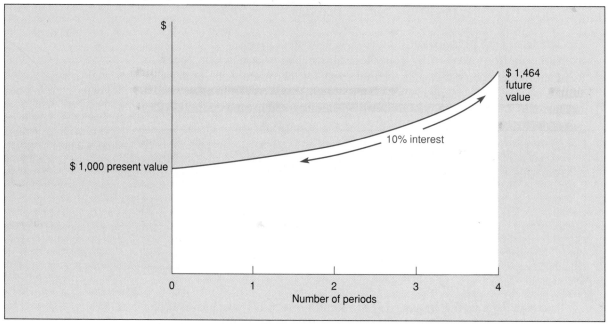

The formula for present value is derived from the original formula for future value.

$$FV = PV(1 + i)^n \qquad \text{Future value}$$

$$PV = FV\left[\frac{1}{(1 + i)^n}\right] \qquad \text{Present value}$$

The present value can be determined by solving for a mathematical solution to the formula above, or by using Table 9–2, the present value of a dollar. In the latter instance, we restate the formula for present value as:

$$PV = FV \times PV_{IF} \qquad\qquad (9\text{–}2)$$

Once again PV_{IF} represents the interest factor found in Table 9–2.

TABLE 9–2
**Present value of $1
(PV$_{IF}$)**

Periods	1%	2%	3%	4%	6%	8%	10%
1	0.990	0.980	0.971	0.962	0.943	0.926	0.909
2	0.980	0.961	0.943	0.925	0.890	0.857	0.826
3	0.971	0.942	0.915	0.889	0.840	0.794	0.751
4	0.961	0.924	0.888	0.855	0.792	0.735	0.683
5	0.951	0.906	0.863	0.822	0.747	0.681	0.621
10	0.905	0.820	0.744	0.676	0.558	0.463	0.386
20	0.820	0.673	0.554	0.456	0.312	0.215	0.149

An expanded table is presented in Appendix B.

Let's demonstrate that the present value of $1,464, based on our assumptions, is $1,000 today.

$$PV = FV \times PV_{IF} \quad (n = 4, i = 10\%) \text{ [Table 9–2]}$$

$$PV = \$1,464 \times 0.683 = \$1,000$$

Our calculations up to now have dealt with single amounts rather than an **annuity,** which may be defined as a series of consecutive payments or receipts of equal amount. The annuity values are generally assumed to occur at the end of each period. If we invest $1,000 at the end of each year for four years and our funds grow at 10 percent, what is the future value of this annuity? We may find the future value for each payment and then total them to find the **future value of an annuity** (Figure 9–2).

Future Value— Annuity

FIGURE 9–2
Compounding process for annuity

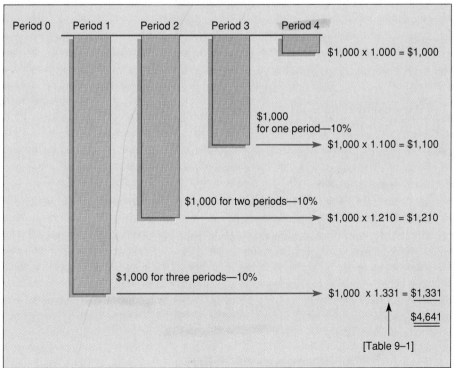

Period 0   Period 1   Period 2   Period 3   Period 4

$1,000 x 1.000 = $1,000

$1,000
for one period—10%
$1,000 x 1.100 = $1,100

$1,000 for two periods—10%
$1,000 x 1.210 = $1,210

$1,000 for three periods—10%
$1,000 x 1.331 = $1,331

$4,641

[Table 9–1]

The future value for the annuity in Figure 9–2 is $4,641. Although this is a four-period annuity, the first $1,000 comes at the *end* of the first period and has but three periods to run, the second $1,000 at the *end* of the second period, with two periods remaining—and so on down to the last $1,000 at the end of the fourth period. The final payment (period 4) is not compounded at all.

Because the process of compounding the individual values is tedious, special tables are also available for annuity computations. We shall refer to Table 9–3, the future value of an annuity of $1. Let us define A as the annuity

TABLE 9–3
Future value of an annuity of $1 (FV$_{IFA}$)

Periods	1%	2%	3%	4%	6%	8%	10%
1	1.000	1.000	1.000	1.000	1.000	1.000	1.000
2	2.010	2.020	2.030	2.040	2.060	2.080	2.100
3	3.030	3.060	3.091	3.122	3.184	3.246	3.310
4	4.060	4.122	4.184	4.246	4.375	4.506	4.641
5	5.101	5.204	5.309	5.416	5.637	5.867	6.105
10	10.462	10.950	11.464	12.006	13.181	14.487	15.937
20	22.019	24.297	26.870	29.778	36.786	45.762	57.275
30	34.785	40.588	47.575	56.085	79.058	113.280	164.490

An expanded table is presented in Appendix C.

value and use Formula 9–3 for the future value of an annuity.[1] Note that the A part of the subscript on both the left and right-hand side of the formula indicates we are dealing with tables for an annuity rather than a single amount. Using Table 9–3:

$$FV_A = A \times FV_{IFA} \qquad (n = 4, i = 10\%) \qquad (9-3)$$
$$FV_A = \$1,000 \times 4.641 = \$4,641$$

If a wealthy relative offered to set aside $2,500 a year for you for the next 20 years, how much would you have to your credit after 20 years if the funds grew at 8 percent?

$$FV_A = A \times FV_{IFA} \qquad (n = 20, i = 8\%)$$
$$FV_A = \$2,500 \times 45.762 = \$114,405$$

A rather tidy sum considering that only a total of $50,000 has been invested over the 20 years.

----

[1]$FV_A = A(1 + i)^{n-1} + A(1 + i)^{n-2} + \ldots A(1 + i)^1 + A(1 + i)^0$

$$= A \left[\frac{(1 + i)^n - 1}{i} \right] = A \times FV_{IFA}$$

To find the **present value of an annuity,** the process is reversed. In theory each individual payment is discounted back to the present and then all of the discounted payments are added up, yielding the present value of the annuity.

TABLE 9–4
**Present value of an
annuity of $1 (PV$_{IFA}$)**

Periods	1%	2%	3%	4%	6%	8%	10%
1	0.990	0.980	0.971	0.962	0.943	0.926	0.909
2	1.970	1.942	1.913	1.886	1.833	1.783	1.736
3	2.941	2.884	2.829	2.775	2.673	2.577	2.487
4	3.902	3.808	3.717	3.630	3.465	3.312	3.170
5	4.853	4.713	4.580	4.452	4.212	3.993	3.791
8	7.652	7.325	7.020	6.773	6.210	5.747	5.335
10	9.471	8.983	8.530	8.111	7.360	6.710	6.145
20	18.046	16.351	14.877	13.590	11.470	9.818	8.514
30	25.808	22.396	19.600	17.292	13.765	11.258	9.427

An expanded table is presented in Appendix D.

Table 9–4 allows us to eliminate extensive calculations and to find our answer directly. In Formula 9–4 the term PV_A refers to the present value of the annuity.[2] Once again, assume A = \$1,000, n = 4, and i = 10 percent—only now we want to know the present value of the annuity. Using Table 9–4:

$$PV_A = A \times PV_{IFA} \qquad (n = 4, i = 10\%) \qquad (9\text{–}4)$$

$$PV_A = \$1,000 \times 3.170 = \$3,170$$

To reinforce your understanding of the material you have just covered, please proceed to the graphical presentation beginning on page 238.

$$^2PV_A = A\left[\frac{1}{(1+i)}\right]^1 + A\left[\frac{1}{(1+i)}\right]^2 + \ldots A\left[\frac{1}{(1+i)}\right]^n = A\left[\frac{1 - \dfrac{1}{(1+i)^n}}{i}\right]$$

$$= A \times PV_{IFA}$$

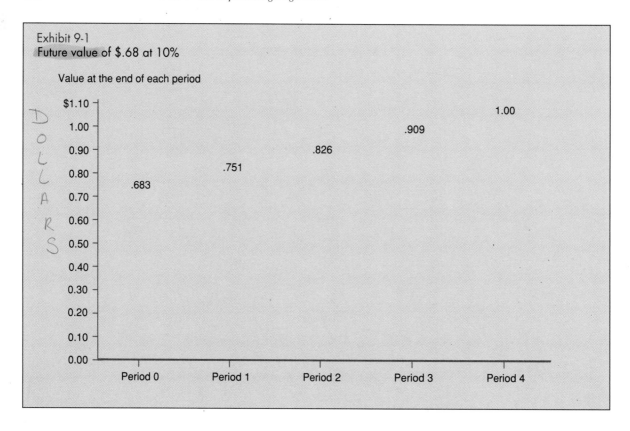

Exhibit 9-1
Future value of $.68 at 10%

Value at the end of each period

Graphical Presentation of Time Value Relationships

This section is designed to supplement the previous discussion of future value, present value, and annuities and to reinforce your understanding of these concepts before you continue into the next chapters. This material is non-mathematical and focuses on time value concepts using a visual approach.

The Relationship between Present Value and Future Value

Earlier in this chapter we presented the future value of a single amount as well as the present value of a single amount and applied the concept of annuities to both future value and present value. In the following special section, we use transparencies to help clarify the relationships between future and present value.

In Exhibits 9–1 and 9–2, we show how the future value and present value of a single amount are inversely related to each other. Future value takes a value today, for example $.68, and computes its value in the future assuming that it earns a rate of return each period. In Exhibit 9–1, the $.68 is invested at 10 percent and grows to $1.00 at the end of period 4. Because we want to avoid large mathematical rounding errors, we actually carry the decimal points 3 places. The $.683 that we invest today (period 0), grows to $.751 after one period, $.826 after two periods, $.909 after three periods and $1.00 at the end of the fourth period. In this example, the $.68 is the present value and the $1.00 is the future value.

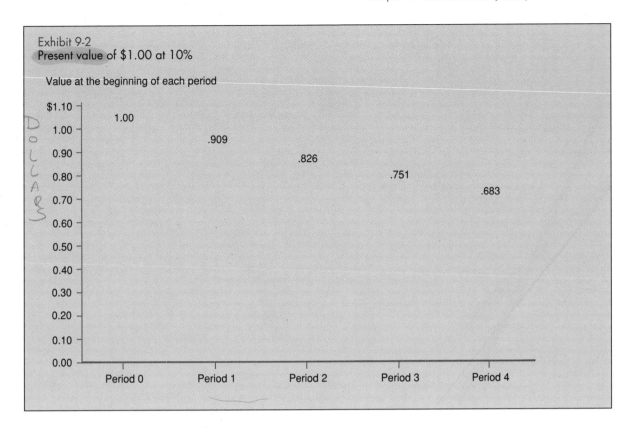

Exhibit 9-2
Present value of $1.00 at 10%

Value at the beginning of each period

If you turn the transparency to Exhibit 9–2, you notice that the future value and present value graphs are the flip side of each other. In the present value table, it becomes clear that if I have $1.00 in period 0, it is worth its present value of $1.00. However, if I have to wait one period to receive my dollar, it is worth only $.909 if I can earn a 10 percent return on my money. You can see this by flipping the transparency back to the future value graph. The $.909 at the end of period 3 will grow to $1.00 during period 4. Or by letting $.909 compound at a 10 percent rate for one period, you have $1.00. Because you can earn a return on your money, $1.00 received in the future is worth less than $1.00 today, and the longer you have to wait to receive the dollar, the less it is worth. For example, if you are to receive $1.00 at the end of four periods, how much is its present value? Flip the transparency to Exhibit 9–2 and you see that the answer is $.68, the same value that we started with in period 0 in the future value graph in Exhibit 9–1. As you change the rate of return that can be earned, the values in Exhibits 9–1 and 9–2 will change, but the relationship will remain the same as presented in this example.

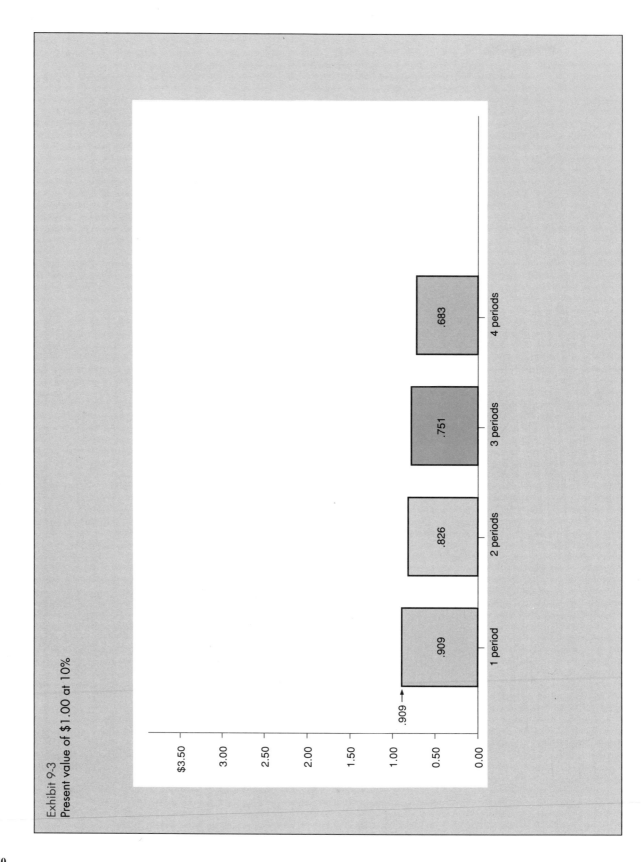

Exhibit 9.3
Present value of $1.00 at 10%

The Relationship between the Present Value of a Single Amount and the Present Value of an Annuity

Exhibit 9–3 shows the relationship between the present value of $1.00 and the present value of a $1.00 annuity. The assumption is that you will receive $1.00 at the end of each period. This is the same concept as a lottery, where you win $2 million over 20 years and receive $100,000 per year for twenty years. In this example we receive only four payments of $1.00 each and we use the transparency format to build up one year at a time.

Looking at Exhibit 9–3 without the transparencies, you see the present value of $1.00 to be received at the end of period 1 is $.909; $1.00 received at the end of period 2 is $.826; $1.00 received at the end of period 3 is $.751; and $1.00 received at the end of period 4 is $.683. These numbers should look very familiar. Exhibit 9–3 has the same values as Exhibit 9–2, except there is no period 0.

Turn the first transparency over Exhibit 9–3. If you are to receive two $1.00 payments, the first at the end of period 1 and the second at the end of period 2, the total present value will simply be the sum of the present value of each $1.00 payment. You can see that the total present value of $1.74 represents the present value of $1.00 to be received at the end of the first period ($.909) and the present value of $1.00 to be received at the end of the second period. The second transparency builds the present value of a three-period annuity equalling $2.49, and the last transparency illustrates the present value of four $1.00 payments equalling $3.17.

This $3.17 is the sum of each present value. The color coding helps illustrate the relationships. The top box is always $.909 and represents the present value of $1.00 received at the end of the first period; the second box from the top is always $.826 and is the present value of the $1.00 received at the end of the second year; the box third from the top is $.751 and is the present value of the $1.00 received at the end of the third year; and finally, the present value of the $1.00 received at the end of the fourth year is $.683. To help solidify this relationship in your memory, look up the present value of $1.00 at 12 percent for periods 1 through 4 in Appendix B. Then create the present value of a $1.00 annuity at 12 percent for two years, three years, and four years. Check your answers in Appendix D. Your answers should match the numbers in Appendix D under the 12 percent column for periods 2 through 4.

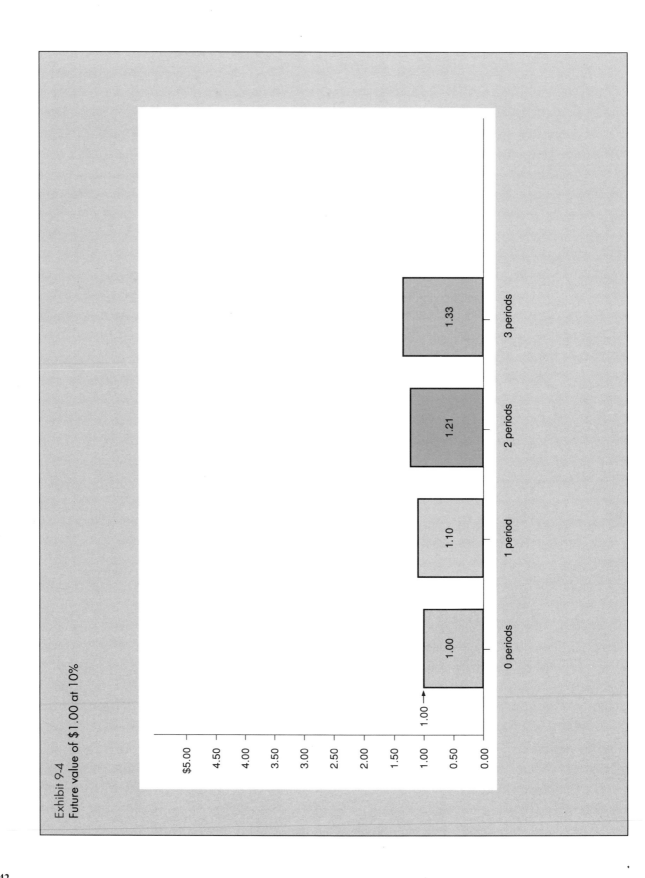

Exhibit 9-4
Future value of $1.00 at 10%

Future Value Related to the Future Value of an Annuity

The next relationship is between the future value of a single sum and the future value of an annuity. We start with Exhibit 9–4, which graphically depicts the future value of $1.00 that is growing at a 10 percent rate of return each period. If we start with a present value of $1.00 today (period 0), at the end of period 1 we will have $1.10; at the end of period 2 we will have $1.21; and at the end of period 3 the $1.00 will have grown to $1.33.

One of the confusing features between the future value of a $1.00 and the future value of a $1.00 annuity is that they have different assumptions concerning the timing of cash flows. The future value of $1.00 (Appendix A) assumes that the $1.00 is invested at the beginning of the period and grows to the end of the period. The future value of an annuity (Appendix C) assumes that $1.00 is invested at the end of the period and grows to the end of the next period. This means that the last $1.00 invested has no time to increase its value by earning a return. This relationship is shown in the transparencies by adding a period 0 to the future value graph and by creating a transparency overlay that replaces the period 0 in the future value with a period 1 for the future value of an annuity.

The calculation for the future value of a $1.00 annuity simply adds together the future value of a series of equal $1.00 investments. When you turn the first transparency, notice the periods have changed to represent the annuity assumptions. Since the last $1.00 invested does not have a chance to compound, the future value of a two-period annuity equals $2.10. This $2.10 comes from adding the $1.00 invested at the end of period 2 plus the first $1.00 that has grown to $1.10. When you flip the second transparency, notice that the future value of a three-period annuity is $3.31. This $3.31 is a combination of the $1.00 invested at the end of period 3, the $1.10 from the second $1.00 invested and $1.21 from the first dollar invested.

Finally, the last transparency demonstrates that the future value of a four-period annuity totals $4.64. The explanation of how each value creates the total is given on the transparency. Since the transparencies are color-coded, you might notice the pattern that exists. The $1.00 amount is always the top box and is the same color. This is the $1.00 that is always invested at the end of the period and has no time to compound. The $1.10 is always the second box from the top and represents the $1.00 that has only been invested for one period, while the $1.21 is always the third box from the top and represents the $1.00 invested for two periods.

Determining the Annuity Value

In our prior discussion of annuities, we assumed the unknown variable was the future value or the present value—with specific information available on the annuity value (A), the interest rate, and the number of periods or years. In certain cases our emphasis may shift to solving for one of these other values (on the assumption that future value or present value is given). For now, we will concentrate on determining an unknown annuity value.

Annuity Equaling a Future Value

Assuming we wish to accumulate $4,641 after four years at a 10 percent interest rate, how much must be set aside at the end of each of the four periods? We take the previously developed statement for the future value of an annuity and solve for A.

$$FV_A = A \times FV_{IFA}$$

$$A = \frac{FV_A}{FV_{IFA}} \qquad\qquad (9\text{--}5)$$

The future value of an annuity (FV_A) is given as $4,641, and FV_{IFA} may be determined from Table 9–3 (future value for an annuity). Whenever you are working with an annuity problem relating to future value, you employ Table 9–3 regardless of the variable that is unknown. For n = 4, and i = 10 percent, FV_{IFA} is 4.641. Thus A equals $1,000.

$$A = \frac{FV_A}{FV_{IFA}} = \frac{\$4,641}{4.641} = \$1,000 \quad \text{—directly from table 9-3}$$

The solution is the exact reverse of that previously presented under the discussion of the future value of an annuity. As a second example, assume the director of the Women's Tennis Association must set aside an equal amount for each of the next 10 years to accumulate $100,000 in retirement funds and the return on deposited funds is 6 percent. Solve for the annual contribution, A.

$$A = \frac{FV_A}{FV_{IFA}} \qquad (n = 10,\ i = 6\%)$$

$$A = \frac{\$100,000}{13.181} = \$7,587$$

directly from table 9-3

Annuity Equaling a Present Value

In this instance, we assume you know the present value and you wish to determine what size annuity can be equated to that amount. Suppose your wealthy uncle presents you with $10,000 now to help you get through the next four years of college. If you are able to earn 6 percent on deposited funds, how many equal payments can you withdraw at the end of each year for four years? We need to know the value of an annuity equal to a given present value. We take the previously developed statement for the present value of an annuity and reverse it to solve for A.

$$PV_A = A \times PV_{IFA}$$

$$A = \frac{PV_A}{PV_{IFA}} \qquad (9\text{--}6)$$

The appropriate table is Table 9–4 (present value of an annuity). We determine an answer of $2,886.

$$A = \frac{PV_A}{PV_{IFA}} \qquad (n = 4, i = 6\%)$$

$$A = \frac{\$10,000}{3.465} = \$2,886$$

The flow of funds would follow the pattern in Table 9–5. Annual interest is based on the beginning balance for each year.

TABLE 9–5
Relationship of present value to annuity

Year	Beginning Balance	Annual Interest (6 percent)	Annual Withdrawal	Ending Balance
1	$10,000.00	$600.00	$2,886.00	$7,714.00
2	7,714.00	462.84	2,886.00	5,290.84
3	5,290.84	317.45	2,886.00	2,722.29
4	2,722.29	163.71	2,886.00	0

The same process can be used to indicate necessary repayments on a loan. Suppose a homeowner signs a $40,000 mortgage to be repaid over 20 years at 8 percent interest. How much must he or she pay annually to eventually liquidate the loan? In other words, what annuity paid over 20 years is the equivalent of a $40,000 present value with an 8 percent interest rate?[3]

$$A = \frac{PV_A}{PV_{IFA}} \qquad (n = 20, i = 8\%)$$

$$A = \frac{\$40,000}{9.818} = \$4,074$$

Part of the payments to the mortgage company will go toward the payment of interest, with the remainder applied to debt reduction, as indicated in Table 9–6.

---

[3] The actual mortgage could be further refined into monthly payments of approximately $340.

TABLE 9–6
**Payoff table for loan
(amortization table)**

Period	Beginning Balance	Annual Payment	Annual Interest (8 percent)	Repayment on Principal	Ending Balance
1	$40,000	$4,074	$3,200	$ 874	$39,126
2	39,126	4,074	3,130	944	38,182
3	38,182	4,074	3,055	1,019	37,163

If this same process is followed over 20 years, the balance will be reduced to zero. The student might note that the homeowner will pay over $41,000 of *interest* during the term of the loan, as indicated below.

Total payments ($4,074 for 20 years)	$81,480
Repayment of principal.	−40,000
Payments applied to interest	$41,480

Determining the Yield on an Investment

In our discussion thus far, we have considered the following time value of money problems.

		Formula	Table	Appendix
Future value — single amount	(9–1)	$FV = PV \times FV_{IF}$	9–1	A
Present value — single amount	(9–2)	$PV = FV \times PV_{IF}$	9–2	B
Future value — annuity	(9–3)	$FV_A = A \times FV_{IFA}$	9–3	C
Present value — annuity.	(9–4)	$PV_A = A \times PV_{IFA}$	9–4	D
Annuity equaling a future value	(9–5)	$A = \dfrac{FV_A}{FV_{IFA}}$	9–3	C
Annuity equaling a present value . . .	(9–6)	$A = \dfrac{PV_A}{PV_{IFA}}$	9–4	D

In each case we knew three out of the four variables and solved for the fourth. We will follow the same procedure again, but now the unknown variable will be i, the interest rate, or yield on the investment.

Yield—Present Value of a Single Amount

An investment producing $1,464 after four years has a present value of $1,000. What is the interest rate, or **yield**, on the investment?

We take the basic formula for the present value of a single amount and rearrange the terms.

$$PV = FV \times PV_{IF}$$

$$PV_{IF} = \frac{PV}{FV} = \frac{\$1,000}{\$1,464} = 0.683 \qquad (9–7)$$

The determination of PV_{IF} does not give us the final answer—but it scales down the problem so we may ascertain the answer from Table 9–2, the present value of $1. A portion of Table 9–2 is reproduced below.

Periods	1%	2%	3%	4%	5%	6%	8%	10%
2. . . .	0.980	0.961	0.943	0.925	0.907	0.890	0.857	0.826
3. . . .	0.971	0.942	0.915	0.889	0.864	0.840	0.794	0.751
4. . . .	0.961	0.924	0.888	0.855	0.823	0.792	0.735	0.683

Read down the left-hand column of the table until you have located the number of periods in question (in this case n = 4), and read across the table for n = 4 until you have located the computed value of PV_{IF} from Formula 9–7. We see that for n = 4 and PV_{IF} equal to 0.683, the interest rate, or yield, is 10 percent. This is the rate that will equate $1,464 received in four years to $1,000 today.

If a PV_{IF} value does not fall under a given interest rate, an approximation is possible. For example, with n = 3 and PV_{IF} = 0.861, 5 percent may be suggested as an approximate answer.

Interpolation may also be used to find a more precise answer. In the above example, we write out the two PV_{IF} values that the designated PV_{IF} (0.861) falls between and take the difference between the two.

PV_{IF} at 5%	0.864
PV_{IF} at 6%	0.840
	0.024

We then find the difference between the PV_{IF} value at the lowest interest rate and the designated PV_{IF} value.

PV_{IF} at 5%	0.864
PV_{IF} designated. . . .	0.861
	0.003

We next express this value (0.003) as a fraction of the preceding value (0.024) and multiply by the difference between the two interest rates (6 percent minus 5 percent). The value is added to the lower interest rate (5 percent) to get a more exact answer of 5.125 percent rather than the estimated 5 percent.

$$5\% + \frac{0.003}{0.024}(1\%) =$$

$$5\% + 0.125(1\%) =$$

$$5\% + 0.125\% = 5.125\%$$

Yield—Present Value of an Annuity

We may also find the yield related to any other problem. Let's look at the present value of an annuity. Take the basic formula for the present value of an annuity, and rearrange the terms.

$$PV_A = A \times PV_{IFA}$$

$$PV_{IFA} = \frac{PV_A}{A} \qquad\qquad (9\text{--}8)$$

The appropriate table is Table 9–4 (the present value of an annuity of $1). Assuming a $10,000 investment will produce $1,490 a year for the next 10 years, what is the yield on the investment?

$$PV_{IFA} = \frac{PV_A}{A} = \frac{\$10,000}{\$1,490} = 6.710$$

If the student will flip back to Table 9–4 and read across the columns for $n = 10$ periods, he or she will see that the yield is 8 percent.

The same type of approximated or interpolated yield that applied to a single amount can also be applied to an annuity when necessary.

Special Considerations in Time Value Analysis

We have assumed interest was compounded or discounted on an annual basis. This assumption will now be relaxed. Contractual arrangements, such as an installment purchase agreement or a corporate bond contract, may call for semiannual, quarterly, or monthly compounding periods. The adjustment to the normal formula is quite simple. To determine n, multiply the number of years by the number of compounding periods during the year. The factor for i is then determined by dividing the quoted annual interest rate by the number of compounding periods.

Case 1—Find the future value of a $1,000 investment after five years at 8 percent annual interest, **compounded semiannually.**

$$n = 5 \times 2 = 10 \qquad i = 8 \text{ percent} \div 2 = 4 \text{ percent}$$

Since the problem calls for the future value of a single amount, the formula is $FV = PV \times FV_{IF}$. Using Table 9–1 for $n = 10$ and $i = 4$ percent, the answer is $1,480.

$$FV = PV \times FV_{IF}$$

$$FV = \$1,000 \times 1.480 = \$1,480$$

Case 2—Find the present value of 20 quarterly payments of $2,000 each to be received over the next five years. The stated interest rate is 8 percent per annum. The problem calls for the present value of an annuity. We again follow the same procedure as in Case 1 in regard to n and i.

$$PV_A = A \times PV_{IFA} \qquad (n = 20, i = 2\%) \quad \text{[Table 9–4]}$$
$$PV_A = A \times \$2{,}000 \times 16.351 = \$32{,}702$$

8 ÷ 4 = 2

Quarterly

Patterns of Payment

Time value of money problems may evolve around a number of different pay-ment or receipt patterns. Not every situation will involve a single amount or an annuity. For example a contract may call for the payment of a different amount each year over a three-year period. To determine present value, each payment is discounted (Table 9–2) to the present and then summed.

(Assume 8% discount rate)

1. $1{,}000 \times 0.926 = \$\ \ 926$
2. $2{,}000 \times 0.857 = \ \ 1{,}714$
3. $3{,}000 \times 0.794 = \ \ \underline{2{,}382}$
$$\$5{,}022$$

A more involved problem might include a combination of single amounts and an annuity. If the annuity will be paid at some time in the future, it is referred to as a deferred annuity and it requires special treatment. Assume the same problem as above, but with an annuity of $1,000 that will be paid at the end of each year from the fourth through the eighth year. With a discount rate of 8 percent, what is the present value of the cash flows?

1. $1,000 ⎫
2.   2,000 ⎬ Present value = $5,022
3.   3,000 ⎭

4. 1,000 ⎫
5. 1,000 ⎪
6. 1,000 ⎬ Five-year annuity
7. 1,000 ⎪
8. 1,000 ⎭

We know the present value of the first three payments is $5,022, but what about the annuity? Let's diagram the five annuity payments.

3,993

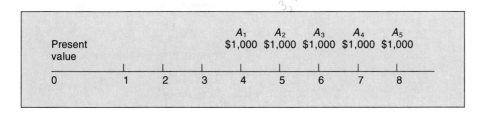

					A_1	A_2	A_3	A_4	A_5
Present value					\$1,000	\$1,000	\$1,000	\$1,000	\$1,000
0	1	2	3	4	5	6	7	8

The information source is Table 9–4, the present value of an annuity of $1. For n = 5, i = 8 percent, the discount factor is 3.993—leaving a "present value" of the annuity of $3,993. However, tabular values only discount to the beginning of the first stated period of an annuity—in this case the beginning of the fourth year, as diagramed below.

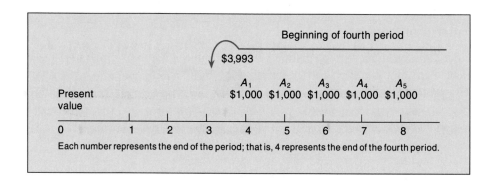

The $3,993 must finally be discounted back to the present. Since this single amount falls at the beginning of the fourth period—in effect, the equivalent of the end of the third period—we discount back for three periods at the stated 8 percent interest rate. Using Table 9–2, we have:

$$PV = FV \times PV_{IF} \qquad (n = 3, i = 8\%)$$
$$PV = \$3,993 \times 0.794 = \$3,170 \text{ (actual present value)}$$

The last step in the discounting process is shown below.

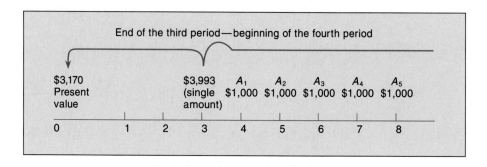

A *second method* for finding the present value of a deferred annuity is to:

1. Find the present value factor of an annuity for the total time period. In this case, where n = 8, i = 8%, the PV_{IFA} is 5.747.
2. Find the present value factor of an annuity for the total time period (8) minus the deferred annuity period (5).

$$8 - 5 = 3$$
$$n = 3, i = 8\%$$

The PV_{IFA} value is 2.577.

3. Subtract the value in step 2 from the value in step 1, and multiply by A.

$$
\begin{array}{r}
5.747 \\
-\ 2.577 \\
\hline
3.170
\end{array}
$$

3.170 × \$1,000 = \$3,170 (present value of the annuity)

\$3,170 is the same answer for the present value of the annuity as that reached by the first method. The present value of the five-year annuity may now be added to the present value of the inflows over the first three years to arrive at the total value.

$$
\begin{array}{r}
\$5,022 \quad \text{First three period flows} \\
+\ 3,170 \quad \text{Five-year annuity} \\
\hline
\$8,192 \quad \text{Total present value}
\end{array}
$$

Special Review of the Chapter

In working a time value of money problem, the student should determine first whether the problem deals with future value or present value and second whether a single sum or an annuity is involved. The major calculations in Chapter 9 are summarized below.

1. *Future value of a single amount.*
   Formula: $FV = PV \times FV_{IF}$
   Table: 9–1 or Appendix A.
   When to use: In determining the future value of a single amount.
   Sample problem: You invest \$1,000 for four years at 10 percent interest. What is the value at the end of the fourth year?

2. *Present value of a single amount.*
   Formula: $PV = FV \times PV_{IF}$
   Table: 9–2 or Appendix B.
   When to use: In determining the present value of an amount to be received in the future.
   Sample problem: You will receive \$1,000 after four years at a discount rate of 10 percent. How much is this worth today?

3. *Future value of an annuity.*
   Formula: $FV_A = A \times FV_{IFA}$
   Table: 9–3 or Appendix C.
   When to use: In determining the future value of a series of consecutive, equal payments (an annuity).
   Sample problem: You will receive \$1,000 at the end of each period for four periods. What is the accumulated value (future worth) at the end of the fourth period if money grows at 10 percent?

4. *Present value of an annuity.*
   Formula: $PV_A = A \times PV_{IFA}$
   Table: 9–4 or Appendix D.
   When to use: In determining the present worth of an annuity.
   Sample problem: You will receive $1,000 at the end of each period
   for four years. At a discount rate of 10 percent, what is the
   current worth?

5. *Annuity equaling a future value.*

$$\text{Formula: } A = \frac{FV_A}{FV_{IFA}}$$

   Table: 9–3 or Appendix C.
   When to use: In determining the size of an annuity that will equal
   a future value.
   Sample problem: You need $1,000 after four periods. With an
   interest rate of 10 percent, how much must be set aside at the end
   of each period to accumulate this amount?

6. *Annuity equaling a present value.*

$$\text{Formula: } A = \frac{PV_A}{PV_{IFA}}$$

   Table: 9–4 or Appendix D.
   When to use: In determining the size of an annuity equal to a
   given present value.
   Sample problems:

   a. What four-year annuity is the equivalent of $1,000 today with an
   interest rate of 10 percent?

   b. You deposit $1,000 today and wish to withdraw funds equally
   over four years. How much can you withdraw at the end of each
   year if funds earn 10 percent?

   c. You borrow $1,000 for four years at 10 percent interest. How
   much must be repaid at the end of each year?

7. *Determining the yield on an investment.*

Formulas	**Tables**	
a. $PV_{IF} = \dfrac{PV}{FV}$	9–2, Appendix B	Yield — present value of a single amount
b. $PV_{IFA} = \dfrac{PV_A}{A}$	9–4, Appendix D	Yield — present value of an annuity

   When to use: In determining the interest rate (i) that will equate an
   investment with future benefits.

Sample problem: You invest $1,000 now, and the funds are expected to increase to $1,360 after four periods. What is the yield on the investment?

$$\text{Use } PV_{IF} = \frac{PV}{FV}$$

8. *Less than annual compounding periods.*

Semiannual	Multiply n × 2	Divide i by 2	then use
Quarterly	Multiply n × 4	Divide i by 4	normal
Monthly	Multiply n × 12	Divide i by 12	formula

When to use: If the compounding period is more (or perhaps less) frequent than once a year.

Sample problem: You invest $1,000 compounded semiannually at 8 percent per annum over four years. Determine the future value.

9. *Patterns of payment—deferred annuity.*

Formulas   **Tables**

$PV_A = A \times PV_{IFA}$ 9–4, Appendix D

$PV = FV \times PV_{IF}$ 9–2, Appendix B   Method 1

When to use: If an annuity begins in the future.

Sample problem: You will receive $1,000 per period, starting at the end of the fourth period and running through the end of the eighth period With a discount rate of 8 percent, determine the present value.

The student is encouraged to work the many problems found at the end of the chapter.

List of Terms

future value 232   future value of an annuity 235
interest factor 233   present value of an annuity 237
present value 234   yield 246
discount rate 234   compounded semiannually 248
annuity 235

Discussion Questions

1. How is the future value (Appendix A) related to the present value of a single sum (Appendix B)?

2. How is the present value of a single sum (Appendix B) related to the present value of an annuity (Appendix D)?

3. Why does money have a time value?

4. Does inflation have anything to do with making a dollar today worth more than a dollar tomorrow?

5. Adjust the annual formula for a future value of a single amount at 12 percent for 10 years to a semiannual compounding formula. What are the interest factors (FV_{IF}) for the two assumptions? Why are they different?

6. If, as an investor, you had a choice of daily, monthly, or quarterly compounding, which would you choose? Why?

7. What is a deferred annuity?

8. List five different financial applications of the time value of money.

Problems

Present value

1. What is the present value of:

   a. $9,000 in 7 years at 8 percent?

   b. $20,000 in 5 years at 10 percent?

   c. $10,000 in 25 years at 6 percent?

   d. $1,000 in 50 years at 16%?

Future value

2. If you invest $9,000 today, how much will you have:

   a. in 2 years at 9 percent?

   b. in 7 years at 12 percent?

   c. in 25 years at 14 percent?

   d. in 25 years at 14 percent (compounded semiannually)?

Present value

3. How much would you have to invest today to receive:

   a. $15,000 in 8 years at 10 percent?

   b. $20,000 in 12 years at 13 percent?

   c. $6,000 each year for 10 years at 9 percent?

   d. $50,000 for 50 years at 7 percent?

Future value

4. If you invest $10,000 per period for the following number of periods, how much would you have?

   a. 6 years at 8 percent

   b. 40 periods at 12 percent

Present value

5. Jean Splicing will receive $8,500 a year for the next 15 years from her trust. If a 7 percent interest rate is applied, what is the current value of the future payments?

Present value

6. "Red" Herring will receive $12,000 a year for the next 18 years as a result of his patent. If a 9 percent rate is applied, should he be willing to sell out his future rights now for $100,000?

7. Larry Doby invests $50,000 in a mint condition 1952 Mickey Mantle Topps baseball card. He expects the card to increase in value 8 percent per year for the next five years. How much will his card be worth after five years?

Future value

8. Dr. Ruth has been secretly depositing $2,500 in her savings account every December starting in 1985. Her account earns 5 percent compounded annually. How much will she have in December 1994? (Assume a deposit is made in 1994.) Make sure to carefully count the years.

Future value

9. At a growth (interest) rate of 9 percent annually, how long will it take for a sum to double? To triple? Select the year that is closest to the correct answer.

Future value

10. If you owe $40,000 at the end of seven years, how much should your creditor accept in payment immediately if she could earn 12 percent on her money?

Present value

11. Les Moore retired as president of Goodman Snack Foods Company but is currently on a consulting contract for $35,000 per year for the next 10 years.

Present value

   a. If Mr. Moore's opportunity cost (potential return) is 10 percent, what is the present value of his consulting contract?

   b. Assuming Mr. Moore will not retire for two more years and will not start to receive his 10 payments until the end of the third year, what would be the value of his deferred annuity?

12. Juan Garza invested $20,000 10 years ago at 12 percent, compounded quarterly. How much has he accumulated?

Compounding quarterly

13. Determine the amount of money in a savings account at the end of five years, given an initial deposit of $5,000 and a 12 percent annual interest rate when interest is compounded (a) annually, (b) semiannually, and (c) quarterly.

Special compounding

14. Your rich uncle has offered you a choice of one of the three following alternatives: $10,000 now; $2,000 a year for eight years; or $24,000 at the end of eight years. Assuming you could earn 11 percent annually, which alternative should you choose? If you could earn 12 percent annually, would you still choose the same alternative?

Alternative present values

15. You need $28,974 at the end of 10 years, and your only investment outlet is an 8 percent long-term certificate of deposit (compounded annually). With the certificate of deposit, you make an initial investment at the beginning of the first year.

Payments required

   a. What single payment could be made at the beginning of the first year to achieve this objective?

   b. What amount could you pay at the end of each year annually for 10 years to achieve this same objective?

16. Carol Travis started a paper route on January 1, 1989. Every three months, she deposits $500 in her bank account, which earns 4 percent

Quarterly compounding

annually but is compounded quarterly. On December 31, 1992, she used the entire balance in her bank account to invest in a contract that pays 9 percent annually. How much will she have on December 31, 1995?

Yield with interpolation

17. On January 1, 1991, Mike Irwin, Jr., bought 100 shares of stock at $14 per share. On December 31, 1993, he sold the stock for $21 per share. What is his annual rate of return? Interpolate to find the exact answer.

Yield

18. Dr. I. N. Stein has just invested $6,250 for his son (age one). The money will be used for his son's education 17 years from now. He calculates that he will need $50,000 for his son's education by the time the boy goes to school. What rate of return will Dr. I. N. Stein need to achieve this goal?

Yield with interpolation

19. Ester Seals has just given an insurance company $41,625. In return, she will receive an annuity of $5,000 for 15 years. At what rate of return must the insurance company invest this $41,625 to make the annual payments? Interpolate.

Solving for an annuity

20. Robert Watts has just retired after 25 years with the electric company. His total pension funds have an accumulated value of $180,000, and his life expectancy is 15 more years. His pension fund manager assumes he can earn a 9 percent return on his assets. What will be his yearly annuity for the next 15 years?

Solving for an annuity

21. Dr. Jordan Rivers, a geography professor, invests $50,000 in a parcel of land that is expected to increase in value by 12 percent per year for the next five years. He will take the proceeds and provide himself with a 10-year annuity. Assuming a 12 percent interest rate, how much will this annuity be?

Solving for an annuity

22. You wish to retire after 18 years, at which time you want to have accumulated enough money to receive an annuity of $14,000 a year for 20 years of retirement. During the period before retirement you can earn 11 percent annually, while after retirement you can earn 8 percent on your money. What annual contributions to the retirement fund will allow you to receive the $14,000 annually?

Deferred annuity

23. Sybil White has just purchased an annuity to begin payment at the end of 1996 (that is the date of the first payment). Assume it is now the beginning of 1994. The annuity is for $8,000 per year and is designed to last 10 years. If the interest rate for this problem is 13 percent, what is the most she should have paid for the annuity?

Yield

24. If you borrow $15,618 and are required to pay back the loan in seven equal annual installments of $3,000, what is the interest rate associated with the loan?

Loan repayment

25. Jim Busby owes $10,000 now. A lender will carry the debt for five more years at 10 percent interest. That is, in this particular case, the amount owed will go up by 10 percent per year for five years. The lender then will require that Jim pay off the loan over the next 12 years at 11 percent interest. What will his annual payment be?

26. If your uncle borrows $60,000 from the bank at 10 percent interest over the seven-year life of the loan, what equal annual payments must be made to discharge the loan, plus pay the bank its required rate of interest (round to the nearest dollar)? How much of his first payment will be applied to interest? To principal? How much of his second payment will be applied to each?

27. Dan Rogers borrows $80,000 at 14 percent interest toward the purchase of a home. His mortgage is for 25 years.

    a. How much will his annual payments be? (Although home payments are usually on a monthly basis, we shall do our analysis on an annual basis for ease of computation. We get a reasonably accurate answer.)

    b. How much interest will he pay over the life of the loan?

    c. How much should he be willing to pay to get out of a 14 percent mortgage and into a 10 percent mortgage with 25 years remaining on the mortgage? Assume current interest rates are 10 percent. Carefully consider the time value of money. Disregard taxes.

28. Your younger sister, Linda, will start college in five years. She has just informed your parents that she wants to go to Hampton University, which will cost $17,000 per year for four years (assumed to come at the end of each year). Anticipating Linda's ambitions, your parents started investing $2,000 per year five years ago and will continue to do so for five more years. How much more will your parents have to invest each year for the next five years to have the necessary funds for Linda's education? Use 10 percent as the appropriate interest rate throughout this problem (for discounting or compounding).

29. Linda (from problem 28) is now 18 years old (five years have passed), and she wants to get married instead of going to school. Your parents have accumulated the necessary funds for her education.

    Instead of her schooling, your parents are paying $8,000 for her upcoming wedding and plan to take a year-end vacation costing $5,000 per year for the next three years.

    How much will your parents have at the end of three years to help you with graduate school, which you will start then? You plan to work on a master's and perhaps a Ph.D. If graduate school costs $14,045 per year, approximately how long will you be able to stay in school based on these funds? Use 10 percent as the appropriate interest rate throughout this problem.

30. You are chairperson of the investment fund for Eastern Football League. You are asked to set up a fund of semiannual payments to be compounded semiannually to accumulate a sum of $100,000 after 10 years at an 8 percent annual rate (20 payments). The first payment into the fund is to occur six months from today, and the last payment is to take place at the end of the 10th year.

    a. Determine how much the semiannual payment should be. (Round to whole numbers.)

On the day after the fourth payment is made (the beginning of the third year) the interest rate goes up to a 10 percent annual rate, and you can earn a 10 percent annual rate on funds that have been accumulated as well as all future payments into the fund. Interest is to be compounded semiannually on all funds.

b. Determine how much the revised semiannual payments should be after this rate change (there are 16 payments and compounding dates). The next payment will be in the middle of the third year. (Round all values to whole numbers.)

Selected References

Bierman, Harold, Jr., Charles P. Bonini, and Warren H. Hausman. *Quantitative Analysis for Business Decisions.* 8th ed. Homewood, Ill.: Richard D. Irwin, 1991.

————, **Seymour Schmidt.** *Financial Management for Decision Making.* New York: Macmillan, 1986.

Black, Fischer. "A Simple Discounting Rule." *Financial Management* 17 (Summer 1988), pp. 7–11.

Cissel, Robert, and Hellen Cissel. *Mathematics in Finance.* 4th ed. Boston: Houghton Mifflin, 1972.

Levy, Haim, and Marshall Sarnat. *Capital Investment and Financial Decisions,* 3rd ed. Englewood Cliffs, N. J.: Prentice Hall, 1986.

Solomon, Ezra. "The Arithmetic of Capital-Budget Decisions." *Journal of Business* 29 (April 1965), pp. 124–29.

CHAPTER 10

Valuation and Rates of Return

CHAPTER CONCEPTS

1 The valuation of a financial asset is based on the present value of future cash flows.

2 The required rate of return in valuing an asset is based on the risk involved.

3 Bond valuation is based on the process of determining the present value of interest payments plus the principal payment at maturity.

4 Stock valuation is based on determining the present value of the future benefits of equity ownership.

5 A price-earnings ratio may also be applied to a firm's earnings to determine value.

In Chapter 9 we considered the basic principles of the time value of money. In this chapter we will use many of those concepts to determine how financial assets (bonds, preferred stock, and common stock) are valued and how investors establish the rates of return they demand. In the next chapter we will use material from this chapter to determine the overall cost of financing to the firm. We merely turn the coin over. Once we know how much bondholders and stockholders demand in the way of rates of return, we then observe what the corporation is required to pay them to attract their funds. The cost of corporate financing (capital) is subsequently used in analyzing whether a project is acceptable for investment or not. These relationships are depicted in Figure 10–1.

FIGURE 10–1
The relationship between time value of money, required return, cost of financing, and investment decisions

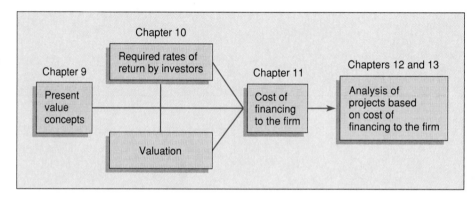

Valuation Concepts

The valuation of a financial asset is based on determining the present value of future cash flows. Thus we need to know the value of future cash flows and the discount rate to be applied to the future cash flows to determine the current value.

The market-determined **required rate of return,** which is the discount rate, depends on the market's perceived level of risk associated with the individual security. Also important is the idea that required rates of return are competitively determined among the many companies seeking financial capital. For example Exxon, due to its low financial risk, relatively high return, and strong market position, is likely to raise debt capital at a significantly lower cost than can Armco Steel or LTV, two financially troubled firms. This implies that investors are willing to accept low return for low risk, and vice versa. The market allocates capital to companies based on risk, efficiency, and expected returns—which are based to a large degree on past performance. The reward to the financial manager for efficient use of capital in the past is a lower required return for investors than that of competing companies that did not manage their financial resources as well.

Throughout the balance of this chapter, we apply concepts of valuation to corporate bonds, preferred stock, and common stock. Although we describe the basic characteristics of each form of security as part of the valuation process, extended discussion of each security is deferred until later chapters.

As previously stated, the value of a financial asset is based on the concept of the present value of future cash flows. Let's apply this approach to bond valuation. A bond provides an annuity stream of interest payments and a $1,000 principal payment at maturity.[1] These cash flows are discounted at Y, the yield to maturity. The value of Y is determined in the bond market and represents the required rate of return for bonds of a given risk and maturity. More will be said about the concept of yield to maturity in the next section.

Valuation of Bonds

The price of a bond is thus equal to the present value of regular interest payments discounted by the yield to maturity added to the present value of the principal (also discounted by the yield to maturity).

This relationship can be expressed mathematically as follows.

$$P_b = \sum_{t=1}^{n} \frac{I_t}{(1 + Y)^t} + \frac{P_n}{(1 + Y)^n} \qquad (10\text{--}1)$$

where

> P_b = Price of the bond
>
> I_t = Interest payments
>
> P_n = Principal payment at maturity
>
> t = Number corresponding to a period; running from 1 to n
>
> n = Number of periods
>
> Y = Yield to maturity (or required rate of return)

The first term in the equation says to take the sum of the present values of the interest payments (I_t); the second term directs you to take the present value of the principal payment at maturity (P_n). The discount rate used throughout the analysis is the yield to maturity (Y). The answer derived is referred to as P_b (the price of the bond). The analysis is carried out for n periods.

Let's assume that I_t (interest payments) equals $100; P_n (principal payment at maturity) equals $1,000; Y (yield to maturity) is 10 percent; and n (total number of periods) equals 20. We could say that P_b (the price of the bond) equals:

$$P_b = \sum_{t=1}^{20} \frac{\$100}{(1 + 0.10)^t} + \frac{\$1,000}{(1 + 0.10)^{20}}$$

Although the price of the bond could be determined with logarithms, it is much simpler to use present value tables. We take the present value of the interest payments and then add this value to the present value of the principal payment at maturity.

---

[1]The assumption is that the bond has a $1,000 par value. If the par value is higher or lower, then this value would be discounted to the present from the maturity date.

Present Value of Interest Payments   In this case we determine the present value of a $100 annuity for 20 years.[2] The discount rate is 10 percent. Using Appendix D, the present value of an annuity, we find the following:

$$PV_A = A \times PV_{IFA} \qquad (n = 20, i = 10\%)$$

$$PV_A = \$100 \times 8.514 = \$851.40$$

Present Value of Principal Payment (Par Value) at Maturity   This single value of $1,000 will be received after 20 years. Note the term *principal payment at maturity* is used interchangeably with *par value* or *face value* of the bond. We discount $1,000 back to the present at 10 percent. Using Appendix B, the present value of a single amount, we find the following:

$$PV = FV \times PV_{IF} \qquad (n = 20, i = 10\%)$$

$$PV = \$1,000 \times .149 = \$149$$

The current price of the bond, based on the present value of interest payments and the present value of the principal payment at maturity, is $1,000.40.

Present value of interest payments	$ 851.40
Present value of principal payment at maturity. .	149.00
Total present value, or price, of the bond . .	$1,000.40

The price of the bond in this case is essentially the same as its par, or stated, value to be received at maturity of $1,000.[3] This is because the annual interest rate is 10 percent (the annual interest payment of $100 divided by $1,000) and the yield to maturity, or discount rate, is also 10 percent. When the interest rate on the bond and the yield to maturity are equal, the bond will trade at par value. Later we shall examine the mathematical effects of varying the yield to maturity above or below the interest rate on the bond. But first let's more fully examine the concept of yield to maturity.

Concept of Yield to Maturity

In the previous example the yield to maturity that was used as the discount rate was 10 percent. The **yield to maturity,** or discount rate, is the required rate of return by bondholders. The bondholder, or any investor for that matter, will allow *three* factors to influence his or her required rate of return.

1. The required **real rate of return**—This is the rate of return the investor demands for giving up current use of the funds on a

---

[2]For now we are using *annual* interest payments for simplicity. Later in the discussion, we will shift to semiannual payments, and more appropriately determine the value of a bond.

[3]The slight difference of $.40 is due to the rounding procedures in the tables.

noninflation-adjusted basis. It is the financial "rent" the investor charges for using his or her funds for one year, five years, or any given period. Although it varies from time to time, historically the real rate of return demanded by investors has been about 2 to 3 percent.

2. **Inflation premium**—In addition to the real rate of return discussed above, the investor requires a premium to compensate for the eroding effect of inflation on the value of the dollar. It would hardly satisfy an investor to have a 3 percent total rate of return in a 5 percent inflationary economy. Under such circumstances, the lender (investor) would be paying the borrower 2 percent (in purchasing power) for use of the funds. This would represent an irrational action. No one wishes to *pay* another party to use his or her funds. The inflation premium added to the real rate of return ensures that this will not happen. The size of the inflation premium will be based on the investor's expectations about future inflation. In the 1980s and early 1990s, the inflation premium has been 3 to 4 percent. In the late 1970s, it was in excess of 10 percent.

 If one combines the real rate of return (part 1) and the inflation premium (part 2), the **risk-free rate of return** is determined. This is the rate that compensates the investor for the current use of his or her funds and for the loss in purchasing power due to inflation, but not for taking risks. As an example, if the real rate of return were 3 percent and the inflation premium were 4 percent, we would say the risk-free rate of return is 7 percent.[4]

3. **Risk premium**—We must now add the risk premium to the risk-free rate of return. This is a premium associated with the special risks of a given investment. Of primary interest to us are two types of risks: **business risk** and **financial risk.** Business risk relates to the inability of the firm to hold its competitive position and maintain stability and growth in its earnings. Financial risk relates to the inability of the firm to meet its debt obligations as they come due. In addition to the two forms of risk mentioned above, the risk premium will be greater or less for different types of investments. For example because bonds possess a contractual obligation for the firm to pay interest to bondholders, they are considered less risky than common stock where no such obligation exists.[5]

 The risk premium of an investment may range from as low as zero on a very short-term U.S. government-backed security to 10 to 15 percent on a gold mining expedition. The typical risk premium is

---

[4]Actually a slightly more accurate representation would be: Risk-free rate = (1 + Real rate of return)(1 + Inflation premium) − 1. We would show: (1.03)(1.04) − 1 = 1.0712 − 1 = .0712 = 7.12 percent.

[5]On the other hand, common stock carries the potential for very high returns when the corporation is quite profitable.

2 to 6 percent. Just as the required real rate of return and the inflation premium change over time, so does the risk premium. For example high-risk corporate bonds (sometimes referred to as junk bonds) normally require a risk premium of about 5 percentage points over the risk-free rate. However, in September 1989 the bottom fell out of the junk bond market as the Campeau Corp., International Resources, and Resorts International began facing difficulties in making their payments. The risk premium almost doubled. As is emphasized in many parts of the text, there is a strong correlation between the risk the investor is taking and the return the investor demands. Supposedly in finance as in other parts of business, "there is no such thing as a free lunch." If you want a higher return, you must take a greater risk.

We shall assume that in the investment we are examining the risk premium is 3 percent. If we add this risk premium to the two components of the risk-free rate of return developed in parts 1 and 2, we arrive at an overall required rate of return of 10 percent.

+ Real rate of return	3%
+ Inflation premium	4
= Risk-free rate	7%
+ Risk premium	3
= Required rate of return	10%

In this instance, we assume we are evaluating the required return on a bond issued by a firm. If the security had been the common stock of the same firm, the risk premium might be 5 to 6 percent and the required rate of return 12 to 13 percent.

Finally, in concluding this section, you should recall that the required rate of return on a bond is effectively the same concept as required yield to maturity.

Changing the Yield to Maturity and the Impact on Bond Valuation

In the earlier bond value calculation, we assumed the interest rate was 10 percent ($100 annual interest on a $1,000 par value bond) and the yield to maturity was also 10 percent. Under those circumstances, the price of the bond was basically equal to par value. Now let's assume conditions in the market cause the yield to maturity to change.

Increase in Inflation Premium   For example assume the inflation premium goes up from 4 to 6 percent. All else remains constant. The required rate of return would now be 12 percent.

+ Real rate of return	3%
+ Inflation premium	6
= Risk-free rate	9%
+ Risk premium	3
= Required rate of return	12%

With the required rate of return, or yield to maturity, now at 12 percent, the price of the bond will change.[6] A bond that pays only 10 percent interest when the required rate of return (yield to maturity) is 12 percent will fall below its current value of approximately $1,000. The new price of the bond, as computed below, is $850.90.

Present value of interest payments—We take the present value of a $100 annuity for 20 years. The discount rate is 12 percent. Using Appendix D:

$$PV_A = A \times PV_{IFA} \qquad (n = 20, i = 12\%)$$

$$PV_A = \$100 \times 7.469 = \$746.90$$

Present value of principal payment at maturity—We take the present value of $1,000 after 20 years. The discount rate is 12 percent. Using Appendix B:

$$PV = FV \times PV_{IF} \qquad (n = 20, i = 12\%)$$

$$PV = \$1,000 \times .104 = \$104$$

Total present value —

Present value of interest payments	$746.90
Present value of principal payment at maturity .	104.00
Total present value, or price, of the bond . .	$850.90

In this example we assumed increasing inflation caused the required rate of return (yield to maturity) to go up and the bond price to fall by approximately $150. The same effect would occur if the business risk increased or the demanded level for the *real* rate of return became higher.

Decrease in Inflation Premium   The opposite effect would happen if the required rate of return went down because of lower inflation, less risk, or other factors. Let's assume the inflation premium declines and the required rate of return (yield to maturity) goes down to 8 percent.

The 20-year bond with the 10 percent interest rate would now sell for $1,196.80.

---

[6]Of course the required rate of return on all other financial assets will also go up proportionally.

Present value of interest payments —

$$PV_A = A \times PV_{IFA} \qquad (n = 20, i = 8\%) \qquad \text{(Appendix D)}$$

$$PV_A = \$100 \times 9.818 = \$981.80$$

Present value of principal payment at maturity —

$$PV = FV \times PV_{IF} \qquad (n = 20, i = 8\%) \qquad \text{(Appendix B)}$$

$$PV = \$1,000 \times .215 = \$215$$

Total present value —

Present value of interest payments	$ 981.80
Present value of principal payment at maturity . .	215.00
Total present value, or price, of the bond . . .	$1,196.80

The bond is now trading at $196.80 over par value. This is certainly the expected result because the bond is paying 10 percent interest when the yield in the market is only 8 percent. The 2 percentage point differential on a $1,000 par value bond represents $20 per year. The investor will receive this differential for the next 20 years. The present value of $20 for the next 20 years at the current market rate of interest of 8 percent is approximately $196.80. This explains why the bond is trading at $196.80 over its stated, or par, value.

The further the yield to maturity on a bond falls from the stated interest rate on the bond, the greater the price change effect will be. This is illustrated in Table 10–1 for the 10 percent interest rate, 20-year bonds discussed in this chapter.

TABLE 10–1
Bond price table

(10 Percent Interest Payment, 20 Years to Maturity)	
Yield to Maturity	**Bond Price**
2%. . . .	$2,308.10
4	1,825.00
6	1,459.00
7	1,317.40
8	1,196.80
9	1,090.90
10	1,000.00
11	920.30
12	850.90
13	789.50
14	735.30
16	643.90
20	513.00
25	407.40

We clearly see the impact that different yields to maturity have on the price of a bond.[7]

Time to Maturity

The impact of a change in yield to maturity on valuation is also affected by the remaining time to maturity. The effect of a bond paying 2 percentage points more or less than the going rate of interest is quite different for a 20-year bond than it is for a 1-year bond. In the latter case, the investor will only be gaining or giving up $2 for one year. That is certainly not the same as having this $20 differential for an extended period. Let's once again return to the 10 percent interest rate bond and show the impact of a 2 percentage point decrease or increase in yield to maturity for varying *times* to maturity. The values are shown in Table 10–2 and graphed in Figure 10–2 on page 268. The upper part of Figure 10–2 shows how the amount (premium) above par value is reduced as the number of years to maturity becomes smaller and smaller. Figure 10–2 should be read from left to right. The lower part of the figure shows how the amount (discount) below par value is reduced with progressively fewer years to maturity. Clearly, the longer the maturity, the greater the impact of changes in yield.

Time Period in Years (of 10 percent bond)	Bond Price with 8 Percent Yield to Maturity	Bond Price with 12 Percent Yield to Maturity
0	$1,000.00	$1,000.00
1	1,018.60	982.30
5	1,080.30	927.50
10	1,134.00	887.00
15	1,170.90	864.11
20	1,196.80	850.90
25	1,213.50	843.30
30	1,224.80	838.50

TABLE 10–2
Impact of time to maturity on bond prices

[7]The reader may observe on page 266 that the impact of a decrease or increase in interest rates is not equal. For example, a 2 percent decrease in interest rates will produce a $196.80 gain in the bond price and an increase of 2 percent causes a $149.10 loss. While price movements are not symmetrical around the price of the bond when the time dimension is the maturity date of the bond, they are symmetrical around the duration of the bond. The duration represents the weighted average time period to recapture the interest and principal on the bond. While these concepts go beyond that appropriate for an introductory finance text, the interested reader may wish to consult Geoffrey A. Hirt and Stanley B. Block, *Fundamentals of Investment Management*, 4th ed. (Homewood, Ill.: Richard D. Irwin, 1993) or Frank K. Reilly, *Investment Analysis and Portfolio Management*, 3rd ed. (Hinsdale, Ill.: Dryden Press, 1989).

FIGURE 10–2
**Relationship between
time to maturity and
bond price***

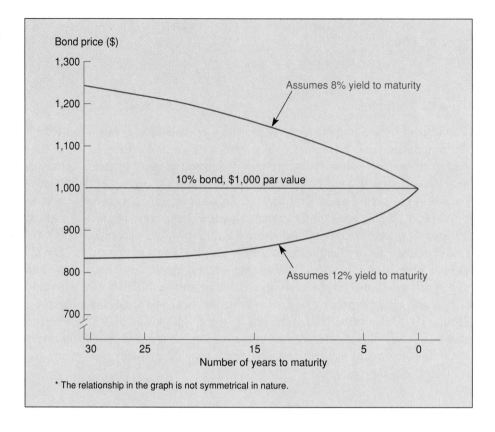

* The relationship in the graph is not symmetrical in nature.

Determining Yield to Maturity from the Bond Price

Until now we have used yield to maturity as well as other factors, such as the interest rate on the bond and number of years to maturity, to determine the price of the bond. We shall now assume we know the price of the bond, the interest rate on the bond, and the years to maturity, and we wish to determine the yield to maturity. Once we have computed this value, we have determined the rate of return that investors are demanding in the marketplace to provide for inflation, risk, and other factors.

Let's once again present Formula 10–1:

$$P_b = \sum_{t=1}^{n} \frac{I_t}{(1 + Y)^t} + \frac{P_n}{(1 + Y)^n}$$

We now try to determine the value of Y, the yield to maturity, that will equate the interest payments (I_t) and the principal payment (P_n) to the price of the bond (P_b). This is similar to the calculations to determine yield in the prior chapter.

Assume a 15-year bond pays \$110 per year (11 percent) in interest and \$1,000 after 15 years in principal repayment. The current price of the bond is \$932.21. We wish to determine the yield to maturity, or discount rate, that equates future flows with the current price.

In this trial and error process, the first step is to choose an initial percentage in the tables to try as the discount rate. Since the bond is trading below the par value of $1,000, we can assume the yield to maturity (discount rate) must be above the quoted interest rate of 11 percent. Let's begin the trial and error process.

A 13 Percent Discount Rate As a first approximation, we might try 13 percent and compute the present value of the bond as follows:

Present value of interest payments —

$$PV_A = A \times PV_{IFA} \qquad (n = 15, i = 13\%) \qquad \text{(Appendix D)}$$
$$PV_A = \$110 \times 6.462 = \$710.82$$

Present value of principal payment at maturity —

$$PV = FV \times PV_{IF} \qquad (n = 15, i = 13\%) \qquad \text{(Appendix B)}$$
$$PV = \$1,000 \times .160 = \$160$$

Total present value —

Present value of interest payments	$710.82
Present value of principal payment at maturity . . .	160.00
Total present value or price of the bond	$870.82

The answer of $870.82 is below the current bond price of $932.21. This indicates we have used too high a discount rate in creating too low a value.

A 12 Percent Discount Rate As a next step in the trial and error process, we will try 12 percent.

Present value of interest payments —

$$PV_A = A \times PV_{IFA} \qquad (n = 15, i = 12\%) \qquad \text{(Appendix D)}$$
$$PV_A = \$110 \times 6.811 = \$749.21$$

Present value of principal payment at maturity —

$$PV = FV \times PV_{IF} \qquad (n = 15, i = 12\%) \qquad \text{(Appendix B)}$$
$$PV = \$1,000 \times .183 = \$183$$

Total present value —

Present value of interest payments	$749.21
Present value of principal payment at maturity .	183.00
Total present value, or price, of the bond . .	$932.21

The answer precisely matches the bond price of $932.21 that we are evaluating. That indicates the correct yield to maturity for the bond is 12 percent. If the computed value were slightly different from the price of the bond, we could use interpolation to arrive at the correct answer. An example of interpolating to derive yield to maturity is presented in Appendix 10A.

Formula for Bond Yield   Because it is tedious to determine the bond yield to maturity through trial and error, an approximate answer can also be found by using Formula 10–2.[8]

$$\text{Approximate yield to maturity } (Y') = \frac{\text{Annual interest payment} + \dfrac{\text{Principal payment} - \text{Price of the bond}}{\text{Number of years to maturity}}}{0.6(\text{Price of the bond}) + 0.4(\text{Principal payment})} \qquad (10\text{–}2)$$

Plugging in the values from the just completed analysis of yield to maturity, we show:

$$Y' = \frac{\$110 + \dfrac{\$1,000 - 932.21}{15}}{0.6(\$932.21) + 0.4(\$1,000)}$$

$$= \frac{\$110 + \dfrac{\$67.79}{15}}{\$559.33 + \$400}$$

$$= \frac{\$110 + \$4.52}{\$959.33}$$

$$= \frac{\$114.52}{\$959.33}$$

$$Y' = 11.94\%.$$

The answer of 11.94 percent is a reasonably good approximation of the exact yield to maturity of 12 percent.[9] We use the prime (') symbol after Y to indicate the answer based on Formula 10–2 is only an approximation.

Note the numerator of Formula 10–2 represents the average annual income over the life of the bond and the denominator represents the average investment. That is, in the numerator, we take the annual interest payment of $110 and add that to the average annual change in the bond value over 15 years, which is computed as $4.52. This provides average annual income of $114.52. In the denominator, we take a *weighted* average of the original price

---

[8]This formula is recommended by Gabriel A. Hawawini and Ashok Vora, "Yield Approximations: A Historical Perspective," *Journal of Finance* 37 (March 1982), pp. 145–56. It tends to provide the best approximation.

[9]The greater the premium or discount and the longer the period to maturity, the less accurate the approximation.

of $932.21 and the final value of $1,000 that we will receive at maturity to get the average investment over the 15-year holding period.[10]

It should be pointed out that, in computing yield to maturity on a bond, financially oriented hand-held calculators[11] and software programs[12] for microcomputers can be extremely helpful. There are also useful bond tables in libraries. Nevertheless, it is important that students also understand the mechanics that go into the calculations.

As we have discussed throughout, the yield to maturity is the required rate of return bondholders demand. More importantly for our purposes here, it also indicates the current cost to the corporation to issue bonds. In the prior example, the corporation had issued bonds at 11 percent, but market conditions changed and the current price of the bond fell to $932.21. At this current price, the ongoing yield to maturity increased to 12 percent (11.94 percent, using the approximation method). If the corporate treasurer were to issue new bonds today, he would have to respond to the current market-demanded rate of 12 percent rather than the initial yield of 11 percent. Only by understanding how investors value bonds in the marketplace can the corporate financial officer properly assess the cost of that source of financing to the corporation.

Semiannual Interest and Bond Prices

We have been assuming that interest was paid annually in our bond analysis. In actuality most bonds pay interest semiannually. Thus a 10 percent interest rate bond may actually pay $50 twice a year instead of $100 annually. To make the conversion from an annual to semiannual analysis, we follow three steps.

1. Divide the annual interest rate by two.
2. Multiply the number of years by two.
3. Divide the annual yield to maturity by two.

Assume a 10 percent, $1,000 par value bond has a maturity of 20 years. The annual yield to maturity is 12 percent. In following the three steps above, we would show:

1. 10%/2 = 5% semiannual interest rate; therefore,
    5% × $1,000 = $50 semiannual interest.
2. 20 × 2 = 40 periods to maturity.
3. 12%/2 = 6% yield to maturity, expressed on a semiannual basis.

---

[10]As indicated by the Hawawini and Vora study (cited in footnote 8), this weighting procedure gives a better approximation than the simple arithmetic mean of the two values.

[11]See Appendix E as an example.

[12]See the Lotus 1–2–3 software package that goes with this text as an example.

In computing the price of the bond issued, on a semiannual analysis, we show:

Present value of interest payments—We take the present value of a $50 annuity for 40 periods. The semiannual discount rate is 6 percent. Using Appendix D:

$$PV_A = A \times PV_{IFA} \qquad (n = 40, i = 6\%)$$

$$PV_A = \$50 \times 15.046 = \$752.30$$

Present value of principal payment at maturity—We take the present value of $1,000 after 40 periods, using a 6 percent discount rate. Note that once we go to a semiannual analysis with the interest payments, we consistently follow the same approach in discounting back the principal payment; otherwise we would be using semiannual and annual calculations on the same bond. Using Appendix B:

$$PV = FV \times PV_{IF} \qquad (n = 40, i = 6\%)$$

$$PV = \$1,000 \times .097 = \$97$$

Total present value—

Present value of interest payments	$752.30
Present value of principal payment at maturity .	97.00
Total present value, or price, of the bond . .	$849.30

The answer of $849.30 is slightly below what we found previously for the same bond, assuming an annual interest rate ($850.90). In terms of accuracy, the semiannual analysis is a more acceptable method and is the method used in bond tables. As is true in many finance texts, the annual interest rate approach is given first for ease of presentation, and then the semiannual basis is given. In the problems at the back of the chapter, you will be asked to do problems on both an annual and semiannual interest payment basis.

Valuation and Preferred Stock

Preferred stock usually represents a **perpetuity** or, in other words, has no maturity date. It is valued in the market without any principal payment since it has no ending life. If preferred stock had a maturity date, the analysis would be similar to that of the preceding bond example. Preferred stock has a fixed dividend payment carrying a higher order of precedence than common stock dividends, but not the binding contractual obligation of interest on debt. Preferred stock, being a hybrid security, has neither the ownership privilege of common stock nor the legally enforceable provisions of debt. To value a perpetuity such as preferred stock, we first consider the formula:

$$P_p = \frac{D_p}{(1 + K_p)^1} + \frac{D_p}{(1 + K_p)^2} + \frac{D_p}{(1 + K_p)^3} + \ldots + \frac{D_p}{(1 + K_p)^\infty} \qquad (10\text{–}3)$$

where

P_p = the price of preferred stock

D_p = the annual dividend for preferred stock (a constant value)

K_p = the required rate of return, or discount rate, applied to preferred stock dividends

Note the formula calls for taking the present value of an infinite stream of constant dividend payments at a discount rate equal to K_p. Because we are dealing with an infinite stream of payments, Formula 10–3 can be reduced to a much more usable form as indicated in Formula 10–4.

$$P_p = \frac{D_p}{K_p} \qquad (10\text{–}4)$$

According to Formula 10–4, all we have to do to find the price of preferred stock (P_p) is to divide the constant annual dividend payment (D_p) by the required rate of return that preferred stockholders are demanding (K_p). For example, if the annual dividend were $10 and the stockholder required a 10 percent rate of return, the price of preferred stock would be $100.

$$P_p = \frac{D_p}{K_p} = \frac{\$10}{.10} = \$100$$

As was true in our bond valuation analysis, if the rate of return required by security holders changes, the value of the financial asset (in this case, preferred stock) will change. You may also recall that the longer the life of an investment, the greater the impact of a change in required rate of return. It is one thing to be locked into a low-paying security for one year when the rate goes up; it is quite another to be locked in for 10 or 20 years. With preferred stock, you have a *perpetual* security, so the impact is at a maximum. Assume in the prior example that because of higher inflation or increased business risk K_p (the required rate of return) increases to 12 percent. The new value for the preferred stock shares is:

$$P_p = \frac{D_p}{K_p} = \frac{\$10}{.12} = \$83.33$$

If the required rate of return were reduced to 8 percent, the opposite effect would occur. The preferred stock price would be computed as:

$$P_p = \frac{D_p}{K_p} = \frac{\$10}{.08} = \$125$$

It is not surprising that preferred stock is now trading well above its original price of $100. It is still offering a $10 dividend (10 percent of the original offering price of $100), and the market is demanding only an 8 percent yield. To match the $10 dividend with the 8 percent rate of return, the market price will advance to $125.

Determining the Required Rate of Return (Yield) from the Market Price

In our analysis of preferred stock, we have used the value of the annual dividend (D_p) and the required rate of return (K_p) to solve for the price of preferred stock (P_p). We could change our analysis to solve for the required rate of return (K_p) as the unknown, given that we knew the annual dividend (D_p) and the preferred stock price (P_p). We take Formula 10–4 and rewrite it as Formula 10–5, where the unknown is the required rate of return (K_p).

$$P_p = \frac{D_p}{K_p} \quad \text{(reverse the position of } K_p \text{ and } P_p\text{)} \tag{10–4}$$

$$K_p = \frac{D_p}{P_p} \tag{10–5}$$

Using Formula 10–5, if the annual preferred dividend (D_p) is \$10 and the price of preferred stock (P_p) is \$100, the required rate of return (yield) would be 10 percent.

$$K_p = \frac{D_p}{P_p} = \frac{\$10}{\$100} = 10\%$$

If the price goes up to \$130, the yield will be only 7.69 percent.

$$K_p = \frac{\$10}{\$130} = 7.69\%$$

We see the higher market price provides quite a decline in the yield.

Valuation of Common Stock

The value of a share of common stock may be interpreted by the shareholder as the *present value* of an expected stream of *future dividends.* Although in the short run stockholders may be influenced by a change in earnings or other variables, the ultimate value of any holding rests with the distribution of earnings in the form of dividend payments. Though the stockholder may benefit from the retention and reinvestment of earnings by the corporation, at some point the earnings must be translated into cash flow for the stockholder. A stock valuation model based on future expected dividends, which is termed a **dividend valuation model,** can be stated as:

$$P_0 = \frac{D_1}{(1 + K_e)^1} + \frac{D_2}{(1 + K_e)^2} + \frac{D_3}{(1 + K_e)^3} + \ldots + \frac{D_\infty}{(1 + K_e)^\infty} \tag{10–6}$$

where

P_0 = Price of stock today

D = Dividend for each year

K_e = the required rate of return for common stock (discount rate)

This formula, with modification, is generally applied to three different circumstances:

1. No growth in dividends.
2. Constant growth in dividends.
3. Variable growth in dividends.

No Growth in Dividends

Under the no-growth circumstance, common stock is very similar to preferred stock. The common stock pays a constant dividend each year. For that reason, we merely translate the terms in Formula 10–5, which applies to preferred stock, to apply to common stock. This is shown as new Formula 10–7.

$$P_0 = \frac{D_0}{K_e} \qquad (10\text{--}7)$$

P_0 = Price of common stock today
D_0 = Current annual common stock dividend (a constant value)
K_e = Required rate of return for common stock

Assume $D_0 = \$1.86$ and $K_e = 12$ percent; the price of the stock would be $15.50:

$$P_0 = \frac{\$1.86}{0.12} = \$15.50$$

A no-growth policy for common stock dividends does not hold much appeal for investors and so is seen infrequently in the real world.

Constant Growth in Dividends

A firm that increases dividends at a constant rate is a more likely circumstance. Perhaps a firm decides to increase its dividends by 5 or 7 percent per year. The general valuation approach is shown in Formula 10–8.

$$P_0 = \frac{D_0(1 + g)^1}{(1 + K_e)^1} + \frac{D_0(1 + g)^2}{(1 + K_e)^2} + \frac{D_0(1 + g)^3}{(1 + K_e)^3} + \ldots + \frac{D_0(1 + g)^\infty}{(1 + K_e)^\infty} \quad (10\text{--}8)$$

where

P_0 = Price of common stock today
$D_0(1 + g)^1$ = Dividend in year 1, D_1
$D_0(1 + g)^2$ = Dividend in year 2, D_2, and so on
g = Constant growth rate in dividends
K_e = Required rate of return for common stock (discount rate)

In other words, the current price of the stock is the present value of the future stream of dividends growing at a constant rate. If we can anticipate the growth pattern of future dividends and determine the discount rate, we can ascertain the price of the stock.

For example, assume the following information:

D_0 = Latest 12-month dividend (assume $1.87)
D_1 = First year, $2.00 (growth rate, 7%)
D_2 = Second year, $2.14 (growth rate, 7%)
D_3 = Third year, $2.29 (growth rate, 7%)
etc.
K_e = Required rate of return (discount rate), 12%

then

$$P_0 = \frac{\$2.00}{(1.12)^1} + \frac{\$2.14}{(1.12)^2} + \frac{\$2.29}{(1.12)^3} + \ldots + \frac{\text{Infinite dividend}}{(1.12)^\infty}$$

To find the price of the stock, we take the present value of each year's dividend. This is no small task when the formula calls for us to take the present value of an *infinite* stream of growing dividends. Fortunately Formula 10–8 can be compressed into a much more usable form if two circumstances are satisfied.

1. The firm must have a constant dividend growth rate (g).
2. The discount rate (K_e) must exceed the growth rate (g).

For most introductory courses in finance, these assumptions are usually made to reduce the complications in the analytical process. This then allows us to reduce or rewrite Formula 10–8 as Formula 10–9. Formula 10–9 is the basic equation for finding the value of common stock and is referred to as the constant growth dividend valuation model.

$$P_0 = \frac{D_1}{K_e - g} \qquad (10\text{–}9)$$

This is an extremely easy formula to use in which:

P_0 = Price of the stock today
D_1 = Dividend at the end of the first year
K_e = Required rate of return (discount rate)
g = Constant growth rate in dividends

Based on the current example:

D_1 = $2.00
K_e = .12
g = .07

and P_0 is computed as:

$$P_0 = \frac{D_1}{K_e - g} = \frac{\$2.00}{0.12 - 0.07} = \frac{\$2.00}{0.05} = \$40$$

Thus, given that the stock has a $2 dividend at the end of the first year, a discount rate of 12 percent, and a constant growth rate of 7 percent, the current price of the stock is $40.

Let's take a closer look at Formula 10–9 and the factors that influence valuation. For example, what is the anticipated effect on valuation if K_e (the required rate of return, or discount rate) increases as a result of inflation or increased risk? Intuitively, we would expect the stock price to decline if investors demand a higher return and the dividend and growth rate remain the same. This is precisely what happens.

If D_1 remains at $2.00 and the growth rate (g) is 7 percent, but K_e increases from 12 percent to 14 percent, using Formula 10–9, the price of the common stock will now be $28.57. This is considerably lower than its earlier value of $40.

$$P_0 = \frac{D_1}{K_e - g} = \frac{\$2.00}{0.14 - 0.07} = \frac{\$2.00}{0.07} = \$28.57$$

Similarly, if the growth rate (g) increases while D_1 and K_e remain constant, the stock price can be expected to increase. Assume $D_1 = \$2.00$, K_e is set at its earlier level of 12 percent, and g increases from 7 percent to 9 percent. Using Formula 10–9 once again, the new price of the stock would be $66.67.

$$P_0 = \frac{D_1}{K_e - g} = \frac{\$2.00}{0.12 - 0.09} = \frac{\$2.00}{0.03} = \$66.67$$

We should not be surprised to see that an increasing growth rate has enhanced the value of the stock.

Stock Valuation Based on Future Stock Value   The discussion of stock valuation to this point has related to the concept of the present value of future dividends. This is a valid concept, but suppose we wish to approach the issue from a slightly different viewpoint. Assume we are going to buy a stock and hold it for three years and then sell it. We wish to know the present value of our investment. This is somewhat like the bond valuation analysis. We will receive a dividend for three years (D_1, D_2, D_3) and then a price (payment) for the stock at the end of three years (P_3). What is the present value of the benefits? What we do is add the present value of three years of dividends and the present value of the stock price after three years. Assuming a constant-growth dividend analysis, the stock price after three years is simply the present value of all future dividends after the third year (from the fourth year on). Thus the current price of the stock in this case is nothing other than the present value of the first three dividends, plus the present value of all future dividends (which is equivalent to the stock price after the third year). Saying the price of the stock is the present value of all future dividends is also the equivalent of saying it is the present value of a dividend stream for a number of years, plus the present value of the price of the stock after that time period. The appropriate formula is still $P_0 = D_1/(K_e - g)$, which we have been using throughout this part of the chapter.

Determining the Required Rate of Return from the Market Price

In our analysis of common stock, we have used the first year's dividend (D_1), the required rate of return (K_e), and the growth rate (g) to solve for the stock price (P_0) based on Formula 10–9.

$$P_0 = \frac{D_1}{K_e - g} \text{ (previously presented Formula 10–9)}$$

We could change the analysis to solve for the required rate of return (K_e) as the unknown, given that we know the first year's dividend (D_1), the stock price (P_0), and the growth rate (g). We take the formula above and algebraically change it to provide Formula 10–10.

$$P_0 = \frac{D_1}{K_e - g} \qquad\qquad (10\text{–}9)$$

$$K_e = \frac{D_1}{P_0} + g \qquad\qquad (10\text{–}10)$$

Formula 10–10 allows us to compute the required return (K_e) from the investment. Returning to the basic data from the common stock example:

K_e = Required rate of return (to be solved)

D_1 = Dividend at the end of the first year, $2.00

P_0 = Price of the stock today, $40

g = Constant growth rate .07, or 7%

$$K_e = \frac{\$2.00}{\$40} + 7\% = 5\% + 7\% = 12\%$$

In this instance we would say the stockholder demands a 12 percent return on his common stock investment. Of particular interest are the individual parts of the formula for K_e that we have been discussing. Let's write out Formula 10–10 again.

$$K_e = \frac{\text{First year's dividend}}{\text{Common stock price}} \left(\frac{D_1}{P_0}\right) + \text{Growth } (g)$$

The first term represents the **dividend yield** the stockholder will receive, and the second term represents the anticipated growth in dividends, earnings, and stock price. While we have been describing the growth rate primarily in terms of dividends, it is assumed the earnings and stock price will also grow at that same rate over the long term if all else holds constant. You should also observe that the formula above represents a total return concept. The stockholder is receiving a current dividend plus anticipated growth in the future. If the dividend yield is low, the growth rate must be high to provide the necessary return. Conversely if the growth rate is low, a high dividend yield will be expected. The concepts of dividend yield and growth are clearly interrelated.

The Price-Earnings Ratio Concept and Valuation

In Chapter 2 we introduced the concept of the price-earnings ratio. The **price-earnings ratio** represents a multiplier applied to current earnings to determine the value of a share of stock in the market. It is considered a pragmatic, everyday approach to valuation. If a stock has earnings per share of $3 and a price-earnings (P/E) ratio of 12 times, it will carry a market value of $36. Another company with the same earnings but a P/E ratio of 15 times will enjoy a market price of $45.

The price-earnings ratio is influenced by the earnings and sales growth of the firm, the risk (or volatility in performance), the debt-equity structure of the firm, the dividend policy, the quality of management, and a number of other factors. Firms that have bright expectations for the future tend to trade at high P/E ratios while the opposite is true of low P/E firms.

For example the average P/E ratio for all New York Stock Exchange firms was 22 in early 1993, but Biogen, a high-tech scientific firm, traded at a P/E of 34 because of unusually bright prospects for the firm. At the same time, Boeing traded at a relatively low P/E of 7 because of less than favorable factors influencing the aerospace industry.

P/E ratios can be looked up in *The Wall Street Journal* or the business section of most newspapers. Quotations from *The Wall Street Journal* are presented in Table 10–3. The first column (Div) after the company symbol (Sym) shows the annual dividend, and the second column (Yld) shows the dividend

TABLE 10–3
Quotations from *The Wall Street Journal*

	52 Weeks Hi	Lo	Stock	Sym	Div	Yld %	PE	Vol 100s	Hi	Lo	Close	Net Chg
	21⅞	12⅝	MexEqIncoFd	MXE	1.53e	9.7	...	435	15¾	15½	15¾	+ ⅜
	34	17⅞	MexicoFd	MXF	2.96e	12.9	...	1025	23⅛	22⅛	23	+ ⅞
	27¾	25	MichConGas pf		2.05	7.9	...	1	26	26	26	+ ½
	4¼	2½	Mickelby	MBC	.06	1.7	6	64	3¾	3⅝	3⅝	...
	24⅜	12⅞	MicronTech	MU	.05e	.2	cc	4539	24¼	23⅛	23⅛	−1
	25⅛	11⅝	MidAmWaste	MAW		...	15	1088	14⅝	13⅝	13¾	− ¼
	20⅝	15¾	MidwRes	MWR	1.16	6.9	23	495	17	16¾	16⅞	+ ⅛
	4¼	2¼	MilestnProp	MPI		...	...	99	4¼	4	4¼	+ ⅜
▲	6⅛	4⅜	MilestnProp pf		.78	12.7	...	258	6¼	6	6⅛	+ ⅛
	39½	27⅛	Millipore	MIL	.52	1.7	21	1170	30	29⅛	29⅞	+ ½
n	26¼	16⅛	MinrlTech	MTX	.03p	.1	...	927	26⅛	24¾	25	− ⅞
	107	85½	MinnMngMfg	MMM	3.20	3.1	18	10306	105⅞	103½	104¼	+3½
▲	35⅝	29⅝	Minn P&L	MPL	1.98f	5.5	16	122	36⅛	35½	36	+ ½
	43⅜	22	MirageResrt	MIR		...	34	3435	42⅞	41⅜	42¾	+1⅝
n	19⅝	13⅝	MitchlEngy A	MNDA	.48	2.7	27	194	17⅝	17⅜	17⅝	+ ⅜
n	18⅝	13	MitchlEngy B	MNDB	.53	3.1	26	523	16⅞	16⅛	16⅞	+ ½
	2⅜	¾	Mitel	MLT		...	...	459	2	1¾	2	+ ¼
	20½	10½	MitsubBk	MBK	.07e	.4	...	124	19⅛	19	19	− ¼
	67⅞	52⅜	Mobil Cp	MOB	3.20	4.9	21	7548	65	64⅛	65	+ ⅞
	37¼	17	MolclrBio	MB		...	dd	95	18½	18¼	18¼	...
	14¼	8⅛	MonarchM	MMO	.20	1.7	...	115	12¼	11⅞	12	+ ¼
n	20⅝	17⅛	MonkAustin	MK		...	...	393	18¾	18½	18½	− ⅛
	71¼	49¾	Monsanto	MTC	2.24	4.1	14	2407	54¾	54⅛	54½	+ ½
	27⅞	23⅝	MontPwr	MTP	1.58f	5.8	13	1360	27¼	26⅞	27¼	+ ⅜
	12⅝	7½	Montedisn	MNT	.44e	5.3	...	294	8⅜	8¼	8¼	+ ¼
	22⅛	19	MontgSt	MTS	1.67e	7.6	...	85	22	21¾	22	− ⅛
	28½	**12⅞**	**MoorcoInt**	**MRC**	**.22**	**1.4**	**12**	**348**	**16⅜**	**14⅝**	**16⅛**	**+1¾**

Source: Reprinted by permission of *THE WALL STREET JOURNAL*, © 1993 Dow Jones & Company, Inc. All Rights Reserved Worldwide. February 5, 1993, p. C4.

yield. This represents the annual dividend divided by the closing stock price. The third column (PE) is of primary interest in that it shows the current price-earnings ratio. For Mobil, it is 21, indicating the current stock price of 65 represents 21 times annual earnings.[13] The remaining columns show the daily volume and the high, low, and closing prices for the day, plus any changes from the previous day.

The dividend valuation approach (based on the present value of dividends) that we have been using throughout the chapter is more theoretically sound than P/E ratios and likely to be used by sophisticated financial analysts. To some extent, the two concepts of P/E ratios and dividend valuation models can be brought together. A stock that has a high required rate of return (K_e) because of its risky nature will generally have a low P/E ratio. Similarly, a stock with a low required rate of return (K_e) because of the predictability of positive future performance will normally have a high P/E ratio. In the first example, both methods provide a low valuation, while in the latter case, both methods provide a high valuation.

Variable Growth in Dividends

In the discussion of common stock valuation, we have considered procedures for firms that had no growth in dividends and for firms that had a constant growth. Most of the discussion and literature in finance assumes a constant growth dividend model. However, there is also a third case, and that is one of variable growth in dividends. The most common variable growth model is one in which the firm experiences supernormal (very rapid) growth for a number of years and then levels off to more normal, constant growth. The **supernormal growth** pattern is often experienced by firms in emerging industries, such as in the early days of electronics or microcomputers.

In evaluating a firm with an initial pattern of supernormal growth, we first take the present value of dividends during the exceptional growth period. We then determine the price of the stock at the end of the supernormal growth period by taking the present value of the normal, constant dividends that follow the supernormal growth period. We discount this price to the present and add it to the present value of the supernormal dividends. This gives us the current price of the stock.

A numerical example of a supernormal growth rate evaluation model is presented in Appendix 10B at the end of this chapter.

Finally, in the discussion of common stock valuation models, readers may ask about the valuation of companies that currently pay no dividends. Since virtually all our discussion has been based on values associated with dividends, how can this "no dividend" circumstance be handled? One approach is

---

[13]The price-earnings ratio is not shown for some companies because they do not have positive earnings on which to base the calculation, or because the preferred stock of the company is shown, in which case, the P/E ratio is not relevant because preferred stock does not have earnings per share as such.

FINANCE IN ACTION

Valuation: What Is Microsoft Really Worth?

In February 1993 Microsoft, the computer software manufacturer, had a total market value of $25 billion (274 million shares outstanding times $91 per share). That exceeds the total value of such U.S. firms as Ford, General Motors, RJR Nabisco, Eastman Kodak, Boeing, 3M, or General Mills. On any given day, the total market value was approximately equal to that of "Big Blue" (IBM). That's not bad for a firm that was initially incorporated in Redmond, Washington, in 1981 and went public in 1986. The stock price that year was between 2 3/8 and 5 3/4.

The founder and CEO of the company, Bill Gates, owns 30 percent of the stock outstanding, giving him a net worth of $7.5 billion. He is the richest man in the United States and can buy and sell H. Ross Perot approximately 2 1/2 times over. It's no surprise that he drives a $380,000 Porsche 959 and lives in a $35 million house.*

Why is Microsoft so highly valued in the marketplace? First of all, it outsells its three largest competitors, Lotus, WordPerfect, and Novell, combined. Its major software product, *Windows,* sold at the rate of 1 million units a month in 1992. Though 1992 was a troubled year for the economy with massive layoffs at Sears, IBM, American Airlines, and elsewhere, Microsoft increased its work force by 2,500 and is rapidly approaching an employment level of 15,000. Earnings per share have grown from $.17 a share in 1986 to approximately $2.40 in 1992.

The company has accomplished this feat with a total-debt-to-total-asset ratio of 17 percent, and *no* long-term debt on its balance sheet. Its return on equity is consistently in the 30 to 40 percent range.

Yet was Microsoft really worth $25 billion ($91 a share) in early 1993? The firm paid no cash dividends. Furthermore it was trading at approximately eight times book value (the net value of the assets on the balance sheet). Its price-earnings ratio fluctuated in the upper stratosphere level of 30 to 35.

Valuation is the most difficult decision the investor must make. Do you go for the great performing company that has a lofty price in the marketplace or do you look for so-called undervalued firms that are out of favor with investors and trading at their annual low values? Each investor must make his or her individual judgment.

*Alan Deutschman, "Bill Gates' Next Challenge," *Fortune,* December 28, 1992, pp. 30–37.

to assume that even for the firm that pays no current dividends, at some point in the future, stockholders will be rewarded with cash dividends. We then take the present value of their deferred dividends.

A second approach to valuing a firm that pays no cash dividend is to take the present value of earnings per share for a number of periods and add that to the present value of a future anticipated stock price. The discount rate applied to future earnings is generally higher than the discount rate applied to future dividends.

Summary and Review of Formulas

The primary emphasis in this chapter is on valuation of financial assets: bonds, preferred stock, and common stock. Regardless of the security being analyzed, valuation is normally based on the concept of determining the present value of future cash flows. Thus we draw on many of the time-value-of-money techniques developed in Chapter 9. Inherent in the valuation process is a determination of rate of return that investors demand. When we have computed this value, we have also identified what it will cost the corporation to raise new capital. Let's specifically review the valuation techniques associated with bonds, preferred stock, and common stock.

Bonds

The price, or current value, of a bond is equal to the present value of interest payments (I_t) over the life of the bond plus the present value of the principal payment (P_n) at maturity. The discount rate used in the analytical process is the yield to maturity (Y). The yield to maturity (required rate of return) is determined in the marketplace by such factors as the *real* rate of return, an inflation premium, and a risk premium.

The equation for bond valuation was presented as Formula 10–1.

$$P_b = \sum_{t=1}^{n} \frac{I_t}{(1 + Y)^t} + \frac{P_n}{(1 + Y)^n} \qquad [10\text{–}1]$$

The actual terms in the equation are solved by the use of present value tables. We say the present value of interest payments is:

$$PV_A = A \times PV_{IFA} \qquad \text{(Appendix D)}$$

The present value of the principal payment at maturity is:

$$PV = FV \times PV_{IF} \qquad \text{(Appendix B)}$$

We add these two values together to determine the price of the bond. We use both annual or semiannual analysis.

The value of the bond will be strongly influenced by the relationship of the yield to maturity in the market to the interest rate on the bond and also the length of time to maturity.

If you know the price of the bond, the size of the interest payments, and the maturity of the bond, you can solve for the yield to maturity through a trial and error approach (discussed in the chapter and expanded in Appendix 10A), by an approximation approach as presented in Formula 10–2, or by using financially oriented calculators (in Appendix E) or appropriate computer software.

Preferred Stock

In determining the value of preferred stock, we are taking the present value of an infinite stream of level dividend payments. This would be a tedious process if the mathematical calculations could not be compressed into a simple formula. The appropriate equation is Formula 10–4.

$$P_p = \frac{D_p}{K_p} \qquad [10\text{–}4]$$

According to Formula 10–4, to find the preferred stock price (P_p) we take the constant annual dividend payment (D_p) and divide this value by the rate of return that preferred stockholders are demanding (K_p).

If, on the other hand, we know the price of the preferred stock and the constant annual dividend payment, we can solve for the required rate of return on preferred stock as:

$$K_p = \frac{D_p}{P_p} \qquad [10\text{--}5]$$

Common Stock

The value of common stock is also based on the concept of the present value of an expected stream of future dividends. Unlike preferred stock, the dividends are not necessarily level. The firm and shareholders may experience:

1. No growth in dividends.
2. Constant growth in dividends.
3. Variable or supernormal growth in dividends.

It is the second circumstance that receives most of the attention in the financial literature. If a firm has constant growth (g) in dividends (D) and the required rate of return (K_e) exceeds the growth rate, Formula 10–9 can be utilized.

$$P_0 = \frac{D_1}{K_e - g} \qquad [10\text{--}9]$$

In using Formula 10–9, all we need to know is the value of the dividend at the end of the first year, the required rate of return, and the discount rate. Most of our valuation calculations with common stock utilize Formula 10–9.

If we need to know the required rate of return (K_e) for common stock, Formula 10–10 can be employed.

$$K_e = \frac{D_1}{P_0} + g \qquad [10\text{--}10]$$

The first term represents the dividend yield on the stock and the second term the growth rate. Together they provide the total return demanded by the investor.

List of Terms

Discussion Questions

1. How is valuation of financial assets by investors related to the cost of financing (cost of capital) for the firm?

2. How is valuation of any financial asset related to future cash flows?

3. Why might investors demand a lower rate of return for an investment in Exxon as compared to Armco Steel or LTV?

4. What are the three factors that influence the required rate of return by investors?

5. If inflationary expectations increase, what is likely to happen to yield to maturity on bonds in the marketplace? What is also likely to happen to the price of bonds?

6. Why is the remaining time to maturity an important factor in evaluating the impact of a change in yield to maturity on bond prices?

7. What are the three adjustments that have to be made in going from annual to semiannual bond analysis?

8. Why is a change in required yield for preferred stock likely to have a greater impact on price than a change in required yield for bonds?

9. What type of dividend pattern for common stock is similar to the dividend payment for preferred stock?

10. What two conditions must be met to go from Formula 10–8 to Formula 10–9 in using the dividend valuation model?

$$P_0 = \frac{D_1}{K_e - g} \qquad [10\text{–}9]$$

11. What two components make up the required rate of return on common stock?

12. What factors might influence a firm's price-earnings ratio?

13. How is the supernormal growth pattern likely to vary from the more normal, constant growth pattern?

14. What approaches can be taken in valuing a firm's stock when there is no cash dividend payment?

Problems

(For the first nine bond problems, assume interest payments are on an annual basis)

Bond value

1. Burns Fire and Casualty Company has $1,000 par value bonds outstanding at 11 percent interest. The bonds will mature in 20 years. Compute the current price of the bonds if the present yield to maturity is:

   a. 6 percent.

   b. 8 percent.

   c. 12 percent.

2. Kilgore Natural Gas has a $1,000 par value bond outstanding that pays 9 percent annual interest. The current yield to maturity on such bonds in the market is 12 percent. Compute the price of the bonds for these maturity dates:

   a. 30 years.

   b. 15 years.

   c. 1 year.

Bond value

3. For problem 2, graph the relationship in a manner similar to the bottom half of Figure 10–2. Also explain why the pattern of price change occurs.

Bond maturity effect

4. Al Simmons calls his broker to inquire about purchasing a bond of Disk Storage Systems. His broker quotes a price of $1,180. Al is concerned that the bond might be overpriced based on the facts involved. The $1,000 par value bond pays 14 percent interest, and it has 25 years remaining until maturity. The current yield to maturity on similar bonds is 12 percent. Compute the new price of the bond and comment on whether you think it is overpriced in the marketplace.

Bond value

5. Westlake Drilling Company issued bonds in 1987 at $1,000 per bond. The bonds had a 30-year life when issued and the annual interest payment was then 11 percent. This return was in line with required returns by bondholders at that point as described below:

Effect of yield to maturity on bond price

Real rate of return . . .	3%
Inflation premium	5
Risk premium.	3
Total return	11%

   Assume that in 1992 the inflation premium is only 2 percent and is appropriately reflected in the required return (or yield to maturity) of the bonds. The bonds have 25 years remaining until maturity. Compute the new price of the bond.

6. Bo Boatler specializes in buying deep discount bonds. These represent bonds that are trading at well below par value. He has his eye on a bond issued by the Quantum Corporation. The $1,000 par value bond pays 5 percent annual interest and has 10 years remaining to maturity. The current yield to maturity on similar bonds is 11 percent.

Profit on bond investment

   a. What is the current price of the bonds?

   b. By what percent will the price of the bonds increase between now and maturity?

   c. What is the annual compound rate of growth in the value of the bonds? (An approximate answer is acceptable.)

7. Bonds issued by the Crane Optical Company have a par value of $1,000, which is also the amount of principal to be paid at maturity. The bonds are currently selling for $850. They have 10 years

Approximate yield to maturity

remaining to maturity. The annual interest payment is 9 percent ($90). Compute the approximate yield to maturity, using Formula 10–2.

Approximate yield to maturity

8. Bonds issued by the West Motel Chain have a par value of $1,000, are selling for $1,100, and have 20 years remaining to maturity. The annual interest payment is 13.5 percent ($135). Compute the approximate yield to maturity, using Formula 10–2.

More exact yield to maturity

9. Optional: For problem 8, use the techniques in Appendix 10A to combine a trial and error approach with interpolation to find a more exact answer. You may choose to use a hand-held calculator instead.

(For the next two problems, assume interest payments are on a semiannual basis.)

Bond value—semiannual analysis

10. Ann Nichols is considering a bond investment in the Southwest Technology Company. The $1,000 bonds have a quoted annual interest rate of 8 percent and the interest is paid semiannually. The yield to maturity on the bonds is 10 percent annual interest. There are 25 years to maturity. Compute the price of the bonds based on semiannual analysis.

Bond value—semiannual analysis

11. You are called in as a financial analyst to appraise the bonds of the Holtz Corporation. The $1,000 par value bonds have a quoted annual interest rate of 14 percent, which is paid semiannually. The yield to maturity on the bonds is 12 percent annual interest. There are 15 years to maturity.

   a. Compute the price of the bonds based on semiannual analysis.

   b. With 10 years remaining to maturity, if yield to maturity goes down substantially to 8 percent, what will be the new price of the bonds?

Preferred stock value

12. The preferred stock of Ultra Corp. pays an annual dividend of $6.30. It has a required rate of return of 9 percent. Compute the price of the preferred stock.

Preferred stock value

13. North Pole Cruise Lines issued preferred stock many years ago. It carries a fixed dividend of $6 per share. With the passage of time, yields have soared from the original 6 percent to 14 percent (yield is the same as required rate of return).

   a. What was the original issue price?

   b. What is the current value of this preferred stock?

   c. If the yield on the Standard & Poor's Preferred Stock Index declines, how will the price of the preferred stock be affected?

Preferred stock rate of return

14. Venus Sportswear Corporation has preferred stock outstanding that pays an annual dividend of $12. It has a price of $110. What is the required rate of return (yield) on the preferred stock?

(All of the following problems pertain to the common stock section of the chapter.)

Common stock value

15. Static Electric Co. currently pays a $2.10 annual cash dividend (D_0). It plans to maintain the dividend at this level for the foreseeable future as

no future growth is anticipated. If the required rate of return by common stockholders (K_e) is 12 percent, what is the price of the common stock?

16. BioScience, Inc., will pay a common stock dividend of $3.20 at the end of the year (D_1). The required return on common stock (K_e) is 14 percent. The firm has a constant growth rate (g) of 9 percent. Compute the current price of the stock (P_0).

Common stock value

17. Friedman Steel Company will pay a dividend of $1.50 per share in the next 12 months (D_1). The required rate of return (K_e) is 10 percent and the constant growth rate is 5 percent.

Common stock value under different conditions

    a. Compute P_0.

(For the remaining questions in this problem all variables remain the same except the one specifically changed. Each question is independent of the others.)

    b. Assume K_e, the required rate of return, goes up to 12 percent, what will be the new value of P_0?

    c. Assume the growth rate (g) goes up to 7 percent, what will be the new value of P_0?

    d. Assume D_1 is $2, what will be the new value of P_0?

18. Maxwell Communications paid a dividend of $3 last year. Over the next 12 months, the dividend is expected to grow at 8 percent, which is the constant growth rate for the firm (g). The new dividend after 12 months will represent D_1. The required rate of return (K_e) is 14 percent. Compute the price of the stock (P_0).

Common stock value

19. Haltom Enterprises has had the following pattern of earnings per share over the last five years:

Common stock value based on determining growth rate

Year	Earnings per Share
1989 . . .	$3.00
1990 . . .	3.18
1991 . . .	3.37
1992 . . .	3.57
1993 . . .	3.78

The earnings per share have grown at a constant rate (on a rounded basis) and will continue to do so in the future. Dividends represent 30 percent of earnings.

    a. Project earnings and dividends for the next year (1994). Round all values in this problem to two places to the right of the decimal point.

    b. If the required rate of return (K_e) is 10 percent, what is the anticipated stock price at the beginning of 1994?

20. A firm pays $4.90 dividend at the end of year one (D_1), has a stock price of $70, and a constant growth rate (g) of 6 percent. Compute the required rate of return.

Common stock required rate of return

Common stock required
rate of return

21. A firm pays a $1.90 dividend at the end of year one (D_1), has a stock price of $40 ($P_0$), and a constant growth rate (g) of 8 percent.

   a. Compute the required rate of return (K_e). Also indicate whether each of the following changes would make the required rate of return (K_e) go up or down. (In each question below, assume only one variable changes at a time. No actual numbers are necessary.)

   b. The dividend payment increases.

   c. The expected growth rate increases.

   d. The stock price increases.

Common stock value
based on PV calculations

22. Cellular Systems paid a $3 dividend last year. The dividend is expected to grow at a constant rate of 5 percent over the next two years. The required rate of return is 12 percent (this will also serve as the discount rate in this problem). Round all values to three places to the right of the decimal point where appropriate.

   a. Compute the anticipated value of the dividends for the next three years. That is, compute D_1, D_2, and D_3; for example, D_1 is $3.15 ($3.00 \times 1.05$). Round all values throughout this problem to three places to the right of the decimal point.

   b. Discount each of these dividends back to the present at a discount rate of 12 percent and then sum them.

   c. Compute the price of the stock at the end of the third year (P_3).

$$P_3 = \frac{D_4}{K_e - g}$$

(D_4 is equal to D_3 times 1.05)

   d. After you have computed P_3, discount it back to the present at a discount rate of 12 percent for three years.

   e. Add together the answers in part b and part d to get P_0, the current value of the stock. This answer represents the present value of the first three periods of dividends, plus the present value of the price of the stock after three periods (which, in turn, represents the value of all future dividends).

   f. Use Formula 10–9 to show that it will provide approximately the same answer as part e.

$$P_0 = \frac{D_1}{K_e - g} \qquad [10\text{–}9]$$

   For Formula 10–9 use $D_1 = 3.15, $K_e = 12$ percent, and $g = 5$ percent. (The slight difference between the answers to part e and part f is due to rounding.)

Selected References

Bernard, Victor L. "Unanticipated Inflation and the Value of the Firm." *Journal of Financial Economics* 15 (March 1986), pp. 285–321.

Bierwag, Gerald O. "Bond Returns, Discrete Stochastic Processes, and Duration." *Journal of Financial Research* 43 (Fall 1987), pp. 191–210.

Estep, Preston W. "A New Method for Valuing Common Stocks." *Financial Analysts Journal* 41 (November–December 1985), pp. 26–33.

Farrell, James L. "The Dividend Discount Model: A Primer." *Financial Analysts Journal* 41 (November–December 1985), pp. 16–25.

Fielitz, Bruce D., and Frederick L. Muller. "A Simplified Approach to Common Stock Valuation." *Financial Analysts Journal* 41 (November-December 1985), pp. 35–41.

Friend, Irwin, and Marshall Blume. "The Demand for Risky Assets." *American Economic Review* 75 (December 1975), p. 900.

Good, Walter R. "When Are Price/Earnings Ratios Too High—or Too Low?" *Financial Analysts Journal* 47 (July–August 1991), pp. 9–12, 15.

Hirt, Geoffrey A., and Stanley B. Block. *Fundamentals of Investment Management.* 4th ed. Homewood, Ill.: Richard D. Irwin, 1993.

McConnell, John J., and Chris J. Muscarella. "Corporate Capital Expenditure Decisions and the Market Value of the Firm." *Journal of Financial Economics (Netherlands),* 14 (September 1985), pp. 399–422.

Reilly, Frank K. *Investment Analysis and Portfolio Management.* 3rd ed. Hinsdale, Ill.: Dryden Press, 1989.

Sinquefield, Rex A. "Are Small-Stock Returns Achievable?" *Financial Analysts Journal* 47 (January–February 1991), pp. 45–50.

Zivney, Terry L., and Donald J. Thompson II. "Relative Stock Prices and the Firm Size Effect." *Journal of Financial Research* 43 (Summer 1987), pp. 99–110.

APPENDIX 10A   The Bond Yield to Maturity Using Interpolation

We will use a numerical example to demonstrate this process. Assume a 20-year bond pays $118 per year (11.8 percent) in interest and $1,000 after 20 years in principal repayment. The current price of the bond is $1,085. We wish to determine the yield to maturity or discount rate that equates the future flows with the current price.

Since the bond is trading above par value at $1,085, we can assume the yield to maturity must be below the quoted interest rate of 11.8 percent (the yield to maturity would be the full 11.8 percent at a bond price of $1,000). As a first approximation, we will try 10 percent. Annual analysis is used.

Present value of interest payments —

$$PV_A = A \times PV_{IFA} \qquad (n = 20, i = 10\%) \qquad \text{(Appendix D)}$$

$$PV_A = \$118 \times 8.514 = \$1,004.65$$

Present value of principal payment at maturity —

$$PV = FV \times PV_{IF} \qquad (n = 20, i = 10\%) \qquad \text{(Appendix B)}$$

$$PV = \$1,000 \times .149 = \$149$$

Total present value —

Present value of interest payments	$1,004.65
Present value of principal payment at maturity. .	149.00
Total present value, or price, of the bond . .	$1,153.65

The discount rate of 10 percent gives us too high a present value in comparison to the current bond price of $1,085. Let's try a higher discount rate to get a lower price. We will use 11 percent.

Present value of interest payments—

$$PV_A = A \times PV_{IFA} \qquad (n = 20, i = 11\%) \qquad \text{(Appendix D)}$$

$$PV_A = \$118 \times 7.963 = \$939.63$$

Present value of principal payment at maturity—

$$PV = FV \times PV_{IF} \qquad (n = 20, i = 11\%) \qquad \text{(Appendix B)}$$

$$PV = \$1,000 \times .124 = \$124$$

Total present value—

Present value of interest payments	$ 939.63
Present value of principal payment at maturity. .	124.00
Total present value, or price, of the bond . .	$1,063.63

The discount rate of 11 percent gives us a value slightly lower than the bond price of $1,085. The rate for the bond must fall between 10 and 11 percent. Using linear interpolation, the answer is 10.76 percent.

$1,153.65 PV @ 10%	$1,153.65 PV @ 10%
1,063.63 PV @ 11%	1,085.00 bond price
$ 90.02	$ 68.65

$$10\% + \frac{\$68.65}{\$90.02}(1\%) = 10\% + .76(1\%) = 10.76\%$$

Problem

10A–1. Bonds issued by the Medford Corporation have a par value of $1,000, are selling for $865, and have 25 years to maturity. The annual interest payment is 8 percent.

Find yield to maturity by combining the trial-and-error approach with interpolation, as shown in this appendix. (Use an assumption of annual interest payments.)

APPENDIX 10B   **Valuation of a Supernormal Growth Firm**

The equation for the valuation of a supernormal growth firm is:

$$P_0 = \sum_{t=1}^{n} \frac{D_t}{(1 + K_e)^t} + P_n \left(\frac{1}{1 + K_e} \right)^n \qquad (10B-1)$$

(Supernormal   (After supernormal
growth   growth period)
period)

Actually the formula is not difficult to use. The first term calls for determining the present value of the dividends using the supernormal growth period. The second term calls for computing the present value of the future stock price as determined at the end of the supernormal growth period. If we add the two, we arrive at the current stock price. We are adding together the two benefits the stockholder will receive: a future stream of dividends during the supernormal growth period and the future stock price.

Let's assume the firm paid a dividend over the last 12 months of $1.67; this represents the current dividend rate. Dividends are expected to grow by 20 percent per year over the supernormal growth period (n) of three years. They will then grow at a normal constant growth rate (g) of 5 percent. The required rate of return (discount rate) as represented by K_e is 9 percent. We first find the present value of the dividends during the supernormal growth period.

1. *Present value of supernormal dividends—*

D_0 = $1.67. We allow this value to grow at 20 percent per year over the three years of supernormal growth.

$D_1 = D_0(1 + .20) = \$1.67(1.20) = \$2.00$

$D_2 = D_1(1 + .20) = \$2.00(1.20) = \$2.40$

$D_3 = D_2(1 + .20) = \$2.40(1.20) = \$2.88$

We then discount these values back at 9 percent to find the present value of dividends during the supernormal growth period.

	Supernormal Dividends	Discount Rate K_e = 9%	Present Value of Dividends during the Supernormal Period
D_1 . . .	$2.00	.917	$1.83
D_2 . . .	2.40	.842	2.02
D_3 . . .	2.88	.772	2.22
			$6.07

The present value of the supernormal dividends is $6.07. We now turn to the future stock price.

2. *Present value of future stock price—*

We first find the future stock price at the end of the supernormal growth period. This is found by taking the present value of the dividends that will be growing at a normal, constant rate after the supernormal period. This will begin *after* the third (and last) period of supernormal growth.

Since after the supernormal growth period the firm is growing at a normal, constant rate (g = 5 percent) and K_e (the discount rate) of 9 percent exceeds the new, constant growth rate of 5 percent, we have fulfilled the two conditions for using the constant dividend growth model after three years. That is, we can apply Formula 10–9 (without subscripts for now).

$$P = \frac{D}{K_e - g}$$

In this case, however, D is really the dividend at the end of the fourth period because this phase of the analysis starts at the beginning of the fourth period and D is supposed to fall at the *end* of the first period of analysis in the formula. Also the price we are solving for now is the price at the beginning of the fourth period, which is the same concept as the price at the end of the third period (P_3).

We thus say:

$$P_3 = \frac{D_4}{K_e - g} \qquad (10B-2)$$

D_4 is equal to the previously determined value for D_3 of $2.88 compounded for one period at the constant growth rate of 5 percent.

$$D_4 = \$2.88(1.05) = \$3.02$$

Also:

$$K_e = .09 \text{ discount rate (required rate of return)}$$

$$g = .05 \text{ constant growth rate}$$

$$P_3 = \frac{D_4}{K_e - g} = \frac{\$3.02}{.09 - .05} = \frac{\$3.02}{.04} = \$75.50$$

This is the value of the stock at the end of the third period. We discount this value back to the present.

Stock Price after Three Years	Discount Rate* $K_e = 9\%$	Present Value of Future Price
$75.50	.772	$58.29

*Note: n is equal to 3.

The present value of the future stock price (P_3) of $75.50 is $58.29.

By adding together the answers in part (1) and part (2) of this appendix, we arrive at the total present value, or price, of the supernormal growth stock.

(1)	Present value of dividends during the normal growth period. .	$ 6.07
(2)	Present value of the future stock price	58.29
	Total present value, or price	$64.36

FIGURE 10B–1   **Stock valuation under supernormal growth analysis**

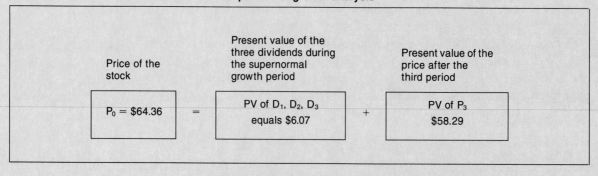

10B–1. Surgical Supplies Corporation paid a dividend of $1.12 over the last 12 months. The dividend is expected to grow at a rate of 25 percent over the next three years (supernormal growth). It will then grow at a normal, constant rate of 7 percent for the foreseeable future. The required rate of return is 12 percent (this will also serve as the discount rate).

 a. Compute the anticipated value of the dividends for the next three years (D_1, D_2, and D_3).

 b. Discount each of these dividends back to the present at a discount rate of 12 percent and then sum them.

 c. Compute the price of the stock at the end of the third year (P_3).

$$P_3 = \frac{D_4}{K_e - g} \quad \text{[Review Appendix 10B for the definition of } D_4\text{]}$$

 d. After you have computed P_3, discount it back to the present at a discount rate of 12 percent for three years.

 e. Add together the answers in part *b* and part *d* to get the current value of the stock. (This answer represents the present value of the first three periods of dividends plus the present value of the price of the stock after three periods.)

Cost of Capital

CHAPTER CONCEPTS

1 The cost of capital represents the overall cost of financing to the firm.

2 The cost of capital is normally the discount rate to use in analyzing an investment.

3 The cost of capital is based on the valuation techniques from the previous chapter and is applied to bonds, preferred stock, and common stock.

4 A firm attempts to find a minimum cost of capital through varying the mix of its sources of financing.

5 The cost of capital may eventually increase as larger amounts of financing are utilized.

Throughout the previous two chapters, a number of references were made to discounting future cash flows in solving for the present value. How do you determine the appropriate interest rate or discount rate in a real situation? Suppose that a young doctor is rendered incapable of practicing medicine due to an auto accident in the last year of his residency. The court determines that he could have made $100,000 a year for the next 30 years. What is the present value of these inflows? We must know the appropriate discount rate. If 10 percent is used, the value is $942,700; with 5 percent, the answer is $1,537,300—over half a million dollars is at stake.

In the corporate finance setting, the more likely circumstance is that an investment will be made today—promising a set of inflows in the future— and we need to know the appropriate discount rate. This chapter sets down the methods and procedures for making such a determination.

First, the student should observe that if we invest money today to receive benefits in the future, we must be absolutely certain we are earning at least as much as it costs us to acquire the funds for investment—that, in essence, is the minimum acceptable return. If funds cost the firm 10 percent, then all projects must be tested to make sure they earn at least 10 percent. By using this as the discount rate, we can ascertain whether we have earned the financial cost of doing business.

The Overall Concept

How does the firm determine the cost of its funds or, more properly stated, the **cost of capital?** Suppose the plant superintendent wishes to borrow money at 6 percent to purchase a conveyor system, while a division manager suggests stock be sold at an effective cost of 12 percent to develop a new product. Not only would it be foolish for each investment to be judged against the specific means of financing used to implement it, but this would also make investment selection decisions inconsistent. For example imagine financing a conveyor system having an 8 percent return with 6 percent debt and also evaluating a new product having an 11 percent return but financed with 12 percent common stock. If projects and financing are matched in this way, the project with the lower return would be accepted and the project with the higher return would be rejected. In reality if stock and debt are sold in equal proportions, the average cost of financing would be 9 percent (one half debt at 6 percent and one half stock at 12 percent). With a 9 percent average cost of financing, we would now reject the 8 percent conveyor system and accept the 11 percent new product. This would be a rational and consistent decision. Though an investment financed by low-cost debt might appear acceptable at first glance, the use of debt might increase the overall risk of the firm and eventually make all forms of financing more expensive. Each project must be measured against the overall cost of funds to the firm. We now consider cost of capital in a broader context.

The determination of cost of capital can best be understood by examining the capital structure of a hypothetical firm, the Baker Corporation, in Table 11–1. Note that the aftertax costs of the individual sources of financing

TABLE 11–1
Cost of capital—Baker Corporation

		(1) Cost (aftertax)	(2) Weights	(3) Weighted Cost
Debt	K_d	7.05%	30%	2.12%
Preferred stock.	K_p	10.94	10	1.09
Common equity (retained earnings)	K_e	12.00	60	7.20
Weighted average cost of capital	K_a			10.41%

are shown, then weights are assigned to each, and finally a weighted average cost is determined. (The costs under consideration are those related to new funds that can be used for future financing, rather than historical costs.) In the remainder of the chapter, each of these procedural steps is examined.

Each element in the capital structure has an explicit or opportunity cost associated with it, herein referred to by the symbol K. These costs are directly related to the valuation concepts developed in the previous chapter. If a reader understands how a security is valued, then there is little problem in determining its cost. The mathematics involved in the cost of capital are not difficult. We begin our analysis with a consideration of the cost of debt.

Cost of Debt

The cost of debt is measured by the interest rate, or yield, paid to bondholders. The simplest case would be a $1,000 bond paying $100 annual interest, thus providing a 10 percent yield. The computation may be more difficult if the bond is priced at a discount or premium from par value. Techniques for computing such bond yields were presented in Chapter 10.

Assume the firm is preparing to issue new debt. To determine the likely cost of the new debt in the marketplace, the firm will compute the yield on its currently outstanding debt. This is not the rate at which the old debt was issued, but the rate that investors are demanding today. Assume the debt issue pays $101.50 per year in interest, has a 20-year life, and is currently selling for $940. To find the current yield to maturity on the debt, we could use the trial and error process described in the previous chapter. That is, we would experiment with discount rates until we found the rate that would equate interest payments of $101.50 for 20 years and a maturity payment of $1,000 with $940 today. A simpler process would be to use Formula 10–2, which gives us the approximate yield to maturity. We reproduce the formula below and relabel it Formula 11–1.

$$\text{Approximate yield to maturity } (Y') = \frac{\text{Annual interest payment} + \dfrac{\text{Principal payment} - \text{Price of the bond}}{\text{Number of years to maturity}}}{0.6(\text{Price of the bond}) + 0.4(\text{Principal payment})} \quad (11\text{–}1)$$

For the bond under discussion, the approximate yield to maturity (Y') would be:

$$Y' = \frac{\$101.50 + \dfrac{\$1,000 - \$940}{20}}{.6(\$940) + .4(\$1,000)}$$

$$= \frac{\$101.50 + \dfrac{60}{20}}{\$564 + \$400}$$

$$Y' = \frac{\$101.50 + \$3}{\$964} = \frac{\$104.50}{\$964} = 10.84\%$$

In many cases you will not have to compute the yield to maturity. It will simply be given to you. The practicing corporate financial manager also can normally consult a source such as Standard & Poor's Bond Guide to determine the yield to maturity on his firm's outstanding debt. An excerpt from this bond guide is presented in Table 11–2. If the firm involved is Louisiana Power & Light, for example, the financial manager could observe that debt maturing in 2000 would have a yield to maturity of 8.94 percent. This is shown in the last column.

TABLE 11–2   **Excerpt from Standard & Poor's Bond Guide**

Once the bond yield is determined through the formula or the tables (or is given to you), you must adjust the yield for tax considerations. Yield to maturity indicates how much the corporation has to pay on a *before tax* basis. But keep in mind the interest payment on debt is a tax-deductible expense. Since interest is tax deductible, its true cost is less than its stated cost because the government is picking up part of the tab by allowing the firm to pay less taxes. The aftertax cost of debt is actually the yield to maturity times one minus the tax rate.[1] This is presented as Formula 11–2.

$$K_d \text{ (Cost of debt)} = Y \text{ (Yield)} (1 - T) \qquad (11\text{--}2)$$

The term *yield* in the formula is interchangeable with yield to maturity or approximate yield to maturity. In using the approximate yield to maturity formula earlier in this section, we determined that the existing yield on the debt was 10.84 percent. We shall assume new debt can be issued at the same going market rate,[2] and that the firm is paying a 35 percent tax (a nice, easy rate with which to work). Applying the tax adjustment factor, the aftertax cost of debt would be 7.05 percent.

$$
\begin{aligned}
K_d \text{ (Cost of debt)} &= Y \text{ (Yield)} (1 - T) \\
&= 10.84\% (1 - .35) \\
&= 10.84\% (.65) \\
&= 7.05\%
\end{aligned}
$$

Please refer back to Table 11–1 and observe in column (1) that the aftertax cost of debt is the 7.05 percent that we have just computed.

Cost of Preferred Stock

The cost of preferred stock is similar to the cost of debt in that a constant annual payment is made, but dissimilar in that there is no maturity date on which a principal payment must be made. Determining the yield on preferred stock is simpler than determining the yield on debt. All you have to do is divide the annual dividend by the current price (this process was discussed in Chapter 10). This represents the rate of return to preferred stockholders as well as the annual cost to the corporation for the preferred stock issue.

---

[1]The yield may also be thought of as representing the interest cost to the firm after considering all selling and distribution costs, though no explicit representation is given above to these costs in relationship to debt. These costs are usually quite small, and they are often bypassed entirely in some types of loans. For those who wish to explicitly include this factor in Formula 11–1, we would have:

$$K_d = [\text{Yield}/(1 - \text{Distribution costs})](1 - T)$$

[2]Actually the rate might be slightly higher to reflect that bonds trading at a discount from par ($940 in this case) generally pay a lower yield to maturity than par value bonds because of potential tax advantages and higher leverage potential. This is not really a major issue in this case.

We need to make one slight alteration to this process by dividing the dividend payment by the *net* price or proceeds received by the firm. Since a new share of preferred stock has a selling cost (**flotation cost**), the proceeds to the firm are equal to the selling price in the market minus the flotation cost. The cost of preferred stock is presented as Formula 11–3.[3]

$$K_p \text{ (Cost of preferred stock)} = \frac{D_p}{P_p - F} \qquad (11\text{--}3)$$

where

$K_p = $ Cost of preferred stock

$D_p = $ The annual dividend on preferred stock

$P_p = $ The price of preferred stock

$F = $ Flotation, or selling cost

In the case of the Baker Corporation, we shall assume the annual dividend is $10.50, the preferred stock price is $100, and the flotation, or selling cost is $4. The effective cost is:

$$K_p = \frac{D_p}{P_p - F} = \frac{\$10.50}{\$100 - 4} = \frac{\$10.50}{\$96} = 10.94\%$$

Because a preferred stock dividend is not a tax-deductible expense, there is no downward tax adjustment.

Please refer back to Table 11–1 and observe in column (1) that 10.94 percent is the value we used for the cost of preferred stock.

Cost of Common Equity

Determining the cost of common stock in the capital structure is a more involved task. The out-of-pocket cost is the cash dividend, but is it prudent to assume the percentage cost of common stock is simply the current year's dividend divided by the market price?

$$\frac{\text{Current dividend}}{\text{Market price}}$$

If such an approach were followed, the common stock costs for selected U.S. corporations in January 1993 would be Disney (.6 percent), Motorola (.7 percent), PepsiCo (1.2 percent), and Marriott (1.3 percent). Ridiculous, you say! If new common stock were assumed to cost such low amounts, the firms would have no need to issue other securities and could profitably finance

---

[3]Note that in Chapter 10, K_p was presented without any adjustment for flotation costs. The instructor may wish to indicate that we have altered the definition slightly. Some may wish to formally add an additional subscript to K_p to indicate we are now talking about the cost of *new* preferred stock. The adjusted symbol would be K_{pn}.

projects that earned only 1 or 2 percent. How then do we find the correct theoretical cost of common stock to the firm?

Valuation Approach

In determining the cost of common stock, the firm must be sensitive to the pricing and performance demands of current and future stockholders. An appropriate approach is to develop a model for valuing common stock and to extract from this model a formula for the required return on common stock.

In Chapter 10 we discussed the constant **dividend valuation model** and said the current price of common stock could be stated to equal:

$$P_0 = \frac{D_1}{K_e - g}$$

where

$$P_0 = \text{Price of the stock today}$$

$$D_1 = \text{Dividend at the end of the first year (or period)}$$

$$K_e = \text{Required rate of return}$$

$$g = \text{Constant growth rate in dividends}$$

We then stated we could arrange the terms in the formula to solve for K_e instead of P_0. This was presented in Formula 10–10. We present the formula once again and relabel it Formula 11–4.

$$K_e = \frac{D_1}{P_0} + g \tag{11-4}$$

The required rate of return (K_e) is equal to the dividend at the end of the first year (D_1), divided by the price of the stock today (P_0), plus a constant growth rate (g). Although the growth rate basically applies to dividends, it is also assumed to apply to earnings and stock price over the long term.

If $D_1 = \$2$, $P_0 = \$40$, and $g = 7\%$, we would say K_e equals 12 percent.

$$K_e = \frac{D_1}{P_0} + g = \frac{\$2}{\$40} + 7\% = 5\% + 7\% = 12\%$$

This means stockholders expect to receive a 5 percent dividend yield on the stock price plus a 7 percent growth in their investment, making a total return of 12 percent.

Alternate Calculation of the Required Return on Common Stock

The required return on common stock can also be calculated by an alternate approach called the capital asset pricing model. This topic is covered in Appendix 11A, so only brief mention will be made at this point. Some accept the capital asset pricing model as an important approach to common stock valuation, while others suggest it is not a valid description of how the real world operates.

Under the **capital asset pricing model (CAPM),** the required return for common stock (or other investments) can be described by the following formula:

$$K_j = R_f + \beta(K_m - R_f) \qquad (11\text{--}5)$$

where

K_j = Required return on common stock

R_f = Risk-free rate of return; usually the current rate on Treasury bill securities

β = Beta coefficient. The beta measures the historical volatility of an individual stock's return relative to a stock market index. A beta greater than 1 indicates greater volatility (price movements) than the market, while the reverse would be true for a beta less than 1.

K_m = Return in the market as measured by an appropriate index

For the Baker Corporation example, we might assume the following values:

$$R_f = 5.5\%$$

$$K_m = 12\%$$

$$\beta = 1.0$$

K_j, based on Formula 11–5, would then equal:

$$K_j = 5.5\% + 1(12\% - 5.5\%) = 5.5\% + 1(6.5\%)$$

$$= 5.5\% + 6.5\% = 12\%$$

In this case we have assumed that K_j (the required return under the capital asset pricing model) would equal K_e (the required return under the dividend valuation model). They are both computed to equal 12 percent. Under this equilibrium circumstance, the dividend valuation model and the capital asset pricing model would produce the same answer.

For now we shall use the dividend valuation model exclusively; that is, we shall use $K_e = D_1/P_0 + g$ in preference to $K_j = R_f + \beta(K_m - R_f)$.

Those who wish to study the capital asset pricing model further are referred to Appendix 11A. This appendix is optional and not required for further reading in the text.

Cost of Retained Earnings

Up to this point, we have discussed the cost (required return) on common stock in a general sense. We have not really specified who is supplying the funds. One obvious supplier of **common stock equity** capital is the purchaser of new shares of common stock. But this is not the only source. For many corporations the most important source of ownership or equity capital is in the form of retained earnings, an internal source of funds.

Accumulated retained earnings represent the past and present earnings of the firm minus previously distributed dividends. Retained earnings, by law, belong to the current stockholders. They can either be paid out to the current stockholders in the form of dividends or reinvested in the firm. As current funds are retained in the firm for reinvestment, they represent a source of equity capital to the firm that is being supplied by the current stockholders. However, they should not be considered as free in nature. An opportunity cost is involved. As previously indicated, the funds could be paid out to the current stockholders in the form of dividends, and then redeployed by the stockholders in other stocks, bonds, real estate, etc. What is the expected rate of return on these alternative investments? That is, what is the opportunity cost? We assume stockholders could at least earn an equivalent return to that provided by their present investment in the firm (on an equal risk basis). This represents $D_1/P_0 + g$. In the security markets, there are thousands of investments from which to choose, so it is not implausible to assume the stockholder can take dividend payments and reinvest them for a comparable yield.

Thus when we compute the cost of retained earnings, this takes us back to the point at which we began our discussion of the cost of common stock. The cost of retained earnings is equivalent to the rate of return on the firm's common stock. This is the opportunity cost. Thus we say the cost of common equity in the form of retained earnings is equal to the required rate of return on the firm's stock.[4]

$$K_e \text{(Cost of common equity in the form of retained earnings)} = \frac{D_1}{P_0} + g \qquad (11\text{–}6)$$

Thus K_e not only represents the required return on common stock as previously defined, but it also represents the cost of equity in the form of retained earnings. It is a symbol that has double significance.

---

[4]One could logically suggest this is not a perfectly equivalent relationship. For example if stockholders receive a distribution of retained earnings in the form of dividends, they will have to pay taxes on the dividends before they can reinvest them in equivalent yield investments. Also the stockholder may incur brokerage costs in the process. For these reasons, one might suggest the opportunity cost of retained earnings is less than the rate of return on the firm's common stock. The authors have generally supported this position in the past. However, the current predominant view is probably that the appropriate cost for retained earnings is equal to the rate of return on the firm's common stock. The strongest argument for this equality position is that, in a publicly traded company, a firm always has the option of buying back its stock in the market. Given that this is the case, it is assured a return of K_e. Thus, the firm should not make a physical asset investment that has an expected equity return of less than K_e. Having presented both sides of the argument, the authors have adopted the equality position in recent editions and have used it throughout this chapter. Nevertheless, some instructors may wish to discuss both sides of the issue. In the event a tax adjustment is made, the cost of retained earnings can be shown as $K_r = K_e(1 - tr)$; where K_r equals the cost of retained earnings, K_e equals the required rate of return on common stock, and tr equals the average stockholder marginal tax rate.

For ease of reference, the terms in Formula 11–6 are reproduced in the box. They are based on prior values presented in this section on the cost of common equity.

K_e = Cost of common equity in the form of retained earnings
D_1 = Dividend at the end of the first year, \$2
P_0 = Price of the stock today, \$40
g = Constant growth rate in dividends, 7%

We arrive at the value of 12%.

$$K_e = \frac{D_1}{P_0} + g = \frac{\$2}{\$40} + 7\% = 5\% + 7\% = 12\%$$

The cost of common equity in the form of retained earnings is equal to 12 percent. Please refer back to Table 11–1 and observe in column (1) that 12 percent is the value we have used for common equity.

Cost of New Common Stock

Let's now consider the other source of equity capital, new common stock. If we are issuing *new* common stock, we must earn a slightly higher return than K_e, which represents the required rate of return of *present* stockholders. The higher return is needed to cover the distribution costs of the new securities. Assume the required return for present stockholders is 12 percent and shares are quoted to the public at \$40. A new distribution of securities must earn slightly more than 12 percent to compensate the corporation for not receiving the full \$40 because of sales commissions and other expenses. The formula for K_e is restated as K_n (the cost of new common stock) to reflect this requirement.

Common stock $\qquad K_e = \dfrac{D_1}{P_0} + g$

New common stock $\qquad K_n = \dfrac{D_1}{P_0 - F} + g \qquad\qquad (11\text{–}7)$

The only new term is F (flotation, or selling costs).
Assume:

$$D_1 = \$2$$
$$P_0 = \$40$$
$$F = \$4$$
$$g = 7\%$$

then

$$K_n = \frac{\$2}{\$40 - \$4} + 7\%$$

$$= \frac{\$2}{\$36} + 7\%$$

$$= 5.6\% + 7\% = 12.6\%$$

The cost of new common stock to the Baker Corporation is 12.6 percent. This value will be used more extensively later in the chapter. New common stock is not assumed to be in the original capital structure for the Baker Corporation presented in Table 11–1.

Overview of Common Stock Costs

For those of you who are suffering from an overexposure to Ks in the computation of cost of common stock, let us boil down the information to the only two common stock formulas that you will be using in the rest of the chapter and in the problems at the back of the chapter.

$$K_e \text{(Cost of common equity in the form of retained earnings)} = \frac{D_1}{P_0} + g$$

$$K_n \text{ (Cost of new common stock)} = \frac{D_1}{P_0 - F} + g$$

The primary emphasis will be on K_e for now, but later in the chapter we will also use K_n when we discuss the marginal cost of capital.

Having established the techniques for computing the cost of the various elements in the capital structure, we must now discuss methods of assigning weights to these costs. We will attempt to weight capital components in accordance with our desire to achieve a minimum overall cost of capital. This represents an **optimum capital structure.** For the purpose of this discussion, Table 11–1 (Cost of Capital for the Baker Corporation) is reproduced below.

Optimal Capital Structure— Weighting Costs

		Cost (aftertax)	Weights	Weighted Cost
Debt	K_d	7.05%	30%	2.12%
Preferred stock.	K_p	10.94	10	1.09
Common equity (retained earnings). . . .	K_e	12.00	60	7.20
Weighted average cost of capital	K_a			10.41%

How does the firm decide on the appropriate weights for debt, preferred stock, and common stock financing? Though debt is the cheapest form of financing, it should be used only within reasonable limits. In the Baker Corporation example, debt carried an aftertax cost of 7.05 percent, while other sources of financing cost at least 10.94 percent. Why not use more debt? The answer is that the use of debt beyond a reasonable point may greatly increase the firm's financial risk and thereby drive up the costs of all sources of financing. For a more complete discussion of the theory related to this point, please see Appendix 11B: Capital Structure Theory and Modigliani and Miller.

Assume you are going to start your own company and are considering three different capital structures. For ease of presentation, only debt and equity (common stock) are being considered. The costs of the components in the capital structure change each time we vary the debt-equity mix (weights).

	Cost (aftertax)	Weights	Weighted Cost
Financial Plan A:			
Debt	6.5%	20%	1.3%
Equity. . . .	12.0	80	9.6
			10.9%
Financial Plan B:			
Debt	7.0%	40%	2.8%
Equity. . . .	12.5	60	7.5
			10.3%
Financial Plan C:			
Debt	9.0%	60%	5.4%
Equity. . . .	15.0	40	6.0
			11.4%

The firm is able to initially reduce the **weighted average cost of capital** with debt financing, but beyond Plan B the continued use of debt becomes unattractive and greatly increases the costs of the sources of financing. Traditional financial theory maintains that there is a U-shaped cost-of-capital curve relative to debt-equity mixes for the firm, as illustrated in Figure 11–1. In this example, the optimum capital structure occurs at a 40 percent debt-to-equity ratio.

Most firms are able to use 30 to 50 percent debt in their capital structure without exceeding norms acceptable to creditors and investors. Distinctions should be made, however, between firms that carry high or low business risks. As discussed in Chapter 5, "Operating and Financial Leverage," a growth firm in a reasonably stable industry can afford to absorb more debt than its counterpart in cyclical industries. Examples of debt use by companies in various industries are presented in Table 11–3.

In determining the appropriate capital mix, the firm generally begins with its present capital structure and ascertains whether its current position is

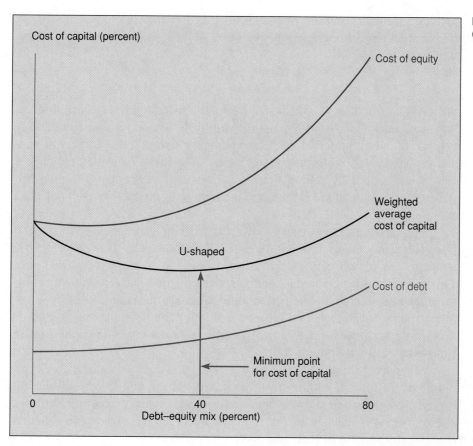

FIGURE 11–1
Cost of capital curve

Cost of capital (percent)

Cost of equity

Weighted average cost of capital

U-shaped

Cost of debt

Minimum point for cost of capital

0   40   80

Debt–equity mix (percent)

TABLE 11–3
Debt as a percentage of total assets

Selected Companies, with Industry Designation	Percent
National Presto (electrical appliances)	19
Liz Claiborne (women's clothing)	23
Diebold (automatic transmissions)	26
Lilly (Eli) & Co. (ethical drugs)	38
Reebok International (footwear)	42
Paramount Communications (motion pictures)	43
Office Depot (office products)	45
Motorola (electronics)	49
Stanley Works (home tools)	54
Alcan Aluminum (aluminum products)	55
Gannett (newspaper and publishing)	56
Fluor (engineering)	58
Playboy Enterprises (entertainment)	60
Fedders (air conditioning)	78
Ford Motor Co. (automobiles)	80
Delta Airlines (air travel)	82

Source: Annual reports, Standard & Poor's *Compustat* tapes, and *Moody's Industrial Manual.*

optimal.[5] If not, subsequent financing should carry the firm toward a mix that is deemed more desirable. Only the costs of new or incremental financing should be considered.

Capital Acquisition and Investment Decision Making

So far the various costs of financial capital and the optimum capital structure have been discussed. **Financial capital,** as you may have figured out, consists of bonds, preferred stock, and common equity. These forms of financial capital appear on the corporate balance sheet under liabilities and equity. The money raised by selling these securities and retaining earnings is invested in the real capital of the firm, the long-term productive assets of plant and equipment.

Long-term funds are usually invested in long-term assets, with several asset-financing mixes possible over the business cycle. Obviously a firm wants to provide all of the necessary financing at the lowest possible cost. This means selling common stock when prices are relatively high to minimize the cost of equity. The financial manager also wants to sell debt at low interest rates. Since there is short-term and long-term debt, the manager needs to know how interest rates move over the business cycle and when to use short-term versus long-term debt.

A firm has to find a balance between debt and equity to achieve its minimum cost of capital. Although we discussed minimizing the overall cost of capital (K_a) at a single debt-to-equity ratio, in reality a firm operates within a relevant range of debt to equity before it becomes penalized with a higher overall cost because of increased risk.

Figure 11–2 shows a theoretical cost-of-capital curve at three different points. As we move from time period t to time period $t + 2$, falling interest rates and rising stock prices cause a downward shift in K_a. This graph illuminates two basic points: (1) the firm wants to keep its debt-to-equity ratio between x and y at all times; and (2) the firm would rather finance its long-term needs at $K_a t + 2$ than at $K_a t$. Corporations are allowed some leeway in the money and capital markets, and it is not uncommon for the debt-to-equity ratio to fluctuate between x and y over a business cycle. The firm that is at point y has lost the flexibility of increasing its debt-to-equity ratio without incurring the penalty of higher capital costs.

Cost of Capital in the Capital Budgeting Decision

The current cost of capital for each source of funds is important when making a capital budgeting decision. Historical costs for past fundings may have very

---

[5]Market value rather than book value should be used—though in practice book value is commonly used.

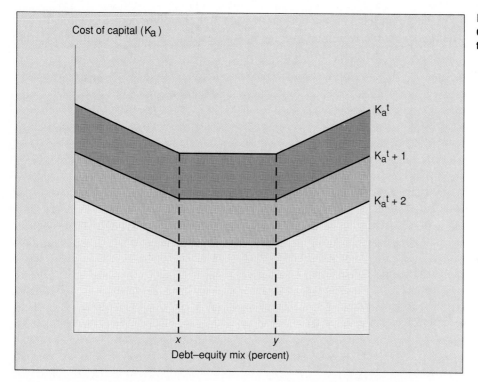

FIGURE 11–2
Cost of capital over time

little to do with current costs against which present returns must be measured. When raising new financial capital, a company will tap the various sources of financing over a reasonable time. Regardless of the particular source of funds the company is using for the purchase of an asset, the required rate of return or discount rate will be the weighted average cost of capital. As long as the company earns its cost of capital, the common stock value of the firm will be maintained, since stockholder expectations are being met. For example, assume the Baker Corporation was considering making an investment in eight projects with the returns and costs shown in Table 11–4.

Projects	Expected Returns	Cost ($ millions)
A. . . .	16.00%	$10
B. . . .	14.00	5
C. . . .	13.50	4
D. . . .	11.80	20
E. . . .	10.65	11
F. . . .	9.50	20
G. . . .	8.60	15
H. . . .	7.00	10
		$95 million

TABLE 11–4
Investment projects available to the Baker Corporation

These projects on the bottom of page 309 could be viewed graphically and merged with the weighted average cost of capital to make a capital budgeting decision, as indicated in Figure 11–3.

FIGURE 11–3
Cost of capital and investment projects for the Baker Corporation

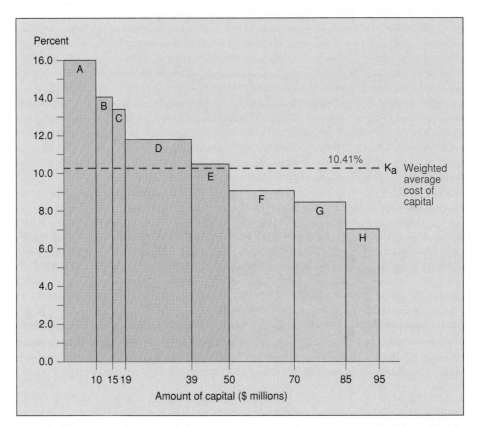

Notice that the Baker Corporation is facing $95 million in potential projects, but given the weighted average cost of capital of 10.41 percent it will choose only projects A through E, or $50 million in new investments. Selecting assets F, G, and H would probably reduce the market value of the common stock because these projects do not provide a return equal to the overall costs of raising funds. The use of the weighted average cost of capital assumes the Baker Corporation is in its optimum capital structure range.

The Marginal Cost of Capital

Nothing guarantees the Baker Corporation that its cost of capital will stay constant for as much money as it wants to raise even if a given capital structure is maintained. If a large amount of financing is desired, the market may demand a higher cost of capital for each amount of funds desired. The point is analogous to the fact that you may be able to go to your relatives and best friends and raise funds for an investment at 10 percent. After you have exhausted the lending or investing power of those closest to you, you will have to look to other sources and the marginal cost of your capital will go up.

As a background for this discussion, the cost of capital table for the Baker Corporation is reproduced again.

		Cost (aftertax)	Weights	Weighted Cost
Debt	K_d	7.05%	30%	2.12%
Preferred stock.	K_p	10.94	10	1.09
Common equity (retained earnings). . . .	K_e	12.00	60	7.20
Weighted average cost of capital	K_a			10.41%

We need to review the nature of the firm's capital structure to explain the concept of **marginal cost of capital** as it applies to the firm. Note the firm has 60 percent of the capital structure in the form of equity capital. The equity (ownership) capital is represented by retained earnings. It is assumed that 60 percent is the amount of equity capital the firm must maintain to keep a balance between fixed income securities and ownership interest. But equity capital in the form of retained earnings cannot grow indefinitely as the firm's capital needs expand. Retained earnings is limited to the amount of past and present earnings that can be redeployed into the investment projects of the firm. Let's assume the Baker Corporation has $23.40 million of retained earnings available for investment. Since retained earnings is to represent 60 percent of the capital structure, there is adequate retained earnings to support a capital structure of up to $39 million. More formally, we say:

$$X = \frac{\text{Retained earnings}}{\text{Percent of retained earnings in the capital structure}} \quad (11\text{--}8)$$

(Where X represents the size of the capital structure that retained earnings will support.)

$$X = \frac{\$23.40 \text{ million}}{.60}$$

$$= \$39 \text{ million}$$

After the first $39 million of capital is raised, retained earnings will no longer be available to provide the 60 percent equity position in the capital structure. Nevertheless lenders and investors will still require that 60 percent of the capital structure be in the form of common equity (ownership) capital. Because of this, *new* common stock will replace retained earnings to provide the 60 percent common equity component for the firm. That is, after $39 million, common equity capital will be in the form of new common stock rather than retained earnings.

In the left-hand portion of Table 11–5, we see the original cost of capital that we have been discussing throughout the chapter. This applies up to $39 million. After $39 million the concept of marginal cost of capital becomes important. The cost of capital goes up as shown on the right-hand portion of the table.

TABLE 11–5   Cost of capital for different amounts of financing

	First $39 Million				Next $11 Million			
		A/T Cost	Wts.	Weighted Cost			A/T Cost	Wts.	Weighted Cost
Debt	K_d	7.05%	.30	2.12%	Debt.	K_d	7.05%	.30	2.12%
Preferred	K_p	10.94	.10	1.09	Preferred	K_p	10.94	.10	1.09
Common equity*	K_e	12.00	.60	7.20	Common equity†	K_n	12.60	.60	7.56
				$K_a = 10.41\%$					$K_{mc} = 10.77\%$

*Retained earnings.   †New common stock.

K_{mc}, in the bottom right-hand portion of the table, represents the *marginal* cost of capital, and it is 10.77 percent after $39 million. The cost of capital has increased after $39 million because common equity is now in the form of new common stock rather than retained earnings. The aftertax (A/T) cost of new common stock is slightly more expensive than retained earnings because of flotation costs (F). The equation for the cost of new common stock was shown earlier in the chapter as Formula 11–7. For the example we are using:

$$K_n = \frac{D_1}{P_0 - F} + g = \frac{\$2}{\$40 - \$4} + 7\%$$

$$= \frac{\$2}{\$36} + 7\% = 5.6\% + 7\% = 12.6\%$$

The flotation cost (F) is $4 and the cost of new common stock is 12.60 percent.

This is higher than the 12 percent cost of retained earnings that we have been using and causes the increase in the marginal cost of capital.

To carry the example a bit further, we will assume the cost of debt of 7.05 percent applies to the first $15 million of debt the firm raises. After that the aftertax cost of debt will rise to 8.60 percent. Since debt represents 30 percent of the capital structure for the Baker Corporation, the cheaper form of debt can be used to support the capital structure up to $50 million. We derive the $50 million by using Formula 11–9.

$$Z = \frac{\text{Amount of lower-cost debt}}{\text{Percent of debt in the capital structure}} \tag{11–9}$$

(Where Z represents the size of the capital structure in which lower-cost debt can be utilized.)

$$Z = \frac{\$15 \text{ million}}{.30}$$

$$= \$50 \text{ million}$$

After the first $50 million of capital is raised, lower-cost debt will no longer be available to provide 30 percent of the capital structure. After $50 million in total financing, the aftertax cost of debt will go up to the previously specified 8.60 percent. The marginal cost of capital for over $50 million in financing is shown in Table 11–6.

Over $50 million				
		Cost (aftertax)	Weights	Weighted Cost
Debt (higher cost)	K_d	8.60%	.30	2.58%
Preferred stock	K_p	10.94	.10	1.09
Common equity (new common stock) . . .	K_n	12.60	.60	7.56
				$K_{mc} = 11.23\%$

TABLE 11–6
Cost of capital for increasing amounts of financing

The change in the cost of debt gives way to a new marginal cost of capital (K_{mc}) of 11.23 percent after $50 million of financing. You should observe that the capital structure with over $50 million of financing reflects not only the change in the cost of debt, but also the continued exclusive use of new common stock to represent common equity capital. This change occurred at $39 million, but must be carried on indefinitely as the capital structure expands.

We could carry on this process by next indicating a change in the cost of preferred stock, or continually increasing the cost of debt or new common stock as more capital is used. For now it is sufficient that you merely observe the basic process. To summarize, we have said the Baker Corporation has a basic weighted average cost of capital of 10.41 percent. This value was developed throughout the chapter and was originally presented in Table 11–1. However, as the firm began to substantially expand its capital structure, the weighted average cost of capital increased. This gave way to the concept of marginal cost of capital. The first increase or break point was at $39 million in which the marginal cost of capital went up to 10.77 percent as a result of replacing retained earnings with new common stock. The second increase or break point was at $50 million in which the marginal cost of capital increased to 11.23 percent as a result of the utilization of more expensive debt. The changes are summarized below.

Amount of Financing	Marginal Cost of Capital
0–$39 million	10.41%
$39–50 million	10.77%
Over $50 million . . .	11.23%

In previously presented Figure 11–3 we showed returns from investments A through H. In Figure 11–4 we reproduce the returns originally shown in Figure 11–3 but include the concept of marginal cost of capital. Observe the increasing cost of capital (dotted lines) in relationship to the decreasing returns (straight lines).

FIGURE 11–4

Marginal cost of capital and Baker Corporation projects

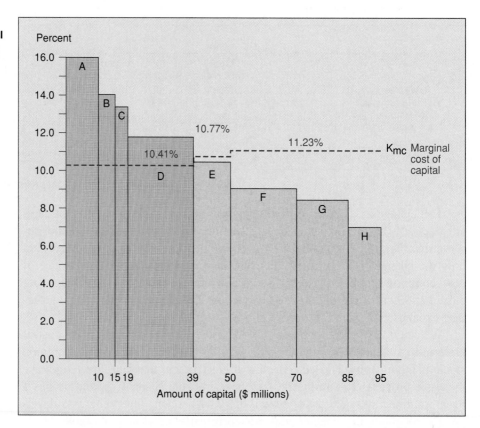

In Figure 11–3 the Baker Corporation was justified in choosing projects A through E for a capital expenditure of $50 million. This is no longer the case in Figure 11–4. Because of the increasing marginal cost of capital, the returns exceed the cost of capital only up to $39 million and now only projects A through D are acceptable.

Although the concept of marginal cost of capital is very important, for most of our capital budgeting decisions in the next chapter, we will assume we are operating on the initial flat part of the marginal cost of capital curve in Figure 11–4, and most of our decisions can be made based on the initial weighted average cost of capital.

Summary

The cost of capital for the firm is determined by computing the costs of various sources of financing and weighting them in proportion to their representation in the capital structure. The cost of each component in the capital structure is closely associated with the valuation of that source. For debt and preferred stock, the cost is directly related to the current yield, with debt adjusted downward to reflect the tax deductible nature of interest.

For common stock, the cost of retained earnings (K_e) is the current dividend yield on the security plus an anticipated rate of growth for the future. Minor adjustments are made to the formula to determine the cost of new common stock. A summary of the Baker Corporation's capital costs is presented in Table 11–7.

TABLE 11–7   **Cost of components in the capital structure**

1. Cost of debt	$K_d = \text{Yield} (1 - T) = 7.05\%$	Yield = 10.84% T = Corporate tax rate, 35%
2. Cost of preferred stock	$K_p = \dfrac{D_p}{P_p - F} = 10.94\%$	D_p = Preferred dividend, \$10.50 P_p = Price of preferred stock, \$100 F = Flotation costs, \$4
3. Cost of common equity (retained earnings)	$K_e = \dfrac{D_1}{P_0} + g = 12\%$	D_1 = First year common dividend, \$2 P_0 = Price of common stock, \$40 g = Growth rate, 7%
4. Cost of new common stock . .	$K_n = \dfrac{D_1}{P_0 - F} + g = 12.60\%$	Same as above, with F = flotation costs, \$4

We weigh the elements in the capital structure in accordance with our desire to achieve a minimum overall cost. While debt is usually the "cheapest" form of financing, excessive debt use may increase the financial risk of the firm and drive up the costs of all sources of financing. The wise financial manager attempts to ascertain what debt component will result in the lowest overall cost of capital. Once this has been determined, the weighted average cost of capital is the discount rate we use in present-valuing future flows to ensure we are earning at least the cost of financing.

The marginal cost of capital is also introduced to explain what happens to a company's cost of capital as it tries to finance a large amount of funds. First the company will use up retained earnings, and the cost of financing will rise as higher-cost new common stock is substituted for retained earnings in order to maintain the optimum capital structure with the appropriate debt-to-equity ratio. Larger amounts of financial capital can also cause the individual means of financing to rise by raising interest rates or by depressing the price of the stock because more is sold than the market wants to absorb.

Review of Formulas

1. K_d (cost of debt) $= Y(1 - T)$ (11–2)
   Y is yield
   T is corporate tax rate

2. K_p (cost of preferred stock) $= \dfrac{D_p}{P_p - F}$ (11–3)
   D_p is the annual dividend on preferred stock
   P_p is the price of preferred stock
   F is flotation, or selling, cost

3. K_e (cost of common equity) $= \dfrac{D_1}{P_0} + g$ (11–4)
   D_1 is dividend at the end of the first year (or period)
   P_0 is the price of the stock today
   g is growth rate in dividends

4. K_j (required return on common stock) $= R_f + \beta(K_m - R_f)$ (11–5)
   R_f is risk-free rate of return
   β is beta coefficient
   K_m is return in the market as measured by the appropriate index

5. K_e (cost of common equity in the form of retained earnings)   (11–6)
   $= \dfrac{D_1}{P_0} + g$
   D_1 is dividend at the end of the first year (or period)
   P_0 is price of the stock today
   g is growth rate in dividends

6. K_n (cost of new common stock) $= \dfrac{D_1}{P_0 - F} + g$ (11–7)
   Same as above with:
   F as flotation, or selling, cost

7. X (size of capital structure that retained earnings will support) $= \dfrac{\text{Retained earnings}}{\text{\% of retained earnings in the capital structure}}$ (11–8)

8. Z (size of capital structure that lower-cost debt will support) $= \dfrac{\text{Amount of lower-cost debt}}{\text{\% of debt in the capital structure}}$ (11–9)

List of Terms

cost of capital 296
flotation costs 300
dividend valuation model 301
capital asset pricing model
  (CAPM) 302
common stock equity 303

optimum capital structure 305
weighted average cost of
  capital 306
financial capital 308
marginal cost of capital 311

Discussion Questions

1. Why do we use the overall cost of capital for investment decisions even when only one source of capital will be used (e.g., debt)?

2. How does the cost of a source of capital relate to the valuation concepts presented in Chapter 10?

3. In computing the cost of capital, do we use the historical costs of existing debt and equity or the current costs as determined in the market? Why?

4. Why is the cost of debt less than the cost of preferred stock if both securities are priced to yield 10 percent in the market?

5. What are the two sources of equity (ownership) capital for the firm?

6. Explain why retained earnings has an opportunity cost associated with it?

7. Why is the cost of retained earnings the equivalent of the firm's own required rate of return on common stock (K_e)?

8. Why is the cost of new common stock (K_n) higher than the cost of retained earnings (K_e)?

9. How are the weights determined to arrive at the optimal weighted average cost of capital?

10. Explain the traditional, U-shaped approach to the cost of capital.

11. Identify other variables (ratios) besides the debt-to-equity ratio that you think will influence a company's cost of capital. You may wish to refer to Chapter 3.

12. It has often been said that if the company can't earn a rate of return greater than the cost of capital it should not make investments. Explain.

13. What effect would inflation have on a company's cost of capital? (Hint: Think about how inflation influences interest rates, stock prices, corporate profits, and growth.)

14. What is the concept of marginal cost of capital?

Problems

Aftertax cost of debt

1. Sullivan Cement Company can issue debt yielding 13 percent. The company is paying a 36 percent tax rate. What is the aftertax cost of debt?

Aftertax cost of debt

2. Calculate the aftertax cost of debt under each of the following conditions.

	Yield	Corporate Tax Rate
a.	8.0%	18%
b.	12.0%	34%
c.	10.6%	15%

Approximate yield to maturity and cost of debt

3. Addison Glass Company has a $1,000 par value bond outstanding with 25 years to maturity. The bond carries an annual interest payment of $88 and is currently selling for $925. Addison is in a 25 percent tax bracket. The firm wishes to know what the aftertax cost of a new bond issue is likely to be. The yield to maturity on the new issue will be the same as the yield to maturity on the old issue because the risk and maturity date will be similar.

   a. Compute the approximate yield to maturity (Formula 11–1) on the old issue and use this as the yield for the new issue.

   b. Make the appropriate tax adjustment to determine the aftertax cost of debt.

Changing rates and cost of debt

4. For Addison Glass Company, described in problem 3, assume the yield on the bonds goes up by one percentage point and that the tax rate is now 40 percent.

   a. What is the new aftertax cost of debt?

   b. Has the aftertax cost of debt gone up or down from problem 3? Explain why.

Real world example and cost of debt

5. Louisville Gas and Electric is planning to issue debt that will mature in 1998. In many respects the issue is similar to currently outstanding debt of the corporation. Using Table 11–2,

   a. Identify the yield to maturity on similarly outstanding debt for the firm, in terms of maturity.

   b. Assume that because the new debt will be issued at par, the required yield to maturity will be 0.15 percent higher than the value determined in part *a.* Add this factor to the answer in *a.* (New issues at par sometimes require a slightly higher yield than old issues that are trading below par. There is less leverage and fewer tax advantages.)

   c. If the firm is in a 30 percent tax bracket, what is the aftertax cost of debt?

6. Burger Queen can sell preferred stock for $70 with an estimated flotation cost of $2.50. The preferred stock is anticipated to pay $6 per share in dividends.

   a. Compute the cost of preferred stock for Burger Queen.

   b. Do we need to make a tax adjustment for the issuing firm?

7. Wallace Container Company issued $100 par value preferred stock 12 years ago. The stock provided a 9 percent yield at the time of issue. The preferred stock is now selling for $72. What is the current yield or cost of preferred stock? (Disregard flotation costs.)

8. The treasurer of BioScience, Inc., is asked to compute the cost of fixed income securities for her corporation. Even before making the calculations, she assumes the aftertax cost of debt is at least 2 percent less than that for preferred stock. Based on the following facts, is she correct?

   Debt can be issued at a yield of 11 percent, and the corporate tax rate is 30 percent. Preferred stock will be priced at $50, and pays a dividend of $4.80. The flotation cost on the preferred stock is $2.10.

9. Murray Motor Company wants you to calculate its cost of common stock. During the next 12 months, the company expects to pay dividends (D_1) of $2.50 per share, and the current price of its common stock is $50 per share. The expected growth rate is 8 percent.

   a. Compute the cost of retained earnings (K_e). Use Formula 11–6.

   b. If a $3 flotation cost is involved, compute the cost of new common stock (K_n). Use Formula 11–7.

10. Compute K_e and K_n under the following circumstances:

    a. $D_1 = \$4.20$, $P_0 = \$55$, $g = 5\%$, $F = \$3.80$

    b. $D_1 = \$0.40$, $P_0 = \$15$, $g = 8\%$, $F = \$1$.

    c. E_1 (earnings at the end of period one) $= \$8$, payout ratio equals 25 percent, $P_0 = \$32$, $g = 5\%$, $F = \$2$.

    d. D_0 (dividend at the beginning of the first period) $= \$3$, growth rate for dividends and earnings $(g) = 9\%$, $P_0 = \$60$, $F = \$3.50$.

11. Business has been good for Keystone Control Systems, as indicated by the four-year growth in earnings per share. The earnings have grown from $1.00 to $1.63.

    a. Use Appendix A at the back of the text to determine the compound annual rate of growth in earnings ($n = 4$).

    b. Based on the growth rate determined in part *a*, project earnings for next year (E_1). Round to two places to the right of the decimal point.

    c. Assume the dividend payout ratio is 40 percent. Compute D_1. Round to two places to the right of the decimal point.

d. The current price of the stock is $50. Using the growth rate (g) from part *a* and D_1 from part *c*, compute K_e.

e. If the flotation cost is $3.75, compute the cost of new common stock (K_n).

Weighted average cost of capital

12. Global Technology's capital structure is as follows:

Debt.	35%
Preferred stock	15
Common equity	50

The aftertax cost of debt is 6.5 percent; the cost of preferred stock is 10 percent; and the cost of common equity (in the form of retained earnings) is 13.5 percent.

Calculate Global Technology's weighted average cost of capital in a manner similar to Table 11–1.

Weighted average cost of capital

13. As an alternative to the capital structure shown in problem 12 for Global Technology, an outside consultant has suggested the following modifications.

Debt.	60%
Preferred stock	5
Common equity	35

Under this new and more debt-oriented arrangement, the aftertax cost of debt is 8.8 percent, the cost of preferred stock is 11 percent, and the cost of common equity (in the form of retained earnings) is 15.6 percent.

Recalculate Global's weighted average cost of capital. Which plan is optimal in terms of minimizing the weighted average cost of capital?

Weighted average cost of capital

14. Given the following information, calculate the weighted average cost of capital for Glamour Girl Cosmetics. Line up the calculations in the order shown in Table 11–1.

Percent of capital structure:	
Debt	40%
Preferred stock	10
Common equity	50
Additional information:	
Bond coupon rate	12%
Bond yield	10%
Dividend, expected common . .	$3.00
Dividend, preferred	$9.20
Price, common	$60.00
Price, preferred.	$99.00
Flotation cost, preferred	$4.00
Corporate growth rate	9%
Corporate tax rate	30%

15. Given the following information, calculate the weighted average cost of capital for Digital Processing, Inc. Line up the calculations in the order shown in Table 11–1.

Weighted average cost of capital

Percent of capital structure:	
Preferred stock.	15%
Common equity	40
Debt	45
Additional information:	
Corporate tax rate	34%
Dividend, preferred.	$8.50
Dividend expected, common . .	$2.50
Price, preferred.	$105.00
Growth rate	7%
Bond yield	9.5%
Flotation cost, preferred	$3.60
Price, common	$75.00

16. Carr Auto Parts is trying to calculate its cost of capital for use in a capital budgeting decision. Mr. Horn, the vice-president of finance, has given you the following information and has asked you to compute the weighted average cost of capital.

Changes in costs and weighted average cost of capital

The company currently has outstanding a bond with a 12 percent coupon rate and a convertible bond with an 8.1 percent rate. The firm has been informed by its investment banker, Axle, Wiell, and Axle, that bonds of equal risk and credit rating are now selling to yield 14 percent. The common stock has a price of $30 and an expected dividend (D_1) of $1.30 per share. The firm's historical growth rate of earnings and dividends per share has been 15.5 percent, but security analysts on Wall Street expect this growth to slow to 12 percent in the future. The preferred stock is selling at $60 per share and carries a dividend of $6.80 per share. The corporate tax rate is 30 percent. The flotation costs are 3 percent of the selling price for preferred stock.

The optimum capital structure for the firm seems to be 45 percent debt, 5 percent preferred stock, and 55 percent common equity in the form of retained earnings.

Compute the cost of capital for the individual components in the capital structure, and then calculate the weighted average cost of capital (similar to Table 11–1).

17. First Tennessee Utility Company faces increasing needs for capital. Fortunately it has an Aa2 credit rating. The corporate tax rate is 36 percent. First Tennessee's treasurer is trying to determine the corporation's current weighted average cost of capital to assess the profitability of capital budgeting projects. Historically the corporation's earnings and dividends per share have increased at about a 6 percent annual rate.

Impact of credit ratings on cost of capital

First Tennessee's common stock is selling at $60 per share, and the company will pay a $4.80 per share dividend (D_1). The company's $100 preferred stock has been yielding 9 percent in the current market. Flotation costs for the company have been estimated by its investment banker to be $1.50 for preferred stock. The company's optimum capital structure is 40 percent debt, 10 percent preferred stock, and 50 percent common equity in the form of retained earnings. Refer to the table below on bond issues for comparative yields on bonds of equal risks to First Tennessee. Compute the answer to questions *a*, *b*, *c*, and *d* from the information given.

Data on Bond Issues

Issue	Moody's Rating	Price	Yield to Maturity
Utilities:			
Balt. G&E 8-3/8's 2006.	Aa1	$975.25	8.60%
New York Tel. Co. 7½s 2009	Aa2	850.75	9.11
Miss. Pow. 9.62s 2008	A1	960.50	9.67
Industrials:			
IBM 9-3/8's 2004	Aaa	$1,050.50	8.50%
May Department St. 7.95s 2002. . . .	Aa3	940.00	11.81
General Mills 9-3/8s 2009	A2	1,030.75	9.05

a. Cost of debt, K_d. (Use the table above—relate to the utility bond credit rating for yield.)

b. Cost of preferred stock, K_p.

c. Cost of common equity in the form of retained earnings, K_e.

d. Weighted average cost of capital.

Marginal cost of capital

18. The Nolan Corporation finds that it is necessary to determine its marginal cost of capital. Nolan's current capital structure calls for 45 percent debt, 15 percent preferred stock, and 40 percent common equity. Initially common equity will be in the form of retained earnings (K_e) and then new common stock (K_n). The costs of the various sources of financing are as follows: debt, 5.6 percent; preferred stock, 9 percent; retained earnings, 12 percent; and new common stock, 13.2 percent.

a. What is the initial weighted average cost of capital? (Include debt, preferred stock, and common equity in the form of retained earnings, K_e.)

b. If the firm has $12 million in retained earnings, at what size capital structure will the firm run out of retained earnings?

c. What will the marginal cost of capital be immediately after that point? (Equity will remain at 40 percent of the capital structure, but will all be in the form of new common stock, K_n.)

d. The 5.6 percent cost of debt referred to above applies only to the first $18 million of debt. After that the cost of debt will be

7.2 percent. At what size capital structure will there be a change in the cost of debt?

e. What will the marginal cost of capital be immediately after that point? (Consider the facts in both parts *c* and *d*.)

19. The Evans Corporation finds it is necessary to determine its marginal cost of capital. Evans' current capital structure calls for 45 percent debt, 15 percent preferred stock, and 40 percent common equity. Initially, common equity will be in the form of retained earnings (K_e) and then new common stock (K_n). The costs of the various sources of financing are as follows: debt, 6.2 percent; preferred stock, 9.4 percent; retained earnings, 12.0 percent; and new common stock, 13.4 percent.

Marginal cost of capital

a. What is the initial weighted average cost of capital? (Include debt, preferred stock, and common equity in the form of retained earnings, K_e.)

b. If the firm has $20 million in retained earnings, at what size capital structure will the firm run out of retained earnings?

c. What will the marginal cost of capital be immediately after that point? (Equity will remain at 40 percent of the capital structure, but will all be in the form of new common stock, K_n.)

d. The 6.2 percent cost of debt referred to above applies only to the first $36 million of debt. After that the cost of debt will be 7.8 percent. At what size capital structure will there be a change in the cost of debt?

e. What will the marginal cost of capital be immediately after that point? (Consider the facts in both parts *c* and *d*.)

COMPREHENSIVE PROBLEMS

Medical Research Corporation is expanding its research and production capacity to introduce a new line of products. Current plans call for the expenditure of $100 million on four projects of equal size ($25 million), but different returns. Project A is in blood clotting proteins and has an expected return of 18 percent. Project B relates to a hepatitis vaccine and carries a potential return of 14 percent. Project C, dealing with a cardiovascular compound, is expected to earn 11.8 percent, and Project D, an investment in orthopedic implants, is expected to show a 10.9 percent return.

Medical Research Corporation
(marginal cost of capital and investment returns)

The firm has $15 million in retained earnings. After a capital structure with $15 million in retained earnings is reached (in which retained earnings represent 60 percent of the financing), all additional equity financing must come in the form of new common stock.

Common stock is selling for $25 per share and underwriting costs are estimated at $3 if new shares are issued. Dividends for the next year will be

$.90 per share (D₁), and earnings and dividends have grown consistently at 11 percent per year.

The yield on comparative bonds has been hovering at 11 percent. The investment banker believes the first $20 million of bonds could be sold to yield 11 percent while additional debt might require a 2 percent premium and be marketed to yield 13 percent. The corporate tax rate is 30 percent. Debt represents 40 percent of the capital structure.

    a. Based on the two sources of financing, what is the initial weighted average cost of capital? (Use K_d and K_e.)

    b. At what size capital structure will the firm run out of retained earnings?

    c. What will the marginal cost of capital be immediately after that point?

    d. At what size capital structure will there be a change in the cost of debt?

    e. What will the marginal cost of capital be immediately after that point?

    f. Based on the information about potential returns on investments in the first paragraph and information on marginal cost of capital (in parts *a*, *c*, and *e*), how large a capital investment budget should the firm use?

    g. Graph the answer determined in part *f.*

Masco Oil and Gas Co. (cost of capital with changing financial needs)
Masco Oil and Gas Company is a very large company with common stock listed on the New York Stock Exchange and bonds traded over the counter. As of the current balance sheet, it has three bond issues outstanding:

$150 million of 10 percent series . . . 2007
$50 million of 7 percent series 2001
$75 million of 5 percent series 1997

The vice-president of finance is planning to sell $75 million of bonds next year to replace the debt due to expire in 1997. Present market yields on similar Baa rated bonds are 12.1 percent. Masco also has $90 million of 7.5 percent noncallable preferred stock outstanding, and it has no intentions of selling any more preferred stock in the future. The preferred stock is currently priced at $80 per share, and its dividend per share is $7.80.

The company has had very volatile earnings, but its dividends per share have had a very stable growth rate of 8 percent and this will continue. The expected dividend (D₁) is $1.90 per share, and the common stock is selling for $40 per share. The company's investment banker has quoted the following flotation costs to Masco: $2.50 per share for preferred stock and $2.20 per share for common stock.

On the advice of its investment banker, Masco has kept its debt at 50 percent of assets and its equity at 50 percent. Masco sees no need to sell either common or preferred stock in the foreseeable future as it generated enough internal funds for its investment needs when these funds are combined with debt financing. Masco's corporate tax rate is 40 percent.

Compute the cost of capital for the following:

a. Bond (debt) (K_d).

b. Preferred stock (K_p).

c. Common equity in the form of retained earnings (K_e).

d. New common stock (K_n).

e. Weighted average cost of capital.

Selected References

Billingsley, Randall S., Robert E. Lamy, M. Wayne Marr, and Rodney G. Thompson. "Split Ratings and Bond Reoffering Yields." *Financial Management* 14 (Summer 1985), pp. 59–66.

————, **Robert E. Lamy, and Rodney G. Thompson.** "The Choice among Debt, Equity, and Convertible Bonds." *Journal of Financial Research* 11 (Spring 1988), pp. 43–55.

Conine, Thomas E., Jr., and Maury Tamarkin. "Divisional Cost of Capital Estimation: Adjusting for Leverage." *Financial Management* 14 (Spring 1986), pp. 54–58.

Dammon, Robert M., and Lemma W. Senbet. "The Effect of Taxes and Depreciation on Corporate Investment and Financial Leverage." *Journal of Finance* 43 (June 1988), pp. 357–73.

Durand, David. *Costs of Debt and Equity Funds for Business: Trends and Problems of Measurement.* Conference on Research in Business Finance. New York: National Bureau of Economic Research, New York, 1952.

————. "Afterthoughts on a Controversy with MM, Plus New Thoughts on Growth and the Cost of Capital." *Financial Management* 18 (Summer 1989), pp. 12–18.

Easterwood, John C., and Palani-Rajan Kadapakkam. "The Role of Private and Public Debt in Corporate Capital Structure." *Financial Management* 20 (Autumn 1991), pp. 49–57.

Frankel, Jeffrey A. "The Japanese Cost of Finance: A Survey." *Financial Management* 20 (Spring 1991), pp. 95–127.

Grosh, Dilik K. "Optimum Capital Restructure Redefined." *Financial Review* 27 (August 1992), pp. 411–29.

Haugen, Robert A., and Lemma W. Senbet. "Bankruptcy and Agency Costs: Their Significance to the Theory of Optimal Capital Structure." *Journal of Financial & Quantitative Analysis* 23 (March 1988), pp. 27–38.

Howe, Keith M., and James H. Patterson. "Capital Investment Decisions under Economies of Scale in Flotation Costs." *Financial Management* 14 (Autumn 1985), pp. 61–69.

Huffman, Gregory W., and Kenneth J. Singleton. "Adjustment Costs and Capital Asset Pricing/Discussion." *Journal of Finance* 40 (July 1985), pp. 691–709.

Miller, Merton H. "Debt and Taxes." *Journal of Finance* 32 (May 1977), pp. 261–73.

Modigliani, Franco, and Merton H. Miller. "The Cost of Capital, Corporation Finance and the Theory of Investment." *American Economic Review* 48 (June 1958), pp. 261–96.

————. "Taxes and the Cost of Capital: A Correction." *American Economic Review* 53 (June 1963), pp. 433–43.

Pinegar, J. Michael, and Lisa Wilbricht. "What Managers Think of Capital Structure Theory: A Survey." *Financial Management* 18 (Winter 1989), pp. 82–91.

Roll, Richard. "A Critique of the Asset Pricing Theory's Test. Part 1: On the Past and Potential Testability of the Theory." *Journal of Financial Economics* 4 (March 1977), pp. 129–76.

————. "Ambiguity When Performance Is Measured by the Securities Market Line." *Journal of Finance* 33 (September 1978), pp. 1051–70.

Sharpe, William F. "Capital Asset Prices: A Theory of Market Equilibrium under Conditions of Risk." *Journal of Finance* 19 (September 1964), pp. 425–42.

Siegel, Jeremy J. "The Application of the DCF Methodology for Determining the Costs of Equity Capital." *Financial Management* 14 (Spring 1985), pp. 46–53.

Taggart, Robert A., Jr. "Consistent Valuation and Cost of Capital Expressions with Corporate and Personal Taxes." *Financial Management* 21 (Autumn 1991), pp. 8–20.

Titman, Sheridan, and Roberto Wessels. "The Determinants of Capital Structure Choice." *Journal of Finance* 43 (March 1988), pp. 1–19.

Weaver, Samuel C. "Divisional Hurdle Rates and the Cost of Capital." *Financial Management* 18 (Spring 1989), pp. 18–25.

Zhu, Yu, and Irwin Friend. "The Effects of Different Taxes on Risky and Risk-Free Investment and on the Cost of Capital." *Journal of Finance* 41 (March 1986), pp. 53–66.

APPENDIX 11A   Cost of Capital and the Capital Asset Pricing Model (Optional)

The Capital Asset Pricing Model

The **capital asset pricing model** (CAPM) relates the risk-return trade-offs of individual assets to market returns. Common stock returns over time have generally been used to test this model since stock prices are widely available and efficiently priced, as are market indexes of stock performance. In theory the CAPM encompasses all assets, but in practice it is difficult to measure returns on all types of assets or to find an all-encompassing market index. For our purposes we will use common stock returns to explain the model and occasionally we will generalize to other assets.

The basic form of the CAPM is a linear relationship between returns on individual stocks and stock market returns over time. By using least squares regression analysis, the return on an individual stock, K_j, is expressed in Formula 11A–1.

$$K_j = \alpha + \beta K_m + e \qquad (11A–1)$$

where

K_j = Return on individual common stock of a company

α = Alpha, the intercept on the y-axis

β = Beta, the coefficient

K_m = Return on the stock market (an index of stock returns is used, usually the Standard & Poor's 500 Index)

e = Error term of the regression equation

As indicated in Table 11A–1 and Figure 11A–1, this equation uses historical data to generate the beta coefficient (β), a measurement of the return performance of a given stock versus the return performance of the market. Assume that we want to calculate a beta for Parts Associates, Inc. (PAI), and that we have the performance data for that company and the market shown in Table 11A–1. The relationship between PAI and the market appears graphically in Figure 11A–1.

The alpha term in Figure 11A–1 of 2.8 percent is the *y* intercept of the linear regression. It is the expected return on PAI stock if returns on the market

TABLE 11A-1
Performance of PAI and the market

Year	Rate of Return on Stock	
	PAI	**Market**
1.	12.0%	10.0%
2.	16.0	18.0
3.	20.0	16.0
4.	16.0	10.0
5.	6.0	8.0
Mean return	14.0%	12.4%
Standard deviation. . . .	4.73%	3.87%

FIGURE 11A-1
Linear regression of returns between PAI and the market

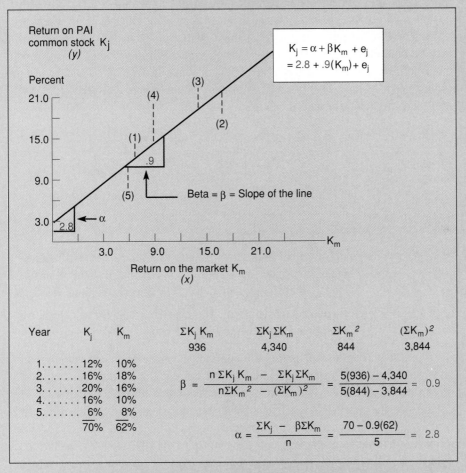

Return on PAI common stock K_j *(y)*

$$K_j = \alpha + \beta K_m + e_j$$
$$= 2.8 + .9(K_m) + e_j$$

Beta = β = Slope of the line

Return on the market K_m *(x)*

Year	K_j	K_m	$\Sigma K_j K_m$	$\Sigma K_j \Sigma K_m$	$\Sigma K_m{}^2$	$(\Sigma K_m)^2$
			936	4,340	844	3,844
1.	12%	10%				
2.	16%	18%				
3.	20%	16%				
4.	16%	10%				
5.	6%	8%				
	70%	62%				

$$\beta = \frac{n\,\Sigma K_j K_m - \Sigma K_j \Sigma K_m}{n\Sigma K_m{}^2 - (\Sigma K_m)^2} = \frac{5(936) - 4,340}{5(844) - 3,844} = 0.9$$

$$\alpha = \frac{\Sigma K_j - \beta\Sigma K_m}{n} = \frac{70 - 0.9(62)}{5} = 2.8$$

are zero. However, if the returns on the market are expected to approximate the historical rate of 12.4 percent, the expected return on PAI would be $K_j = 2.8 + 0.9(12.4) = 14.0$ percent. This maintains the historical relationship. If the returns on the market are expected to rise to 18 percent next year, expected return on PAI would be $K_j = 2.8 + 0.9(18.0) = 19$ percent.

Notice that we are talking in terms of expectations. The CAPM is an expectational (ex ante) model, and there is no guarantee historical data will reoccur. One area of empirical testing involves the stability and predictability of the beta coefficient based on historical data. Research has indicated that betas are more useful in a portfolio context (for groupings of stocks) because the betas of individual stocks are less stable from period to period than portfolio betas. In addition, research indicates betas of individual common stocks have the tendency to approach 1.0 over time.

The Security Market Line

The capital asset pricing model evolved from Formula 11A–1 into a **market risk premium** model where the basic assumption is that, for investors to take more risk, they must be compensated by larger expected returns. Investors should also not accept returns that are less than they can get from a riskless asset. For CAPM purposes it is assumed that short-term U.S. Treasury bills may be considered a riskless asset.[1] When viewed in this context, an investor must achieve an extra return above that obtainable from a Treasury bill in order to induce the assumption of more risk. This brings us to the more common and theoretically useful model:

$$K_j = R_f + \beta(K_m - R_f) \qquad (11A-2)$$

where

$$R_f = \text{Risk-free rate of return}$$

$$\beta = \text{Beta coefficient from Formula 11A–1}$$

$$K_m = \text{Return on the market index}$$

$K_m - R_f =$ Premium or excess return of the market versus the risk-free rate (since the market is riskier than R_f, the assumption is that the expected K_m will be greater than R_f)

$\beta(K_m - R_f) =$ Expected return above the risk-free rate for the stock of Company j, given the level of risk

The model centers on "beta," the coefficient of the premium demanded by an investor to invest in an individual stock. For each individual security, **beta** measures the sensitivity (volatility) of the security's return to the market. By definition, the market has a beta of 1.0, so that if an individual company's beta is 1.0, it can expect to have returns as volatile as the market and total returns equal to the market. A company with a beta of 2.0 would be twice as volatile as the market and would be expected to generate more returns, whereas a company with a beta of 0.5 would be half as volatile as the market.

The term $(K_m - R_f)$ indicates common stock is expected to generate a rate of return higher than the return on a U.S. Treasury bill. This makes sense since common stock has more risk. Research by Roger Ibbottson shows that this risk premium over the last 65 years is close to 6.5 percent on average

---

[1] A number of studies have also indicated that longer-term government securities may appropriately represent R_f (the risk-free rate).

but exhibits a wide standard deviation.[2] In the actual application of the CAPM to cost of capital, companies often will use this historical risk premium in their calculations. In our example we use 6.5 percent to represent the expected $(K_m - R_f)$.

For example, assuming the risk-free rate is 5.5 percent and the market risk premium $(K_m - R_f)$ is 6.5 percent, the following returns would occur with betas of 2.0, 1.0, and 0.5:

$$K_2 = 5.5\% + 2.0(6.5\%) = 5.5\% + 13.0\% = 18.5\%$$

$$K_1 = 5.5\% + 1.0(6.5\%) = 5.5\% + 6.5\% = 12.0\%$$

$$K_{.5} = 5.5\% + 0.5(6.5\%) = 5.5\% + 3.25\% = 8.75\%$$

The beta term measures the riskiness of an investment relative to the market. To outperform the market, one would have to assume more risk by selecting assets with betas greater than 1.0. Another way of looking at the risk-return trade-off would be that if less risk than the market is desired, an investor would choose assets with a beta of less than 1.0. Beta is a good measure of a stock's risk when the stock is combined into a portfolio, and therefore it has some bearing on the assets that a company acquires for its portfolio of real capital.

In Figure 11A–1, individual stock returns were compared to market returns and the beta from Formula 11A–1 was shown. From Formula 11A–2, the risk-premium model, a generalized risk-return graph called the **security market line** (SML) can be constructed that identifies the risk-return trade-off of any common stock (asset) relative to the company's beta. This is shown in Figure 11A–2.

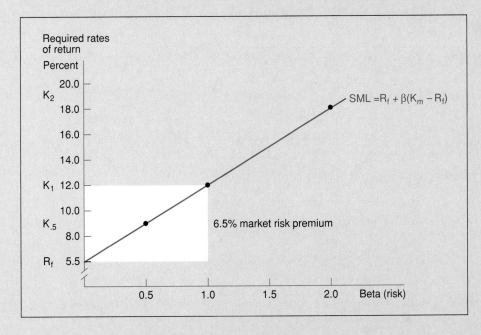

FIGURE 11A–2
The security market line (SML)

___

[2]Ibbotson Associates, *Stocks, Bonds, Bills and Inflation: 1992 Yearbook* (Chicago: Ibbotson Associates and Capital Market Research Center, 1992).

The required return for all securities can be expressed as the risk-free rate plus a premium for risk. Thus we see that a stock with a beta of 1.0 would have a risk premium of 6.5 percent added to the risk-free rate of 5.5 percent to provide a required return of 12 percent. Since a beta of 1.0 implies risk equal to the stock market, the return is also at the overall market rate. If the beta is 2.0, twice the market risk premium of 6.5 percent must be earned and we add 13 percent to the risk-free rate of 5.5 percent to determine the required return of 18.5 percent. For a beta of 0.5, the required return is 8.75 percent.

Cost of Capital Considerations

When calculating the cost of capital for common stock, remember that K_e is equal to the expected total return from the dividend yield and capital gains.

$$K_e = \frac{D_1}{P_0} + g$$

K_e is the return required by investors based on expectations of future dividends and growth. The SML provides the same information, but in a market-related risk-return model. As required returns rise, prices must fall to adjust to the new equilibrium return level, and as required returns fall, prices rise. Stock markets are generally efficient, and when stock prices are in equilibrium, the K_e derived from the dividend model will be equal to K_j derived from the SML.

The SML helps us to identify several circumstances that can cause the cost of capital to change. Figure 11–2 in Chapter 11 examined required rates of returns over time with changing interest rates and stock prices. Figure 11A–3 does basically the same thing, only through the SML format.

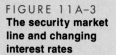

FIGURE 11A–3
The security market line and changing interest rates

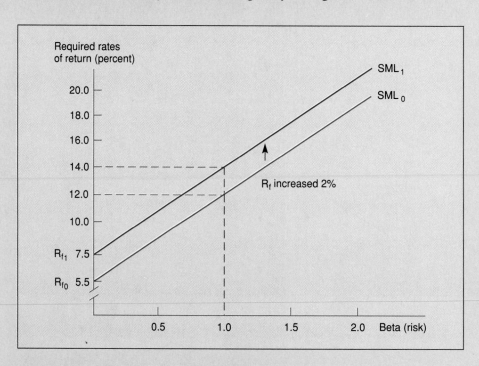

When interest rates increase from the initial period (R_{f1} versus R_{f0}), the security market line in the next period is parallel to SML_0, but higher. What this means is that required rates of return have risen for every level of risk, as investors desire to maintain their risk premium over the risk-free rate.

One very important variable influencing interest rates is the rate of inflation. As inflation increases, lenders try to maintain their real dollar purchasing power, so they increase the required interest rates to offset inflation. The risk-free rate can be thought of as:

$$R_f = RR + IP$$

where

RR is the real rate of return on a riskless government security when inflation is zero.

IP is an inflation premium that compensates lenders (investors) for loss of purchasing power.

An upward shift in the SML indicates that the prices of all assets will shift downward as interest rates move up. In Chapter 10, "Valuation and Rates of Return," this was demonstrated in the discussion that showed that when market interest rates went up, bond prices adjusted downward to make up for the lower coupon rate (interest payment) on the old bonds.

Another factor affecting the cost of capital is a change in risk preferences by investors. As investors become more pessimistic about the economy, they require larger premiums for assuming risks. Even though the historical average market risk premium may be close to 6.5 percent, this is not stable and investors' changing attitudes can have a big impact on the market risk premium. For example the 1987 stock market crash on October 19 (a 22.6 percent decline in one day) had to be somewhat influenced by investors' quick move to a more risk-averse attitude. This risk aversion shows up in higher required stock returns and lower stock prices. For example, if investors raise their market risk premium to 8 percent, the required rates of return from the original equations will increase as follows:

$$K_2 = 5.5\% + 2.0(8.0\%) = 5.5\% + 16.0\% = 21.5\%$$

$$K_1 = 5.5\% + 1.0(8.0\%) = 5.5\% + 8.0\% = 13.5\%$$

$$K_{.5} = 5.5\% + 0.5(8.0\%) = 5.5\% + 4.0\% = 9.5\%$$

The change in the market risk premium will cause the required market return (beta = 1.00) to be 13.5 percent instead of the 12 percent from Figure 11A–2. Any asset riskier than the market would have a larger increase in the required return. For example, a stock with a beta of 2.0 would need to generate a 21.5 percent return, instead of the 18.5 percent in Figure 11A–2. The overall shape of the new security market line (SML_1) is shown in Figure 11A–4. Note the higher slope for SML_1, in comparison to SML_0.

In many instances rising interest rates and pessimistic investors go hand in hand, so the SML may change its slope and intercept at the same time. This combined effect would cause severe drops in the prices of risky assets and much larger required rates of return for such assets.

FIGURE 11A–4
**The security market
line and changing
investor expectations**

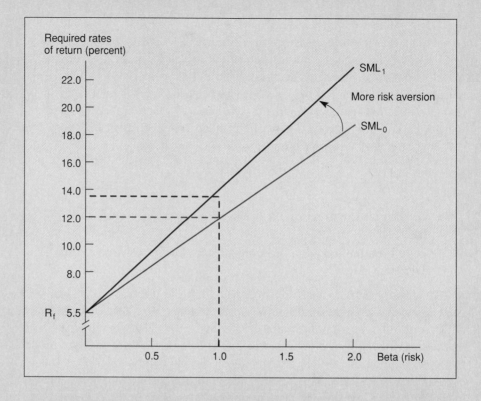

The capital asset pricing model and the security market line have been
presented to further your understanding of market-related events that impact
the firm's cost of capital, such as market returns and risk, changing interest
rates, and changing risk preferences.

While the capital asset pricing model has received criticism because of
the difficulties of dealing with the betas of individual securities and because
of the problems involved in consistently constructing the appropriate slope of
the SML to represent reality, it provides some interesting insights into risk-
return measurement.

List of Terms

capital asset pricing model 326	**beta** 328
market risk premium 328	**security market line** 329

Discussion Questions

11A–1. How does the capital asset pricing model help explain changing
costs of capital?

11A–2. Why does K_e approximate K_j, or why does $D_1/(P_0 - g)$
approximate $R_f + \beta(K_m - R_f)$?

11A–3. How does the SML react to changes in the rate of interest, changes in the rate of inflation, and changing investor expectations?

Problems

11A–1. Assume that $R_f = 5$ percent and $K_m = 10.5$ percent. Compute K_j for the following betas, using Formula 11A–2.

    a. 0.6

    b. 1.3

    c. 1.9

Capital asset pricing model

11A–2. In the preceding problem, assume an increase in interest rates changes R_f to 6.0 percent, and the market risk premium $(K_m - R_f)$ changes to 7.0 percent. Compute K_j for the three betas of 0.6, 1.3, and 1.9.

Capital asset pricing model

APPENDIX 11B   Capital Structure Theory and Modigliani and Miller

The foundation supporting cost of capital theories was primarily developed by Professors Modigliani and Miller in the late 1950s and mid-1960s.[1] They actually went through an evolutionary process in which they proposed many different theories and conclusions about cost of capital.

However, before we discuss Modigliani and Miller, we will briefly touch on the work of David Durand in the early 1950s, which was the first written attempt to describe the effect of financial leverage on cost of capital and valuation. Professor Durand described three different theories of cost of capital: the net income (NI) approach, the net operating income (NOI) approach, and the traditional approach.[2]

Under the **net income (NI) approach,** it is assumed the firm can raise all the funds it desires at a constant cost of equity and debt. Since debt tends to have a lower cost than equity, the more debt utilized the lower the overall cost of capital and the higher the evaluation of the firm as indicated in Figure 11B–1.

Under the net income (NI) approach, the firm would be foolish not to use 100 percent debt to minimize cost of capital and maximize valuation. However, the assumption of constant cost of all forms of financing regardless of the level of utilization was severely challenged by practitioners.

Net Income (NI) Approach

---

[1]Franco Modigliani and Merton H. Miller, "The Cost of Capital, Corporation Finance and the Theory of Investment," *American Economic Review,* June 1958, and "Taxes and the Cost of Capital: A Correction," *American Economic Review,* June 1963, pp. 433–43.

[2]See David Durand, "Costs of Debt and Equity Funds for Business: Trends and Problems of Measurement," *Conference on Research in Business Finance,* National Bureau of Economic Research, New York, 1952.

**Net income (NI)
approach**

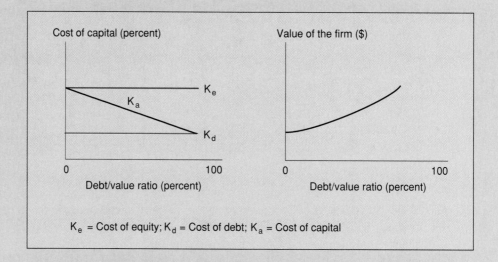

K_e = Cost of equity; K_d = Cost of debt; K_a = Cost of capital

Net Operating Income (NOI) Approach

A second approach covered by Professor Durand was the **net operating income (NOI) approach.** Under this proposition, the low cost of debt is assumed to remain constant with greater debt utilization, but the cost of equity increases to such an extent that the cost of capital remains unchanged. Essentially only operating income matters, and how you finance it makes no difference in terms of cost of capital or valuation. In Figure 11B–2, we see the effects of the net operating income (NOI) approach.

**Net operating income
(NOI) approach**

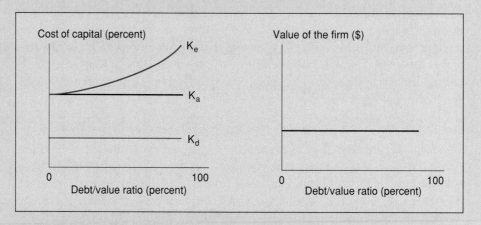

Finally Professor Durand described the **traditional approach.** This falls somewhere between the net income (NI) approach and the net operating income (NOI) approach, in which there are benefits from increased debt utilization, but only up to a point. After that point the cost of capital begins to turn up and the valuation of the firm begins to turn down. A graphic presentation of the traditional approach is seen in Figure 11B–3.

The student will perhaps realize that the traditional approach described by Durand in 1952 is very similar to what is accepted today (as described in the main body of the chapter), but the many theories of Modigliani and Miller had a major impact as we went from 1952 to the currently existing theory.

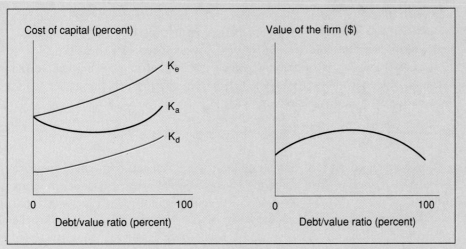

FIGURE 11B-3
Traditional approach as described by Durand

The approaches described by Durand were largely unsupported by theories and mathematical proofs. The major contribution by Modigliani and Miller (M&M) was to add economic and financial theories to naive assumptions. Although it is beyond the scope of this text to go through all the various mathematical proofs of M&M, their basic positions will be presented.

    Under the initial Modigliani and Miller approach, it is assumed the value of the firm and its cost of capital are independent of the means of financing. This is very similar to the NOI approach described by Durand, but the rationale for arriving at this conclusion is different.

    M&M stipulate that the value of the firm equals the following:

$$V = \frac{EBIT}{K_a} \qquad (11B\text{-}1)$$

where

$$V = \text{Value}$$
$$EBIT = \text{Earnings before interest and taxes}$$
$$K_a = \text{Cost of capital}$$

They further stipulate that:

$$K_a = K_{eu} \qquad (11B\text{-}2)$$

K_{eu} represents the cost of equity for an unleveraged firm (one with no debt).

    But what if a firm decides to include debt in its capital structure? Then the cost of equity for this leveraged firm will increase by a risk premium to compensate for the additional risk associated with the debt.

$$K_{eL} = K_{eu} + \text{Risk premium} \qquad (11B\text{-}3)$$
$$K_{eL} = K_{eu} + (K_{eu} - I)(D/S)$$

K_{eL} represents the cost of equity to the leveraged firm, I is the interest rate on the debt, D is the amount of debt financing, and S is the amount of stock

Modigliani and Miller's Initial Approach

(equity) financing. The actual symbols aren't really very important. The important point to observe in Formula 11B–3 is that a risk premium is associated with the cost of equity financing (K_e) when leverage is involved.

M&M thus say a firm cannot reduce the cost of capital or increase the valuation of the firm, because any benefits from cheaper debt are offset by the increased cost of equity financing. That is:

$$K_{eL} = K_{eu} + \text{Risk premium}$$

M&M then go on to demonstrate that, if a leveraged firm could increase its value over another firm not using leverage (when all else is equal in terms of operating performance), then investors would simply sell off the overpriced leveraged firm and use **homemade leverage** (borrow on their own) to buy the underpriced, unleveraged firm's stock. Since both firms are equal in terms of operating performance, investors would simply arbitrage between the values of the two to bring them into equilibrium (sell the overpriced firm and buy the underpriced one using their own personally borrowed funds as part of the process).

In summary, under the initial M&M hypothesis, the value of a firm and its cost of capital are unaffected by the firm's capital structure.

Modigliani and Miller with the Introduction of Corporate Taxes

As is true of many economic models, M&M made a number of assumptions in their initial theory of cost of capital that simplified the analysis. The most critical simplifying assumption was to ignore the impact of corporate taxes on the cost of capital to the firm (Durand made similar simplifying assumptions). Once M&M began to consider the effect of taxes, their whole outlook changed. Because interest on debt is a tax-deductible expense, the tax effect greatly reduces the cost of debt and the associated cost of capital. Furthermore, with a reduced cost of capital, there is an increased valuation for the firm.

A key adjustment to the basic valuation formula is that:

$$V_L = V_U + TD \tag{11B–4}$$

Formula 11B–4 says that the value of a leveraged firm (V_L) is equal to the value of an unleveraged firm (V_U), plus an amount equal to the corporate tax rate (T) times the amount of debt (D) the firm has. If an unleveraged firm has a value of $1,000,000 ($V_U$), then a leveraged firm with $400,000 in debt and a tax rate of 34 percent will have a value of $1,136,000.

$$
\begin{aligned}
V_L = V_U &+ TD \\
&= \$1,000,000 + 0.34(\$400,000) \\
&= \$1,000,000 + 136,000 \\
&= \$1,136,000
\end{aligned}
$$

A firm with $600,000 in debt will have a value of $1,204,000 and so on.

$$V_L = V_U + TD$$
$$= \$1,000,000 + 0.34(\$600,000)$$
$$= \$1,000,000 + \$204,000$$
$$= \$1,204,000$$

Graphically, we are led to the positions presented in Figure 11B–4.

As can be viewed in Figure 11B–4, once corporate taxes are introduced, it is assumed that every increment of debt will reduce the cost of capital, eventually down to the cost of debt itself. Furthermore, the more debt a firm has, the higher its valuation will be.[3]

Under the second version of M&M, every firm should be 100 percent (perhaps 99.9 percent) financed by debt to lower its cost of capital and increase its valuation.

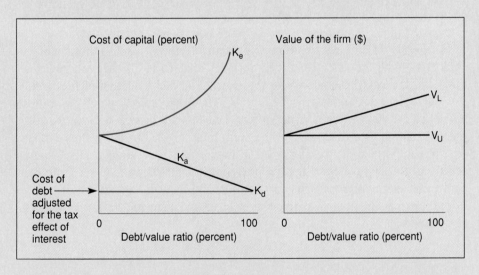

FIGURE 11B–4
Modigliani and Miller with corporate taxes

Modigliani and Miller with Bankruptcy Considerations

Since no firm or investor in the real world operates on the basis of the just described M&M hypothesis, there must be some missing variables. One of the disadvantages of heavy borrowing is that the firm may eventually go bankrupt (a topic discussed in Appendix 16A). A firm that does not borrow at all has *no* such threat. All things being equal, the threat of bankruptcy increases as the amount of borrowing increases.

When bankruptcy occurs, the firm may be forced to sell assets at a fraction of their value. Furthermore, there is likely to be substantial legal fees,

---

[3]The only constraint to this proposition is that the amount of debt cannot exceed the amount of assets.

court costs, and administrative expenses. Even if a firm does not go bankrupt but is on the verge of bankruptcy, customers may be hesitant to do business with the firm. Suppliers may demand advanced payments and so on.

Also as a firm increases the amount of debt it has, there are likely to be restrictive covenants or provisions in debt agreements that hinder normal operations (the current ratio must be at a given level or no new projects can be undertaken without lender approval).

All of these bankruptcy-related considerations have an implicit cost. If the potential cost of bankruptcy were $10 million, then the probability of that bankruptcy must also be considered. If the firm has no debt, then the probability of bankruptcy is zero and the obvious cost is zero. If the firm has 50 percent debt, there may be a 10 percent probability of bankruptcy and the expected cost is $1 million ($10 million × 10 percent). Finally, with 90 percent debt, there may be a 25 percent probability of bankruptcy and the expected cost is $2,500,000 ($10,000,000 × 25 percent). Once these expected costs of bankruptcy are present valued, they must be deducted from the current, unadjusted value of the firm to determine true value. Similarly the expected value of the threat of future bankruptcy also tends to increase the cost of capital to the firm as progressively more debt is utilized.

In Figure 11B–5 we combine the effect of the corporate tax advantage (M&M II) with the effect of the bankruptcy threat (M&M III) to show the impact of financial leverage on the cost of capital and valuation of the firm.

As you can see in Panel A of Figure 11B–5, the curve, which combines the tax effect with the bankruptcy effect, takes us all the way back to the initial proposition first discussed in the main body of the chapter, which is that cost of capital tends to be U-shaped in nature. We have simply added some additional theory to support this proposition. In Panel B we also see from the curve that the combined effect of taxation and bankruptcy allows the firm to maximize valuation at a given debt level and then the valuation begins to diminish.

The Miller Model

As if to temporarily confuse an already settled issue, Professor Miller announced at the annual meeting of the American Finance Association in 1976 that he was rejecting his own latest version of the M&M hypothesis (M&M III, as indicated by the curved lines in Figure 11B–5).[4] His new premise was that he had considered corporate taxes but not personal taxes in the earlier M&M models. He suggested that, when one began considering personal taxes in the process, stock ownership had substantial advantages over debt ownership. Why? Because, at the time, gains from stock ownership were potentially taxed at a much lower rate than interest income, due to the capital gains component that was part of the anticipated return to stockholders. Long-term capital gains

---

[4]Merton H. Miller, "Debt and Taxes," *Journal of Finance* 32 (May 1977), pp. 261–75.

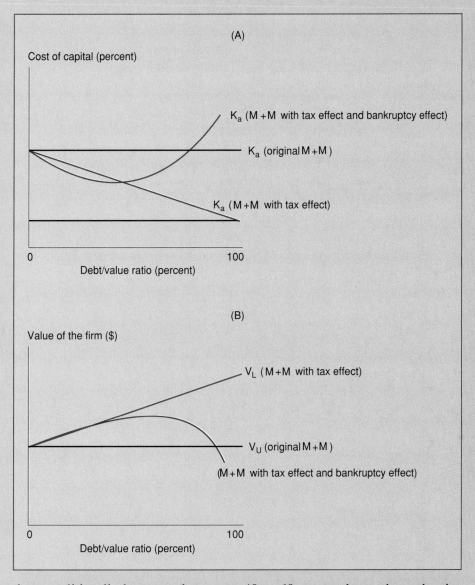

(A)

Cost of capital (percent)

K_a (M +M with tax effect and bankruptcy effect)

K_a (original M + M)

K_a (M + M with tax effect)

0   100

Debt/value ratio (percent)

(B)

Value of the firm ($)

V_L (M + M with tax effect)

V_U (original M + M)

(M + M with tax effect and bankruptcy effect)

0   100

Debt/value ratio (percent)

FIGURE 11B–5
Combined impact of the corporate tax effect and bankruptcy effect on valuation and cost of capital

have traditionally been taxed at a rate 40 to 60 percent lower than other income. Miller said that once you factored all tax considerations (corporate and personal) into the analysis, there was not an overall advantage to debt utilization to the firm and, therefore, the cost of capital was unaffected by the capital structure of the firm.

Subsequent research has partially taken issue with Professor Miller. Fortunately, from a theoretical viewpoint, the Tax Reform Act of 1986, the Deficit Reduction Act of 1990, and subsequent tax legislation have made the tax treatment of capital gains almost equal to other forms of income (except for the wealthiest people). Therefore, the personal tax effect enunciated by Professor Miller in 1976 has now been largely negated and we can somewhat safely return to the U-shaped approach generally described in this chapter and in this appendix.

List of Terms

net income (NI) approach 333
net operating income (NOI)
    approach 334

traditional approach 334
homemade leverage 336

Discussion Questions

11B–1. What is the difference between the net income (NI) approach, the net operating income (NOI) approach, and the traditional approach?

11B–2. Under the initial Modigliani and Miller approach, does the use of debt affect the cost of capital? Explain.

11B–3. How do corporate taxes and bankruptcy considerations change the initial Modigliani and Miller approach? What is the net effect?

The Capital Budgeting Decision

CHAPTER CONCEPTS

1 A capital budgeting decision represents a long-term investment decision.

2 Cash flow rather than earnings is used in the capital budgeting decision.

3 The three methods of ranking investments are the payback method, the internal rate of return, and net present value.

4 The discount or cutoff rate is normally the cost of capital.

5 The two primary cash inflows analyzed in a capital budgeting decision are the aftertax operating benefits and the tax shield benefits of depreciation.

The decision on capital outlays is among the most significant a firm has to make. A decision to build a new plant or expand into a foreign market may influence the performance of the firm over the next decade. The airline industry has shown a tendency to expand in excess of its needs, while other industries have insufficient capacity. The auto industry has often miscalculated its product mix and has had to shift down from one car size to another at an enormous expense.

The capital budgeting decision involves the planning of expenditures for a project with a life of at least one year, and usually considerably longer. In the public utilities sector, a time horizon of 25 years is not unusual. The capital expenditure decision requires extensive planning to ensure that engineering and marketing information is available, product design is completed, necessary patents are acquired, and the capital markets are tapped for the necessary funds. Throughout this chapter we will use techniques developed under the discussion of the time value of money to equate future flows to the present, while using the cost of capital as the basic discount rate.

As the time horizon moves farther into the future, uncertainty becomes a greater hazard. The manager is uncertain about annual costs and inflows, product life, interest rates, economic conditions, and technological change. A good example of the vagueness of the marketplace can be observed in the pocket calculator industry going back to the mid-1970s. A number of firms tooled up in the early 1970s in the hope of being first to break through the $100 price range for pocket calculators, assuming that penetration of the $100 barrier would bring a larger market share and high profitability. However, technological advancement, price cutting, and the appearance of Texas Instruments in the consumer market drove prices down by 60 to 90 percent and made the $100 pocket calculator a museum piece. Rapid Data Systems, the first entry into the under-$100 market, went into bankruptcy. The same type of change, though less dramatic, can be viewed in the personal computer industry of the 1980s and early 1990s. IBM and Apple took the early lead in product development and had no difficulty selling their products in the $2,000 to $5,000 range. As Tandy, Compaq, and foreign competitors moved into the market, prices not only dropped by 50 percent, but also consumer demand for quality went up. Not all new developments are so perilous, and a number of techniques, which will be treated in the next chapter, have been devised to cope with the impact of uncertainty on decision making.

In this chapter capital budgeting is studied under the following major topical headings: administrative considerations, accounting flows versus cash flows, methods of ranking investment proposals, selection strategy, capital rationing, combining cash flow analysis and selection strategy, and the replacement decision. Later in the chapter, taxes and their impact on depreciation and capital budgeting decisions are emphasized.

Administrative Considerations

A good capital budgeting program requires that a number of steps be taken in the decision-making process.

FINANCE IN ACTION

The First Step in Capital Budgeting Is Developing an Idea to Analyze: Just Ask Sony Corporation

Before an analyst can apply the many types of techniques for capital budgeting described in this chapter, there first must be an idea. Sony Corporation of Japan is a master at creating new products.

The firm started in 1946 in a post-World War II bombed-out department store. By 1992 the firm was doing over $30 billion a year in sales. In a February 1992 article in *Fortune* magazine, the author proclaimed that Sony "reigns unchallenged as the most consistently innovative consumer electronics enterprise on the planet."*

The evidence can be found in the creation and development of such Sony products as the pocket-size transistor radio, the VCR, the camcorder, and the Walkman portable cassette player. The firm employs 9,000 engineers and scientists and develops or vastly improves

1,000 products a year. The latter number translates into four major product developments per business day.

Sony recruits employees from engineering schools in Japan's major universities, but it does not necessarily look for the student with the highest grades. Rather Sony selects students who are inquisitive, optimistic (a "can do" attitude), and have diverse interests.

Employees are free to move around in the company without getting permission from their supervisors. If you have an idea, you go with it. The ultimate goal is to father (or mother) a new Sony project. People work and dream overtime to start the new high-tech wave of the future.

*Brenton R. Schlender, "How Sony Keeps the Magic Going," *Fortune,* February 24, 1992, p. 76.

1. Search for and discovery of investment opportunities.
2. Collection of data.
3. Evaluation and decision making.
4. Reevaluation and adjustment.

The search for new opportunities is often the least emphasized, though perhaps the most important, of the four steps. The collection of data should go beyond engineering data and market surveys and should attempt to capture the relative likelihood of the occurrence of various events. The probabilities of increases or slumps in product demand may be evaluated from statistical analysis, while other outcomes may be estimated subjectively.

After all data have been collected and evaluated, the final decision must be made. Generally determinations involving relatively small amounts will be made at the department or division level, while major expenditures can be approved only by top management. A constant monitoring of the results of a given decision may indicate that a new set of probabilities must be developed, based on first-year experience, and the initial decision to choose Product A over Product B must be reevaluated and perhaps reversed. The preceding factors are illustrated in Figure 12–1.

FIGURE 12–1
Capital budgeting procedures

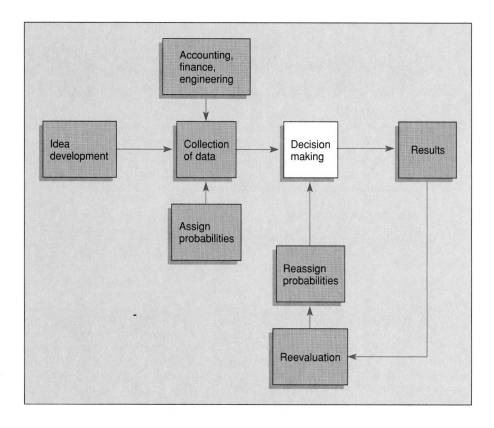

Accounting Flows versus Cash Flows

In most capital budgeting decisions the emphasis is on **cash flow,** rather than reported income. Let us consider the logic of using cash flow in the capital budgeting process. Because depreciation does not represent an actual expenditure of funds in arriving at profit, it is added back to profit to determine the amount of cash flow generated.[1] Assume the Alston Corporation has $50,000 of new equipment to be depreciated at $5,000 per year. The firm has $20,000 in earnings before depreciation and taxes and pays 35 percent in taxes. The information is presented in Table 12–1.

The firm shows $9,750 in earnings after taxes, but it adds back the non-cash deduction of $5,000 in depreciation to arrive at a cash flow figure of $14,750. The logic of adding back depreciation becomes even greater if we consider the impact of *$20,000* in depreciation for the Alston Corp. (Table 12–2). Net earnings before and after taxes are zero, but the company has $20,000 cash in the bank.

To the capital budgeting specialist, the use of cash flow figures is well accepted. However, top management does not always take a similar viewpoint. Assume you are the president of a firm listed on the New York Stock Exchange and must select between two alternatives. Proposal A will provide

[1]As explained in Chapter 2, depreciation is not a new source of funds (except in tax savings) but represents a noncash outlay to be added back.

TABLE 12-1
**Cash flow for Alston
Corporation**

Earnings before depreciation and taxes (cash inflow)	$20,000
Depreciation (noncash expense) . . .	5,000
Earnings before taxes	15,000
Taxes (cash outflow)	5,250
Earnings after taxes	9,750
Depreciation	+ 5,000
Cash flow	$14,750
Cash inflow (EBDT)	$20,000
Cash outflow (taxes)	− 5,250
Cash flow	$14,750

**Alternative method of
cash flow calculation**

TABLE 12-2
**Revised cash flow for
Alston Corporation**

Earnings before depreciation and taxes . . .	$20,000
Depreciation	20,000
Earnings before taxes	0
Taxes	0
Earnings after taxes	0
Depreciation	+20,000
Cash flow	$20,000

zero in aftertax earnings and $100,000 in cash flow, while Proposal B, calling for no depreciation, will provide $50,000 in aftertax earnings and cash flow. As president of a publicly traded firm, you have security analysts constantly penciling in their projections of your earnings for the next quarter, and you fear your stock may drop dramatically if earnings are too low by even a small amount. Although Proposal A is superior, you may be more sensitive to aftertax earnings than to cash flow and you may therefore select Proposal B. Perhaps you are also overly concerned about the short-term impact of a decision rather than the long-term economic benefits that might accrue.

The student must be sensitive to executives' concessions to short-term pressures. Nevertheless in the material that follows, the emphasis is on the use of proper evaluation techniques to make the best economic choice and assure long-term wealth maximization.

Methods of Ranking Investment Proposals

Three widely used methods for evaluating capital expenditures will be considered, along with the shortcomings and advantages of each.

1. Payback method.
2. Internal rate of return.
3. Net present value.

The first method, while not conceptually sound, is often used. Approaches 2 and 3 are more acceptable, and one or the other should be applied to most situations.

Payback Method

Under the **payback** method, we compute the time required to recoup the initial investment. Assume we are called on to select between Investment A and Investment B in Table 12–3.

	Cash Inflows (of $10,000 investment)	
Year	**Investment A**	**Investment B**
1 . . .	$5,000	$1,500
2 . . .	5,000	2,000
3 . . .	2,000	2,500
4 . . .		5,000
5 . . .		5,000

The payback period for Investment A is 2 years, while Investment B requires 3.8 years. In the latter case, we recover $6,000 in the first three years, leaving us with the need for another $4,000 to recoup the full $10,000 investment. Since the fourth year has a total inflow of $5,000, $4,000 represents 0.8 of that value. Thus the payback period for Investment B is 3.8 years.

In using the payback method to select Investment A, two important considerations are ignored. First there is no consideration of inflows after the cutoff period. The $2,000 in year 3 for Investment A is ignored, as is the $5,000 in year 5 for Investment B. Even if the $5,000 were $50,000, it would have no impact on the decision under the payback method.

Second the method fails to consider the concept of the time value of money. If we had two $10,000 investments with the following inflow patterns, the payback method would rank them equally.

Year	Early Returns	Late Returns
1	$9,000	$1,000
2	1,000	9,000
3	1,000	1,000

Although both investments have a payback period of two years, the first alternative is clearly superior because the $9,000 comes in the first year rather than the second.

The payback method does have some features that help to explain its use by U.S. corporations. It is easy to understand, and it emphasizes liquidity. An investment must recoup the initial investment quickly or it will not qualify (most corporations use a maximum time horizon of three to five years). A rapid payback may be particularly important to firms in industries characterized by rapid technological developments.

Nevertheless the payback method, concentrating as it does on only the initial years of investment, fails to discern the optimum or most economic solution to a capital budgeting problem. The analyst is therefore required to consider the more theoretically correct methods.

Internal Rate of Return

The **internal rate of return (IRR)** calls for determining the yield on an investment, that is, calculating the interest rate that equates the cash outflows (cost) of an investment with the subsequent cash inflows. The simplest case would be an investment of $100 that provides $120 after one year, or a 20 percent internal rate of return. For more complicated situations, we use Appendix B (present value of a single amount) and Appendix D (present value of an annuity) and the techniques described in Chapter 9, "The Time Value of Money." For example a $1,000 investment returning an annuity of $244 per year for five years provides an internal rate of return of 7 percent, as indicated by the following calculations.

1. First divide the investment (present value) by the annuity.

$$\frac{\text{(Investment)}}{\text{(Annuity)}} = \frac{\$1,000}{\$244} = 4.1 \; (PV_{IFA})$$

2. Then proceed to Appendix D (present value of an annuity). The factor of 4.1 for five years indicates a yield of 7 percent.

Whenever an annuity is being evaluated, annuity interest factors (PV_{IFA}) can be used to find the final IRR solution. If an uneven cash inflow is involved, we are not so lucky. We need to use a trial and error method. The first question is, Where do we start? What interest rate should we pick for our first trial? Assume we are once again called on to evaluate the two investment alternatives in Table 12–3, only this time using the internal rate of return to rank the two projects. Because neither proposal represents a precise annuity stream, we must use the trial and error approach to determine an answer. We begin with Investment A.

Year	Cash Inflows (of $10,000 investment)	
	Investment A	Investment B
1 . . .	$5,000	$1,500
2 . . .	5,000	2,000
3 . . .	2,000	2,500
4 . . .		5,000
5 . . .		5,000

1. To find a beginning value to start our first trial, average the inflows as if we were really getting an annuity.

$$\begin{array}{r} \$\,5,000 \\ 5,000 \\ \underline{2,000} \\ \$12,000 \div 3 = \$4,000 \end{array}$$

2. Then divide the investment by the "assumed" annuity value in step 1.

$$\frac{\text{(Investment)}}{\text{(Annuity)}} = \frac{\$10,000}{\$4,000} = 2.5 \; (PV_{IFA})$$

3. Proceed to Appendix D to arrrive at a *first approximation* of the internal rate of return, using:

$$PV_{IFA} \text{ factor} = 2.5$$

$$n \text{ (period)} = 3$$

The factor falls between 9 and 10 percent. This is only a first approximation—our actual answer will be closer to 10 percent or higher because our method of averaging cash flows theoretically moved receipts from the first two years into the last year. This averaging understates the actual internal rate of return. The same method would overstate the IRR for Investment B because it would move cash from the last two years into the first three years. Since we know that cash flows in the early years are worth more and increase our return, we can usually gauge whether our first approximation is overstated or understated.

4. We now enter into a trial and error process to arrive at an answer. Because these cash flows are uneven rather than an annuity, we need to use Appendix B. We will begin with 10 percent and then try 12 percent.

Year	10 percent	Year	12 percent
1	$5,000 × 0.909 = $ 4,545	1	$5,000 × 0.893 = $4,465
2	5,000 × 0.826 = 4,130	2	5,000 × 0.797 = 3,985
3	2,000 × 0.751 = 1,502	3	2,000 × 0.712 = 1,424
	$10,177		$9,874

At 10 percent, the present value of the inflows exceeds $10,000 — we therefore use a higher discount rate.

At 12 percent, the present value of the inflows is less than $10,000 — thus the discount rate is too high.

The answer must fall between 10 percent and 12 percent, indicating an approximate answer of 11 percent.

If we want to be more accurate, the results can be *interpolated.* Because the internal rate of return is determined when the present value of the inflows (PV_1) equals the present value of the outflows (PV_0), we need to find a discount rate that equates the PV_1 to the cost of $10,000 ($PV_0$). The total difference in present values between 10 percent and 12 percent is $303.

$10,177 . . .	PV₁ @ 10%	$10,177 . . .	PV₁ @ 10%
− 9,874	PV₁ @ 12%	−10,000 . . .	(cost)
$ 303		$ 177	

The solution at 10 percent is $177 away from $10,000. Actually the solution is ($177/$303) percent of the way between 10 and 12 percent. Since there is a

2 percentage point difference between the two rates used to evaluate the cash inflows, we need to multiply the fraction by 2 percent and then add our answer to 10 percent for the final answer of:

$$10\% + (\$177/\$303)(2\%) = 11.17\% \text{ IRR}$$

In Investment B the same process will yield an answer of 14.33 percent (you may wish to confirm this).

The use of the internal rate of return calls for the prudent selection of Investment B in preference to Investment A, the exact opposite of the conclusion reached under the payback method.

	Investment A	Investment B	Selection
Payback method	2 years	3.8 years	Quicker payback: Investment A
Internal rate of return. . .	11.17%	14.33%	Higher yield: Investment B

The final selection of any project under the internal rate of return method will also depend on the yield exceeding some minimum cost standard, such as the cost of capital to the firm.

Net Present Value

The final method of investment selection is to determine the **net present value** of an investment. This is done by discounting back the inflows over the life of the investment to determine whether they equal or exceed the required investment. The basic discount rate is usually the cost of capital to the firm. Thus inflows that arrive in later years must provide a return that at least equals the cost of financing those returns. If we once again evaluate Investments A and B—using an assumed cost of capital or a discount rate of 10 percent—we arrive at the following figures for net present value.

$10,000 Investment, 10 Percent Discount Rate				
Year	**Investment A**	**Year**	**Investment B**	
1	$5,000 × 0.909 = $ 4,545	1	$1,500 × 0.909 = $ 1,364	
2	5,000 × 0.826 = 4,130	2	2,000 × 0.826 = 1,652	
3	2,000 × 0.751 = 1,502	3	2,500 × 0.751 = 1,878	
	$10,177	4	5,000 × 0.683 = 3,415	
		5	5,000 × 0.621 = 3,105	
			$11,414	
Present value of inflows.	$10,177	Present value of inflows	$11,414	
Present value of outflows	−10,000	Present value of outflows. . . .	−10,000	
Net present value	$ 177	Net present value	$ 1,414	

While both proposals appear to be acceptable, Investment B has a considerably higher net present value than Investment A.[2] Under most circumstances the net present value and internal rate of return methods give theoretically correct answers, and the subsequent discussion will be restricted to these two approaches. A summary of the various conclusions reached under the three methods is presented in Table 12–4.

TABLE 12–4
Capital budgeting results

	Investment A	Investment B	Selection
Payback method	2 years	3.8 years	Quicker payout: Investment A
Internal rate of return . .	11.17%	14.33%	Higher yield: Investment B
Net present value. . . .	$177	$1,414	Higher net present value: Investment B

Selection Strategy

In both the internal rate of return and net present value methods, the profitability must equal or exceed the cost of capital for the project to be potentially acceptable. However, other distinctions are necessary—namely, whether the projects are *mutually exclusive or not*. If investments are **mutually exclusive,** the selection of one alternative will preclude the selection of any other alternative. Assume we are going to build a specialized assembly plant in the Midwest and four major cities are under consideration, only one of which will be picked. In this situation we select the alternative with the highest acceptable yield or the highest net present value and disregard all others. Even if certain locations provide a marginal return in excess of the cost of capital, assumed to be 10 percent, they will be rejected. In the table below, the possible alternatives are presented.

Mutually Exclusive Alternatives

	IRR	Net Present Value
Dayton.	15%	$ 300
Columbus	12	200
St. Paul	11	100
Cost of capital	10	—
Gary.	9	(100)

Among the mutually exclusive alternatives, only Dayton would be selected. If the alternatives were not mutually exclusive (much-needed multiple

---

[2]A further possible refinement under the net present value method is to compute a profitability index.

$$\text{Profitability index} = \frac{\text{Present value of the inflows}}{\text{Present value of the outflows}}$$

For Investment A the profitability index is 1.0177 ($10,177/$10,000) and for Investment B it is 1.1414 ($11,414/$10,000). The profitability index can be helpful in comparing returns from different size investments by placing them on a common measuring standard. This was not necessary in this example.

retail outlets), we would accept all of the alternatives that provide a return in excess of our cost of capital, and only Gary would be rejected.

Applying this logic to Investments A and B in the prior discussion and assuming a cost of capital of 10 percent, only Investment B would be accepted if the alternatives were mutually exclusive, while both would clearly qualify if they were not mutually exclusive.

	Investment A	Investment B	Accepted if Mutually Exclusive	Accepted if Not Mutually Exclusive
Internal rate of return . .	11.17%	14.33%	B	A, B
Net present value	$177	$1,414	B	A, B

The discussion to this point has assumed the internal rate of return and net present value methods will call for the same decision. Although this is generally true, there are exceptions. Two rules may be stated:

1. Both methods will accept or reject the same investments based on minimum return or cost of capital criteria. If an investment has a positive net present value, it will also have a yield in excess of the cost of capital.
2. In certain limited cases, however, the two methods may give different answers in selecting the best investment from a range of acceptable alternatives.

Reinvestment Assumption

It is only under this second state of events that a preference for one method over the other must be established. A prime characteristic of the internal rate of return is the **reinvestment assumption** that all inflows can be reinvested at the yield from a given investment. For example, in the case of the aforementioned Investment A yielding 11.17 percent, the assumption is made that the dollar amounts coming in each year can be reinvested at that rate. For Investment B, with a 14.33 percent internal rate of return, the new funds are assumed to be reinvested at this high rate. The relationships are presented in Table 12–5.

TABLE 12–5   **The reinvestment assumption—internal rate of return ($10,000 investment)**

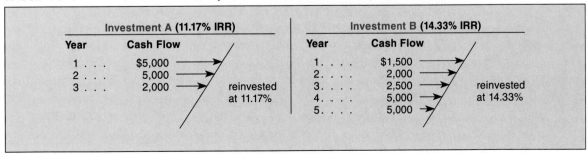

For investments with a very high IRR, it may be unrealistic to assume that reinvestment can occur at an equally high rate. The net present value method, depicted in Table 12–6, makes the more conservative assumption that each inflow can be reinvested at the cost of capital or discount rate.

TABLE 12–6   The reinvestment assumption—net present value ($10,000 investment)

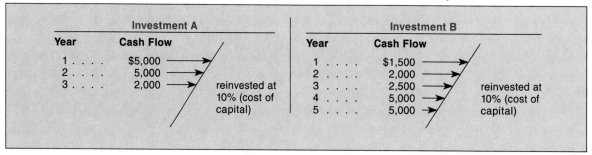

The reinvestment assumption under the net present value method allows for a certain consistency. Inflows from each project are assumed to have the same (though conservative) investment opportunity. Although this may not be an accurate picture for all firms, net present value is generally the preferred method.

Capital Rationing

At times management may place an artificial constraint on the amount of funds that can be invested in a given period. This is known as **capital rationing.** The executive planning committee may emerge from a lengthy capital budgeting session to announce that only $5 million may be spent on new capital projects this year. Although $5 million may represent a large sum, it is still an artificially determined constraint and not the product of marginal analysis, in which the return for each proposal is related to the cost of capital for the firm, and projects with positive net present values are accepted.

A firm may adopt a posture of capital rationing because it is fearful of growth or hesitant to use external sources of financing (perhaps debt). In a strictly economic sense, capital rationing hinders a firm from achieving maximum profitability. With capital rationing as indicated in Table 12–7,

TABLE 12–7
Capital rationing

	Project	Investment	Total Investment	Net Present Value
Capital rationing solution →	A	$2,000,000		$400,000
	B	2,000,000		380,000
	C	1,000,000	$5,000,000	150,000
	D	1,000,000		100,000
Best solution →	E	800,000	6,800,000	40,000
	F	800,000		(30,000)

acceptable projects must be ranked, and only those with the highest positive net present value are accepted.

Under capital rationing, only Projects A through C, calling for $5 million in investment, will be accepted. Although Projects D and E have returns exceeding the cost of funds, as evidenced by a positive net present value, they will not be accepted with the capital rationing assumption.

An interesting way to summarize the characteristics of an investment is through the use of the **net present value profile.** The profile allows us to graphically portray the net present value of a project at different discount rates. Let's apply the profile to the investments we have been discussing. The projects are summarized again below.

Net Present Value Profile

| Year | Cash Inflows (of $10,000 investment) | |
	Investment A	Investment B
1	$5,000	$1,500
2	5,000	2,000
3	2,000	2,500
4		5,000
5		5,000

To apply the net present value profile, you need to know *three* characteristics about an investment:

1. *The net present value at a zero discount rate.* That is easy to determine. A zero discount rate means no discount rate. The values simply retain their original value. For Investment A the net present value would be $2,000 ($5,000 + $5,000 + $2,000 − $10,000). For Investment B the answer is $6,000 ($1,500 + $2,000 + $2,500 + $5,000 + $5,000 − $10,000).
2. *The net present value as determined by a normal discount rate* (such as the cost of capital). For these two investments, we use a discount rate of 10 percent. As previously summarized in Table 12–4, the net present values for the two investments at that discount rate are $177 for Investment A and $1,414 for Investment B.
3. *The internal rate of return for the investments.* Once again referring to Table 12–4, we see the internal rate of return is 11.17 percent for Investment A and 14.33 percent for Investment B. The reader should also realize the internal rate of return is the discount rate that allows the project to have a net present value of zero. This characteristic will become more important when we present our graphic display.

We summarize the information about discount rates and net present values for each investment at the top of page 354 and graphically in Figure 12–2 on the same page.

Investment A	
Discount Rate	**Net Present Value**
0	$2,000
10%	177
11.17% (IRR)	0

Investment B	
Discount Rate	**Net Present Value**
0	$6,000
10%	1,414
14.33% (IRR) . . .	0

FIGURE 12–2
Net present value profile

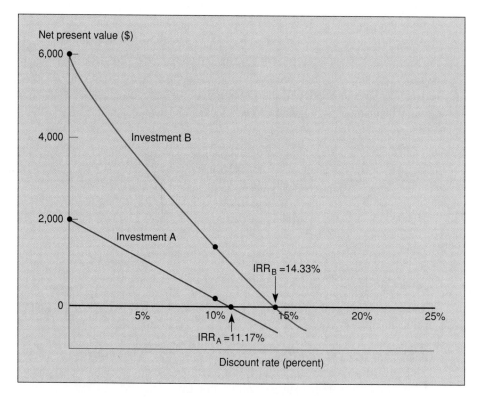

Note that in Figure 12–2 we have graphed the three points for each invest-ment. For Investment A we showed a $2,000 net present value at a zero dis-count rate, a $177 net present value at a 10 percent discount rate, and a zero net present value at an 11.17 percent discount rate. We then connected the points. The same procedure was applied to Investment B. The reader can also visually approximately what the net present value for the investment projects would be at other discount rates (such as 5 percent).

In the current example, the net present value of Investment B was superior to Investment A at every point. This is not always the case in comparing projects. To illustrate let's introduce a new project, Investment C, and then compare it with Investment B.

Investment C ($10,000 Investment)	
Year	**Cash Inflows**
1	$9,000
2	3,000
3	1,200

Characteristics of Investment C

1. The net present value at a zero discount rate for this project is $3,200 ($9,000 + $3,000 + $1,200 − $10,000).
2. The net present value at a 10 percent discount rate is $1,560.
3. The internal rate of return is 22.51 percent.

You could compute these values for yourself, but that is not necessary at this point.

Comparing Investment B to Investment C in Figure 12–3, we observe that at low discount rates, Investment B has a higher net present value than Investment C. However, at high discount rates, Investment C has a higher net present value than Investment B. The actual crossover point can be viewed as approximately 8.7 percent. That is to say, if you had to choose between Investment B and Investment C, your answers would depend on the discount rate. At low rates (below 8.7 percent), you would opt for Investment B. At higher rates (above 8.7 percent), you would select Investment C. Since the cost of capital is presumed to be 10 percent, you would probably prefer Investment C, but keep in mind the cost of capital can change.

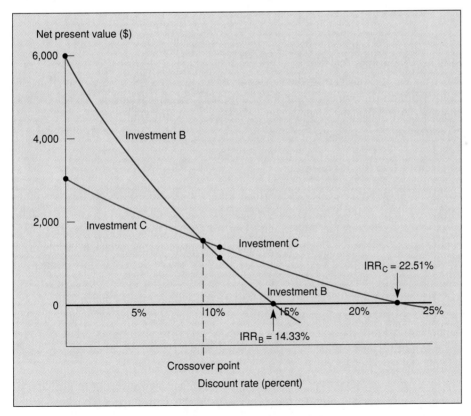

FIGURE 12–3
Net present value profile with crossover

Why does Investment B do well compared to Investment C at low discount rates and relatively poorly compared to Investment C at high discount rates? This difference is related to the timing of inflows. Let's examine the inflows.

	Cash inflows (of $10,000 investment)	
Year	Investment B	Investment C
1 . . .	$1,500	$9,000
2 . . .	2,000	3,000
3 . . .	2,500	1,200
4 . . .	5,000	
5 . . .	5,000	

Investment B has heavy late inflows ($5,000 in both the fourth and fifth years) and these are more strongly penalized by high discount rates. Investment C has extremely high early inflows and these hold up well with high discount rates.

As previously mentioned in the chapter, if the investments are nonmutually exclusive or there is not capital rationing, we would probably accept both Investment B and Investment C at discount rates below 14.33 percent, because they both would have positive net present values. If we can select only one, the decision may well turn on the discount rate. Observe in Figure 12–3 on page 355, at a discount rate of 5 percent, we would select Investment B, at 10 percent we would select Investment C, and so on. The net present value profile helps us make such decisions. Now back to basic capital budgeting issues.

Combining Cash Flow Analysis and Selection Strategy

Many of the points that we have covered thus far will be reviewed in the context of a capital budgeting decision, in which we determine the annual cash flows from an investment and compare them to the initial outlay. To be able to analyze a wide variety of cash flow patterns, we shall first consider the types of allowable depreciation.

The Rules for Depreciation

Under the Tax Reform Act of 1986, assets are classified according to eight categories that determine the allowable rate of depreciation write-off. Each class is referred to as an "ACRS category." ACRS stands for **accelerated cost recovery system** and is a carryover term from prior tax legislation. Some references are also made to ADR, which stands for **asset depreciation range,** or the expected physical life of the asset or class of assets. For example an asset may have a midpoint of its ADR of four years, which means the middle of its expected useful life is four years. Most assets can be written off more rapidly than the midpoint of their ADR. An asset with a midpoint of its ADR of four years might be written off over three years. Table 12–8 shows the various categories for depreciation.

It is not necessary that you become an expert in determining the category in which an asset belongs. In problems at the end of this material you will be given enough information to easily make a determination.

Each of the eight categories in Table 12–8 has its own rate of depreciation that you apply to the purchase price of the asset. These rates are shown in Table 12–9 and are developed with the use of the half-year convention, which treats all property as if it were placed in service in midyear. The half-year

TABLE 12-8
Categories for depreciation write-off

Class	
3-year ACRS	All property with ADR midpoints of four years or less. Autos and light trucks are *excluded* from this category.
5-year ACRS	Property with ADR midpoints of more than 4, but less than 10 years. Key assets in this category include automobiles, light trucks, and technological equipment such as computers and research-related properties.
7-year ACRS	Property with ADR midpoints of 10 years or more, but less than 16 years. Most types of manufacturing equipment would fall into this category, as would office furniture and fixtures.
10-year ACRS	Property with ADR midpoints of 16 years or more, but less than 20 years. Petroleum refining products, railroad tank cars, and manufactured homes fall into this group.
15-year ACRS	Property with ADR midpoints of 20 years or more, but less than 25 years. Land improvement, pipeline distribution, telephone distribution, and sewage treatment plants all belong in this category.
20-year ACRS	Property with ADR midpoints of 25 years or more (with the exception of real estate, which is treated separately). Key investments in this category include electric and gas utility property and sewer pipes.
27½-year write-off	This is the first of two categories for real estate (real property). Investments in residential real estate fall into this category.
31½-year write-off	This is the second real estate category and includes all nonresidential real estate. Examples include office buildings, warehouses, and shopping centers.

TABLE 12-9   **Depreciation percentages (expressed in decimals)**

Depreciation Year	3-Year ACRS	5-Year ACRS	7-Year ACRS	10-Year ACRS	15-Year ACRS	20-Year ACRS
1	.333	.200	.143	.100	.050	.038
2	.445	.320	.245	.180	.095	.072
3	.148	.192	.175	.144	.086	.067
4	.074	.115	.125	.115	.077	.062
5		.115	.089	.092	.069	.057
6		.058	.089	.074	.062	.053
7			.089	.066	.059	.045
8			.045	.066	.059	.045
9				.065	.059	.045
10				.065	.059	.045
11				.033	.059	.045
12					.059	.045
13					.059	.045
14					.059	.045
15					.059	.045
16					.030	.045
17						.045
18						.045
19						.045
20						.045
21						.017
	1.000	1.000	1.000	1.000	1.000	1.000

convention is also extended to the sale or retirement of an asset. Thus for three-year ACRS depreciation, there are four years of depreciation to be taken as demonstrated at the top of page 358.

Year 1. . . .	1/2 year
Year 2. . . .	1 year
Year 3. . . .	1 year
Year 4. . . .	1/2 year
	3-year ACRS depreciation

For five-year ACRS depreciation, there are six years of depreciation to be taken and so on.

Let's return to Table 12–9 and assume you purchase a $50,000 asset that falls in the five-year ACRS category. How much would your depreciation be for the next six years? (Don't forget that we get an extra year because of the half-year convention.) The depreciation schedule is shown in Table 12–10.

TABLE 12–10
Depreciation schedule

(1) Year	(2) Depreciation Base	(3) Percentage Depreciation (Table 12–9)	(4) Annual Depreciation
1 . . .	$50,000	.200	$10,000
2 . . .	50,000	.320	16,000
3 . . .	50,000	.192	9,600
4 . . .	50,000	.115	5,750
5 . . .	50,000	.115	5,750
6 . . .	50,000	.058	2,900
		Total Depreciation	$50,000

The Tax Rate

In analyzing investment decisions, a corporate tax rate must be considered. As mentioned in Chapter 2, the rate has been changed four times since 1980, and it is almost certain to be changed two or three more times between now and the year 2000. Although the maximum quoted federal corporate tax rate is now in the mid-30 percent range, very few pay this rate. Smaller corporations and those with big tax breaks for research and development, new asset purchases, or natural resource development may only pay taxes at a 15 to 20 percent rate. Larger corporations with foreign tax obligations and special state levies may pay effective total taxes of 40 percent or more. In the following examples, we shall use a rate of 35 percent for ease of calculation, but remember the rate varies from situation to situation and from time period to time period. In the problems at the back of the chapter, you will be given a variety of tax rates with which to work.

Actual Investment Decision

Assume in the $50,000 depreciation analysis shown in Table 12–10 that we are given additional facts and asked to make an investment decision about whether this asset should be purchased or not. We shall assume we are purchasing a piece of machinery that will have a six-year productive life. It will produce income of $18,500 before deductions for depreciation and taxes for the first three years. In the last three years, the income before depreciation and taxes will be $12,000. Furthermore we will assume a corporate tax rate of 35 percent and a cost of capital of 10 percent for the analysis. The annual cash flow related to the machinery is presented in Table 12–11. For each year we subtract depreciation from "earnings before depreciation and taxes" to arrive at earnings before taxes. We then subtract the taxes to determine earnings after taxes. Finally depreciation is added back in to arrive at cash flow. The cash flow starts at $15,525 in the first year and ends at $8,815 in the last year.

TABLE 12–11   **Cash flow related to the purchase of machinery**

	Year 1	Year 2	Year 3	Year 4	Year 5	Year 6
Earnings before depreciation and taxes (EBDT)	$18,500	$18,500	$18,500	$12,000	$12,000	$12,000
Depreciation (from Table 12–10)	10,000	16,000	9,600	5,750	5,750	2,900
Earnings before taxes	8,500	2,500	8,900	6,250	6,250	9,100
Taxes (35%)	2,975	875	3,115	2,188	2,188	3,185
Earnings after taxes	5,525	1,625	5,785	4,062	4,062	5,915
+ Depreciation	10,000	16,000	9,600	5,750	5,750	2,900
Cash flow	$15,525	$17,625	$15,385	$ 9,812	$ 9,812	$ 8,815

Having determined the annual cash flows, we now are in a position to discount the values back to the present at the previously specified cost of capital, 10 percent. The analysis is presented in Table 12–12. At the bottom of the same table, the present value of the inflows is compared to the present value of the outflows (simply the cost of the asset) to arrive at a new present value of $7,991. On the basis of the analysis, it appears that the asset should be purchased.

TABLE 12–12
Net present value analysis

Year	Cash Flow (inflows)	Present Value Factor (10%)	Present Value
1.	$15,525	.909	$14,112
2.	17,625	.826	14,558
3.	15,385	.751	11,554
4.	9,812	.683	6,702
5.	9,812	.621	6,093
6.	8,815	.564	4,972
			$57,991

Present value of inflows	$57,991
Present value of outflows (cost)	50,000
Net present value	$ 7,991

So far our analysis has centered on an investment that is being considered as a net addition to the present plant and equipment. However, many investment

The Replacement Decision

decisions occur because of new technology, and these are considered **replacement decisions.** The financial manager often needs to determine whether a new machine with advanced technology can do the job better than the machine being used at present.

These replacement decisions include several additions to the basic investment situation. For example we need to include the sale of the old machine in our analysis. This sale will produce a cash inflow that partially offsets the purchase price of the new machine. In addition the sale of the old machine will usually have tax consequences. Some of the cash inflow from the sale will be taxable if the old machine is sold for more than book value. If it is sold for less than book value, this will be considered a loss and will provide a tax benefit.

The replacement decision can be analyzed by using a total analysis of both the old and new machine or by using an incremental analysis that emphasizes the changes in cash flows between the old and the new machine. We will emphasize the incremental approach.

Assume the Bradley Corporation purchased a computer two years ago for $120,000. The asset is being depreciated under the five-year ACRS schedule shown in Table 12–9, which implies a six-year write-off because of the half-year convention. We will assume the old computer can be sold for $37,600. A new computer will cost $180,000 and will also be written off using the five-year ACRS schedule in Table 12–9.

The new computer will provide cost savings and operating benefits over the old computer of $42,000 per year for the next six years. These cost savings and operating benefits are the equivalent of increased earnings before depreciation and taxes. The firm has a 35 percent tax rate and a 10 percent cost of capital.

First we need to determine the net cost of the new computer. We will take the purchase price of the new computer ($180,000) and subtract the cash inflow from the sale of the old computer.

Sale of Old Asset

The cash inflow from the sale of the old computer is based on the sale price as well as the related tax factors. To determine these tax factors, we first compute the book value of the old computer and compare this figure to the sale price to determine if there is a taxable gain or loss. The book value of the old computer is shown in Table 12–13.

TABLE 12–13
Book value of old computer

Year	Depreciation Base	Percentage Depreciation (Table 12–9)	Annual Depreciation
1 . . .	$120,000	.200	$24,000
2 . . .	120,000	.320	38,400
Total depreciation to date			$62,400
Purchase price			$120,000
Total depreciation to date			62,400
Book value			$ 57,600

Since the book value of the old computer is $57,600 and the sale price (previously given) is $37,600, there will be a $20,000 loss.

Book value	$57,600
Sales price	37,600
Tax loss on sale	$20,000

This loss can be written off against other income for the corporation.[3] The Bradley Corporation has a 35 percent tax rate, so the tax write-off is worth $7,000.

Tax loss on sale	$20,000
Tax rate	35%
Tax benefit	$ 7,000

We now add the tax benefit to the sale price to arrive at the cash inflow from the sale of the old computer.

Sale price of old computer	$37,600
Tax benefit from sale	$ 7,000
Cash inflow from sale of old computer . . .	$44,600

The computation of the cash inflow figure allows us to compute the net cost of the new computer. The purchase price of $180,000, minus the cash inflow from the sale of the old computer, provides a value of $135,400 as indicated in Table 12–14.

TABLE 12–14
Net cost of new computer

Price of new computer	$180,000
− Cash flow from sale of old computer . . .	44,600
Net cost of new computer	$135,400

The question then becomes: Are the incremental gains from the new computer compared to the old computer large enough to justify the net cost of $135,400? We will assume that both will be operative over the next six years, although the old computer will run out of depreciation in four more years. We will base our cash flow analysis on (*a*) the incremental gain in depreciation and the related tax shield benefits and (*b*) cost savings.

---

[3] Note that had there been a capital gain instead of a loss, it is automatically taxed at the corporation's normal tax rate.

Incremental Depreciation

The annual depreciation on the new computer will be:

Year	Depreciation Base	Percentage Depreciation (Table 12–9)	Annual Depreciation
1 . . .	$180,000	.200	$ 36,000
2 . . .	180,000	.320	57,600
3 . . .	180,000	.192	34,560
4 . . .	180,000	.115	20,700
5 . . .	180,000	.115	20,700
6 . . .	180,000	.058	10,440
			$180,000

The annual depreciation on the old computer for the remaining four years would be:

Year*	Depreciation Base	Percentage Depreciation (Table 12–9)	Annual Depreciation
1 . . .	$120,000	.192	$23,040
2 . . .	120,000	.115	13,800
3 . . .	120,000	.115	13,800
4 . . .	120,000	.058	6,960

*The next four years represent the last four years for the old computer, which is already two years old.

In Table 12–15 we bring together the depreciation on the old and new computers to determine **incremental depreciation** and the related tax shield benefits. Since depreciation shields other income from being taxed, the tax shield benefits are worth the amount being depreciated times the tax rate. For example in year one, $12,960 in incremental depreciation will keep $12,960 from being taxed, and with the firm in a 35 percent tax bracket, this represents a tax savings of $4,536. The same type of analysis applies to each subsequent year.

TABLE 12–15
Analysis of incremental depreciation benefits

(1) Year	(2) Depreciation on New Computer	(3) Depreciation on Old Computer	(4) Incremental Depreciation	(5) Tax Rate	(6) Tax Shield Benefits
1 . . .	$36,000	$23,040	$12,960	.35	$ 4,536
2 . . .	57,600	13,800	43,800	.35	15,330
3 . . .	34,560	13,800	20,760	.35	7,266
4 . . .	20,700	6,960	13,740	.35	4,809
5 . . .	20,700		20,700	.35	7,245
6 . . .	10,440		10,440	.35	3,645

Cost Savings

The second type of benefit relates to cost savings from the new computer. As previously stated these savings are assumed to be $42,000 for the next six years. The aftertax benefits are shown in Table 12–16.

TABLE 12–16
Analysis of incremental cost savings benefits

(1) Year	(2) Cost Savings	(3) 1 − Tax Rate	(4) Aftertax Savings
1 . . .	$42,000	.65	$27,300
2 . . .	42,000	.65	27,300
3 . . .	42,000	.65	27,300
4 . . .	42,000	.65	27,300
5 . . .	42,000	.65	27,300
6 . . .	42,000	.65	27,300

As indicated in Table 12–16, we take the cost savings in column 2 and multiply by one minus the tax rate. This indicates the value of the savings on an aftertax basis.

We now combine the incremental tax shield benefits from depreciation (Table 12–15) and the aftertax cost savings (Table 12–16) to arrive at total annual benefits in Table 12–17 (column 4). These benefits are discounted to the present at a 10 percent cost of capital. The present value of the inflows is $150,945 as indicated at the bottom of column 6 in Table 12–17.

TABLE 12–17   **Present value of the total incremental benefits**

(1) Year	(2) Tax Shield Benefits from Depreciation (from Table 12–15)	(3) Aftertax Cost Savings (from Table 12–16)	(4) Total Annual Benefits	(5) Present Value Factor (10%)	(6) Present Value
1 . . .	$ 4,536	$27,300	$31,836	.909	$ 28,939
2 . . .	15,330	27,300	42,630	.826	35,212
3 . . .	7,266	27,300	34,566	.751	25,959
4 . . .	4,809	27,300	32,109	.683	21,930
5 . . .	7,245	27,300	34,545	.621	21,452
6 . . .	3,645	27,300	30,945	.564	17,453
		Present value of incremental benefits			$150,945

We now are in a position to compare the present value of incremental benefits of $150,945 from Table 12–17 to the net cost of the new computer of $135,400 from Table 12–14.

Present value of incremental benefits	$150,945
Net cost of new computer	135,400
Net present value	$ 15,545

Clearly there is a positive net present value, and the purchase of the computer should be recommended on the basis of the financial analysis. Of course there may be other subjective factors to consider as well.

Investment Tax Credits

No coverage of capital budgeting would be complete without some discussion of investment tax credits (ITCs). An **investment tax credit** allows a firm to directly deduct a percentage of the purchase price of an asset against its income tax obligation. For example a company that purchases a $100,000 asset that qualifies for a 7 percent investment tax credit would be able to immediately deduct $7,000 from its tax bill. The remaining $93,000 would then be depreciated over the life of the asset.

A tax credit has a much greater tax benefit than depreciation or other types of tax-deductible expenses. A $7,000 tax credit directly saves $7,000 in taxes (or, said another way, provides $7,000 in cash flow). For a company in a 30 percent tax bracket, it would require $23,333 in depreciation to accomplish the same goal. The $23,333 would save a like amount from being taxed and that, in turn, would save the company $7,000 in taxes (30 percent × $23,333). For a company being taxed at 25 percent, it would require $28,000 in depreciation to equal a $7,000 tax credit.

President John Kennedy initiated the use of investment tax credits to stimulate investments by business in the early 1960s. Since then investment tax credits have been eliminated and then reintroduced five times. A new investment tax credit immediately stimulates investment by business in a weak economy. Each time, however, the investment tax credit losses its punch after a couple of years (everyone makes most of their tax-motivated investments by then). The government then decides the investment tax credit is draining tax revenue and it is eliminated. The authors wish you to be familiar with the concept of the investment tax credit because it will undoubtedly come and go many times over your business career.

Summary

The capital budgeting decision involves the planning of expenditures for a project with a life of at least one year and usually considerably longer. Although top management is often anxious about the impact of decisions on short-term reported income, the planning of capital expenditures dictates a longer time horizon. Three primary methods are used to analyze capital investment proposals: the payback method, the internal rate of return, and the net present value. The first method is unsound, while the last two are acceptable, with net present value deserving our greatest attention. The net present value method uses the cost of capital as the discount rate.

Investment alternatives may be classified as either mutually exclusive or nonmutually exclusive. If they are mutually exclusive, the selection of one alternative will preclude the selection of all other alternatives, and projects with a positive net present value may be eliminated in favor of projects with an even higher net present value. The same is also true under capital rationing, a less than desirable method in which management arbitrarily determines the maximum amount that can be invested in any time period. The student must carefully define each situation and apply the appropriate capital budgeting technique. Tax considerations are also a major factor in capital budgeting decisions. In this chapter the impact of tax legislation on depreciation and related factors is considered in the analysis. In Chapter 13 we will examine how risk fits into the capital budgeting decision-making process.

List of Terms

cash flow 344
payback 346
internal rate of return 347
net present value 349
mutually exclusive 350
reinvestment assumption 351
capital rationing 352
net present value profile 353

accelerated cost recovery system
 (ACRS) 356
asset depreciation range
 (ADR) 356
replacement decision 360
incremental depreciation 362
investment tax credit 364

Discussion Questions

1. What are the important administrative considerations in the capital budgeting process?
2. Why does capital budgeting rely for analysis on cash flows rather than on net income?
3. What are the weaknesses of the payback method?
4. What is normally used as the discount rate in the net present value method?
5. What does the term *mutually exclusive investments* mean?
6. If a corporation has projects that will earn more than the cost of capital, should it ration capital? Shouldn't it be able to find external funds and thus increase its wealth?
7. What is the net present value profile? What three points (characteristics) should be determined to compute the profile?
8. How does an asset's ADR (asset depreciation range) relate to its ACRS category?
9. What is an investment tax credit? Why is it more valuable to a corporation than other types of tax-deductible items?

Problems

1. Assume a corporation has earnings before depreciation and taxes of $90,000 and depreciation of $40,000, and it has a 30 percent tax rate. Compute its cash flow.

   Cash flow

2. *a.* In problem 1, how much would cash flow be if there were only $10,000 in depreciation? All other factors are the same.

   Cash flow

  b. How much cash flow is lost due to the reduced depreciation between problems 1 and 2*a*?

Payback method

3. Assume a $40,000 investment and the following cash flows for two alternatives:

Year	Investment X	Investment Y
1. . . .	$ 6,000	$15,000
2. . . .	8,000	20,000
3. . . .	9,000	10,000
4. . . .	17,000	—
5. . . .	20,000	—

  Which of the alternatives would you select under the payback method?

Payback method

4. Referring back to problem 3, if the inflow in the fifth year for Investment X were $20,000,000 instead of $20,000, would your answer change under the payback method?

Internal rate of return

5. You buy a new piece of equipment for $16,980, and you receive a cash inflow of $3,000 per year for 12 years. What is the internal rate of return?

Internal rate of return

6. Warner Business Products is considering the purchase of a new machine at a cost of $11,070. The machine will provide $2,000 per year in cash flow for eight years. Warner's cost of capital is 13 percent. Using the internal rate of return method, evaluate this project and indicate whether it should be undertaken.

Net present value method

7. Aerospace Dynamics will invest $110,000 in a project that will produce the following cash flows. The cost of capital is 11 percent. Should the project be undertaken? (Note: the fourth year's cash flow is negative.)

Year	Cash Flow
1	$ 36,000
2	44,000
3	38,000
4	(44,000)
5	81,000

Net present value method

8. The Horizon Corporation will invest $60,000 in a temporary project that will generate the following cash inflows for the next three years.

Year	Cash Flow
1	$15,000
2	25,000
3	40,000

  The firm will also be required to spend $10,000 to close the project at the end of the three years. If the cost of capital is 10 percent, should the investment be undertaken?

9. Skyline Corp. will invest $130,000 in a project that will not begin to produce returns until after the third year. From the end of the 3rd year until the end of the 12th year (10 periods), the annual cash flow will be $34,000. If the cost of capital is 12 percent, should this project be undertaken?

Net present value method

10. The Ogden Corporation makes an investment of $25,000, which yields the following cash flows:

Net present value and internal rate of return methods

Year	Cash Flow
1	$ 5,000
2	5,000
3	8,000
4	9,000
5	10,000

   a. What is the present value with a 9 percent discount rate (cost of capital)?

   b. What is the internal rate of return? Use the interpolation procedure shown in this chapter.

   c. In this problem would you make the same decision in parts *a* and *b*?

11. The Danforth Tire Company is considering the purchase of a new machine that would increase the speed of manufacturing tires and save money. The net cost of the new machine is $66,000. The annual cash flows have the following projections.

Net present value and internal rate of return methods

Year	Cash Flow
1	$21,000
2	29,000
3	36,000
4	16,000
5	8,000

   a. If the cost of capital is 10 percent, what is the net present value?

   b. What is the internal rate of return?

   c. Should the project be accepted? Why?

12. You are asked to evaluate the following two projects for Adventures Club, Inc. Using the net present value method, combined with the profitability index approach described in footnote 2 of this chapter, which project would you select? Use a discount rate of 12 percent.

Use of profitability index

Project X (trips to Disneyland) ($10,000 Investment)		Project Y (International Film Festivals) ($22,000 Investment)	
Year	Cash Flow	Year	Cash Flow
1	$4,000	1	$10,800
2	5,000	2	9,600
3	4,200	3	6,000
4	3,600	4	7,000

Reinvestment rate
assumption in capital
budgeting

13. Cablevision, Inc., will invest $48,000 in a project. The firm's discount rate (cost of capital) is 9 percent. The investment will provide the following inflows:

1	. . .	$10,000
2	. . .	10,000
3	. . .	16,000
4	. . .	19,000
5	. . .	20,000

The internal rate of return is 15 percent.

a. If the reinvestment assumption of the net present value method is used, what will be the total value of the inflows after five years? (Assume the inflows come at the end of each year.)

b. If the reinvestment assumption of the internal rate of return method is used, what will be the total value of the inflows after five years?

c. Generally is one investment assumption likely to be better than another?

Capital rationing and
mutually exclusive
investments

14. Oliver Stone and Rock Company uses a process of capital rationing in its decision making. The firm's cost of capital is 12 percent. It will invest only $80,000 this year. It has determined the internal rate of return for each of the following projects:

Project	Project Size	Percent of Internal Rate of Return
A	$15,000	14%
B	25,000	19
C	30,000	10
D	25,000	16.5
E	20,000	21
F	15,000	11
G	25,000	18
H	10,000	17.5

a. Pick out the projects that the firm should accept.

b. If projects B and G are mutually exclusive, how would that affect your overall answer? That is, which projects would you accept in spending the $80,000?

Net present value profile

15. Miller Electronics is considering two new investments. Project C calls for the purchase of a coolant recovery system. Project H represents the investment in a heat recovery system. The firm wishes to use a net present value profile in comparing the projects. The investment and cash flow patterns are as follows:

Project C ($25,000 Investment)		Project H ($25,000 Investment)	
Year	Cash Flow	Year	Cash Flow
1	$ 6,000	1	$20,000
2	7,000	2	6,000
3	9,000	3	5,000
4	13,000		

 a. Determine the net present value of the projects based on a zero discount rate.

 b. Determine the net present value of the projects based on a 9 percent discount rate.

 c. The internal rate of return on Project C is 13.01 percent, and the internal rate of return on Project H is 15.68 percent. Graph a net present value profile for the two investments similar to Figure 12–3. (Use a scale up to $10,000 on the vertical axis, with $2,000 increments. Use a scale up to 20 percent on the horizontal axis, with 5 percent increments.)

 d. If the two projects are not mutually exclusive, what would your acceptance or rejection decision be if the cost of capital (discount rate) is 8 percent? (Use the net present value profile for your decision; no actual numbers are necessary.)

 e. If the two projects are mutually exclusive (the selection of one precludes the selection of the other), what would be your decision if the cost of capital is (1) 5 percent, (2) 13 percent, (3) 19 percent? Use the net present value profile for your answer.

16. Software Systems is considering an investment of $20,000, which produces the following inflows:

Net present value profile

Year	Cash Flow
1. . .	$11,000
2. . .	9,000
3. . .	5,800

 You are going to use the net present value profile to approximate the value for the internal rate of return. Please follow these steps:

 a. Determine the net present value of the project based on a zero discount rate.

 b. Determine the net present value of the project based on a 10 percent discount rate.

 c. Determine the net present value of the project based on a 20 percent discount rate (it will be negative).

 d. Draw a net present value profile for the investment (use a scale up to $6,000 on the vertical axis, with $2,000 increments. Use a scale up

to 20 percent on the horizontal axis, with 5 percent increments.).
Observe the discount rate at which the net present value is zero.
This is an approximation of the internal rate of return on the project.

e. Actually compute the internal rate of return based on the interpolation
procedure presented in this chapter. Compare your answers in
parts *d* and *e*.

ACRS depreciation and
cash flow

17. Howell Magnetics Corporation is going to purchase an asset for
$400,000 that will produce $180,000 per year for the next four years in
earnings before depreciation and taxes. The asset will be depreciated
using the three-year ACRS depreciation schedule in Table 12–9. (This
represents four years of depreciation based on the half-year convention.)
The firm is in a 34 percent tax bracket. Fill in the schedule below for
the next four years. (You need to first determine annual depreciation.)

Earnings before depreciation and taxes	_____
Depreciation	_____
Earnings before taxes	_____
Taxes	_____
Earnings after taxes	_____
+ Depreciation	_____
Cash flow	_____

ACRS depreciation
categories

18. Assume $80,000 is going to be invested in each of the following
assets. Using Table 12–8 and Table 12–9, indicate the dollar amount of
the first year's depreciation.

a. Computers

b. Petroleum refining product

c. Office furniture

d. Pipeline distribution

ACRS depreciation and
net present value

19. The Keystone Corporation will purchase an asset that qualifies for
three-year ACRS depreciation. The cost is $60,000 and the asset will
provide the following stream of earnings before depreciation and taxes
for the next four years:

Year 1	$27,000
Year 2	30,000
Year 3	23,000
Year 4	15,000

The firm is in a 36 percent tax bracket and has an 11 percent cost
of capital. Should it purchase the asset?

ACRS depreciation and
net present value

20. Oregon Forest Products will acquire new equipment that falls under the
five-year ACRS category. The cost is $300,000. If the equipment is
purchased, the following earnings before depreciation and taxes will be
generated for the next six years.

Year 1 . . .	$112,000
Year 2 . . .	105,000
Year 3 . . .	82,000
Year 4 . . .	53,000
Year 5 . . .	37,000
Year 6 . . .	32,000

The firm is in a 30 percent tax bracket and has a 14 percent cost of capital. Should Oregon Forest Products purchase the equipment? Use the net present value method.

21. The Thorpe Corporation is considering the purchase of manufacturing equipment with a 10-year midpoint in its asset depreciation range (ADR). Carefully refer to Table 12–8 to determine in what depreciation category the asset falls. (Hint: it is not 10 years.) The asset will cost $80,000, and it will produce earnings before depreciation and taxes of $28,000 per year for three years, and then $12,000 a year for seven more years. The firm has a tax rate of 34 percent. With a cost of capital of 12 percent, should it purchase the asset? In doing your analysis, if you have years in which there is no depreciation, merely enter a zero for depreciation.

ACRS depreciation and net present value

22. The Spartan Technology Company has a proposed contract with the Digital Systems Company of Michigan. The initial investment in land and equipment will be $120,000. Of this amount $70,000 is subject to five-year ACRS depreciation. The balance is in nondepreciable property. The contract covers six years. At the end of six years, the nondepreciable assets will be sold for $50,000. The depreciated assets will have zero resale value.

Working capital requirements in capital budgeting

The contract will require an investment of $55,000 in working capital at the beginning of the first year, and, of this amount, $25,000 will be returned to the Spartan Technology Company after six years.

The investment will produce $50,000 in income before depreciation and taxes for each of the six years. The corporation is in a 40 percent tax bracket and has a 10 percent cost of capital.

Should the investment be undertaken? Use the net present value method.

23. An asset was purchased three years ago for $140,000. It falls into the five-year category for ACRS depreciation. The firm is in a 35 percent tax bracket. Compute the:

Tax losses and gains in capital budgeting

  a. Tax loss on the sale and the related tax benefit if the asset is sold for $15,320.

  b. Gain and related tax on the sale if the asset is sold for $58,820. (Refer to footnote 3.)

COMPREHENSIVE PROBLEMS

Graphic Systems
(Replacement decision analysis)

Graphic Systems purchased a computerized graphing device two years ago for $80,000. It falls into the five-year category for ACRS depreciation. The equipment can be currently sold for $28,400.

A new piece of equipment will cost $210,000. It falls into the five-year category for ACRS depreciation.

Assume the new equipment would provide the following stream of added cost savings for the next six years.

Year	Cost Savings
1. . .	$76,000
2. . .	66,000
3. . .	62,000
4. . .	60,000
5. . .	56,000
6. . .	42,000

The tax rate is 34 percent and the cost of capital is 12 percent.

a. What is the book value of the old equipment?

b. What is the tax loss on the sale of the old equipment?

c. What is the tax benefit from the sale?

d. What is the cash inflow from the sale of the old equipment?

e. What is the net cost of the new equipment? (Include the inflow from the sale of the old equipment.)

f. Determine the depreciation schedule for the new equipment.

g. Determine the depreciation schedule for the remaining years of the old equipment.

h. Determine the incremental depreciation between the old and new equipment and the related tax shield benefits.

i. Compute the aftertax benefits of the cost savings.

j. Add the depreciation tax shield benefits and the aftertax cost savings, and determine the present value. (See Table 12–17 as an example.)

k. Compare the present value of the incremental benefits (j) to the net cost of the new equipment (e). Should the replacement be undertaken?

Woodruff Corporation
(Replacement decision analysis)

The Woodruff Corporation purchased a piece of equipment three years ago for $230,000. It has an asset depreciation range (ADR) midpoint of eight years. The new equipment can be sold for $90,000.

A new piece of equipment will cost $320,000. It also has an ADR of eight years.

Assume the old and new equipment would provide the following operating gains (or losses) over the next six years.

	New Equipment	Old Equipment
1 . . .	$80,000	$25,000
2 . . .	76,000	16,000
3 . . .	70,000	9,000
4 . . .	60,000	8,000
5 . . .	50,000	6,000
6 . . .	45,000	(7,000)

The firm has a 36 percent tax rate and a 9 percent cost of capital. Should the new equipment be purchased to replace the old equipment?

Selected References

Brick, Ivan, and Daniel G. Weaver. "A Comparison of Capital Budgeting Techniques in Identifying Profitable Investments." *Financial Management* 13 (Winter 1984), pp. 29–39.

Brigham, Eugene F., and T. Craig Tapley. "Financial Leverage and the Use of the Net Present Value Investment Criterion: A Reexamination." *Financial Management* 14 (Summer 1985), pp. 48–52.

Durand, David. "Comprehensiveness in Capital Budgeting." *Financial Management* 10 (Winter 1981), pp. 7–13.

Eccles, Robert G., and Philip J. Pyburn. "Creating a Comprehensive System to Measure Performance." *Management Accounting* 74 (October 1992), pp. 41–51.

Golbe, Devra L., and Barry Schacter. "The Net Present Value Rule and an Algorithm for Maintaining a Constant Debt–Equity Ratio." *Financial Management* 14 (Summer 1985), pp. 53–58.

Howe, Keith M. "Does Inflationary Change Affect Capital Asset Life?" *Financial Management* 16 (Summer 1987), pp. 63–67.

Lipscomb, Joseph. "Real Estate Capital Budgeting." *The Real Estate Appraiser and Analyst* 48 (Summer 1982), pp. 23–31.

McDaniel, William R., Daniel E. McCarty, and Kenneth A. Jessell. "Discounted Cash Flow with Explicit Reinvestment Rates: Tutorial and Extension." *Financial Review* 23 (August 1988), pp. 369–85.

Miller, Edward M. "The Competitive Market Assumption and Capital Budgeting Criteria." *Financial Management* 16 (Winter 1987), pp. 22–28.

Pruitt, Stephen W., and Lawrence J. Gitman. "Capital Budgeting Forecasts Biases: Evidence from the Fortune 500." *Financial Management* 16 (Winter 1986), pp. 15–22.

Rappaport, Alfred, and Robert A. Taggert, Jr. "The Evaluation of Capital Expenditure Proposals under Inflation." *Financial Management* 11 (Spring 1982), pp. 5–13.

Ross, Marc. "Capital Budgeting Practices of Twelve Large Manufacturers." *Financial Management* 15 (1986), pp. 15–22.

Statman, Meir, and Tyzoon T. Tyebjee. "Optimistic Capital Budgeting Forecasts: An Experiment." *Financial Management* 14 (Autumn 1985), pp. 27–33.

Woods, John C., and Maury R. Randall. "The Net Present Value of Future Investment Opportunities: Its Impact on Shareholder Wealth and Implications for Capital Budgeting Theory." *Financial Management* 18 (Summer 1989), pp. 85–92.

Risk and Capital Budgeting

CHAPTER CONCEPTS

1 The concept of risk is based on uncertainty about future outcomes.

2 Most investors are risk-averse, which means they dislike uncertainty.

3 Because investors dislike uncertainty, they will require higher rates of return from risky projects.

4 Simulation models and decision trees can be used to help assess the risk of an investment.

5 Not only the risk of an individual project must be considered, but also how the project affects the total risk of the firm.

No one area is more essential to financial decision making than the evaluation and management of risk. The price of a firm's stock is to a large degree influenced by the amount of risk investors perceive to be inherent in the firm. A company is constantly trying to achieve the appropriate mix between profitability and risk to satisfy those with a stake in its affairs and to achieve wealth maximization for shareholders.

The difficulty is not in finding viable investment alternatives but in determining an appropriate position on the risk-return scale. Would a firm prefer a 25 percent potential return on a new product in Eastern Europe or a safe 8 percent return on an extension of its current product line in its home territory? The question can only be answered in terms of profitability, the risk position of the firm, and management and stockholder disposition toward risk. In this chapter we examine additional definitions of risk, its measurement and its incorporation into the *capital budgeting* process, and the basic tenets of portfolio theory.

Definition of Risk in Capital Budgeting

Risk may be defined in terms of the variability of possible outcomes from a given investment. If funds are invested in a 30-day U.S. government obligation, the outcome is certain and there is no variability—hence no risk. If we invest the same funds in a gold-mining expedition to the deepest wilds of Africa, the variability of possible outcomes is great and we say the project is replete with risk.

The student should observe that risk is measured not only in terms of losses but also in terms of uncertainty.[1] We say gold mining carries a high degree of risk not just because you may lose your money but also because there is a wide range of possible outcomes. Observe in Figure 13–1 examples of three investments with different risk characteristics. Note that in each case the distributions are centered on the same expected value ($20,000), but the variability (risk) increases as we move from Investment A to Investment C. Because you may *gain* or *lose* the most in Investment C, it is clearly the riskiest of the three.

The Concept of Risk-Averse

A basic assumption in financial theory is that most investors and managers are **risk-averse**—that is, for a given situation they would prefer relative certainty to uncertainty. In Figure 13–1 they would prefer Investment A over Investments B and C, although all three investments have the same expected value of $20,000. You are probably risk-averse too. Assume you have saved $1,000 toward your last year in college and are challenged to flip a coin,

---

[1]We use the term *uncertainty* in its normal sense, rather than in the more formalized sense in which it is sometimes used in decision theory to indicate that insufficient evidence is available to estimate a probability distribution.

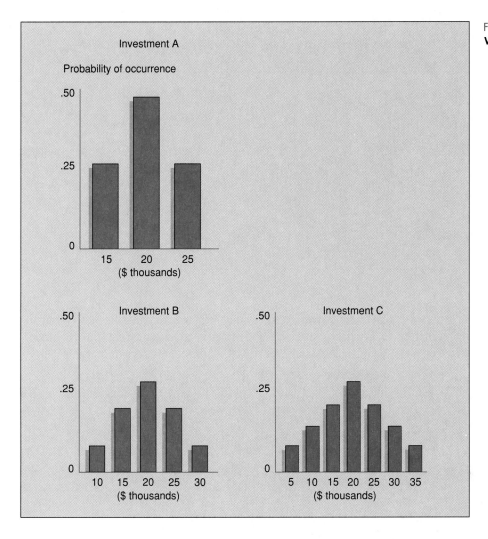

FIGURE 13–1
Variability and risk

double or nothing. Heads, you end up with $2,000; tails, you are broke. Given that you are not enrolled at the University of Nevada at Las Vegas or that you are not an inveterate gambler, you will probably stay with your certain $1,000.

This is not to say investors or businesspeople are unwilling to take risks—but rather they will require a higher expected value or return for risky investments. In Figure 13–2, we compare a low-risk proposal with an expected value of $20,000 to a high-risk proposal with an expected value of $30,000. The higher expected return may compensate the investor for absorbing greater risk.

Throughout the chapter we will develop methods for incorporating a higher demanded return for risky investments. For Evel Knievel in the 1970s, it was $7 million to jump over the Snake River Canyon—for a corporation it may be a bonus return of 5 percent over the cost of capital.

FIGURE 13–2
Risk-return trade-off

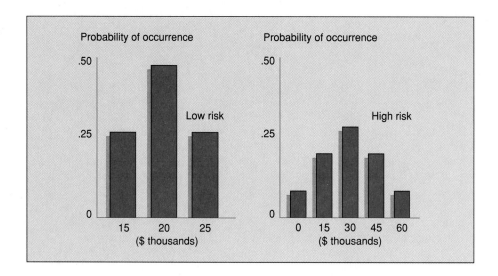

Actual Measurement of Risk

A number of basic statistical devices may be used to measure the extent of risk inherent in any given situation. Assume we are examining an investment with the possible outcomes and probability of outcomes shown in Table 13–1.

TABLE 13–1
Probability distribution of outcomes

Outcome	Probability of Outcome	Assumptions
$300 . . .	.2	Pessimistic
600 . . .	.6	Moderately successful
900 . . .	.2	Optimistic

The probabilities in Table 13–1 may be based on past experience, industry ratios and trends, interviews with company executives, and sophisticated simulation techniques. The probability values may be easy to determine for the introduction of a mechanical stamping process in which the manufacturer has 10 years of past data, but difficult to assess for a new product in a foreign market. In any event we force ourselves into a valuable analytical process.

With the data before us, we compute two important statistical measures—the expected value and the standard deviation. The **expected value** is a weighted average of the outcomes (D) times their probabilities (P).

$$\overline{D} \text{ (expected value)} = \Sigma \, DP \qquad (13\text{–}1)$$

$$
\begin{array}{ccc}
D & P & DP \\
300 \times .2 = & \$\ 60 \\
600 \times .6 = & 360 \\
900 \times .2 = & \underline{180} \\
& \$600 = \Sigma\, DP
\end{array}
$$

The expected value ($\overline{D}$) is $600. We then compute the **standard devia-tion**—the measure of dispersion or variability around the expected value:

$$\sigma \text{ (standard deviation)} = \sqrt{\Sigma (D - \overline{D})^2 P} \qquad (13\text{--}2)$$

The following steps should be taken:

Step 1: Subtract the Expected Value ($\overline{D}$) from Each Outcome (D)			Step 2: Square ($D - \overline{D}$)	Step 3: Multiply by P and Sum			Step 4: Determine the Square Root
D	$\overline{D}$	($D - \overline{D}$)	($D - \overline{D}$)^2	P	($D - \overline{D}$)^{2}P		
300 − 600 =		−300	90,000	× .20 =	18,000		
600 − 600 =		0	0	× .60 =	0		
900 − 600 =		+300	90,000	× .20 =	18,000		
					36,000		$\sqrt{36,000} = \$190$

The standard deviation of $190 gives us a rough average measure of how far each of the three outcomes falls away from the expected value. Generally, the larger the standard deviation (or spread of outcomes), the greater is the risk, as indicated in Figure 13–3 on page 380.

The student will note that in Figure 13–3 we compare the standard devia-tion of three investments with the same expected value of $600. If the ex-pected values of the investments were different (such as $600 versus $6,000), a direct comparison of the standard deviations for each distribution would not be helpful in measuring risk. In Figure 13–4, also on page 380, we show such an occurrence.

Note that the investment in Panel A of Figure 13–4 appears to have a high standard deviation, but not when related to the expected value of the distribu-tion. A standard deviation of $600 on an investment with an expected value of $6,000 may indicate less risk than a standard deviation of $190 on an invest-ment with an expected value of only $600.

We can eliminate the size difficulty by developing a third measure, the **coefficient of variation** (V). This term calls for nothing more difficult than dividing the standard deviation of an investment by the expected value. Gen-erally, the larger the coefficient of variation, the greater is the risk.

$$\text{Coefficient of variation (V)} = \frac{\sigma}{\overline{D}} \qquad (13\text{--}3)$$

For the investments in Panels A and B of Figure 13–4, we show:

$$
\begin{array}{cc}
A & B \\
\dfrac{600}{6,000} = .10 & \dfrac{190}{600} = .317
\end{array}
$$

We have correctly identified the second investment as carrying the greater risk.

FIGURE 13–3
Probability distribution with differing degrees of risk

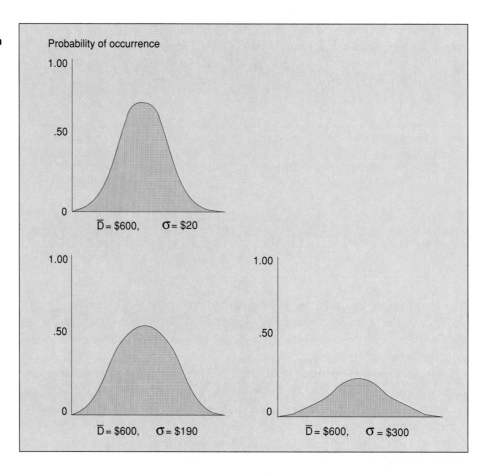

FIGURE 13–4

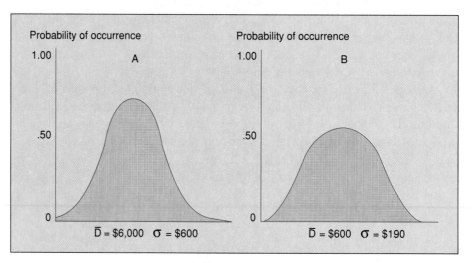

Another risk measure, the **beta** (β), is widely used with portfolios of common stock. Beta measures the volatility of returns on an individual stock relative to the stock market index of returns, such as the Standard & Poor's 500

Stock Index.[2] A common stock with a beta of 1.0 is said to be of equal risk with the market. Stocks with betas greater than 1.0 are riskier than the market, while stocks with betas of less than 1.0 are less risky than the market. Table 13–2 presents a sample of betas for several well-known companies from 1987 to 1992.

Company Name	Beta
Tucson Electric Power	0.65
Carolina Power & Lighting	0.70
Litton Industries	0.75
Tootsie Roll	0.85
Quaker Oats	0.95
Standard & Poor's 500 Stock Index	1.00
Procter & Gamble	1.05
General Motors	1.15
Southwest Airlines	1.35
Merrill Lynch	1.65
Roberts Pharmaceutical	1.90

TABLE 13–2
Betas for a five-year period (1987–1992)

Risk and the Capital Budgeting Process

How can risk analysis be used effectively in the capital budgeting process? In Chapter 12 we made no distinction between risky and nonrisky events.[3] We showed the amount of the investment and the annual returns—making no comment about the riskiness or likelihood of achieving these returns. We know that enlightened investors and managers need further information. A $1,400 investment that produces "certain" returns of $600 a year for three years is not the same as a $1,400 investment that produces returns with an expected value of $600 for three years—but a high coefficient of variation. Investors, being risk-averse by nature, will apply a stiffer test to the second investment. How can this new criterion be applied to the capital budgeting process?

Risk-Adjusted Discount Rate

A favored approach to adjust for risk is to use different discount rates for proposals with different risk levels. Thus we use **risk-adjusted discount rates.** A project that carries a normal amount of risk and does not change the overall risk composure of the firm should be discounted at the cost of capital. Investments carrying greater than normal risk will be discounted at a higher rate, and so on. In Figure 13–5 on page 382 we show a possible risk-discount rate trade-off scheme. Risk is assumed to be measured by the coefficient of variation (V).

The normal risk for the firm is represented by a coefficient of variation of 0.30. An investment with this risk would be discounted at the firm's normal cost of capital of 10 percent. As the firm selects riskier projects, for

---

[2]Other market measures may also be used.

[3]Our assumption was that the risk factor could be considered constant for various investments.

FIGURE 13–5
**Relationship of risk to
discount rate**

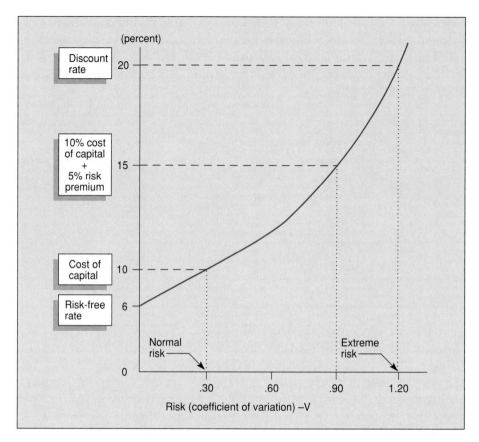

example, with a V of 0.90, a risk premium of 5 percent is added to compensate for an increase in V of 0.60 (from .30 to .90). If the company selects a project with a coefficient of variation of 1.20, it will now add another 5 percent risk premium for this additional V of 0.30. Notice that the same risk premium of 5 percent was added for a smaller increase in risk. This is an example of being increasingly risk-averse at higher levels of risk and potential return.

Increasing Risk over Time

Our ability to forecast accurately diminishes as we forecast farther out in time. As the time horizon becomes longer, more uncertainty enters the forecast. The decline in oil prices sharply curtailed the search for petroleum and left many drillers in serious financial condition in the 1980s after years of expanding drilling activity. Conversely the users of petroleum products were hurt in 1990 when the conflict in the Middle East caused oil prices to skyrocket. Airlines and auto manufacturers had to reevaluate decisions made many years ago that were based on more stable energy prices. The downfall of real estate investments in many sectors of the country in the late 1980s and early 1990s is another example. Only a few years before, investors in the Sunbelt states were fighting over opportunities to get into hot deals. Many of these deals went sour when office and shopping center vacancy rates climbed to 20 to 25 percent in Dallas, Houston, Atlanta, and elsewhere. These unexpected events create a higher standard deviation in cash flows and increase the risk associated with long-lived projects. Figure 13–6 depicts the relationship between risk and time.

Even though a forecast of cash flows shows a constant expected value, Figure 13–6 shows that the range of outcomes and probabilities increases as we move from year 2 to year 10. The standard deviations increase for each forecast of cash flow. If cash flows were forecast as easily for each period, all distributions would look like the first one for year 2. Using progressively higher discount rates to compensate for risk tends to penalize late flows more than early flows, and this is consistent with the notion that risk is greater for longer-term cash flows than for near-term cash flows.

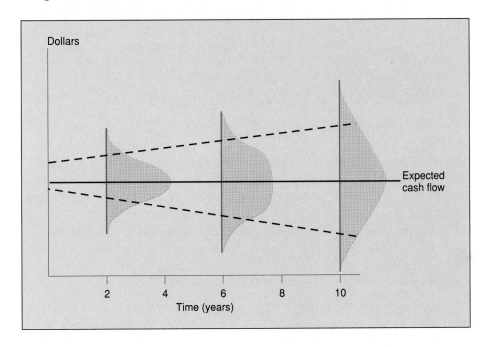

FIGURE 13–6
Risk over time

Qualitative Measures

Rather than relate the discount rate—or required return—to the coefficient of variation or possibly the beta, management may wish to set up risk classes based on qualitative considerations. Examples are presented in Table 13–3. Once again we are equating the discount rate to the perceived risk.

	Discount Rate
Low or no risk (repair to old machinery)	6%
Moderate risk (new equipment).	8
Normal risk (addition to normal product line) . . .	10
Risky (new product in related market)	12
High risk (completely new market)	16
Highest risk (new product in foreign market) . . .	20

TABLE 13–3
Risk categories and associated discount rates

Example—Risk-Adjusted Discount Rate In Chapter 12 we compared two $10,000 investment alternatives and indicated that each had a positive net present value (at a 10 percent cost of capital). The analysis is reproduced in Table 13–4.

TABLE 13–4
Capital budgeting analysis

Year	Investment A (10% discount rate)	Year	Investment B (10% discount rate)
1. . . .	$5,000 × 0.909 = $ 4,545	1	$1,500 × 0.909 = $ 1,364
2. . . .	5,000 × 0.826 = 4,130	2	2,000 × 0.826 = 1,652
3. . . .	2,000 × 0.751 = 1,502	3	2,500 × 0.751 = 1,878
	$10,177	4	5,000 × 0.683 = 3,415
		5	5,000 × 0.621 = 3,105
			$11,414
Present value of inflows . . . $10,177		Present value of inflows $11,414	
Investment. . . . . −10,000		Investment . . . . −10,000	
Net present value . . . . . . $ 177		Net present value . . . . . . $ 1,414	

Though both proposals are acceptable, if they were mutually exclusive, only Investment B would be undertaken. But what if we add a risk dimension to the problem? Assume Investment A calls for an addition to the normal product line and is assigned a discount rate of 10 percent. Further assume that Investment B represents a new product in a foreign market and must carry a 20 percent discount to adjust for the large risk component. As indicated in Table 13–5 our answers are reversed and Investment A is now the only acceptable alternative.

TABLE 13–5
Capital budgeting decision adjusted for risk

Year	Investment A (10% discount rate)	Year	Investment B (20% discount rate)
1. . . .	$5,000 × 0.909 = $ 4,545	1. . . .	$1,500 × 0.833 = $ 1,250
2. . . .	5,000 × 0.826 = 4,130	2. . . .	2,000 × 0.694 = 1,388
3. . . .	2,000 × 0.751 = 1,502	3. . . .	2,500 × 0.579 = 1,448
	$10,177	4. . . .	5,000 × 0.482 = 2,410
		5. . . .	5,000 × 0.402 = 2,010
			$ 8,506
Present value of inflows . . $10,177		Present value of inflows . . . $ 8,506	
Investment . . . . −10,000		Investment. . . . . −10,000	
Net present value. . . . . . $ 177		Net present value . . . . . . $ (1,494)	

Other methods besides the risk-adjusted discount rate approach are also used to evaluate risk in the capital budgeting process. The spectrum runs from a seat-of-the-pants "executive preference" approach to sophisticated computer-based statistical analysis. All methods, however, include a common approach—that is, they must recognize the riskiness of a given investment proposal and make an appropriate adjustment for risk.[4]

Computers make it possible to simulate various economic and financial outcomes, using a large number of variables. Thus **simulation** is one way of dealing with the uncertainty involved in forecasting the outcomes of capital budgeting projects or other types of decisions. A Monte Carlo simulation model uses random variables for inputs. By programming the computer to randomly select inputs from probability distributions, the outcomes generated by a simulation are distributed about a mean, and instead of generating one return or net present value, a range of outcomes with standard deviations is provided. A simulation model relies on repetition of the same random process as many as several hundred times. Since the inputs are representative of what one might encounter in the real world, many possible combinations of returns are generated.

Simulation Models

One of the benefits of simulation is its ability to test various possible combinations of events. This sensitivity testing allows the planner to ask "what if" questions, such as: What will happen to the returns on this project if oil prices go up? go down? What effect will a 5 percent increase in interest rates have on the net present value of this project? The analyst can use the simulation process to test possible changes in economic policy, sales levels, inflation, or any other variable included in the modeling process. Some simulation models are driven by sales forecasts with assumptions to derive income statements and balance sheets. Others generate probability acceptance curves for capital budgeting decisions by informing the analyst about the probabilities of having a positive net present value.

For example, each distribution in Figure 13–7 on page 386 will have a value picked randomly and used for one simulation. The simulation will be run many times, each time selecting a new random variable to generate the final probability distribution for the net present value (at the bottom of Figure 13–7). For that probability distribution, the expected values are on the horizontal axis and the probability of occurrence is on the vertical axis. The outcomes also indicate something about the riskiness of the project, which is indicated by the overall dispersion.

Decision Trees

Decision trees help lay out the sequence of decisions that can be made and present a tabular or graphical comparison resembling the branches of a tree,

---

[4]As an example, each value might be penalized for lack of certainty (adjusted for risk) and then a risk-free discount rate might be applied to the resultant values. This is termed the *certainty equivalent approach.* In practice the expected value for a given year is multiplied by a percentage figure indicating the degree of certainty and then translated back to the present at a risk-free discount rate (less than the cost of capital). Items with a high degree of certainty are multiplied by 100 percent, less certain items by 75 percent, and so on down the scale.

FIGURE 13–7
Simulation flow chart

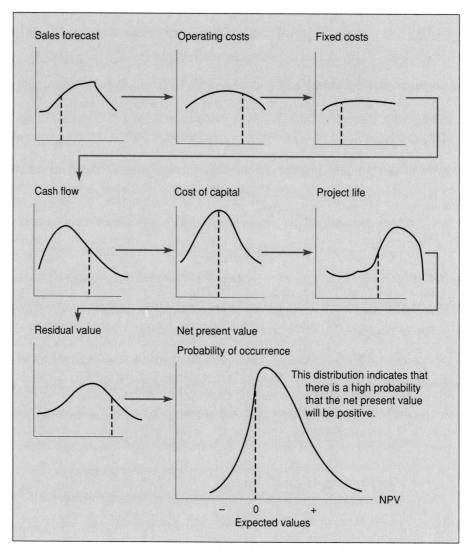

which highlight the differences between investment choices. In Figure 13–8 we examine a semiconductor firm considering two choices: (*a*) expanding the production of semiconductors for sale to end users of these tiny chips or (*b*) entering the highly competitive home computer market by using the firm's technology. The cost of both projects is the same $60 million, but the net present value (NPV) and risk are different.

If the firm expands its semiconductor capacity (Project A), it is assured of some demand so a high likelihood of a positive rate of return exists. The market demand for these products is volatile over time, but long-run growth seems to be a reasonable expectation as the United States increases the emphasis on technology. If the firm expands into the home computer market (Project B), it faces stiff competition from many existing firms. It stands to lose more money if expected sales are low than it would under option A; but it

FIGURE 13-8   **Decision trees**

	(1) Expected Sales	(2) Probability	(3) Present Value of Cash Flow from Sales ($ millions)	(4) Initial Cost ($ millions)	(5) NPV (3) − (4) ($ millions)	(6) Expected NPV (2) × (5) ($ millions)
Expand semiconductor capacity	High	.50	$100	$60	$40	$20.00
	Moderate	.25	75	60	15	3.75
	Low	.25	40	60	(20)	(5.00)
					Expected NPV =	$18.75 ($ millions)
Enter home computer market	High	.20	$200	$60	$140	$28.00
	Moderate	.50	75	60	15	7.50
	Low	.30	25	60	(35)	(10.50)
					Expected NPV =	$25.00 ($ millions)

A

Start

B

will make more if sales are high. Even though Project B has a higher expected NPV than Project A (last column in Figure 13–8), its extra risk does not make for an easy choice. More analysis would have to be done before management made the final decision between these two projects. Nevertheless the decision tree provides for an important analytical process.

The Portfolio Effect

Up to this point, we have been primarily concerned with the risk inherent in an *individual* investment proposal. While this approach is useful, we also need to consider the impact of a given investment on the overall risk of the firm—the **portfolio effect.** For example we might undertake an investment in the building products industry that appears to carry a high degree of risk— but if our primary business is the manufacture of electronic components for industrial use, we may diminish the overall risk exposure of the firm. Why? Because electronic component sales expand when the economy does well and falter in a recession. The building products industry reacts in the opposite fashion—performing poorly in boom periods and generally reacting well in recessionary periods. By investing in the building products industry, an electronic components manufacturer could smooth the cyclical fluctuations inherent in its business and reduce overall risk exposure, as indicated in Figure 13–9 on page 388.

The risk-reduction phenomenon is demonstrated by a less dispersed probability distribution. We say the standard deviation for the entire company (the portfolio of investments) has been reduced.

FIGURE 13-9
Portfolio considerations in evaluating risk

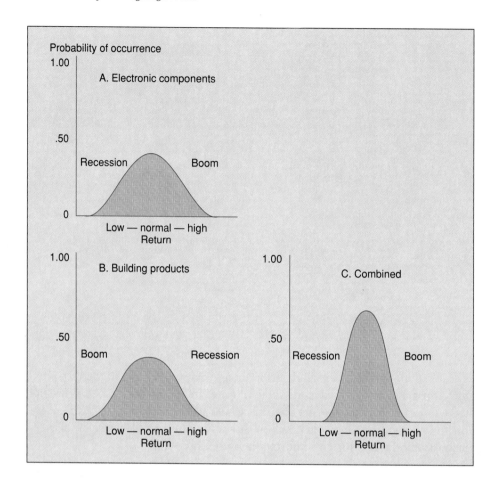

Portfolio Risk

Whether or not a given investment will change the overall risk of the firm depends on its relationships to other investments. If one airline purchases another, there is very little risk reduction. Highly correlated investments—that is, projects that move in the same direction in good times as well as bad—do little or nothing to diversify away risk. Projects moving in opposite directions (building products and electronic components) are referred to as being negatively correlated and provide a high degree of risk reduction.

Finally projects that are totally uncorrelated provide some overall reduction in portfolio risk—though not as much as negatively correlated investments. For example if a beer manufacturer purchases a textile firm, the projects are neither positively nor negatively correlated; but the purchase will reduce the overall risk of the firm simply through the "law of large numbers." If you have enough unrelated projects going on at one time, good and bad events will probably even out.

The extent of correlation among projects is represented by a new term called the **coefficient of correlation**—a measure that may take on values anywhere from -1 to $+1$.[5] Examples are presented in Table 13–6.

TABLE 13–6
Measures of correlation

Coefficient of Correlation	Condition	Example	Impact on Risk
-1 . . .	Negative correlation	Electronic components, building products	Large risk reduction
0 . . .	No correlation	Beer, textile	Some risk reduction
$+1$ . . .	Positive correlation	Two airlines	No risk reduction

In the real world, few investment combinations take on values as extreme as -1 or $+1$, or for that matter exactly 0. The more likely case is a point somewhere between, such as $-.2$ negative correlation or $+.3$ positive correlation, as indicated along the continuum in Figure 13–10.

The fact that risk can be reduced by combining risky assets with low or negatively correlated assets can be seen in the example of Conglomerate, Inc., in Table 13–7 on page 390. Conglomerate has fairly average returns and standard deviations of returns. The company is considering the purchase of two separate but large companies with sales and assets equal to its own. Management is struggling with the decision since both companies have a 14 percent rate of return, which is 2 percentage points higher than that of Conglomerate, and they have the same standard deviation of returns as that of Conglomerate, at 2.82 percent. This information is presented in the first three columns of Table 13–7.

Since management desires to reduce risk (σ) and to increase returns at the same time, it decides to analyze the results of each combination.[6] These are shown in the last two columns in Table 13–7. A combination with Positive

---

[5]Coefficient of correlation is not to be confused with coefficient of variation, a term used earlier in the chapter.

[6]In Chapter 20 you will evaluate a merger situation in which there is no increase in earnings, only a reduction in the standard deviation. Because the lower risk may mean a higher price-earnings ratio, this could be beneficial.

TABLE 13–7   **Rates of return for Conglomerate, Inc. and two merger candidates**

Year	(1) Conglomerate, Inc.	(2) Positive Correlation, Inc. +1.0	(3) Negative Correlation, Inc. −.9	(1) + (2) Conglomerate, Inc. + Positive Correlation, Inc.	(1) + (3) Conglomerate, Inc. + Negative Correlation, Inc.
1	14%	16%	10%	15%	12%
2	10	12	16	11	13
3	8	10	18	9	13
4	12	14	14	13	13
5	16	18	12	17	14
Mean return	12%	14%	14%	13%	13%
Standard deviation of returns (σ)	2.82%	2.82%	2.82%	2.82%	.63%
Correlation coefficients with Conglomerate, Inc.				+1.0	−.9

Correlation, Inc., increases the mean return for Conglomerate, Inc., to 13 percent but maintains the same standard deviation of returns (no risk reduction) because the coefficient of correlation is +1.0 and no diversification benefits are achieved. A combination with Negative Correlation, Inc., also increases the mean return to 13 percent, but it reduces the standard deviation of returns to 0.63 percent, a significant reduction in risk. This occurs because of the offsetting relationship of returns between the two companies, as evidenced by the coefficient of correlation of −.9 (bottom row of Table 13–7). When one company has high returns, the other has low returns, and vice versa.

Evaluation of Combinations

The firm should evaluate all possible combinations of projects, determining which will provide the best trade-off between risk and return. In Figure 13–11 we see a number of alternatives that might be available to a given firm. Each point represents a combination of different possible investments. For example point F might represent a semiconductor manufacturer combining three different types of semiconductors, plus two types of computers, and two products in unrelated fields. In choosing between the various points or combinations, management should have two primary objectives:

1. Achieve the highest possible return at a given risk level.
2. Provide the lowest possible risk at a given return level.

All the best opportunities will fall along the leftmost sector of the diagram (line C–F–G). Each point on the line satisfies the two objectives of the firm. Any point to the right is less desirable.

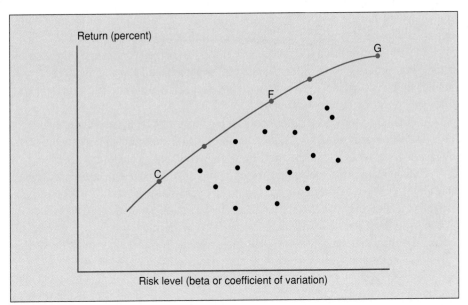

FIGURE 13-11
Risk–return trade-offs

After we have developed our best risk-return line, known in the financial literature as the **"efficient frontier,"** we must determine where on the line our firm should be. There is no universally correct answer. To the extent we are willing to take large risks for superior returns, we will opt for some point on the upper portion of the line—such as G. A more conservative selection might be C or F.

The Share Price Effect

The firm must be sensitive to the wishes and demands of shareholders. To the extent that unnecessary or undesirable risks are taken, a higher discount rate and lower valuation may be assigned to the stock in the market. Higher profits, resulting from risky ventures, could have a result opposite from that intended. In raising the coefficient of variation, or beta, we could be lowering the overall valuation of the firm.

The aversion of investors to nonpredictability (and the associated risk) is confirmed by observing the relative valuation given to cyclical stocks versus highly predictable growth stocks in the market. Metals, autos, and housing stocks generally trade at an earnings multiplier well below that for industries with level, predictable performance, such as drugs, soft drinks, and even alcohol or cigarettes. Each company must carefully analyze its own situation to determine the appropriate trade-off between risk and return. The changing desires and objectives of investors tend to make the task somewhat more difficult.

Summary

Risk may be defined as the potential variability of the outcomes from an investment. The less predictable the outcomes, the greater is the risk. Both management and investors tend to be risk-averse—that is, all things being equal, they would prefer to take less risk, rather than greater risk.

The most commonly employed method to adjust for risk in the capital budgeting process is to alter the discount rate based on the perceived risk level. High-risk projects will carry a risk premium, producing a discount rate well in excess of the cost of capital.

In assessing the risk components in a given project, management may rely on simulation techniques to generate probabilities of possible outcomes and decision trees to help isolate the key variables to be evaluated.

Management must consider not only the risk inherent in a given project, but also the impact of a new project on the overall risk of the firm (the portfolio effect). Negatively correlated projects have the most favorable effect on smoothing business cycle fluctuations. The firm may wish to consider all combinations and variations of possible projects and to select only those that provide a total risk-return trade-off consistent with its goals.

Review of Formulas

1. $\overline{D}$ (expected value) $= \Sigma\, DP$ (13–1)

    D is outcome

    P is probability of outcome

2. σ (standard deviation) $= \sqrt{\Sigma\, (D - \overline{D})^2 P}$ (13–2)

    D is outcome

    $\overline{D}$ is expected value

    P is probability of outcome

3. V (coefficient of variation) $= \dfrac{\sigma}{\overline{D}}$ (13–3)

    σ is standard deviation

    $\overline{D}$ is expected value

List of Terms

risk 376

risk-averse 376

expected value 378

standard deviation 379

coefficient of variation 379

beta 380

risk-adjusted discount rate 381

simulation 385

decision trees 385

portfolio effect 387

coefficient of correlation 389

efficient frontier 391

Discussion Questions

1. If corporate managers are risk-averse, does this mean they will not take risks? Explain.

2. Discuss the concept of risk and how it might be measured.

3. When is the coefficient of variation a better measure of risk than the standard deviation?

4. Explain how the concept of risk can be incorporated into the capital budgeting process.

5. If risk is to be analyzed in a qualitative way, place the following investment decisions in order from the lowest risk to the highest risk:

   a. New equipment.

   b. New market.

   c. Repair old machinery.

   d. New product in a foreign market.

   e. New product in a related market.

   f. Addition to a new product line.

6. Assume a company, correlated with the economy, is evaluating six projects, of which two are positively correlated with the economy, two are negatively correlated, and two are not correlated with it at all. Which two projects would you select to minimize the company's overall risk?

7. Assume a firm has several hundred possible investments and that it wants to analyze the risk-return trade-off for portfolios of 20 projects. How should it proceed with the evaluation?

8. Explain the effect of the risk-return trade-off on the market value of common stock.

9. What is the purpose of using simulation analysis?

10. Why might an analyst set up a decision tree in attempting to make a decision?

Problems

1. Myers Business Systems is evaluating the introduction of a new product. The possible levels of unit sales and the probabilities of occurrence are given.

   Expected value and standard deviation

Possible Market Reaction	Sales in Units	Probabilities
Low response.	20	.10
Moderate response . . .	40	.30
High response	55	.40
Very high response . . .	70	.20

   a. What is the expected value of unit sales for the new product?

   b. What is the standard deviation of unit sales?

Coefficient of variation

2. Five investment alternatives have the following returns and standard deviations of returns.

Alternative	Returns: Expected Value	Standard Deviation
A.	$ 5,000	$1,200
B.	4,000	600
C.	4,000	800
D.	8,000	3,200
E.	10,000	900

Using the coefficient of variation, rank the five alternatives from lowest risk to highest risk.

Coefficient of variation

3. In problem 2, if you were to choose between Alternative B and C only, would you need to use the coefficient of variation? Why?

Coefficient of variation

4. Possible outcomes for three investment alternatives and their probabilities of occurrence are given below.

	Alternative 1		Alternative 2		Alternative 3	
	Outcomes	Probability	Outcomes	Probability	Outcomes	Probability
Failure	50	.2	90	.3	80	.4
Acceptable	80	.4	160	.5	200	.5
Successful	120	.4	200	.2	400	.1

Rank the three alternatives in terms of risk (compute the coefficient of variation).

Coefficient of variation and investment decision

5. Bridgets Modeling Studios is considering opening in a new location in Miami. An aftertax cash flow of $120 per day (expected value) is projected for each of the two locations being evaluated.

Which of these sites would you select based on the distribution of these cash flows (use the coefficient of variation as your measure of risk):

Site A		Site B	
Probability	Cash Flows	Probability	Cash Flows
.15	$ 80	.10	$ 50
.50	110	.20	80
.30	140	.40	120
.05	220	.20	160
		.10	190
Expected value	$120	Expected value	$120

Risk-adjusted discount rate

6. Dixie Dynamite Company is evaluating two methods of blowing up old buildings for commercial purposes over the next five years. Method one (implosion) is relatively low in risk for this business and will carry

a 12 percent discount rate. Method two (explosion) is less expensive to perform but more dangerous and will call for a higher discount rate of 16 percent. Either method will require an initial capital outlay of $75,000. The inflows from projected business over the next five years are given below. Which method should be selected using net present value analysis?

Years	Method 1	Method 2
1. . . .	$18,000	$20,000
2. . . .	24,000	25,000
3. . . .	34,000	35,000
4. . . .	26,000	28,000
5. . . .	14,000	15,000

7. Larry's Athletic Lounge is planning an expansion program to increase the sophistication of the exercise equipment. Larry is considering some new equipment priced at $20,000 with an estimated life of five years. Larry is not sure how many members the new equipment will attract, but he estimates his increased yearly cash flows for each of the next five years will have the following probability distribution. Larry's cost of capital is 14 percent.

Expected value with net present value and internal rate of return

P (probability)	Cash Flow
.2	$2,400
.4	4,800
.3	6,000
.1	7,200

   a. What is the expected cash flow?
   b. What is the expected net present value and internal rate of return?
   c. Should Larry buy the new equipment?

8. Silverado Mining Company is analyzing the purchase of two silver mines. Only one investment will be made. The Alaska mine will cost $2,000,000 and will produce $400,000 per year in years 5 through 15 and $800,000 per year in years 16 through 25. The Montana mine will cost $2,400,000 and will produce $300,000 per year for the next 25 years. The cost of capital is 10 percent.

Deferred cash flows and risk-adjusted discount rate

   a. Which investment should be made? (Note: in looking up present value factors for this problem, you need to work with the concept of a deferred annuity for the Alaska mine. The returns in years 5 through 15 actually represent 11 years; the returns in years 16 through 25 represent 10 years.)
   b. If the Alaska mine justifies an extra 5 percent premium over the normal cost of capital because of its riskiness and relative uncertainty of flows, does the investment decision change?

Coefficient of variation
and investment decision

9. Mr. Monty Terry, a real estate investor, is trying to decide about two potential small shopping center purchases. His choices are the Wrigley Village and Crosley Square. The anticipated annual cash inflows from each are as follows:

Wrigley Village		Crosley Square	
Yearly Aftertax Cash Inflow (in thousands)	Probability	Yearly Aftertax Cash Inflow (in thousands)	Probability
10. . . .	.1	20. . .	.1
30. . . .	.2	30. . .	.3
40. . . .	.3	35. . .	.4
50. . . .	.3	50. . .	.2
60. . . .	.1		

a. Find the expected value of the cash flow for each shopping center.

b. What is the coefficient of variation for each shopping center?

c. Which shopping center has more risk?

Risk-adjusted discount
rate

10. Referring to problem 9, Mr. Terry is likely to hold the shopping center of his choice for 25 years and will use this period for decision-making purposes. Either shopping center can be purchased for $300,000.
Mr. Terry uses a risk-adjusted discount rate approach when evaluating investments. His scale is related to the coefficient of variation (for other types of investments, he also considers other measures).

Coefficient of Variation	Discount Rate
0–0.30	8%
0.31–0.60	11 (cost of capital)
0.61–0.90	14
Over 0.90	18

a. Compute the risk-adjusted net present value for Wrigley Village and Crosley Square using cash flow figures (in thousands) from the previous problem.

b. Which investment should Mr. Terry accept if the two investments are mutually exclusive? If the investments are not mutually exclusive and no capital rationing is involved, how would your decision be affected?

Decision tree analysis

11. Roper Fashions is preparing a strategy for the fall season. One option is to go to a highly imaginative new, four gold button sport coat with special emblems on the front pocket. The all-wool product would be available for both males and females. A second option would be to produce a traditional blue blazer line. The marketing research department has determined that the new, four gold button coat and traditional blue blazer line offer the probabilities of outcomes and related cash flows shown at the top of page 397.

	New Coat			Blazer	
Expected Sales	Probability	Present Value of Cash Flows from Sales	Probability	Present Value of Cash Flows from Sales	
Fantastic . . .	.5	$130,000	.3	$65,000	
Moderate . . .	.2	70,000	.4	50,000	
Dismal.	.3	0	.3	35,000	

The initial cost to get into the new coat line is $50,000 in designs, equipment, and inventory. The blazer line would carry an initial cost of $30,000.

a. Diagram a complete decision tree of the possible outcomes similar to Figure 13–8. Take the analysis all the way through the process of computing expected NPV (last column) for each investment.

b. Given the analysis in part *a*, would you automatically make the investment indicated?

12. When returns from a project can be assumed to be normally distributed, such as those shown in Figure 13–6 (represented by a symmetrical, bell-shaped curve), the areas under the curve can be determined from statistical tables based on standard deviations. For example, 68.26 percent of the distribution will fall within one standard deviation of the expected value $(\overline{D} \pm 1\sigma)$. Similarly 95.44 percent will fall within two standard deviations $(\overline{D} \pm 2\sigma)$, and so on. An abbreviated table of areas under the normal curve is shown here.

Probability analysis with a normal curve distribution

Number of σs from Expected Value	+ or −	+ and −
0.5	0.1915	0.3830
1.0	0.3413	0.6826
1.5	0.4332	0.8664
1.96	0.4750	0.9500
2.0	0.4772	0.9544

Assume Project A has an expected value of $40,000 and a standard deviation (σ) of $8,000.

a. What is the probability the outcome will be between $32,000 and $48,000?

b. What is the probability the outcome will be between $28,000 and $52,000?

c. What is the probability the outcome will be greater than $32,000?

d. What is the probability the outcome will be less than $55,680?

e. What is the probability the outcome will be less than $32,000 or greater than $52,000?

13. The Palo Alto Microchip Corporation projects a pattern of inflows from the investment shown at the top of page 398. The inflows are spread over time to reflect delayed benefits. Each year is independent of the others.

Increasing risk over time

Year 1		Year 5		Year 10	
Cash Inflow	Probability	Cash Inflow	Probability	Cash Inflow	Probability
50	.20	40	.25	30	.30
60	.60	60	.50	60	.40
70	.20	80	.25	90	.30

The expected value for all three years is $60.

a. Compute the standard deviation for each of the three years.

b. Diagram the expected values and standard deviations for each of the three years in a manner similar to Figure 13–6.

c. Assuming a 5 percent and 10 percent discount rate, complete the table for present value factors.

Year	PV_{IF} 5 Percent	PV_{IF} 10 Percent	Difference
1	0.952	0.909	0.043
5	_____	_____	_____
10	_____	_____	_____

d. Is the increasing risk over time, as diagrammed in part b, consistent with the larger differences in PV_{IF}s over time as computed in part c?

e. Assume the initial investment is $110. What is the net present value of the expected values of $60 for the investment at a 10 percent discount rate? Should the investment be accepted?

Portfolio effect of a merger

14. Gifford Western Wear makes blue jeans and cowboy shirts. It has seven manufacturing outlets in Texas, Oklahoma, and New Mexico. It is seeking to diversify its business and lower its risk. It is examining three companies—a toy company, a boot company, and a highly exclusive jewelry store chain. Each of these companies can be bought at the same multiple of earnings. The following represents information about all the companies.

Company	Correlation with Gifford Western Wear	Sales ($ millions)	Average Earnings ($ millions)	Standard Deviation in Earnings ($ millions)
Gifford Western Wear . . .	+1.0	$150	$10	$3
Toy Company	+.2	150	10	6
Boot Company	+.9	150	10	5
Jewelry Company	−.6	150	10	7

a. Discuss what would happen to Gifford Western Wear's portfolio risk-return if it bought Toy Company? Boot Company? Jewelry Company? Pay particular attention to the first column of correlation data.

b. If you were going to buy one company, which would you choose? Why?

c. If you wanted to buy two companies, which would you choose? Why?

15. Hooper Chemical Company, a major chemical firm that uses such raw materials as carbon and petroleum as part of its production process, is examining a plastics firm to add to its operations. Before the acquisition the normal expected outcomes for the firm were as follows:

Portfolio effect of a merger

	Outcomes ($ millions)	Probability
Recession.	$20	.30
Normal economy . .	40	.40
Strong economy. . .	60	.30

After the acquisition the expected outcomes for the firm would be:

	Outcomes ($ millions)	Probability
Recession.	$10	.3
Normal economy . .	40	.4
Strong economy. . .	80	.3

a. Compute the expected value, standard deviation, and coefficient of variation before the acquisition.

b. After the acquisition these values are as follows:

Expected value	43.0 ($ millions)
Standard deviation.	27.2 ($ millions)
Coefficient of variation . . .	.633

Comment on whether this acquisition appears desirable to you.

c. Do you think the firm's stock price is likely to go up as a result of this acquisition?

d. If the firm were interested in reducing its risk exposure, which of the following three industries would you advise it to consider for an acquisition? Briefly comment on your answer.

(1) Chemical company

(2) Oil company

(3) Computer company

16. Mr. Boone is looking at a number of different types of investments for his portfolio. He identifies eight possible investments.

Efficient frontier

	Return	Risk		Return	Risk
A . .	10%	1.5%	E . .	14%	4.0%
B . .	11	3.0	F . .	14	5.0
C . .	13	3.5	G . .	15	5.5
D . .	13	4.0	H . .	17	7.0

a. Graph the data in a manner similar to Figure 13–11. Use the following axes for your data.

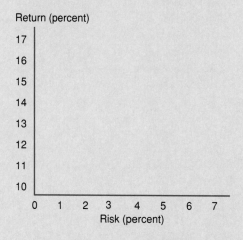

b. Draw a curved line representing the efficient frontier.
c. What two objectives do points on the efficient frontier satisfy?
d. Is there one point on the efficient frontier that is best for all investors?

COMPREHENSIVE PROBLEMS

Tobacco Company of America
(portfolio effect of a merger)

Tobacco Company of America is a very stable billion-dollar company with sales growth of about 5 percent per year in good or bad economic conditions. Because of this stability (a correlation coefficient with the economy of +.3 and a standard deviation of sales of about 5 percent from the mean), Mr. Weed, the vice-president of finance, thinks the company can absorb some small risky company that could add quite a bit of return without increasing the company's risk very much. He is trying to decide which of two companies below he will buy. Tobacco Company of America's cost of capital is 10 percent.

Computer Whiz Company (cost $75 million)		American Micro-Technology (cost $75 million)	
Probability	Aftertax Cash Flows for 10 Years ($ millions)	Probability	Aftertax Cash Flows for 10 Years ($ millions)
.3	$ 6	.2	$ (1)
.3	10	.2	3
.2	16	.2	10
.2	25	.3	25
		.1	31

a. What is the expected cash flow from both companies?
b. Which company has the lower coefficient of variation?
c. Compute the net present value of each company.

d. Which company would you pick, based on net present values?

e. Would you change your mind if you added the risk dimensions to the problem? Explain.

f. What if Computer Whiz had a correlation coefficient with the economy of +.5 and AMT had one of −.1? Which of the companies would give you the best portfolio effects for risk reduction?

g. What might be the effect of the acquisitions on the market value of Tobacco Company's stock?

Ace Trucking Company (investment decision based on probability analysis)

Ace Trucking Company is considering buying 50 new diesel trucks that are 15 percent more fuel-efficient than the ones the firm is now using. Mr. King, the president, has found that the company uses an average of 10 million gallons of diesel fuel per year at a price of $1.20 per gallon. If he can cut fuel consumption by 15 percent, he will save $1,800,000 per year (1,500,000 gallons times $1.20).

Mr. King assumes the price of diesel fuel is an external market force he cannot control and any increased costs of fuel will be passed on to the shipper through higher rates endorsed by the Interstate Commerce Commission. If this is true, then fuel efficiency would save more money as the price of diesel fuel rises (at $1.30 per gallon, he would save $1,950,000 in total if he buys the new trucks).

Mr. King has come up with two possible forecasts as shown below—each of which he believes has about a 50 percent chance of coming true. Under assumption one, diesel prices will stay relatively low; under assumption two, diesel prices will rise considerably.

Fifty new trucks will cost Ace Trucking $5 million. Under a special provision from the Interstate Commerce Commission, the allowable depreciation will be 25 percent in year one, 38 percent in year two, and 37 percent in year three. The firm has a tax rate of 40 percent and a cost of capital of 11 percent.

a. First compute the yearly expected costs of diesel fuel for both assumption one (relatively low prices) and assumption two (high prices) from the forecasts below.

Forecast for assumption one:

Probability (same for each year)	Price of Diesel Fuel per Gallon		
	Year 1	Year 2	Year 3
.1. . . .	$ .70	$ .90	$1.00
.2. . . .	.90	1.10	1.20
.3. . . .	1.00	1.20	1.30
.2. . . .	1.20	1.45	1.50
.2. . . .	1.30	1.55	1.70

Forecast for assumption two:

Probability (same for each year)	Price of Diesel Fuel per Gallon		
	Year 1	Year 2	Year 3
.1. . . .	$1.30	$1.50	$1.90
.3. . . .	1.40	1.70	2.20
.4. . . .	1.90	2.30	2.70
.2. . . .	2.30	2.50	3.00

b. What will be the dollar savings in diesel expenses each year for assumption one and for assumption two?

c. Find the increased cash flow after taxes for both forecasts.

d. Compute the net present value of the truck purchases for each fuel forecast assumption and the combined net present value (that is, weigh the NPVs by .5).

e. If you were Mr. King, would you go ahead with this capital investment?

f. How sensitive to fuel prices is this capital investment?

Selected References

Brigham, Eugene F., Dilip K. Shome, and Steve R. Vinson. "The Risk Premium Approach to Measuring a Utility's Cost of Equity." *Financial Management* 14 (Spring 1985), pp. 33–45.

Brown, Keith C., W. V. Harlow, and M. Seha Tinic. "Risk Aversion, Uncertain Information, and Market Efficiency." *Journal of Financial Economics* (Netherlands) 22 (December 1988), pp. 355–85.

Butler, J. S., and Barry Schachter. "The Investment Decision: Estimation Risk and Risk Adjusted Discount Rates." *Financial Management* 18 (Winter 1989), pp. 13–22.

Chen, Son-Nan, and William T. Moore. "Investment Decisions under Uncertainty: Application and Estimation Risk in the Hiller Approach." *Journal of Financial and Quantitative Analysis* 17 (September 1982), pp. 425–37.

Fabozzi, Frank J. "The Use of Operations Research Techniques for Capital Budgeting Decisions: A Sample Survey." *Journal of Operations Research Society* 29 (1978), pp. 39–42.

Green, Richard C., and Sanjay Stivastava. "Risk Aversion and Arbitrage." *Journal of Finance* 40 (March 1985), pp. 39–42.

Hertz, David B. "Investment Policies That Pay Off." *Harvard Business Review* 46 (January–February 1968), pp. 96–108.

————. "Risk Analysis in Capital Investment." *Harvard Business Review* 22 (January–February 1964), pp. 95–106.

Logue, Dennis E., and T. Craig Tapley. "Performance Monitoring and the Timing of Cash Flows." *Financial Management* 14 (Autumn 1986), pp. 34–39.

Markowitz, Harry. "Portfolio Selection." *Journal of Finance* 7 (March 1952), pp. 77–91.

Neyens, Andrew W., and Ruth Lane Neyens. "Decision Tree Analysis: Formalizing the Workout Decision." *Journal of Commercial Lending* 75 (September 1992), pp. 6–22.

Sick, Gordon A. "A Certainty-Equivalent Approach to Capital Budgeting Forecasts." *Financial Management* 15 (Winter 1986), pp. 22–32.

P A R T

5

Long-Term Financing

INTRODUCTION

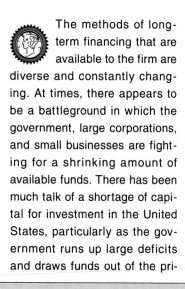

The methods of long-term financing that are available to the firm are diverse and constantly changing. At times, there appears to be a battleground in which the government, large corporations, and small businesses are fighting for a shrinking amount of available funds. There has been much talk of a shortage of capital for investment in the United States, particularly as the government runs up large deficits and draws funds out of the pri-

vate sector. • Fortunately, foreign investors have been supplying a large amount of the capital needed by the U.S. government and American businesses. Only time will tell whether financial capital will be readily available during the 1990s. One thing is certain: the supply and demand for financial capital is occurring in an international market. Most of the following chapters have an increased amount of material on the international impact of this trend. • In Chapter 14 we take a close look at the security mar-

kets, with an eye toward major changes that are taking place. In the next chapter, we examine the actual process of selling securities to the public through an investment banker. The investment banker serves as the middleman between the corporation and the public. As part of our discussion of investment banking, we also consider the advantages and disadvantages of going public—that is, of selling corporate stock to the general public in the over-the-counter market or through an organized exchange—rather than main-

taining ownership in private hands. H. Ross Perot, at one time depicted by *Fortune* magazine as the "Fastest Richest Texan Ever," is studied in the context of going public during the market hysteria of an earlier time period. An offering of additional shares by Chrysler Corporation in 1993 also illustrates how a company can positively affect the demand for its shares. • In Chapters 16 and 17, we study the advantages, disadvantages, and limitations of long-term debt, preferred stock, and common stock. Although the analysis is developed primarily from the corporate viewpoint (should the issue take place or not?), the investor's viewpoint is also considered. Under long-term debt financing, we also consider the lease alternative to "borrowing funds and purchasing the asset outright." • In Chapter 18, we examine a critically important decision for a corporation: whether it should pay out retained earnings in the form of dividends or hold the funds in the corporation for financing future projects. Retained earnings represent an important form of internal long-term financing and must be related to the growth and the life cycle of the firm. In each case, the impact of dividend policy on stockholder expectations and market value maximization must be considered. • Corporate securities that may be converted into common stock or that have special provisions for the purchase of common stock are considered in Chapter 19. The investment features of convertibles and warrants are evaluated along with their potential usage in corporate finance.

Capital Markets

CHAPTER CONCEPTS

1 The capital markets are made up of securities that have a life of one year or longer (often much longer).

2 The primary participants raising funds in the capital markets are the U.S. Treasury; other agencies of the federal, state, and local governments; and corporations.

3 The United States is a three-sector economy in which households, corporations, and governmental units allocate funds between themselves.

4 Security markets are considered to be efficient when prices adjust rapidly to new information.

5 Security legislation is intended to protect investors against fraud, manipulation, and illegal insider trading.

Security markets are generally separated into short-term and long-term markets. The short-term markets comprise securities with maturities of one year or less and are referred to as **money markets.** The securities most commonly traded in these markets, such as Treasury bills, commercial paper, and negotiable certificates of deposit, were previously discussed under working capital and cash management and will not be covered again.

The long-term markets are called **capital markets** and consist of securities having maturities greater than one year. The most common corporate securities in this category are bonds, common stock, preferred stock, and convertible securities. These securities are found on the firm's balance sheet under the designation long-term liabilities and equities. Taken together, these long-term securities comprise the firm's capital structure.

In this chapter, we will be looking at how the capital markets are organized and integrated into the corporate and economic system of the United States. Capital markets are becoming increasingly international as suppliers of financial capital seek out the best risk-return opportunities from among the major industrialized countries in the global economy.

The globalization of capital markets is particularly important for large U.S. multinational corporations that use these markets to raise capital for both domestic and international operations. We start with a global overview of markets and then discuss the U.S. capital markets more fully.

International Capital Markets

During the 1980s, international capital markets have increased in importance. Since 1990 the iron curtain collapsed, the two Germanys reunited, and at the beginning of 1993, the European Community implemented a more competitive and tariff-free Europe. On top of these events, economic growth in the Pacific Rim countries and Japan has continued to expand. These events combine to create an international demand and need for capital. The result is an increase in the growth and development of capital markets worldwide. The U.S. capital markets are still the most important in the world, but there is very strong competition from the Japanese, German, and British markets.

More often, companies search the international markets for opportunities to raise debt capital at the lowest cost. Corporations list their common stock the world over to increase liquidity for their stockholders and to provide opportunities for the potential sale of new stock in foreign countries. While these developments are also very important to investors (suppliers of capital), our focus in this chapter is primarily on corporations.

Figure 14–1 provides a worldwide overview of the capital markets in the early 1990s. At the time the total world capital market was over $20 trillion. International (foreign) equity made up 24.9 percent of the total, and international bonds, 26.4 percent. U.S. equities comprised only 13.5 percent of this world capital pool, while U.S. bonds made up 20.9 percent. The balance was made up of real estate, cash equivalents, and venture capital.

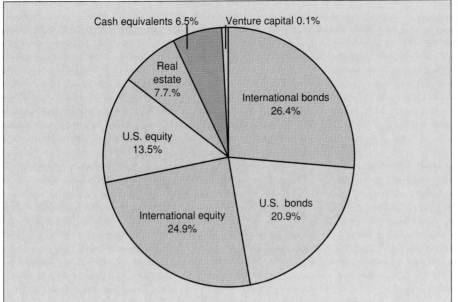

FIGURE 14–1
Percentage breakdown of worldwide capital

Competition for Funds in the U.S. Capital Markets

In order to put U.S. corporate securities into perspective, it is necessary to look at other securities available in the capital markets. The federal government, government agencies, state governments, and local municipalities all compete with one another for a limited supply of financial capital. The capital markets serve as a way of allocating the available capital to the most efficient user. Therefore the ultimate investor must choose among many kinds of securities, both corporate and noncorporate. Before investors part with their money, they desire to maximize their return for any given level of risk, and thus the expected return from the universe of securities acts as an allocating mechanism in the markets.

The corporate and noncorporate capital markets are large. The total annual dollars of new securities issued with maturities of more than one year rose from $76 billion in 1970 to $717 billion in 1986 and then fell somewhat over the next few years before setting a new high at $800 billion in 1992. The decline in funds raised after 1986 is largely the result of the October stock market crashes in 1987 and 1989 as well as the collapse of the junk bond market in 1989 and 1990. However, the continued decline of interest rates with the recession of 1990–91 motivated corporations to raise record amounts of external funds in 1991 and 1992 at a low cost.

The billions of dollars referred to above are still a sizable sum of money to be raised in one year, and they do not include the tremendous amount of funds raised in the short-term money markets. Figure 14–2 depicts the specific composition of long-term funds raised from 1970 through 1992. We will discuss the items in this exhibit in detail.

FIGURE 14–2   **Composition of long-term funds raised**

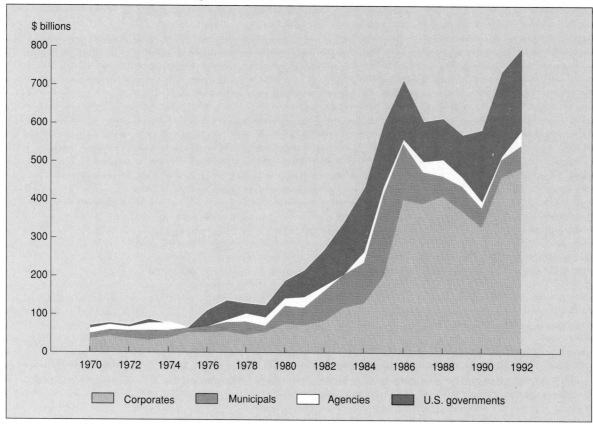

Government Securities

U.S. Government Securities   In accordance with government fiscal policy, the U.S. Treasury manages the federal government's debt in order to balance the inflows and outflows. When deficits are incurred, the Treasury can sell short-term or long-term securities to finance the shortfall. In Figure 14–2 only long-term financing is depicted.

Over the total 23-year period shown in Figure 14–2, long-term **U.S. government securities** averaged 24 percent of the total. From 1970 through 1975, however, long-term financing by the Treasury averaged only about 2.0 percent as the Treasury primarily used short-term Treasury bills for its cash needs during this period. Between 1980 and 1992, the use of long-term U.S. government financing has averaged close to 22 percent as the U.S. government ran up large deficits. The recessions of the early 1980s and a string of $100 to $300 billion-plus deficits from 1982 through the present caused the U.S. government to be a large demander of long-term capital, particularly in 1984 and 1985, averaging almost 39 percent of total long-term funds raised for those two years.[1]

In 1992 the country elected Bill Clinton president, partly on his pledge to reduce the government deficit by 50 percent during his term. Only time will tell if he will be successful in delivering on this promise.

Foreign investors, notably from Japan and Germany, have supplied capital to finance the U.S. deficit. At the end of 1992, the total gross public debt of the United States was $4.177 trillion, and 11 percent was held by foreigners. Given the higher interest rates in Germany during the 1990s and its need to rebuild East Germany, it is understandable that Germany has decreased its holding of U.S. government debt. The Japanese have also decreased their holdings of U.S. debt due to the first economic slowdown in Japan in the last 20 years.

Federally Sponsored Credit Agencies   The **federally sponsored credit agencies** are governmental units that issue their securities on a separate basis from the U.S. Treasury government issues previously discussed. Although the securities are not directly backed by the U.S. Treasury, no issue has ever failed. The Federal Home Loan Banks (FHLB) have the most debt outstanding at $136 billion and have moved ahead of the Federal National Mortgage Association (Fannie Mae) in size. Fannie Mae is included as a government-sponsored agency even though it is currently a privately run corporation. It still maintains a quasi-agency relationship with the United States, based on its original government charter. Both of these agencies are involved in the housing market, and a third credit agency called the Resolution Trust Corporation was established in 1989 by the Financial Institutions Reform, Recovery, and Enforcement Act of 1989. This agency was set up to help finance the large losses run up by the savings and loan industry and to cover potential losses to depositors of up to $300 billion. This number is an uncertain estimate at the time of this writing, and some projections are higher. In any event the Resolution Trust Corporation has the potential to be the biggest borrower of all credit agencies within the next decade.

Another large federal agency is the group of 37 Farm Credit Banks. The depressed farm economy has created many problems for farm lenders as farmers have defaulted on their loans. The Farm Credit System sustained losses of $2.7 billion in 1985 and $1.9 billion in 1986. Since 1986, outstanding indebtedness in the Farm Credit System has declined by $8 billion and the farm economy has recovered somewhat, thus averting what was once thought to be an inevitable collapse of this agency's credit financing ability. From 1970 to 1992, the three aforementioned agencies and the other federally sponsored agencies averaged 9.4 percent of the long-term financing shown in

---

[1]When short-term U.S. government financing is added to long-term U.S. government financing, the amounts greatly increase.

Figure 14–2. Long-term financing for government-sponsored agencies has been rather inconsistent, rising from 1.5 percent in 1975 to 16.4 percent in 1978 and accounting for 1.2 percent of total long-term financing in 1991.

State and Local Issues　　These issues are referred to as **municipal securities** or tax exempt offerings, because the interest on them is normally exempt from federal income taxes and from state taxes in the state of issue. During the 1970–92 period, state and local municipalities accounted for about the same percentage of long-term funds raised at 24 percent as the U.S. government. This is illustrated in Figure 14–2. When huge federal deficits began to mushroom in 1980, long-term municipal financing fell into third place behind U.S. Treasury and corporate financing. In 1985 federal income tax reform was considered in the U.S. Congress, which threatened to eliminate the tax exclusion for interest on municipal bonds beginning in 1986. This caused a swell of new municipal offerings in order to lock in favored tax treatment in 1985. The total volume of funds raised by state and municipal governments amounted to $214 billion or 35.5 percent of the funds raised in 1985. The tax law revisions in 1986 maintained the deductability of interest on municipal bonds, but the lower marginal tax rates removed a large incentive for individuals and corporations to purchase these "tax-free" bonds, and they accounted for only 9.3 percent of total long-term funds raised from 1987 through 1992. In 1993 President Clinton introduced new tax legislation to raise taxes, and the municipal bond market attracted billions of dollars of investors' money.

Corporate Securities

Corporate Bonds　　One misconception held by many investors is that corporate bond markets are dominated in size by the market for common stocks. This is far from the truth. In the new issues corporate market, bonds averaged 77.9 percent of all long-term corporate securities sold from 1970 through 1992. Bonds as a percentage of total corporate issues have ranged from highs of 92.7 percent in 1990 to a low of 57 percent in 1983. In 1974 stock prices reached their lowest levels of the decade, and bonds were the dominant source of external corporate financing in that year with almost 84 percent of the total. The low point of bond financing was reached in 1983. Stock prices soared after having been low for some time and corporations rushed to increase equity financing. Interest rates began falling in 1982 and continued their decline through the record quarter of 1993. Once rates came down significantly, companies began refinancing high-cost debt with lower-cost debt as well as raising new debt capital. From 1984 through 1992, long-term funds raised through corporate bonds averaged a very high 86 percent of total corporate funds raised.

In general when interest rates are expected to rise, financial managers try to lock in long-term financing at low costs and balance the company's debt structure toward more long-term debt and away from short-term debt. Not all the increase in debt financing during this period can be tied to falling interest rates. Part of this higher-than-average bond financing was the result of increased use of high-yield junk bonds for mergers, acquisitions, takeovers, and leveraged buyouts such as RJR Nabisco's $25 billion leveraged buyout.

Preferred Stock   Preferred stock is the least used of all long-term corporate securities. It has averaged only 4.9 percent of long-term corporate financing for the period from 1970 to 1992. The major reason for the small amount of financing by preferred stock is that the dividend is not deductible to the corporation before income taxes, as is bond interest.

Common Stock   The sale of common stock from 1970 through 1992 averaged 17.2 percent of total corporate long-term financing. When total long-term funds including government financing are considered, common stock accounted for only about 8 percent of all long-term financing. This small percentage of new common stock financing illustrates that corporations do not regularly rely on common stocks as a major source of funds. During 1990, corporate financing in general fell $100 billion from the 1986 peak, and common stock accounted for only 6 percent of total corporate financing for the smallest percentage during the 22 years from 1970 to 1992. With falling interest rates and rising stock prices, total financing did reach high levels in 1992, estimated at $481 billion. Figure 14–3 provides comparative data on the use of various financing alternatives by U.S. corporations.

FIGURE 14–3   **Long-term corporate financing**

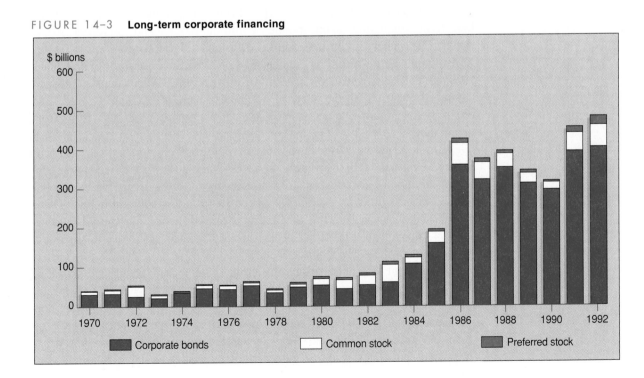

Equity Financing in General   When financing by common stock and preferred stock is combined, one industry has historically stood out, at least until recently. Stock financing of any significance from 1970 through 1982 was done by utility companies. Utilities accounted for an average of 41.7 percent of the stock financing during this time period. In 1974 utilities sold 61 percent of all stock offerings and, in the following five years, averaged over 50 percent of the total stock financing.

The pattern began to change in 1982. From 1982 to 1986, other firms besides public utilities were also heavy users of equity capital, and utilities accounted for only 7 percent of total stock issues. Manufacturing companies accounted for almost 22 percent of equity financing during this period, and other industries were also important. However, real estate and financial companies were by far the largest users of new equity, accounting for 22 percent of equity raised in 1982 and rising steadily to 50 percent by 1992. The increased dependence on equity financing for the financial segment of the economy can be expected to continue. Banks, investment bankers, and retail stockbrokers all need more equity capital to compete in global financial markets dominated by large financial companies. The new tax laws have also made debt less advantageous to the real estate industry and have increased the need for equity capital in this industry segment.

Internal versus External Sources of Funds

So far we have discussed how corporations raise funds externally through long-term financing, using bonds, common stock, and preferred stock. Another extremely important source of funds to the corporation is **internally generated funds** as represented by retained earnings and cash flow added back from depreciation. In our previous discussions of cost of capital (Chapter 11), the cost of retained earnings was considered, and our capital budgeting decisions (Chapter 12) also included cash flow from depreciation.

A look at Figure 14–4 shows that corporations have increased their reliance on external funds beginning in 1983. During the rising bull market for stocks and bonds, corporations took advantage of high security prices and liquid security markets to issue new issues of common stock and bonds. These rising markets, as well as low profitability, caused the use of external funds to reach 47 percent of total funds raised in 1986 and to stay close to historical highs through the early 1990s.

What about the composition of internal funds that make up the balance of the financing in Figure 14–4? A surprising thing for many people is that retained earnings do not account for the majority of internal funds used by corporations. Figure 14–5 shows that, on average, retained earnings made up about 30 percent of internal funds generated during the 1970s. The other 70 percent came from internally generated funds such as depreciation and deferred taxes.

FIGURE 14–4   **External versus internal funds raised**

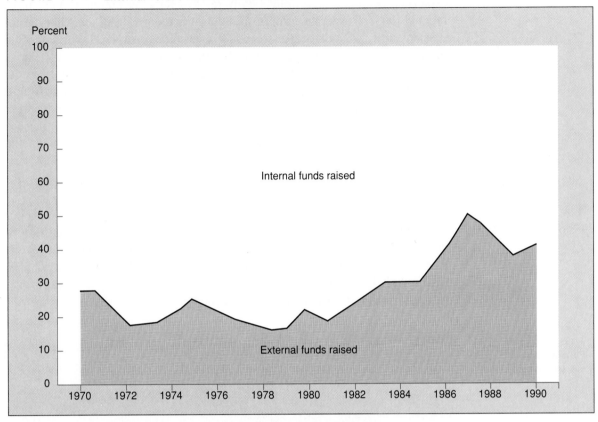

FIGURE 14–5   **Retained earnings (as a percentage of internal funds)**

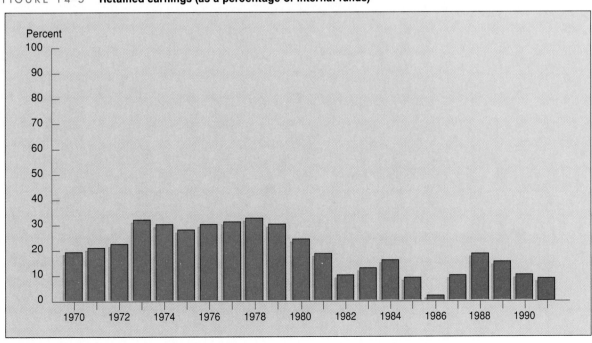

The ability of retained earnings to provide internal funds for corporate expansion declined more dramatically in the 1980s, averaging 12 percent of internal funds. Corporate earnings did not fully recover from the 1980–81 recession until 1987 and, after reaching a new peak in 1988, turned down through 1992. Low earnings, coupled with accelerated depreciation methods and higher dividends, created an internal funds flow derived mainly from depreciation benefits. Retained earnings accounted for less than 1 percent of all internal funds in 1986 (because of depressed profits) and about 7.5 percent in 1991. The decline in funds from retained earnings exerted a large influence on corporations, increasing the need for external funds during the 1980s and into the 1990s.

The Supply of Capital Funds

Having discussed the major users of capital in the U.S. economy, we turn our attention to the suppliers of capital. In a **three-sector economy,** consisting of business, government, and households, the major supplier of funds for investment is the household sector. Corporations and the federal government have traditionally been net demanders of funds. Figure 14–6 diagrams the flow of funds through our basic three-sector economy.

FIGURE 14–6
Flow of funds through the economy

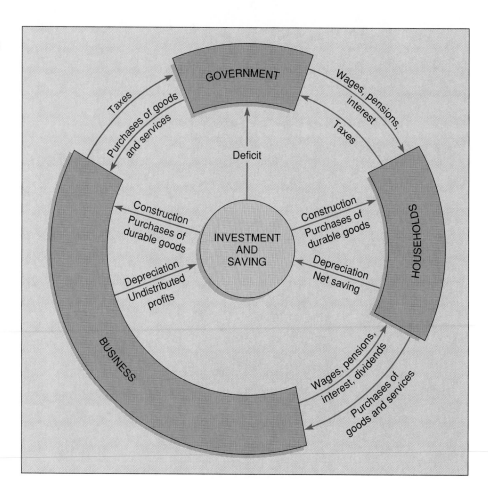

As households receive wages and transfer payments from the government and wages and dividends from corporations, they generally save some portion of their income. These savings are usually funneled to **financial intermediaries** that, in turn, make investments in the capital markets with the funds received from the household sector. This is known as indirect investment. The types of financial institutions that channel funds into the capital markets are specialized and diverse. Funds may flow into commercial banks, savings and loans, mutual savings banks, and credit unions. Households may also purchase mutual fund shares, invest in life insurance, or participate in some form of private pension plan or profit sharing. All these financial institutions act as intermediaries; they help make the flow of funds from one sector of the economy to another very efficient and competitive. Without intermediaries, the cost of funds would be higher, and the efficient allocation of funds to the best users at the lowest cost would not occur.

The international saver and investor has also become a critical supplier to the U.S. capital markets, as previously pointed out.

The Role of the Security Markets

Security markets exist to aid the allocation of capital among households, corporations, and governmental units, with financial institutions acting as intermediaries. Just as financial institutions specialize in their services and investments, so are the capital markets divided into many functional subsets, with each specific market serving a certain type of security. For example the common stocks of some of the largest corporations are traded on the New York Stock Exchange, whereas government securities are traded by government security dealers in the over-the-counter markets.

Once a security is sold for the first time as an original offering, the security trades in its appropriate market among all kinds of investors. This trading activity is known as **secondary trading,** since funds flow among investors, rather than to the corporation. Secondary trading provides liquidity to investors and keeps prices competitive among alternative security investments.

Security markets provide liquidity in two ways. First, they enable corporations to raise funds by selling new issues of securities rapidly and at fair, competitive prices. Second, they allow the investor who purchases securities to sell them with relative ease and speed and thereby to turn a paper asset into cash. Ask yourself the question, "Would I buy securities if there were no place to sell them?" You would probably think twice before committing funds to an illiquid investment. Without markets, corporations and governmental units would not be able to raise the large amounts of capital necessary for economic growth.

The competitive structure and organization of the security markets have changed considerably since the early 1970s. In this section we present the current organization of the markets and provide an update of significant events of the last few years. The most common division of security markets is

The Organization of the Security Markets

between organized exchanges and over-the-counter markets. Each will be examined separately.

The Organized Exchanges

Organized exchanges are either national or regional in scope. Each exchange has a central location where all buyers and sellers meet in an auction market to transact purchases and sales. Buyers and sellers are not actually present on the floor of the exchange but are represented by **brokers** who act as their agents. These brokers are registered members of the exchange. On the **New York Stock Exchange,** the number of members has been fixed at 1,366 since 1953, while the **American Stock Exchange** has a fixed limit of 650 members.

The New York Stock Exchange (NYSE) and the American Stock Exchange (AMEX) are national exchanges, and each is governed by an elected board of directors, of whom half are public directors and the other half industry representatives. Although the Chicago and Pacific Coast exchanges are the largest of the so-called **regional stock exchanges,** they trade primarily in issues of large national companies. Some of the smaller exchanges, such as the Detroit, Boston, Cincinnati, and PBW,[2] are more regional in the sense that most of the companies listed on them are headquartered or do their principal business in the region in which the exchange is located. These smaller exchanges account for a very small percentage of trading in listed securities.

Securities can only be listed and traded on an exchange with the approval of the board of the exchange. Until October 1976 the NYSE and AMEX were mutually exclusive and did not allow shares of stock to be listed on both exchanges. Under prodding from the Securities and Exchange Commission (SEC), both exchanges agreed to allow dual listing so securities could be traded on both exchanges simultaneously. Currently no companies maintain dual listing on the NYSE and AMEX. Dual listing has long been common between the NYSE and the regional exchanges. Approximately 90 percent of the stocks traded on the Chicago and Pacific exchanges are also traded on the NYSE. This means the shares of many large companies can be purchased on several different exchanges, which helps to make prices more competitive and the markets more efficient in establishing prices.

Although **dual trading** has been common for many years, brokers on the floor of an exchange did not have immediate price information from the other markets. To make prices of all competitive trades in the same stock available to all market participants at the same time, the SEC pressured for creation of a consolidated tape, which became reality on June 16, 1975. The consolidated tape presents the prices and volume of all shares traded on the regional exchanges and the NYSE. This information is visible to all brokers on the floor of each exchange and allows traders on each exchange to follow the activity and prices on all other exchanges, as well as any over-the-counter trades in

---

[2]The PBW was formed by a merger of the Philadelphia, Baltimore, and Washington exchanges.

listed securities. Because of the consolidated tape, prices are more competitive and efficient.

The New York Stock Exchange

Size and Liquidity   The NYSE is the largest and most important of all the exchanges. In 1992 it accounted for almost 82 percent of the volume of all listed stocks on the consolidated tapes and 65 percent of total trades. Liquidity provided by the NYSE is also evident by the fact that the average daily share trading volume during 1992 was 202 million shares. By the end of 1992, companies listed on the NYSE had over 115 billion shares of stock listed on the exchange, their worth being close to $4 trillion. We can see that the NYSE is certainly an important mechanism in the flow of funds among investors of all types (though there is much new competition coming into play).

Listing Requirements   Each organized exchange has some minimum **listing requirement** that a company must meet before the exchange will agree to trade its securities. Most of the largest U.S. companies are traded on the NYSE, as its listing requirements are more stringent than those of the AMEX or the regionals.

Although each case is decided on its own merits, according to the *NYSE Fact Book,* the minimum requirements for a company to be listed on the New York Stock Exchange for the first time are as follows:

1. Demonstrated earning power under competitive conditions of: *either* $2.5 million before federal income taxes for the most recent year and $2 million pre-tax for each of the preceding two years, *or* an aggregate for the last three fiscal years of $6.5 million *together with* a minimum in the most recent fiscal year of $4.5 million. (All three years must be profitable.)
2. Net tangible assets of $18 million, but greater emphasis is placed on the aggregate market value of the common stock.
3. Market value of publicly held shares, at least equal to $18 million.
4. A total of 1,100,000 common shares publicly held.
5. *Either* 2,000 holders of 100 shares or more, *or* 2,200 total stockholders *together with* average monthly trading volume (for the most recent six months) of 100,000 shares.

Corporations desiring to be listed on exchanges have decided that public availability of the stock on an exchange will benefit their shareholders. The benefits will occur either by providing liquidity to owners or by allowing the company a more viable means for raising external capital for growth and expansion. The company must pay annual listing fees to the exchange and additional fees based on the number of shares traded each year.

The New York Stock Exchange also has the authority to remove (delist) or suspend a security from trading when the security fails to meet certain criteria. There is much latitude in these decisions, but generally a company's security may be considered for delisting if there are fewer than 1,200 round-lot (100 share) owners, 600,000 shares or fewer in public hands, and market value of the security is less than $5 million. A company that easily exceeded these standards on first being listed may fall below them during hard times.

Foreign Exchanges

As the industrialized world has grown, capital markets around the world have increased in size and importance. As a sign of the international capital markets, large U.S. international companies—such as IBM, Sears, and McDonald's—trade on the Tokyo and Frankfurt stock exchanges; and many foreign companies trade on the New York Stock Exchange—such as Sony and TDK of Japan; British Petroleum, Royal Dutch Petroleum, and Phillips G.N.V. of the Netherlands; and BMW and Siemens of Germany.

Table 14–1 lists the major global stock markets by country, alphabetically. Not all are large but most are flourishing, with growing volume, new listings, and increased interest by investors worldwide.

TABLE 14–1
Global stock markets

Australia	Mexico
Austria	Netherlands
Belgium	Norway
Canada	Singapore/Malaysia
Denmark	Spain
France	Sweden
Germany	Swizerland
Hong Kong	United Kingdom
Italy	United States
Japan	

As more companies have their common stock listed on exchanges around the world, the easier it will be for trading to be continuous for 24 hours per day. Already several exchanges have linked their trading floors so trading can be maintained at all hours of the day. For example, the Chicago Mercantile Exchange, which specializes in metals, foreign exchange currencies, and interest rate futures contracts, has instituted 24-hour computer trading by linking with Reuters Holding PLC. This new system, called Globex, enables customers around the world to trade financial futures products when their own exchange is closed. Other systems patterned after this could begin to show up in stock and bond markets during the next few years.

The Over-the-Counter Markets

Corporations trading in the **over-the-counter market (OTC)** are referred to as unlisted. This is primarily a domestic market. There is no central location for the OTC market; instead, a network of **dealers** all over the country is linked by computer display terminals, telephones, and teletypes. The difference between *dealers* in the OTC markets and *brokers* on exchanges is that dealers own the securities they trade, while brokers act as agents for the buyers and sellers. Dealers are much like any wholesaler or retailer who possesses an inventory of goods. They price the goods to reflect their cost and to manage their inventory by seeking a balance between supply and demand.

Many dealers make markets in the same security, and this creates very competitive prices. With the advent of a centralized computer to keep track of all trades and prices, dealers have up-to-the-minute price information on all competing dealers. Many people currently think that the structure of the OTC market is more competitive and cost efficient than organized exchanges.

At least 5,000 stocks are actively traded over the counter, but the average price of the securities is low, so the dollar volume of the stocks traded is not as great as that of the organized exchanges. The OTC markets are supervised by the **National Association of Securities Dealers (NASD).** In recent years the NASD has divided the OTC market into various groupings based on size and trading requirements. The segment with the biggest companies is called the **NASDAQ National Market,** followed by the **NASDAQ Small-Cap Market.** These categories make it easier to distinguish between various sized companies. The NASDAQ National Market includes such companies as Apple Computer, MCI Communications, Intel, Coors, Lotus Development, and so on, while the NASDAQ Small-Cap Market includes smaller firms. The Small-Caps could include companies centered in one city or state with little national ownership or small developmental companies, with stock priced as low as 25 cents per share, or companies that are closely held by the founders, with very few shares available for trading. The NASDAQ estimates that at least 600 companies trading on the previously mentioned National Market would meet the listing requirements of the New York Stock Exchange.

Although the AMEX and NYSE both trade corporate bonds and a small number of government securities, the bulk of all bond trading is done over-the-counter. Trading in government bonds, notes, and Treasury bills through government security dealers makes the OTC the largest market for security transactions in total dollars (though the NYSE is clearly the largest for just stocks).

Market Efficiency

We have mentioned competitive and efficient markets in this chapter, but so far we have not given any criteria to judge whether the U.S. securities markets are indeed competitive and efficient.

Criteria of Efficiency

There are several concepts of **market efficiency** and there are many degrees of efficiency, depending on which market we are talking about. Markets in general are efficient when: (1) prices adjust rapidly to new information; (2) there is a continuous market, in which each successive trade is made at a price close to the previous price (the faster that the price responds to new information and the smaller the differences in price changes, the more efficient the market); and (3) the market can absorb large dollar amounts of securities without destabilizing the price.

A key variable affecting efficiency is the certainty of the income stream. The more certain the expected income, the less volatile price movements will be. Fixed income securities, with known maturities, have reasonably efficient markets. The most efficient market is that for U.S. government securities, with the short-term Treasury bill market being exemplary. Corporate bond markets are somewhat efficient, but less so than government bond markets. A question that is still widely debated and researched by academics is the degree of efficiency for common stock.

The Efficient Market Hypothesis

If stock markets are efficient, it is very difficult for investors to select portfolios of common stocks that can outperform the stock market in general. The efficient market hypothesis is stated in three forms—the weak, semistrong, and strong.

The weak form simply states that past price information is unrelated to future prices, and that trends cannot be predicted and taken advantage of by investors. The semistrong form states that prices currently reflect all *public* information. Most of the research in this area focuses on changes in public information and on the measurement of how rapidly prices converge to a new equilibrium after new information has been released. The strong form states that all information, *both private and public,* is immediately reflected in stock prices.

Generally researchers have indicated that markets are somewhat efficient in the weak and semistrong sense, but not in the strong sense (private, insider information is valuable—though generally illegal to use for quick profits).

Our objective in bringing up this subject is to make you aware that much current research is focused on the measurement of market efficiency. As communications systems advance, information gets disseminated faster and more accurately. Furthermore, securities laws are forcing fuller disclosure of corporate data. It would appear that our security markets are generally efficient, but not perfect, in digesting information and adjusting stock prices.

Regulation of the Security Markets

Organized securities markets are regulated by the Securities and Exchange Commission (SEC) and by the self-regulation of the exchanges. The OTC market is controlled by the National Association of Securities Dealers. Three major laws govern the sale and subsequent trading of securities. The Securities Act of 1933 pertains to new issues of securities, while the Securities Exchange Act of 1934 deals with trading in the securities markets. The latest major legislation is the Securities Acts Amendments of 1975, whose main emphasis is on a national securities market. The primary purpose of these laws is to protect unwary investors from fraud and manipulation and to make the markets more competitive and efficient by forcing corporations to make relevant investment information public.

Securities Act of 1933

The **Securities Act of 1933** was enacted after congressional investigations of the abuses present in the securities markets during the 1929 crash. Its primary purpose was to provide full disclosure of all pertinent investment information whenever a corporation sold a new issue of securities. For this reason, it is sometimes referred to as the truth-in-securities act. The Securities Act of 1933 has several important features, which follow:

1. All offerings except government bonds and bank stocks that are to be sold in more than one state must be registered with the SEC.[3]
2. The registration statement must be filed 20 days in advance of the date of sale and must include detailed corporate information.[4] If the SEC finds the information misleading, incomplete, or inaccurate, it will delay the offering until the registration statement is corrected. The SEC in no way certifies that the security is fairly priced, but only that the information seems to be accurate.
3. All new issues of securities must be accompanied by a prospectus containing the same information appearing in the registration statement. Usually included in the prospectus are a list of directors and officers; their salaries, stock options, and shareholdings; financial reports certified by a CPA; a list of the underwriters; the purpose and use of the funds to be provided from the sales of securities; and any other reasonable information that investors may need before they can wisely invest their money. A preliminary prospectus may be distributed to potential buyers before the offering date, but it will not contain the offering price or the underwriting fees. It is called a "red herring" because stamped on the front in red letters are the words *preliminary prospectus.*
4. For the first time, officers of the company and other experts preparing the prospectus or the registration statement could be sued for penalties and recovery of realized losses if any information presented was fraudulent, factually wrong, or omitted.

Securities Exchange Act of 1934

This act created the **Securities and Exchange Commission** to enforce the securities laws. The SEC was empowered to regulate the securities markets

---

[3]Actually the SEC was not established until 1934. References to the SEC in this section refer to 1934 to the present. The FTC performed these functions in 1933.

[4]Shelf registration, which was initiated by the SEC in 1982, changes this provision somewhat. Shelf registration is discussed in Chapter 15.

and those companies listed on the exchanges. Specifically, the major points of the **Securities Exchange Act of 1934** are:

1. Guidelines for insider trading were established. Insiders must hold securities for at least six months before they can sell them. This is to prevent them from taking quick advantage of information, which could result in a short-term profit. All short-term profits are payable to the corporation.[5] Insiders were at first generally thought to be officers, directors, employees, or relatives. In the late 1960s, however, the SEC widened its interpretation to include anyone having information that was not public knowledge. This could include security analysts, loan officers, large institutional holders, and many others who had business dealings with the firm.

2. The Federal Reserve's Board of Governors became responsible for setting margin requirements to determine how much credit would be available to purchasers of securities.

3. Manipulation of securities by conspiracies among investors was prohibited.

4. The SEC was given control over the proxy procedures of corporations (a proxy is an absent stockholder's vote).

5. In its regulation of companies traded on the markets, the SEC required that certain reports be filed periodically. Corporations must file quarterly financial statements and annual 10K reports with the SEC and send annual reports to stockholders. The 10K report has more financial data than the annual report and can be very useful to an investor or a loan officer. Most companies will now send 10K reports to stockholders on request.

6. The act required all security exchanges to register with the SEC. In this capacity, the SEC supervises and regulates many pertinent organizational aspects of exchanges, such as the mechanics of listing and trading.

Securities Acts Amendments of 1975

The major focus of the **Securities Acts Amendments of 1975** was to direct the SEC to supervise the development of a national securities market. No exact structure was put forth, but the law did assume that any national market would make extensive use of computers and electronic communication devices. In addition the law prohibited fixed commissions on public transactions and also prohibited banks, insurance companies, and other financial institutions from buying stock exchange memberships to save commission costs

---

[5] In the mid-1980s, Congress and the SEC passed legislation to make the penalty three times the size of the gain.

FINANCE IN ACTION

Security Regulation as We Move into the Next Century

The major security laws that were passed in the 1930s were needed to restore confidence in the stock market. After the great market crash of 1929, investors felt they needed a watchdog in the form of the Securities and Exchange Commission to look over their interests. No longer could companies easily lie or mislead investors about their earnings or growth prospects. Not only the corporation but also the officers and directors of the corporation were made liable for fraud.

In the 1970s and 1980s, there was a backlash against government regulation in all forms. The airline, banking, and savings and loan industries were given new freedoms and flexibility that they had not previously enjoyed. However, as taxpayers were asked to bail out the savings and loan industry (at the rate of $2,000 per person over the next 30 years), many clamored for *re-regulation* of the financial services industry so that the same disaster would not reoccur among banks, insurance companies, or even stock brokerage firms.

Where do we stand today, and more importantly, where will we stand as we move into the 21st century? In regard to the securities markets, it is a basic fact that tight regulation will simply not work as it once did. Why? The answer is globalization of the securities markets. Ultimately, Washington will be forced to lessen long-standing tough disclosure and accounting standards to be in harmony with the rest of the world. Otherwise, firms and investors will take their business to London, Tokyo, Paris, and elsewhere. To a certain extent, they already have. The value of U.S. private pension fund assets invested abroad has grown from $21 billion in 1980 to over $250 billion.* Firms such as IBM and Exxon have listed their securities on foreign stock exchanges throughout the world. A similar movement to U.S. security markets by foreign firms has been slow because of our tougher standards.

In time, a *stateless* electronic market trading world-class securities is likely to develop. By the year 2000, the emphasis will not be so much on domestic rules and regulations but on acceptable international methods and standards of performance.

*"The Future of Wall Street; Why Our Financial System Will Never Be the Same," *Business Week,* November 5, 1990, pp. 119–32.

for their own institutional transactions. This act is a worthwhile addition to the securities laws, since it fosters greater competition and more efficient prices. Much progress has already been made on the national market system as mandated by this act.

Current Legislative Issues

In the early 1990s, a wave of new legislation is also being considered to further deal with the abuses of insider trading. The scandals surrounding the massive profits accumulated by Wall Street traders Ivan Boesky, Mike Milken, Dennis Levine, and others, as a result of using improperly acquired information, has triggered the congressional interest. While most of these people have been successfully prosecuted, a fear remains that the small trader may be at a competitive disadvantage when it comes to privileged information.

Another development of the late 1980s and early 1990s has been the use of **program trading** by large institutional investors (such as mutual funds, pension funds, and bank trust departments). Program trading means that computer-based trigger points in the market are established by these traders for unusually big orders to buy or sell securities. If a large number of institutional investors engage in program trading at the same time (and all are either buying or selling), there is the potential for a market crash (such as on October 19, 1987) or an incredible market rise. Many government regulators are looking into the process of program trading, with an eye toward future legislation. To some extent the securities industry itself has tried to head off government regulation in this area by placing limits (so-called collars) on the amount that the market can move before the use of program trading is temporarily suspended.

Summary

In this chapter we presented the concept of a capital market, in which corporations compete for funds not only among themselves but also with governmental units of all kinds. Corporations account for a significant percent of all funds raised in the capital market, and most of that is obtained through the sale of corporate debt. We also depicted a three-sector economy, consisting of households, corporations, and governmental units, and showed how funds flow through the capital markets from suppliers of funds to the ultimate users. This process is highly dependent on the efficiency of the financial institutions that act as intermediaries in channeling the funds to the most productive users.

Security markets are divided into organized exchanges and over-the-counter markets. Brokers act as agents for stock exchange transactions, and dealers make markets in over-the-counter stocks at their own risk as owners of the securities they trade. The New York Stock Exchange is the largest of the organized exchanges. We explored some of its major characteristics, such as its relative size, the liquidity it provides corporations and investors, and its requirements for listing securities. Although the OTC market for stock is not as large as that of the organized exchanges, a majority of corporate bond trades and almost all trades in municipal and federal government securities are transacted over-the-counter. Foreign markets are also becoming increasingly important.

Throughout this chapter we have tried to present the concept of efficient markets doing an important job in allocating financial capital. We find that the existing markets provide liquidity for both the corporation and the investor, and that they are efficient in adjusting to new information. Because of the laws governing the markets, much information is available for investors, and this in itself creates more competitive prices. In the future, we expect even more efficient markets, with a national market system using the best of both the NYSE and OTC trading systems.

money markets 408
capital markets 408
U.S. government securities 410
federally sponsored credit
   agencies 411
municipal securities 412
internally generated funds 414
three-sector economy 416
financial intermediaries 417
secondary trading 417
brokers 418
New York Stock Exchange 418
American Stock Exchange 418
regional stock exchanges 418
dual trading 418
listing requirement 419
over-the-counter market
   (OTC) 420

dealer 420
National Association of Security
   Dealers (NASD) 421
NASDAQ National Market 421
NASDAQ Small-Cap
   Market 421
Market efficiency 421
Securities Act of 1933 423
Securities and Exchange
   Commission 423
Securities Exchange Act of
   1934 424
Securities Acts Amendments of
   1975 424
program trading 426

1. What is the difference between the money and the capital markets?
2. Why do firms list their securities on foreign capital markets?
3. Is the international equity market larger than the U.S. equity market?
4. Name the major competitors for funds in the U.S. capital markets.
5. Are federally sponsored credit agency issues directly backed by the U.S. Treasury?
6. What has been the percentage composition of long-term financing (bonds, preferred stock, and common stock) by corporations from 1970 through 1992?
7. What industries were the largest users of equity capital between 1982 and 1992? What industry has previously been the largest user?
8. Explain the role of financial intermediaries in the flow of funds through the economy.
9. Discuss the importance of security markets for both the corporation and the stockholder or bondholder.
10. What is the difference between organized exchanges and over-the-counter markets?
11. Why does the New York Stock Exchange have listing requirements? What are the major requirements? How do they compare with the listing requirements of the other exchanges?
12. How would you define efficient security markets?

13. The efficient market hypothesis is interpreted in a weak form, a semistrong form, and a strong form. How can we differentiate its various forms?

14. Why is the 24-hour trading day becoming progressively more important?

15. Discuss the major implications of the Securities Act of 1933 and the Securities Exchange Act of 1934.

16. Why has there been a renewed interest in regulating insider trading in the 1980s and early 1990s?

Problem

Financial markets

1. Go to the latest issue of the *Federal Reserve Bulletin* and see whether you can update Figures 14–2 and 14–3.

Selected References

Baker, H. Kent, and Richard B. Edelman. "The Effect of Spread and Volume of Switching to the NASDAQ Market System." *Financial Analysts Journal* 83 (January–February 1992), pp. 83–86.

Conroy, Robert M., and Richard J. Rendleman, Jr. "A Test of Market Efficiency in Government Bonds." *Journal of Portfolio Management* 13 (Summer 1987), pp. 57–64.

Cowan, Arnold R., Richard B. Carter, Frederick H. Dark, and Ajai K. Singh. "Explaining the NYSE Listing of NASDAQ Firms." *Financial Management* 21 (Winter 1992), pp. 73–86.

Feinberg, Phyllis. "$200-Billion Foreign Exchange Market Serves Even All-Domestic Firms." *Corporate Cashflow* 10 (July 1989), pp. 50–53.

Gamble, Richard H. "Capital Markets Enter the 1990s: The Outlook." *Corporate Cashflow* 10 (December 1989), pp. 24–33.

Howe, John S., and Kathryn Kelm. "The Stock Price Impacts of Overseas Listings." *Financial Management* 16 (Autumn 1987), pp. 51–56.

Jensen, Michael C. "Some Anomalous Evidence Regarding Market Efficiency." *Journal of Financial Economics* 5 (June–September 1978).

Marsh, Paul. "The Choice between Equity and Debt: An Empirical Study." *Journal of Finance* 37 (March 1982), pp. 121–44.

Modhavan, Ananth. "Trading Mechanisms in Securities Markets." *Journal of Finance* 47 (June 1992), pp. 607–41.

Oppenheimer, Henry, and Gary Schlarbaum. "Investing with Ben Graham: An Ex Ante Test of the Efficient Markets Hypothesis." *Journal of Financial and Quantitative Analysis* 16 (September 1981), pp. 341–60.

Sanger, Gary C., and John J. McConnell. "Stock Exchange Listings, Firm Value, and Security Market Efficiency: The Impact of NASDAQ." *Journal of Financial & Quantitative Analysis* 21 (March 1986), pp. 1–25.

Selected issues of the *Federal Reserve Bulletin*.

Sweeney, Richard J., and Arthur D. Worga. "The Pricing of Interest Rate Risk: Evidence from the Stock Market." *Journal of Finance* 41 (June 1986), pp. 393–410.

nies even choose to sell their own securities directly. Both the "best efforts" and "direct" methods account for a relatively small portion of total offerings.

Market Maker   During distribution and for a limited time after, the investment banker may make a market in a given security—that is, engage in the buying and selling of the security to ensure a liquid market. The investment banker may also provide research on the firm to encourage active investor interest.

Advisor   The investment banker may advise clients on a continuing basis about the types of securities to be sold, the number of shares or units for distribution, and the timing of the sale. A company considering a stock issuance to the public may be persuaded, in counsel with an investment banker, to borrow the funds from an insurance company or, if stock is to be sold, to wait for two more quarters of earnings before going to the market. The investment banker also provides important advisory services in the area of mergers and acquisitions, leveraged buyouts, and corporate restructuring.

Agency Functions   The investment banker may act as an **agent** for a corporation that wishes to place its securities privately with an insurance company, a pension fund, or a wealthy individual. In this instance the investment banker will shop around among potential investors and negotiate the best possible deal for the corporation.

The Distribution Process

The actual distribution process requires the active participation of a number of parties. The principal or **managing investment banker** will call on other investment banking houses to share the burden of risk and to aid in the distribution. To this end, they will form an **underwriting syndicate** comprising as few as 2 or as many as 100 investment banking houses. In Figure 15–1 on page 432, we see a typical case in which a hypothetical firm, the Maxwell Corporation, wishes to issue 250,000 additional shares of stock with Merrill Lynch as the managing underwriter and an underwriting syndicate of 15 firms.

The underwriting syndicate will purchase shares from the Maxwell Corporation and distribute them through the channels of distribution. Syndicate members will act as wholesalers in distributing the shares to brokers and dealers who will eventually sell the shares to the public. Large investment banking houses may be vertically integrated, acting as underwriter-dealer-broker and capturing all fees and commissions.

The Spread   The **underwriting spread** represents the total compensation for those who participate in the distribution process. If the public or retail price is $21.50 and the managing investment banker pays a price of $20.00 to the issuing company, we say there is a total spread of $1.50. The $1.50 may be divided up among the participants, as indicated in Figure 15–2.

Note that the lower a party falls in the distribution process, the higher the price for shares. The managing investment banker pays $20, while dealers pay

FIGURE 15–1
**Distribution process in
investment banking**

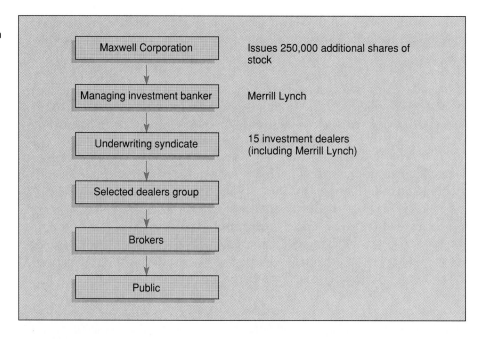

FIGURE 15–1
**Distribution process in
investment banking**

FIGURE 15–2
**Allocation of
underwriting spread**

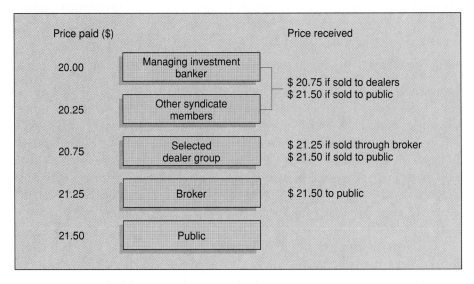

$20.75. Also, the farther down the line the securities are resold, the higher is the potential profit. If the managing investment banker resells to dealers, he makes 75 cents per share; if he resells to the public, he makes $1.50.

The total spread of $1.50 in the present case represents 7 percent of the offering price ($1.50/$21.50). Generally, the larger the dollar value of an issue, the smaller the spread is as a percentage of the offering price. Percentage figures on underwriting spreads for U.S. corporations are presented in Table 15–1. Because there is more uncertainty in the market reaction to common stock, a larger spread often exists for common stock than for other types of offerings.

Since the Maxwell Corporation stock issue is for $5.375 million (250,000 shares × $21.50), the 7 percent spread is in line with SEC figures in

TABLE 15–1
Underwriting compensation as a percentage of proceeds

Size of Issue ($ millions)	Spread	
	Common Stock	Debt
Under 0.5	11.3%	7.4%
0.5–0.9	9.7	7.2
1.0–1.9	8.6	7.0
2.0–4.9	7.4	4.2
5.0–9.9	6.7	1.5
10.0–19.9	6.2	1.0
20.0–49.9	4.9	1.0
50.0 and over . . .	2.3	0.8

Source: Securities and Exchange Commission data.

Table 15–1. It should be noted that the issuer bears not only the "give-up" expense of the spread in the underwriting process but also out-of-pocket costs related to legal and accounting fees, printing expenses, and so forth. As indicated in Table 15–2, when the spread plus the out-of-pocket costs are considered, the total cost of a new issue is rather high. Of course substantial benefits may be received in return.

TABLE 15–2
Total costs to issue stock (percentage of total proceeds)

Size of Issue ($ millions)	Common Stock		
	Spread	Out-of-Pocket Cost*	Total Expense
Under 0.5	11.3%	7.3%	18.6%
0.5–0.9	9.7	4.9	14.6
1.0–1.9	8.6	3.0	11.6
2.0–4.9	7.4	1.7	9.1
5.0–9.9	6.7	1.0	7.7
10.0–19.9	6.2	0.6	6.8
20.0–49.9	4.9	0.8	5.7
50.0 and over . . .	2.3	0.3	2.6

*Out-of-pocket cost of debts is approximately the same.
Source: Securities and Exchange Commission data.

Pricing the Security

Because the syndicate members purchase the stock for redistribution in the marketing channels, they must be careful about the pricing of the stock. When a stock is sold to the public for the first time (i.e., the firm is going public), the managing investment banker will do an in-depth analysis of the company to determine its value. The study will include an analysis of the firm's industry, financial characteristics, and anticipated earnings and dividend-paying capability. Based on appropriate valuation techniques, a price will be tentatively assigned and will be compared to that enjoyed by similar firms in a given industry. If the industry's average price-earnings ratio is 12, the firm should not stray too far from this norm. Anticipated public demand will also be a major factor in pricing a new issue.

The great majority of the issues handled by investment bankers are, however, additional issues of stocks or bonds for companies already trading

FINANCE IN ACTION

Investment Banks Pocket $6.76 Billion in Fees

Disclosed fees from new issue underwriting

Manager	Full-Year 1992			Full-Year 1991	
	Amount ($ millions)	Market Share	Number of Issues	Amount ($ millions)	Rank
Merrill Lynch	$1,418.5	21.0%	834	$844.2	1
Goldman Sachs	914.5	13.5	534	701.7	2
Lehman Brothers	659.5	9.8	503	345.2	5
Morgan Stanley	616.4	9.1	356	479.4	3
First Boston	484.2	7.2	381	341.1	6
Salomon Brothers	328.1	4.9	268	289.6	7
Donaldson Lufkin	238.2	3.5	117	71.5	13
Alex. Brown	208.2	3.1	60	447.7	4
PaineWebber	191.4	2.8	109	115.1	8
Prudential Securities	191.1	2.8	107	96.4	10
Top 10	$5,250.4	77.7%	3,269	$3,731.9	—
Industry total	$6,756.0	100.0%	5,157	$4,665.0	—

Source: Securities Data Co.

Wall Street investment banks pocketed a record $6.76 billion in underwriting fees in 1992, propelling the securities industry to its most profitable year ever. Last year's underwriting fee level easily eclipsed the prior record of $5.07 billion, set in 1986, according to Securities Data Co., and is 45 percent higher than 1991's level. Wall Street earns fees by buying new securities from corporate issuers and reselling them to the public at a markup.

"In real estate, it's location, location, location. In underwriting fees, it's volume, volume, volume," says Michael D. Madden, co-head of investment banking at Lehman Brothers. "Everybody enjoyed a record equity-underwriting year and that translated into record fees."

This fee explosion helped to boost brokerage firms to record profits in 1992, analysts say. Amid the boom in stock and bond underwriting and trading, Wall Street securities firms earned record pretax profits totaling as much as $7 billion in 1992, according to estimates from the Securities Industry Association, a trade group. That is 20 percent higher than the prior profit record, set in 1991.

Merrill snared the No. 1 spot in the underwriting-fee race for the fifth straight year. The nation's largest brokerage firm earned a record $1.4 billion in fees for a 21 percent market share, stemming from Merrill's broad-based dominance of the underwriting market.

The fee table provides the best gauge to how much Wall Street investment banks generate from underwriting new stocks and bonds. But the rankings don't necessarily correlate with the actual profits earned from underwriting among securities firms, investment bankers say. The numbers reflect only disclosed fees; on many deals, particularly mortgage-backed and derivatives transactions, fees aren't fully shown.

Full credit for fees is given to the lead manager in an underwriting syndicate. But in reality, those fees typically are spread among several investment banks in the deal. This typically translates into lead managers keeping about 50 percent of the underwriting fee, with the co-managers sharing the rest, investment bankers say.

Moreover, lead managers end up keeping only part of the fee. About 60 percent of an underwriting fee goes to the firm's operating profit before taxes and bonuses; the other 40 percent typically is eaten up by legal, administrative, and sales expenses, the bankers say.

Stock transactions often are many times as profitable as the typical bond deal, investment bankers say. Indeed, Wall Street firms typically have to manage as much as $150 billion of bond underwritings to generate $100 million of revenue, say investment bankers.

Source: Michael Siconolfi, "Investment Banks Pocket $6.76 Billion in Fees," *The Wall Street Journal*, January 4, 1993, p. R38. Reprinted by permission of THE WALL STREET JOURNAL, © 1993 Dow Jones & Company, Inc. All Rights Reserved Worldwide.

publicly. When additional shares are to be issued, the investment bankers will generally set the price at slightly below the current market value. This process, known as **underpricing**, will help ensure a receptive market for the securities.

At times an investment banker will also handle large blocks of securities for existing stockholders. Because the number of shares may be too large to trade in normal channels, the investment banker will manage the issue and underprice the stock below current prices to the public. Such a process is known as a secondary offering, in contrast to a primary offering, in which new corporate securities are sold.

Dilution

A problem a company faces when issuing additional securities is the actual or perceived **dilution of earnings** effect on shares currently outstanding. In the case of the Maxwell Corporation, the 250,000 new shares may represent a 10 percent increment to shares currently in existence. Perhaps the firm had earnings of $5 million on 2,500,000 shares before the offering, indicating earnings per share of $2. With 250,000 new shares to be issued, earnings per share will temporarily slip to $1.82.

The proceeds from the sale of new shares may well be expected to provide the increased earnings necessary to bring earnings back to at least $2. While financial theory dictates that a new equity issue should not be undertaken if it diminishes the overall wealth of current stockholders, there may be a perceived time lag in the recovery of earnings per share as a result of the increased shares outstanding. For this reason, there may be a temporary weakness in a stock when an issue of additional shares is proposed. In most cases this is overcome with time.

Market Stabilization

Another problem may set in when the actual public distribution begins— namely, unanticipated weakness in the stock or bond market. Since the sales group normally has made a firm commitment to purchase stock at a given price for redistribution, it is essential that the price of the stock remain relatively strong. Syndicate members, committed to purchasing the stock at $20 or better, could be in trouble if the sales price fell to $19 or $18. The managing investment banker is generally responsible for stabilizing the offering during the distribution period and may accomplish this by repurchasing securities as the market price moves below the initial public offering price of $21.50.

The period of **market stabilization** usually lasts two or three days after the initial offering, but it may extend up to 30 days for difficult-to-distribute securities. In a very poor market environment, stabilization may be virtually impossible to achieve. As a classic example, when Federal Reserve Board Chairman Paul Volcker announced an extreme credit-tightening policy in October 1979, newly underwritten, high-quality IBM bond prices fell dramatically, and Salomon Brothers and other investment bankers got trapped into approximately $10 million in losses. The bonds later recovered in value, but the investment bankers had already taken their losses.

Aftermarket

The investment banker is also interested in how well the underwritten security behaves after the distribution period—for the banker's ultimate reputation rests on bringing strong securities to the market. This is particularly true of initial public offerings.

Research has indicated that initial public offerings often do well in the immediate **aftermarket**. For example one study examined approximately 500 firms and determined there were 10.9 percent excess returns one week after issue (excess returns refers to movement in the price of the stock above and beyond the market). There were also positive excess returns of 11.6 percent for a full month after issue, but a negative market-adjusted performance of −3.0 percent one full year after issue.[1] Because the managing underwriter may underprice the issue initially to ensure a successful offering, often the value jumps after the issue first goes public. However, the efficiency of the market eventually takes hold, and sustained long-term performance depends on the quality of the issue and the market conditions at play.

Changes in the Investment Banking Industry

Investment banking is becoming more internationally oriented, with U.S. investment bankers and foreign investment bankers underwriting securities in the United States, Europe, and Asia.

In the early 1980s, nonbrokerage firms moved into the brokerage area through acquisitions and, at the same time, absorbed these firms' investment banking activities. The merger of Prudential Insurance Company with Bache Halsey Stuart Shields was the first of these types of mergers. Sears acquired Dean Witter Reynolds. American Express purchased Shearson Loeb Rhoades and E. F. Hutton brokerage operations and Lehman Brothers investment bankers.

By 1993 the mergers within the industry had not turned out as positively as expected. American Express sold Shearson's retail brokerage business to Primerica, and Sears sold a portion of Dean Witter (including the Discover Card) to the public with plans to eventually distribute the rest to Sears' shareholders.

Nevertheless the industry is still highly concentrated; the 10 largest investment bankers controlled 87.4 percent of the volume in 1992. The top three firms in 1992—Merrill Lynch, Goldman Sachs, and Lehman Brothers—did over 40 percent of the total business.

Shelf Registration

In February 1982, the Securities and Exchange Commission began allowing a new filing process, called shelf registration, under SEC Rule 415. **Shelf registration** permits large companies, such as Exxon or Citicorp, to file one comprehensive registration statement, which outlines the firm's financing

---

[1] Frank K. Reilly, "New Issues Revisited," *Financial Management* 6 (Winter 1977), pp. 28–42. Similar studies have confirmed these results.

plans for up to the next two years. Then, when market conditions seem appropriate, the firm can issue the securities without further SEC approval. Future issues are thought to be sitting on the shelf, waiting for the appropriate time to appear.

Shelf registration is at variance with the traditional requirement that security issuers file a detailed registration statement for SEC review and approval every time they plan a sale. Whether investors are deprived of important "current" information as a result of shelf registration is difficult to judge. While shelf registration was started on an experimental basis by the SEC in 1982, it has now become a permanent part of the underwriting process. Shelf registration has been most frequently used with debt issues, with relatively less utilization in the equity markets (corporations do not wish to announce equity dilution in advance).

Shelf registration has contributed to the concentrated nature of the investment banking business, previously discussed. The strong firms are acquiring more and more business and, in some cases, are less dependent on large syndications to handle debt issues. Only investment banking firms with a big capital base and substantial expertise are in a position to benefit from this new registration process.

Public versus Private Financing

Our discussion to this point has assumed the firm was distributing stocks or bonds in the public markets (through the organized exchanges or over the counter, as explained in Chapter 14). However, many companies, by choice or circumstance, prefer to remain private—restricting their financial activities to direct negotiations with bankers, insurance companies, and so forth. Let us evaluate the advantages and the disadvantages of **public placement** versus private financing and then explore the avenues open to a privately financed firm.

Advantages of Being Public

First of all, the corporation may tap the security markets for a greater amount of funds by selling securities directly to the public. With over 50 million individual stockholders in the country, combined with thousands of institutional investors, the greatest pool of funds is channeled toward publicly traded securities. Furthermore, the attendant prestige of a public security may be helpful in bank negotiations, executive recruitment, and the marketing of products. Some corporations listed on the New York Stock Exchange actually allow stockholders a discount on the purchase of their products.

Stockholders of a heretofore private corporation may also sell part of their holdings if the corporation decides to go public. A million-share offering may contain 500,000 authorized but unissued corporate shares (a primary offering) and 500,000 existing stockholder shares (a secondary offering). The stockholder is able to achieve a higher degree of liquidity and to diversify his or her portfolio. A publicly traded stock with an established price may also be helpful for estate planning.

Finally, going public allows the firm to play the merger game, using marketable securities for the purchase of other firms. The high visibility of a public offering may even make the firm a potential recipient of attractive offers for its own securities. (This may not be viewed as an advantage by firms that do not wish to be acquired.)

Disadvantages of Being Public

The company must make all information available to the public through SEC and state filings. Not only is this tedious, time consuming, and expensive, but also important corporate information on profit margins and product lines must be divulged. The president must adapt to being a public relations representative to all interested members of the securities industry.

Another disadvantage of being public is the tremendous pressure for short-term performance placed on the firm by security analysts and large institutional investors. Quarter-to-quarter earnings reports can become more important to top management than providing a long-run stewardship for the company. A capital budgeting decision calling for the selection of Alternative A—carrying a million dollars higher net present value than Alternative B—may be discarded in favor of the latter because Alternative B adds two cents more to next quarter's earnings per share.

In a number of cases, the blessings of having a publicly quoted security may become quite the opposite. Although a security may have had an enthusiastic reception in a strong "new-issues" market, such as that of 1961–62, 1967–68, or 1981–83, a dramatic erosion in value may later occur, causing embarrassment and anxiety for stockholders and employers.

A final disadvantage is the high cost of going public. As indicated in previously presented Table 15–2 on page 433, for issues under a million dollars the underwriting spread plus the out-of-pocket cost may run in the 15 to 18 percent range.

Public Offerings

A Classic Example of Instant Wealth—EDS Goes Public

In September 1968, Ross Perot took EDS public, and within one month he found himself worth $300 million. This was no small accomplishment for a man who, six years earlier, had been an IBM salesman with only a few thousand dollars in the bank and a degree from the Naval Academy.

The original EDS offering—managed by P.W. Presprich, a New York investment banker—was at 118 times current earnings (the norm was 10 to 12 times earnings). After one month in the hot new-issues market of 1967–68, the stock was trading at over 200 times earnings. A company with earnings of only $1.5 million had a market value well over $300 million, exceeding many of Fortune's 500 largest companies. By 1970 EDS had a total market value of $1.5 billion. All of this was accomplished by a firm with a few hundred employees.

It is interesting to note that Perot's main concern in the initial pricing of his stock was not to set too low a value. In the strong new-issues market of the period, too many computer issues, which had been underpriced when they first crossed the tape, quickly doubled or tripled in price. Perot considered this an irrevocable loss to original shareholders, who initially sold large blocks of their holdings. He was determined to avoid this by fully pricing his stock and trading only a small percentage of the total capitalization on the initial offering (only 650,000 shares out of 11.5 million). Even at a price-earnings ratio of 118 at initial trading, the stock jumped from $16.50 to $23 in one day.[2]

In the bear markets of the 1970s, EDS suffered more than most companies, and its stock price declined from a high of $161 per share in 1970 to a low of $12½ in 1974. Total market value retreated from a high of $1.5 billion to about $200 million. After the stock price recovered over the next decade, Perot sold EDS to General Motors Corporation in 1984 for $2.5 billion, and stockholders received Class E common stock of General Motors (discussed more fully in Chapter 17). Perot became the largest single shareholder of General Motors through his ownership of Class E shares and was elected to the board of directors. By 1986 GM tired of Perot's criticism of corporate policy and, in a very controversial move, bought out his shares of stock and he resigned from the board. By 1992, this hard-driving Texan was a candidate for the U.S. presidency and won 19 percent of the total vote as an independent.

Chrysler Corporation

The automobile industry reported losing years from 1989 through 1991, but by the fourth quarter of 1992, things were starting to look up for the economy and the automobile industry. Chrysler's stock had hit a low of $12 per share but rebounded to almost $40 per share on good earnings news and the optimistic reception of its new series of 1993 cars. With this strong performance, Chrysler's board of directors decided to sell new shares of stock to help increase the company's equity capital and lower the debt-to-equity ratio.

In February 1993 Chrysler Corporation issued 52 million shares of common stock at $38.75 per share to raise almost $2 billion after underwriting charges. The global offering was managed by Credit Suisse First Boston Group and included 41.86 million shares sold in the United States and 10.14 million shares sold abroad.

Figure 15–3 on page 440 is the advertisement for the Chrysler Corporation offering and depicts many of the characteristics of the distribution process discussed early in the chapter. The lead underwriter is CS First Boston listed right below the price of $38.75. On the following lines, the syndicate of investment bankers responsible for the selling and distribution of the common stock are listed by size of their position. For example, the underwriters immediately following CS First Boston such as Merrill Lynch & Co., Morgan Stanley & Co., and Salomon Brothers Inc. are responsible for millions of shares, while those companies listed on the last line of the first box, such as Muriel Siebert & Co., Inc., SoundView Financial Group, Inc., and

---

[2]A. M. Louis, "Fastest Richest Texan Ever," *Fortune*, November 1968, pp. 168–70.

FIGURE 15-3

This announcement is neither an offer to sell nor a solicitation of offers to buy any of these securities. The offering is made only by the Prospectus, copies of which may be obtained in any State in which this announcement is circulated only from such of the undersigned as may legally offer these securities in such State.

NEW ISSUE   February 3, 1993

$2,015,000,000

CHRYSLER CORPORATION

52,000,000 Shares
Common Stock
($1.00 par value)

Price $38.75 Per Share

Global Coordinator of the Offerings
CS First Boston Group

United States Offering
41,860,000 Shares

The First Boston Corporation

Merrill Lynch & Co.

Morgan Stanley & Co.
Incorporated

Lehman Brothers   **Salomon Brothers Inc**

J.P. Morgan Securities Inc.

PaineWebber Incorporated

Smith Barney, Harris Upham & Co.
Incorporated

S.G. Warburg Securities   Bear, Stearns & Co. Inc.   Sanford C. Bernstein & Co., Inc.   Alex. Brown & Sons   BT Securities Corporation
Credit Lyonnais Securities (USA) Inc.   Daiwa Securities America Inc.   Dillon, Read & Co. Inc.   Donaldson, Lufkin & Jenrette
                                                                                                                    Securities Corporation
A. G. Edwards & Sons, Inc.   Furman Selz   Goldman, Sachs & Co.   Invemed Associates, Inc.   Kidder, Peabody & Co.   Lazard Frères & Co.
                               Incorporated   Incorporated
Montgomery Securities   Oppenheimer & Co., Inc.   Prudential Securities Incorporated   RBC Dominion Securities Corporation
ScotiaMcLeod (USA) Inc.   Société Générale   SBCI Swiss Bank Corporation   UBS Securities Inc.
                            Securities Corporation   Investment banking
Wertheim Schroder & Co.   Dean Witter Reynolds Inc.   Wood Gundy Corp.   Allen & Company
Incorporated   Incorporated
Advest, Inc.   Robert W. Baird & Co.   William Blair & Company   J.C. Bradford & Co.   Cowen & Company   Dain Bosworth
                 Incorporated   Incorporated
First of Michigan Corporation   Howard, Weil, Labouisse, Freidrichs   Janney Montgomery Scott Inc.   Kemper Securities, Inc.
                                  Incorporated
Ladenburg, Thalmann & Co. Inc.   Legg Mason Wood Walker   McDonald & Company   Morgan Keegan & Company, Inc.   Piper Jaffray Inc.
                                   Incorporated   Securities, Inc.
Rauscher Pierce Refsnes, Inc.   Raymond James & Associates, Inc.   The Robinson-Humphrey Company, Inc.   Serfin Securities, Inc.
Stephens Inc.   Stifel, Nicolaus & Company   Sutro & Co. Incorporated   Tucker Anthony   Wheat First Butcher & Singer
                  Incorporated   Incorporated   Capital Markets
George K. Baum & Company   M♦R♦Beal & Company   The Chapman Company   The Chicago Corporation   Crowell, Weedon & Co.
Fahnestock & Co. Inc.   Gabelli & Company, Inc.   Gerard Klauer Mattison & Co., Inc.   Gruntal & Co., Incorporated   Interstate/Johnson Lane
                                                                                                                               Corporation
Edward D. Jones & Co.   C.J. Lawrence Inc.   WR Lazard, Laidlaw & Mead Inc.   Mabon Securities Corp.
Neuberger & Berman   The Ohio Company   Pryor, McClendon, Counts & Co., Inc.   Ragen MacKenzie   Roney & Co.
                                                                                      Incorporated
AIBC Investment Services Corporation   Apex Securities, Inc.   Doley Securities, Inc.   Dominick & Dominick   First Equity Corporation
                                                                                             Incorporated   of Florida
Howard Gary & Company   Grigsby Brandford & Co. Inc.   Keane Securities Co., Inc.   Luther, Smith & Small, Inc.
Jason MacKenzie Securities, Inc.   Pennsylvania Merchant Group Ltd   Samuel A. Ramirez & Co. Inc.
Muriel Siebert & Co., Inc.   SoundView Financial Group, Inc.   Sturdivant & Co., Inc.

International Offering
10,140,000 Shares

Credit Suisse First Boston Limited

Merrill Lynch International Limited   **Morgan Stanley International**

Salomon Brothers International Limited   **Swiss Bank Corporation**   **S.G. Warburg Securities**

ABN AMRO Bank N.V.   Credit Lyonnais Securities   Daiwa Europe Limited
Dresdner Bank   UBS Phillips & Drew Securities Limited
Aktiengesellschaft
Barclays de Zoete Wedd Limited   Cazenove & Co.   Commerzbank Aktiengesellschaft   Kleinwort Benson Limited
NatWest Securities Limited   Nikko Europe plc   Paribas Capital Markets   Société Générale

Sturdivant & Co., Inc., are responsible for only thousands of shares. The international portion of the offering, shown on the bottom box, includes many international giants such as Swiss Bank Corporation, ABN AMRO (a Dutch bank), Credit Lyonnais Securities (French), Daiwa Europe (Japanese), Dresdner Bank (German), and NatWest Securities (British).

Private placement refers to the selling of securities directly to insurance companies, pension funds, and wealthy individuals, rather than through the security markets. This financing device may be employed by a growing firm that wishes to avoid or defer an initial public stock offering or by a publicly traded company that wishes to incorporate private funds into its financing package. Private placement usually takes the form of a debt instrument.

Private Placement

Figure 15–4 presents the history of publicly and privately placed bonds since 1976 and includes bonds sold abroad since 1986. Publicly placed bonds are the most popular method of raising debt capital; but as new bond issues increased during 1986–91, privately placed bonds also increased in use and accounted for 19 percent of the total of all offerings in Figure 15–4. The inclusion of foreign bond offerings also points out the increasing importance of the international market as a source of capital for U.S. companies. Foreign bond issues equaled 7 percent of the debt capital raised.

The advantages of private placement are worthy of note. First, there is no lengthy, expensive registration process with the SEC. Second, the firm has greater flexibility in negotiating with one or a handful of insurance companies, pension funds, or bankers than is possible in a public offering. Because there is no SEC registration or underwriting, the initial costs of a private

FIGURE 15–4   **Public versus private placement of bonds**

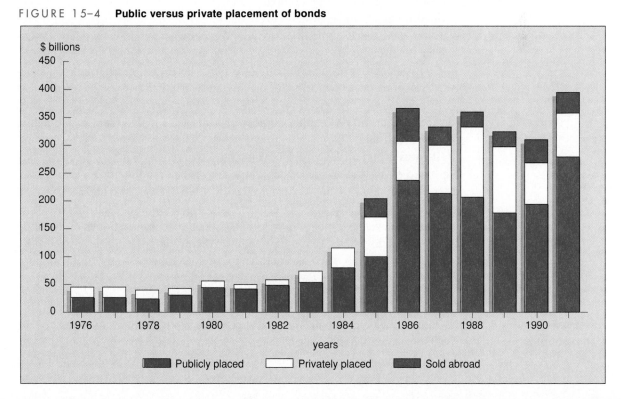

placement may be considerably lower than those of a public issue. However, the interest rate is usually higher to compensate the investor for holding a less liquid obligation.

Going Private and Leveraged Buyouts

Throughout the years, there have always been some public firms **going private.** In the 1970s, a number of firms gave up their public listings to be private, but these were usually small firms. Management figured it could save several hundred thousand dollars a year in annual report expenses, legal and auditing fees, and security analysts meetings—a significant amount for a small company.

In the 1980s, however, very large corporations began going private and not just to save several hundred thousand dollars. More likely they had a long-term strategy in mind.

There are basically two ways to accomplish going private. A publicly owned company can be purchased by a private company, or the company can re-purchase all publicly traded shares from the stockholders. Both methods have been in vogue and are accomplished through the use of a leveraged buyout. In a **leveraged buyout,** either the management or some other investor group borrows the needed cash to repurchase all the shares of the company. After the repurchase, the company exists with a lot of debt and heavy interest expense.

Usually management of the private company must sell assets to reduce the debt load, and a corporate **restructuring** occurs, wherein divisions and products are sold and assets redeployed into new, higher-return areas. As specialists in the valuation of assets, investment bankers try to determine the "breakup value" of a large company. This is its value if all its divisions were divided up and sold separately. Over the long run, these strategies can be rewarding, and these companies may again become publicly owned. For example, Beatrice Foods went private in 1986 for $6.2 billion. One year later, it sold various pieces of the company—Avis, Coke Bottling, International Playtex, and other assets worth $6 billion and still had assets left valued at $4 billion for a public offering. Leslie Fay, an apparel firm, bought its shares for $58 million in 1982 and a number of years later resold them to the public for $360 million.

However, not all leveraged buyouts have worked as planned. Because they are based on the heavy use of debt, any shortfall in a company's performance after the buyout can prove disastrous. In 1990 Chase Manhattan Corp., a major lender in the leveraged buyout market, was desperately selling part of its $4.6 billion leveraged buyout portfolio at a deep discount in hopes of avoiding future problems. Also, firms that enthusiastically approached leveraged buyouts a few years ago, such as Southland Corp. (7-Eleven stores) and Campeau Corp. (department stores) were facing bankruptcy.

A Look at Investment Banking Deals

No look at investment banking would be complete without an overview of the five biggest deals that were put together during a given year (see Table 15–3). The really interesting information is found in the last two columns. While the

TABLE 15-3 **Biggest deals of 1991**

RANK		VALUE (000) % of Book Value	TRANSACTION	FINANCIAL INTERMEDIARIES (Client)	FEE (000)	FEE as % of Deal
1	AT&T acquires NCR	$7,377,596 406%	Acquisition for stock, September 19	MORGAN STANLEY (AT&T)	$13,280	.18%
				DILLON READ GOLDMAN SACHS (NCR)	$17,866 $17,866	.24% .24%
2	GTE acquires CONTEL	$6,728,719 401%	Acquisition for stock, March 14	MERRILL LYNCH PAINE WEBBER (GTE)	$6,000 $6,000	.09% .09%
				GOLDMAN SACHS SALOMON BROTHERS (Contel)	$5,000 $5,000	.07% .07%
3	NCNB (banking) acquires C&S/SOVRAN (banking)	$4,661,630 156%	Acquisition for stock, December 31	JAMES D. WOLFENSOHN MERRILL LYNCH MORGAN STANLEY SALOMAN BROTHERS (NCNB)	$7,000 $2,000 $11,000 $2,000	.15% .04% .24% .04%
				DILLON READ FIRST BOSTON LEHMAN BROTHERS (C&S/Sovran)	$2,000 $14,000 $3,850	.04% .30% .08%
4	ALLIANZ AKTIENGESELLSCHAFT HOLDING (German insurance company) acquires FIREMAN'S FUND INSURANCE from FUND AMERICAN COS.	$2,909,000 N.A.	Acquisition for cash, January 2	LAZARD FRÈRES (Allianz Aktiengesellschaft Holding)	N.A.	—
				LEHMAN BROTHERS (Fund American Cos.)	N.A.	—
5	TIME WARNER issues rights to common stock	$2,760,000 44%	Offering of rights to purchase 34.5 million shares, July 15	SALOMAN BROTHERS* GOLDMAN SACHS MERRILL LYNCH	$117,638	4.26%

N.A. Not available.
*Lead manager.
Source: Kathleeen Carroll Smyth, *Fortune*, January 27, 1992, pp. 105.

fees paid primarily to investment bankers as a percent of the deal (last column) appear to be small, note the dollar amounts in the next-to-last column. In the first transaction involving AT&T's $7 billion acquisition of NCR, the three investment banking firms had total fees of over $49 million. The third place deal, between NCNB and C&S/SOVRAN netted the seven investment banking firms $41.85 million.

Summary

The role of the investment banker is critical to the distribution of securities in the U.S. economy. The investment banker serves as an underwriter or risk taker by purchasing the securities from the issuing corporation and redistributing them to the public, and he or she may continue to maintain a market in the distributed securities long after they have been sold to the public. The investment banking firm can also help a company sell a new issue on a "best-efforts" basis. Investment bankers also serve as advisors to corporations and have become more important to corporations in the 1980s and early 1990s in providing advice on mergers, acquisitions, and leveraged buyouts, and on resisting hostile takeover attempts.

The advantages of selling securities in the public markets must be weighed against the disadvantages. While going public may give the corporation and major stockholders greater access to funds as well as additional prestige, these advantages quickly disappear in a down market. Furthermore the corporation must open its books to the public and orient itself to the short-term emphasis of investors.

Investment bankers have become larger, and the industry is consolidated into fewer firms. The industry is dominated by a few large investment bankers able to take down large blocks of securities and compete in a more international market. Shelf registration has also become an alternative to public syndications, particularly with debt issues, and is advantageous to the larger investment bankers.

Private placement—or the direct distribution of securities to large insurance companies, pension funds, and wealthy individuals—bypasses the rigors of SEC registration and allows more flexibility in terms. A number of corporations actually changed their structure from public to private during the bear market of 1973–74. This trend has become evident again two decades later, with many large companies going private through leveraged buyouts. However, a number of these companies publicly distributed their shares a year or two later.

List of Terms

investment banker 430
underwrite 430
best efforts 430

agent 431
managing investment
  banker 431

Discussion Questions

1. In what way is an investment banker a risk taker?
2. What is the purpose of market stabilization activities during the distribution process?
3. Discuss how an underwriting syndicate decreases risk for each underwriter and at the same time facilitates the distribution process.
4. Discuss the reason for the differences between underwriting spreads for stocks and bonds.
5. Explain how the price-earnings ratio is related to the pricing of a new security issue and the dilution effect.
6. What is shelf registration? How does it differ from the traditional requirements for security offerings?
7. Comment on the market performance of companies going public, both immediately after the offering has been made and some time later. Relate this to research that has been done in this area.
8. Describe the mergers between nonbrokerage firms and brokerage firms that occurred in the early 1980s. How successful have these been?
9. Discuss the benefits accruing to a company that is traded in the public securities markets.
10. What are some reasons a corporation may prefer to remain privately held?
11. If a company were looking for capital by way of a private placement, where would it look for funds?
12. How does a leveraged buyout work? What does the debt structure of the firm normally look like after a leveraged buyout? What might be done to reduce the debt?
13. How might a leveraged buyout eventually lead to high returns for companies?

Problems

1. Louisiana Timber Company currently has 5 million shares of stock outstanding and will report earnings of $9,000,000 in the current year. The company is considering the issuance of 1 million additional shares that will net $40 per share to the corporation.

    a. What is the immediate dilution potential for this new stock issue?

Dilution effect of stock issue

b. Assume the Louisiana Timber Co. can earn 11 percent on the proceeds of the stock issue in time to include it in the current year's results. Should the new issue be undertaken based on earnings per share?

Dilution effect of stock issue

2. In problem 1, if the 1 million additional shares can only be issued at $32 per share and the company can earn 5.0 percent on the proceeds, should the new issue be undertaken based on earnings per share?

Underwriting spread

3. Blaine and Company is the managing investment banker for a major new underwriting. The price of the stock to the investment banker is $24 per share. Other syndicate members may buy the stock for $24.30. The price to the selected dealers group is $24.90, with a price to brokers of $25.32. The price to the public is $25.60.

   a. If Blaine and Company sells its shares to the dealer group, what will the percentage return be?

   b. If Blaine and Company performs the dealer's function also and sells to brokers, what will the percentage return be?

   c. If Blaine and Company fully integrates its operation and sells directly to the public, what will its percentage return be?

Market stabilization and risk

4. Lynch Brothers is the managing underwriter for a 1 million share issue by Overcharge Healthcare Inc. Lynch Brothers is "handling" 10 percent of the issue. Its price is $30, and the price to the public is $31.50.

   Lynch also provides the market stabilization function. During the issuance, the market for the stock turned soft, and Lynch was forced to repurchase 45,000 shares in the open market at an average price of $29.90. It later sold the shares at an average value of $26.

   Compute Lynch Brothers' overall gain or loss from managing the issue.

Underwriting costs

5. Skyway Airlines will issue stock at a retail (public) price of $15. The company will receive $13.80 per share.

   a. What is the spread on the issue in percentage terms?

   b. If Skyway Airlines demands receiving a net price only $.75 below the public price suggested in part a, what will the spread be in percentage terms?

   c. To hold the spread down to 3 percent based on the public price in part a, what net amount should Skyway Airlines receive?

Underwriting costs

6. Winston Sporting Goods is considering a public offering of common stock. Its investment banker has informed the company that the retail price will be $18 per share for 600,000 shares. The company will receive $16.50 per share and will incur $150,000 in registration, accounting, and printing fees.

   a. What is the spread on this issue in percentage terms? What are the total expenses of the issue as a percentage of total value (at retail)?

   b. If the firm wanted to net $18 million from this issue, how many shares must be sold?

7. Richmond Rent-A-Car is about to go public. The investment banking firm of Tinkers, Evers and Chance is attempting to price the issue. The car rental industry generally trades at a 10 percent discount below the P/E ratio on the Standard & Poor's 500 Stock Index. Assume that index currently has a P/E ratio of 20. The firm can be compared to the car rental industry as follows: P/E ratio for new public issue

	Richmond	Car Rental Industry
Growth rate in earnings per share . .	15 percent	10 percent
Consistency of performance	Increased earnings 4 out of 5 years	Increased earnings 3 out of 5 years
Debt to total assets	52 percent	39 percent
Turnover of product	Slightly below average	Average
Quality of management	High	Average

Assume, in assessing the initial P/E ratio, the investment banker will first determine the appropriate industry P/E based on the Standard & Poor's 500 Index. Then a half point will be added to the P/E ratio for each case in which Richmond Rent-A-Car is superior to the industry norm, and a half point will be deducted for an inferior comparison. On this basis, what should the initial P/E be for the firm?

8. The investment banking firm of Luther King, Inc., will use a dividend valuation model to appraise the shares of the Pyramid Corporation. Dividends (D_1) at the end of the current year will be $1.20. The growth rate (g) is 9 percent and the discount rate (K_e) is 13 percent. Dividend valuation model for new public issue

   a. Using Formula 10–9 from Chapter 10, what should be the price of the stock to the public?

   b. If there is a 6 percent total underwriting spread on the stock, how much will the issuing corporation receive?

   c. If the issuing corporation requires a net price of $29 (proceeds to the corporation) and there is a 6 percent underwriting spread, what should be the price of the stock to the public? (Round to two places to the right of the decimal point.)

9. The Alston Corporation needs to raise $1 million of debt on a 20-year issue. If it places the bonds privately, the interest rate will be 11 percent, and $25,000 in out-of-pocket costs will be incurred. For a public issue, the interest rate will be 10 percent, and the underwriting spread will be 5 percent. There will be $75,000 in out-of-pocket costs. Comparison of private and public debt offering

   Assume interest on the debt is paid semiannually, and the debt will be outstanding for the full 20 years, at which time it will be repaid.

   Which plan offers the higher net present value? For each plan, compare the net amount of funds initially available—inflow—to the present value of future payments of interest and principal to determine net present value. Assume the stated discount rate is 12 percent annually, but use 6 percent semiannually throughout the analysis. (Disregard taxes.)

Features associated with a
stock distribution

10. Warner Drug Co. has a net income of $18 million and 9 million shares outstanding. Its common stock is currently selling for $30 per share. Warner plans to sell common stock to set up a major new production facility with a net cost of $21,280,000. The production facility will not produce a profit for one year, and then it is expected to earn a 16 percent return on the investment. Roth and Stern, an investment banking firm, plans to sell the issue to the public for $28 per share with a spread of 5 percent.

   a. How many shares of stock must be sold to net $21,280,000? (Note: No out-of-pocket costs must be considered in this problem.)

   b. Why is the investment banker selling the stock at less than its current market price?

   c. What are the earnings per share (EPS) and the price-earnings ratio before the issue (based on a stock price of $30)? What will be the price per share immediately after the sale of stock if the P/E stays constant? (based on including the additional shares computed in part *a*).

   d. Compute the EPS and the price (P/E stays constant) after the new production facility begins to produce a profit.

   e. Are the shareholders better off because of the sale of stock and the resultant investment? What other financing strategy could the company have tried to increase earnings per share?

Dilution and rates of
return

11. The Presley Corporation is about to go public. It currently has aftertax earnings of $7,500,000, and 2,500,000 shares are owned by the present stockholders (the Presley family). The new public issue will represent 600,000 new shares. The new shares will be priced to the public at $20 per share, with a 5 percent spread on the offering price. There will also be $200,000 in out-of-pocket costs to the corporation.

   a. Compute the net proceeds to the Presley Corporation.

   b. Compute the earnings per share immediately before the stock issue.

   c. Compute the earnings per share immediately after the stock issue.

   d. Determine what rate of return must be earned on the net proceeds to the corporation so there will not be a dilution in earnings per share during the year of going public.

   e. Determine what rate of return must be earned on the proceeds to the corporation so there will be a 5 percent increase in earnings per share during the year of going public.

Aftermarket for new
public issue

12. B. P. Hart has a chance to participate in a new public offering by Cardiovascular Systems, Inc. His broker informs him demand for the 800,000 shares to be issued is very strong. His broker's firm is assigned 20,000 shares in the distribution and will allow Hart, a relatively good customer, 1.5 percent of its 20,000 share allocation.

   The initial offering price is $40 per share. There is a strong aftermarket, and the stock goes to $44 one week after issue. After the first full month after issue, Mr. Hart is pleased to observe his shares are selling for $46.25. He is content to place his shares in a lockbox and eventually use their anticipated increased value to help send his son to college many years in the future. However, one year after the distribution, he looks up the shares in *The Wall Street Journal* and finds they are trading at $38.50.

a. Compute the total dollar profit or loss on Mr. Hart's shares one week, one month, and one year after the purchase. In each case compute the profit or loss against the initial purchase price.

b. Also compute this percentage gain or loss from the initial $40 price and compare this to the results that might be expected in an investment of this nature based on prior research. Assume the overall stock market was basically unchanged during the period of observation.

c. Why might a new public issue be expected to have a strong aftermarket?

13. The management of Rowe Boat Co. decided to go private in 1992 by buying all 2 million outstanding shares at $16.50 per share. By 1994 management had restructured the company by selling the scuba diving division for $7.5 million, the pleasure cruise division for $9 million, and the military contract aqua division for $11 million.

    Because these divisions had been only marginally profitable, Rowe Boat is a stronger company after the restructuring. Rowe is now able to concentrate exclusively on the construction of new boats and will generate earnings per share of $1.20 this year. Investment bankers have contacted the firm and indicated that, if it returned the public market, the 2 million shares it purchased to go private could now be reissued to the public at a P/E ratio of 15 times earnings per share.

a. What was the initial total cost to Rowe Boat Co. to go private?

b. What is the total value to the company from (1) the proceeds of the divisions that were sold as well as (2) the current value of the 2 million shares (based on current earnings and an anticipated P/E of 15)?

c. What is the percentage return to the management of Rowe Boat Co. from the restructuring? Use answers from parts *a* and *b* to determine this value.

Leveraged buyout

COMPREHENSIVE PROBLEM

The Anton Corporation, a manufacturer of radar control equipment, is planning to sell its shares to the general public for the first time. The firm's investment banker is working with the Anton Corporation in determining a number

Anton Corporation
(impact of new public offering)

of items. Information on the Anton Corporation follows:

ANTON CORPORATION
Income Statement
For the Year 199X

Sales (all on credit)	$22,428,000
Cost of goods sold	16,228,000
Gross profit	6,200,000
Selling and administrative expenses. . .	2,659,400
Operating profit	3,540,600
Interest expense	370,600
Net income before tax	3,170,000
Taxes	1,442,000
Net income	$ 1,728,000

Balance Sheet
As of December 31, 199X

Assets

Cash	$ 150,000
Marketable securities	100,000
Accounts receivable	2,000,000
Inventory	3,800,000
Total current assets	6,050,000
Net plant and equipment	6,750,000
Total assets	$12,800,000

Liabilities and Stockholders' Equity

Accounts payable	$ 1,000,000
Notes payable	1,200,000
Total current liabilities	2,200,000
Long-term liabilities	2,380,000
Total liabilities	4,580,000
Common stock (1,200,000 shares at $1 par)	1,200,000
Capital paid in excess of par	2,800,000
Retained earnings	4,220,000
Total stockholders' equity	8,220,000
Total liabilities and stockholders' equity	$12,800,000

The new public offering will be at 10 times the earnings per share.

a. Assume that 500,000 new corporate shares will be issued to the general public. What will earnings per share immediately after the public offering be? (Round to two places to the right of the decimal point.) Based on the price-earnings ratio of 10, what will the initial price of the stock be? Use earnings per share after the distribution in the calculation.

b. Assuming an underwriting spread of 7 percent and out-of-pocket costs of $150,000, what will net proceeds to the corporation be?

  c. What return must the corporation earn on the net proceeds to equal the earnings per share before the offering? How does this compare with current return on the total assets on the balance sheet?

  d. Now assume that, of the initial 500,000-share distribution, 250,000 shares belong to current stockholders and 250,000 are new corporate shares, and these will be added to the 1,200,000 corporate shares currently outstanding. What will earnings per share immediately after the public offering be? What will the initial market price of the stock be? Assume a price-earnings ratio of 10 and use earnings per share after the distribution in the calculation.

  e. Assuming an underwriting spread of 7 percent and out-of-pocket costs of $150,000, what will net proceeds to the corporation be?

  f. What return must the corporation now earn on the net proceeds to equal earnings per share before the offering? How does this compare with current return on the total assets on the balance sheet?

Selected References

Barry, Christopher. "Initial Public Offering Underpricing: The Issuer's View—A Comment." *Journal of Finance* 44 (September 1989), pp. 1099–1103.

————, **Chris Muscarella, and Michael Vetsuypens.** "Underwriter Warrants, Underwriter Compensation and Cost of Going Public." *Journal of Financial Economics* 18 (March 1991), pp. 113–35.

Block, Stanley B., and Marjorie T. Stanley. "The Price Movement Pattern and Financial Characteristics of Companies Approaching the Unseasoned Securities Market in the Late 1970s." *Financial Management* 9 (Winter 1980), pp. 30–36.

Ferreira, Eurico, Michael F. Spivey, and Charles E. Edwards. "Pricing New Issues and Seasoned Preferred Stock: A Comparison of Valuation Models." *Financial Management* 21 (Summer 1992), pp. 52–62.

Hayes, Samuel L., III. "The Transformation of Investment Banking." *Harvard Business Review* 57 (January–February 1979), pp. 153–70.

Hess, Alan C., and Peter A. Frost. "Tests for Price Effects of New Issues of Seasoned Securities." *Journal of Finance* 37 (March 1982), pp. 11–25.

Ibbotson, Roger G. "Price Performance of Common Stock New Issues." *Journal of Financial Economics* 2 (September 1975), pp. 253–72.

Michel, Allen, Israel Shaked, and You-Tay Lee. "An Evaluation of Investment Banker Investment Advice: The Shareholders' Perspective." *Financial Management* 20 (Summer 1991), pp. 40–49.

Moore, Nathan H., David R. Peterson, and Pamela P. Peterson. "Shelf Registration and Stockholder Wealth: A Comparison of Shelf and Traditional Equity Offerings." *Journal of Finance* 41 (June 1986), pp. 451–63.

Reilly, Frank K. "New Issues Revisited." *Financial Management* 6 (Winter 1977), pp. 28–42.

Ritler, Jay R. "The Long-Term Performance of Initial Public Offerings." *Journal of Finance* 46 (March 1991), pp. 3–27.

Rogowski, Robert J., and Eric H. Sorensen. "Deregulation in Investment Banking: Shelf Registration, Structure, and Performance." *Financial Management* 14 (Spring 1985), pp. 5–15.

Long-Term Debt and Lease Financing

CHAPTER CONCEPTS

1 Analyzing long-term debt requires a consideration of the collateral pledged, method of repayment, and other key factors.

2 Bond yields and prices are influenced by how bonds are rated by major bond rating agencies.

3 An important corporate decision is whether to call in and reissue debt (refund the obligation) when interest rates decline.

4 Innovative bond forms are represented by zero-coupon rate bonds and floating rate bonds.

5 Long-term lease obligations have many similar characteristics to debt and are recognized as a form of indirect debt by the accounting profession.

The Shakespearean advice of "Neither a borrower nor a lender be" hardly applies to corporate financial management. The virtues and drawbacks of debt usage were considered in Chapter 5, "Operating and Financial Leverage," and in Chapter 11, "The Cost of Capital." One can only surmise that today's financial managers, many of whom were educated in the 1960s and 1970s, remember the advantages a bit better than the disadvantages. Debt usage has been at unprecedented levels in the 1980s and early 1990s. In Chapter 16 we consider the importance of debt in the U.S. economy, the nature of long-term debt instruments, the mechanics of bond yields and pricing, and the decision to call back or refund an existing bond issue. Finally lease financing will be considered as a special case of long-term debt financing. We give particular attention to accounting rules that affect leasing.

The Expanding Role of Debt

Corporate debt has increased dramatically since World War II. This growth is related to rapid business expansion, the inflationary impact on the economy, and, at times, inadequate funds generated from the internal operations of business firms. The expansion of the U.S. economy has placed pressure on U.S. corporations to raise capital and will continue to do so. In this context a new set of rules has been developed for evaluating corporate bond issues. Much deterioration in borrowing qualifications has occurred. In 1977 the average U.S. manufacturing corporation had its interest payments covered by operating earnings at a rate of eight times (operating earnings were eight times as great as interest). By the early 1990s the ratio had diminished to less than three times. Nor has this been a short-term, cyclical phenomenon, but rather a long-term process of deterioration, as indicated in Figure 16–1. With the declining interest-paying capabilities of U.S. corporations, the

FIGURE 16–1   **Times interest earned for Standard & Poor's Industrials**

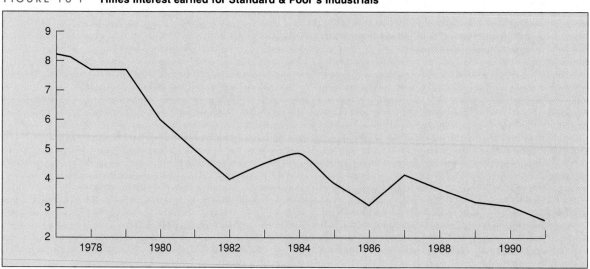

Source: *S&P Analyst's Handbook* (1992).

debt contract between corporate borrowers and lenders has become increasingly important.

The corporate bond represents the basic long-term debt instrument for most large U.S. corporations. The bond agreement specifies such basic items as the par value, the coupon rate, and the maturity date.

The Debt Contract

Par Value   The initial value of the bond. The **par value** is sometimes referred to as the principal or face value. Most corporate bonds are initially traded in $1,000 units.

Coupon Rate   This is the actual interest rate on the bond, usually payable in semiannual installments. To the extent that interest rates in the market go above or below the coupon rate after the bond has been issued, the market price of the bond will change from the par value.

Maturity Date   The **maturity date** is the final date on which repayment of the bond principal is due.

The bond agreement is supplemented by a much longer document termed a bond **indenture**. The indenture, often containing over 100 pages of complicated legal wording, covers every detail surrounding the bond issue—including collateral pledged, methods of repayment, restrictions on the corporation, and procedures for initiating claims against the corporation. The corporation appoints a financially independent trustee to administer the provisions of the bond indenture under the guidelines of the Trust Indenture Act of 1939. Let's examine two items of interest in any bond agreement: the security provisions of the bond and the methods of repayment.

Security Provisions

A **secured debt** is one in which specific assets are pledged to bondholders in the event of default. Only infrequently are pledged assets actually sold and the proceeds distributed to bondholders. Typically the defaulting corporation is reorganized and existing claims are partially satisfied by issuing new securities to the participating parties. The stronger and better secured the initial claim, the higher the quality of the new security to be received in exchange. When a defaulting corporation is reorganized for failure to meet obligations, existing management may be terminated and, in extreme cases, held legally responsible for any imprudent actions.

A number of terms are used to denote collateralized or secured debt. Under a **mortgage agreement,** real property (plant and equipment) is pledged as security for the loan. A mortgage may be *senior* or *junior* in nature, with the former requiring satisfaction of claims before payment is given to the latter. Bondholders may also attach an **after-acquired property clause,** requiring that any new property be placed under the original mortgage.

The student should realize not all secured debt will carry every protective feature, but rather represents a carefully negotiated position including some safeguards and rejecting others. Generally, the greater the protection offered a given class of bondholders, the lower is the interest rate on the bond. Bondholders are willing to assume some degree of risk to receive a higher yield.

Unsecured Debt

A number of corporations issue debt that is not secured by a specific claim to assets. In Wall Street jargon, the name **debenture** refers to a long-term, unsecured corporate bond. Among the major participants in debenture offerings are such prestigious firms as American Telephone & Telegraph, Exxon, International Paper, and Dow Chemical. Because of the legal problems associated with "specific" asset claims in a secured bond offering, the trend is to issue unsecured debt—allowing the bondholder a general claim against the corporation, rather than a specific lien against an asset.

Even unsecured debt may be divided between high-ranking and subordinated debt. A **subordinated debenture** is an unsecured bond in which payment to the holder will occur only after designated senior debenture holders are satisfied. The hierarchy of creditor obligations for secured as well as unsecured debt is presented in Figure 16–2, along with consideration of the position of stockholders. For a further discussion of payment of

FIGURE 16–2
Priority of claims

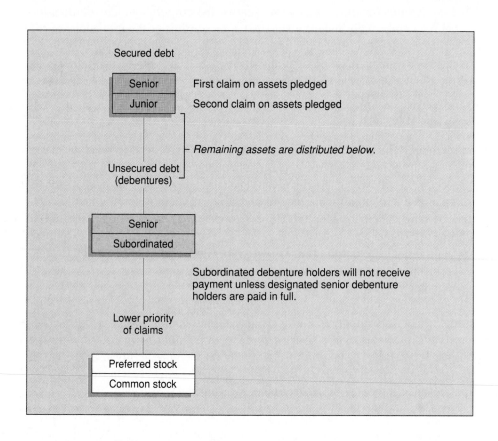

FINANCE IN ACTION

Continental Airline Bonds: Don't Forget to Read the Fine Print

In March of 1987 Continental Airlines issued $350 million of bonds that were secured by 53 planes and 55 spare engines having a total appraised value of $467 million. Bonds of this type are common in the airline industry and are sometimes referred to as equipment bonds or equipment trust certificates. Investors in general assume the equipment listed as collateral for the bond will protect them from default, and therefore they agree to lend money at a rate lower than those of unsecured bonds of equal risk. What bondholders found out after Continental declared bankruptcy in 1990 was that Continental put its oldest and least salable planes into the asset pool used as collateral.

The $467 million in planes appeared to more than secure the bond issue and provided 4.7 times the indebtedness of the $100 million in first-class bonds. This particular bond issue had three classes of bondholders: first class, second class, and third class. It was assumed that the first-class bondholders were most protected because they could claim the whole asset pool as collateral while the third-class bondholders were at more risk because they would be satisfied only after the first two classes of bondholders had been paid off.

Now that bankruptcy has occurred, many investors realize they failed to read the fine print in the bond indenture (or didn't understand the implications) that stated Continental could remove several planes from the collateral pool of 53 planes and sell the planes to raise cash. If Continental did exercise this option and sold planes, it was required to either replace the planes or buy back bonds. After selling planes for about $167 million, Continental repurchased bonds at a discount in the open market. Because it could retire $167 million in par value at a discount, Continental paid much less than $167 million in cash to reduce this liability on the balance sheet. It then used the leftover dollars for other corporate purposes rather than protecting the bondholders. Because the third-class bonds were the riskiest, they were also selling at the biggest discount from par value and Continental was able to maximize its bond repurchase program by buying third-class rather than first-class bonds. Continental also repurchased a big amount of the second-class bonds and in the end Continental took more money out of the asset pool than it put back into it.

The biggest travesty was that the first-class bondholders, who were supposed to be the most secure, found themselves unprotected by the asset pool. What was left were mostly old models that were not fuel efficient and had very little value in the resale market. The moral of the story might be that just because times are good when you buy bonds doesn't mean they will stay that way. Covenants are there to protect the investor when times are bad and it doesn't make sense to overlook permissive covenants with the hope of squeezing out a slightly higher interest rate. The investor may be trading off significant protection for very little "extra" return.

Source: Linda Sandler, "Continental Air Bonds' Terms Spur Turbulence," *The Wall Street Journal*, December 17, 1990, pp. C1–C2.

claims and the hierarchy of obligations, the reader should see Appendix 16A, "Financial Alternatives for Distressed Firms," which also covers bankruptcy considerations.

Methods of Repayment

The method of repayment for bond issues may not always call for one lump-sum disbursement at the maturity date. Some Canadian and British government bonds are perpetual in nature. More interestingly, West Shore Railroad 4 percent bonds are not scheduled to mature until 2361 (almost 400 years in the future). Nevertheless most bonds have some orderly or preplanned system of repayment. In addition to the simplest arrangement—a single-sum payment at maturity—bonds may be retired by serial payments, through sinking-fund provisions, through conversion, or by a call feature.

Serial Payments   Bonds with **serial payment** provisions are paid off in installments over the life of the issue. Each bond has its own predetermined date of maturity and receives interest only to that point. Although the total issue may span over 20 years, 15 or 20 different maturity dates may be assigned specific dollar amounts.

Sinking-Fund Provision   A less structured but more popular method of debt retirement is through the use of a **sinking fund.** Under this arrangement semiannual or annual contributions are made by the corporation into a fund administered by a trustee for purposes of debt retirement. The trustee takes the proceeds and purchases bonds from willing sellers. If no willing sellers are available, a lottery system may be used among outstanding bondholders.

Conversion   A more subtle method of reducing debt outstanding is to provide for debt conversion into common stock. Although this feature is exercised at the option of the bondholder, a number of incentives or penalties may be utilized to encourage conversion. The mechanics of convertible bond trading are discussed at length in Chapter 19, "Convertibles and Warrants."

Call Feature   A **call provision** allows the corporation to retire or force in the debt issue before maturity. The corporation will pay a premium over par value of 5 to 10 percent—a bargain value to the corporation if bond prices are up. Modern call provisions usually do not take effect until the bond has been outstanding at least 5 to 10 years. Often the call provision declines over time, usually by 0.5 to 1 percent per year after the call period begins. A corporation may decide to call in outstanding debt issues when interest rates on new securities are considerably lower than those on previously issued debt (let's get the high-cost, old debt off the books).

An Example: Exxon Corp. 6½ Percent Bond

Now that we have covered the key features of the bond indenture, let us examine an existing bond. Table 16–1 presents a page from *Moody's Bond Record* of December 1992. We find that Exxon Corporation has a 6.5 percent debenture due in 1998. The bond carried Moody's highest rating of Aaa. More specific features of this bond are found in Table 16–2 from *Standard & Poor's Corporate Records.*

As we can see in Table 16–2 on page 460, the 6.5 percent bond was originally sold July 15, 1968, and had an original authorized offering of $250 million. As of December 31, 1992, $151 million were still outstanding. The

TABLE 16-1 **Moody's bond record**

CUSIP	ISSUE	MOODY'S RATING	INTEREST DATES	CURRENT CALL PRICE	CALL DATE	SINK FUND PROV	CURRENT PRICE	YIELD TO MAT.	1992 HIGH	1992 LOW	AMT. OUTST. MIL. $	ISSUED	PRICE	YLD.
293567AP	•ENSERCH CORP. nts. 11.375 1995	Baa2 r	M&S15	100.00	fr 9-15-92	No	100 1/4 bid	11.27	103	100	95.69	9-1-85	100.00	11.38
293567AE	s.f.deb. 7.50 1996	Baa2 r	J&D 1	101.21	to 11-30-92	Yes	101 bid	7.20	101 1/8	97 3/4	15.34	12-14-71	99.75	7.52
293567AR	nts. 8.00 1997	Baa2 r	M&S 15	N.C.	----	No	103 1/2 bid	7.07	104	100 1/4	100	3-10-92	99.78	8.05
293567AF •	s.f.deb. 7.65 1998	Baa2 r	M&S15	101.59	to 3-14-93	Yes	95 1/2 bid	8.67	99	94 3/8	12.6	3-13-73	100.00	7.65
293567AG •	s.f.deb. 8.95 1999	Baa2 r	M&S15	102.24	to 3-14-93	Yes	100 3/8 bid	8.87	100	98	29.38	3-28-74	100.00	8.95
293567AJ •	s.f.deb. 8.75 2001	Baa2 r	A&O 1	103.28	to 9-30-92	Yes	101 1/2 bid	8.51	102	100 1/2	24.0	10-6-76	100.00	8.75
293567AS	nts. 8.875 2001	Baa2 r	M&S 15	106.51	fr 3-15-93	No	103 7/8 bid	8.22	104	97 7/8	100	3-10-92	99.10	9.05
293567AK •	s.f.deb. 8.50 2002	Baa2 r	M&N15	103.44	to 11-14-92	Yes	100 bid	8.49	101	98 1/2	29.23	11-8-77	99.75	8.52
294037AA	Environdyne Ind., Inc. sub.nts. 13.50 1996	Ca r	J&D 15	105.25	to 6-14-92	No	55 1/2 bid	----	57 1/2	40 1/2	100	6-10-86	100.00	12.00
294037AB	sr.nts. 0.00 1997[1]	Caa r	[2]N.P.	112.08	to 7-31-92	No	----	flat	----	----	250	7-31-89	49.84	
294037AC	sr.sub.deb. 14.00 2001	Ca r	F&A 1	110.00	to 7-31-92	Yes	68 1/2 bid	----	69 3/8	51	200	7-28-89	100.00	14.00
29409KAA	Envirosource, Inc. ext. 14.00 1990[3]	Caa r	JAJ&O1	N.C.	----	No	----	----	----	----	151.7	10-14-88	100.00	14.00
268748AB	EOA Consumer Fin. Corp. asset-bkd.ctf. B 9.15 1994[4]	Aaa r	MJS&D15	100.00	to 3-15-94	No	100 1/8 bid	9.03	----	----	354.8	9-23-88	99.93	
293932AB	Epic Healthcare Group Inc sr.sub.nts. 15.00 2001	B3 r	F&A 1	105.62	fr 2-1-94	Yes	111 bid	12.83	113	110	103.6	2-8-89	00.00	
29425DAA	Epic Holdings, Inc. sr.nts. 12.00 2002[5]	B3	A30&O31	104.45	fr 9-30-93	No	----	----	56	56	250	3-24-92	56.02	23.63
294432AA	Equimark Corp. sub.cap.nts. 12.875 1999	B3 r	F&A 15	106.50	fr 8-15-92	No	50 bid	----	50	50	50.0	8-13-87	99.54	12.96
294497AF	•EQUIT. RESOURCES INC. deb. 9.00 1996[6]	A1 r	J&D15	100.79	to 6-14-93	Yes	100 3/8 bid	8.88	102 7/8	99 1/8	9.630	6-15-71	100.00	9.00
294549AA	Equit. Resources Inc. deb. 8.25 1996	A1 r	J&J 1	N.C.	----	No	106 1/2 bid	6.32	107	101 3/4	75.0	6-27-86	100.00	8.25
294549AD •	deb. 7.50 1999	A1 r	J&J 1	N.C.	----	No	99 1/4 bid	7.64	99	97	75.0	6-29-87	100.00	7.50
294549AB	deb. 9.90 2013	A1 r	A&O 15	103.65	fr 4-15-98	Yes	109 1/8 bid	8.91	109 1/8	104	75.0	4-6-88	97.40	10.19
294510AA	Equitable Of Iowa Co, Inc nts. 9.30 1998	A3	J&D 1	N.C.	----	No	----	----	----	----	50.0	3-26-91	100.00	
295569AP	Erie R.R. 1st 7.00 1980[7]	Caa	[8]†9-1-72	100.00	to 9-1-80	Yes	----	flat	----	----	11.0	9-24-41		
297015AA	Essex Group, Inc. sr.sub.deb. 12.375 2000	B2 r	M&N 15	106.00	fr 5-15-93	Yes	107 bid	11.01	107	104	140	5-18-88	100.00	12.38
297425AB	•Esterline sub.deb. 12.50 1995	N.R. r	A&O 1	100.30	to 3-31-93	Yes	----	----	----	----	2.13	1974		
297659AA	Ethyl Corp. nts. 11.00 1995	A2 r	M&N1	100.00	fr 11-1-92	No	101 1/4 bid	10.50	104 1/8	101 1/4	100	10-23-85	100.00	11.00
297659AC	nts. 9.80 1998	A2 r	M&S 15	100.00	fr 9-15-95	No	110 1/2 bid	7.60	111	107 5/8	200	9-16-88	100.00	9.80
297659AB	s.f.deb. 9.375 2016	A2 r	J&D 15	§106.69	to 12-14-92	Yes	106 5/8 bid	8.70	106 5/8	100 3/4	116.2	Ref. fr. 12-15-96 @ 104.46		
302051AA	Exide Corp. sr.sub.nts. 12.875 1997	Caa r	J&D 15	105.00	to 6-14-93	Yes	104 1/4 bid	11.70	104 1/4	94	135	6-17-87	99.25	13.01
302150AN	Export Devel. Corp. nts. 8.625 1992	Aaa r	M&N 12	N.C.	----	No	101 1/4 bid	3.78	103 1/8	101 1/8	150	11-5-87	99.62	8.72
302150AQ	nts. 8.15 1993	Aaa	M&N 15	N.C.	----	No	104 7/8 bid	4.18	105 1/8	103 1/4	200	11-5-90	99.90	8.19
302150AP	nts. 8.125 1999	Aaa	F&A 10	N.C.	----	No	108 1/2 bid	6.58	108 5/8	102	200	8-2-89	99.63	8.18
302289AN	Exxon Cap. Corp. nts. 6.50 1999[9]	Aaa	J&J 15	N.C.	----	No	100 1/8 bid	6.46	100 1/4	99 5/8	250	7-7-92	99.43	6.60
302289AF •	gtd.nts. 8.25 1994[9]	Aaa r	A&O 15	N.C.	----	No	105 5/8 bid	5.50	109	103 3/4	199	10-12-89	99.75	8.31
302289AH	nts. 8.00 1995[9]	Aaa r	J&D 1	N.C.	----	No	107 7/8 bid	5.37	108 1/4	104	250	12-7-90	100.00	8.00
302289AJ	gtd.nts. 7.75 1996[9]	Aaa r	F&A 14	N.C.	----	No	106 1/2 bid	5.66	107	102 3/4	100	2-1-91	99.80	7.80
302289AK	gtd.nts. 7.875 1996[9]	Aaa r	A&O 15	N.C.	----	No	107 3/8 bid	5.63	107 3/4	103 3/8	250	4-15-91	99.89	7.90
302289AL	nts. 7.875 1997	Aaa r	F&A 15	N.C.	----	No	106 1/2 bid	6.32	107	102 3/8	250	8-13-91	99.69	7.94
302289AG	gtd.nts. 8.25 1999[9]	Aaa r	M&N 1	N.C.	----	No	109 3/8 bid	6.59	109 1/2	102 3/4	200	10-24-89	99.60	8.31
302290AA	•Exxon Corp. deb. 6.00 1997	Aaa r	M&N 1	100.13	to 10-31-92	Yes	99 3/4 bid	6.05	100 3/4	94 1/4	156.5	10-25-67	100.00	6.00
302290AB •	deb. 6.50 1998	Aaa r	J&J15	100.25	to 7-14-93	Yes	100 3/8 sale	6.42	101	95 3/8	151.3	7-11-68	100.00	6.50
302292AG	•Exxon Pipeline s.f.deb. 5.625 1997[10]	Aaa r	J&D 1	100.00	to 6-1-97	Yes	97 bid	6.35	95 7/8	92 1/8	11.5	6-14-67	99.25	5.68
302292AH •	s.f.deb. 6.625 1998	Aaa r	J&D 1	100.75	to 11-30-92	Yes	100 sale	6.62	100	97	37.0	12-11-68	100.00	6.62
302292AE •	gtd.deb. 8.25 2001	Aaa r	M&S 1	101.55	to 2-28-93	Yes	101 1/4 bid	8.03	102 3/8	101 1/8	245	2-26-76	99.50	
302293AB	•Exxon Shipping Co. gtd.deb. 7.50 2011[11]	Aaa r	A&O 1	100.00	to 10-1-11	Yes	98 1/4 bid	7.67	100	97	150	10-6-86	99.70	
302293AA	deb. 0.00 2012[12]	Aaa r	[13]N.P.	100.00	to 9-1-12	No	20 1/8 bid	8.14	20 1/8	17 5/8	560	9-17-82	27.00	
269288AA	EZ Communications, Inc. sr.sub.nts. 12.70 1996	N.R. r	M&N 1	104.00	to 10-31-92	No	97 1/2 bid	13.49	97 1/2	83 1/2	50.0	10-31-86	100.00	12.70
303261AB	Fair Lanes, Inc. sr.nts. 11.875 1997	B1	F&A 15	N.C.	----	No	101 1/2 bid	11.47	101 1/2	101 1/2	138	2-18-92	99.50	12.00
303698AA	•Fairchild Corp. sub.nts. 12.25 1996[14]	B3 r	M&S15	104.08	to 3-14-93	No	100 sale	12.25	100	83 1/2	60.0	3-6-86	95.86	13.00
303698AB	sub.deb. 12.00 2002[15]	B3 r	M&S 15	N.C.	----	No	----	----	----	----	160	9-23-87	00.00	
303698AC •	sub.deb. 13.125 2006	B3 r	M&S15	105.25	to 3-14-93	Yes	90 1/2 sale	14.76	93 7/8	76 1/8	75.0	3-6-86	95.77	13.75
303698AD	jr.sub.deb. 13.00 2007	B3	M&S 1	N.C.	----	No	85 7/8 sale	15.46	85 7/8	76	102	9-23-87	00.00	
303711AG	Fairchild Indust. nts. F 12.25 1993	B2	F&A15	N.C.	----	No	----	----	----	----	2.200	2-15-83	100.00	12.25
----	nts. D 12.25 1993	B2	J&J15	100.00	to 1-15-93	No	----	----	----	----	15.0	1-13-83		
303711AJ	sr.nts. 12.375 1994	B2	M&N15	102.75	to 11-14-92	Yes	----	----	----	----	6.000	11-20-84	100.00	12.38
303711AE	deb. B 13.75 1997	B2	M&N1	103.11	to 11-1-92	Yes	----	----	----	----	13.5	11-9-82		
303711AB •	sub.deb. 9.75 1998	B3 r	A&O 1	100.00	to 4-1-98	Yes	84 1/4 bid	13.85	85	70	5.195	1978		
304231AE	•Fairfield Commun. sr.sub.nts. 13.25 1992	Ca r	†10-31-90	101.89	to 10-30-92	No	44 bid	flat	46	31	40.0	11-5-85	100.00	13.25
304231AC ♦	sub.deb. 15.125 1997	Ca r	†8-15-90	100.00	to 2-15-97	Yes	---- bid	flat	----	03 1/8	15.9	2-11-82		
305902AA	Falcon Cable Systems Co. sr.sub.deb. 14.375 2000	N.R. r	J&D15	102.50	to 12-14-91	Yes	----	----	----	----	50.0	12-17-85	100.00	14.38
307353AB	♦Far West Sav. & Ln. zero cpn. 0.00 1995	N.R. r	[16]N.P.	N.C.	----	No	---- bid	----	----	----	30.0	11-16-82	25.00	11.63
307617AA	Farley, Inc. sr.sub.nts. 14.625 1995[17]	N.R. r	F&A 15	[18] N.C.	----	No	----	----	----	----	250	2-9-88	100.00	14.63
307617AB	sub.nts. 15.625 1998	N.R. r	F&A 15	106.94	fr 2-15-93	Yes	28 bid	----	29	17	000	2-9-87	100.00	15.63
30766RAE	Farm Credit Sys Fin'l bonds 9.20 2005	Aaa	M&S 27	N.C.	----	No	----	----	----	----	89.0	9-21-90	100.00	9.20
309594AA	Farmers Group, Inc. 1st 8.25 1996	A2 r	J&J 15	N.C.	----	No	103 7/8 bid	7.09	104 1/4	99 5/8	200	7-21-86	100.00	8.25
313035AA	Fay's Drug Co., Inc. sub.deb. 13.75 2005	Ba3 r	M&N 15	103.00	to 5-14-93	Yes	105 bid	12.94	----	----	27.8	5-23-85	100.00	13.75
----	FCC National Bank dep.nts. 8.00 1994	A2	M&S 15	N.C.	----	No	----	----	----	----	100	3-6-91	99.58	
313309AC	Federal Express sr.nts. 8.125 1993	Baa3	F&A 15	N.C.	----	No	101 3/8 bid	5.45	102 3/4	101 1/4	100	2-10-88	99.63	8.22
313309AG	sr.nts. 9.20 1994	Baa3 r	M&N 15	[19] N.C.	----	No	105 5/8 bid	6.50	106 5/8	102 1/2	150	11-13-89	100.00	9.20
313309AA	sr.nts. 10.625 1995	Baa3 r	F&A15	100.00	fr 8-15-92	No	100 1/4 bid	10.52	102 3/4	100 1/8	100	8-20-85	99.50	10.71
313309AE	nts. 9.75 1996	Baa3 r	M&N 15	[20] N.C.	----	No	107 5/8 bid	7.39	108 1/8	103 3/8	150	5-18-89	99.70	9.81
313309AD	sr.nts. 10.00 1999	Baa3	A&O 15	[20] N.C.	----	No	107 7/8 bid	8.41	108 5/8	103 1/8	100	4-18-89	99.38	10.10
313309AH	nts. 9.875 2002	Baa3	A&O 1	N.C.	----	No	107 3/4 bid	8.66	109	97 3/8	175	3-23-92	99.28	9.98
313309AF	s.f.deb. 9.625 2019	Baa3 r	A&O 15	103.78	fr 10-15-99	Yes	98 1/8 bid	9.82	98 1/2	93 3/8	100	10-10-89	97.94	9.84
313309AJ	Federal Express Corp. deb. 9.65 2012	Baa3	J&D 15	N.C.	----	No	101 5/8 bid	9.45	101 5/8	99 1/2	300	6-19-92	99.55	9.70
313693AE	Federal Paper Board Co., deb. 8.125 2002	Baa3	J&J 1	N.C.	----	No	101 5/8 bid	7.88	101 5/8	100 1/2	125	6-29-92	100.00	8.88
313693AF	deb. 8.875 2012	Baa3	J&J 1	N.C.	----	No	101 1/2 bid	8.71	101 1/2	99 3/4	50.0	6-29-92	99.76	8.16
313693AC	Federal Paper-Brd. sub.deb. 13.00 2000	Ba3 r	J&D15	100.00	to 6-14-93	Yes	----	----	----	----	125	6-20-85	99.00	13.15
313693AD	deb. 10.00 2011	Baa3	A&O 15	N.C.	----	No	110 5/8 bid	8.82	110 5/8	100 3/4	200	4-16-91	100.00	10.00
313747AB	FEDERAL REALTY INVEST. TR sr.nts. 8.65 1996	Baa2 r	A&O 1	101.00	fr 4-1-93	No	99 5/8 bid	8.75	100	95	40.0	3-27-86	100.00	8.65
313549AD	•Federal-Mogul Corp. nts. 8.375 1993	Ba1 r	A&O 1	N.C.	----	No	101 1/2 bid	7.01	101 1/2	98	100	10-1-86	100.00	8.38
313549AA •	s.f.deb. 7.50 1998	Ba1 r	J&J15	100.38	to 1-14-93	Yes	93 1/4 bid	9.09	95	93	5.293	2-6-73	100.00	7.50
313549AC •	s.f.deb. 13.00 2005	Ba1 r	F&A15	106.50	to 8-14-91	Yes	105 5/8 bid	12.12	106 1/4	105 5/8	30.4			
314099AK	Federated Dept. St. nts. 9.375 1992[21]	N.R. r	†11-1-90	N.C.	----	No	100 1/4 bid	flat	104 3/8	87	200	10-22-87	100.00	9.38
314099AA	s.f.deb. 8.375 1995[22]	N.R. r	†1-15-90	100.00	to 9-14-92	No	----	flat	----	----	15.0	9-23-70	100.00	8.37
314099AJ	nts. 7.875 1996	Caa r	†12-15-90	100.00	fr 12-15-93	No	100 5/8 bid	flat	100 5/8	84	200	12-18-86	99.25	7.99
314099AN	sr.sub.deb. 16.00 2000	Ca r	†11-1-90	112.00	to 10-31-92	Yes	10 3/8 bid	flat	10 3/8	06 1/2	500	11-4-88	100.00	16.00
314099AB	s.f.deb. 7.125 2002	N.R. r	†3-15-90	101.19	to 3-14-93	Yes	----	flat	----	----	32.5	3-23-72	99.63	7.16
314099AM	sub.deb. 17.75 2004[23]	Ca r	[24]†1-1-90	105.00	fr 11-1-93	Yes	02 1/4 bid	flat	02 1/2	01 3/4	306.2	11-1-88	42.89	
314099AC	s.f.deb. 10.25 2010	N.R. r	†6-15-90	104.88	to 6-14-93	Yes	100 3/4 bid	flat	105	78 3/4	39.7	6-11-80	99.12	
314099AE	s.f.deb. 10.625 2013	N.R. r	†5-1-90	§105.71	to 4-30-93	Yes	----	flat	----	----	13.9	Ref. fr. 5-1-93 @ 105.19		
314099AF	s.f.deb. 9.50 2016	Caa r	†3-1-90	§106.65	to 2-28-93	Yes	101 3/4 bid	flat	105	85 1/2	100	Ref. fr. 3-1-96 @ 104.75		
315290AE	Ferrellgas Inc. sr.sub.deb. 11.625 2003	B2	J&D 15	N.C.	----	No	102 1/2 bid	11.23	102 1/2	100	250	12-5-91	98.42	11.88

[1]Discount, semi-annual int. payments begin 8-1-94, coupon rate of 14 1 /2%. [2]Due 8-1-97. [3]Reset nt.. [4]Asset bkd. LOC Credit Suisse. [5]Deferred Cpn. [6]Form. Equitable Gas Co. [7]Ohio Div. [8]Due 5-1-80. [9]Gtd. by Exxon Corp. [10]Form. Humble Pipeline. Gtd. by Exxon Corp. [11]Int. rt. thru 10-1-93, gtd. by Exxon Corp. [12]Gtd. Def.Int. Deb. Gtd. by Exxon Corp. Exch. offer for co.'s 6 5/8 gtd . nts. due 1998 and 7.40% gtd. nts. due 2002. [13]Ea. $270 princ. amt. will have int. payment at mat. of $730. [14]Form. Banner Industries. [15]Intermediate . [16]Due 3-7-95. [17]Ext. Reset Nts. [18]Callable under circumstances specified in the in denture. [19]Except for conditions specified in the indenture. [20]Callable at the option of the holder. [21]Co. filed for Chap. 11. [22]Acq. by Campeau Corp. [23]Discount. [24]Fr. 11-1-93.

Notes: Moody's ratings are subject to change. Because of the possible time lapse between Moody's assignment or change of a rating and your use of this monthly publication, we suggest you verify the current rating of any security or issuer in which you are interested. For standard abbreviations and symbols, see page 5.

Source: *Moody's Bond Record*, December 1992, p. 31.

TABLE 16–2
Exxon corporation debentures

6½% DEBENTURES; Due July 15, 1998
(S&P Rating AAA; at Aug. 31, 1992)

Authorized. $250,000,000
Outstanding (Dec. 31, 1991)   151,000,000
Retired or in treas   99,000,000
    ORIGINALLY ISSUED under the title Standard Oil Co. (New Jersey).
    INDENTURE DATED July 15, 1968. INTEREST PAYABLE Jan. & July 15, to holders registered the preceding Dec. 31 & June 30, respectively. PRINCIPAL & INTEREST PAYABLE at trustee's office. INTEREST GRACE PERIOD—90 days.
    TRUSTEE & REGISTRAR—Citibank, N.A., New York.
    DENOMINATIONS—Fully registered, $1,000 and multiples thereof.
    SINKING FUND requires retirement at 100 & int. of $6,000,000 Debs. each July 15, 1987–97, Co. having noncumulative option to redeem up to a like amount more each year. Optional payments may not be used to reduce mandatory requirements.
    REDEEMABLE OTHERWISE on 30 days' notice, at the following prices & int., thru each July 14, with price declining each year after to 100:
1993 . . . . 100¼   After 100
    SECURITY—Same as 6% Debs.
    LISTED—NYSE:

1991	. . .	99¾	88	1990	. . .	90	82¾
1989	. . .	89½	79¾	1988	. . .	86¾	80¾

Source: *Standard & Poor's Corporate Records*, December 1992, p. 8350.

sinking-fund requirement indicates that retirement of a minimum of $6 million was to begin on July 15, 1987, and continue through July 15, 1997. An additional $6 million could also be retired on each date, but Exxon was still required to retire the minimum amount the following year. From the bond price listing at the bottom of Table 16–2, it is clear that the bond sold at less than 100 percent of par in 1988 through 1991. The low prices occurred because market interest rates were higher than the coupon rate on Exxon's debentures.

The information in Table 16–2 also provides other pertinent information found in the indenture, such as the interest payment dates, denominations of each bond, and call features (listed under "redeemable otherwise").

Bond Prices, Yields, and Ratings

The financial manager must be sensitive to interest rate changes and price movements in the bond market. The treasurer's interpretation of market conditions will influence the timing of new issues, the coupon rate offered, and the maturity date. Lest the student of finance think bonds maintain stable long-term price patterns, he or she need merely consider bond pricing during the five-year period 1967–72. When the market interest rate on outstanding 30-year, Aaa corporate bonds went from 5.10 percent to 8.10 percent, the average price of existing bonds dropped 36 percent. A conservative investor would be quite disillusioned to see a $1,000, 5.10 percent bond now quoted at

$640.[1] Though most bonds are virtually certain to be redeemed at their face value at maturity ($1,000 in this case), this is small consolation to the bond-holder who has many decades to wait. Of course, at times, bonds also greatly increase in value, such as in 1982, 1984–85, and 1990–92.

As indicated above and in Chapter 10, the price of a bond is intimately tied to current interest rates. A bond paying 5.10 percent ($51 a year) will fare quite poorly when the going market rate is 8.10 percent ($81 a year). To maintain a market in the older issue, the price is adjusted downward to reflect current market demands. The longer the life of the issue, the greater the influence of interest rate changes on the price of the bond.[2] The same process will work in reverse if interest rates go down. A 30-year, $1,000 bond initially issued to yield 8.10 percent would go up to $1,500 if interest rates declined to 5.10 percent (assuming the bond is not callable). A further illustration of interest rate effects on bond prices is presented in Table 16–3 for a bond paying 12 percent interest. Observe that not only interest rates in the market but also years to maturity have a strong influence on bond prices.

	Rate in the Market (percent) — Yield to Maturity*				
Years to Maturity	**8%**	**10%**	**12%**	**14%**	**16%**
1 . . .	$1,038.16	$1,018.54	$1,000	$981.48	$963.98
15 . . .	1,345.52	1,153.32	1,000	875.54	774.48
25 . . .	1,429.92	1,182.36	1,000	862.06	754.98

Interest rates and bond prices (the bond pays 12 percent interest)

*The prices in the table are based on semiannual interest, but you enter it with annual values.

TABLE 16–3
Bond price table

From 1940 through the early 1980s, the pattern has been for long-term interest rates to move upward (Figure 16–3). However, long-term interest rates have been declining since 1982.

Bond Yields

Bond yields are quoted on three different bases: **coupon rate, current yield,** and **yield to maturity.** We will apply each to a $1,000 par value bond paying $100 per year interest for 10 years. The bond is currently priced at $900.

Coupon Rate (Nominal Yield) Stated interest payment divided by the par value.

$$\frac{\$100}{\$1,000} = 10\%$$

---

[1]Bond prices are generally quoted as a percentage of original par value. In this case the quote would read 64.

[2]This is known as Malkiel's second theory of bonds. In fact it is only completely true when the coupon rate of the bond equals or is greater than the original discount rate.

FIGURE 16–3   **Long-term yields on debt**

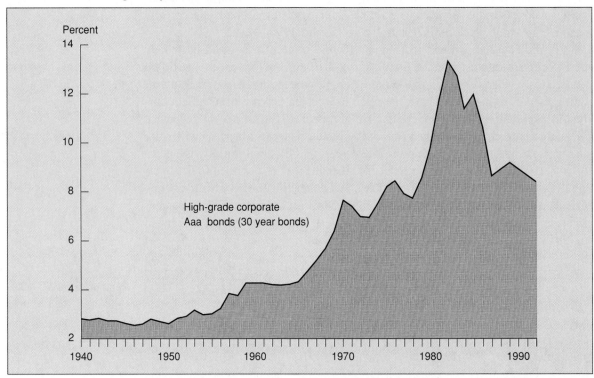

Current Yield   Stated interest payment divided by the current price of the bond.

$$\frac{\$100}{\$900} = 11.11\%$$

Yield to Maturity   The yield to maturity is the interest rate that will equate future interest payments and the payment at maturity to the current market price. This represents the concept of the internal rate of return. In the present case, an interest rate of approximately 11.70 percent will equate interest payments of $100 for 10 years and a final payment of $1,000 to the current price of $900. A simple formula may be used to approximate yield to maturity.[3] This formula was initially presented in Chapter 10.

$$\text{Approximate yield to maturity (Y')} = \frac{\text{Annual interest payment} + \dfrac{\text{Principal payment} - \text{Price of the bond}}{\text{Number of years to maturity}}}{0.6 \,(\text{Price of the bond}) + 0.4 \,(\text{Principal payment})} \quad (16\text{–}1)$$

----

[3]The exact answer can be found through Appendix E covering financial calculators at the back of the text.

$$Y' = \frac{\$100 + \dfrac{\$1,000 - 900}{10}}{0.6\ (\$900) + 0.4\ (\$1,000)}$$

$$= \frac{\$100 + \dfrac{\$100}{10}}{\$540 + \$400}$$

$$Y' = \frac{\$100 + \$10}{\$940} = \frac{\$110}{\$940} = \boxed{11.70\%}$$

Extensive bond tables indicating yield to maturity are also available. When financial analysts speak of bond yields, the general assumption is that they are speaking of yield to maturity. This is deemed to be the most significant measure of return.

Bond Ratings

Both the issuing corporation and the investor are concerned about the rating their bond is assigned by the two major bond rating agencies—Moody's Investor Service and Standard & Poor's Corporation. The higher the rating assigned a given issue, the lower the required interest payments are to satisfy potential investors. This is because highly rated bonds carry lower risk. A major industrial corporation may be able to issue a 30-year bond at 8 percent yield to maturity because it is rated Aaa, whereas a smaller, regional firm may only qualify for a B rating and be forced to pay 11 or 12 percent.

As an example of **bond rating** systems, Moody's Investor Service provides the following nine categories of ranking:

Aaa   Aa   A   Baa   Ba   B   Caa   Ca   C

The first two categories represent the highest quality (for example, 3M and Procter & Gamble); the next two, medium to high quality; and so on. Beginning in 1982, Moody's began applying numerical modifiers to categories Aa through B: 1 is the highest in a category, 2 is the midrange, and 3 is the lowest. Thus, a Aa2 rating means the bond is in the midrange of Aa. Standard & Poor's has a similar letter system with + and − modifiers.

Bonds receive ratings based on the corporation's ability to make interest payments, its consistency of performance, its size, its debt-equity ratio, its working capital position, and a number of other factors. The yield spread between higher- and lower-rated bonds changes with the economy. If investors are pessimistic about economic events, they will accept as much as 3 percent less return to go into securities of very high quality, whereas in more normal times the spread may be only 1.5 percent.

Examining Actual Bond Ratings

Three actual bond offerings are presented in Table 16–4 to illustrate the various terms we have used.

TABLE 16–4   **Outstanding bond issues (January 1993)**

Name	Coupon	Type of Bond	Rating	Price	Yield to Maturity
Jos. E. Seagram & Son.	8.35%	Debenture due 2006	A2	$1,060	7.63%
Turner Broadcasting System . .	12.00%	Senior subordinated debenture due 2001	B1	$1,110	10.08%
Philadelphia Electric Co.	8.75%	First mortgage bonds and refundable due 2022	Baa1	$1,026	8.50%

Source: *Moody's Bond Record,* January 1993.

Recall, the true return on a bond issue is measured by yield to maturity (the last column of Table 16–4). The Joseph E Seagram & Son bonds are unsecured, as indicated by the term *debenture*. The bonds are rated A2, or middle investment grade. The bonds carry a market price of $1,060 because the interest rate at time of issue (8.35 percent) is higher than the demanded yield to maturity of 7.63 percent in January 1993 for bonds of equal quality and maturity. The Turner Broadcasting System bond is a senior subordinated debenture with a rating of B1 (junk bond quality) and a high yield to maturity of 10.08 percent. The Philadelphia Electric Company bond is a mortgage against plant and equipment. It can be refunded if the company desires. The meaning and benefits of refunding are made clear in the following section.

The Refunding Decision

Assume you are the financial vice president for a corporation that has issued bonds at 11.75 percent, only to witness a drop in interest rates to 9.5 percent. If you believe interest rates will rise rather than sink further, you may wish to redeem the expensive 11.75 percent bonds and issue new debt at the prevailing 9.5 percent rate. This process is labeled a **refunding** operation. It is made feasible by the call provision that enables a corporation to buy back bonds at close to par, rather than at high market values, when interest rates are declining. Although long-term interest rates tended to move up in the last few decades, recently there were periods of decline in interest rates that provided an excellent environment for refunding.

A Capital Budgeting Problem

The refunding decision involves outflows in the form of financing costs related to redeeming and reissuing securities, and inflows represented by savings in annual interest costs and some tax savings. In the present case, we shall assume the corporation issued $10 million worth of 11.75 percent debt with a 25-year maturity and the debt has been on the books for five years. The corporation now has the opportunity to buy back the old debt at 10 percent above par (the call premium) and to issue new debt at 9.5 percent interest with a 20-year life. The underwriting cost for the old issue was $125,000, and the underwriting cost for the new issue is $200,000. We shall also assume the corporation is in the 35 percent tax bracket and uses a 6 percent discount rate for refunding decisions. Since the savings from a refunding decision are certain—unlike the savings from most other capital budgeting decisions—we use the aftertax cost of new debt as the discount rate, rather than the more generalized cost of capital.[4] Actually, in this case, the aftertax cost of new debt is 9.5 percent $\times$ (1 − Tax rate), or 9.5% $\times$ 0.65 = 6.18%. We round to 6 percent. The facts in this example are restated below.

	Old Issue	New Issue
Size	$10,000,000	$10,000,000
Interest rate.	11.75%	9.5%
Total life	25 years	20 years
Remaining life.	20 years	20 years
Call premium	10%	—
Underwriting costs	$125,000	$200,000

Tax bracket. . . .	35%
Discount rate	6%

Let's go through the capital budgeting process of defining our outflows and inflows and determining the net percent value.

Step A—Outflow Considerations

1. *Payment of call premium*—The first outflow is the 10 percent call premium on $10 million, or $1 million. This prepayment penalty is necessary to call in the original issue. Being an *out-of-pocket* tax-deductible expense, the $1 million cash expenditure will cost us only $650,000 on an aftertax basis. We multiply the expense by (1 − Tax rate) to get the aftertax cost.

$$\$1,000,000(1 - T) = \$1,000,000(1 - 0.35) = \$650,000$$

Net cost of call premium = $650,000

2. *Underwriting cost on new issue*—The second outflow is the $200,000 underwriting cost on the new issue. The actual cost is somewhat less because the payment is tax deductible, though the write-off must be spread over the life of the bond. While the actual $200,000 is being spent now, equal tax deductions of $10,000 a year will occur over the next 20 years (in a manner similar to depreciation).

---

[4]A minority opinion would be that there is sufficient similarity between the bond refunding decision and other capital budgeting decisions to disallow any specialized treatment. Also note that although the bondholders must still bear some risk of default, for which they are compensated, the corporation assumes no risk.

The tax savings from a *non-cash* write-off equal the amount times the tax rate. For a company in the 35 percent tax bracket, $10,000 of annual tax deductions will provide $3,500 of tax savings each year for the next 20 years. The present value of these savings is the present value of a $3,500 annuity for 20 years at 6 percent interest:

$$\$3,500 \times 11.470 \ (n = 20, \ i = 6\%) = \$40,145$$

The net cost of underwriting the new issue is the actual expenditure now, minus the present value of future tax savings:

Actual expenditure	$200,000
− PV of future tax savings . . .	40,145
Net cost of underwriting expense on the new issue . . .	$159,855

Step B—Inflow Considerations

The major inflows in the refunding decision are related to the reduction of annual interest expense and the immediate write-off of the underwriting cost on the old issue.

3. *Cost savings in lower interest rates*—The corporation will enjoy a 2.25 percentage point drop in interest rates, from 11.75 percent to 9.50 percent, on $10 million of bonds.

11.75% × $10,000,000. . . .	$1,175,000
9.50% × $10,000,000. . . .	950,000
Savings	$ 225,000

Since we are in the 35 percent tax bracket, this is equivalent to $146,250 of aftertax benefits per year for 20 years. We have taken the savings and multiplied by one minus the tax rate to get the aftertax benefits.

$$\$225,000(1 - T)$$
$$\$225,000(1 - 0.35)$$
$$\$146,250$$

Applying a 6 percent discount rate for a 20-year annuity:

$$\$146,250 \times 11.470 \ (n = 20, i = 6\%) = \$1,677,488$$

Cost savings in lower interest rates. . . . $1,677,488

4. *Underwriting cost on old issue*—There is a further cost savings related to immediately writing off the remaining underwriting costs on the old bonds. Note that the initial amount of $125,000 was spent five years ago and was to be written off for tax purposes over

25 years at $5,000 per year. Since five years have passed, $100,000 of old underwriting costs have not been amortized.

Original amount	$125,000
Written off over five years	25,000
Unamortized old underwriting costs . . .	$100,000

A tax benefit is associated with the immediate write-off of old underwriting costs, which we shall consider shortly.

Note, however, that this is not a total gain. We would have gotten the $100,000 additional write-off eventually if we had not called in the old bonds. By calling them in now, we simply take the write-off sooner. If we extended the write-off over the remaining life, we would have taken $5,000 a year for 20 years. Discounting this value, we show:

$$\$5,000 \times 11.470 \ (n = 20, i = 6\%) = \$57,350$$

Thus, we are getting a write-off of $100,000 now, rather than a present value of future write-offs of $57,350. The gain in immediate tax write-offs is $42,650. The tax savings from a *non-cash* tax write-off equal the amount times the tax rate. Since we are in the 35 percent tax bracket, our savings from this write-off are $14,928.

Immediate write-off	$100,000
− PV of future write-off	57,350
Gain from immediate write-off	$ 42,650

$$\$42,650(T)$$
$$42,650(.35) = \$14,928$$

Net gain from the underwriting on the old issue $14,928

Step C—Net Present Value

We now compare our outflows and our inflows.

Outflows		Inflows	
1. Net cost of call premium	$650,000	3. Cost savings in lower interest rates	$1,677,488
2. Net cost of under- writing expense on new issue	159,855	4. Net gain from under- writing cost on old issue	14,928
	$809,855		$1,692,416

Present value of inflows	$1,692,416
Present value of outflows . . .	809,855
Net present value	$ 882,561

The refunding decision has a positive net present value, suggesting that interest rates have dropped to a sufficiently low level to indicate refunding is in order. The only question is, Will interest rates go lower—indicating an even better time for refunding? There is no easy answer for this consideration.

A number of other factors could be plugged into the problem. For example, there could be overlapping time periods in the refunding procedure when both issues are outstanding and the firm is paying double interest (hopefully for less than a month). The dollar amount, however, tends to be small and is not included in the analysis.

In working problems, the student should have minimum difficulty if he or she follows the four suggested calculations. In each of the four calculations we had the following tax implications:

1. Payment of call premium—the cost equals the amount times (1 − Tax rate) for this *cash tax-deductible expense.*

2. Underwriting costs on new issue—we pay an amount now and then amortize it over the life of the bond for tax purposes. This subsequent amortization is similar to depreciation and represents a *non-cash write-off* of a tax-deductible expense. The tax saving from the amortization is equal to the amount times the tax rate.

3. Cost savings in lower interest rates—cost savings are like any form of income, and we will retain the cost savings times (1 − Tax rate).

4. Underwriting cost on old issue—once again, the writing off of underwriting costs represents a *non-cash write-off* of a tax-deductible expense. The tax savings from the amortization are equal to the amount times the tax rate.

Innovative Forms of Bond Financing

As interest rates continued to show increasing volatility in the 1980s, two innovative forms of bond financing became very popular. We shall examine the zero-coupon rate bond and the floating rate bond.

The zero-coupon rate bond, as the name implies, does not pay interest. It is, however, sold at a deep discount from face value. The return to the investor is the difference between the investor's cost and the face value received at the end of the life of the bond. For example, in early 1982, BankAmerica Corporation offered $1,000 zero-coupon rate bonds with maturities of 5, 8, and 10 years. The 5-year bonds were sold for $500, the 8-year bonds for $333.33, and the 10-year bonds for $250. All three provided an initial yield to maturity (through gain in value) of approximately 14.75 percent. A dramatic case of a zero-coupon bond was an issue offered by PepsiCo, Inc., in 1982, in which the maturities ranged from 6 to 30 years. The 30-year $1,000 par value issue could be purchased for $26.43, providing a yield of approximately 12.75 percent. The purchase price per bond of $26.43 represents only 2.643 percent of the par value. A million dollars worth of these 30-year bonds could be initially purchased for a mere $26,430.

The advantage to the corporation is that there is immediate cash inflow to the corporation, without any outflow until the bonds mature. Furthermore, the difference between the initial bond price and the maturity value may be amortized for tax purposes by the corporation over the life of the bond. This means the corporation will be taking annual deductions without current cash outflow.

From the investor's viewpoint, the zero-coupon bonds allow him or her to lock in a multiplier of the initial investment. For example, investors may know they will get four times their investment after a specified number of years. The major drawback is that the annual increase in the value of bonds is taxable as ordinary income as it accrues, even though the bondholder does not get any cash flow until maturity. For this reason most investors in zero-coupon rate bonds have tax-exempt or tax-deferred status (pension funds, foundations, charitable organizations, individual retirement accounts, and the like).

The prices of the bonds tend to be highly volatile because of changes in interest rates. Even though the bonds provide no annual interest payment, there is still an initial yield to maturity that may prove to be too high or too low with changes in the marketplace.

In the 1980s, Merrill Lynch and Salomon Brothers and other brokerage houses began offering a variation of the zero-coupon rate bond through selling future interests in government securities. The securities, which are held in custody for the benefit of investors, are sold at a fraction of face value and ultimately redeemed at full value. The investor receives a multiple of the original investment and no interest. These securities tend to be long term (20 to 30 years) when originally offered.

When interest rates drop to relatively low levels as they have in the 1990s, zero-coupon bonds lose their advantage to investors and suffer the risk of declining prices if rates rise again. Companies are more than willing to sell low coupon bonds when rates are down.

The top part of Table 16–5 contains examples of two zero-coupon bonds from Shearson Lehman Brothers and J.P. Morgan & Co. The bonds sell at a large discount from par since they do not come due until 1998. The main difference between the price of the two bonds comes from the difference in ratings rather than maturity.

A second type of innovative bond issue is the **floating rate bond** (already popular in European capital markets). In this case, instead of a change in the

TABLE 16–5 **Zero-coupon and floating rate bonds**

	Rating	Coupon	Maturity	Price	Yield to Maturity
Zero-coupon bonds:					
Shearson Lehman Brothers . .	A3	0.00%	1998	$641.30	8.42%
J.P. Morgan & Co.	Aa2	0.00%	1998	687.50	7.39%
Floating rate bonds:					
Chemical Banking Corp.	Baa3	6.50%	2004	952.50	7.11%
Source: *Moody's Bond Record,* January 1993.					

price of the bond, the interest rate paid on the bond changes with market conditions (usually monthly or quarterly). Thus, a bond that was initially issued to pay 9 percent may lower the interest payments to 6 percent during some years and raise them to 12 percent in others. The interest rate is usually tied to some overall market rate, such as the yield on Treasury bonds (perhaps 120 percent of the going yield on long-term Treasury bonds).

An example of a floating rate bond is the Chemical Banking Corp. bond presented at the bottom of Table 16–5 on page 469.

The advantage to investors in floating rate bonds is that they have a constant (or almost constant) market value for the security, even though interest rates vary. An exception is that floating rate bonds often have broad limits that interest payments cannot exceed. For example, the interest rate on a 9 percent initial offering may not be allowed to go over 16 percent or below 4 percent. If long-term interest rates dictated an interest payment of 20 percent, the payment would still remain at 16 percent. This could cause some short-term loss in market value. To date, floating rate bonds have been relatively free of this problem.

Zero-coupon rate bonds and floating rate bonds still represent a relatively small percentage of the total market of new debt offerings. Nevertheless, they should be part of a basic understanding of long-term debt instruments.

Advantages and Disadvantages of Debt

The financial manager must consider whether debt will contribute to or detract from the firm's operations. In certain industries, such as airlines, very heavy debt utilization is a way of life, whereas in other industries (drugs, photographic equipment) reliance is placed on other forms of capital.

Benefits of Debt

The advantages of debt may be enumerated as:

1. Interest payments are tax deductible. Because the maximum corporate tax rate is in the mid-30 percent range, the effective aftertax cost of interest is approximately two thirds of the dollar amount expended.
2. The financial obligation is clearly specified and of a fixed nature (with the exception of floating rate bonds). Contrast this with selling an ownership interest in which stockholders have open-ended participation in the sharing of profits.
3. In an inflationary economy, debt may be paid back with "cheaper dollars." A $1,000 bond obligation may be repaid in 10 or 20 years with dollars that have shrunk in value by 50 or 60 percent. In terms of "real dollars," or purchasing power equivalents, one might argue that the corporation should be asked to repay something in excess of $2,000. Presumably, high interest rates in inflationary periods

compensate the lender for loss in purchasing power, but this is not always the case.

4. The use of debt, up to a prudent point, may lower the cost of capital to the firm. To the extent that debt does not strain the risk position of the firm, its low aftertax cost may aid in reducing the weighted overall cost of financing to the firm.

Drawbacks of Debt

Finally, we must consider the disadvantages of debt:

1. Interest and principal payment obligations are set by contract and must be met, regardless of the economic position of the firm.

2. Both indenture agreements may place burdensome restrictions on the firm, such as maintenance of working capital at a given level, limits on future debt offerings, and guidelines for dividend policy. Although bondholders generally do not have the right to vote, they may take virtual control of the firm if important indenture provisions are not met.

3. Utilized beyond a given point, debt may depress outstanding common stock values.

Eurobond Market

A market with an increasing presence in world capital markets is in Eurobonds. A **Eurobond** may be defined as a bond payable in the borrower's currency but sold outside the borrower's country. The Eurobond is usually sold by an international syndicate of investment bankers and includes bonds sold by companies in Switzerland, Japan, Netherlands, Germany, the United States, and Britain, to name the most popular countries. An example might be a bond of a U.S. company, payable in dollars and sold in London, Paris, Tokyo, or Frankfurt. Disclosure requirements in the Eurobond market are less demanding than those of the Securities and Exchange Commission or other domestic regulatory agencies. Examples of several Eurobonds are presented in Table 16–6.

TABLE 16–6 **Examples of Eurobonds**

	Rating	Coupon	Maturity	Amount Outstanding ($ millions)	Currency Denomination*
Merrill Lynch & Co., Inc.**	A1	0.00%	2000	100.0	DM
Nippon Telephone & Telegraph	Aaa	10.25%	2001	200.0	U.S.$
Nissan Motor Co., Ltd.	A2	7.50%	1996	100.0	ECU
Petro-Canada.	Baa1	9.25%	2021	300.0	U.S.$
Philip Morris Cos..	A2	6.00%	1996	133.1	DM
Procter & Gamble Co.	Aa2	10.88%	2001	200.0	C$

*DM is Deutsche Mark, ECU is Eurocurrency, and C$ is Canadian dollar.
**These are zero-coupon rate bonds.
Source: *Moody's Bond Record*, January 1993.

Leasing as a Form of Debt

When a corporation contracts to lease an oil tanker or a computer and signs a noncancelable, long-term agreement, the transaction has all the characteristics of a debt obligation. Long-term leasing was not recognized as a debt obligation in the early post–World War II period, but since the mid-60s there has been a strong movement by the accounting profession to force companies to fully divulge all information about leasing obligations and to indicate the equivalent debt characteristics.

This position was made official for financial reporting purposes as a result of Statement 13, issued by the Financial Accounting Standard Board (FASB) in November 1976. This statement said certain types of leases must be shown as long-term obligations on the financial statements of the firm. Before FASB Statement 13, lease obligations could merely be divulged in footnotes to financial statements, and large lease obligations did not have to be included in the debt structure (except for the upcoming payment). Consider the case of Firm ABC, whose balance sheet is shown in Table 16–7.

TABLE 16–7
**Balance sheet
($ millions)**

Current assets	$ 50	Current liabilities	$ 50
Fixed assets	150	Long-term liabilities	50
		Total liabilities	100
		Stockholders' equity	100
Total assets	$200	Total liabilities and stockholders' equity	$200

Before the issuance of FASB Statement 13, a footnote to the financial statements might have indicated a lease obligation of $12 million a year for the next 15 years, with a present value of $100 million. With the issuance of FASB Statement 13, this information has, of necessity, been moved directly to the balance sheet, as indicated in Table 16–8.

TABLE 16–8
**Revised balance sheet
($ millions)**

Current assets	$ 50	Current liabilities	$ 50
Fixed assets	150	Long-term liabilities	50
Leased property under capital lease* . . .	100	Obligation under capital lease*	100
		Total liabilities	200
		Stockholders' equity	100
Total assets	$300	Total liabilities and stockholders' equity . . .	$300

*See text below.

We see that both a new asset and a new liability have been created, as indicated by the asterisks. The essence of this treatment is that a long-term, noncancelable lease is tantamount to purchasing the asset with borrowed funds, and this should be reflected on the balance sheet. Note that between the original balance sheet (Table 16–7) and the revised balance sheet (Table 16–8), the total-debt-to-total-assets ratio has gone from 50 percent to 66.7 percent.

$$\text{Original:} \quad \frac{\text{Total debt}}{\text{Total assets}} = \frac{\$100 \text{ million}}{\$200 \text{ million}} = 50\%$$

$$\text{Revised:} \quad \frac{\text{Total debt}}{\text{Total assets}} = \frac{\$200 \text{ million}}{\$300 \text{ million}} = 66.7\%$$

Though this represents a substantial increase in the ratio, the impact on the firm's credit rating or stock price may be minimal. To the extent that the financial markets are efficient, the information was *already* known by analysts who took the data from footnotes or other sources and made their own adjustments. Nevertheless, corporate financial officers fought long, hard, and unsuccessfully to keep the lease obligation off the balance sheet. They tend to be much less convinced about the efficiency of the marketplace.

Capital Lease versus Operating Lease

Not all leases must be capitalized (present-valued) and placed on the balance sheet. This treatment is necessary only when substantially all the benefits and risks of ownership are transferred in a lease. Under these circumstances, we have a **capital lease** (also referred to as a financing lease). Identification as a capital lease and the attendant financial treatment are required whenever any *one* of the four following conditions is present:

1. The arrangement transfers ownership of the property to the lessee (the leasing party) by the end of the lease term.
2. The lease contains a bargain purchase price at the end of the lease. The option price will have to be sufficiently low so exercise of the option appears reasonably certain.
3. The lease term is equal to 75 percent or more of the estimated life of the leased property.
4. The present value of the minimum lease payments equals 90 percent or more of the fair value of the leased property at the inception of the lease.[5]

A lease that does not meet any of these four criteria is not regarded as a *capital* lease, but as an **operating lease.** An operating lease is usually short term and is often cancelable at the option of the lessee. Furthermore, the lessor (the owner of the asset) may provide for the maintenance and upkeep of the

---

[5]The discount rate used for this test is the leasing firm's new cost of borrowing or the lessor's (the firm that owns the asset) implied rate of return under the lease. The lower of the two must be used when both are known.

asset, since he or she is likely to get it back. An operating lease does not require the *capitalization*, or presentation, of the full obligation on the balance sheet. Operating leases are used most frequently with such assets as automobiles and office equipment, while capital leases are used with oil drilling equipment, airplanes and rail equipment, certain forms of real estate, and other long-term assets. The greatest volume of leasing obligations is represented by capital leases.

Income Statement Effect

The capital lease calls not only for present-valuing the lease obligation on the balance sheet but also for treating the arrangement for income statement purposes as if it were somewhat similar to a purchase-borrowing arrangement. Thus, under a capital lease, the intangible asset account previously shown in Table 16–8 as "Leased property under capital lease" is amortized or written off over the life of the lease with an annual expense deduction. Also, the liability account shown in Table 16–8 as "Obligation under capital lease" is written off through regular amortization, with an implied interest expense on the remaining balance. Thus, for financial reporting purposes the annual deductions are amortization of the asset, plus the implied interest expense on the remaining present value of the liability. Though the actual development of these values and accounting rules is best deferred to an accounting course, the finance student should understand the close similarity between a capital lease and borrowing to purchase an asset, for financial reporting purposes.

An operating lease, on the other hand, usually calls for an annual expense deduction equal to the lease payment, with no specific amortization, as is indicated in Appendix 16B, "Lease versus Purchase Decision," at the end of this chapter.

Advantages of Leasing

Why is leasing so popular? It has emerged as a $100 billion-plus industry, with such firms as Clark Equipment, Citicorp, and U.S. Leasing International providing an enormous amount of financing. Major reasons for the popularity of leasing include the following:

1. The lessee may lack sufficient funds or the credit capability to purchase the asset from a manufacturer, who is willing, however, to accept a lease arrangement or to arrange a lease obligation with a third party.
2. The provisions of a lease obligation may be substantially less restrictive than those of a bond indenture.
3. There may be no down payment requirement, as would generally be the case in the purchase of an asset (leasing allows for a larger indirect loan).

4. The lessor may possess particular expertise in a given industry—allowing for expert product selection, maintenance, and eventual resale. Through this process, the negative effects of obsolescence may be reduced.

5. Creditor claims on certain types of leases, such as real estate, are restricted in bankruptcy and reorganization proceedings. Leases on chattels (non-real estate items) have no such limitation.

There are also some tax factors to be considered. Where one party to a lease is in a higher tax bracket than the other party, certain tax advantages, such as depreciation write-off or research-related tax credits, may be better utilized. For example, a wealthy party may purchase an asset for tax purposes, then lease the asset to another party in a lower tax bracket for actual use. Also, lease payments on the use of land are tax deductible, whereas land ownership does not allow a similar deduction for depreciation. It should be pointed out that tax advantages related to leasing were reduced somewhat with the passage of the Tax Reform Act of 1986.

Finally, a firm may wish to engage in a sale-leaseback arrangement, in which assets already owned by the lessee are sold to the lessor and then leased back. This process provides the lessee with an infusion of capital, while allowing the lessee to continue to use the asset. Even though the dollar costs of a leasing arrangement are often higher than the dollar costs of owning an asset, the advantages cited above may outweigh the direct cost factors.

Summary

The use of debt financing by corporations has grown very rapidly since the end of World War II, and the quality of corporate debt coverage has deteriorated.

Corporate bonds may be secured by a lien on a specific asset or may carry an unsecured designation, indicating the bondholder possesses a general claim against the corporation. A special discussion of the hierarchy of claims for firms in financial distress is presented in Appendix 16A.

Bond prices have been in a steady decline for the last few decades, due to rising interest rates. Nevertheless, recent downturns in interest rates have afforded an excellent opportunity for refunding—that is, replacing high-interest-rate bonds with lower-interest-rate bonds. The financial manager must consider whether the savings in interest will compensate for the additional cost of calling in the old issue and selling a new one.

Finally, the long-term, noncancelable lease should be considered as a special debt form available to the corporation. It is capitalized on the balance sheet to represent both a debt and an asset account and is amortized on a regular basis. Leasing offers a means of financing in which lessor expertise and other financial benefits can be imparted to the lessee (leasing party).

A lease versus purchase decision for an operating lease is presented in Appendix 16B.

List of Terms

par value 455
maturity date 455
indenture 455
secured debt 455
mortgage agreement 455
after-acquired property
  clause 455
debenture 456
subordinated debenture 456
serial payment 458
sinking fund 458

call provision 458
coupon rate 461
current yield 461
yield to maturity 461
bond rating 463
refunding 464
zero-coupon rate bond 468
floating rate bond 469
Eurobond 471
capital lease 473
operating lease 473

Discussion Questions

1. Corporate debt has been expanding very dramatically since World War II. What has been the impact on interest coverage, particularly since 1977?

2. What are some basic features of bond agreements?

3. What is the difference between a bond agreement and a bond indenture?

4. Discuss the relationship between the coupon rate (original interest rate at time of issue) on a bond and its security provisions.

5. Take the following list of securities and arrange them in order of their priority of claims:

Preferred stock	Senior debenture
Subordinated debenture	Senior secured debt
Common stock	Junior secured debt

6. What method of "bond repayment" reduces debt and increases the amount of common stock outstanding?

7. What is the purpose of serial repayments and sinking funds?

8. Under what circumstances would a call on a bond be exercised by a corporation? What is the purpose of a deferred call?

9. Discuss the relationship between bond prices and interest rates. What impact do changing interest rates have on the price of long-term bonds versus short-term bonds?

10. What is the difference between the following yields: coupon rate, current yield, yield to maturity?

11. How does the bond rating affect the interest rate paid by a corporation on its bonds?

12. Bonds of different risk classes will have a spread between their interest rates. Is this spread always the same? Why?

13. Explain how the bond refunding problem is similar to a capital budgeting decision.

14. What cost of capital is generally used in evaluating a bond refunding decision? Why?

15. Explain how the zero-coupon rate bond provides return to the investor. What are the advantages to the corporation?

16. Explain how floating rate bonds can save the investor from potential embarrassments in portfolio valuation.

17. Discuss the advantages and disadvantages of debt.

18. What is a Eurobond?

19. What do we mean by capitalizing lease payments?

20. Explain the close parallel between a capital lease and the borrow-purchase decision from the viewpoint of both the balance sheet and the income statement.

Problems

(Assume the par value of the bonds in the following problems is $1,000 unless otherwise specified.)

1. The Pioneer Petroleum Corporation has a bond outstanding with an $85 annual interest payment, a market price of $800, and a maturity date in five years. Find the following: *Bond yields*

   a. The coupon rate.

   b. The current rate.

   c. The approximate yield to maturity.

2. Harold Reese must choose between two bonds: *Bond yields*

   Bond X pays $95 annual interest and has a market value of $900. It has 10 years to maturity.

   Bond Z pays $95 annual interest and has a market value of $920. It has two years to maturity.

   a. Compute the current yield on both bonds.

   b. Which bond should he select based on your answer to part *a*?

   c. A drawback of current yield is that it does not consider the total life of the bond. For example, the approximate yield to maturity on Bond X is 11.17 percent. What is the approximate yield to maturity on Bond Z?

   d. Has your answer changed between part *b* and *c* of this question?

3. The Southeast Investment Fund buys 70 bonds of the Hillary Bakery Corporation through its broker. The bonds pay 9 percent annual   *Bond value*

interest. The yield to maturity (market rate of interest) is 12 percent. The bonds have a 25-year maturity. Using an assumption of semiannual interest payments:

  a. Compute the price of a bond (refer to "semiannual interest and bond prices" in Chapter 10 for review if necessary).

  b. Compute the total value of the 70 bonds.

Bond value

4. Barry, Sanders & Co. pays a 12 percent coupon rate on debentures due in 20 years. The current yield to maturity on bonds of similar risk is 10 percent. The bonds are currently callable at $1,060. The theoretical value of the bonds will be equal to the present value of the expected cash flow from the bonds. This is the normal definition we use.

  a. Find the theoretical market value of the bonds using semiannual analysis.

  b. Do you think the bonds will sell for the price you arrived at in part *a?* Why?

Effect of bond rating change

5. The yield to maturity for 25-year bonds is as follows for four different bond rating categories.

Aaa	9.4%	Aa2	10.0%
Aa1	9.6%	Aa3	10.2%

  The bonds of Evans Corporation were rated as Aa1 and issued at par a few weeks ago. The bonds have just been downgraded to Aa2. Determine the new price of the bonds, assuming a 25-year maturity and semiannual interest payments. As a first step, use the data above as a guide to appropriate interest rates for bonds with different ratings.

Interest rates and bond ratings

6. Twenty-five-year B-rated bonds of Parker Optical Company were initially issued at a 12 percent yield. After 10 years the bonds have been upgraded to Aa2. Such bonds are currently yielding 10 percent. Use Table 16–3 to determine the price of the bonds with 15 years remaining to maturity. (You do not need the bond ratings to enter the table; just use the basic facts of the problem).

Interest rates and bond ratings

7. A previously issued Aa1, 20-year industrial bond provides a return one third higher than the prime interest rate of 6 percent. Previously issued public utility bonds provide a yield of three-fourths of a percentage point higher than previously issued industrial bonds of equal quality. Finally, new issues of Aa1 public utility bonds pay one-fourth of a percentage point more than previously issued public utility bonds.

  What should the interest rate be on a newly issued Aa1 public utility bond?

Zero-coupon bond values

8. A 15-year, $1,000 par value zero-coupon rate bond is to be issued to yield 12 percent.

  a. What should be the initial price of the bond? (Take the present value of $1,000 for 15 years at 12 percent using Appendix B.)

  b. If immediately upon issue, interest rates dropped to 10 percent, what would be the value of the zero-coupon rate bond?

   c. If immediately upon issue, interest rates increased to 14 percent, what would be the value of the zero-coupon rate bond?

9. Fourteen years ago, the U.S. Aluminum Corporation borrowed $9,900,000. Since then, cumulative inflation has been 98 percent (a compound rate of approximately 5 percent per year).

   a. When the firm repays the original $9,900,000 loan this year, what will be the effective purchasing power of the $9,900,000? (Hint: divide the loan amount by one plus cumulative inflation.)

   b. To maintain the original $9,900,000 purchasing power, how much should the lender be repaid? (Hint: multiply the loan amount by one plus cumulative inflation.)

   c. If the lender knows he will receive only $9,900,000 in payment after 14 years, how might he be compensated for the loss in purchasing power? A descriptive answer is acceptable.

Effect of inflation on purchasing power of bond

10. A $1,000 par value bond was issued 25 years ago at a 12 percent coupon rate. It currently has 15 years remaining to maturity. Interest rates on similar debt obligations are now 8 percent.

    a. What is the current price of the bond? (Look up the answer in Table 16–3.)

    b. Assume Ms. Bright bought the bond three years ago, when it had a price of $1,050. What is her dollar profit based on the bond's current price?

    c. Further assume Ms. Bright paid 30 percent of the purchase price in cash and borrowed the rest (known as buying on margin). She used the interest payments from the bond to cover the interest costs on the loan. How much of the purchase price of $1,050 did Ms. Bright pay in cash?

    d. What is Ms. Bright's percentage return on her cash investment? Divide the answer to part *b* by the answer to part *c.*

    e. Explain why her return is so high.

Profit potential associated with margin

11. The Delta Corporation has a $20 million bond obligation outstanding, which it is considering refunding. Though the bonds were initially issued at 13 percent, the interest rates on similar issues have declined to 11.5 percent. The bonds were originally issued for 20 years and have 16 years remaining. The new issue would be for 16 years. There is a 9 percent call premium on the old issue. The underwriting cost on the new $20,000,000 issue is $560,000, and the underwriting cost on the old issue was $400,000. The company is in a 40 percent tax bracket, and it will use a 7 percent discount rate (rounded aftertax cost of debt) to analyze the refunding decision. Should the old issue be refunded with new debt?

Refunding decision

12. The Sunbelt Corporation has $40 million of bonds outstanding that were issued at a coupon rate of 12 7/8 percent seven years ago. Interest rates have fallen to 12 percent. Mr. Heath, the vice-president of

Refunding decision

finance, does not expect rates to fall any further. The bonds have 18 years left to maturity, and Mr. Heath would like to refund the bonds with a new issue of equal amount also having 18 years to maturity. The Sunbelt Corporation has a tax rate of 36 percent. The underwriting cost on the old issue was 2.5 percent of the total bond value. The underwriting cost on the new issue will be 1.8 percent of the total bond value. The original bond indenture contained a five-year protection against a call, with an 8 percent call premium starting in the sixth year and scheduled to decline by one-half percent each year thereafter (consider the bond to be seven years old for purposes of computing the premium). Assume the discount rate is equal to the aftertax cost of new debt rounded up to the nearest whole number. Should the Sunbelt Corporation refund the old issue?

Call premium

13. In problem 12, what would be the aftertax cost of the call premium at the end of Year 11 (in dollar value)?

Capital lease or operating lease

14. The Richmond Corporation has just signed a 144-month lease on an asset with an 18-year life. The minimum lease payments are $3,000 per month ($36,000 per year) and are to be discounted back to the present at an 8 percent annual discount rate. The estimated fair value of the property is $290,000. Should the lease be recorded as a capital lease or an operating lease?

Balance sheet effect of leases

15. The Bradley Corporation has heavy lease commitments. Before FASB Statement No. 13, it merely footnoted lease obligations in the balance sheet, which appeared as follows:

BRADLEY CORPORATION
($ millions)

Current assets . . .	$150	Current liabilities	$ 50
Fixed assets	250	Long-term liabilities	100
		Total liabilities	150
		Stockholders' equity	250
		Total liabilities and	
Total assets	$400	stockholders' equity . . .	$400

The footnotes stated that the company had $22 million in annual capital lease obligations over the next 20 years.

a. Discount these annual lease obligations back to the present at a 7 percent discount rate (round to the nearest million dollars).

b. Construct a revised balance sheet that includes lease obligations, as in Table 16–8.

c. Compute total debt to total assets on the original and revised balance sheets.

d. Compute total debt to equity on the original and revised balance sheets.

    e. In an efficient capital market environment, should the consequences of FASB Statement No. 13, as viewed in the answers to parts *c* and *d,* change stock prices and credit ratings?

    f. Comment on management's perception of market efficiency (the viewpoint of the financial officer).

16. The Lollar Corporation plans to lease an $800,000 asset to the Pierce Corporation. The lease will be for 12 years.

    a. If the Lollar Corporation desires a 10 percent return on its investment, how much should the lease payments be?

    b. If the Lollar Corporation is able to generate $120,000 in immediate tax shield benefits from the asset to be purchased for the lease arrangement and will pass the benefits along to the Pierce Corporation in the form of lower lease payments, how much should the revised lease payments be? Continue to assume the Lollar Corporation desires a 10 percent return on the 12-year lease.

Determining size of lease payments

Selected References

Brennan, Michael J., and Eduardo S. Schwartz. "Bond Pricing and Market Efficiency." *Financial Analysts Journal* 38 (September–October 1982), pp. 49–56.

Brick, Ivan, William Fung, and Marti Subrahmanyam. "Leasing and Financial Intermediation: Comparative Tax Advantages." *Financial Management* 16 (Spring 1987), pp. 55–59.

Cason, Roger L. "Leasing, Asset Lives, and Uncertainty: A Practitioner's Comments." *Financial Management* 16 (Summer 1987), pp. 13–16.

Collins, Robert A. "An Empirical Comparison of Bankruptcy Prediction Models." *Financial Management* 9 (Summer 1980), pp. 52–57.

Dambolena, Ismael G., and Joel M. Shulman. "A Primary Rule for Detecting Bankruptcy: Watch the Cash." *Financial Analysts Journal* 44 (September–October 1988), pp. 74–78.

Davis, Stephen J. "Leasing as a Financing Tool." *Cash Flow* 7 (September 1986), pp. 41–42.

Eckbo, B. Espen. "Valuation Effects of Corporate Debt Offerings." *Journal of Financial Economics* (Netherlands) 15 (January–February 1986), pp. 119–51.

Ederington, Louis H. "Why Split Ratings Occur." *Financial Management* 15 (Spring 1986), pp. 37–47.

Ferri, Michael G. "An Empirical Examination of Determinants of Bond Yield Spreads." *Financial Management* 7 (August 1978), pp. 40–46.

Johnson, Dana J. "The Risk Behavior of Equity of Firms Approaching Bankruptcy." *Journal of Financial Research* 12 (Spring 1989), pp. 33–50.

Kalotay, Andrew J., and George W. Williams. "The Management and Valuation of Bonds with Sinking Fund Provisions." *Financial Analysts Journal* 48 (March–April 1992), pp. 59–67.

Mauer, David C., Amir Barnea, and Chang-Soo Kim. "Valuation of Callable Bonds under Progressive Personal Taxes and Interest Rate Uncertainty." *Financial Management* 20 (Summer 1991), pp. 50–59.

Mukherjee, Tarun, K. "A Survey of Corporate Leasing Analysis." *Financial Management* 20 (Autumn 1991), pp. 96–107.

Robbins, Edward Henry, and John D. Schatzberg. "Callable Bonds: A Risk-Reducing Signalling Mechanism." *Journal of Finance* 4 (September 1986), pp. 935–49.

Schall, Lawrence D. "Analytic Issues in Lease vs. Purchase Decisions." *Financial Management* 16 (Summer 1987), pp. 17–22.

Turnbull, Stuart M. "Swaps: A Zero Sum Game?" *Financial Management* 16 (Spring 1987), pp. 15–21.

Weingartner, H. Martin. "Leasing, Assets Lives and Uncertainty: Guides to Decision Making." *Financial Management* 16 (Summer 1987), pp. 5–12.

APPENDIX 16A   **Financial Alternatives for Distressed Firms**

A firm may be in financial distress because of **technical insolvency** or bankruptcy. The first term refers to a firm's inability to pay its bills as they come due. Thus, a firm may be technically insolvent, even though it has a positive net worth; there simply may not be sufficient liquid assets to meet current obligations. The second term, **bankruptcy,** indicates the market value of a firm's assets are less than its liabilities and the firm has a negative net worth. Under the law, either technical insolvency or bankruptcy may be adjudged as a financial failure of the business firm.

Many firms do not fall into either category but are still suffering from extreme financial difficulties. Perhaps they are rapidly approaching a situation in which they cannot pay their bills or their net worth will soon be negative.

Firms in the types of financial difficulty discussed in the first two paragraphs may participate in out-of-court settlements or in-court settlements through formal bankruptcy proceedings under the National Bankruptcy Act.

Out-of-court settlements, where possible, allow the firm and its creditors to bypass certain lengthy and expensive legal procedures. If an agreement cannot be reached on a voluntary basis between a firm and its creditors, in-court procedures will be necessary.

Out-of-Court Settlement

Out-of-court settlements may take many forms. Four alternatives will be examined. The first is an **extension,** in which creditors agree to allow the firm more time to meet its financial obligations. A new repayment schedule will be developed, subject to the acceptance of the creditors.

A second alternative is a **composition,** under which creditors agree to accept a fractional settlement of their original claim. They may be willing to do this because they believe the firm is unable to meet its total obligations and they wish to avoid formal bankruptcy procedures. In the case of either a proposed extension or a composition, some creditors may not agree to go along with the arrangements. If their claims are relatively small, major creditors may allow them to be paid off immediately and in full to hold the agreement together. If their claims are large, no out-of-court settlement may be possible, and formal bankruptcy proceedings may be necessary.

A third type of out-of-court settlement may take the form of a **creditor committee** established to run the business. Here the parties involved assume management can no longer effectively conduct the affairs of the firm. Once the creditors' claims have been partially or fully settled, a new management team may be brought in to replace the creditor committee. The outgoing management may be willing to accept the imposition of a creditor committee only when formal bankruptcy proceedings appear likely and they wish to avoid that stigma. Sometimes creditors are unwilling to form such a committee because they fear lawsuits from other dissatisfied creditors or from common or preferred stockholders.

A fourth type of out-of-court settlement is an **assignment**, in which assets are liquidated without going through formal court action. To effect an assignment, creditors must agree on liquidation values and the relative priority of claims. This is not an easy task.

In actuality, there may be combinations of two or more of the above-described out-of-court procedures. For example, there may be an extension as well as a composition, or a creditor committee may help to establish one or more of the alternatives.

When it is apparent an out-of-court settlement cannot be reached, the next step is formal bankruptcy. Bankruptcy proceedings may be initiated voluntarily by the company or, alternatively, by creditors.

In-Court Settlements— Formal Bankruptcy

Once the firm falls under formal bankruptcy proceedings, a referee is appointed by the court to oversee the activities. The referee becomes the arbitrator of the proceedings, whose actions and decisions are final, subject only to review by the court. A trustee will also be selected to properly determine the assets and liabilities of the firm and to carry out a plan of reorganization or liquidation for the firm.

Reorganization

If the firm is to be reorganized (under the Bankruptcy Act's Chapter 11 restructuring), the plan must prove to be fair and feasible. An **internal reorganization** calls for an evaluation of current management and operating policies. If current management is shown to be incompetent, it will probably be discharged and replaced by new management. An evaluation and possible redesign of the current capital structure is also necessary. If the firm is top-heavy with debt (as is normally the case), alternate securities, such as preferred or common stock, may replace part of the debt.[1] Any restructuring must be fair to all parties involved.

An **external reorganization,** in which a merger partner is found for the firm, may also be considered. The surviving firm must be deemed strong enough to carry out the financial and management obligations of the joint entities. Old creditors and stockholders may be asked to make concessions to ensure that a feasible arrangement is established. Their motivation is that they hope to come out further ahead than if such a reorganization were not

---

[1]Another possibility is income bonds, in which interest is payable only if earned.

undertaken. Ideally the firm should be merged with a strong firm in its own industry, although this is not always possible. The savings and loan and banking industries have been particularly adept at merging weaker firms with stronger firms within the industry.

Liquidation

A **liquidation** or sale of assets may be recommended when an internal or external reorganization does not appear possible and it is determined that the assets of the firm are worth more in liquidation than through a reorganization. Priority of claims becomes extremely important in a liquidation, because it is unlikely that all parties will be fully satisfied in their demands.

The priority of claims in a bankruptcy liquidation is as follows:

1. Cost of administering the bankruptcy procedures (lawyers get in line first).
2. Wages due workers if earned within three months of filing the bankruptcy petition. The maximum amount is $600 per worker.
3. Taxes due at the federal, state, or local level.
4. Secured creditors to the extent that designated assets are sold to meet their claims. Secured claims that exceed the sales value of the pledged assets are placed in the same category as other general creditor claims.
5. General or unsecured creditors are next in line. Examples of claims in this category are those held by debenture (unsecured bond) holders, trade creditors, and bankers who have made unsecured loans.

   There may be senior and subordinated positions within category 5, indicating that subordinated debt holders must turn over their claims to senior debt holders until complete restitution is made to the higher-ranked category. Subordinated debenture holders may keep the balance if anything is left over after that payment.
6. Preferred stockholders.
7. Common stockholders.

The priority of claims 4 through 7 is similar to that presented in Figure 16–2 of the chapter.

Let us examine a typical situation to determine "who" should receive "what" under a liquidation in bankruptcy. Assume the Mitchell Corporation has a book value and liquidation value as shown in Table 16A–1. Liabilities and stockholders' claims are also presented.

We see that the liquidation value of the assets is far less than the book value ($700,000 versus $1,300,000). Also the liquidation value of the assets will not cover the total value of liabilities ($700,000 compared to $1,100,000).

TABLE 16A-1
Financial data for the Mitchell Corporation

Assets

	Book Value	Liquidation Value
Accounts receivable	$ 200,000	$160,000
Inventory.	410,000	240,000
Machinery and equipment	240,000	100,000
Building and plant	450,000	200,000
	$1,300,000	$700,000

Liabilities and Stockholders' Claims

Liabilities:	
Accounts payable	$ 300,000
First lien, secured by machinery and equipment*	200,000
Senior unsecured debt	400,000
Subordinated debentures.	200,000
Total liabilities	1,100,000
Stockholders' claims:	
Preferred stock.	50,000
Common stock.	150,000
Total stockholders' claims	200,000
Total liabilities and stockholders' claims	$1,300,000

*A lien represents a potential claim against property. The lien holder has a secured interest in the property.

Since all liability claims will not be met, it is evident that lower-ranked preferred stockholders and common stockholders will receive nothing.

Before a specific allocation is made to the creditors (those with liability claims), the three highest priority levels in bankruptcy must first be covered. That would include the cost of administering the proceedings, allowable past wages due to workers, and overdue taxes. For the Mitchell Corporation, we shall assume these total $100,000. Since the liquidation value of assets was $700,000, that would leave $600,000 to cover creditor demands, as indicated in the left-hand column of Table 16A–2.

Before we attempt to allocate the values in the left-hand column of Table 16A–2 to the right-hand column, we must first identify any creditor

TABLE 16A-2   **Asset values and claims**

Assets		Creditor Claims	
Asset values in liquidation . . .	$700,000	Accounts payable	$ 300,000
Administrative costs, wages, and taxes	−100,000	First lien, secured by machinery and equipment . . .	200,000
Remaining asset values	$600,000	Senior unsecured debt	400,000
		Subordinated debentures.	200,000
		Total liabilities	$1,100,000

claims that are secured by the pledge of a specific asset. In the present case, there is a first lien on the machinery and equipment of $200,000. Referring back to Table 16A–1, we observe that the machinery and equipment have a liquidation value of only $100,000. The secured debt holders will receive $100,000, with the balance of their claim placed in the same category as the unsecured debt holders. In Table 16A–3, we show asset values available for unsatisfied secured claims and unsecured debt (top portion) and the extent of the remaining claims (bottom portion).

TABLE 16A–3
Asset values available for unsatisfied secured claims and unsecured debt holders—and their remaining claims

Asset values:	
Asset values in liquidation	$ 700,000
Administrative costs, wages, and taxes . . .	100,000
Remaining asset values	600,000
Payment to secured creditors	−100,000
Amount available to unsatisfied	
secured claims and unsecured debt . . .	$ 500,000
Remaining claims of unsatisfied	
secured debt and unsecured debt:	
Secured debt (unsatisfied first lien).	$ 100,000
Accounts payable	300,000
Senior unsecured debt.	400,000
Subordinated debentures	200,000
	$1,000,000

In comparing the available asset values and claims in Table 16A–3, it appears that the settlement on the remaining claims should be at a 50 percent rate ($500,000/$1,000,000). The allocation will take place in the manner presented in Table 16A–4.

TABLE 16A–4
Allocation procedures for unsatisfied secured claims and unsecured debt

(1) Category	(2) Amount of Claim	(3) Initial Allocation (50%)	(4) Amount Received
Secured debt (unsatisfied 1st lien) . .	$ 100,000	$ 50,000	$ 50,000
Accounts payable	300,000	150,000	150,000
Senior unsecured debt	400,000	200,000	300,000
Subordinated debentures	200,000	100,000	0
	$1,000,000	$500,000	$500,000

Each category receives 50 percent as an initial allocation. However, the subordinated debenture holders must transfer their $100,000 initial allocation to the senior debt holders in recognition of their preferential position. The secured debt holders and those having accounts payable claims are not part of the senior-subordinated arrangement and, thus, hold their initial allocation position.

Finally, in Table 16A–5, we show the total amounts of claims, the amount received, and the percent of the claim that was satisfied.

TABLE 16A–5
Payments and percent of claims

(1) Category	(2) Total Amount of Claim	(3) Amount Received	(4) Percent of Claim Satisfied
Secured debt (1st lien)	$200,000	$150,000	75%
Accounts payable	300,000	150,000	50
Senior unsecured debt	400,000	300,000	75
Subordinated debentures. . . .	200,000	0	0

The $150,000 in column (3) for secured debt represents the $100,000 from the sale of machinery and equipment, and $50,000 from the allocation process in Table 16A–4. The secured debt holders and senior-unsecured debt holders come out on top in terms of percent of claim satisfied (it is coincidental that they are equal). Furthermore, the subordinated debt holders and, as previously mentioned, the preferred and common stockholders receive nothing. Naturally, allocations in bankruptcy will vary from circumstance to circumstance. Working problem 16A–1 will help to reinforce many of the liquidation procedure concepts discussed in this section.

List of Terms

technical insolvency 482
bankruptcy 482
extension 482
composition 482
creditor committee 482

assignment 483
internal reorganization 483
external reorganization 483
liquidation 484

Discussion Questions

16A–1. What is the difference between technical insolvency and bankruptcy?

16A–2. What are four types of out-of-court settlements? Briefly describe each.

16A–3. What is the difference between an internal reorganization and an external reorganization under formal bankruptcy procedures?

16A–4. What are the first three priority items under liquidation in bankruptcy?

Problem

16A–1. The trustee in the bankruptcy settlement for Immobile Corporation lists the following book values and liquidation values for the assets

Settlement of claims in bankruptcy liquidation

of the corporation. Liabilities and stockholders' claims are also shown below.

	Book Value	Liquidation Value
Assets		
Accounts receivable	$1,000,000	$ 700,000
Inventory.	1,100,000	600,000
Machinery and equipment	800,000	400,000
Building and plant	3,000,000	1,800,000
	$5,900,000	$3,500,000
Liabilities and Stockholders' Claims		
Liabilities:		
Accounts payable	$2,000,000	
First lien, secured by		
machinery and equipment . . .	650,000	
Senior unsecured debt	1,300,000	
Subordinated debentures.	1,450,000	
Total liabilities	5,400,000	
Stockholders' claims:		
Preferred stock.	100,000	
Common stock	400,000	
Total stockholders' claims . . .	500,000	
Total liabilities and		
stockholders' claims	$5,900,000	

a. Compute the difference between the liquidation value of the assets and the liabilities.

b. Based on the answer to part a, will preferred stock or common stock participate in the distribution?

c. Assuming the administrative costs of bankruptcy, workers' allowable wages, and unpaid taxes add up to $300,000, what is the total of remaining asset value available to cover secured and unsecured claims?

d. After the machinery and equipment are sold to partially cover the first lien secured claim, how much will be available from the remaining asset liquidation values to cover unsatisfied secured claims and unsecured debt?

e. List the remaining asset claims of unsatisfied secured debt holders and unsecured debt holders in a manner similar to that shown at the bottom portion of Table 16A–3.

f. Compute a ratio of your answers in part d and part e. This will indicate the initial allocation ratio.

g. List the remaining claims (unsatisfied secured and unsecured) and make an initial allocation and final allocation similar to that shown in Table 16A–4. Subordinated debenture holders may keep the balance after full payment is made to senior debt holders.

h. Show the relationship of amount received to total amount of claim in a similar fashion to that of Table 16A–5. (Remember to use the sales [liquidation] value for machinery and equipment plus the allocation amount in part *g* to arrive at the total received on secured debt.)

APPENDIX 16B **Lease versus Purchase Decision**

The classic lease versus purchase decision does not fit a *capital* leasing decision given the existence of FASB Statement 13 and the similar financial accounting and tax treatment accorded to a capital lease and borrowing to purchase. Nevertheless, the classic lease versus purchase decision is still appropriate for the short-term *operating lease*.

Assume a firm is considering the purchase of a $6,000 asset in the three-year ACRS category (with a four-year write-off) or entering into two sequential operating leases, for two years each. Under the operating leases, the annual payments would be $1,400 on the first lease and $2,600 on the second lease. If a firm purchased the asset, it would pay $1,893 annually to amortize a $6,000 loan over four years at 10 percent interest. This is based on the use of Appendix D for the present value of an annuity.

$$A = \frac{PV_A}{PV_{IFA}} = \frac{\$6,000}{3.170} = \$1,893 \qquad (n = 4, i = 10\%)$$

The firm is in a 30 percent tax bracket. In doing our analysis, we look first at the aftertax costs of the operating lease arrangements in Table 16B–1. The tax shield in column (2) indicates the amount the lease payments will save us in taxes. In column (3) we see the net aftertax cost of the lease arrangement.

TABLE 16B–1
Aftertax cost of operating leases

Year	(1) Payment	(2) Tax Shield 30% of (1)	(3) Aftertax Cost
1	$1,400	$420	$ 980
2	1,400	420	980
3	2,600	780	1,820
4	2,600	780	1,820

For the borrowing and purchasing decision, we must consider not only the amount of the payment but also separate out those items that are tax deductible. First we consider interest and then depreciation.

In Table 16B–2, we show an amortization table to pay off a $6,000 loan over four years at 10 percent interest with $1,893 annual payments. In column (1) we show the beginning balance for each year. This is followed by the annual payment in column (2). We then show the amount of interest we

TABLE 16B-2
Amortization table

	(1)	(2)	(3)	(4)	(5)
	Beginning	Annual	Annual Interest	Repayment of Principal	Ending Balance
Year	Balance	Payment	10% of (1)	(2) − (3)	(1) − (4)
1. . . .	$6,000	$1,893	$600	$1,293	$4,707
2. . . .	4,707	1,893	471	1,422	3,285
3. . . .	3,285	1,893	329	1,564	1,721
4. . . .	1,721	1,893	172	1,721	0

will pay on the beginning balance at a 10 percent rate in column (3). In column (4) we subtract the interest payment from the annual payment to determine how much is applied directly to the repayment of principal. In column (5) we subtract the repayment of principal from the beginning balance to get the year-end balance.

After determining our interest payment schedule, we look at the depreciation schedule that would apply to the borrow-purchase decision. Using the three-year ACRS depreciation category (with the associated four-year write-off), the asset is depreciated at the rates indicated in Table 16B–3.

TABLE 16B-3
Depreciation schedule

Year	Depreciation Base	Depreciation Percentage	Depreciation
1 . . .	$6,000	.333	$1,998
2 . . .	6,000	.445	2,670
3 . . .	6,000	.148	888
4 . . .	6,000	.074	444
			$6,000

We now bring our interest and depreciation schedules together in Table 16B–4 to determine the aftertax cost, or cash outflow, associated with the borrow-purchase decision.

TABLE 16B–4   Aftertax cost of borrow–purchase

	(1)	(2)	(3)	(4)	(5)	(6)
				Total Tax Deductions	Tax Shield	Net After-tax Cost
Year	Payment	Interest	Depreciation	(2) + (3)	30% × (4)	(1) − (5)
1	$1,893	$600	$1,998	$2,598	$779	$1,114
2	1,893	471	2,670	3,141	942	951
3	1,893	329	888	1,217	365	1,528
4	1,893	172	444	616	185	1,708

The interest and depreciation charges are tax-deductible expenses and provide a tax shield against other income. The total deductions in column (4) are multiplied by the tax rate of 30 percent to show the tax shield benefits in column (5). In column (6), we subtract the tax shield from the payments to get the net aftertax cost, or cash outflow.

Finally, we compare the cash outflows from leasing to the cash outflows from borrowing and purchasing. To consider the time value of money, we discount the annual values at an interest rate of 7 percent. This is the aftertax cost of debt to the firm, and it is computed by multiplying the interest rate of 10 percent by (1 − Tax rate). Because the costs associated with both leasing and borrowing are contractual and certain, we use the aftertax cost of debt as the discount rate, rather than the normal cost of capital. The overall analysis is presented in Table 16B–5.

TABLE 16B-5   **Net present-value comparison**

Year	Aftertax Cost of Leasing	Present-value Factor at 7%	Present Value	Aftertax Cost of Borrow-Purchase	Present-Value Factor at 7%	Present Value
1	$ 980	0.935	$ 916	$1,114	0.935	$1,042
2	980	0.873	856	951	0.873	830
3	1,820	0.816	1,485	1,528	0.816	1,247
4	1,820	0.763	1,389	1,708	0.763	1,303
			4,646			4,422

The borrow-purchase alternative has a lower present value of aftertax costs ($4,422 versus $4,646), which would appear to make it the more desirable alternative. However, many of the previously discussed qualitative factors that support leasing must also be considered in the decision-making process.

Problem

Lease versus purchase decision

16B–1. Edison Electronics is considering whether to borrow funds and purchase an asset or to lease the asset under an operating lease arrangement. If it purchases the asset, the cost will be $8,000. It can borrow funds for four years at 12 percent interest. The firm will use the three-year ACRS depreciation category (with the associated four-year write-off). Assume a tax rate of 35 percent.

The other alternative is to sign two operating leases, one with payments of $2,100 for the first two years and the other with payments of $3,700 for the last two years. In your analysis, round all values to the nearest dollar.

a. Compute the aftertax cost of the leases for the four years.

b. Compute the annual payment for the loan (round to the nearest dollar).

c. Compute the amortization schedule for the loan. (Disregard a small difference from a zero balance at the end of the loan due to rounding.)

d. Determine the depreciation schedule (see Table 12–9).

e. Compute the aftertax cost of the borrow-purchase alternative.

f. Compute the present value of the aftertax cost of the two alternatives. Use a discount rate of 8 percent.

g. Which alternative should be selected, based on minimizing the present value of aftertax costs?

Common and Preferred Stock Financing

CHAPTER CONCEPTS

1 Common stockholders are the owners of the corporation and therefore have a claim to undistributed income, the right to elect the board of directors, and other privileges.

2 Cumulative voting provides minority stockholders with the potential for some representation on the board of directors.

3 A rights offering gives current stockholders a first option to purchase new shares.

4 Poison pills and other similar provisions may make it difficult for outsiders to take over a corporation against management's wishes.

5 Preferred stock is an intermediate type of security that falls somewhere between debt and common stock.

The ultimate ownership of the firm resides in **common stock,** whether it is in the form of all outstanding shares of a closely held corporation or one share of AT&T. In terms of legal distinctions, it is the common stockholder alone who directly controls the business. While control of the company is legally in the shareholders' hands, it is practically wielded by management on an everyday basis. It is also important to realize that large creditors may exert tremendous pressure on a firm to meet certain standards of financial performance, even though the creditor has no voting power.

Although there are over 50 million common stockholders in the United States, increasingly ownership is being held by large institutional interests, such as pension funds, mutual funds, or bank trust departments, rather than the individual investor. As would be expected, management has become increasingly sensitive to these large stockholders who may side with corporate raiders in voting their shares for or against merger offers or takeover attempts (these topics are covered in Chapter 20). Table 17–1 presents a list of major companies with high percentages of common stock owned by institutions at the end of September 1992. Institutional investors owned 51.7 percent of General Electric, worth $34.587 billion, and 74.4 percent of Intel Corp., a maker of microprocessors and computer chips. In the previous edition, IBM had the largest holding of institutional investors but due to a disastrous 1992,

TABLE 17–1
Institutional ownership of U.S. companies

Stock	Number of Institutions	Percent Owned	Ownership in $ Millions
General Electric	767	51.7%	$34,587
Exxon Corp.	735	38.7%	30,720
Coca-Cola Co.	648	51.9%	27,539
Merck & Co.	741	51.6%	26,357
IBM	721	43.5%	20,606
Wal-Mart Stores	590	29.7%	20,201
AT&T.	704	32.8%	19,130
Bristol-Myers Squibb	744	51.1%	16,878
PepsiCo Inc.	672	54.9%	16,487
Pfizer Inc.	601	64.4%	15,895
GTE Corp.	630	48.3%	15,281
Procter & Gamble Co.	588	44.5%	14,928
Minnesota Mining & Mfg. . . .	600	65.2%	14,624
Royal Dutch Petroleum	545	28.2%	13,815
Amoco	623	52.3%	13,697
Du Pont Co.	571	40.1%	12,737
American Home Products . .	658	59.6%	12,462
Atlantic Richfield	577	57.4%	11,001
Ford Motor Co.	445	56.5%	10,887
Intel Corp.	457	74.4%	10,101
Texaco Inc..	536	58.5%	9,699
Dow Chemical	489	51.5%	7,866
American Express	429	62.1%	6,485
Pacific Telesis Group	513	35.2%	6,341
Boeing	483	40.6%	5,065

Source: Compact disclosure; data as of September 30, 1992.

the stock price plummeted and the institutions reduced their holdings to 43.5 percent.

Preferred stock plays a secondary role in financing the corporate enterprise. It represents a hybrid security, combining some of the features of debt and common stock. Though preferred stockholders do not have an ownership interest in the firm, they do have a priority of claims to dividends that is superior to that of common stockholders.

To understand the rights and characteristics of the different means of financing, we shall examine the powers accorded to shareholders under each arrangement. In the case of common stock everything revolves around three key rights: the residual claim to income, the voting right, and the right to purchase new shares. We shall examine each of these in detail and then consider the rights of preferred stockholders.

All income that is not paid out to creditors or preferred stockholders automatically belongs to common stockholders. Thus we say they have a **residual claim to income.** This is true regardless of whether these residual funds are actually paid out in dividends or retained in the corporation. A firm that earns $10 million before capital costs and pays $1 million in interest to bondholders and a like amount in dividends to preferred stockholders will have $8 million available for common stockholders.[1] Perhaps half of that will be paid out as common stock dividends and the balance will be reinvested in the business for the benefit of stockholders, with the hope of providing even greater income, dividends, and price appreciation in the future.

Of course, it should be pointed out the common stockholder does not have a legal or enforceable claim to dividends. Whereas a bondholder may force the corporation into bankruptcy for failure to make interest payments, the common stockholder must accept circumstances as they are or attempt to change management if a new dividend policy is desired.

Occasionally a company will have several classes of common stock outstanding that carry different rights to dividends and income. For example, Turner Broadcasting, Dow Jones Co., and Ford Motor Company all have two separate classes of common stock that differentiate the shares of founders from other stockholders and grant preferential rights to founders. General Motors may have the most unusual classes of stock with its Class E and Class H shares. In October 1984 GM acquired Electronic Data Systems (EDS) for cash and General Motors Class E common stock for a total of $2.5 billion and, in 1985, acquired Hughes Aircraft for cash and Class H common stock for a total of $5.8 billion.

Both Class E and Class H common stock are distinct from the regular GM common shares in both voting and dividend rights. These companies are traded on the New York Stock Exchange as subsidiaries of GM with minority

Common Stockholders' Claim to Income

---

[1]Tax consequences related to interest payments are ignored for the present.

public ownership. Their prices are based on their own earnings and dividends rather than on the performance of General Motors. By March 1993 the Class E shares were worth $6.1 billion and the Class H shares were worth $2.3 billion. The owners of Class E shares have fared much better than those of General Motors common stock[2] since 1984. Dividends for Class E have grown consistently, and the Class E stock has had three (two for one) splits since 1984.

The Voting Right

Because common stockholders are the owners of the firm, they are accorded the right to vote in the election of the board of directors and on all other major issues. Common stockholders may cast their ballots as they see fit on a given issue, or assign a **proxy,** or "power to cast their ballot," to management or some outside contesting group. As mentioned in the previous section, some corporations have different classes of common stock with unequal voting rights. In the case of General Motors' Class E and H stock, not only are dividends unequal but voting rights are also unequal. Regular General Motors common stock is entitled to one vote per share, while each GM Class E share is entitled to 0.25 votes per share and each Class H share is entitled to 0.50 vote per share. At future designated time periods, both Class E and H shares will be exchangeable for GM common shares at exchange rates based on future earnings.

Perhaps the Ford Motor Company is the biggest and best example of "founders" stock. Class B shares were used to differentiate the original **founders' shares** and those shares sold to the public. The founders wanted to preserve their control of the company while at the same time raise new capital for expansion. The regular common stock (no specific class) has one vote and is entitled to elect 60 percent of the board of directors, and the Class B shares have one vote but are entitled, as a class of shareholders, to elect 40 percent of the board of directors as long as there are at least 30,375,000 Class B shares outstanding. There are currently 129 owners of Class B stock, which is reserved solely for Ford family members or their descendants, trusts, or appointed interests. As of September 1992 there were 452.1 million shares of Ford common stock outstanding and 35.4 million shares of Class B. The Ford family has a very important position in Henry Ford's company without owning more than about 8 percent of the current outstanding stock. Both common and Class B stock share in dividends equally, and no stock dividends may be given unless to both common and Class B in proportion to their ownership. Class B is convertible into regular common on a share-for-share basis.

While common stockholders and the different classes of common stock that they own may, at times, have different voting rights, they do have a vote. Bondholders and preferred stockholders may vote only when a violation of their corporate agreement exists and a subsequent acceleration of their rights takes place. For example, Continental Illinois Corporation, the Chicago banking

---

[2]GM common stock has been basically flat from 1984 to March 1993.

FINANCE IN ACTION

Keeping Control of the Company

The dilema for many owners who start their own business is dealing with the success of the company. The company grows, it prospers, it needs more capital, and eventually the owner takes the company public. Now that the public owns a piece of the company, shares are no longer totally controlled by the founders. In many cases the original owners attempt to ensure their continued control even after they have fewer shares than the public. They do this in many ways. The Chandler family of Times Mirror is one of those founding families who created several classes of common shares as a way of controlling the large communications company they built.

In 1987 the company's authorized common stock was changed to 300,000,000 Series A common shares, 100,000,000 Series B common shares, and 150,000,000 Series C common shares. As of November 1992, there were 94.8 million Series A shares outstanding (market value of $3.2 billion) and 33.8 million Series C shares outstanding (market value of $1.1 billion) and no Series B shares currently issued. Times Mirror's 1991 annual report states:

> Shares of Series A and Series C common stock are identical, except with respect to voting rights, restrictions on transfer of

Series C shares, and the right to convert Series C shares into shares of Series A common stock. Each share is entitled to 1 vote per share for Series A common stock and to 10 votes per share for Series C common stock. The Series C shares are subject to mandatory conversion into Series A shares upon transfer to any person other than a "Permitted Transferee" as defined in the company's Certificate of Incorporation or upon the occurrence of certain regulatory events.

Through these different classes of common stock, the Chandler family and related trusts exercised majority control of the voting power. In addition to Series A and C, they even thought ahead for the potential dilution of voting power through the sale of new shares. In the event new shares are sold through an underwritten public offering or issued for acquisitions, they would be Series B common shares having only one tenth of a vote per share. The three classes of common stock at Times Mirror are perhaps one of the more complex schemes to maintain voting control by a founding family. The Ford Motor Company mentioned in the text is another example of a well-known family with the same strategy of voting control.

giant on the edge of bankruptcy in 1984, failed to pay dividends on one series of preferred stock for five quarters from July 1, 1984, to September 30, 1985. The preferred stockholder agreement stated that failure to pay dividends for six consecutive quarters would result in the preferred stockholders being able to elect two directors to the board to represent their interests. Continental Illinois declared a preferred dividend in November 1985 to pay all current and past dividends on two classes of preferred stock, thus avoiding the special voting privilege for preferred stockholders. The bank continued to recover and instituted dividends on common stock in 1990.

Cumulative Voting

The most important voting matter is the election of the board of directors. As indicated in Chapter 1, the board has primary responsibility for the stewardship of the corporation. If illegal or imprudent decisions are made, the board can be held legally accountable. Furthermore, members of the board of directors normally serve on a number of important subcommittees of the corporation, such as the audit committee, the long-range financial planning committee, and the salary and compensation committee. The board may be elected through the familiar majority rule system or by cumulative voting. Under **majority voting,** any group of stockholders owning over 50 percent of the common stock may elect all of the directors. Under **cumulative voting,** it is possible for those who hold less than a 50 percent interest to elect some of the directors. The provision for some minority interests on the board is important to those who, at times, wish to challenge the prerogatives of management.

The issue of the type of voting has become more important to stockholders and management with the threat of takeovers, leveraged buyouts, and other challenges to management's control of the firm. In many cases large minority stockholders, seeking a say in the operations and direction of the company, desire seats on the board of directors. To further their goals several have gotten stockholders to vote on the issue of cumulative voting at the annual meeting.

How does this cumulative voting process work? A stockholder gets one vote for each share of stock he or she owns times one vote for each director to be elected. The stockholder may then accumulate votes in favor of a specified number of directors.

Assume there are 10,000 shares outstanding, you own 1,001, and nine directors are to be elected. Your total number of votes under a cumulative election system is:

Number of shares owned	1,001
Number of directors to be elected	9
Number of votes	9,009

Let us assume you cast all your votes for the one director of your choice. With nine directors to be elected, there is no way for the owners of the remaining shares to exclude you from electing a person to one of the top nine positions. If you own 1,001 shares, the majority interest could control a maximum of 8,999 shares. This would entitle them to 80,991 votes.

Number of shares owned (majority)	8,999
Number of directors to be elected	9
Number of votes (majority)	80,991

These 80,991 votes cannot be spread thinly enough over nine candidates to stop you from electing your one director. If they are spread evenly, each of the majority's nine choices will receive 8,999 votes (80,991/9). Your choice is assured 9,009 votes as previously indicated. Because the nine top vote-getters win, you will claim one position. Note that candidates do not run head-on against each other (such as Place A or Place B on the ballot), but rather that the top nine candidates are accorded directorships.

To determine the number of shares needed to elect a given number of directors under cumulative voting, the following formula is used:

$$\frac{\text{Shares}}{\text{required}} = \frac{\begin{array}{c}\text{Number of directors desired} \times \\ \text{Total number of shares outstanding}\end{array}}{\begin{array}{c}\text{Total number of directors to be} \\ \text{elected} + 1\end{array}} + 1 \qquad (17\text{--}1)$$

The formula reaffirms that in the previous instance 1,001 shares would elect one director.

$$\frac{1 \times 10,000}{9 + 1} + 1 = \frac{10,000}{10} + 1 = 1,001$$

If three director positions out of nine are desired, 3,001 shares are necessary.

$$\frac{3 \times 10,000}{9 + 1} + 1 = \frac{30,000}{10} + 1 = 3,001$$

Note that, with approximately 30 percent of the shares outstanding, a minority interest can control one third of the board. If instead of cumulative voting a majority rule system were utilized, a minority interest could elect no one. The group that controlled 5,001 or more shares out of 10,000 would elect every director.

As a restatement of the problem: If we know the number of minority shares outstanding under cumulative voting and wish to determine how many directors that can be elected, we use the formula:

Number of directors that can be elected

$$= \frac{\begin{array}{c}(\text{Shares owned} - 1) \times \\ (\text{Total number of directors to be elected} + 1)\end{array}}{(\text{Total number of shares outstanding})} \qquad (17\text{--}2)$$

Plugging 3,001 shares into the formula, we show:

$$\frac{(3,001 - 1)(9 + 1)}{10,000} = \frac{3,000(10)}{10,000} = 3$$

If the formula yields an uneven number of directors, such as 3.3 or 3.8, you always round down to the nearest whole number (i.e., 3).

It is not surprising that 22 states require cumulative voting in preference to majority rule, that 18 consider it permissible as part of the corporate charter, and that only 10 make no provision for its use. Such consumer-oriented states as California, Illinois, and Michigan require cumulative voting procedures.

**The Right
to Purchase
New Shares**

In addition to a claim to residual income and the right to vote for directors, the common stockholders may also enjoy a privileged position in the offering of new securities. If the corporate charter contains a **preemptive right** provision, holders of common stock must be given the first option to purchase new shares. While only two states specifically require the use of preemptive rights, most other states allow for the inclusion of a **rights offering** in the corporation charter.

The preemptive right provision ensures that management cannot subvert the position of present stockholders by selling shares to outside interests without first offering them to current shareholders. If such protection were not afforded, a 20 percent stockholder might find his or her interest reduced to 10 percent through the distribution of new shares to outsiders. Not only would voting rights be diluted, but proportionate claims to earnings per share would be reduced.

The Use of Rights in Financing

Many corporations also engage in a preemptive rights offering to tap a built-in market for new securities—the current investors. Let us assume the Watson Corporation has 9 million shares outstanding and the current market price is $40 a share (the total market value is $360 million). Watson needs to raise $30 million for new plant and equipment and will sell 1 million new shares at $30 per share.[3] As part of the process, it will use a rights offering in which each old shareholder receives a first option to participate in the purchase of new shares.

Each old shareholder will receive one right for each share of stock owned and may combine a specified number of rights plus $30 cash to buy a new share of stock. Let us consider these questions:

1. How many rights should be necessary to purchase one new share of stock?
2. What is the monetary value of these rights?

Rights Required   Since 9 million shares are currently outstanding and 1 million new shares will be issued, the ratio of old to new shares is 9 to 1. On this basis, the old stockholder may combine nine rights plus $30 cash to purchase one new share of stock.

A stockholder with 90 shares of stock would receive an equivalent number of rights, which could be applied toward the purchase of 10 shares of stock at $30 per share. As indicated later in the discussion, stockholders may choose to sell their rights, rather than exercise them in the purchase of new shares.

---

[3]If this were not a rights offering, the discount from the current market price would be much smaller. The new shares might sell for $38 or $39.

Monetary Value of a Right   Anything that contributes toward the privilege of purchasing a considerably higher priced stock for $30 per share must have some market value. Consider the following two-step analysis.

Nine old shares sold at $40 per share, or for $360; now one new share will be introduced for $30. Thus, we have a total market value of $390 spread over 10 shares. After the rights offering has been completed, the average value of a share is theoretically equal to $39.[4]

Nine old shares sold at $40 per share	$360
One new share will sell at $30 per share . . .	30
Total value of 10 shares	$390
Average value of one share	$ 39

The rights offering thus entitles the holder to buy a stock that should carry a value of $39 (after the transactions have been completed) for $30. With a differential between the anticipated price and the subscription price of $9 and nine rights required to participate in the purchase of one share, the value of a right in this case is $1.

Average value of one share	$39
Subscription price	30
Differential.	$ 9
Rights required to buy one share. . . .	9

Formulas have been developed to determine the value of a right under any circumstance. Before they are presented, let us examine two new terms that will be part of the calculations—*rights-on* and *ex-rights*. When a rights offering is announced, a stock initially trades **rights-on;** that is, if you buy the stock, you will also acquire a right toward a future purchase of the stock. After a certain period (say four weeks) the stock goes **ex-rights**—when you buy the stock you no longer get a right toward future purchase of stock. Consider the following:

Date	Value of Stock	Value of Right
March 1: Stock trades rights-on	$40	$1 (part of $40)
April 1: Stock trades ex-rights	39	$1
April 30: End of subscription period	39	—

Once the ex-rights period is reached, the stock will go down by the theoretical value of the right. The remaining value ($39) is the ex-rights value.

[4]A number of variables may intervene to change the value. This is a "best" approximation.

Though there is a time period remaining between the ex-rights date (April 1) and the end of the subscription period (April 30), the market assumes the dilution has already occurred. Thus, the ex-rights value reflects precisely the same value as can be expected when the new, underpriced $30 stock issue is sold. In effect, it projects the future impact of the cheaper shares on the stock price.

The formula for the value of the right when the stock is trading rights-on is:

$$R = \frac{M_o - S}{N + 1} \qquad (17\text{--}3)$$

where

$$M_o = \text{Market value—rights-on, \$40}$$
$$S = \text{Subscription price, \$30}$$
$$N = \text{Number of rights required to purchase a new share of stock; in this case, 9}$$

$$\frac{\$40 - \$30}{9 + 1} = \frac{\$10}{10} = \$1$$

Using Formula 17–3 we determine that the value of a right in the Watson Corporation offering is $1. An alternative formula giving precisely the same answer is:

$$R = \frac{M_e - S}{N} \qquad (17\text{--}4)$$

The only new term is M_e, the market value of the stock when the shares are trading ex-rights. We show:

$$R = \frac{\$39 - \$30}{9} = \frac{\$9}{9} = \$1$$

These are all theoretical relationships, which may be altered somewhat in reality. If there is great enthusiasm for the new issue, the market value of the right may exceed the initial theoretical value (perhaps the right will trade for 1⅜).

Effect of Rights on Stockholder's Position

At first glance a rights offering appears to bring great benefits to stockholders. But is this really the case? Does a shareholder really benefit from being able to buy a stock that is initially $40 (and later $39) for $30? Don't answer too quickly!

Think of it this way: Assume 100 people own shares of stock in a corporation and one day decide to sell new shares to themselves at 25 percent below current value. They cannot really enhance their wealth by selling their own stock more cheaply to themselves. What is gained by purchasing inexpensive new shares is lost by diluting existing outstanding shares.

Take the case of Stockholder A, who owns nine shares before the rights offering and also has $30 in cash. His holdings would appear as follows:

Nine old shares at $40. . . .	$360
Cash	30
Total value	$390

If he receives and exercises nine rights to buy one new share at $30, his portfolio will contain:

Ten shares at $39 (diluted value)	$390
Cash.	0
Total value	$390

Clearly he is no better off. A second alternative would be for him to sell his rights in the market and stay with his position of owning only nine shares and holding cash.

Nine shares at $39 (diluted value). . . .	$351
Proceeds from sale of nine rights	9
Cash.	30
Total value	$390

As indicated above, whether he chooses to exercise his rights or not, the stock will still go down to a lower value (others are still diluting). Once again, his overall value remains constant. The value received for the rights ($9) exactly equals the extent of dilution in the value of the original nine shares.

The only foolish action would be for the stockholder to throw away the rights as worthless securities. He would then suffer the pains of dilution without the offset from the sale of the rights.

Nine shares at $39 (diluted value). . . .	$351
Cash.	30
Total value	$381

Empirical evidence indicates this careless activity occurs 1 to 2 percent of the time.

Desirable Features of Rights Offerings

The student may ask, If the stockholder is no better off in terms of total valuation, why undertake a rights offering? There are a number of possible advantages.

As previously indicated, by giving current stockholders a first option to purchase new shares, we protect their current position in regard to voting rights and claims to earnings. Of equal importance, the use of a rights offering gives the firm a built-in market for new security issues. Because of this built-in base, distribution costs are likely to be considerably lower than under a straight public issue in which investment bankers must underwrite the full risk of distribution.[5]

Also, a rights offering may generate more interest in the market than would a straight public issue. There is a market not only for the stock but also for the rights. Because the subscription price is normally set 15 to 25 percent below current value, there is the "nonreal" appearance of a bargain, creating further interest in the offering.

A last advantage of a rights offering over a straight stock issue is that stock purchased through a rights offering carries lower margin requirements. The **margin requirement** specifies the amount of cash or equity that must be deposited with a brokerage house or a bank, with the balance of funds eligible for borrowing. Though not all investors wish to purchase on margin, those who do so prefer to put down a minimum amount. While normal stock purchases may require a 50 percent margin (half cash, half borrowed), stock purchased under a rights offering may be bought with as little as 25 percent down, depending on the current requirements of the Federal Reserve Board.

Poison Pills

During the 1980s, a new wrinkle was added to the meaning of rights when firms began receiving merger and acquisition proposals from companies interested in acquiring voting control of the firm. The management of many firms did not want to give up control of the company, and so they devised a method of making the firm very unattractive to a potential acquisition-minded company. As you can tell from our discussion of voting provisions, a company using majority voting needs to control only over 50 percent of the voting shares to exercise total control. Management of companies considered potential takeover targets began to develop defensive tactics in fending off these unwanted mergers. One widely used strategy is called the *poison pill.*

A **poison pill** is a rights offer made to existing shareholders of Company X with the sole purpose of making it more difficult for another firm to acquire Company X. Most poison pills have a trigger point. When a potential buyer accumulates a given percentage of the common stock (for example, 25 percent), the other shareholders may receive rights to purchase additional shares from the company, generally at very low prices. If the rights are exercised by shareholders, this increases the total shares outstanding and dilutes the potential buyer's ownership percentage. Poison pill strategies often do not

---

[5]Though investment bankers generally participate in a rights offering as well, their fees are less because of the smaller risk factor.

have to be voted on by shareholders to be put into place. At International Paper Company, however, the poison pill issue was put on the proxy ballot and 76 percent of the voting shareholders sided with management to maintain the poison pill defense. This was surprising, because many institutional investors are opposed to the pill. They believe it lowers the potential for maximizing shareholder value by discouraging potential high takeover bids.

Having discussed bonds (in Chapter 16) and common stock, we are prepared to look at this intermediate or hybrid form of security known as **preferred stock.** You may question the validity of the term *preferred,* for preferred stock does not possess any of the most desirable characteristics of debt or common stock. In the case of debt, bondholders have a contractual claim against the corporation for the payment of interest and may throw the corporation into bankruptcy if payment is not forthcoming. Common stockholders are the owners of the firm and have a residual claim to all income not paid out to others. Preferred stockholders are merely entitled to receive a stipulated dividend and, generally, must receive the dividend before the payment of dividends to common stockholders. However, their right to annual dividends is not mandatory for the corporation, as is true of interest on debt, and the corporation may forgo preferred dividends when this is deemed necessary.

For example, XYZ Corporation might issue 9 percent preferred stock with a $100 par value. Under normal circumstances, the corporation would pay the $9 per share dividend. Let us also assume it has $1,000 bonds carrying 9.2 percent interest and shares of common stock with a market value of $50, normally paying a $1 cash dividend. The 9.2 percent interest *must* be paid on the bonds. The $9 in preferred dividends has to be paid before the $1 dividend on common, but both may be waived without threat of bankruptcy. The common stockholder is the last in line to receive payment, but the stockholder's potential participation is unlimited. Instead of getting a $1 dividend, the investor may someday receive many times that much.

Preferred Stock Financing

Justification for Preferred Stock

Because preferred stock has few unique characteristics, why might the corporation issue it and, equally important, why are investors willing to purchase the security?

Most corporations that issue preferred stock do so to achieve a balance in their capital structure. It is a means of expanding the capital base of the firm without diluting the common stock ownership position or incurring contractual debt obligations. Firms that are heavy users of debt, such as public utilities and capital goods producers, may go to preferred stock to balance their sources of financing.

Even here, there may be a drawback. While interest payments on debt are tax deductible, preferred stock dividends are not. Thus, the interest cost on 10 percent debt may be only 6.5 to 7 percent on an aftertax cost basis, while the aftertax cost on 10 percent preferred stock would be the stated amount. A firm issuing the preferred stock may be willing to pay the higher aftertax cost to assure investors it has a balanced capital structure and because preferred stock may have a positive effect on the costs of the other sources of funds in the capital structure.

Investor Interest   Primary purchasers of preferred stock are corporate investors, insurance companies, and pension funds. To the corporate investor, preferred stock offers a very attractive advantage over bonds. The tax law provides that any corporation that receives either preferred or common dividends from another corporation must add only 30 percent of such dividends to its taxable income. Thus, 70 percent of such dividends are exempt from taxation. On a preferred stock issue paying a 10 percent dividend, only 30 percent would be taxable. By contrast, the interest of bonds is usually taxable to the recipient except for municipal bond interest.

For example, if we take the 1992 figures for Aa bond yields and preferred stock yields in Table 17–2 and adjust them for aftertax yields to a corporation,

Year	Aa Bond Yields	High-Grade Preferred Stock Yields	Yield Spread Bonds/Preferred Stock
1977	8.24	7.60	0.64
1978	8.92	8.25	0.67
1979	10.46	9.50	0.96
1980	12.50	10.57	1.93
1981	14.75	12.36	2.39
1982	14.41	12.53	1.88
1983	12.42	11.02	1.40
1984	13.31	11.59	1.72
1985	11.82	10.49	1.33
1986	9.47	8.76	0.71
1987	9.68	8.37	1.31
1988	9.94	9.23	0.71
1989	9.46	9.05	0.41
1990	9.56	8.96	0.60
1991	9.05	8.17	0.88
1992	8.46	7.45	1.01

the advantage of preferred stock ownership to these investors is evident. Since interest on bonds receives no tax reduction, the aftertax bond yield must be adjusted by the corporation's marginal tax rate.

In this example we shall use a rate of 35 percent.

$$\text{Aftertax bond yield} = \text{Before tax bond yield} \times (1 - \text{Tax rate})$$

$$= 8.46\% \times (1 - .35)$$

$$= 5.50\%$$

For preferred stock the adjustment also includes the advantageous 30 percent taxing provision.

$$\frac{\text{Aftertax}}{\text{preferred yield}} = \text{Before tax preferred stock yield} \times [1 - (\text{Tax rate})(.30)]$$

$$= 7.45\% \times [1 - (.35)(.30)]$$

$$= 7.45\% \times (1 - .105)$$

$$= 7.45\% \times .895$$

$$= 6.67\%$$

The aftertax yield on preferred stock is higher than the aftertax bond yield even though the bond has the higher before-tax yield. Because of this tax consideration, it is not surprising that corporations are able to issue preferred stock at a slightly lower yield than debt. As indicated in Table 17–2 (last column), preferred stock has been trading at a ½ to 2½ percent lower yield than comparable bonds since the late 1970s.

Summary of Tax Considerations Tax considerations for preferred stock work in two opposite directions. First, they make the aftertax cost of debt cheaper than preferred stock to the issuing corporation because interest is deductible to the payer. (This is true even though the quoted rate may be higher.) Second, tax considerations generally make the receipt of preferred dividends more valuable than corporate bond interest to corporate investors because 70 percent of the dividend is exempt from taxation.

A preferred stock issue contains a number of stipulations and provisions that define the stockholder's claim to income and assets.

Provisions Associated with Preferred Stock

1. Cumulative Dividends Most issues are **cumulative preferred stock** and have a cumulative claim to dividends. That is, if preferred stock dividends are not paid in any one year, they accumulate and must be paid in total before common stockholders can receive dividends. If preferred stock carries a $10 cash dividend and the company does not pay dividends for three years, preferred stockholders must receive the full $30 before common stockholders can receive anything.

The cumulative dividend feature makes a corporation very aware of its obligation to preferred stockholders. When a financially troubled corporation has missed a number of dividend payments under a cumulative arrangement, there may be a financial recapitalization of the corporation in which preferred stockholders receive new securities in place of the dividend arrearage. Assume the corporation has now missed five years of dividends under a $10 a year obligation and the company still remains in a poor cash position. Preferred stockholders may be offered $50 or more in new common stock for forgiveness of the missed dividend payments. Preferred stockholders may be willing to cooperate in order to receive some potential benefit for the future.

2. Conversion Feature   Like certain forms of debt, preferred stock may be convertible into common shares. Thus, $100 in preferred stock may be convertible into x number of shares of common stock at the option of the holder. One new wrinkle on convertible preferreds is the use of **convertible exchangeable preferreds** that allow the company to force conversion from convertible preferred stock into convertible debt. This can be used to allow the company to take advantage of falling interest rates or to allow the company to change preferred dividends into tax-deductible interest payments when it is to the company's advantage to do so.

The topic of convertibility is discussed at length in Chapter 19, "Convertibles and Warrants."

3. Call Feature   Also, preferred stock, like debt, may be callable; that is the corporation may retire the security before maturity at some small premium over par. This, of course, accrues to the advantage of the corporation and to the disadvantage of the preferred stockholder. A preferred issue carrying a call provision will be accorded a slightly higher yield than a similar issue without this feature. The same type of refunding decision applied to debt obligations in Chapter 16 could also be applied to preferred stock.

4. Participation Provision   A *small* percentage of preferred stock issues are **participating preferreds;** that is they may participate over and above the quoted yield when the corporation is enjoying a particularly good year. Once the common stock dividend equals the preferred stock dividend, the two classes of securities may share equally in additional payouts.

5. Floating Rate   Beginning in 1982, a few preferred stock issuers made the dividend adjustable in nature and these are classified as **floating rate preferred stock.** These issuers include such firms as Alcoa, U.S. Steel, and BankAmerica Corporation. Typically the dividend is changed on a quarterly basis, based on current market conditions. Because the dividend rate only changes quarterly, there is still some possibility of a small price change between dividend adjustment dates. Nevertheless, it is less than the price change for regular preferred stock.

Investors that participate in floating rate preferred stock do so for two reasons: to minimize the risk of price changes and to take advantage of the tax benefits associated with preferred stock corporate ownership. The price stability actually makes floating rate preferred stock the equivalent of a safe short-term investment even though preferred stock is normally thought of as long term in nature.

6. Dutch Auction Preferred Stock   **Dutch auction preferred stock** is similar to floating rate preferred stock—but is a short-term instrument. The security matures every seven weeks and is sold (reauctioned) at a subsequent bidding. The concept of Dutch auction means the stock is issued to the bidder willing to accept the lowest yield and then to the next lowest bidder and so on until all the preferred stock is sold. This is much like the Treasury bill auc-

Chapter 17 Common and Preferred Stock Financing

tions held by the Federal Reserve Bank. This auction process at short-term intervals allows investors to keep up with the changing interest rates in the short-term market. Some corporate investors like Dutch auction preferred stock because it allows them to invest at short-term rates and take advantage of the tax benefits available to them with preferred stock investments.

7. Par Value A final important feature associated with preferred stock is par value. Unlike the par value of common stock, which is often only a small percentage of the actual value, the par value of preferred stock is set at the anticipated market value at the time of issue. The par value establishes the amount due to preferred stockholders in the event of liquidation. Also, the par value of preferred stock determines the base against which the percentage or dollar return on preferred stock is computed. Thus, 10 percent preferred stock would indicate $10 a year in preferred dividends if the par value were $100, but only $5 annually if the par value were $50.

In Table 17–3, we compare the characteristics of common stock, preferred stock, and bonds. The student should carefully consider the comparative advantages and disadvantages of each.

Comparing Features of Common and Preferred Stock and Debt

TABLE 17–3 **Features of alternative security issues**

	Common Stock	Preferred Stock	Bonds
1. Ownership and control of the firm	Belongs to common stockholders through voting right and residual claim to income	Limited rights when dividends are missed	Limited rights under default in interest payments
2. Obligation to provide return	None	Must receive payment before common stockholder	Contractual obligation
3. Claim to assets in bankruptcy	Lowest claim of any security holder	Bondholders and creditors must be satisfied first	Highest claim
4. Cost of distribution	Highest	Moderate	Lowest
5. Risk–return trade-off	Highest risk, highest return (at least in theory)	Moderate risk, moderate return	Lowest risk, moderate return
6. Tax status of payment by corporation	Not deductible	Not deductible	Tax deductible Cost = Interest payment × (1 − Tax rate)
7. Tax status of payment to recipient	70 percent of dividend to another corporation is tax exempt	Same as common stock	Municipal bond interest is tax exempt

In terms of the risk-return features of these three classes of securities and also of the other investments discussed in Chapter 7, we might expect the risk-return patterns depicted in Figure 17–1. The lowest return is obtained from savings accounts, and the highest return and risk are generally associated with common stock. In between, we note that short-term instruments generally, though not always, provide lower returns than longer-term instruments. We also observe that government securities pay lower returns than issues originated by corporations, because of the lower risk involved. Next on the scale after government issues is preferred stock. This hybrid form of security generally pays a lower return than even well-secured corporate debt instruments, because of the 70 percent tax-exempt status of preferred stock dividends to corporate purchasers. Thus, the focus on preferred stock is not just on risk-return trade-offs but also on aftertax return.[6]

FIGURE 17–1
Risk and expected return for various security classes

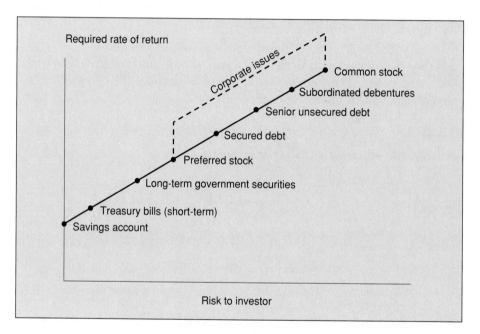

Next, we observe increasingly high return requirements on debt, based on the presence or absence of security provisions and the priority of claims on unsecured debt. At the top of the scale is common stock. Because of its lowest priority of claim in the corporation and its volatile price movement, it has the highest demanded return.

While extensive research has tended to validate these general patterns,[7] short-term or even intermediate-term reversals have occurred, in which investments with lower risk have outperformed investments at the higher end of the risk scale.

---

[6]In a strict sense, preferred stock does not belong on the straight line because of its unique tax characteristics.

[7]Ibbotson Associates, *Stocks, Bonds, Bills and Inflation: 1992 Yearbook* (Chicago: Ibbotson Associates Capital Management Research Center, 1992).

Summary

While common stock is owned by over 50 million individual investors, institutional ownership through mutual funds, pension funds, insurance companies, and bank trusts is increasing every year.

Common stock ownership carries three primary rights or privileges. First, there is a residual claim to income. All funds not paid out to other classes of securities automatically belong to the common stockholder; the firm may then choose to pay out these residual funds in dividends or to reinvest them for the benefit of common stockholders. Different classes of stock may carry different dividends. There are also cases, such as the new GM Class E and H stock, where dividends are tied to the performance of a subsidiary company.

Because common stockholders are the ultimate owners of the firm, they alone have the privilege of voting. There may be more than one class of stock, each having differing voting rights. The key example where voting rights are not equal is usually founders' stock, such as in Ford Motor Company's Class B stock and Times Mirror Series A, Series B, and Series C common stock. The General Motors' Class E and H stock also have different rights as a result of acquisitions by General Motors.

To expand the role of minority stockholders, many corporations use a system of cumulative voting, in which each stockholder has voting power equal to the number of shares owned times the number of directors to be elected. By cumulating votes for a small number of selected directors, minority stockholders are able to have representation on the board.

Common stockholders may also enjoy a first option to purchase new shares. This privilege is extended through the procedure known as a rights offering. A shareholder receives one right for each share of stock owned and may combine a certain number of rights, plus cash, to purchase a new share. While the cash or subscription price is usually somewhat below the current market price, the stockholder neither gains nor loses through the process.

A hybrid, or intermediate, security, falling between debt and common stock, is preferred stock. Preferred stockholders are entitled to receive a stipulated dividend and must receive this dividend before any payment is made to common stockholders. Preferred dividends usually accumulate if they are not paid in a given year, though preferred stockholders cannot initiate bankruptcy proceedings or seek legal redress if nonpayment occurs.

Finally, common stock, preferred stock, bonds, and other securities tend to receive returns over the long run in accordance with risk, with corporate issues generally paying a higher return than government securities.

Review of Formulas

$$1. \quad \frac{\text{Shares}}{\text{required}} = \frac{\text{Number of directors desired} \times \text{Total number of shares outstanding}}{\text{Total number of directors to be elected} + 1} + 1 \qquad (17\text{--}1)$$

2. Number of directors that can be elected

$$= \frac{(\text{Shares owned} - 1) \times (\text{Total number of directors to be elected} + 1)}{(\text{Total number of shares outstanding})} \qquad (17\text{--}2)$$

3. $R = \dfrac{M_o - S}{N + 1}$ \hfill (17--3)

R is the value of a right

M_o is the market value of the stock—rights-on (stock carries a right)

S is the subscription price

N is the number of rights required to purchase a new share of stock

4. $R = \dfrac{M_e - S}{N}$ \hfill (17--4)

R is the value of a right

M_e is the market value of stock—ex-rights (stock no longer carries a right)

S is the subscription price

N is number of rights required to purchase a new share of stock

---

List of Terms

common stock 494
residual claim to income 495
proxy 496
founders' shares 496
majority voting 498
cumulative voting 498
preemptive right 500
rights offering 500
rights-on 501
ex-rights 501

margin requirement 504
poison pill 504
preferred stock 505
cumulative preferred stock 507
convertible exchangeable
   preferreds 508
participating preferreds 508
floating rate preferred stock 508
Dutch auction preferred
   stock 508

Discussion Questions

1. Why has corporate management become increasingly sensitive to the desires of large institutional investors?

2. Why might a corporation use a special category such as founders' stock in issuing common stock?

3. What is the purpose of cumulative voting? Are there any disadvantages to management?

4. How does the preemptive right protect stockholders from dilution?

5. If common stockholders are the *owners* of the company, why do they have the last claim on assets and a residual claim on income?

6. During a rights offering, the underlying stock is said to sell "rights-on" and "ex-rights." Explain the meaning of these terms and their significance to current stockholders and potential stockholders.

7. Why might management use a poison pill strategy?

8. Preferred stock is often referred to as a hybrid security. What is meant by this term?

9. What is the most likely explanation for the use of preferred stock from a corporate viewpoint?

10. If preferred stock is riskier than bonds, why has preferred stock had lower yields than bonds in recent years?

11. Why is the cumulative feature of preferred stock particularly important to preferred stockholders?

12. A small amount of preferred stock is participating. What would your reaction be if someone said common stock is also participating?

13. What is an advantage of floating rate preferred stock for the risk-averse investor?

14. Put an X by the security that has the feature best related to the following considerations. You may wish to refer to Table 17–3.

	Common Stock	Preferred Stock	Bonds
a. Ownership and control of the firm			
b. Obligation to provide return			
c. Claims to assets in bankruptcy			
d. High cost of distribution			
e. Highest return			
f. Highest risk			

Problems

1. Mr. Thomas owns 6,001 shares of the Piston Corp. There are 12 seats on the company board of directors, and the company has a total of 78,000 shares outstanding. The Piston Corp. utilizes cumulative voting.

   Can Mr. Thomas elect himself to the board when the vote to elect 12 directors is held next week? (Use Formula 17–2 to determine if he can elect one director.)

   Cumulative voting

2. Boston Fishery has been experiencing declining earnings, but has just announced a 50 percent salary increase for its top executives. A dissident group of stockholders wants to oust the existing board of directors. There are currently 11 directors and 60,000 shares of stock

   Dissident stockholder group and cumulative voting

outstanding. Mr. Bass, the president of the company, has the full support of the existing board. The dissident stockholders control proxies for 20,001 shares. Mr. Bass is worried about losing his job.

a. Under cumulative voting procedures, how many directors can the dissident stockholders elect with the proxies they now hold? How many directors could they elect under majority rule with these proxies?

b. How many shares (or proxies) are needed to elect six directors under cumulative voting?

Dissident stockholder group and cumulative voting

3. Galaxy Corporation is holding a stockholders meeting next month. Mr. Starr is the president of the company and has the support of the existing board of directors. All nine members of the board are up for reelection. Mr. Kramer is a dissident stockholder. He controls proxies for 30,001 shares. Mr. Starr and his friends on the board control 50,001 shares. Other stockholders, whose loyalties are unknown, will be voting the remaining 19,998 shares. The company uses cumulative voting.

a. How many directors can Mr. Kramer be sure of electing?

b. How many directors can Mr. Starr and his friends be sure of electing?

c. How many directors could Mr. Kramer elect if he obtains all the proxies for the uncommitted votes? (Uneven values must be *rounded down* to the nearest whole number regardless of the amount.)

Cumulative voting

4. In problem 3, if 12 directors were to be elected, and Mr. Starr and his friends had 50,001 shares and Mr. Kramer had 30,001 shares plus half the uncommitted votes, how many directors could Mr. Kramer elect?

Different classes of voting stock

5. Higgins Metal Company was established in 1980. Four years later the company went public. At that time Henry Higgins, the original owner, decided to establish two classes of stock. The first represents Class A founders' stock and is entitled to 10 votes per share. The normally traded common stock, designated as Class B, is entitled to one vote per share. In late 1993 Mr. Andrews was considering purchasing shares in Higgins Metal Company. While he knew founders' shares were not present in many companies, he decided to buy the shares anyway because of a new high-technology melting process the company had developed.

Of the 1,400,000 total shares currently outstanding, the original founder's family owns 52,525 shares. What is the percentage of the founder's family votes compared to the Class B votes?

Rights offering

6. Grantland Rice Co. has issued rights to its shareholders. The subscription price is $45 and four rights are needed along with the subscription price to buy one of the new shares. The stock is selling for $55 rights-on.

a. What would be the value of one right?

b. If the stock goes ex-rights, what would the new stock price be?

7. Harmon Candy Co. has announced a rights offering for its shareholders. Cindy Barr owns 500 shares of Harmon Candy Co. stock. Five rights plus $62 cash are needed to buy one of the new shares. The stock is currently selling for $70 rights-on.

   a. What is the value of a right?

   b. How many of the new shares could Cindy buy if she exercised all her rights? How much cash would this require?

   c. Cindy doesn't know if she wants to exercise her rights or sell them. What alternative would have the most beneficial effect on her wealth?

Procedures associated with a rights offering

8. Roy Randall has $9,000 to invest. He has been looking at Barton Petroleum common stock. Barton has issued a rights offering to its common stockholders. Six rights plus $51 cash will buy one new share. Barton's stock is selling for $60 ex-rights.

   a. How many rights could Roy buy with his $9,000? Alternatively, how many shares of stock could he buy with the same $9,000 at $60 per share?

   b. If Roy invests his $9,000 in Barton rights and the price of Barton stock rises to $72 per share ex-rights, what would his dollar profit on the rights be? (First compute profits per right.)

   c. If Roy invests his $9,000 in Barton stock and the price of the stock rises to $72 per share ex-rights, what would his total dollar profit be?

   d. What would be the answer to part *b* if the price of Barton's stock falls to $45 per share ex-rights instead of rising to $72?

   e. What would the answer be to part *c* if the price of Barton's stock falls to $45 per share ex-rights?

Investing in rights

9. Mr. and Mrs. Anderson own five shares of Magic Tricks Corporation common stock. The market value of the stock is $60. They also have $48 in cash. They have just received word of a rights offering. One new share of stock can be purchased at $48 for each five shares currently owned (based on five rights).

   a. What is the value of a right?

   b. What is the value of the Andersons' portfolio before the rights offering? (Portfolio in this question represents stock plus cash.)

   c. If the Andersons participate in the rights offering, what will be the value of their portfolio, based on the diluted value (ex-rights) of the stock?

   d. If they sell their five rights but keep their stock at its diluted value and hold on to their cash, what will be the value of their portfolio?

Effects of rights on stockholder position

10. Kristy Fashions, Inc., has 4.5 million shares of common stock outstanding. The current market price of Kristy Fashions common stock is $60 per share rights-on. The company's net income this year is $18 million. A rights offering has been announced in which

Effect of rights on earnings and the P/E ratio

450,000 new shares will be sold at $55 per share. The subscription price of $55 plus 10 rights is needed to buy one of the new shares.

a. What are the earnings per share and price-earnings ratio before the new shares are sold via the rights offering?

b. What would the earnings per share be immediately after the rights offering? What would the price-earnings ratio be immediately after the rights offering? (Assume there is no change in the market value of the common stock, except for the change that occurs when the stock begins trading ex-rights.) Round all answers to two places to the right of the decimal point.

Aftertax comparison of preferred stock and other investments

11. The Shelton Corporation has some excess cash that it would like to invest in marketable securities for a long-term hold. Its vice-president of finance is considering three investments (Shelton Corporation is in a 36 percent tax bracket). Which one should he select based on aftertax return: (*a*) Treasury bonds at a 7 percent yield; (*b*) corporate bonds at a 10 percent yield; or (*c*) preferred stock at an 8 percent yield?

12. Silicon Industries has a cumulative preferred stock issue outstanding, which has a stated annual dividend of $8 per share. The company has been losing money and has not paid preferred dividends for the last four years. There are 260,000 shares of preferred stock outstanding and 500,000 shares of common stock.

a. How much is the company behind in preferred dividends?

b. If Silicon Industries earns $7,500,000 in the coming year after taxes and before dividends, and this is all paid out to the preferred stockholders, how much will the company be in arrears (behind in payments)? Keep in mind that the coming year would represent the fifth year.

c. How much, if any, would be available in common stock dividends in the coming year if $7,500,000 is earned as explained in part *b*?

Preferred stock dividends in arrears

13. Industrial Gas Company is four years in arrears on cumulative preferred stock dividends. There are 650,000 preferred shares outstanding, and the annual dividend is $7 per share. The vice-president of finance sees no real hope of paying the dividends in arrears. He is devising a plan to compensate the preferred stockholders for 90 percent of the dividends in arrears.

a. How much should the compensation be?

b. Industrial Gas Company will compensate the preferred stockholders in the form of bonds paying 12 percent interest in a market environment in which the going rate of interest is 14 percent. The bonds will have a 25-year maturity. Using the bond valuation table in Chapter 16 (Table 16–3), indicate the market value of a $1,000 par value bond.

c. Based on market value, how many bonds must be issued to provide the compensation determined in part *a*? (Round to the nearest whole number.)

14. The treasurer of Garcia Mexican Food Restaurants (a corporation) currently has $100,000 invested in preferred stock yielding 7.5 percent. He appreciates the tax advantages of preferred stock and is considering buying $100,000 more with borrowed funds. The cost of the borrowed funds is 9.5 percent. He suggests this proposal to his board of directors. The directors are somewhat concerned by the fact that the treasurer is paying 2 percent more for funds than he is earning. The firm is in a 34 percent tax bracket.

Borrowing funds to purchase preferred stock

   a. Compute the amount of the aftertax income from the additional preferred stock if it is purchased.

   b. Compute the aftertax borrowing cost to purchase the additional preferred stock. That is, multiply the interest cost times $(1 - T)$.

   c. Should the treasurer proceed with his proposal?

   d. If interest rates and dividend yields in the market go up six months after a decision to purchase is made, what impact will this have on the outcome?

15. Referring back to the original information in problem 14, if the yield on the $100,000 of preferred stock is still 7.5 percent and the borrowing cost remains 9.5 percent, but the tax rate is only 20 percent, is this a feasible investment?

Effect of changing tax rates on preferred stock investments

16. Hailey Transmission has two classes of preferred stock: floating rate preferred stock and straight (normal) preferred stock. Both issues have a par value of $100. The floating rate preferred stock pays an annual dividend yield of 7 percent, and the straight preferred stock pays 8 percent. Since the issuance of the two securities, interest rates have gone up by 3 percent for each issue. Both securities will pay their year-end dividend today.

Floating rate preferred stock

   a. What is the price of the floating rate preferred stock likely to be?

   b. What is the price of the straight preferred stock likely to be? Refer back to Chapter 10 and use Formula 10–4 to answer this question.

COMPREHENSIVE PROBLEMS

The Crandall Corporation currently has 100,000 shares outstanding that are selling at $50 per share. It needs to raise $900,000. Net income after taxes is $500,000. Its vice-president of finance and its investment banker have decided on a rights offering, but are not sure how much to discount the subscription price from the current market value. Discounts of 10 percent, 20 percent, and 40 percent have been suggested. Common stock is the sole means of financing for the Crandall Corporation.

Crandall Corporation
(rights offering and the impact on shareholders)

   a. For each discount, determine the subscription price, the number of shares to be issued, and the number of rights required to purchase one share. (Round to one place after the decimal point where necessary.)

b. Determine the value of one right under each of the plans. (Round to two places after the decimal point.)

c. Compute the earnings per share before and immediately after the rights offering under a 10 percent discount from the subscription price.

d. By what percentage has the number of shares outstanding increased?

e. Stockholder X has 100 shares before the rights offering and participated by buying 20 new shares. Compute his total claim to earnings both before and after the rights offering (that is, multiply shares by the earnings per share figures computed in part c).

f. Should Stockholder X be satisfied with this claim over a longer period of time?

Snyder Meat Packing Co.
(cumulative voting with staggered terms of directors)

Snyder Meat Packing Co. is a small firm that has been very profitable over the past five years and has also exhibited a strong earnings growth trend. Mr. Snyder owns 35 percent of the 3 million shares of common stock outstanding, but he is nevertheless worried about being taken over by a larger firm in the future. He has read some articles in *The Wall Street Journal* about techniques used to discourage forced mergers and takeovers. The firm currently uses majority voting for nine directors. Mr. Snyder wonders which of the following proposals would make it easier for him to reject a takeover bid.

a. What would be the effect of cumulative voting?

b. What would be accomplished if shareholders could vote for only one third of the directors every year (staggered terms)?

c. Should Mr. Snyder reduce or increase the number of directors? Does the answer to this question depend on majority rule or cumulative voting?

Selected References

Bhagat, Sanjai, James A. Brickley, and Ronald C. Lease. "The Authorization of Additional Common Stock: An Empirical Investigation." *Financial Management* 15 (Autumn 1986), pp. 45–53.

Davidson, Wallace N., III, and John L. Glascock. "The Announcement Effects of Preferred Stock Re-Ratings." *Journal of Financial Research* 36 (Winter 1985), pp. 317–26.

Fisher, Lawrence, and James H. Lorie. *A Half Century of Returns on Common Stocks and Bonds.* Chicago: University of Chicago Graduate School of Business, 1977.

Grossman, Sanford J., and Oliver D. Hart. "One Share–One Vote and the Market for Corporate Control." *Journal of Financial Economics* (Netherlands) 20 (January–March 1988), pp. 175–202.

Ibbotson Associates. *Stocks, Bonds, Bills and Inflation: 1992 Yearbook.* Chicago: Ibbotson Associates Capital Management Research Center, 1992.

Linn, Scott C., and Michael J. Pinegar. "The Effect of Issuing Preferred Stock on Common and Preferred Stockholder Wealth." *Journal of Financial Economics* (Netherlands) 22 (October 1988), pp. 155–84.

Logue, Dennis E., and James K. Seward. "The Time Warner Rights Offering and the Destruction of Stockholder Value." *Financial Analysts Journal* 48 (March–April 1992), pp. 37–45.

Malatesta, Paul H., and Ralph A. Walkling. "Poison Pill Securities: Stockholder Wealth, Profitability, and Ownership Structure." *Journal of Financial Economics* (Netherlands) 20 (January–March 1988), pp. 347–76.

Mikkelson, Wayne H., and Megan Patch. "Stock Price Effects and Costs of Secondary Distributions." *Journal of Financial Economics* (Netherlands) 14 (June 1985), pp. 165–94.

Moyer, R. Charles, Ramesh Rao, and Phillip M. Sisneros. "Substitutes for Voting Rights: Evidence from Dual Class Recapitalizations." *Financial Management* 21 (Autumn 1992), pp. 35–47.

Paré, Terence P. "How to Know When to Buy Stocks." *Fortune* 126 (Fall 1992), pp. 79–83.

Pinegar, J. Michael, and Ronald C. Lease. "The Impact of Preferred-for-Common Exchange Offers on Firm Value." *Journal of Finance* 41 (September 1986), pp. 795–814.

Winger, Berhard J., Carl R. Chen, John D. Martin, J. William Petty, and Steven Hayden. "Adjustable Rate Preferred Stock." *Financial Management* 15 (Spring 1986), pp. 48–57.

CHAPTER 18

Dividend Policy and Retained Earnings

CHAPTER CONCEPTS

1 Corporate management must decide what to do with retained earnings: pay them out as dividends or reinvest them in future projects.

2 Many other factors also influence dividend policy such as legal rules, the cash position of the firm, the tax position of shareholders, and so on.

3 Stock dividends and stock splits provide common stockholders with new shares, but their value must be carefully assessed.

4 Some firms make a decision to repurchase their shares in the marketplace rather than increase dividends.

A successful owner of a small business must continually decide what to do with the profits his or her firm has generated. One option is to reinvest in the business—purchasing new plant and equipment, expanding inventory, and perhaps hiring new employees. Another alternative, however, is to withdraw the funds from the business and invest them elsewhere. Prospective uses might include buying other stocks and bonds, purchasing a second business, or perhaps spending a lost weekend in Las Vegas.

A corporation and its stockholders must face the same type of decision. Should funds associated with profits be retained in the business or paid out to stockholders in the form of dividends?

The Marginal Principle of Retained Earnings

In theory, corporate directors should ask, "How can the best use of the funds be made?" The rate of return that the corporation can achieve on retained earnings for the benefit of stockholders must be compared to what stockholders could earn if the funds were paid to them in dividends. This is known as the **marginal principle of retained earnings.** Each potential project to be financed by internally generated funds must provide a higher rate of return than the stockholder could achieve on other investments. We speak of this as the opportunity cost of using stockholder funds.

Life Cycle Growth and Dividends

One of the major influences on dividends is the corporate growth rate in sales and the subsequent return on assets. Figure 18–1 shows a corporate **life cycle** and the corresponding dividend policy that is most likely to be found at each stage. A small firm in the initial stages of development (Stage I) pays no dividends because it needs all its profits (if there are any) for reinvestment in new productive assets. If the firm is successful in the marketplace, the demand for its products will create growth in sales, earnings, and assets, and the firm will move into Stage II. At this stage sales and returns on assets will be growing at an increasing rate, and earnings will still be reinvested. In the early part of Stage II, stock dividends (distribution of additional shares) may be instituted and, in the latter part of Stage II, *low* cash dividends may be started to inform investors that the firm is profitable but cash is needed for internal acquisition.

After the growth period the firm enters Stage III. The expansion of sales continues, but at a decreasing rate, and returns on investment may decline as more competition enters the market and tries to take away the firm's market share. During this period the firm is more and more capable of paying cash dividends, as the asset expansion rate slows and external funds become more readily available. Stock dividends and stock splits are still common in the expansion phase, and the dividend payout ratio usually increases from a low level of 5 to 15 percent of earnings to a moderate level of 25 to 40 percent of earnings. Finally, at Stage IV, maturity, the firm maintains a stable growth rate in sales similar to that of the economy as a whole; and, when risk premi-

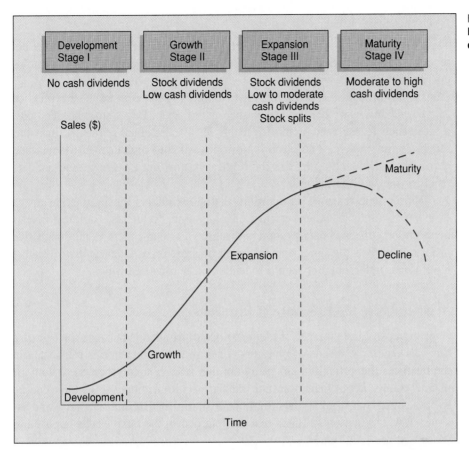

FIGURE 18–1
**Life cycle growth and
dividend policy**

ums are considered, its returns on assets level out to those of the industry and the economy. In unfortunate cases firms suffer declines in sales if product innovation and diversification have not occurred over the years. In Stage IV, assuming maturity rather than decline, dividends might range from 40 to 60 percent of earnings. These percentages will be different from industry to industry, depending on the individual characteristics of the company, such as operating and financial leverage and the volatility of sales and earnings over the business cycle.

As the chapter continues, more will be said about stock dividends, stock splits, the availability of external funds, and other variables that affect the dividend policy of the firm.

Dividends as a Passive Variable

In the preceding analysis, dividends were used as a passive decision variable: They are to be paid out only if the corporation cannot make better use of the funds for the benefit of stockholders. The active decision variable is retained earnings. Management decides how much retained earnings will be spent for internal corporate needs, and the residual (the amount left after internal expenditures) is paid to the stockholders in cash dividends.

An Incomplete Theory

The only problem with the **residual theory of dividends** is that we have not recognized how stockholders feel about receiving dividends. If the stockholders' only concern is with achieving the highest return on their investment, either in the form of *corporate retained earnings remaining in the business* or as *current dividends paid out,* then there is no issue. But if stockholders have a preference for current funds, for example, over retained earnings, then our theory is incomplete. The issue is not only whether reinvestment of retained earnings or dividends provides the highest return, but also how stockholders react to the two alternatives.

While some researchers maintain that stockholders are indifferent to the division of funds between retained earnings and dividends[1] (holding investment opportunities constant), others disagree.[2] Though there is no conclusive proof one way or the other, the judgment of most researchers is that investors have some preference between dividends and retained earnings.

Arguments for the Relevance of Dividends

A strong case can be made for the relevance of dividends because they *resolve uncertainty* in the minds of investors. Though retained earnings reinvested in the business theoretically belong to common stockholders, there is still an air of uncertainty about their eventual translation into dividends. Thus, it can be hypothesized that stockholders might apply a higher discount rate (K_e) and assign a lower valuation to funds that are retained in the business as opposed to those that are paid out.[3]

It is also argued that dividends may be viewed more favorably than retained earnings because of the **information content of dividends.** In essence the corporation is telling the stockholder, "We are having a good year, and we wish to share the benefits with you." If the dividend per share is raised, then the information content of the dividend increase is quite positive while a reduction in the dividend generally has a negative information content. Even though the corporation may be able to generate the same or higher returns with the funds than the stockholder and perhaps provide even greater dividends in the future, some researchers find that "in an uncertain world in which verbal statements can be ignored or misinterpreted, dividend action does provide a clear-cut means of making a statement that speaks louder than a thousand words."[4]

---

[1]Merton H. Miller and Franco Modigliani, "Dividend Policy, Growth and Valuation of Shares," *Journal of Business* 34 (October 1961), pp. 411–33. Under conditions of perfect capital markets with an absence of taxes and flotation costs, it is argued that the sum of discounted value per share after dividend payments equals the total valuation before dividend payments.

[2]Myron J. Gordon, "Optimum Investment and Financing Policy," *Journal of Finance* 18 (May 1963), pp. 264–72; and John Lintner, "Dividends, Earnings, Leverage, Stock Prices, and the Supply of Capital to the Corporation," *Review of Economics and Statistics* 44 (August 1962), pp. 243–69.

[3]Ibid.

[4]Ezra Solomon, *The Theory of Financial Management* (New York: Columbia University Press, 1963),

The relevance of dividends in policy determination can also be argued from the viewpoint that the optimum dividend payout rate should be low. Because certain stockholders may be in high tax brackets, retention of funds in excess of investment needs might be recommended to defer the potential tax obligation.

The primary contention in arguing for the relevance of dividend policy is that stockholders' needs and preferences go beyond the *marginal principal of retained earnings.* The issue is not only who can best utilize the funds (the corporation or the stockholder) but also what are the stockholders' preferences. In practice it appears that most corporations adhere to the following logic. First investment opportunities relative to a required return (marginal analysis) are determined. This is then tempered by some subjective notion of stockholders' desires. Corporations with unusual growth prospects and high rates of return on internal investments generally pay a relatively low dividend (the small amount may be paid out only for its informational content). For the more mature firm, an analysis of both investment opportunities and stockholder preferences may indicate that a higher rate of payout is necessary. Examples of dividend policies of selected major U.S. corporations are presented in Table 18–1. Notice that the high-growth firms have a propensity to retain earnings rather than pay dividends, while the slow-growth firms have a rather large payout ratio. The normal payout has been approximately 50 percent of aftertax earnings in the post–World War II period.

TABLE 18–1
Corporate dividend policy

	Historical Growth in EPS (1988–92)	Estimated Growth in EPS* (1995–97)	Dividend Payout as Percent of Aftertax Earnings (1992)
Category 1—Rapid Growth			
Harley-Davidson	39%	20%	0%
Toys 'R' Us	21%	17%	0%
Microsoft	54%	29%	0%
Dell Computer.	51%	31%	0%
Category 2—Slow Growth			
Exxon Corp.	3%	6%	74%
Bell South	1%	6%	82%
Southwest Bell	3%	9%	67%
Royal Dutch Petroleum	8%	5%	71%

*Estimated growth from various issues of *Value Line Investment Survey.*

Dividend Stability

In considering stockholder desires in dividend policy, a primary factor is the maintenance of stability in dividend payments. Thus corporate management must not only ask, "How many profitable investments do we have this year?" It must also ask, "What has been the pattern of dividend payments in the last few years?" Though earnings may change from year to year, the dollar amount of cash dividends tends to be much more stable, increasing in value only as new permanent levels of income are achieved. Note in Figure 18–2

FIGURE 18-2   **Corporate profits and dividends for manufacturing corporations**

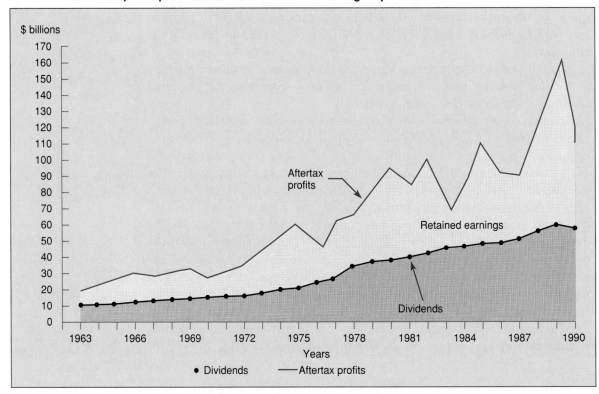

the considerably greater volatility of aftertax profits (earnings) compared to dividends for U.S. manufacturing corporations.

By maintaining a record of relatively stable dividends, corporate management hopes to lower the discount rate (K_e) applied to future dividends of the firm, thus raising the value of the firm. The operative rule appears to be that a stockholder would much prefer to receive $1 a year for three years, rather than 75 cents for the first year, $1.50 for the second year, and 75 cents for the third year—for the same total of $3. Once again, we temper our policy of marginal analysis of retained earnings to include a notion of stockholder preference, with the emphasis on stability of dividends.

Other Factors Influencing Dividend Policy

Corporate management must also consider the legal basis of dividends, the cash flow position of the firm, and the corporation's access to capital markets. Other factors that must be considered include management's desire for control and the tax and financial position of shareholders. Each is briefly discussed.

Legal Rules

Most states forbid firms to pay dividends that would impair the initial capital contributions to the firm. For this reason dividends may be distributed only from past and current earnings. To pay dividends in excess of this amount would mean the corporation is returning to investors their original capital contribution (raiding the capital). If the ABC Company has the following statement of net worth, the maximum dividend payment would be $20 million.

Common stock (1 million shares at $10 par value)*. .	$10,000,000
Retained earnings	20,000,000
Net worth	$30,000,000

*If there is a "paid-in capital in excess of par" account, some states will allow additional dividend payments against capital, while others will not. To simplify the problem for now, paid-in capital in excess of par is not considered.

Why all the concern about impairing permanent capital? Since the firm is going to pay dividends only to those who contributed capital in the first place, what is the problem? Clearly there is no abuse to the stockholders, but what about the creditors? They have extended credit on the assumption that a given capital base would remain intact throughout the life of the loan. While they may not object to the payment of dividends from past and current earnings, they must have the protection of keeping contributed capital in place.[5]

Even the laws against having dividends exceed the total of past and current earnings (retained earnings) may be inadequate to protect creditors. Because retained earnings is merely an accounting concept and in no way certifies the current liquidity of the firm, a company paying dividends equal to retained earnings may, in certain cases, jeopardize the operation of the firm. Let us examine Table 18–2.

TABLE 18–2   **Dividend policy considerations**

Cash	$ 1,000,000	Debt	$10,000,000
Accounts receivable . . .	4,000,000	Common stock	10,000,000
Inventory	15,000,000	Retained earnings	15,000,000
Plant and equipment . . .	15,000,000		$35,000,000
	$35,000,000		
		Current earnings	$ 1,500,000
		Potential dividends	15,000,000

Theoretically management could pay up to $15,000,000 in dividends by selling assets even though current earnings are only $1,500,000. In most cases such frivolous action would not be taken; but the mere possibility encourages creditors to closely watch the balance sheets of corporate debtors and, at times, to impose additional limits on dividend payments as a condition for the granting of credit.

---

[5]Of course, on liquidation of the corporation, the contributed capital to the firm may be returned to common stockholders after creditor obligations are met. Normally stockholders who need to recoup all or part of their contributed capital sell their shares to someone else.

Cash Position of the Firm

Not only do retained earnings fail to portray the liquidity position of the firm, but there are also limitations to the use of current earnings to indicate liquidity. As described in Chapter 4, "Financial Forecasting," a growth firm producing the greatest gains in earnings may be in the poorest cash position. As sales and earnings expand rapidly, there is an accompanying buildup in receivables and inventory that may far outstrip cash flow generated through earnings. Note that the cash balance of $1,000,000 in Table 18–2 represents only two thirds of current earnings of $1,500,000. A firm must do a complete funds flow analysis before establishing a dividend policy.

Access to Capital Markets

The medium-to-large-size firm with a good record of performance may have relatively easy access to the financial markets. A company in such a position may be willing to pay dividends now, knowing it can sell new common stock or bonds in the future if funds are needed. Some corporations may even issue debt or stock *now* and use part of the proceeds to ensure the maintenance of current dividends. Though this policy seems at variance with the concept of a dividend as a reward, management may justify its action on the basis of maintaining stable dividends. In the era of the 1980s and early 1990s, only a relatively small percentage of firms had sufficient ease of entry to the capital markets to modify their dividend policy in this regard. Many firms may actually defer the payment of dividends, because they know they will have difficulty in going to the capital markets for more funds.

Desire for Control

Management must also consider the effect of the dividend policy on its collective ability to maintain control. The directors and officers of a small, closely held firm may be hesitant to pay any dividends for fear of diluting the cash position of the firm and forcing the owners to look to outside investors for financing. The funds may be available only through venture capital sources who wish to have a large say in corporate operations.

A larger firm with a broad base of shareholders may face a different type of threat in regard to dividend policy. Stockholders, spoiled by a past record of dividend payments, may demand the ouster of management if dividends are withheld.

Tax Position of Shareholders

While the payment of a cash dividend is generally taxable to the recipient, some feel the burden much more heavily than others. To the wealthy doctor or lawyer, dividend income can be taxed in the 30 to 40 percent range. Even the average taxpayer will probably pay a 15 to 20 percent tax. Contrast this with the corporate recipient (such as General Motors owning Xerox stock), in which

70 percent of the dividend payment is tax exempt. Furthermore, many large institutional investors, such as pension funds and charitable organizations, are tax exempt.

Because of differences among investors' tax rates, certain investor preferences for dividends versus capital gains have been observed in the market. This investor behavior is called the **clientele effect.** Investors in high marginal tax brackets usually prefer companies that reinvest most of their earnings, thus creating more growth in earnings and stock prices and enabling them to pay taxes sometimes *well into the future.* Companies following these dividend policies will most probably be found in the growth and expansion stages (see Figure 18–1). Investors in lower marginal tax brackets will have a greater preference for dividends, since the tax penalty is less at lower marginal tax rates. The clientele effect is also used to explain the advantages of a stable dividend policy that makes investors more certain about the type of return they will receive.

One additional point is important. About every four or five years, Congress (with the president's urging) enacts a new tax law. Shareholders react to the changing tax laws by adjusting their preferences for dividends or capital gains and corporations' boards of directors are sensitive to shareholder preferences for income versus growth.

Now that we have examined the many factors that influence dividend policy, let us track the actual procedures for announcing and paying a dividend. Though dividends are quoted on an annual basis, the payments actually take place over four quarters during the year. For example in 1993, General Electric was expected to pay an annual cash dividend of $2.52. This meant stockholders could expect to receive 63 cents a quarter in dividends. If we divide the annual dividend per share by the current stock price, the result is called the **dividend yield,** which is the percentage return provided by the cash dividend on the current market price. Because General Electric was selling at $91 per share in April 1993, the dividend yield at that time was 2.77 percent ($2.52/$91). Also because General Electric had expected earnings per share of $6.00 for 1993, the **dividend payout** ratio was expected to be 42 percent ($2.52/$6.00).

Three key dates are associated with the declaration of a quarterly dividend: the ex-dividend date, the holder-of-record date, and the payment date.

We must begin with the **holder-of-record date.** On this date the firm examines its books to determine who is entitled to a cash dividend. To have your name included on the corporate books, you must have bought or owned the stock before the **ex-dividend date,** which is four business days before the holder-of-record date. If you bought the stock on the ex-dividend date or later, your name will eventually be transferred to the corporate books, but you will have bought the stock without the quarterly dividend privilege. Thus we say you bought the stock ex-dividend.[6] As an example, a stock with a

Dividend Payment Procedures

---

[6]In this case the old stockholder will receive the dividend.

holder-of-record date of March 5 will go ex-dividend on March 1. You must buy the stock by the last day of February to get the dividend. Investors are very conscious of the date on which the stock goes ex-dividend, and the value of the stock may go down by the value of the quarterly dividend on the ex-dividend date (all other things being equal). Finally, in our example, we might assume the **dividend payment date** is April 2 and checks will go out to entitled stockholders on or about this time.

Stock Dividend

A **stock dividend** represents a distribution of additional shares to common stockholders. The typical size of such dividends is in the 10 percent range, so a stockholder with 10 shares might receive 1 new share in the form of a stock dividend. Larger distributions of 20 to 25 percent or more are usually considered to have the characteristics of a stock split, a topic to be discussed later in the chapter.

Accounting Considerations for a Stock Dividend

Assume that before the declaration of a stock dividend, the XYZ Corporation has the net worth position indicated in Table 18–3.

TABLE 18–3
XYZ Corporation's financial position before stock dividend

Capital accounts	Common stock (1,000,000 shares at $10 par) . .	$10,000,000
	Capital in excess of par	5,000,000
	Retained earnings	15,000,000
	Net worth	$30,000,000

If a 10 percent stock dividend is declared, shares outstanding will increase by 100,000 (10 percent times 1,000,000 shares). An accounting transfer will occur between retained earnings and the two capital stock accounts based on the market value of the stock dividend. If the stock is selling at $15 a share, we will asign $1,000,000 to common stock (100,000 shares times $10 par) and $500,000 to capital in excess of par. The net worth position of XYZ after the transfer is shown in Table 18–4.

TABLE 18–4
XYZ Corporation's financial position after stock dividend

Capital accounts	Common stock (1,100,000 shares at $10)	$11,000,000
	Capital in excess of par	5,500,000
	Retained earnings	13,500,000
	Net worth	$30,000,000

Value to the Investor

An appropriate question might be: Is a stock dividend of real value to the investor? Suppose your finance class collectively purchased $1,000 worth of assets and issued 10 shares of stock to each class member. Three days later it is announced that each stockholder will receive an extra share. Has anyone benefited from the stock dividend? Of course not! The asset base remains the same ($1,000), and your proportionate ownership in the business is unchanged (everyone got the same new share). You merely have more paper to tell you what you already knew.

The same logic is essentially true in the corporate setting. In the case of the XYZ Corporation, shown in Tables 18–3 and 18–4, we assumed 1 million shares were outstanding before the stock dividend and 1.1 million shares afterward. Now let us assume the corporation had aftertax earnings of $6.6 million. Without the stock dividend, earnings per share would be $6.60, and with the dividend $6.00.

$$\text{Earnings per share} = \frac{\text{Earnings after taxes}}{\text{Shares outstanding}}$$

Without stock dividend:

$$= \frac{\$6.6 \text{ million}}{1 \text{ million shares}} = \$6.60$$

With stock dividend:

$$= \frac{\$6.6 \text{ million}}{1.1 \text{ million shares}} = \$6.00 \atop (10\% \text{ decline})$$

Earnings per share have gone down by exactly the same percentage that shares outstanding increased. For further illustration, assuming that Stockholder A had 10 shares before the stock dividend and 11 afterward, what are his or her total claims to earnings? As expected, they remain the same, at $66.

$$\text{Claim to earnings} = \text{Shares} \times \text{Earnings per share}$$

Without stock dividend:

$$10 \times \$6.60 = \$66$$

With stock dividend:

$$11 \times \$6.00 = \$66$$

Taking the analogy one step further, assuming the stock sold at 20 times earnings before and after the stock dividend, what is the total market value of the portfolio in each case?

$$\text{Total market value} = \text{Shares} \times \left(\frac{\text{Price-earnings}}{\text{ratio}} \times \frac{\text{Earnings per}}{\text{share}} \right)$$

Without stock dividend:

$$10 \times (20 \times \$6.60)$$
$$10 \times \$132 = \$1,320$$

With stock dividend:

$$11 \times (20 \times \$6.00)$$
$$11 \times \$120 = \$1,320$$

The total market value is unchanged. Note that if the stockholder sells the 11th share to acquire cash, his or her stock portfolio will be worth $120 less than it was worth before the stock dividend.

Possible Value of Stock Dividends

There are limited circumstances under which a stock dividend may be more than a financial sleight of hand. If, at the time a stock dividend is declared, the cash dividend per share remains constant, the stockholder will receive greater total cash dividends. Assume the annual cash dividend for the XYZ Corporation will remain $1 per share even though earnings per share decline from $6.60 to $6.00. In this instance a stockholder moving from 10 to 11 shares as the result of a stock dividend has a $1 increase in total dividends. The overall value of his total shares may then increase in response to larger dividends.

Use of Stock Dividends

Stock dividends are most frequently used by growth companies as a form of "informational content" in explaining the retention of funds for reinvestment purposes. This was indicated in the discussion of the life cycle of the firm earlier in the chapter. A corporation president may state, "Instead of doing more in the way of cash dividends, we are providing a stock dividend. The funds remaining in the corporation will be used for highly profitable investment opportunities." The market reaction to such an approach may be neutral or slightly positive.

A second use of stock dividends may be to camouflage the inability of the corporation to pay cash dividends and to cover up the ineffectiveness of management in generating cash flow. The president may proclaim, "Though we are unable to pay cash dividends, we wish to reward you with a 15 percent stock dividend." Well-informed investors are likely to react very negatively.

Stock Splits

A **stock split** is similar to a stock dividend, only more shares are distributed. For example, a two-for-one stock split would double the number of shares outstanding. In general, the rules of the New York Stock Exchange and the Financial Accounting Standards Board encourage distributions in excess of 20 to 25 percent to be handled as stock splits.

The accounting treatment for a stock split is somewhat different from that for a stock dividend, in that there is no transfer of funds from retained earnings to the capital accounts but merely a reduction in par value and a proportionate increase in the number of shares outstanding. For example, a two-for-one stock split for the XYZ Corporation would necessitate the accounting adjustments shown in Table 18–5 on page 534.

FINANCE IN ACTION

The Baby Bells and Stock Splits

Because of antitrust proceedings against American Telephone & Telegraph (AT&T), the courts forced AT&T to divest itself of its local phone companies by "spinning off" shares to AT&T's stockholders. On November 21, 1983, the "baby Bells" began trading on the New York Stock Exchange as separate companies along with AT&T. The divestiture of the baby Bells created seven regional phone companies responsible for local phone service with AT&T providing only long-distance service and manufacturing under its Bell Laboratories division.

The changes in communications since 1983 have been quite dramatic and so has the growth in the regional phone companies' stock prices. AT&T common stock was always widely held by individual investors who generally prefer common stock at a price range of between $30 and $80 per share. Since the regional phone companies inherited the same set of stockholders, management assumed the same stockholder preferences existed. As the price of the baby Bells' common stock rose in the bull market of the 1980s, several stock splits or stock dividends initiated by management kept prices in the $30 to $80 range and increased the number of shares outstanding. One result is increased liquidity to stockholders through a broader ownership base of stockholders. Stock

splits not only cause the stock price to be adjusted downward in proportion to the number of new shares, but they also have the same adjustment effect on earnings per share and dividends per share.

In general, most companies are prone to either split their shares or offer sizable stock dividends when the price of the stock rises much above $100 per share. Companies that trade above $100 and those like Berkshire Hathaway that trade for $10,000 to $12,000 per share have stockholders who are primarily institutional investors who are not as sensitive to the level of stock prices as are individual investors.

The following table tracks AT&T and the seven regional phone companies. Some companies' stock prices have performed better than others but they seem to have performed about the same as Ma Bell (AT&T). The table highlights their stock splits, stock prices, shares outstanding, institutional ownership, and total number of shareholders. It appears that most of these phone companies started with about 100 million shares outstanding and every one of them has had at least one stock split since they began trading in late 1983. It is also clear that individual investors still hold the majority of each company's common stock.

Company	Opening Price 11/21/83 Adj. for Splits and Stock Dividends	Stock Price 4/6/93	Stock Splits	Shares Outstanding 1983 (in millions)	1992	Institutional Ownership	Total Shareholders (millions)
AT&T	19.00	57.375	none	1088.962	1335.609	33%	2.60
Ameritech	21.00	77.375	3 for 2, 1/23/87 2 for 1, 1/23/89	88.75	269.08	29%	1.04
Bell Atlantic	16.38	55.125	2 for 1, 4/17/86 2 for 1, 5/1/90	99.88	432.91	29%	1.10
Bell South	19.75	56.5	3 for 1, 5/22/84 3 for 2, 2/23/87	107.07	493.63	25%	1.30
Nynex	30.25	90.875	2 for 1, 4/30/86	100.77	206.12	36%	1.10
Pacific Telesis	12.88	48.25	2 for 1, 6/9/86 2 for 1, 3/24/87	101.92	404.35	36%	1.10
Southwestern Bell	20.63	78	3 for 1, 5/22/87	100.23	299.65	37%	1.05
U.S. West	14.00	43.75	2 for 1, 5/28/86 2 for 1, 5/2/90	93.78	413.40	40%	0.90

TABLE 18–5
XYZ Corporation before and after stock split

Before	
Common stock (1 million shares at $10 par) . .	$10,000,000
Capital in excess of par	5,000,000
Retained earnings	15,000,000
	$30,000,000
After	
Common stock (2 million shares at $5 par) . .	$10,000,000
Capital in excess of par	5,000,000
Retained earnings	15,000,000
	$30,000,000

In this case all adjustments are in the common stock account. Because the number of shares are doubled and the par value halved, the market price of the stock should drop proportionately. There has been much discussion in the financial literature about the impact of a split on overall stock value. While there might be some positive benefit, that benefit is virtually impossible to capture after the split has been announced. Perhaps a $66 stock will drop only to $36 after a two-for-one split, but one must act very early in the process to benefit.

The primary purpose of a stock split is to lower the price of a security into a more popular trading range. A stock selling for over $50 per share may be excluded from consideration by many small investors. Splits are popular because only the stronger companies that have witnessed substantial growth in market price are in a position to participate in them.

As examples, during 1990 Coca-Cola and Harley-Davidson split their common stock two for one because rising earnings over the previous five years had pushed the stock price higher than management wanted in order to maintain liquid trading and also keep the price within reach of the individual investor.

In the real world example on page 533, we provide a look at stock splits and the regional phone companies since the AT&T breakup.

Repurchase of Stock as an Alternative to Dividends

A firm with excess cash and inadequate investment opportunities may choose to make a **corporate stock repurchase** of its own shares in the market, rather than pay a cash dividend. For this reason, the stock repurchase decision may be thought of as an alternative to the payment of cash dividends.

The benefits to the stockholder are equal under either alternative, at least in theory. For purposes of study, assume the Morgan Corporation's financial position may be described by the data in Table 18–6.

The firm has $2 million in excess cash, and it wishes to compare the value to stockholders of a $2 cash dividend (on the million shares outstanding) as opposed to spending the funds to repurchase shares in the market. If the cash dividend is paid, the shareholder will have $30 in stock and the $2 cash dividend. On the other hand, the $2 million may be used to repurchase

TABLE 18–6
**Financial data of
Morgan Corporation**

Earnings after taxes	$3,000,000
Shares	1,000,000
Earnings per share	$3
Price-earnings ratio	10
Market price per share	$30
Excess cash	$2,000,000

shares at slightly over market value (to induce sale).[7] The overall benefit to stockholders is that earnings per share will go up as the number of shares outstanding is decreased. If the price-earnings ratio of the stock remains constant, then the price of the stock should also go up. If a purchase price of $32 is used to induce sale, then 62,500 shares will be purchased.

$$\frac{\text{Excess funds}}{\text{Purchase price per share}} = \frac{\$2,000,000}{\$32} = 62,500 \text{ shares}$$

Total shares outstanding are reduced to 937,500 (1,000,000 − 62,500). Revised earnings per share for the Morgan Corporation become:

$$\frac{\text{Earnings after taxes}}{\text{Shares}} = \frac{\$3,000,000}{937,500} = \$3.20$$

Since the price-earnings ratio for the stock is 10, the market value of the stock should go to $32. Thus we see that the consequences of the two alternatives are presumed to be the same.

(1) **Funds Used for Cash Dividend**	(2) **Funds Used to Repurchase Stock**
Market value per share $30	
Cash dividend per share. . . . <u>2</u>	
$32	Market value per share $32

In either instance the total value is presumed to be $32. Theoretically the stockholder would be indifferent with respect to the two alternatives.

Before passage of the Tax Reform Act of 1986, a clear tax advantage would have been associated with the repurchase decision, because the $2 gain could possibly qualify as a long-term capital gain. Such gains were taxed at 40 percent of the normal rate. Since capital gains now receive only minimal preferential tax treatment, the aftertax consequences of a $2 dividend or $2 increase in value are not as significant.[8] Nevertheless, there are valid reasons for stock repurchases.

---

[7]To derive the desired equality between the two alternatives, the purchase price for the new shares should equal the current market price plus the proposed cash dividend under the first alternative ($30 + $2 = $32).

[8]It can be pointed out that the capital gains treatment can be deferred until the stock is sold. The tax on the cash dividend, on the other hand, is immediately due.

Other Reasons for Repurchase

In addition to using the repurchase decision as an alternative to cash dividends, corporate management may acquire its own shares in the market, because it believes they are selling at a low price. A corporation president who sees his firm's stock decline by 25 to 30 percent over a six-month period may determine the stock is the best investment available to the corporation.

By repurchasing shares the corporation can maintain a constant demand for its own securities and, perhaps, stave off further decline. Stock repurchases by corporations were partially credited with stabilizing the stock market after the 508-point crash on October 19, 1987.

In Table 18–7 we see some enormous stock repurchases announced by major U.S. corporations during the crash year of 1987. In many cases compa-

TABLE 18–7   **Stock repurchases**

	Biggest Announced Stock Buybacks of 1987					
Company	**Common Shares (in millions)**	**Value**		**Company**	**Common Shares (in millions)**	**Value**
General Motors	64.0	$4.72 billion		Procter & Gamble	10.0	810.0 million
Santa Fe Southern Pacific	60.0	3.38 billion		Salomon	21.3	808.7 million
Ford	27.9	2.00 billion		Hewlett-Packard	15.3	750.0 million
Coca-Cola	40.0	1.80 billion		Nynex	10.0	736.3 million
Henley Group	64.5	1.76 billion		Chrysler	27.0	729.0 million
Gencorp	12.5	1.63 billion		Burlington Industries	8.0	640.0 million
IBM	12.9	1.57 billion		Monsanto	8.0	627.0 million
American Express	40.0	1.35 billion		ITT	10.0	625.0 million
Allied-Signal	25.0	1.11 billion		Hospital Corp. of America	12.0	612.0 million
Owens-Illinois	20.0	1.11 billion		Atlantic Richfield	8.3	600.0 million
J.C. Penney	20.0	1.04 billion		Schlumberger	20.0	595.0 million
Hercules	15.0	1.02 billion		Tektronix	15.6	593.2 million
IC Industries	30.8	1.00 billion		Boeing	15.0	592.5 million
Merck	5.4	1.00 billion		Kimberly-Clark	9.0	547.5 million
Philip Morris	10.0	933.5 million		Kraft	10.0	547.5 million
Bristol-Myers	25.0	925.0 million		Eaton	8.5	500.0 million
NCR	14.0	825.3 million		Kmart	17.9	500.0 million

Note: Figures represent announcements, not actual purchases, and may include more than one announcement. Values are actual dollar amounts when available or estimates based on closing prices before announcements. Reprinted by permission of *The Wall Street Journal,* © Dow Jones and Company, Inc., January 4, 1987, p. 8B. All rights reserved.
Source: Merrill Lynch & Co.

nies may take years to complete stock repurchases, and they may time the repurchase depending on stock price behavior. During 1992 Coca-Cola and Philip Morris, companies featured in Table 18–7, announced buybacks that would continue throughout 1993 and longer. Figure 18–3 gives a multi-

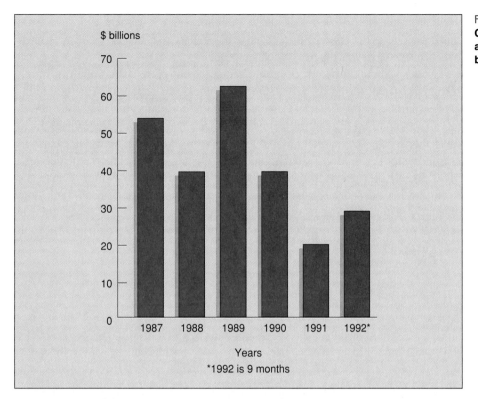

FIGURE 18–3
Common stock buyback announcements (in billions of dollars)

year perspective on the dollars expended on corporate share repurchases from 1987 through the third quarter of 1992.

Reacquired shares may also be used for employee stock options or as part of a tender offer in a merger or an acquisition. Firms may also reacquire part of their shares as a protective device against being taken over as a merger candidate.

There is one caveat for firms that continually repurchase their own shares. Some analysts may view the action as a noncreative use of funds. The analysts may say, "Why aren't the funds being used to develop new products or to modernize plant and equipment?" Thus it is important that the corporation carefully communicate the reason(s) for the repurchase decision to analysts and shareholders—such as the fact that the stock is a great bargain at its current price.

Dividend Reinvestment Plans

Years ago, many companies started **dividend reinvestment plans** for their shareholders. These plans take various forms, but basically they provide the investor with an opportunity to buy additional shares of stock with the cash dividend paid by the company. Some plans will sell treasury stock or authorized but unissued shares to the stockholders. With this type of plan, the company is the beneficiary of increased cash flow, since dividends paid are returned to the company for reinvestment in common stock. These types of plans have been very popular with cash-short public utilities, and very often very often public utilities will allow shareholders a 5 percent discount from market value at the time of purchase. This is justified, because no investment banking or underwriting fees need be paid.

Under a second popular dividend reinvestment plan, the company's transfer agent, usually a bank, buys shares of stock in the market for the stockholder. This plan provides no cash flow for the company; but it is a service to the shareholder, who benefits from much lower transaction costs, the right to own fractional shares, and more flexibility in choosing between cash and common stock. Usually a shareholder can also add cash payments of between $500 and $1,000 per month to his or her dividend payments and receive the same lower transaction costs. Shareholder accounts are kept at the bank, and quarterly statements are provided. Shares will be sent out to stockholders on request or will be sold on request for a commission that is usually lower than that charged by a broker.

Summary

The first consideration in the establishment of a dividend policy is the firm's ability to reinvest the funds versus that of the stockholder. To the extent that the firm is able to earn a higher return, reinvestment of retained earnings may be justified. However, we must temper this "highest return theory" with a consideration of stockholder preferences and the firm's need for earnings retention and growth as presented in the life cycle growth curve.

Stockholders may be given a greater payout than the optimum determined by rational analysis in order to resolve their uncertainty about the future and for informational content purposes. Conversely stockholders may prefer a greater than normal retention in order to defer the income tax obligation associated with cash dividends. Another important consideration in establishing a dividend policy may be the stockholders' desire for steady dividend payments.

Other factors influencing dividend policy are legal rules relating to maximum payment, the cash position of the firm, and the firm's access to capital markets. One must also consider the desire for control by corporate management and stockholders.

An alternative (or a supplement) to cash dividends may be the use of stock dividends and stock splits. While neither of these financing devices directly changes the intrinsic value of the stockholders' position, they may provide communication to stockholders and bring the stock price into a more acceptable trading range. A stock dividend may take on some actual value when total cash dividends are allowed to increase. Nevertheless, the alert investor will watch for abuses of stock dividends—situations in which the corporation indicates that something of great value is occurring when, in fact, the new shares that are created merely represent the same proportionate interest for each shareholder.

The decision to repurchase shares may be thought of as an alternative to the payment of a cash dividend. Decreasing shares outstanding will cause earnings per share, and perhaps the market price, to go up. The increase in the market price may be equated to the size of the cash dividend forgone.

Many firms are now offering stockholders the option of reinvesting cash dividends in the company's common stock. Cash-short companies have been using dividend reinvestment plans to raise external funds. Other companies simply provide a service to stockholders by allowing them to purchase shares in the market for low transaction costs.

List of Terms

marginal principle of retained
   earnings   522
life cycle   522
residual theory of dividends   524
information content of
   dividends   524
clientele effect   529
dividend yield   529

dividend payout   529
holder-of-record date   529
ex-dividend date   529
dividend payment date   530
stock dividend   530
stock split   532
corporate stock repurchase   534
dividend reinvestment plans   537

Discussion Questions

1. How does the marginal principle of retained earnings relate to the returns that a stockholder may make in other investments?
2. Discuss the difference between a passive and an active dividend policy.
3. How does the stockholder, in general, feel about the relevance of dividends?
4. Explain the relationship between a company's growth possibilities and its dividend policy.
5. Since initial contributed capital theoretically belongs to the stockholders, why are there legal restrictions on paying out the funds to the stockholders?
6. Discuss how desire for control may influence a firm's willingness to pay dividends.
7. If you buy stock on the ex-dividend date, will you receive the upcoming quarterly dividend?
8. How is a stock split (versus a stock dividend) treated on the financial statements of a corporation?
9. Why might a stock dividend or a stock split be of limited value to an investor?
10. Does it make sense for a corporation to repurchase its own stock? Explain.
11. What advantages to the corporation and the stockholder do dividend reinvestment plans offer?

Problems

Payout ratio

1. Moon and Sons, Inc., earned $120 million last year and retained $72 million. What is the payout ratio?

Dividends and retained earnings

2. Swank Clothiers earned $640 million last year and had a 30 percent payout ratio. How much did the firm add to its retained earnings?

Policy on payout ratio

3. In doing a five-year analysis of future dividends, Newell Labs, Inc., is considering the following two plans. The values represent dividends per share.

Year	Plan A	Plan B
1	$2.50	$ .80
2	2.55	3.30
3	2.50	.35
4	2.65	2.80
5	2.65	6.60

   a. How much in total dividends per share will be paid under each plan over the five years?

   b. Ms. Carter, the vice-president of finance, suggests that stockholders often prefer a stable dividend policy to a highly variable one. She will assume stockholders apply a lower discount rate to dividends that are stable. The discount rate to be used for Plan A is 10 percent; the discount rate for Plan B is 12 percent. Which plan will provide the higher present value for the future dividends? (Round to two places to the right of the decimal point.)

Growth and dividend policy

4. The following companies have different financial statistics. What dividend policies would you recommend for them? Explain your reasons.

	Mathews Co.	Aaron Corp.
Growth rate in sales and earnings	5%	20%
Cash as a percentage of total assets. . .	15%	2%

Dividend yield

5. The stock of the Pills Berry Corporation is currently selling at $60 per share. The firm pays a dividend of $1.80 per share.

   a. What is the annual dividend yield?

   b. If the firm has a payout rate of 50 percent, what is the firm's P/E ratio?

Dividend yield

6. The shares of Dyer Drilling Co. sell for $60. The firm has a P/E ratio of 15. Forty percent of earnings are paid out in dividends. What is the dividend yield?

Dividends and taxation

7. Goren Bridge Construction Co. has two important stockholders: Ms. Queen and the Ace Corporation. Ms. Queen is in a 31 percent

marginal tax bracket, while the Ace Corporation is in a 36 percent bracket.

   a. If Ms. Queen receives $3.80 in cash dividends, how much in taxes (per share) will she pay?

   b. If the Ace Corporation receives $3.80 in cash dividends, how much in taxes (per share) will it pay? (Please review the partial exemption accorded to corporate recipients of cash dividends in Table 17–3.) Round all answers to two places to the right of the decimal point.

8. Peabody Mining Company's common stock is selling for $50 the day before the stock goes ex-dividend. The annual dividend yield is 5.6 percent, and dividends are distributed quarterly. Based solely on the impact of the cash dividend, by how much should the stock go down on the ex-dividend date? What will the new price of the stock be?

        Ex-dividends and stock price

9. Below are the earnings per share and the dividends per share of three companies.

        Payout ratio patterns

Alpha Co.		Beta Co.		Delta Co.	
EPS	**DPS**	**EPS**	**DPS**	**EPS**	**DPS**
$4.00	$2.00	$4.00	$2.00	$4.00	$2.00
4.20	2.10	4.20	2.00	4.20	1.50
4.80	2.40	4.80	2.00	4.80	2.00
5.60	2.80	5.60	2.00	5.60	3.00
6.00	3.00	6.00	2.30	6.00	2.00

   a. What are the payout ratios for each company on an annual basis?

   b. Can you explain some of the reasons for such differences in payout patterns?

   c. Which company would you prefer to own as a stockholder? Why? What other kinds of information would you want before you invested your money?

10. Sun Energy Company has the following capital section in its balance sheet. Its stock is currently selling for $5 per share.

        Stock dividend and cash dividend

Common stock (100,000 shares at $1 par) . . .	$100,000
Capital in excess of par	100,000
Retained earnings	200,000
	$400,000

The firm intends to first declare a 10 percent stock dividend and then pay a 30-cent cash dividend (which also causes a reduction of retained earnings). Show the capital section of the balance sheet after the first transaction and then after the second transaction.

Cash dividend policy

11. Rolex Discount Jewelers is trying to determine the maximum amount of cash dividends it can pay this year. Assume its balance sheet is as follows:

Assets	
Cash	$ 350,000
Accounts receivable	900,000
Fixed assets.	1,150,000
Total assets	$2,400,000
Liabilities and Stockholders' Equity	
Accounts payable	$ 395,000
Long-term notes payable.	330,000
Common stock (250,000 shares at $3 par)	750,000
Retained earnings	925,000
Total liabilities and stockholders' equity . . .	$2,400,000

a. From a legal perspective, what is the maximum amount of dividends per share the firm could pay? Is this realistic?

b. In terms of cash availability, what is the maximum amount of dividends per share the firm could pay?

c. Assume the firm earned an 18 percent return on stockholders' equity. If the board wishes to pay out 50 percent of earnings in the form of dividends, how much will dividends per share be?

Dividends and stockholder wealth maximization

12. The Vinson Corporation has earnings of $500,000, with 250,000 shares outstanding. Its P/E ratio is 20. The firm is holding $300,000 of funds to invest or pay out in dividends. If the funds are retained, the aftertax return on investment will be 15 percent, and this will add to present earnings. The 15 percent is the normal return anticipated for the corporation, and the P/E ratio would remain unchanged. If the funds are paid out in the form of dividends, the P/E ratio will increase by 10 percent, because the stockholders in this corporation have a preference for dividends over retained earnings. Which plan will maximize the market value of the stock?

Stock split and its effect

13. The Wallace Corporation has done very well in the stock market during the last three years—its stock has risen from $18 per share to $44 per share. Its current statement of net worth is:

Common stock (3 million shares issued at a par value of $10 per share, 9 million shares authorized)	$30,000,000
Paid-in capital in excess of par.	15,000,000
Retained earnings	45,000,000
Net worth	$90,000,000

a. What changes would occur in the statement of net worth after a two-for-one stock split?

b. What would the statement of net worth look like after a three-for-one stock split?

c. Assume Wallace Corporation earned $6 million. What would its earnings per share be before and after the two-for-one stock split?

d. What would the price per share be before and after the two-for-one and the three-for-one stock splits? (Assume the price-earnings ratio of 22 stays the same.)

e. Should a stock split change the price-earnings ratio for Wallace?

14. Slick Products sells marked playing cards to blackjack dealers. It has not paid a dividend in many years but is currently contemplating some kind of dividend. The capital accounts for the firm are:

Stock dividend and its effect

Common stock (150,000 shares at $1 par) . .	$150,000
Capital paid in excess of par	150,000
Retained earnings.	400,000
Net worth	$700,000

The company's stock is selling for $6 per share, and it earned $0.60 per share this year, indicating a P/E ratio of 10.

a. What adjustments would have to be made to the capital accounts for a 10 percent stock dividend?

b. What adjustments would be made to EPS and the stock price? (Assume the P/E ratio remains constant.)

c. How many shares would an investor end up with if he or she originally had 100 shares?

d. What is the investor's total investment worth before and after the stock dividend if the P/E ratio remains constant? (There may be a small difference due to rounding.)

e. Has Slick Products pulled a magic trick, or has it given the investor something of value? Explain.

15. The Lomax Corporation has $4 million in earnings after taxes and 1 million shares outstanding. The stock trades at a P/E of 10. The firm has $3 million in excess cash.

Cash dividend versus stock repurchase

a. Compute the current price of the stock.

b. If the $3 million is used to pay dividends, how much will dividends per share be?

c. If the $3 million is used to repurchase shares in the market at a premium price of $43 per share, how many shares will be reacquired? (Round to the nearest share.)

d. What will the new earnings per share be? (Round to the nearest cent.)

e. If the P/E remains constant, what will the new price of the securities be? By how much, in terms of dollars, did the repurchase increase the stock price?

f. Has the stockholder's total wealth changed as a result of the stock repurchase as opposed to the cash dividend?

g. Given the passage of recent tax legislation, is there any major tax advantage to capital appreciation versus the receipt of cash dividends?

h. What are some other reasons a corporation may wish to repurchase its own shares in the market?

Retaining funds versus paying them out

16. The Majestic Corporation has the following pattern of net income each year and associated capital expenditure projects for which the firm can earn a higher return than the stockholders could earn if the funds were paid out in the form of dividends.

Year	Net Income	Profitable Capital Expenditure
1	$ 5 million	$4 million
2	8 million	6 million
3	10 million	8 million
4	7 million	7 million
5	12 million	5 million

The Majestic Corporation has 1 million shares outstanding (the following questions are separate from each other).

a. If the marginal principle of retained earnings is applied, how much in total cash dividends will be paid over the five years?

b. If the firm simply uses a payout ratio of 40 percent of net income, how much in total cash dividends will be paid?

c. If the firm pays a 10 percent stock dividend in years 2 through 5 and also pays a cash dividend of $2.50 per share for each of the five years, how much in total dividends will be paid?

d. Assume the payout ratio in each year is to be 30 percent of net income and the firm will pay a 20 percent stock dividend in years 2 through 5, how much will dividends per share for each year be?

Selected References

Ang, James S. "Do Dividends Matter? A Review of Corporate Dividend Theories and Evidence." *Monograph Series in Finance and Economics* (1987), pp. 1–58.

Asquith, Paul, and David W. Mullins, Jr. "Signaling With Dividends, Stock Purchases, and Equity Issues." *Financial Management* 15 (Autumn 1986), p. 2744.

Baker, H. Kent, Gail E. Farrelly, and Richard B. Edelman. "A Survey of Management Views on Dividend Policy." *Financial Management* 14 (Autumn 1985), pp. 78–84.

Born, Jeffery A., James T. Moser, and Dennis T. Officer. "Changes in Dividend Policy and Subsequent Earnings." *Journal of Portfolio Management* 14 (Summer 1988), pp. 56–62.

Chang, Rosita P., and Ghon S. Rhee. "The Impact of Personal Taxes on Corporate Dividend Policy and Capital Structure Decisions." *Financial Management* 19 (Summer 1990), pp. 21–31.

De Angelo, Harry, Linda De Angelo, and Douglas J. Skinner. "Dividends and Losses." *Journal of Finance* 47 (December 1992), pp. 1837–63.

Gehr, Adam K., Jr. "A Bias in Dividend Discount Models." *Financial Analysts Journal* 48 (January–February 1992), pp. 75–80.

Gordon, Myron J. "Optimum Investment and Financing Policy." *Journal of Finance* 18 (May 1963), pp. 264–72.

Grinblatt, Mark S., Ronald W. Masulis, and Sheridan Titman. "The Valuation Effect of Stock Splits and Stock Dividends." *Journal of Financial Economics* 13 (December 1984), pp. 461–90.

Healy, Paul M., and Krishna G. Palepu. "Earnings Information Conveyed by Dividend Initiations and Omissions." *Journal of Financial Economics* 21 (September 1988), pp. 149–75.

Impson, C. Michael, and Imre Karafiath. "A Note on the Stock Market Reaction to Dividend Announcements." *Financial Review* 27 (May 1992), pp. 259–71.

Kalay, Avner. "Stockholder–Bondholder Conflict and Dividend Constraints." *Journal of Financial Economics* 59 (July 1982), pp. 211–33.

Lintner, John. "Distribution of Income of Corporations among Dividends, Retained Earnings, and Taxes." *American Economic Review* 46 (May 1956), pp. 97–113.

Miller, Merton H., and Franco Modigliani. "Dividend Policy, Growth, and the Valuation of Shares." *Journal of Business* 34 (October 1961), pp. 411–33.

Pettit, R. Richardson. "Dividend Announcements, Security Performance, and Capital Market Efficiency." *Journal of Finance* 27 (December 1972), pp. 993–1007.

Scholes, Myron S., and Mark A. Wolfson. "Decentralized Investment Banking: The Case of Discount Dividend-Reinvestment and Stock-Purchase Plans." *Journal of Financial Economics* 24 (September 1989), pp. 7–35.

Solomon, Ezra. *The Theory of Financial Management.* New York: Columbia University Press, 1963.

Talmor, Eli, and Sheridan Titman. "Taxes and Dividend Policy." *Financial Management* 19 (Summer 1990), pp. 32–35.

Convertibles and Warrants

CHAPTER CONCEPTS

1 Convertible securities can be converted to common stock at the option of the owner.

2 Because these securities can be converted to common stock, they may move with the value of common stock.

3 Another feature of convertibles is that they receive a fixed rate of return before being converted.

4 Warrants are similar to convertibles in that they give the warrant holder the right to acquire common stock.

5 Accountants require that the potential effect of convertibles and warrants on earnings per share be reported on the income statement.

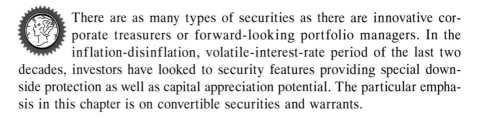 There are as many types of securities as there are innovative corporate treasurers or forward-looking portfolio managers. In the inflation-disinflation, volatile-interest-rate period of the last two decades, investors have looked to security features providing special downside protection as well as capital appreciation potential. The particular emphasis in this chapter is on convertible securities and warrants.

Convertible Securities

A **convertible security** is a bond or share of preferred stock that can be converted, at the option of the holder, into common stock. Thus the owner has a fixed income security that can be transferred into common stock if and when the affairs of the firm indicate such a conversion is desirable. Even though convertible securities are most often converted into common stock, during the 1980s and early 1990s, some convertible preferred stock was created that was exchangeable, in turn, into convertible bonds, which were then convertible into common stock. Additionally, when a company is merged with another company, sometimes the convertible securities of the acquired company may become convertible into common stock of the surviving company. While these departures from the norm are interesting, in this chapter, we focus on convertible bonds (debentures) that result in the potential for common stock ownership and recognize that the same principles apply to other forms of convertibles.

When a convertible debenture is initially issued, a **conversion ratio** to common stock is specified. The ratio indicates the number of shares of common stock into which the debentures may be converted. Assume that in 1993 the Williams Company issued $10 million of 25-year, 6 percent convertible debentures, with each $1,000 bond convertible into 20 shares of common stock. The conversion ratio of 20 may also be expressed in terms of a **conversion price.** To arrive at the conversion price, we divide the par value of the bond by the conversion ratio of 20. In the case of the Williams Company, the conversion price is $50. Conversely the conversion ratio may also be found by dividing the par value by the conversion price ($1,000/$50 = 20).

Value of the Convertible Bond

As a first consideration in evaluating a convertible bond, we must examine the value of the conversion privilege. In the above case, we might assume that the common stock is selling at $45 per share, so the total **conversion value** is $900 ($45 × 20). Nevertheless, the bond may sell for par or face value ($1,000) in anticipation of future developments in the common stock and because interest payments are being received on the bonds. With the bond selling for $1,000 and a $900 conversion value, the bond would have a $100 **conversion premium,** representing the dollar difference between market value and conversion value. The conversion premium generally will be influenced by the expectations of future performance of the common stock. If investors are optimistic about the prospects of the common stock, the premium may be large.

If the price of the common stock really takes off and goes to $60 per share, the conversion privilege becomes quite valuable. The bonds, which are convertible into 20 shares, will go up to at least $1,200 and perhaps more. Note that you do not have to convert to common immediately, but may enjoy the movement of the convertible in concert with the common.

What happens if the common stock goes in the opposite direction? Assume that instead of going from $45 to $60 the common stock simply drops from $45 to $25—what will happen to the value of the convertible debentures? We know the value of a convertible bond will go down in response to the drop in the common stock, but will it fall all the way to its conversion value of $500 (20 × $25 per share)? The answer is clearly no, because the debenture still has value as an interest-bearing security. If the going market rate of interest in straight debt issues of similar maturity (25 years) and quality is 8 percent, we would say the debenture has a pure bond value of $785.46.[1] The **pure bond value** equals the value of a bond that has no conversion features but has the same risk as the convertible bond being evaluated. Thus a convertible bond has a **floor value**,[2] but no upside limitation. The price pattern for the convertible bond is depicted in Figure 19–1.

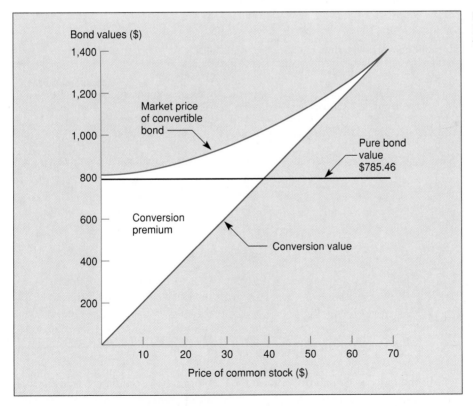

FIGURE 19–1
Price movement pattern for a convertible bond

---

[1]Based on discounting procedures covered in Chapter 10, "Valuation and Rates of Return." Semiannual interest payments are assumed.

[2]The floor value can change if interest rates in the market change. For ease of presentation, we shall assume they are constant for now.

We see the effect on the convertible bond price as the common stock price, shown along the X axis, is assumed to change. Note that the floor (pure bond) value for the convertible is well above the conversion value when the common stock price is very low. As the common stock price moves to higher levels, the convertible bond moves together with the conversion value. Representative information on outstanding convertible bonds is presented in Table 19–1.

Many of the bonds in Table 19–1 are good examples of what is meant by floor value. Notice that for the bonds of Anacomp, Bally, Sterling Software, and Time Warner, the conversion value is less than the pure bond value. As the common stock prices fell, the conversion values declined accordingly, but, because the companies maintained their coupon payments, the market prices of the bonds were equal to the pure bond value or sold above the pure bond value because of expectations of potential rising stock prices. In other words, the pure bond value kept the market price of the bond from falling to the low conversion value levels. This pure bond value is the floor value. This is best illustrated by the Bally Manufacturing bond in Table 19–1 due in 1998 where the market price equals the pure bond value of $790 and the conversion value is only $228.50. If interest rates were to rise, the Bally bond's market value would decline with the pure bond value.

TABLE 19–1   **Pricing pattern for convertible bonds outstanding, April 1993**

Issue, Coupon, and Maturity	Moody's Bond Rating	Conversion Value	Market Value of Bond	Pure Bond Value	Yield to Maturity on Bond	Market Rate for Bond of Similar Maturity and Quality
American Bankers Ins.. . . . . 5.75, 2001	No Rating	$1,337.60	$1,322.50	$1,000	1.50%	5.75%
Anacomp, Inc.. . . . . 13.875, 2002	B3	214.30	1,030.50	1,000	13.60%	13.75%
Bally Mfg. 6.0, 1998	Caa	228.50	790.00	790	11.60%	11.60%
Corning Glass 6.5, 2006	A2	2,662.00	2,698.80	880	NMF*	8.00%
J. P. Morgan. 4.75, 1998	Aa1	3,362.50	3,371.50	880	NMF*	7.25%
Sterling Software 5.75, 2003	B1	696.60	945.00	700	6.60%	10.71%
Time Warner 8.75, 2015	Ba2	641.90	1,047.50	840	8.60%	10.65%

*Not meaningful.
Source: *Value Line Convertibles,* April 12, 1993; *Moody's Bond Record,* March 1993.

In the case of Corning Glass and J. P. Morgan, the bonds are trading well above their pure bond values, indicating their conversion privilege is very valuable and their interest payments are probably not a factor in establishing the bonds' price. Note the J. P. Morgan bond. Since the conversion value ($3,362.50) is greater than the pure bond value ($880) by $2,482.50, we can assume the market price of the bond is being supported by the expectations of a rising stock price. Given the $2,482.50 difference, the pure bond value does not act as a floor value in this common stock price range. Instead the stock price is the deciding factor in determining the bond's market price. The Time Warner bond has a conversion value lower than the pure bond value and a market price higher than the pure bond value. In this case the pure bond value acts as a partial floor value, and the expectation that the stock price might go up also helps create a market price that is at a premium to both the pure bond value and conversion value. A decline in either the pure bond value or the stock price would cause the market value of the Time Warner convertible bond to decrease.

Is This Fool's Gold?

Have we repealed the old risk-return trade-off principle—to get superior returns, we must take larger than normal risks? With convertible bonds, we appear to limit our risk while maximizing our return potential.

Although there is some truth to this statement, there are many qualifications. For example once convertible debentures begin going up in value, say to $1,100 or $1,200, the downside protection becomes pretty meaningless. In the case of the Williams Company in our earlier example in Figure 19–1 at the top of page 550, the floor is at $785.46. If an investor were to buy the convertible bond at $1,200, he would be exposed to $414.54 in potential losses (hardly adequate protection for a true risk averter). Also if interest rates in the market rise, the floor value, or pure bond value, could fall, creating more downside risk.

A second drawback with convertible bonds is that the purchaser is invariably asked to accept below-market rates of interest on the debt instrument. The interest rate on convertibles is generally one third below that for instruments in a similar risk class at time of issue. In the sophisticated environment of the bond and stock markets, one seldom gets an additional benefit without having to suffer a corresponding disadvantage.

The student will also recall that the purchaser of a convertible bond normally pays a premium over the conversion value. For example if a $1,000 bond were convertible into 20 shares of common at $45 per share, a $100 conversion premium might be involved initially. If the same $1,000 were invested directly in common stock at $45 per share, 22.2 shares could be purchased. If the shares go up in value, we have 2.2 more shares on which to garner a profit.

Lastly convertibles may suffer from the attachment of a call provision giving the corporation the option of redeeming the bonds at a specified price above par ($1,000) in the future. In a subsequent section, we will see how the corporation can use this device to force the conversion of the bonds into common stock.

None of these negatives is meant to detract from the fact that convertibles carry some inherently attractive features if they are purchased with appropriate objectives in mind. If the investor wants downside protection, he or she should search out convertible bonds trading below par, perhaps within 10 to 15 percent of the floor value. Though a fairly large move in the stock may be necessary to generate upside profit, the investor has the desired protection and some hope for capital appreciation.

Advantages and Disadvantages to the Corporation

Having established the fundamental characteristics of the convertible secuity from the *investor* viewpoint, let us now turn the coin over and examine the factors a corporate financial officer must consider in weighing the advisability of a convertible offer for the firm.

Not only has it been established that the interest rate paid on convertible issues is lower than that paid on a straight debt instrument, but also the convertible feature may be the only device for allowing smaller corporations access to the bond market. In this day of debt-ridden corporate balance sheets, investor acceptance of new debt may be contingent on a special sweetener, such as the ability to convert to common.

Convertible debentures are also attractive to a corporation that believes its stock is currently undervalued. You will recall in the case of the Williams Company, $1,000 bonds were convertible into 20 shares of common stock at a conversion price of $50. Since the common stock had a current price of $45 and new shares of stock might be sold at only $44,[3] the corporation effectively received $6 over current market price, assuming future conversion. Of course, one can also argue that if the firm had delayed the issuance of common stock or convertibles for a year or two, the stock might have gone up from $45 to $60 and new common stock might have been sold at this lofty price.

To translate this to overall numbers for the firm, if a corporation needs $10 million in funds and offers straight stock now at a net price of $44, it must issue 227,273 shares ($10 million shares/$44). With convertibles, the number of shares potentially issued is only 200,000 shares ($10 million/$50). Finally if no stock or convertible bonds are issued now and the stock goes up to a level at which new shares can be offered at a net price of $60, only 166,667 shares will be required ($10 million/$60).

Table 19–2 demonstrates the company's ability to sell stock at premium prices through the use of convertible bonds. The typical convertible bond,

TABLE 19–2
Characteristics of convertible bonds

Yield to maturity	8.5%
Years to maturity	22.9
Size	$50.4 million
Investment value grade	Ba Moody's Rating
Initial premium over conversion value	20.0%

[3]There is always a bit of underpricing to ensure the success of a new offering.

according to *Value Line Convertibles,* had a 20 percent conversion premium at issue. The table also provides a composite picture of the yield to maturity, years to maturity, size, and investment rating. Notice that the average size of convertibles is quite small, with an average offering of only $50.4 million per issue. The typical nonconvertible issue is well in excess of $100 million. This is, partially, because many small companies with less than a top-grade credit rating are primary issuers of convertible bonds.

Another matter of concern to the corporation is the accounting treatment accorded to convertibles. In the funny-money days of the conglomerate merger movement of the 1960s, corporate management often chose convertible securities over common stock, because the convertibles had a nondilutive effect on earnings per share. As is indicated in a later section on reporting earnings for convertibles, the rules were changed in 1969, and this is no longer the case.

Inherent in a convertible issue is the presumed ability of the corporation to force the security holder to convert the present instrument to common stock. We will examine this process.

Forcing Conversion

How does a corporation, desirous of shifting outstanding debt to common stock, force conversion? The principal device is the call provision, as discussed in Chapter 16, "Long-Term Debt and Lease Financing." When the value of the common stock goes up, the convertible security will move in a similar fashion. Table 19–3 indicates that convertible debentures may go up substantially in value. Some particularly successful convertibles have more than quadrupled in price.

If one of these companies wanted to call in the bonds to force conversion, this is how it would work. As an example we will use Bank of New York's 7.5 percent bond due in 2001, the first bond listed in Table 19–3. At the time of issue, the corporation established a future privilege for calling in the bond

TABLE 19–3   **Successful convertible bonds not yet called as of April 1993**

Issue, Coupon, and Maturity	Moody's Bond Rating	Current Market Price	1993 Price Range High	1993 Price Range Low	Current Call Price	Current Yield	Dividend Yield
Bank of New York Co. 7.5, 2001	Baa1	$1,455.00	$1,610.00	$1,440.00	$1,037.50	5.15%	2.70%
Greyhound Lines. 8.5, 2007	B3	1,540.00	1,540.00	1,140.00	1,059.50	5.50%	nil
Hercules Inc.. . . . . 6.5, 1999	A3	2,110.60	1,560.00	1,400.00	1,006.50	3.10%	3.00%
International Gaming Tech.. 5.5, 2001	B1	4,050.00	4,050.00	3,240.00	844.14	1.40%	nil
Piedmont Natural Gas . . . 12.00, 2000	A2	3,088.75	3,088.75	2,741.25	1,043.70	3.90%	nil
PNC Financial Corp.. . . . . 8.25, 2008	A3	2,738.75	2,738.75	2,380.00	1,008.30	3.00%	3.20%

Source: *Value Line Convertibles,* April 12, 1993; *Moody's Bond Record,* March 1993.

at 10 percent above par value—thus the $1,000 debenture was initially redeemable at $1,100. Most bonds have an initial 5 to 10 percent call premium, which declines over time. The Bank of New York bond has risen in value to $1,455.00 per $1,000 bond. The call price has declined annually from its initial value of $1,100 to its current level of $1,037.50. An owner of this bond is entitled to 25.575 shares of stock worth $1,451.38[4] or accepting a call price of $1,037.50. Any rational bondholder will take the 25.575 shares of Bank of New York common stock and thus the higher value. This demonstrates the derivation of the term **forced conversion.** By calling the bond, the Bank of New York would force conversion of debt to equity. This would improve the composition of the balance sheet by decreasing the debt-to-asset ratio. It is also worth noting that the dividend payment on common stock may require less cash outflow than the interest payment on debt, even though interest payments are tax deductible.

Conversion may also be encouraged through a **step-up in the conversion price** over time. When the bond is issued, the contract may specify the following conversion provisions:

	Conversion Price	Conversion Ratio
First five years . . .	$40	25.0 shares
Next three years . .	45	22.2 shares
Next two years . . .	50	20.0 shares
Next five years . . .	55	18.2 shares

At the end of each time period, there is a strong inducement to convert rather than accept an adjustment to a higher conversion price and a lower conversion ratio.

Euro-Convertible Bonds

Over the past 20 years, many companies have been selling convertible bonds to foreign investors, particularly in Europe.[5] The Eurobonds are dollar denominated and sold primarily in Western Europe. Foreign investors like **convertible Eurobonds** because they have the safety of a bond but the chance to grow with U.S. stock prices since they are convertible into a U.S. firm's stock. U.S. companies like Eurobonds because they skirt U.S. capital transfer restrictions and allow companies to raise dollars outside of the United States. Table 19–4 presents some selected convertible Eurobonds.

In the last several years a new phenomenon has occurred in the Euro-convertible bond market. Foreign companies, most notably Japanese compa-

[4]The common stock shares were selling at $56.75. Thus the conversion value was $1,451.38 (25.575 × $56.75). This is also within $4 of the current market price.

[5]Steve Dawson, "A Somber Fifteenth Euro-Convertible Bond Reunion," *Journal of Portfolio Management,* Winter 1985, pp. 85–87.

TABLE 19–4
Selected issues of convertible Eurobonds, April 1993

Issue, Coupon, and Maturity	Moody's Bond Rating	Conversion Value	Market Value of Bond	Call Price
American Brands cv. eurodeb. 7.75, 2002	A3	$1,058.20	$1,120.00	$1,038.75
Eastman Kodak Co. euro c.s.d. 6.375, 2001	Baa1	1,046.00	1,065.00	1,038.20
Genentech, Inc. euro c.s.d. 5.0, 2002	Baa3	474.10	900.00	1,000.00
Goodyear Tire & Rubber Co. cv. eurodeb. 6.875, 2003	Ba1	915.90	1,035.00	1,020.00

Source: *Value Line Convertibles,* April 12, 1993; *Moody's Bond Record,* March 1993.

nies with operations in the United States, have begun to sell Euro-convertible bonds to finance their U.S. operations. Mitsubishi, Bank of Tokyo, and Sony, to name a few, have Euro-convertible bonds outstanding with par values and interest payments in dollars but conversion values expressed in Japanese yen since that is the denominated value of the underlying common stock.

Accounting Considerations with Convertibles

Before 1969 the full impact of the conversion privilege as it applied to convertible securities, warrants (long-term options to buy stock), and other dilutive securities was not adequately reflected in reported earnings per share. Since all of these securities may generate additional common stock in the future, the potential effect of dilution should be considered. Let us examine the unadjusted (for conversion) financial statements of the XYZ Corporation in Table 19–5.

TABLE 19–5

XYZ CORPORATION

1. *Capital section of balance sheet:*

Common stock (1 million shares at $10 par)	$10,000,000
4.5% convertible debentures (10,000 debentures of $1,000; convertible into 40 shares per bond, or a total of 400,000 shares)	10,000,000
Retained earnings	20,000,000
Net worth	$40,000,000

2. *Condensed income statement:*

Earnings before interest and taxes	$ 2,450,000
Interest (4.5% of $10 million)	450,000
Earnings before taxes	2,000,000
Taxes (50%)	1,000,000
Earnings after taxes	$ 1,000,000

3. *Earnings per share:*

$$\frac{\text{Earnings after taxes}}{\text{Shares of common outstanding}} = \frac{\$1,000,000}{1,000,000} = \$1$$

An analyst would hardly be satisfied in accepting the unadjusted earnings per share figure of $1 for the XYZ Corporation. In computing earnings per share, we have not accounted for the 400,000 additional shares of common stock that could be created by converting the bonds. How then do we provide this full disclosure? According to Accounting Principles Board Opinion 15, issued by the American Institute of Certified Public Accountants in 1969 and amended by the Financial Accounting Standards Board's Statement 55 in 1982, we need to compute earnings per share using two different methods when there is potential dilution of a material nature.

1.
$$\text{Primary earnings per share} = \frac{\text{Adjusted earnings after taxes}}{\text{Shares outstanding} + \text{Common stock equivalents}} \quad (19\text{--}1)$$

Common stock equivalents include warrants, other options, and any *convertible securities that paid less than two thirds of the average Aa bond yield at time of issue.*

2.
$$\text{Fully diluted earnings per share} = \frac{\text{Adjusted earnings after taxes}}{\text{Shares outstanding} + \text{Common stock equivalents} + \textit{All convertibles regardless of the interest rate}} \quad (19\text{--}2)$$

The intent in computing both **primary** and **fully diluted earnings per share** is to consider the effect of potential dilution. Common stock equivalents represent those securities that are capable of generating new shares of common stock in the future.[6] Note that convertible securities may or may not be required in computing primary earnings per share, depending on rates, but must be included in computing fully diluted earnings per share.

In the case of the XYZ Corporation in Table 19–5, the convertibles pay 4.5 percent interest. We shall assume that the average Aa bond yield at time of issue was 9 percent, so they are considered as common stock equivalents and are included in both primary and fully diluted earnings per share.

We get new earnings per share for the XYZ Corporation by assuming 400,000 new shares will be created from potential conversion, while at the same time allowing for the reduction in interest payments that would occur as a result of the conversion of the debt to common stock. Since before-tax interest payments on the convertibles are $450,000 for the XYZ Corporation and a 50 percent tax rate is assumed, the aftertax cost is $225,000. The assumption is that this aftertax interest cost will be saved and can be added back to income. Making the appropriate adjustment to the numerator and denominator, we show adjusted earnings per share.

---

[6]Warrants and options are similar to convertibles in that they may be used to acquire common stock. Warrants are discussed in the next section.

$$\text{Primary earnings per share*} = \frac{\text{Adjusted earnings after taxes}}{\text{Shares outstanding} + \text{Common stock equivalents}}$$

$$= \frac{\overset{\textit{Reported earnings}}{\$1,000,000} + \overset{\textit{Interest savings}}{\$225,000}}{1,000,000 + 400,000} = \frac{\$1,225,000}{1,400,000} = \$0.88$$

*Same as fully diluted in this instance.

We see a 12-cent reduction from the earnings per share figure of $1 in Table 19–5. The new figure is the value that a sophisticated security analyst would use.

A **warrant** is an option to buy a stated number of shares of stock at a specified price over a given time period. For example the warrants of Magma Copper, shown in Table 19–6, enable the holder to buy one share of stock at a price of $8.50 any time between April 1993 and November 1995. If the price of Magma Copper common stock goes to $20 or $30 during this period, the warrants will be quite valuable.

Financing through Warrants

TABLE 19–6 **Relationships determining warrant prices, April 1993**

(1) Firm: Place of Warrant Listing and Stock Listing*	(2) Warrant Price	(3) Stock Price	(4) Exercise Price	(5) Number of Shares	(6) Intrinsic Value	(7) Speculative Premium	(8) Due Date
Anacomp Inc. . . . . . . NYSE, OTC	$2.50	$3.75	$1.84	1.000	$1.91	$0.59	11/11/00
Biogen . . . . OTC, OTC	$13.50	$26.63	$20.00	1.000	$6.63	$6.87	06/30/94
Genzyme Corp. . . . . . OTC, OTC	$16.50	$31.75	$19.00	1.000	$12.75	$3.75	12/31/94
Intel (Step Up Warrant)† . OTC, OTC	$23.88	$110.13	$143.00	1.000	none	$0.00	03/13/98
Magma Copper. . . . . . AMEX, AMEX	$9.00	$13.75	$8.50	1.000	$5.25	$3.75	11/30/95
Metropolitan Financial . . NYSE, OTC	$16.50	$19.25	$5.21	1.000	$14.04	$2.46	11/19/00
Smith International A . . . NYSE, OTC	$2.38	$9.75	$8.28	1.000	$1.47	$0.91	02/28/95

*OTC = over-the-counter market; NYSE = New York Stock Exchange; AMEX = American Stock Exchange.
†Exercise price rises to $149 on 5/15/94, to $155 on 3/15/95, to $161 on 3/15/96, and $167 on 3/15/97. Last expiration on 3/13/98.
Source: *Value Line Convertibles,* April 12, 1993.

Warrants are sometimes issued as a **financial sweetener** in a bond offering, and they may enable the firm to issue debt when this would not be otherwise feasible. The warrants are usually detachable from the bond issue, have their own market price, and are generally traded on the New York Stock Exchange or American Stock Exchange. After warrants are exercised, the initial debt to which they are attached remains in existence.

Because a warrant is dependent on the market movement of the underlying common stock and has no "security value" as such, it is highly speculative. If the common stock of the firm is volatile, the value of the warrants may change dramatically.

Tri-Continental Corporation warrants went from ⅟₃₂ to 75¾, while United Airlines warrants moved from 4½ to 126. Of course this is not a one-way street, as holders of LTV warrants will attest as they saw their holdings dip from 83 to 2¼.

Valuation of Warrants

Because the value of a warrant is closely tied to the underlying stock price, we can develop a formula for the **intrinsic value** of a warrant.

$$I = (M - E) \times N \qquad (19\text{--}3)$$

where

I = Intrinsic value of a warrant

M = Market value of common stock

E = Exercise price of a warrant

N = Number of shares each warrant entitles the holder to purchase

Using the data from Table 19–6, we see that Magma Copper common stock is trading at $13.75 in April 1993. Each warrant carries with it the option to purchase one share of Magma Copper common stock at the **exercise price** of $8.50 per share until November 30, 1995. Using Formula 19–3 the intrinsic value is $5.25 or ($13.75 − $8.50) × 1. Since the warrant has time to run and is an effective vehicle for speculative trading, it is selling at $9.00 per warrant. This is $3.75 more than its intrinsic value, and represents a speculative premium well over the warrant's intrinsic value. Investors are willing to pay a premium because a small percentage gain in the stock price may generate large percentage increases in the warrant price. Formula 19–4 demonstrates the calculation of the **speculative premium.**

$$S = W - I \qquad (19\text{--}4)$$

where

S = Speculative premium

W = Warrant price

I = Intrinsic value

For Magma Cooper we use the formula to show the previously stipulated speculative premium of $3.75.

$$\$3.75 = \$9.00 - \$5.25$$

Even if Magma's common stock price were trading at less than the $8.50 exercise price, the warrant might still have some value in the market. Speculators might purchase the warrant in the hope that the common stock would increase sufficiently to make the option provision valuable. As an example the warrants of Intel in Table 19–6 on page 557 are selling at $23.88 despite a stock price almost $33 below the exercise price. Notice that the intrinsic value of the Intel warrant is zero (none) and is not negative when the market price is less than the exercise price. A warrant cannot have a negative intrinsic value. If Intel, the largest manufacturer of computer microchips, continues to rise over the next several years as it has done during 1992 and 1993, the stock price could easily move through the exercise price and the warrant would have an intrinsic value. However, if an investor in Intel warrants pays the current warrant price of $23.88, the common stock would have to rise to $166.88 ($143 + 23.88) to break even on the investment.[7] Because Intel has been known to double in less than a year during profitable times, investors may be willing to speculate that its price will go well above the exercise price before it expires in 1998. There is more than enough potential profit to entice speculators to buy a warrant with a zero intrinsic value. It is this potential to participate in the growth of the common stock that makes warrants attractive additions to bond offerings. Bond investors are often willing to accept lower interest rates on bonds that carry warrants because they know the warrants have potential value that could be far in excess of a larger coupon rate.

The typical relationship between the warrant price and intrinsic value of a warrant is depicted in Figure 19–2. We assume the warrant entitles the holder

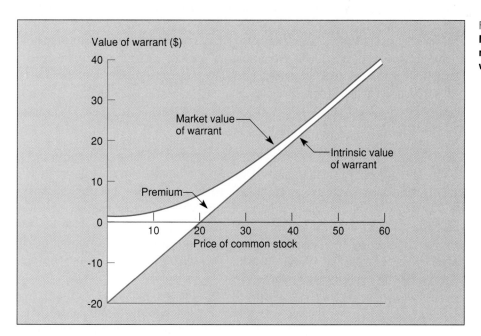

FIGURE 19–2
Market price relationships for a warrant

---

[7]Actually the break-even level becomes even larger as the exercise price goes up.

to purchase one new share of common at $20. Note that, although the intrinsic value of the warrant is theoretically negative at a common stock price between 0 and 20, the warrant still carries some value in the market. Also observe that the difference between the market price of the warrant and its intrinsic value is diminished at the upper ranges of value. Two reasons may be offered for the declining premium.

First the speculator loses the ability to use leverage to generate high returns as the price of the stock goes up. When the price of the stock is relatively low, say $25, and the warrant is in the $5 range, a 10-point movement in the stock could mean a 200 percent gain in the value of the warrant, as indicated in the left-hand panel of Table 19–7.

TABLE 19–7
Leverage in valuing warrants

Low Stock Price	High Stock Price
Stock price, $25; warrant price, $5*	Stock price, $50; warrant price, $30
+ 10-point movement in stock price	+ 10-point movement in stock price
New warrant price, $15 (10-point gain)	New warrant price, $40 (10-point gain)
Percentage gain in warrant $= \dfrac{\$10}{\$5} \times 100 = 200\%$	Percentage gain in warrant $= \dfrac{\$10}{\$30} \times 100 = 33\%$

*The warrant price would, of course, be greater than $5, because of the speculative premium. Nevertheless, we use $5 for ease of computation.

At the upper levels of stock value, much of this leverage is lost. At a stock value of $50 and a warrant value of approximately $30, a 10-point movement in the stock would produce only a 33 percent gain in the warrant as indicated in the right panel of Table 19–7.

Another reason speculators pay a very low premium at higher stock prices is that there is less downside protection. A warrant selling at $30 when the stock price is $50 is more vulnerable to downside movement than is a $5 to $10 warrant when the stock is in the 20s.

Use of Warrants in Corporate Finance

Let us judge the suitability of warrants for corporate financing purposes. As previously indicated, warrants may allow for the issuance of debt under difficult circumstances. While a straight debt issue may not be acceptable or may be accepted only at extremely high rates, the same security may be well received because detachable warrants are included. Warrants may also be included as an add-on in a merger or acquisition agreement. A firm might offer $20 million in cash plus 10,000 warrants in exchange for all the outstanding shares of the acquisition candidate.

The use of warrants has traditionally been associated with such aggressive high-flying firms as speculative real estate investment companies, airlines, and conglomerates. However, in the 1970s staid and venerable American Telephone & Telegraph came out with a $1.57 billion debt offering, sweetened by the use of warrants.

As a financing device for creating new common stock, warrants may not be as desirable as convertible securities. A corporation with convertible debentures outstanding may force the conversion of debt to common stock through a call, while no similar device is available to the firm with warrants.[8] The only possible inducement might be a step-up in option price—whereby the warrant holder pays a progressively higher option price if he does not exercise by a given date.

As with convertible securities, the potential dilutive effect of warrants must be considered. All warrants are included in computing both primary and fully diluted earnings per share.[9] The accountant must compute the number of new shares that could be created by the exercise of all warrants, with the provision that the total can be reduced by the assumed use of the cash proceeds to purchase a partially offsetting amount of shares at the market price. Assume that warrants to purchase 10,000 shares at $20 are outstanding and that the current price of the stock is $50. We show the following:

Accounting Considerations with Warrants

---

1. New shares created 10,000
2. Reduction of shares from cash proceeds (computed below) . . 4,000
   Cash proceeds—10,000 shares at $20 = $200,000
   Current price of stock— $50
   Assumed reduction in shares outstanding from
     cash proceeds = $200,000/$50 = 4,000
3. Assumed net increase in shares from exercise
   of warrants (10,000 − 4,000) 6,000

In computing earnings per share, we will add 6,000 shares to the denominator, with no adjustment to the numerator. This of course will lead to some dilution in earnings per share. Its importance must be interpreted by the financial manager and security analyst.

Summary

A number of security devices related to the debt and common stock of the firm are popular. Each security offers downside protection or upside potential, or a combination of these features.

A convertible security is a bond or share of preferred stock that can be converted into common stock at the option of the holder. Thus the holder has a fixed income security that will not go below a minimum amount because of the interest or dividend payment feature and, at the same time, he or she has a

---

[8] A number of later financing devices can blur this distinction. See Jerry Miller, "Accounting for Warrants and Convertible Bonds," *Management Accounting*, January 1973, pp. 26–28.

[9] Under most circumstances, if the market price is below the option price, dilution need not be considered. APB Opinion 15, par. 35.

security that is potentially convertible to common stock. If the common stock goes up in value, the convertible security will appreciate as well. From a corporate viewpoint, the firm may force conversion to common stock through a call feature and thus achieve a balanced capital structure. Interest rates on convertibles are usually lower than those on straight debt issues.

A warrant is an option to buy a stated number of shares of stock at a specified price over a given time period. The warrant has a large potential for appreciation if the stock goes up in value. Warrants are used primarily as sweeteners for debt instruments or as add-ons in merger tender offers. When warrants are exercised, the basic debt instrument to which they may be attached is not eliminated, as is the case for a convertible debenture. The potential dilutive effect of warrants and convertible securities must be considered in computing earnings per share.

Review of Formulas

1. Primary earnings per share $=\dfrac{\text{Adjusted earnings after taxes}}{\text{Shares outstanding + Common stock equivalents}}$ (19–1)

2. Fully diluted earnings per share $=\dfrac{\text{Adjusted earnings after taxes}}{\text{Shares outstanding + Common stock equivalents + } \textit{All convertibles regardless of the interest rate}}$ (19–2)

3. Intrinsic value of a warrant

$$I = (M - E) \times N \qquad (19\text{–}3)$$

where

I = Intrinsic value of a warrant

M = Market value of common stock

E = Exercise price of a warrant

N = Number of shares each warrant entitles
the holder to purchase

4. Speculative premium of a warrant

$$S = W - I \qquad (19\text{–}4)$$

where

S = Speculative premium

W = Warrant price

I = Intrinsic value

Discussion Questions

1. How can a company force conversion of a convertible bond?

2. What are the basic advantages to the corporation of issuing convertible securities?

3. Why are investors willing to pay a premium over the theoretical value (pure bond value or conversion value)?

4. Why is it said that convertible securities have a floor price?

5. The price of Gordon Corporation 5½ 2018 convertible bonds is $1,390. For the Marshall Corporation, the 6⅜ 2017 convertible bonds are selling at $730.

   a. Explain what factors might cause their prices to be different from their par value of $1,000.

   b. What will happen to each bond's value if long-term interest rates decline?

6. What is meant by a step-up in the conversion price?

7. Explain the difference between primary earnings per share and fully diluted earnings per share.

8. Explain how convertible bonds and warrants are similar and different.

9. Explain why warrants generally are issued (why are they used in corporate finance?).

10. What are the reasons that warrants sell above their intrinsic value?

Problems

Value of warrants

1. Hanson Toy Co. has warrants outstanding that allow the holder to purchase 1.5 shares of stock per warrant at $22 per share (option price). The common stock is currently selling for $28, while the warrant is selling for $12.25 per share.

   a. What is the intrinsic (minimum) value of this warrant?

b. What is the speculative premium on this warrant?

c. What should happen to the speculative premium as the expiration date approaches?

(Assume all bonds in the following problems have a par value of $1,000.)

Features of a convertible bond

2. Plunkett Gym Equipment, Inc., has a $1,000 par value convertible bond outstanding that can be converted into 25 shares of common stock. The common stock is currently selling for $34.75 a share, and the convertible bond is selling for $960.

a. What is the conversion value of the bond?

b. What is the conversion premium?

c. What is the conversion price?

Price of a convertible bond

3. The bonds of Goldman Sack Co. have a conversion premium of $55. Their conversion price is $40. The common stock price is $42. What is the price of the convertible bonds?

Conversion premium for a bond

4. Iowa Meat Packers, Inc., has a convertible bond quoted on the NYSE bond market at 85. (Bond quotes represent percentage of par value. Thus 70 represents $700, 80 represents $800 and so on.) It matures in 15 years and carries a coupon rate of 6½ percent. The conversion price is $20, and the common stock is currently selling for $12 per share on the NYSE.

a. Compute the conversion premium.

b. At what price does the common stock need to sell for the conversion value to be equal to the current bond price?

Conversion value and pure bond value

5. Hughes Technology has a convertible bond outstanding, trading in the marketplace at $835. The par value is $1,000, the coupon rate is 9 percent, and the bond matures in 25 years. The conversion ratio is 20, and the company's common stock is selling for $41 per share. Interest is paid semiannually.

a. What is the conversion value?

b. If similar bonds, which are not convertible, are currently yielding 12 percent, what is the pure bond value of this convertible bond? (Use semiannual analysis as described in Chapter 10.)

Current yield on a convertible bond

6. Western Pipeline, Inc., has been very successful in the last five years. Its $1,000 par value convertible bonds have a conversion ratio of 28. The bonds have a quoted interest rate of 5 percent a year. The firm's common stock is currently selling for $43.50 per share. The current bond price has a conversion premium of $10 over the conversion value.

a. What is the current price of the bond?

b. What is the current yield on the bond (annual interest divided by the bond's market price)?

c. If the common stock price goes down to $22.50 and the conversion premium goes up to $100, what will be the new current yield on the bond?

7. Eastern Digital Corp. has a convertible bond outstanding with a coupon rate of 9 percent and a maturity date of 20 years. It is rated Aa, and competitive, nonconvertible bonds of the same risk class carry a 10 percent return. The conversion ratio is 40. Currently the common stock is selling for $18.25 per share on the New York Stock Exchange.

   a. What is the conversion price?

   b. What is the conversion value?

   c. Compute the pure bond value. (Use semiannual analysis.)

   d. Draw a graph that includes the floor price and the conversion value but not the convertible bond price. For the stock price on the horizontal axis, use 10, 20, 30, 40, and 50.

   e. Which will influence the bond price more—the pure bond value (floor value) or the conversion premium?

Conversion value versus pure bond value

8. Defense Systems, Inc., has convertible bonds outstanding that are callable at $1,070. The bonds are convertible into 33 shares of common stock. The stock is currently selling for $39.25 per share.

   a. If the firm announces it is going to call the bonds at $1,070, what action are bondholders likely to take and why?

   b. Assume that instead of the call feature, the firm has the right to drop the conversion ratio from 33 down to 30 after 5 years and down to 27 after 10 years. If the bonds have been outstanding for 4 years and 11 months, what will the price of the bonds be if the stock price is $40? Assume the bonds carry no conversion premium.

   c. Further assume you anticipate in two months that the common stock price will be up to $42.50. Considering the conversion feature, should you convert now or continue to hold the bond for at least two more months?

Call feature with a convertible bond

9. Assume you can buy a warrant for $5 that gives you the option to buy one share of common stock at $14 per share. The stock is currently selling at $16 per share.

   a. What is the intrinsic value of the warrant?

   b. What is the speculative premium on the warrant?

   c. If the stock rises to $24 per share and the warrant sells at its theoretical value without a premium, what will be the percentage increase in the stock price and the warrant price if you bought the stock and the warrant at the prices stated above? Explain this relationship.

Price appreciation with a warrant

10. The Redford Investment Company bought 100 Cinema Corp. warrants one year ago and would like to exercise them today. The warrants were purchased for $24 each, and they expire when trading ends today (assume there is no speculative premium left). Cinema Corp. common stock is selling today for $50 per share. The option price is $30 and

Profit potential with a warrant

each warrant entitles the holder to purchase two shares of stock, each at the option price.

a. If the warrants are exercised today, what would the Redford Investment Company's dollar profit or loss be?

b. What is the Redford Investment Company's percentage rate of return?

Comparing returns on warrants and common stock

11. Assume in problem 10, Cinema Corp. common stock was selling for $40 per share when the Redford Investment Company bought the warrants.

a. What was the intrinsic value of a warrant at that time?

b. What was the speculative premium per warrant when the warrants were purchased?

c. What would the Redford Investment Company's total dollar profit or loss have been had it invested the $2,400 directly in Cinema Corp.'s common stock one year ago at $40 per share and sold it today at $50 per share?

d. What would the percentage rate of return be on this common stock investment? Compare this to the rate of return on the warrant investment computed in problem 10b.

Return calculations with warrants

12. Harvey Cunningham has $1,200 to invest in the market. He is considering buying 48 shares of the Eagle Corporation at $25 per share. His broker suggests he may wish to consider purchasing warrants instead. The warrants are selling for $6, and each warrant allows him to purchase one share of Eagle Corporation common stock at $23 per share.

a. How many warrants can Mr. Cunningham purchase for the same $1,200?

b. If the price of the stock goes to $35, what would be his total dollar and percentage return on the stock?

c. At the time the stock goes to $35, the speculative premium on the warrant goes to zero (though the intrinsic value of the warrant goes up). What would be Mr. Cunningham's total dollar and percentage return on the warrant?

d. Assuming the speculative premium remains $4 over the intrinsic value, how far would the price of the stock have to fall before the warrant has no value?

Primary earnings per share with convertibles

13. Hughes Technology has net income of $450,000 in the current fiscal year. There are 100,000 shares of common stock outstanding along with convertible bonds, which have a total face value of $1,200,000. The $1,200,000 is represented by 1,200 different $1,000 bonds. Each $1,000 bond pays 6 percent interest and was issued when the average Aa bond yield was 10 percent. The conversion ratio is 20. The firm is in a 34 percent tax bracket. Calculate Hughes' primary earnings per share in accordance with APB Opinion No. 15. Note: To get aftertax savings in interest, multiply the before-tax figure by $(1 - T)$.

14. Using information from problem 13, assume the average Aa bond yield was 8 percent instead of 10 percent at the time the convertible bonds were issued. All other facts are the same.

    a. What are the primary earnings per share for Hughes Technology?

    b. Indicate the value for fully diluted earnings per share.

15. Meyers Business Systems has 2 million shares of stock outstanding. It also has two convertible bond issues outstanding with terms as follows:

1.	9 percent convertible, 1998	$12,000,000
2.	10 percent convertible, 2006	$15,000,000

    The issue with the 9 percent coupon rate was first sold when average Aa bonds were yielding 12 percent and is convertible into 300,000 shares. The issue with the 10 percent coupon rate was first sold when average Aa bonds were yielding 15.5 percent and is convertible into 400,000 shares. Earnings after taxes are $4 million and the tax rate is 50 percent.

    a. Compute both primary and fully diluted earnings per share for Meyers.

    b. Now assume Meyers also has warrants outstanding, which allow the holder to buy 100,000 shares of stock at $20 per share. The stock is currently selling for $40 per share. Compute primary earnings per share considering the possible impact of both the warrants and convertibles.

16. Tulsa Drilling Company has $1 million in 11 percent convertible bonds outstanding. Each bond has a $1,000 par value. The conversion ratio is 40, the stock price is $32, and the bond matures in 10 years. The bonds are currently selling at a conversion premium of $70 over the conversion value.

    a. If the price of Tulsa Drilling Company common stock rises to $42 on this date next year, what would your rate of return be if you bought a convertible bond today and sold it in one year? Assume that on this date next year, the conversion premium has shrunk from $70 to $20.

    b. Assume the yield on similar nonconvertible bonds has fallen to 8 percent at the time of sale. What would the pure bond value be at that point? (Use semiannual analysis.) Would the pure bond value have a significant effect on valuation then?

Primary and fully diluted earnings per share with convertibles

Dilution with both convertibles and warrants

Conversion value and changing pure bond value

COMPREHENSIVE PROBLEMS

The Furgeson Corporation has 1,000 convertible bonds ($1,000 par value) outstanding, each of which may be converted to 50 shares ($20 conversion price). The $1 million worth of bonds has 15 years to maturity. The current

Furgeson Corporation (rates of return on convertible bond investments)

price of the stock is $25 per share. Furgeson's net income in the most recent fiscal year was $300,000. The bonds pay 12 percent interest and were issued when the average Aa bond rate was 13 percent. The corporation has 150,000 shares of common stock outstanding. Current market rates on long-term bonds of equal quality are 14 percent. A 30 percent tax rate is assumed.

a. Compute fully diluted earnings per share.

b. Assume the bonds currently sell at a 5 percent conversion premium over straight conversion value (based on a stock price of $25). However, as the price of the stock increases from $25 to $35 due to new events, there will be an increase in the bond price, but zero conversion premium. Under these circumstances, determine the rate of return on a convertible bond investment after this price change, based on the appreciation in value.

c. Now assume the stock price fell to $15 per share because a competitor introduced a new product. Would the straight conversion value be greater than the pure bond value, based on the interest rates stated above? (See Table 16–3 in Chapter 16 to get the bond value without having to go through the actual computation.)

d. In the case of part c, if the convertible traded at a 20 percent premium over the straight conversion value, would the convertible be priced above the pure bond value?

e. If long-term interest rates in the market go down to 10 percent, while the stock price is at $26, with a 4 percent conversion premium, what would the difference be between the market price of the convertible bond and the pure bond value? Assume 15 years to maturity, and once again use Table 16–3 for part of your answer.

f. If Furgeson were able to retire the convertibles and replace them with 40,000 shares of common stock selling at $25 per share and paying a 6.5 percent dividend yield (dividend to price ratio), would the aftertax cash outflow related to the convertible be greater or less than the cash outflow related to the stock?

I. M. Stern, Inc.
(a call decision with
convertible bonds)

I. M. Stern, Inc., (IMS) has $30 million of convertible bonds outstanding (30,000 bonds at $1,000 par value) with a coupon rate of 10 percent. Interest rates are currently 8 percent for bonds of equal risk. The bonds were originally sold when the average Aa rate was 12 percent, and they have 25 years left to maturity. The bonds may be called at a 10 percent premium over par as well as converted into 25 shares of common stock. The tax rate for the company is 40 percent.

The firm's common stock is currently selling for $49 per share, and it pays a dividend of $4. The expected income for the company is $42 million with 5 million shares of common stock currently outstanding.

Thoroughly analyze this bond and determine whether IMS should call the bond at the 10 percent call premium. In your analysis, consider the following:

a. The impact of the call on primary and fully diluted earnings per share and the common stock price (assume the call forces conversion).

b. The consequences of your decision on financing flexibility.

c. The net change in cash outflows to the company as a result of the call and conversion.

Selected References

Altman, Edward I. "The Convertible Debt Market: Are Returns Worth the Risk?" *Financial Analysts Journal* 45 (July–August 1989), pp. 23–31.

Billingsley, Randall S., Robert E. Lamy, and G. Rodney Thompson. "Valuation of Primary Issue Convertible Bonds." *Journal of Financial Research* 39 (Fall 1986), pp. 251–60.

Calamos, John P. "Investment Opportunities in New-Issue Convertible Bonds." *Cash Flow* 8 (February 1987), pp. 35–37.

Chen, K. C., R. Stephen Sears, and Manucher Shahrokhi. "Pricing Nikkei Put Warrants: Some Empirical Evidence." *Journal of Financial Research* 15 (Fall 1992), pp. 231–51.

Cowan, Arnold R., Nandkumar Nayar, and Ajai K. Singh. "Underwriting Calls of Convertible Securities." *Journal of Financial Economics* 31 (April 1992), p. 269–78.

Dawson, Steve. "A Somber Fifteenth Euro-Convertible Bond Reunion." *Journal of Portfolio Management* (Winter 1985), pp. 85–87.

Dunn, Kenneth B., and Kenneth M. Eades. "Voluntary Conversion of Convertible Securities and the Optimal Call Strategy." *Journal of Financial Economics* 23 (August 1989), pp. 273–301.

Janjigian, Vahan. "The Leverage Changing Consequences of Convertible Debt Financing." *Financial Management* 16 (Autumn 1987), pp. 15–21.

Leonard, David C., and Michael E. Solt. "On Using the Black-Scholes Model to Value Warrants." *Journal of Financial Research* 13 (Summer 1990), pp. 81–92.

Mais, Eric L., William T. Moore, and Ronald C. Rogers. "A Re-Examination of Shareholder Wealth Effects of Calls of Convertible Preferred Stock." *Journal of Finance* 44 (December 1989), pp. 1401–10.

Marr, Wayne M., and G. Rodney Thompson. "The Pricing of New Convertible Bond Issues." *Financial Management* 13 (Summer 1984), pp. 38–40.

Miller, Jerry. "Accounting for Warrants and Convertible Bonds." *Management Accounting,* January 1973, pp. 26–28.

Schwartz, Eduardo S. "The Valuation of Warrants: Implementing a New Approach." *Journal of Financial Economics* 4 (January 1977), pp. 79–94.

Stein, Jeremy C. "Convertible Securities as Backdoor Equity Financing." *Journal of Financial Economics* 32 (August 1992), pp. 3–21.

Vu, Joseph D. "An Empirical Investigation of Calls of Non-Convertible Bonds." *Journal of Financial Economics* 16 (June 1986), pp. 235–65.

P A R T

6

Expanding the Perspective of Corporate Finance Planning

INTRODUCTION

The final two topics, mergers and international finance, are particularly appropriate for the current financial environment. Both have achieved increasing importance as financial managers have attempted to grow and diversify away from traditional product lines and across international borders. • Mergers have long been recognized as offering the potential for risk reduction by combining diversified firms under common con-trol. However, the achievement of such risk reduction can be an elusive process, as overly optimistic planners often find obstacles in their way. The successful merger must be based on realistic expectations and a careful consideration of postmerger performance. We shall evaluate both of these factors in Chapter 20. • The latest merger wave was somewhat unique in that it was populated by such high-quality acquiring firms as Du Pont, General Electric, and Colgate Palmolive. It is also unusual in that many of the merg-ers were unfriendly. That is, the acquired firm did not necessarily wish to be taken over by the acquiring firm. • In the merger chapter, we examine the significant financial and management variables that influence the merger decision, including the price paid, the accounting implications, the stock market effect, and the motivations of the participating parties. The chapter provides an overview of many topics discussed earlier in the text. • The importance of the multinational business firm is considered in Chapter 21. In an

ever shrinking world, the financial manager must be prepared to make decisions that have worldwide effects. As the business firm moves into foreign markets and deals in deutsche marks, Swiss francs, and Japanese yen, the foreign exchange implications of decisions must also be considered. A firm may suddenly have to receive a future payment in a currency that is rapidly declining in value. How is this to be handled? The international financial manager must understand his or her options. • Although foreign investments may carry unusual political and economic risks, they also allow for expanded market potential. Local customs and requirements in regard to taxation and payment of dividends must be carefully examined. • The importance of European Community (EC) 92 is also considered, along with other developments around the world. • Finally international financing arrangements, such as the Eurodollar market and Eurobond market, which were previously touched on in Part 3, are given expanded coverage.

Also the relationship of the multinational firm to foreign stock markets is considered.

External Growth through Mergers

1 Firms engage in mergers for financial motives and to increase operating efficiency.

2 Companies may be acquired through cash purchases or by one company exchanging its shares for another company's shares.

3 The potential impact of the merger on earnings per share and stock value must be carefully assessed.

4 The diversification benefits of a merger should be evaluated.

5 Some buyouts are unfriendly and are strongly opposed by the potential candidate.

Many of the previously discussed points regarding financial planning, risk-return analysis, valuation, capital budgeting, and portfolio management can be examined in the very meaningful context of mergers and acquisitions. To this extent Chapter 20 may be thought of as an integrative chapter for much of the material discussed throughout the text.

There have been a number of major merger movements in the industrial history of the United States, beginning in the late 1890s with the development of the oil, railroad, tobacco, and steel industries and culminating with the merger mania of the late 1970s and 1980s. This last wave of mergers is of particular interest to us because it has significantly influenced the current corporate environment.

The major theme of this latest merger movement is that it is cheaper to acquire other companies than it is to expand through new product development or the purchase of new plant and equipment.

A second significant feature of the modern merger boom has been that the major participants are no longer the "urge to merge" gunslinger conglomerate giants of the 1960s, but rather old and conservative corporations, such as Du Pont, General Electric, and Colgate Palmolive. In addition foreign acquirers, such as British Petroleum, have come on the scene in a big way as foreign companies have opted for U.S. investments. Foreigners seem to be attracted to U.S. companies because of the relatively stable political climate and the fear that the United States will impose import restrictions. This has caused foreigners to either undertake joint ventures with U.S. companies, buy U.S. companies, or build U.S. facilities.

A final development of the latest merger movement has been the unfriendly buyout, in which a major acquiring company identifies a target company and attempts to acquire it without management approval. At first this activity was centered in the oil industry, with unfriendly takeover attempts by T. Boone Pickens of Gulf Oil, Phillips Petroleum, and Union Oil of California (Unocal). Phillips Petroleum and Unocal fended off the takeover by restructuring their balance sheet with a heavy debt load and with strategies designed to reduce the value of the company if the takeover were successful. These self-emasculating strategies are also a form of a poison pill. Gulf was bought by white knight Chevron for a then record $13.3 billion in 1984. Also Texaco bought Getty Oil Company for $10.1 billion right out from under Pennzoil Company. This merger resulted in a lawsuit by Pennzoil, in which the Texas courts ruled in favor of Pennzoil and declared a judgment against Texaco of $10.3 billion. This caused Texaco to file bankruptcy and eventually settle the suit for $3 billion (the largest such payment in U.S. history). Table 20–1 lists the 13 biggest acquisitions of the last decade.

After oil prices tended to drift lower, corporate raiders began looking for other targets with undervalued assets and found companies like MGM, ABC, and Prentice Hall in the fields of movies, broadcasting, and publishing. Then the move was on to retail stores, where hidden real estate values were thought

TABLE 20–1
Largest acquisitions of the past decade

	Target	Buyer	Cost ($ billions)	Year
1.	RJR Nabisco.	Kohlberg Kravis Roberts	$24.7	1989
2.	Kraft.	Philip Morris	13.4	1988
3.	Gulf	Chevron	13.3	1984
4.	Warner Communications . . .	Time Warner	12.6	1990
5.	Squibb.	Bristol-Myers	12.1	1989
6.	Getty	Texaco	10.1	1984
7.	SmithKline.	Beecham	7.9	1989
8.	Standard Oil	British Petroleum	7.8	1987
9.	NCR Corp.	AT&T	7.5	1991
10.	Warner	Time	7.0	1989
11.	MCA Inc.	Matsushita	6.9	1991
12.	Contel Corp.	GTE Corp.	6.8	1991
13.	Security Pacific Corp.	BankAmerica Corp.	5.5	1992

to exist. The wheel next turned to food companies with the acquisition of Kraft and General Foods by Philip Morris. A 10-year rundown of merger activity is presented in Table 20–2.

TABLE 20–2
Ten-year merger completion record: 1983–1992

Year	Number of Transactions	Percent Change (prior year)	Value ($ billions)	Percent Change (prior year)
1983. . .	1,812	—	$ 48.9	—
1984. . .	2,416	+33.3	121.1	+147.7
1985. . .	2,773	+14.8	141.3	+ 16.7
1986. . .	3,803	+37.1	200.7	+ 42.0
1987. . .	3,150	+17.2	171.5	− 14.6
1988. . .	3,310	+ 5.1	232.4	+ 35.5
1989. . .	3,061	− 7.5	244.1	+ 5.0
1990. . .	3,154	+ 3.0	164.3	− 32.7
1991. . .	2,117	−32.9	98.0	− 40.3
1992. . .	2,199	+ 3.9	81.5	− 16.8

Source: "1991 Profile," *Mergers and Acquisitions,* May–June 1992, and "M&A Scoreboard," *Mergers and Acquisitions,* March–April 1993.

By the early 1990s, the merger mania had slowed somewhat. This was due to the difficulty in finding financing as investors and bankers became more cautious about the success of proposed deals in an uncertain economic environment. Nevertheless the corporate merger is still an important topic for discussion, and history has shown that the next major wave of mergers is never far off.

In the following sections, we examine the motives for business combinations; the establishment of negotiated terms of exchange, with the associated accounting implications; and the stock market effect of mergers (including unfriendly takeovers). The final section of the chapter presents the use of holding companies.

FINANCE IN ACTION

Reverse LBOs

During the 1980s leveraged buyouts of publicly listed companies were the rage. In a leveraged buyout, the buyer uses debt to buy all the outstanding common stock of the public company, which then becomes privately held by the new owners who are now in hock up to their ears. Many times the new owners are the old management team who persuaded a lending group to help them buy the company's common stock. Sometimes the new owners are professional buyout specialists such as Kohlberg Kravis Roberts & Co., the firm that helped complete the $24.7 billion leveraged buyout of RJR Nabisco in 1989. Of course most new owners hope to pay off the debt by selling assets and improving cash flow by eliminating corporate

court supervision. Others have returned to the public market with sales of stock. This process has been called a *reverse LBO*. Here are some summary results from 70 LBOs that sold shares between August 31, 1991, and August 31, 1992. The percentage gain or loss reflects the performance of each company's stock price from the time it reentered the public market until August 31, 1992. The average return for the 70 reverse LBOs was 4.2 percent, but the stock price of 38 out of the 70 closed below their initial offering prices by August 31, 1992. Many large banks* such as Bankers Trust ($60.5 billion), Manufacturers Hanover ($44.1 billion), Citicorp ($37.3 billion), and Chase Manhattan ($30.1 billion), who were the four leading lenders for LBOs between 1985

Biggest Winners among Reverse LBOs		Biggest Losers among Reverse LBOs	
Perrigo	+98.4%	Health O Meter Products	−58.0%
Comp USA	+79.2%	Buttrey Food & Drug	−57.1%
R. P. Scherer	+70.1%	Alliance Imaging	−55.9%
Tetra Tech	+66.7%	Menley & James	−54.8%
Lincare Hldg.	+58.9%	AGCO	−48.2%

inefficiency. Their final objective is to end up owning a profitable company that they can then take public again for a nice profit.

Now that the 1990s are here, we have a view of the success and failure of some of these leveraged buyouts. Several, such as Federated Department Stores, Macy's, and Revco Drugs, ended up in bankruptcy and are recovering under

through the first half of 1992, are still recovering from the disappointments and negative returns from this activity. LBOs are still occurring but at a small fraction of the pace of the frantic 1980s.

* Dollar amount after the bank name is the amount of loans made for LBOs from 1985 to 1992.

Motives for Business Combinations

A business combination may take the form of either a merger or a consolidation. A **merger** is defined as a combination of two or more companies in which the resulting firm maintains the identity of the acquiring company. In a **consolidation** two or more companies are combined to form a new entity. A consolidation might be utilized when the firms are of equal size and market power. For purposes of our discussion, the primary emphasis will be on mergers, though virtually all of the principles presented could apply to consolidations as well.

Financial Motives

The motives for mergers and consolidations are both financial and nonfinancial in nature. We examine the financial motives first. As discussed in Chapter 13, a merger allows the acquiring firm to enjoy a potentially desirable **portfolio effect** by achieving risk reduction while perhaps maintaining the firm's rate of return. If two firms that benefit from opposite phases of the business cycle combine, their variability in performance may be reduced. Risk-averse investors may then discount the future performance of the merged firm at a lower rate and thus assign it a higher valuation than was assigned to the separate firms. The same point can be made in regard to multinational mergers. Through merger, a firm that has holdings in diverse economic and political climates can enjoy some reduction in the risks that derive from foreign exchange translation, government politics, military takeovers, and localized recessions.

While the portfolio diversification effect of a merger is intellectually appealing—with each firm becoming a mini-mutual fund unto itself—the practicalities of the situation can become quite complicated. No doubt one of the major forces of the merger wave of the mid-to-late 1960s was the desire of the conglomerates for diversification. The lessons we have learned from the LTVs, the Littons, and others is that too much diversification can strain the operating capabilities of the firm. As one form of evidence on the lack of success of some of these earlier mergers, the ratio of divestitures[1] to new acquisitions was only 11 percent in 1967, but it rose to over 50 percent a generation later. The stock market reaction to divestitures may actually be positive when it can be shown that management is freeing itself from an unwanted or unprofitable division.[2]

A second financial motive is the improved financing posture that a merger can create as a result of expansion. Larger firms may enjoy greater access to financial markets and thus be in a better position to raise debt and equity capital. Such firms may also be able to attract larger and more prestigious investment bankers to handle future financing.

Greater financing capability may also be inherent in the merger itself. This is likely to be the case if the acquired firm has a strong cash position or a low debt-equity ratio that can be used to expand borrowing by the acquiring company.

---

[1] A divestiture is a spin-off or a sell-off of a subsidiary or a division.

[2] J. Fred Weston, "Divestitures: Mistakes or Learning," *Journal of Applied Corporate Finance* 4 (Summer 1989), pp. 68–76.

A final financial motive is the **tax loss carry-forward** that might be available in a merger if one of the firms has previously sustained a tax loss.

In the following example, we assume all the losses can be carried forward. Firm A acquires Firm B, which has a $220,000 tax loss carry-forward. We look at Firm A's financial position before and after the merger. The assumption is that the firm has a 40 percent tax rate.

The tax shield value of a carry-forward is equal to the loss involved times the tax rate ($220,000 × 40 percent = $88,000). Based on the carry-forward, the company can reduce its total taxes from $120,000 to $32,000, and thus it could pay $88,000 for the carry-forward alone (this is on a nondiscounted basis).

	1992	1993	1994	Total Values
Firm A (without merger):				
Before-tax income	$100,000	$100,000	$100,000	$300,000
Taxes (40%)	40,000	40,000	40,000	120,000
Income available to stockholders	$ 60,000	$ 60,000	$ 60,000	$180,000
Firm A (with merger and associated tax benefits):				
Before-tax income	$100,000	$100,000	$100,000	$300,000
Tax loss carry-forward	100,000	100,000	20,000	220,000
Net taxable income	0	0	80,000	80,000
Taxes (40%)	0	0	32,000	32,000
Income available to stockholders	$100,000	$100,000	$ 68,000*	$268,000

*Before tax income minus taxes ($100,000 − $32,000 = $68,000).

As would be expected, income available to stockholders also has gone up by $88,000 ($268,000 − $180,000 = $88,000). Of course Firm B's anticipated operating gains and losses for future years must also be considered in analyzing the deal.

Nonfinancial Motives

The nonfinancial motives for mergers and consolidations include the desire to expand management and marketing capabilities as well as the acquisition of new products. Particularly popular industries in the latest merger movement—in addition to energy-related companies—have been companies in entertainment, retailing, food products, and financial services.

While mergers may be directed toward either **horizontal integration** (that is, the acquisition of competitors) or **vertical integration** (the acquisition of buyers or sellers of goods and services to the company), antitrust policy generally precludes the elimination of competition. For this reason mergers are often with companies in allied but not directly related fields. The pure conglomerate merger of firms in totally unrelated firms is still undertaken, but less frequently than in the past.

Perhaps the greatest management motive for a merger is the possible synergistic effect. **Synergy** is said to occur when the whole is greater than the sum of the parts. This "2 + 2 = 5" effect may be the result of eliminating overlapping functions in production and marketing as well as meshing together various engineering capabilities. In terms of planning related to mergers, there is often a tendency to overestimate the possible synergistic benefits that might accrue.[3]

Motives of Selling Stockholders

Most of our discussion has revolved around the motives of the acquiring firm that initiates a merger. Likewise the selling stockholders may be motivated by a desire to receive the acquiring company's stock—which may have greater acceptability or activity in the marketplace than the stock they hold. Also when cash is offered instead of stock, this gives the selling stockholders an opportunity to diversify their holdings into many new investments. As will be discussed later in the chapter, the selling stockholders generally receive an attractive price for their stock that may well exceed its current market or book value.

In addition officers of the selling company may receive attractive post-merger management contracts as well as directorships in the acquiring firm. In some circumstances they may be allowed to operate the company as a highly autonomous subsidiary after the merger (though this is probably the exception).[4]

A final motive of the selling stockholders may simply be the bias against smaller businesses that has developed in this country and around the world. Real clout in the financial markets may dictate being part of a larger organization. These motives should not be taken as evidence that all or even most officers or directors of smaller firms wish to sell out—a matter that we shall examine further when we discuss negotiated offers versus takeover attempts.

Terms of Exchange

In determining the price that will be paid for a potential acquisition, a number of factors are considered, including earnings, dividends, and growth potential. We shall divide our analysis between cash purchases and stock-for-stock exchanges, in which the acquiring company trades stock rather than paying cash for the acquired firm.

Cash Purchases

The cash purchase of another company can be viewed within the context of a capital budgeting decision. Instead of purchasing new plant or machinery, the

---

[3]T. Hogarty, "The Profitability of Corporate Mergers," *Journal of Business* 43 (July 1970), pp. 317–27.

[4]This is most likely to happen when the acquiring firm is a foreign company.

purchaser has opted to acquire a *going concern*. For example assume the Invest Corporation is analyzing the acquisition of the Sell Corporation for $1 million. The Sell Corporation has expected cash flow (aftertax earnings plus depreciation) of $100,000 per year for the next 5 years and $150,000 per year for the 6th through the 20th year. Furthermore the synergistic benefits of the merger (in this case, combining production facilities) will add $10,000 per year to cash flow. Finally the Sell Corporation has a $50,000 tax loss carryforward that can be used immediately by the Invest Corporation. Assuming a 40 percent tax rate, the $50,000 loss carry-forward will shield $20,000 of profit from taxes immediately. The Invest Corporation has a 10 percent cost of capital, and this is assumed to remain stable with the merger. Our analysis would be as follows:

Cash outflow:

Purchase price	$1,000,000
Less tax shield benefit	
from tax loss carry-forward ($50,000 × 40%) . . .	20,000
Net cash outflow.	$ 980,000

Cash inflows:

Years 1–5: $100,000   Cash inflow
              10,000   Synergistic benefit
            $110,000   Total cash inflow

Present value of $110,000 × 3.791 . . . . $ 417,010

Years 6–20: $150,000   Cash inflow
              10,000   Synergistic benefit
            $160,000   Total cash inflow

Present value of $160,000 × 4.723   755,680
         Total present value of inflows. $1,172,690

The present value factor for the first five years (3.791) is based on n = 5, i = 10 percent, and can be found in Appendix D. For the 6th through the 20th year, we take the present value factor in Appendix D for n = 20, i = 10 percent, and subtract from this the present value factor for n = 5, i = 10 percent. This allows us to isolate the 6th through the 20th year with a factor of 4.723 (8.515 − 3.791).

The net present value of the investment is:

Total present value of inflows . . .	$1,172,690
Net cash outflow.	980,000
Net present value	$ 192,690

The acquisition appears to represent a desirable alternative for the expenditure of cash, with a positive net present value of $192,690. In the market environment of the last two decades, some firms could be purchased at a value below the replacement costs of their assets and thus represented a potentially desirable capital investment. As an extreme example, Anaconda Copper had an asset replacement value of $1.3 billion when the firm was purchased by Atlantic Richfield for $684 million.

Stock-for-Stock Exchange

On a stock-for-stock exchange, we use a somewhat different analytical approach, emphasizing the earnings per share impact of exchanging securities (and ultimately the market valuation of those earnings). The analysis is primarily from the viewpoint of the acquiring firm. The shareholders of the acquired firm are concerned mainly about the initial price they are paid for their shares and about the outlook for the acquiring firm.

Assume that Expand Corporation is considering the acquisition of Small Corporation. Significant financial information on the firms before the merger is provided in Table 20–3.

	Small Corporation	Expand Corporation
Total earnings	$200,000	$500,000
Number of shares of stock outstanding.	50,000	200,000
Earnings per share	$4.00	$2.50
Price–earnings ratio (P/E) . . .	7.5×	12×
Market price per share	$30.00	$30.00

TABLE 20-3
Financial data on potential merging firms

We begin our analysis with the assumption that one share of Expand Corporation ($30) will be traded for one share of Small Corporation ($30). (In actuality Small Corporation will probably demand more than $30 per share because the acquired firm usually gets some premium over the current market value. We will later consider the impact of paying such a premium.)

If 50,000 new shares of Expand Corporation are traded in exchange for all the old shares of Small Corporation, Expand Corporation will then have 250,000 shares outstanding. At the same time, its claim to earnings will go to $700,000 when the two firms are combined. Postmerger earnings per share will be $2.80 for the Expand Corporation, as indicated in Table 20–4.

TABLE 20-4
Postmerger earnings per share

Total earnings: Small ($200,000) + Expand ($500,000) .	$700,000
Shares outstanding in surviving corporation: Old (200,000) + New (50,000).	250,000

$$\text{New earnings per share for Expand Corporation} = \frac{\$700,000}{250,000} = \$2.80$$

A number of observations are worthy of note. First the earnings per share of Expand Corporation have increased as a result of the merger, rising from $2.50 to $2.80. This has occurred because Expand Corporation's P/E ratio was higher than that of Small Corporation at the time of the merger (12.0 versus 7.5) as previously presented in Table 20–3. Whenever a firm acquires another entity whose P/E ratio is lower than its own, there is an immediate increase in earnings per share.

Of course if Expand Corporation pays a price higher than Small Corporation's current market value, which is typically the case, it may be paying equal to or more than its own current P/E ratio for Small Corporation. For example at a price of $48 per share for Small Corporation, Expand Corporation will be paying 12 times Small Corporation's earnings, which is exactly the current P/E ratio of Expand Corporation. Under these circumstances there will be no change in postmerger earnings per share for Expand Corporation.

Endless possibilities can occur in mergers based on stock-for-stock exchanges. Even if the acquiring company increases its immediate earnings per share as a result of the merger, it may slow its future growth rate if it is buying a less aggressive company. Conversely the acquiring company may dilute immediate postmerger earnings per share but increase its potential growth rate for the future as a result of acquiring a rapidly growing company.

The ultimate test of a merger rests with its ability to maximize the market value of the acquiring firm. This is sometimes a difficult goal to achieve but is the measure of the success of a merger.

Portfolio Effect

Inherent in all of our discussion is the importance of the merger's portfolio effect on the risk-return posture of the firm. The reduction or increase in risk may influence the P/E ratio as much as the change in the growth rate. To the extent that we are diminishing the overall risk of the firm in a merger, the post-merger P/E ratio and market value may increase even if the potential earnings growth is unchanged. Business risk reduction may be achieved through acquiring another firm that is influenced by a set of factors in the business cycle opposite from those that influence our own firm, while financial risk reduction may be achieved by restructuring our postmerger financial arrangements to include less debt.

Perhaps Expand Corporation may be diversifying from a heavy manufacturing industry into the real estate/housing industry. While heavy manufacturing industries move with the business cycle, the real estate/housing industry tends to be countercyclical. Even though the expected value of earnings per share may remain relatively constant as a result of the merger, the standard deviation of possible outcomes may decline as a result of risk reduction through diversification, as is indicated in Figure 20–1.

We see that the expected value of the earnings per share has remained constant in this instance but the standard deviation has gone down. Because

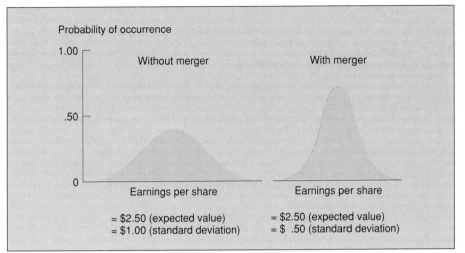

FIGURE 20–1
**Risk-reduction
portfolio benefits**

there is less risk in the corporation, the investor may be willing to assign a higher valuation, thus increasing the price-earnings ratio.

Accounting Considerations in Mergers and Acquisitions

The role of financial accounting has significance in the area of mergers and acquisitions. When a price substantially above book value is paid for a potential acquisition, goodwill may be created on the books of the acquiring firm and the writing off of this goodwill over time can have a negative impact on earnings per share. Many firms try to avoid the creation of goodwill. Let's see what the issues and the options are.

A merger can be treated on the books of the acquiring firm as either a pooling of interests or a purchase of assets. Under a **pooling of interests,** the financial statements of the firms are combined, subject to some minor adjustments, and no goodwill is created. To qualify for a pooling of interests, certain criteria must be met, such as:

1. The acquiring corporation issues only common stock, with rights identical to its old outstanding voting stock, in exchange for substantially all of the other company's voting stock.
2. The acquired firm's stockholders maintain an ownership position in the surviving firm.
3. The combined entity does not intend to dispose of a significant portion of the assets of the combined companies within two years.
4. The combination is effected in a single transaction.[5]

Goodwill may be created when the second type of merger recording—a purchase of assets—is used. Because of the criteria described above (particularly items 1 and 2), a purchase of assets treatment, rather than a pooling

---

[5]Accounting Principles Board, "Business Combinations," APB Opinion 16 (New York: AICPA, 1970). A number of lesser criteria are also involved.

of interests treatment, is generally necessary when the tender offer is in cash, bonds, preferred stock, or common stock with restricted rights. Under a **purchase of assets** accounting treatment, any excess of purchase price over book value must be recorded as goodwill and written off over a maximum period of 40 years. If a company purchases a firm with a $4 million book value (net worth) for $6 million, $2 million of goodwill is created on the books of the acquiring company, and it must be written off over a maximum period of 40 years. This would cause a $50,000-per-year reduction in reported earnings ($2 million/40 years). Because the writing off of goodwill is not a tax-deductible expense, the firm suffers the full amount of the deduction without any tax relief. Under a pooling of interests accounting treatment, you will recall, goodwill is not created.

The main reason we look at the pooling of interests versus the purchase of assets accounting treatment is to recognize the potentially beneficial effect to a corporation of exchanging common stock, rather than nonequity compensation (cash, bonds, preferred stock, and so on), and thus perhaps qualifying as a pooling of interests. Common stock also more readily qualifies a merger for a tax-free exchange under Section 368(a) of the Internal Revenue Code. Under a tax-free exchange, the stockholders of the acquired firm may defer a tax obligation until the newly acquired shares have actually been sold. Thus there would be no immediate tax for trading a share of stock in Growth Corporation that was purchased 10 years ago at $5 for $30 in Expand Corporation stock. If and when the Expand Corporation stock is sold, the tax will be recognized at the newly established sales price. If the tender offer were $30 in cash, there would be an immediate tax obligation.

In analyzing accounting and tax considerations, we see that the acquiring corporation has some inducement to offer common stock to qualify for a pooling of interests when the exchange offer exceeds book value; also the stockholders of the acquired firm have some incentive to receive common stock when the exchange offer exceeds their initial cost basis to avoid immediate taxes. During the 1960s and part of the 1970s, common stock, often supplemented by convertible securities and warrants, was a frequently used mode of exchange.[6] In the merger movement of the last two decades, cash offers came into vogue.

Why? First stockholders of the acquired firms became somewhat disenchanted with the postmerger performances of acquiring companies' common stock. For this reason they have been willing to take cash, pay a tax, and invest in a new and diversified set of investments. Acquiring corporations have gone along with the cash tender offer pattern, despite the requirement for purchase of assets accounting treatment, in order to satisfy the demands of selling stockholders.[7]

---

[6]The popularity of the last two items was reduced somewhat by Accounting Principles Board Opinion 15, "Earnings per Share," issued by the AICPA in May 1969, which required tough standards for the dilutive effects of convertibles and warrants, as described in Chapter 19.

[7]Also where a substantial postmerger asset write-up is possible, the corporation may acquire a beneficial tax base for depreciation, rather than nontax-deductible goodwill.

Also by using cash instead of stock, a corporation may diminish the perceived dilutive effect of a merger. If Small Corporation or Growth Corporation had been acquired for straight cash by Expand Corporation, no new shares would have been issued and earnings per share would have gone up proportionately by the amount of new aftertax earnings. This latter argument tends to be weakened by recognition of the fact that cash tendered in a merger has a substantial capital cost associated with it and, furthermore, that new shares of stock may later have to be authorized and sold to finance the cash drain.

Negotiated versus Tendered Offers

Traditionally mergers have been negotiated in a friendly atmosphere between officers and directors of the participating corporations. Product lines, quality of assets, and future growth prospects are discussed, and eventually an exchange ratio is hammered out and reported to the investment community and the financial press.

As previously mentioned, the merger wave of the late 1970s and the 1980s helped to create a whole new atmosphere. The **takeover tender offer,** in which a company attempts to acquire a target firm against its will, has come into vogue. One of the most notorious examples was the announced intent of American Express to take over McGraw-Hill in early 1979. At that time McGraw-Hill was selling at $26 per share. The initial American Express offer was for $34, and eventually the offer went up to $40. McGraw-Hill fought off the offer by maintaining that American Express would obstruct the independent character required of a publisher. McGraw-Hill discouraged the unwelcome offer from American Express, but many small McGraw-Hill stockholders sued the publisher, claiming the calling off of the merger caused them to lose an opportunity to advance the cash value of their holdings.

Not all companies can fend off the unwanted advances of suitors. An entire vocabulary has developed on Wall Street around the concept of the target takeover. For example the **Saturday night special** refers to a surprise offer made just before the market closes for the weekend and takes the target company's officers by surprise. By the time the officers can react, the impact of the offer has already occurred. Perhaps a stock is trading at $20 and an unfriendly offer comes in at $28. Though the offer may please the company's stockholders, its management faces the dangers of seeing the company going down the wrong path in a merger and perhaps being personally ousted.

To avoid an unfriendly takeover, management may turn to a **white knight** for salvation. A white knight represents a third firm that management calls on to help it avoid the initial unwanted tender offer. For example in 1978 Babcock and Wilcox received an unsolicited takeover bid from United Technologies to purchase its stock at $42 per share. Since the stock was currently selling at 34¾, this was not a bad offer. However, the company turned to J. Ray McDermott & Company as a friendly suitor. After a bidding war, Babcock and Wilcox was eventually purchased by McDermott for $65 a share. Under similar circumstances in the 1980s, Conoco turned to Du Pont as a suitor after being pursued on an unfriendly basis by Seagrams and others.

Also Marathon Oil merged with U.S. Steel to avoid an unfriendly tender offer from Mobil Oil. The biggest white knight was Chevron Corporation, which "saved" Gulf Oil from T. Boone Pickens at a cost of $13.3 billion.

Many firms that wish to avoid takeovers have moved their corporate offices to states that have tough prenotification and protection provisions in regard to takeover offers. Other companies have bought portions of their own shares to restrict the amount of stock available for a takeover or have encouraged employees to buy stock under corporate pension plans. Other protective measures include increasing dividends to keep stockholders happy and staggering the election of members of the board of directors to make outside power plays more difficult to initiate. Possible target companies have also bought up other companies to increase their own size and make themselves more expensive and less vulnerable. One of the key rules for avoiding a targeted takeover is to never get caught with too large a cash position. A firm with large cash balances serves as an ideal target for a leveraged takeover. The acquiring company can negotiate a bank loan based on the target company's assets and then to go into the marketplace to make a cash tender offer. For example, CIT Financial left itself wide open when it sold a banking subsidiary for $425 million. At that point CIT had cash balances equal to $20 per share for shares that had a market value in the $30 to $40 range. RCA bought the company for $65 per share.

Also the poison pill, discussed at some length in Chapter 17, is an effective device for protection. It may give those in an entrenched position the ability to accumulate new shares at well below the market price in order to increase their percentage of ownership. This privilege is usually triggered when an unwanted outside group accumulates a certain percentage of the shares outstanding (such as 25 percent).

While a takeover bid may not appeal to management, it may be enticing to stockholders, as previously indicated. Herein lies the basic problem. The bidding may get so high that stockholders demand action. The desire of management to maintain the status quo can conflict with the objective of stockholder wealth maximization.

Premium Offers and Stock Price Movements

Until the latest merger wave, the average premium paid over market value in a merger or acquisition was of the magnitude of 20–25 percent.[8] In the merger movement of the late 1970s and 1980s, the average **merger premium** appears to have been closer to 50–60 percent.[9]

Many of the companies acquired in the latest merger movement have tended to be of unusually high quality and thus have commanded a high premium. The motivation of the acquiring company in making the purchase

---

[8]William A. Alberts and Joel E. Segall, *The Corporate Merger* (Chicago: University of Chicago Press, 1966), pp. 117–18. Also George D. McCarthy, *Acquisitions and Mergers* (New York: Ronald Press, 1963), pp. 92–102.

[9]Selected issues of *Mergers and Acquisitions,* 1981–90.

was often not to turn around a poor performance, but to take advantage of the superior market or product position of the acquired company.

Many acquisition candidates represented some of the most interesting stock market performers of the decade. Often the daily volume leaders and outstanding price movers were acquisition candidates. Researchers have found that potential acquirees have superior price performance on a risk-adjusted basis.[10] It is not surprising that a company that is offered a large premium over its current market value has a major upside movement. The only problem for the investor is that much of this activity may occur before the public announcement of the merger offer. If a firm is selling at $25 per share when informal negotiations begin, it may be $34 by the time an announced offer of $40 is made. Still there are good profits to be made if the merger goes through.

A group of investors who specialize in merger situations came into high visibility in the late 1970s and the 1980s. Known as **ARBs (arbitrageurs),** their strategy is to purchase the stock of the acquisition candidate in the hope of being bought out at the tender offer price. In the prior example, they would accumulate stock at between $34 and $38 in the hope of selling out at $40. The ARBs often become the allies of acquiring companies because their profits (and their avoidance of losses) are dependent on the merger's actual completion.

In a stock-for-stock exchange, an arbitrageur may attempt to protect his or her profit position by buying the stock of the acquisition candidate and, at the same time, short-selling the stock of the acquirer. A short sell is a current sale of stock that is not owned, with the intention of acquiring the stock in the future to close out the position. The arbitrageur buys the acquiree's stock at $34 and simultaneously short-sells the acquiring company's stock at $40. When the merger has been consummated, the arbitrageur will trade the acquiree's stock for a share of the acquiring company's stock and use the stock to cover the $40 short position. Thus the selling price is preestablished at $40 and the buy price at $34. Even if the acquiring company's stock goes up or *down* from $40 after the merger has been announced, the sale price and profit spread have been established.

The only problem with this strategy or of any merger-related investment strategy is that the merger may be called off. In that case the merger candidate's stock, which shot up from $25 to $34, may fall back to $25, and the Johnny-come-lately investor would lose $9 per share.[11] In Table 20–5, we consider the case of three canceled mergers. Of course if a new suitor comes along shortly after cancellation (or causes the original cancellation), the price may quickly rebound.

All this information on price movement patterns has significance to corporate financial managers, who must understand and react to the motivations

---

[10]Gershon Mandelker, "Risk and Return: The Case of Merging Firms," *Journal of Financial Economics* 1 (December 1974), pp. 303–35. Mandelker found the merger effect beginning to influence the acquiree's stock seven months before consummation of the merger, with the cumulative average residual (excess returns) moving positively at that point. A number of later studies have also confirmed this type of finding.

[11]The arbitrageur also would not have new stock of the acquiring company to cover his short position, since there would be no exchange of shares.

TABLE 20–5   **Stock movement of potential acquirees**

Acquirer — Potential Acquiree	Preannouncement	One Day after Announcement	One Day after Cancellation
Mead Corp. — Occidental Petroleum . . .	20⅜	33¼	23¼
Olin Corp. — Celanese	16	23¾	16¾
Chicago Rivet — MITE	20¾	28⅛	20¾

of investors. For example once the ARBs have established their investment position, these arbitrageurs will do everything possible to see that the merger goes through. This, at a minimum, will include voting all their shares in favor of a merger. On a more active basis, it may encompass a strategy of influencing other large stockholders, and it could ultimately include an attempt to discredit the management of a target company in the eyes of shareholders.

Two-Step Buyout

Another merger ploy that has been undertaken in the recent merger movement is the **two-step buyout.** Under this plan the acquiring company attempts to gain control by offering a very high cash price for 51 percent of the shares outstanding. At the same time, it announces a second, lower price that will be paid, either in cash, stock, or bonds, later. As an example, an acquiring company may offer stockholders of a takeover target company a $70 cash offer that can be executed in the next 20 days (for 51 percent of the shares outstanding). Subsequent to that time period, the selling stockholders will receive $57.50 in preferred stock for each share.

This buyout procedure accomplishes two purposes. First it provides a strong inducement to stockholders to quickly react to the offer. Those who delay must accept a lower price. Second it allows the acquiring company to pay a lower total price than if a single offer is made. In the example above, a single offer may have been made for $68 a share. Assume 1 million shares are outstanding. The single offer has a total price tag of $68,000,000, while the two-step offer would have called for only $63,875,000.

Single offer:
      1,000,000 shares at $68 = $68,000,000

Two-step offer:
      510,000 shares (51%) at $70   = $35,700,000
      490,000 shares (49%) at $57.50 = <u> 28,175,000</u>
                                                              $63,875,000

An example of a two-step buyout was the Mobil Oil attempt to acquire 51 percent of Marathon Oil shares at a price of $126 in cash, with a subsequent offer to buy the rest of the shares for $90 face value debentures. In this case Marathon Oil decided to sell to U.S. Steel, which also made a two-step offer of $125 in cash or $100 in notes to later sellers. Incidentally, before the bidding began, Marathon Oil was selling for $60 a share.

The SEC has continued to keep a close eye on the two-step buyout. Government regulators fear that smaller stockholders may not be sophisticated enough to compete with arbitrageurs or institutional investors in rapidly tendering shares to ensure receipt of the higher price. The SEC has emphasized the need for a pro rata processing of stockholder orders, in which each stockholder receives an equal percentage of shares tendered.

The holding company achieved its greatest popularity in the early part of the 20th century, and it is still in evidence today in a number of industries, particularly in public utilities. A **holding company** is one that has control over one or more other firms. To establish voting control, the holding company may own less than a majority interest but can determine policy because of widely spread minority interests among the other stockholders.

> **Holding Companies**

The primary advantage of the holding company is that it affords unusual opportunities for leverage. Assume Giant Holding Corporation has the investment interests in Companies A, B, and C that are shown in Table 20–6. All numbers are assumed to represent millions of dollars. Also assume Giant Holding Corporation has effective voting control of the three companies

TABLE 20–6
Assets, liabilities, and stockholders' equity of Giant Holding Corporation and related companies (in $ millions)

GIANT HOLDING CORPORATION

Assets		Liabilities and Stockholders' Equity	
Common stockholdings:			
Company A.	$10	Long-term debt	$15
Company B.	15	Preferred stock.	10
Company C	20	Common stock equity	20
	$45		$45

COMPANY A

Assets		Liabilities and Stockholders' Equity	
Current assets	$ 50	Current liabilities.	$ 20
Plant and equipment	50	Long-term debt	30
	$100	Common stock equity	50
			$100

COMPANY B

Assets		Liabilities and Stockholders' Equity	
Current assets	$ 60	Current liabilities.	$ 10
Plant and equipment	60	Long-term debt	70
	$120	Common stock equity	40
			$120

COMPANY C

Assets		Liabilities and Stockholders' Equity	
Current assets	$ 80	Current liabilities.	$ 20
Plant and equipment	120	Long-term debt	100
	$200	Common stock equity	80
			$200

because of the widely dispersed interests of these companies' other owners. It owns 20 percent of the equity of Company A, as indicated by Giant Holding Corporation's balance sheet holding of $10 million in Company A (an asset) and Company A's common stock equity account of $50 million. In the case of Company B, the ratio is 37.5 percent ($15 million/$40 million), while for Company C it is 25 percent ($20 million/$80 million). Through these interlocking positions, Giant Holding Corporation controls $420 million in assets (the combined assets of the three companies). Note that it is doing this with only $20 million of common stock equity in its own firm. Its equity to "assets controlled" ratio is 4.8 percent ($20 million/$420 million). If we really want to get creative, we can assume that another holding company has control of Giant Holding Corporation with only a small investment in it, thus creating additional levels of ownership.

The holding company device also benefits from the isolation of the "legal" risks of the firms. Theoretically, if Company C loses money, this will not *legally* affect the other firms, because Company C is a separate legal entity with separate shareholders.

Drawbacks

The drawbacks are those inherent in any pyramiding arrangement.[12] Although Companies A, B, and C are separate legal entities, and one cannot force the bankruptcy of another, an indirect chain effect could be disastrous. For example if Company A has a bad year, it may be unable to pay dividends to the holding company, which, in turn, may be unable to pay interest on the $15 million it has in long-term debt. The more complicated the arrangement, the more vulnerable the operation is to reversals.

The holding company also suffers from the problem of multiple taxation. For example Company A must pay taxes on its profits and then declare dividends to the holding company, which are also partially taxable. Although there is a 70 percent exemption on dividends paid to another corporation, the 30 percent additional tax bite is still significant,[13] particularly when one considers that the stockholders of the holding company will have to pay a third tax on the dividends declared to them.

The administrative problems and procedures of a holding company are also worthy of note. With multiple managements, boards of directors, dividend policies, and reporting systems, the expenses are high and the opportunities for problems substantial.

Summary

Corporations may seek external growth through mergers to reduce risk, to improve access to the financial markets through increased size, or to obtain tax carry-forward benefits. A merger may also expand the marketing and manage-

---

[12]There are also many serious legal questions associated with holding companies.

[13]Only if the holding company has an 80 percent or greater ownership interest can the second tax be avoided.

ment capabilities of the firm and allow for new product development. While some mergers promise synergistic benefits (the $2 + 2 = 5$ effect), this can be an elusive feature, with initial expectations exceeding subsequent realities.

The *cash* purchase of another corporation takes on many of the characteristics of a classical capital budgeting decision. In a *stock-for-stock* exchange, there is often a trade-off between immediate gain or dilution in earnings per share and future growth. If a firm buys another firm with a P/E ratio lower than its own, there is an immediate increase in earnings per share, but the long-term earnings growth prospects must also be considered. The ultimate objective of a merger, as is true of any financial decision, is stockholder wealth maximization, and the immediate and delayed effects of the merger must be evaluated in this context.

The accounting considerations in a merger are also important. Where the purchase price exceeds the book value of the acquired firm (after postmerger asset value adjustments), goodwill may be created, which must be written off directly against future earnings per share. To avoid goodwill creation, the merger may be treated as a pooling of interests rather than a purchase of assets if certain restrictive conditions are met. For example stock must be tendered rather than cash, debt, preferred stock, or other financial instruments.

In the merger wave of the late 1970s and the 1980s, the unsolicited tender offer for a target company gained in popularity. Offers were made at values well in excess of the current market price, and management of the target company became trapped in the dilemma of maintaining its current position versus agreeing to the wishes of the acquiring company, the arbitrageurs, and even the target company's own stockholders.

Finally the holding company is viewed as a means of accumulating large asset control with a minimum equity investment through leveraging the investment. However, many tax, administrative, and legal problems are inherent in this form of organization.

List of Terms

merger 576	purchase of assets 584
consolidation 576	takeover tender offer 585
portfolio effect 577	Saturday night special 585
tax loss carry-forward 578	white knight 585
horizontal integration 578	merger premium 586
vertical integration 578	ARBs (arbitrageurs) 587
synergy 579	two-step buyout 588
pooling of interests 583	holding company 589
goodwill 583	

Discussion Questions

1. What is the difference between a merger and a consolidation?
2. Why might the portfolio effect of a merger provide a higher valuation for the participating firms?

3. If a firm wishes to achieve immediate appreciation in earnings per share as a result of a merger, how can this be best accomplished in terms of exchange variables? What is a possible drawback to this approach in terms of long-range considerations?

4. What is the essential difference between a pooling of interests and a purchase of assets accounting treatment of a merger? Is goodwill amortization a tax-deductible expense?

5. If Ford Motor Company were to merge with Chrysler Corporation, suggest three forms of synergy that might occur.

6. Generally a stockholder of the selling corporation will demand a higher price if cash consideration is tendered. Explain why this might be the case.

7. It is possible for the postmerger P/E ratio to move in a direction opposite to that of the immediate postmerger earnings per share. Explain why this could happen.

8. Explain why unusually high premiums have been paid in the latest merger movement.

9. Suggest some ways in which firms have tried to avoid being part of a target takeover.

10. Why do management and stockholders often have divergent viewpoints about the desirability of a takeover?

11. How does a merger arbitrageur benefit from a possible merger? What is the danger in being a merger arbitrageur? Explain.

12. Compare the use of leverage in a holding company to the concept of operating and financial leverage explained in Chapter 5. What tax problems related to dividends does a holding company have?

13. What is the purpose(s) of the two-step buyout from the viewpoint of the acquiring company?

Problems

Tax loss carry-forward

1. The Clark Corporation desires to expand. It is considering a cash purchase of Kent Enterprises for $3,000,000. Kent has a $700,000 tax loss carry-forward that could be used immediately by the Clark Corporation, which is paying taxes at the rate of 30 percent. Kent will provide $420,000 per year in cash flow (aftertax income plus depreciation) for the next 20 years. If the Clark Corporation has a cost of capital of 13 percent, should the merger be undertaken?

Tax loss carry-forward

2. Assume the Citrus Corporation is considering the acquisition of Orange Juice, Inc. The latter has a $500,000 tax loss carry-forward. Projected earnings for the Citrus Corporation are as follows:

	1994	1995	1996	Total Values
Before-tax income . .	$200,000	$250,000	$380,000	$830,000
Taxes (40%)	80,000	100,000	152,000	332,000
Income available to stockholders. . .	$120,000	$150,000	$228,000	$498,000

a. How much will the total taxes of Citrus Corporation be reduced as a result of the tax loss carry-forward?

b. How much will the total income available to stockholders be for the three years if the acquisition occurs? Use the same format as that on the bottom half of the illustration on page 578.

3. Texas Investments, Inc., is considering a cash acquisition of Bubba Brewing Co. for $2,200,000. Bubba Brewing will provide the following pattern of cash inflows and synergistic benefits for the next 20 years. There is no tax loss carry-forward.

Cash acquisition with deferred benefits

	Years		
	1–5	6–15	16–20
Cash inflow (aftertax)	$220,000	$240,000	$280,000
Synergistic benefits (aftertax) . .	$ 20,000	$ 22,000	$ 40,000

The cost of capital for the acquiring firm is 12 percent. Should the merger be undertaken? (If you have difficulty with delayed time value of money problems, consult Chapter 9.)

4. Assume the following financial data for the Barker Corporation and Howell Enterprises.

Impact of a merger on earnings per share

	Barker Corporation	Howell Enterprises
Total earnings.	$400,000	$1,200,000
Number of shares of stock outstanding.	200,000	1,000,000
Earnings per share	$2.00	$1.20
Price-earnings ratio (P/E). . .	12×	20×
Market price per share	$24.00	$24.00

a. If all the shares of the Barker Corporation are exchanged for shares of the Howell Enterprises on a share-for-share basis, what will postmerger earnings per share be for Howell Enterprises? Use an approach similar to Table 20–4.

b. Explain why the earnings per share of Howell Enterprises changed.

c. Can we necessarily assume Howell Enterprises is better or worse off?

Two-step buyout

5. The Clinton Corporation is considering a two-step buyout of Gore Environmental Systems. The latter firm has 2 million shares outstanding and its stock price is currently $20 per share. In the two-step buyout, Clinton Corporation will offer to buy 51 percent of Gore's shares outstanding for $34 in cash and the balance in a second offer of 980,000 convertible preferred stock shares; each share of preferred stock would be valued at 45 percent over Gore's common stock current value. Mr. Bentsen, a newcomer to the management team at Clinton Corporation, suggests that only one offer for all Gore's shares be made at $32.50 per share. Compare the total costs of the two alternatives. Which is preferred in terms of minimizing costs?

Future tax obligation to selling stockholder

6. Gil Whitaker helped start Marshall Engineering Company in 1953. At the time he purchased 200,000 shares of stock at one dollar per share. In 1994, he has the opportunity to sell his interest in the company to Beta Technology for $40 a share. His tax rate would be 28 percent.

   a. If he sells his interest, what will be the value for before-tax profit, taxes, and aftertax profit?

   b. Assume, instead of cash, he accepts stock valued at $40 per share. He holds the stock for five years and then sells it for $72.50 (the stock pays no cash dividends). What will be the value for before-tax profit, taxes, and aftertax profit?

   c. Using an 11 percent discount rate, compare the aftertax profit figure in part b to part a. (That is, discount back the answer in part b for five years and compare it to the answer in part a.)

Portfolio effect of a merger

7. Assume the Knight Corporation is considering the acquisition of Day, Inc. The expected earnings per share for the Knight Corporation will be $4.00 with or without the merger. However, the standard deviation of the earnings will go from $2.40 to $1.60 with the merger because the two firms are negatively correlated.

   a. Compute the coefficient of variation for the Knight Corporation before and after the merger (consult Chapter 13 to review statistical concepts if necessary).

   b. Discuss the possible impact on Knight's postmerger P/E ratio, assuming investors are risk-averse.

Portfolio considerations and risk aversion

8. Bork Construction Company is considering two mergers. The first is with Firm A in its own volatile industry, whereas the second is a merger with Firm B in an industry that moves in the opposite direction (and will tend to level out performance due to negative correlation).

Bork Construction Merger with Firm A		Bork Construction Merger with Firm B	
Possible Earnings ($ in millions)	Probability	Possible Earnings ($ in millions)	Probability
10	.30	$30	.25
40	.40	40	.50
70	.30	50	.25

a. Compute the mean, standard deviation, and coefficient of variation for both investments (consult Chapter 13 to review statistical concepts if necessary).

b. Assuming investors are risk-averse, which alternatives can be expected to bring the higher valuation?

9. Wright Aerospace is considering the acquisition of Columbus Shipping Corporation. The book value of the Columbus Shipping Corporation is $30 million, and Wright Aerospace is willing to pay $90 million in cash and preferred stock. No upward adjustment of asset values is anticipated. Wright Aerospace Corporation has 2 million shares outstanding. A purchase of assets financial recording will be used, with a 40-year write-off of goodwill.

Purchase of assets with goodwill amortization

a. How much will the annual amortization be?

b. How much will the annual amortization be on a per share basis?

c. Is any tax benefit involved?

d. Explain how the recording of goodwill could have been avoided.

10. The New York Power Corporation, a holding company, has investments in three other firms. Values are expressed in millions of dollars.

Holding company control

MANTLE CORPORATION

Assets		Liabilities and Stockholders' Equity	
Current assets.	$100	Current liabilities	$ 50
Plant and equipment . .	200	Long-term debt	150
	$300	Common stock equity . .	100
			$300

MAYS CORPORATION

Assets		Liabilities and Stockholders' Equity	
Current assets.	$150	Current liabilities	$150
Plant and equipment . .	250	Long-term debt	100
	$400	Common stock equity . .	150
			$400

SNIDER CORPORATION

Assets		Liabilities and Stockholders' Equity	
Current assets.	$175	Current liabilities	$ 50
Plant and equipment . .	275	Long-term debt	200
	$450	Common stock equity . .	200
			$450

The New York Power Corporation has voting control of the three other corporations with the following investment interests in each: 20 percent of the equity in Mantle Corporation, 30 percent of the equity in Mays Corporation, and 25 percent of the equity in the Snider Corporation.

a. Fill in the table below for the New York Power Company's investments in the three companies.

Common stockholdings:	
Mantle Corporation	_____
Mays Corporation	_____
Snider Corporation	_____
Total	_____

b. Fill in the table below for the New York Power Corporation's liabilities and stockholders' equity. Liabilities are equal to 80 percent of the total assets in part *a*, with the balance in stockholders' equity.

Liabilities and Stockholders' Equity	
Liabilities	_____
Stockholders' equity . . .	_____
Total	_____

c. Compute the ratio of the New York Power Corporation's stockholders' equity to the total holding company assets for the three corporations.

Selected References

Agrawal, Anup, Jeffrey F. Jaffe, and Gershon N. Mandelker. "The Post-Merger Performance of Acquiring Firms: A Reexamination of an Anomaly." *Journal of Finance* 47 (September 1992), pp. 1605–21.

Alberts, William A., and Joel E. Segall. *The Corporate Merger.* Chicago: University of Chicago Press, 1966 and 1974.

Amihud, Yakov, Baruch Lev, and Nickolaos G. Travlos. "Corporate Control and the Choice of Investment Financing: The Case of Corporate Acquisitions." *Journal of Finance* 45 (June 1990), pp. 603–16.

Bradley, James W., and Donald H. Korn. "Acquisition and Merger Trends Affecting the Portfolio Manager." *Financial Analysts Journal* 33 (November–December 1977), pp. 65–70.

Boot, Arnoud W. A. "Why Hang on to Losers? Divestitures and Takeovers." *Journal of Finance* 47 (September 1992), pp. 1401–23.

Conn, Robert L., and James F. Nielson. "An Empirical Test of the Larson–Gonedes Exchange Ratio Determination Model." *Journal of Finance* 32 (June 1977), pp. 749–59.

Davidson, Wallace N., III, Sharon Hatten Garrison, and Glen V. Henderson, Jr. "Examining Merger Synergy with the Capital Asset Pricing Model." *Financial Review* 22 (May 1987), pp. 233–48.

Dodd, Peter, and Richard Ruback. "Tender Offers and Stockholder Returns." *Journal of Financial Economics* 5 (December 1977), pp. 351–73.

Fabozzi, Frank J., Michael G. Ferri, Dessa T. Fabozzi, and Julia Tucker. "A Note on Unsuccessful Tender Offers and Stockholder Returns." *Journal of Finance* 43 (December 1988), pp. 1275–83.

Healy, Paul M., Krishna G. Palepu, and Richard S. Ruback. "Does Corporate Performance Improve after Mergers?" *Journal of Financial Economics* 31 (April 1992), pp. 133–75.

Hogarty, T. "The Profitability of Corporate Mergers." *Journal of Business* 43 (July 1970), pp. 317–27.

Jarrell, Gregg A., and Annette B. Poulsen. "The Returns to Acquiring Firms in Tender Offers: Evidence from Three Decades." *Financial Management* 18 (Autumn 1989), pp. 12–19.

Larson, Kermit D., and Nicholas J. Gonedes. "Business Combinations: An Exchange Ratio Determination Model." *Accounting Review* 44 (October 1969), pp. 720–28.

Lewellen, Wilbur, Claudio Loderer, and Ahron Rosenfeld. "Mergers, Executive Risk Reduction, and Stockholder Wealth." *Journal of Financial and Quantitative Analysis* 24 (December 1989), pp. 459–72.

Mandelker, Gershon N. "Risk and Return: The Case of Merging Firms." *Journal of Financial Economics* 1 (December 1974), pp. 303–35.

Mitchell, Mark L. "The Value of Corporate Takeovers." *Financial Analysts Journal* (January–February 1991), pp. 21–31.

Reilly, Frank K. "What Determines the Ratio of Exchange in Corporate Mergers?" *Financial Analysts Journal* 18 (November–December 1962), pp. 47–50.

Ryngaert, Michael D. "Firm Valuation, Takeover Defenses, and the Delaware Supreme Court." *Financial Management* 18 (Autumn 1989), pp. 20–28.

Stulz, Rene M., Ralph A. Walkling, and Moon H. Song. "The Distribution of Target Ownership and the Division of Gains in Successful Takeovers." *Journal of Finance* 45 (July 1990), pp. 817–33.

Weston, J. Fred. "Divestitures: Mistakes or Learning?" *Journal of Applied Corporate Finance* 4 (Summer 1989), pp. 68–76.

International Financial Management

1 The multinational corporation is one that crosses international borders to gain expanded markets.

2 A company operating in many foreign countries must consider the effect of exchage rates on its profitability and cash flow.

3 Foreign exchange risk can be hedged or reduced.

4 Political risk must be carefully assessed in making a foreign investment decision.

5 The potential ways for financing international operations are much greater than for domestic operations and should be carefully considered.

During the post–World War II era, advances in communications and transportation systems brought people everywhere closer together. In this shrinking world, it became easier to interact with others through trade, regardless of geographic origin, location, or nationality. The political systems that emerged from World War II also contributed to the establishment of trade relations between nations. Under the Marshall Plan, the United States helped the war-torn nations of Western Europe rebuild their economies. Western Europe, Canada, and Japan experienced sustainable growth under the economic leadership of the United States. As the economies of Western nations grew in this manner, their trade relations were also strengthened. Concurrently European nations formed the European Common Market in an effort to promote better trade relations among themselves. Technology and capital also started to flow from the United States to the allied countries. Thus the United States became the dominant partner in the world economy.

Today the world economy is more integrated than ever, and nations are dependent on one another for many valuable and scarce resources. Just as the United States is dependent on Saudi Arabia for part of its oil, the Saudis are dependent on the United States for computers, aircraft, and military hardware. The former Soviet Union has accepted a more market-based economy in contrast to total government control and is actively seeking trading relationships and support from the rest of the world. This growing interdependence necessitates the development of sound international business relations, which, in turn, will enhance the prospects for future international cooperation and understanding. It is virtually impossible for any country to isolate itself from the impact of international developments in an integrated world economy.

In no time during the post–World War II period has the world come closer together than in the 1990s. Capitalism seems to thrive on a worldwide scale. The same can be said for cooperation in the North American continent as the United States, Mexico, and Canada move ever closer together in their economic linkage. The "Wall" has come down between East and West Germany, and Western Europe is seeking a new age of harmony and cooperation in the form of European Community (EC) 1992.

The significance of international business operations becomes more apparent if we look at the size of foreign sales relative to the domestic sales for major American corporations. Table 21–1 shows that, in such companies as Colgate-Palmolive, CPC International, Exxon, Gillette, and Mobil, foreign sales accounted for over 60 percent of total sales in 1992. Also you should note the importance of foreign profits and foreign assets. Just as foreign operations affect the performance of American business firms, developments in international financial markets also affect our lifestyles. If you took a summer trip to Sweden in 1992, you might have been pleased to discover how much cheaper hotels, food, and recreation were compared to a few short years ago. The primary reason was the strong increase in the dollar relative to the Swedish krona. Of course Swedish citizens would have been disappointed to find out their currency would buy less in the United States. These types of events occur daily throughout the world.

TABLE 21-1
**1992 data on
international activities
of selected U.S.
corporations**

	Foreign Sales (percent of total sales)	Foreign Operating Profit (percent of total operating profit)	Foreign Assets (percent of total assets)
Chevron	38.2%	87.4%	31.3%
Colgate-Palmolive	63.8	58.4	49.3
CPC International	62.7	52.9	64.9
Digital Equipment	59.8	NA	52.9
Exxon	75.9	84.2	58.4
Gillette	68.1	67.4	67.7
Goodyear Tire and Rubber	42.9	NA	40.2
Hewlett-Packard	54.2	33.2	45.9
H. J. Heinz	41.9	46.7	46.2
Johnson & Johnson	49.8	53.9	46.3
Kellogg	41.1	36.0	47.8
Merck	46.3	20.0	30.6
Mobil	68.1	86.3	56.6
3M	48.5	33.8	42.2
PPG Industries	36.1	35.7	34.0
Sara Lee	30.7	60.7	41.4
Texaco	49.9	57.6	28.6
Xerox	44.3	64.3	21.3

   This chapter deals with the dimensions of doing business worldwide. We believe this chapter provides a basis for understanding the complexities of international financial decisions. Such an understanding is important whether you work for a multinational manufacturing firm, a large commercial bank, a major brokerage firm, or any firm involved in international transactions.

   International business operations, by their very nature, are complex, risky, and require special understanding. Many major U.S. banks have had to learn the lessons of international finance through painful experience. In the worldwide recession of 1991–92, many less-developed Third World countries had trouble repaying their debt obligations as their exports dropped. The ingenuity of world financial institutions was challenged (and continues to be challenged) to avoid disaster.

   The following section of this chapter describes the international business firm and its environment. Then foreign exchange rates and the variables influencing foreign currency values are explained, and strategies dealing with foreign exchange risk are examined. Finally international financing sources, including the Eurodollar market, the Eurobond market, and foreign equity markets, are discussed.

The Multinational Corporation: Nature and Environment

The focus of international financial management has been the multinational corporation (MNC). One might ask, just what is a **multinational corporation?** Some definitions of a multinational corporation require that a minimum percentage (often 30 percent or more) of a firm's business activities be carried on outside its national borders. For our understanding, however, a firm doing business across its national borders is considered a multinational enterprise. Multinational corporations can take several forms. Four are briefly examined.

Exporter   An MNC could produce a product domestically and export some of that production to one or more foreign markets. This is, perhaps, the least risky method—reaping the benefits of foreign demand without committing any long-term investment to that foreign country.

Licensing Agreement   A firm with exporting operations may get into trouble when a foreign government imposes or substantially raises an import tariff to a level at which the exporter cannot compete effectively with the local domestic manufacturers. The foreign government may even ban all imports at times. When this happens the exporting firm may grant a license to an independent local producer to use the firm's technology in return for a license fee or a royalty. In essence, then, the MNC will be exporting technology, rather than the product, to that foreign country.

Joint Venture   As an alternative to licensing, the MNC may establish a joint venture with a local foreign manufacturer. The legal, political, and economic environments around the globe are more conducive to the joint venture arrangement than any of the other modes of operation. Historical evidence also suggests that a joint venture with a local entrepreneur exposes the firm to the least amount of political risk. This position is preferred by most business firms and by foreign governments as well.

Fully Owned Foreign Subsidiary   Although the joint venture form is desirable for many reasons, it may be hard to find a willing and cooperative local entrepreneur with sufficient capital to participate. Under these conditions the MNC may have to go it alone. For political reasons, however, a wholly owned foreign subsidiary is becoming more of a rarity in the 1990s. The reader must keep in mind that whenever we mention a *foreign affiliate* in the ensuing discussion, it could be a joint venture or a fully owned subsidiary.

As the firm crosses its national borders, it faces an environment that is riskier and more complex than its domestic surroundings. Sometimes the social and political environment can be hostile. Despite these difficult challenges, foreign affiliates often are more profitable than domestic businesses. A purely domestic firm faces several basic risks, such as the risk related to maintaining sales and market share, the financial risk of too much leverage, the risk of a poor equity market, and so on. In addition to these types of risks, the foreign affiliate is exposed to foreign exchange risk and political risk. While the foreign affiliate experiences a larger amount of risk than a domestic firm, it actually lowers the portfolio risk of its parent corporation by stabilizing the combined operating cash flows for the MNC. This risk reduction occurs because foreign and domestic economies are less than perfectly correlated.

Foreign business operations are more complex because the host country's economy may be different from the domestic economy. The rate of inflation in many foreign countries is likely to be higher than in the United States. The rules of taxation are different. The structure and operation of financial markets and institutions also vary from country to country, as do financial policies and practices. The presence of a foreign affiliate benefits the host country's economy. Foreign affiliates have been a decisive factor in shaping the pattern of trade, investment, and the flow of technology between nations. They can have a significant positive impact on a host country's economic growth, employment, trade, and balance of payments. This positive contribution, however, is occasionally overshadowed by allegations of wrongdoing. For example some host countries have charged that foreign affiliates subverted their governments and caused instability of their currencies in international money and foreign exchange markets. The less-developed countries (LDCs) have, at times, alleged that foreign businesses exploit their labor with low wages. The multinational companies are also under constant criticism in their home countries where labor unions charge the MNCs with exporting jobs, capital, and technology to foreign nations while avoiding their fair share of taxes. Despite all these criticisms, the multinational companies have managed to survive and prosper. The MNC is well positioned to take advantage of imperfections in the global markets. Furthermore, since current global resource distribution favors the MNC's survival and growth, it may be concluded that the multinational corporation is here to stay.

Foreign Exchange Rates

Suppose you are planning to spend a semester in Paris studying the French culture. To put your plan into operation you will need French currency, that is, French francs (FF), so you can pay for your expenses during your stay. How many French francs you can obtain for $1,000 will depend on the exchange rate at that time. The relationship between the values of two currencies is known as the **exchange rate.** The exchange rate between U.S. dollars and French francs is stated as dollars per franc or francs per dollar. For example the quotation of $0.18 per franc is the same as FF5.56 per dollar. At this exchange rate you can purchase 5,560 French francs with $1,000. *The Wall Street Journal* publishes exchange rates of major foreign currencies each day. The names of some countries' currencies and their exchange rates relative to the U.S. dollar are shown in Table 21–2 on page 604. This table shows dollars (fractions of dollars) that one can exchange for each unit of foreign currency ($/currency). As you may notice from this table, the exchange rates change. By comparing exchange rates between August 1, 1990, and January 1, 1993, you will observe that most currencies decreased in value relative to the dollar. That is the foreign currency would buy fewer dollars (fractions of dollars) in January 1993 than in August 1990. The German deutsche mark was the equivalent of .6305 dollars in August 1990 but decreased to .6102 dollars in January 1993. By taking the reciprocal of these two values, we could say the

TABLE 21–2
**Selected currencies
and exchange rates.
Dollar (fractions of
dollar) that one can
exchange for each
unit of foreign currency
($/currency)**

Country	Currency	August 1, 1990	January 1, 1993
Austria.	schilling	0.0894	0.0868
Belgium	franc	0.0260	0.0297
Britain	pound	1.8565	1.5145
Denmark.	krone	.1649	0.1572
France.	franc	.1915	0.1801
Germany.	deutsche mark	.6305	0.6102
India	rupee	.0571	0.0348
Italy	lira	.0005	0.0007
Japan	yen	.0068	0.0081
Mexico.	peso	.3000	0.3206
Netherlands . . .	guilder	.5587	0.5426
Portugal	escudo	.0071	0.0068
South Africa . . .	rand	.3859	0.3263
Spain	peseta	.0102	0.0086
Sweden	krona	.1719	0.1388
Switzerland . . .	franc	.7383	0.6780

dollar was worth 1.59 (1 ÷ .6305) deutsche marks in August 1990 and increased to 1.64 (1 ÷ .6102) deutsche marks in January 1993.

The dollar was not stronger against all currencies, as also indicated in Table 21–2. Countries that had increasing buying power relative to the dollar include Japan, Mexico, and Belgium. The relative strength of the dollar to other currencies changes many times over a business cycle.

Factors Influencing Exchange Rates

The present international monetary system consists of a mixture of "freely" floating exchange rates and fixed rates. The currencies of the major trading partners of the United States are traded in free markets. In such a market the exchange rate between two currencies is determined by the supply of, and the demand for, those currencies. This activity, however, is subject to intervention by many countries' central banks. Factors that tend to increase the supply or decrease the demand schedule for a given currency will bring down the value of that currency in foreign exchange markets. Similarly the factors that tend to decrease the supply or increase the demand for a currency will raise the value of that currency. Since fluctuations in currency values result in foreign exchange risk, the financial executive must understand the factors causing these changes in currency values. Although the value of a currency is determined by the aggregate supply and demand for that currency, this alone does not help our financial manager understand or predict the changes in exchange rates. Fundamental factors, such as inflation, interest rates, balance of payments, and government policies, are quite important in explaining both the short-term and long-term fluctuations of a currency value.

Inflation   A parity between the purchasing powers of two currencies establishes the rate of exchange between the two currencies. Suppose it takes $1.00

to buy one dozen apples in New York and 2.50 deutsche marks to buy the same apples in Frankfurt, Germany. Then the rate of exchange between the U.S. dollar and deutsche mark is DM2.50/$1.00 or $0.40/DM. If prices of apples double in New York while the prices in Frankfurt remain the same, you know that the purchasing power of a dollar in New York will drop 50 percent. Consequently, you will be able to exchange $1.00 for only DM 1.25 in foreign currency markets (or receive $0.80 per DM). Currency exchange rates tend to vary inversely with their respective purchasing powers to provide the same or similar purchasing power in each country. This is called the **purchasing power parity theory.** When the inflation rate differential between two countries changes, the exchange rate also adjusts to correspond to the relative purchasing powers of the countries.

Interest Rates   Another economic variable that has a significant influence on exchange rates is interest rates. As a student of finance, you should know that investment capital flows in the direction of higher yield for a given level of risk. This flow of short-term capital between money markets occurs because investors seek equilibrium through arbitrage buying and selling. If investors can earn 6 percent interest per year in Country X and 10 percent per year in Country Y, they will prefer to invest in Country Y, provided the inflation rate and risk are the same in both countries. Thus interest rates and exchange rates adjust until the foreign exchange market and the money market reach equilibrium. This interplay between interest rate differentials and exchange rates is called the **interest rate parity theory.**

Balance of Payments   The term **balance of payments** refers to a system of government accounts that catalogs the flow of economic transactions between the residents of one country and the residents of other countries. (The balance of payments statement for the United States is prepared by the U.S. Department of Commerce quarterly and annually.) It resembles the funds statement presented in Chapter 2 and tracks the country's exports and imports as well as the flow of capital and gifts. When a country sells (exports) more goods and services to foreign countries than it purchases (imports) from abroad, it will have a surplus in its balance of trade. Japan, through its aggressive competition in world markets, exports more goods than it imports and has been enjoying a trade surplus for quite some time. Since the foreigners who buy Japanese goods are expected to pay their bills in yen, the demand for yen and, consequently, its value increases in foreign currency markets. On the other hand, continuous deficits in the balance of payments are expected to depress the value of a currency because such deficits would increase the supply of that currency relative to the demand. This has sometimes been the case with the U.S. dollar.

Government Policies   A national government may, through its central bank, intervene in the foreign exchange market, buying and selling currencies as it sees fit to support the value of its currency relative to others. Sometimes a given country may deliberately pursue a policy of maintaining an undervalued currency in order to promote cheap exports. In Communist countries the currency values are set by government decree. Even in some free market countries, the central banks fix the exchange rates, subject to periodic review and adjustment. Some nations affect the foreign exchange rate indirectly by restricting the flow of funds into and out of the country. Monetary and fiscal policies also affect the currency value in foreign exchange markets. For example expansionary monetary policy and excessive government spending are primary causes of inflation, and continual use of such policies eventually reduces the value of the country's currency.

Other Factors   A pronounced and extended stock market rally in a country attracts investment capital from other countries, thus creating a huge demand by foreigners for that country's currency. This increased demand is expected to increase the value of that currency. Similarly a significant drop in demand for a country's principal exports worldwide is expected to result in a corresponding decline in the value of its currency. The South African rand is an example from recent history. A precipitous drop in gold prices is cited as the reason for the depreciation of this currency during the 1980s and early 1990s. Political turmoil in a country often drives capital out of the country into stable countries. A mass exodus of capital, due to the fear of political risk, undermines the value of a country's currency in the foreign exchange market. Also widespread labor strikes that may appear to weaken the nation's economy will depress its currency value.

Although a wide variety of factors that can influence exchange rates have been discussed, a few words of caution are in order. All of these variables will not necessarily influence all currencies to the same degree. Some factors may have an overriding influence on one currency's value, while their influence on another currency may be negligible at that time.

Spot Rates and Forward Rates

When you look into a major financial newspaper (e.g., *The Wall Street Journal*), you will discover that two exchange rates exist simultaneously for most major currencies—the spot rate and the forward rate. The **spot rate** for a currency is the exchange rate at which the currency is traded for immediate delivery. For example you walk into a local commercial bank and ask for French francs. The banker will indicate the rate at which the franc is selling, say FF 5.56/$. If you like the rate, you buy 5,560 francs with $1,000 and walk out the door. This is a spot market transaction at the retail level. The trading of currencies for future delivery is called a forward market transaction. Suppose IBM Corporation expects to receive FF 60 million from a French customer 30 days from now. It is not certain, however, what these francs will be worth in dollars 30 days from today. To eliminate this uncertainty, IBM calls a bank and offers to sell FF 60 million for U.S. dollars 30 days from now. In their negotiation the two parties may agree on an exchange rate of FF 6/$. Since the exchange rate is established for future delivery, it is a **forward rate.** After 30 days IBM delivers FF 60 million to the bank and receives $10 million. The difference between spot and forward exchange rates, expressed in dollars per unit of foreign curency, may be seen in the following typical values.

Rates	Deutsche Mark (DM) ($/DM)	British Pound (£) ($/£)
Spot	$0.6102	$1.5145
30-day forward	0.6115	1.5038
90-day forward	0.6138	1.5031
180-day forward . . .	0.6172	1.4917

The forward exchange rate of a currency is slightly different from the spot rate prevailing at that time. Since the forward rate deals with a future time, the expectations regarding the future value of that currency are reflected in the forward rate. Forward rates may be greater than the current spot rate (premium) or less than the current spot rate (discount). The table above shows forward rates on the deutsche mark were at a premium in relation to the spot rate, while the forward rates for the British pound were at a discount from the spot rate. This means the participants in the foreign exchange market expected the deutsche mark to appreciate relative to the U.S. dollar in the future and the British pound to depreciate against the dollar. The discount or premium is usually expressed as an annualized percentage deviation from the spot rate. The percentage discount or premium is computed with the following formula:

$$\begin{matrix} \text{Forward} \\ \text{premium} \\ \text{(or discount)} \end{matrix} = \frac{\text{Forward rate} - \text{Spot rate}}{\text{Spot rate}} \times \frac{12}{\begin{matrix} \text{Length of} \\ \text{forward contract} \\ \text{(in months)} \end{matrix}} \times 100 \qquad (21\text{--}1)$$

For example the 90-day forward contract in deutsche marks was selling at a 2.36 percent premium:

$$\left(\frac{0.6138 - 0.6102}{0.6102} \right) \times \frac{12}{3} \times 100 = 2.3599\%$$

while the 90-day forward contract in pounds was trading at a 3.01 percent discount:

$$\left(\frac{1.5031 - 1.5145}{1.5145} \right) \times \frac{12}{3} \times 100 = 3.0109\% \text{ (discount)}$$

Normally the forward premium or discount is between 0.5 percent and 10 percent.

The spot and forward transactions are said to occur in the over-the-counter market. Foreign currency dealers (usually large commercial banks) and their customers (importers, exporters, investors, multinational firms, and so on) negotiate the exchange rate, the length of the forward contract, and the commission in a mutually agreeable fashion. Although the length of a typical forward contract may generally vary between one month and six months, contracts for longer maturities are not uncommon. The dealers, however, may require higher returns for longer contracts.

Cross Rates Since currencies are quoted against the U.S. dollar in *The Wall Street Journal,* sometimes it may be necessary to work out the **cross rates** for other currencies than the dollar.[1] For example on January 1, 1993, the Swedish krona was selling for $0.1388 and the British pound was selling for $1.5145. The cross rate between the krona and the pound is 10.91 (kronas/pounds). In determining this value, we show that one dollar will buy 7.205 kronas (1 ÷ 0.1388) and a pound is equal to $1.5145 dollars. Thus 7.205 Swedish kronas per *dollar* times 1.5145 *dollars* per pound equals 10.91 Swedish kronas per pound.

Managing Foreign Exchange Risk

When the parties associated with a commercial transaction are located in the same country, the transaction is denominated in a single currency. International transactions inevitably involve more than one currency (because the parties are residents of different countries). Since most foreign currency values fluctuate from time to time, the monetary value of an international transaction measured in either the seller's currency or the buyer's currency is likely to change when payment is delayed. As a result the seller may receive less revenue than expected or the buyer may have to pay more than the expected amount for the merchandise. Thus the term **foreign exchange risk** refers to the possibility of a drop in revenue or an increase in cost in an international transaction due to a change in foreign exchange rates. Importers, exporters, investors, and multinational firms are all exposed to this foreign exchange risk.

The international monetary system has undergone a significant change over the last 20 years. The free trading Western nations basically went from a fixed exchange rate system to a "freely" floating rate system. For the most part, the new system proved its agility and resilience during the most turbulent years of oil price hikes and hyperinflation of the last two decades. The free market exchange rates responded and adjusted well to these adverse conditions. Consequently the exchange rates fluctuated over a much wider range than before. The increased volatility of exchange markets forced many multinational firms, importers, and exporters to pay more attention to the function of foreign exchange risk management.

The foreign exchange risk of a multinational company is divided into two types of exposure. They are: accounting or translation exposure and transaction exposure. An MNC's foreign assets and liabilities, which are denominated

---

[1]Some cross rate quotations are also given in *The Wall Street Journal.* However, many currencies are not covered.

in foreign currency units, are exposed to losses and gains due to changing exchange rates. This is called accounting or **translation exposure.** The amount of loss or gain resulting from this form of exposure and the treatment of it in the parent company's books depends on the accounting rules established by the parent company's government. In the United States, the rules are spelled out in Financial Accounting Standards Board Statement 52 (FASB 52). Under FASB 52 all foreign currency denominated assets and liabilities are converted at the rate of exchange in effect on the date of balance sheet preparation. An unrealized translation gain or loss is held in an equity reserve account while the realized gain or loss is incorporated in the parent's consolidated income statement for that period. Thus FASB 52 reduces the impact of accounting exposure resulting from the translation of a foreign subsidiary's balance sheet on reported earnings of multinational firms.

However, foreign exchange gains and losses resulting from international transactions, which reflect **transaction exposure,** are shown in the income statement for the current period. As a consequence of these transactional gains and losses, the volatility of reported earnings per share increases. Three different strategies can be used to minimize this transaction exposure.

1. Hedging in the forward exchange market.
2. Hedging in the money market.
3. Hedging in the currency futures market.

Forward Exchange Market Hedge   To see how the transaction exposure can be covered in forward markets, suppose Electricitie de France, an electric company in France, purchased a large generator from General Electric of the United States for FF 9.250 million on October 26, 1992, and GE was promised the payment in French francs in 90 days. Since GE is now exposed to exchange risk by agreeing to receive the payment in French francs in the future, it is up to GE to find a way to reduce this exposure. One simple method is to hedge the exposure in the forward exchange market. On October 26, 1992, to establish the forward cover, GE sells a forward contract to deliver the FF 9.250 million, 90 days from now in exchange for $1.660 million. On January 25, 1993, GE receives payment from Electricitie de France and delivers the FF 9.250 million to the bank that signed the contract. In return the bank delivers $1.660 million to GE. Thus, through this international transaction, GE receives the same dollar amount it expected three months ago regardless of what happened to the value of French francs in the interim. In contrast, if the sale had been invoiced in U.S. dollars, Electricitie de France, not GE, would have been exposed to the exchange risk.

Money Market Hedge   A second way to have eliminated transaction exposure in the previous example would have been to borrow money in French francs and then convert it to U.S. dollars immediately. When the accounts receivable from the sale is collected three months later, the loan is cleared with the proceeds. In this case GE's strategy consists of the following steps. On October 26, 1992:

1. Borrow FF 8.980,582—(FF 9,250,000/1.03) = FF 8,980,582—at the rate of 12 percent per year for three months. You borrow less than the full amount of FF 9,250,000 in recognition of the fact that interest must be paid on the loan. Twelve percent interest for 90 days translates into 3 percent. Thus FF 9,250,000 is divided by 1.03 to arrive at the size of the loan before the interest payment.
2. Convert the French francs into the U.S. dollars in the spot market.

Then on January 25, 1993 (90 days later):

3. Receive the payment FF 9,250,000 from Electricitie de France.
4. Clear the loan with the proceeds received from Electricitie de France.

The money market hedge basically calls for matching the exposed asset (accounts receivable) with a liability (loan payable) in the same currency. Some firms prefer this money market hedge because of the early availability of funds possible with this method.

Currency Futures Market Hedge   Transaction exposure associated with a foreign currency can also be covered in the futures market with a **currency futures contract.** The International Monetary Market (IMM) of the Chicago Mercantile Exchange began trading in futures contracts in foreign currencies on May 16, 1972. Trading in currency futures contracts also made a debut on the London International Financial Futures Exchange (LIFFE) in September 1982. Other markets have also developed around the world. Just as futures contracts are traded in corn, wheat, hogs, and beans, foreign currency futures contracts are traded in these markets. Although the futures market and forward market are similar in concept, they differ in their operations. To illustrate the hedging process in the currency futures market, suppose that in June the Chicago-based Continental Illinois National Bank considers lending 500,000 deutsche marks to a German subsidiary of a U.S. parent company for six months. The bank purchases the deutsche marks in the spot market, delivers them to the borrower, and simultaneously hedges its transaction exposure by selling December contracts in deutsche marks for the same amount. In December when the loan is cleared, the bank sells the deutsche marks in the spot market and buys back the December deutsche mark contracts. The transactions are illustrated as follows for the spot and futures market:[2]

---

[2]For purposes of this example, we assumed the deutsche mark was trading at a discount in the futures market. Had it been trading at a premium, the hedge would have been even more attractive.

Date	Spot Market	Futures Market
June 1.	Buys 500,000 deutsche marks (DM) at $0.6100/DM = $305,000	Sells DM 500,000 for December delivery at $0.6090 = $304,500
December 1 . . .	Sells DM 500,000 at 0.6070 = $303,500	Buys DM 500,000 at $0.6070/DM = $303,500
	Loss $1,500	Gain $1,000

While the loan was outstanding, the deutsche mark dropped its value in relation to the U.S. dollar. Had the bank remained unhedged, it would have lost $1,500 in the spot market. By hedging in the futures market, the bank reduced the loss to only $500. A $1,000 gain in the futures market was used to cancel all but $500 of the $1,500 loss in the spot market.

Hedging is not the only means companies have for protecting themselves against foreign exchange risk. Over the years multinational companies have developed elaborate foreign asset management programs, which involve such strategies as switching cash and other current assets into strong currencies, while piling up debt and other liabilities in depreciating currencies. Companies also encourage the quick collection of bills in weak currencies by offering sizable discounts, while extending liberal credit in strong currencies.

Foreign Investment Decisions

It is estimated from the *Directory of American Firms Operating in Foreign Countries* that more than 4,000 U.S. firms have one or more foreign affiliates. Several explanations are offered for the move to foreign soil. First, with the emergence of trading blocks like the common market in Europe, American firms feared their goods might face import tariffs in those countries. To avoid such trade barriers, U.S. firms started manufacturing in foreign countries. The second factor was the lower production costs overseas. Firms were motivated by the significantly lower wage costs prevailing in foreign countries. Firms in labor-intensive industries, such as textiles and electronics, moved some of their operations to countries where labor was cheap. Third superior American technology gave U.S. firms an easy access to oil exploration, mining, and manufacturing in many developing nations. A fourth advantage relates to taxes. The U.S.-based multinational firms can postpone payment of U.S. taxes on income earned abroad until such income is actually repatriated (forwarded) to the parent company. This tax deferral provision can be used by an MNC to minimize its tax liability. Some countries, like Israel, Ireland, and South Africa, offer special tax incentives for foreign firms that establish operations there.[3] Although the benefits of lower taxes and lower wage costs and the

---

[3]Tax advantages for multinational corporations are being challenged by the Clinton administration and are likely to be significantly less in the future.

technological gap have diminished in recent years, the average rate of return on U.S. investment abroad continues to be higher than on U.S. domestic investments.

The decision to invest in a foreign country by a firm operating in an oligopolistic industry is also motivated by strategic considerations. When a competitor undertakes a direct foreign investment, other companies quickly follow with defensive investments in the same foreign country. Foreign investments undertaken by U.S. tire and rubber companies are classic examples of this competitive reaction. Wherever you find a Firestone subsidiary in a foreign country, you are likely to see a Goodyear affiliate also operating in that country.

Many academicians believe international diversification of risks is also an important motivation for direct foreign investment. The basic premise of portfolio theory in finance is that an investor can reduce the risk level of a portfolio by combining those investments whose returns are less than perfectly positively correlated. In addition to domestic diversification, it is shown in Figure 21–1 that further reduction in investment risk can be achieved by diversifying across national boundaries. International stocks, in Figure 21–1, show a consistently lower percentage of risk compared to any given number of U.S. stocks in a portfolio. It is argued, however, that institutional and

FIGURE 21–1
Risk reduction from international diversification

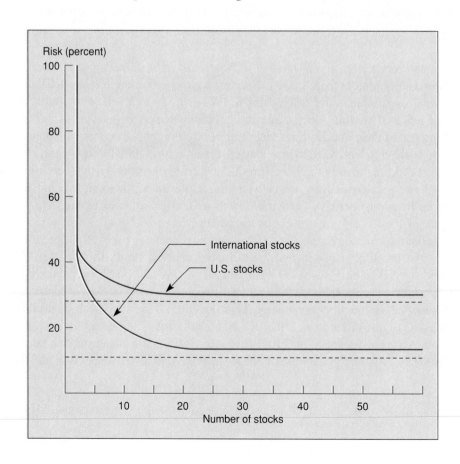

political constraints, language barriers, and lack of adequate information on foreign investments prevent investors from diversifying across nations. Multinational firms, on the other hand, through their unique position around the world, derive the benefits of international diversification. This argument has been weakened somewhat by the introduction of international mutual funds.

While U.S.-based firms took the lead in establishing overseas subsidiaries during the 1950s and 1960s, European and Japanese firms started this activity in the 1970s and have continued into the 1990s. The flow of foreign direct investment into the United States has proceeded at a rapid rate. These investments employ millions of people. It is evident that the United States is becoming an attractive site for foreign investment. In addition to the international diversification and strategic considerations, many other factors are responsible for this rapid inflow of foreign capital into the United States. Increased foreign labor costs in some countries and saturated overseas markets in others are partly responsible. In Japan an acute shortage of land suitable for industrial development and a near total dependence on imported oil prompted some of their firms to locate in the United States. In Germany a large number of paid holidays, restrictions limiting labor layoffs, and worker participation in management decision making caused many firms to look favorably at the United States. Political stability, large market size, and access to advanced technology are other primary motivating factors for firms to establish operations in the United States. Also large balance of payments deficits have spread hundreds of millions of dollars around the world for potential reinvestment in the United States, particularly by the Japanese.

To some extent foreign investors in the U.S. Treasury bond market have been bankrolling enormous budget deficits that the government has been running up. When the U.S. government began falling $150 to $200 billion into the red on an annual basis in the 1980s, many analysts thought this would surely mean high inflation, high interest rates, and perhaps a recession. They also were sure there would be a "shortage of capital" for investment because of large government borrowing to finance the deficits. For the most part, foreign investors from Japan, Western Europe, Canada, and elsewhere have bailed the government out by supplying the necessary capital. Of course this now means the United States is more dependent on flows of foreign capital into the country. We must satisfy our "outside" investors or face the unpleasant consequences. In a decade we have gone from being the largest lender in the world to the largest borrower. The United States does not have the flexibility to manage monetary policy and interest rates with only a concern for domestic consequences; the world is now our frame of reference.

Analysis of Political Risk

Business firms tend to make direct investments in foreign countries for a relatively long time. Because of the time necessary to recover the initial investment, they do not intend to liquidate their investments quickly. The government may change hands several times during the foreign firm's tenure in that country; and, when a new government takes over, it may not be as friendly or as cooperative as the previous administration. An unfriendly government can interfere with the foreign affiliate in many ways. It may impose foreign exchange restrictions, or the foreign ownership share may be limited to a set percentage of the total. **Repatriation** (transfer) of a subsidiary's profit to the parent company may be blocked, at least temporarily; and, in the extreme case, the government may even **expropriate** (take over) the foreign subsidiary's assets. The multinational company may experience a sizable loss of income or property, or both, as a result of this political interference. Many well-known U.S. firms, like Anaconda, ITT, and Occidental Petroleum, have lost hundreds of millions of dollars in politically unstable countries. Over the last decade, more than 60 percent of U.S. companies doing business abroad suffered some form of politically inflicted damage. Therefore analysis of foreign political risk is gaining more attention in multinational firms.

The best approach to protection against political risk is to thoroughly investigate the country's political stability long before the firm makes any investment in that country. Companies have been using different methods for assessing political risk. Some firms hire consultants to provide them with a report of political-risk analysis. Others form their own advisory committees (little state departments) consisting of top-level managers from headquarters and foreign subsidiaries. After ascertaining the country's political-risk level, the multinational firm can use one of the following strategies to guard against such risk:

1. One strategy is to establish a joint venture with a local entrepreneur. By bringing a local partner into the deal, the MNC not only limits its financial exposure but also minimizes antiforeign feelings.

2. Another risk-management tactic is to enter into a joint venture, preferably with firms from other countries. For example Chevron may pursue its oil production operation in Zaire in association with Royal Dutch Petroleum and Nigerian National Petroleum as partners. The foreign government will be more hesitant to antagonize a number of partner-firms of many nationalities at the same time.

3. When the perceived political-risk level is high, insurance against such risks can be obtained in advance. **Overseas Private Investment Corporation (OPIC),** a federal government agency, sells insurance policies to qualified firms. This agency insures against losses due to inconvertibility into dollars of amounts invested in a foreign country. Policies are also available from OPIC to insure against expropriation and against losses due to war or revolution. Many firms have used this service over the years. Greenlaw, Inc., a Florida-based firm, insured its fruit-processing plant in the Dominican Republic through OPIC. Private insurance companies, such as Lloyds of London, American International Group Inc., CIGNA, and others, issue similar policies to cover political risk.

FINANCE IN ACTION

India: A New Player in the Global Economy

Of India's population of 870 million, 300 million are considered to be in the broad middle class. That figure is appealing to multinational companies seeking to enter new markets.

The government is encouraging international trade as well. Tariffs, while averaging a high of 80 percent, are on their way down and should be around 25 percent in the next few years.* In a 15-month period in the early 1990s, the government's Foreign Investment Promotion Board approved new investments adding up to $1.3 billion by such companies as General Motors, Du Pont, BMW, Kellogg, and Coca-Cola. In the past such action, if taken at all, would have required many years for completion with an endless amount of red tape. Furthermore India is now allowing foreign companies to take stakes of greater than 50 percent in privately run operations. Also foreign institutional investors are being allowed to trade on the once restricted Indian Stock Exchange.

Another consideration for foreign firms investing in India is that the country has an unusually large pool of English-speaking managers and technicians, who take unusual pride in their performance. Of all the countries in the world, only the United States and Russia have a larger scientific and technical work force.

As an example of the changed environment, IBM, which pulled out of India in the 1970s due to restrictive regulatory policy, has joined a $20 million joint venture with India's Tota group to make computers and develop related software. Bank of America, which is also a player in India, anticipates that the number of credit card holders could go from 750,000 in the early 1990s to 30 million by the end of the decade. Such an environment is very appealing to multinational corporations that face mature or shrinking markets in other parts of the world.

*Rahul Jacob, "India Is Open for Business," *Fortune*, November 16, 1992, pp. 128–30.

Political-risk umbrella policies do not come cheaply. Coverage for projects in "fairly safe" countries can cost anywhere from 0.3 percent to 12 percent of the insured values per year. Needless to say, the coverage is more expensive or unavailable in troubled countries. OPIC's rates are lower than those of private insurers, and its policies extend for up to 20 years, compared to three years or less for private insurance policies.

European Community 1992

One segment of the world that is attempting to reduce political risk and facilitate trade is Europe through **European Community (EC) 1992.** Under the EC 92 arrangement, 12 major European countries are breaking down nationalistic barriers between themselves and forming a common bond to achieve economic progress. Participating countries are Belgium, Denmark, France, Germany, Greece, Great Britain, Ireland, Italy, Luxembourg, Netherlands, Portugal, and Spain. While December 31, 1992, was the official date for the opening of EC 92, the development began many years ago and will continue through the beginning of the next century.

The major provisions initially intended for EC 92 included:

- Elimination of border controls.
- Common standards for trade and commerce.
- Integrated financial markets.
- Mobility of labor markets.
- Common European air traffic control system.
- Shared telecommunication and information services.
- Recognition of individual country licensing.

While progress in a number of these areas has occurred, there is still much strain and disagreement among the participating countries and only time will tell whether the goals of EC 92 will be met.

Financing International Business Operations

When the parties to an international transaction are well known to each other and the countries involved are politically stable, sales are generally made on credit, as is customary in domestic business operations. However, if a foreign importer is relatively new or the political environment is volatile, or both, the possibility of nonpayment by the importer is worrisome for the exporter. To reduce the risk of nonpayment, an exporter may request that the importer furnish a letter of credit. The importer's bank normally issues the **letter of credit,** in which the bank promises to subsequently pay the money for the merchandise. For example, assume Archer Daniels Midland (ADM) is negotiating with a South Korean trading company to export soybean meal. The two parties agree on price, method of shipment, timing of shipment, destination point, and the like. Once the basic terms of sale have been agreed to, the South Korean trading company (importer) applies for a letter of credit from its commercial bank in Seoul. The Korean bank, if it so desires, issues such a letter of credit, which specifies in detail all the steps that must be completed by the American exporter before payment is made. If ADM complies with all specifications in the letter of credit and submits to the Korean bank the proper documentation to prove that it has done so, the Korean bank guarantees the payment on the due date. On that date the American firm is paid by the Korean bank, not by the buyer of the goods. Therefore all the credit risk to the exporter is absorbed by the importer's bank, which is in a good position to evaluate the creditworthiness of the importing firm.

The exporter who requires cash payment or a letter of credit from foreign buyers of marginal credit standing is likely to lose orders to competitors. Instead of risking the loss of business, American firms can find an alternative way to reduce the risk of nonpayment by foreign customers. This alternative method consists of obtaining export credit insurance. The insurance policy provides assurance to the exporter that should the foreign customer default on payment, the insurance company will pay for the shipment. The **Foreign Credit Insurance Association (FCIA),** a private association of 60 U.S. insurance firms, provides this kind of insurance to exporting firms.

Funding of Transactions

Assistance in the funding of foreign transactions may take many forms.

Eximbank (Export-Import Bank)   This agency of the U.S. government facilitates the financing of U.S. exports through its miscellaneous programs. In its direct loan program, the **Eximbank** lends money to foreign purchasers of U.S. goods, such as aircraft, electrical equipment, heavy machinery, computers, and the like. The Eximbank also purchases eligible medium-term obligations of foreign buyers of U.S. goods at a discount from face value. In this discount program, private banks and other lenders are able to rediscount (sell at a lower price) promissory notes and drafts acquired from foreign customers of U.S. firms.

Loans from the Parent Company or a Sister Affiliate   An apparent source of funds for a foreign affiliate is its parent company or its sister affiliates. In addition to contributing equity capital, the parent company often provides loans of varying maturities to its foreign affiliate. Although the simplest arrangement is a direct loan from the parent to the foreign subsidiary, such a loan is rarely extended because of foreign exchange risk, political risk, and tax treatment. Instead the loans are often channeled through an intermediary to a foreign affiliate. Parallel loans and fronting loans are two examples of such indirect loan arrangements between a parent company and its foreign affiliate. A typical parallel loan arrangement is depicted in Figure 21–2.

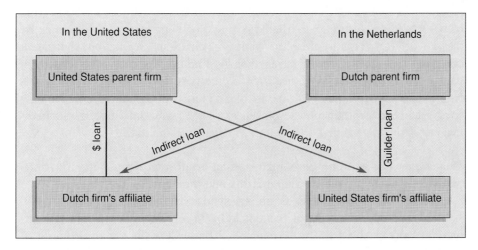

FIGURE 21–2
A parallel loan arrangement

In this illustration of a **parallel loan,** an American firm wanting to lend funds to its Dutch affiliate locates a Dutch parent firm, which wants to transfer funds to its U.S. affiliate. Avoiding the exchange markets, the U.S. parent lends dollars to the Dutch affiliate in the United States, while the Dutch parent lends guilders to the American affiliate in the Netherlands. At maturity the two loans would each be repaid to the original lender. Notice that neither loan carries any foreign exchange risk in this arrangement. In essence both parent firms are providing indirect loans to their affiliates.

A **fronting loan** is simply a parent's loan to its foreign subsidiary channeled through a financial intermediary, usually a large international bank. A schematic of a fronting loan is shown in Figure 21–3.

FIGURE 21–3
**A fronting loan
arrangement**

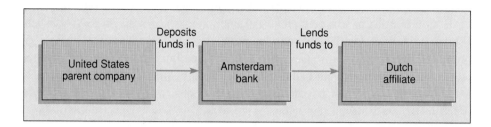

In the example the U.S. parent company deposits funds in an Amsterdam bank and that bank lends the same amount to the U.S. firm's affiliate in the Netherlands. In this manner the bank fronts for the parent by extending a risk-free (fully collateralized) loan to the foreign affiliate. In the event of political turmoil, the foreign government is more likely to allow the American subsidiary to repay the loan to a large international bank than to allow the same affiliate to repay the loan to its parent company. Thus the parent company reduces its political risk substantially by using a fronting loan instead of transferring funds directly to its foreign affiliate.

Even though the parent company would prefer that its foreign subsidiary maintain its own financial arrangements, many banks are apprehensive about lending to a foreign affiliate without a parent guarantee. In fact a large portion of bank lending to foreign affiliates is based on some sort of a guarantee by the parent firm. Usually, because of its multinational reputation, the parent company has a better credit rating than its foreign affiliates. The lender advances funds on the basis of the parent's creditworthiness even though the affiliate is expected to pay back the loan. The terms of a parent guarantee may vary greatly, depending on the closeness of the parent-affiliate ties, parent-lender relations, and the home country's legal jurisdiction.

Eurodollar Loans   The Eurodollar market is an important source of short-term loans for many multinational firms and their foreign affiliates.

Eurodollars are simply U.S. dollars deposited in European banks. A substantial portion of these deposits are held by European branches of U.S. commercial banks. About 85 to 90 percent of these deposits are in the form of term deposits with the banks for a specific maturity and at a fixed interest rate. The remaining 10 to 15 percent of these deposits represent negotiable certificates of deposit with maturities varying from one week to five years or longer. However, maturities of three months, six months, and one year are most common in this market.

Since the early 1960s, the Eurodollar market has established itself as a significant part of world credit markets. The participants in these markets are diverse in character and geographically widespread. Hundreds of corporations and banks, mostly from the United States, Canada, Western Europe, and Japan, are regular borrowers and depositors in this market.

U.S. firms have more than doubled their borrowings in the Eurodollar market during the early 1990s. The lower costs and greater credit availability of the Eurodollar market continue to attract borrowers. The lower borrowing costs in the Eurodollar market are often attributed to the smaller overhead costs for lending banks and the absence of a compensating balance requirement. The lending rate for borrowers in the Eurodollar market is based on the **London Interbank Offered Rate (LIBOR),** which is the interest rate for large deposits. Interest rates on loans are calculated by adding premiums to this basic rate. The size of this premium varies from 0.25 percent to 0.50 percent, depending on the customer, length of the loan period, size of the loan, and so on. For example, Northern Indiana Public Service Company obtained a $75 million, three-year loan from Merrill Lynch International Bank. The utility company paid 0.375 points above LIBOR for the first two years and 0.50 points above for the final year of the loan. Over the years borrowing in the Eurodollar market has been one eighth to seven eighths of a percentage point cheaper than borrowing at the U.S. prime interest rate. During a recent peak interest rate period in the United States, many cost-conscious domestic borrowers fled to the Eurodollar market. Having seen this trend, some U.S. banks began offering their customers the option of taking a LIBOR-based rate in lieu of the prime rate in order to stay competitive.

Lending in the Eurodollar market is done almost exclusively by commercial banks. Large Eurocurrency loans are often syndicated by a group of participating banks. The loan agreement is put together by a lead bank known as the manager, which is usually one of the largest U.S. or European banks. The manager charges the borrower a once-and-for-all fee or commission of 0.25 percent to 1 percent of the loan value. A portion of this fee is kept by the lead bank and the remainder is shared by all the participating banks. The aim of forming a syndicate is to diversify the risk, which would be too large for any single bank to handle by itself. Multicurrency loans and revolving credit arrangements can also be negotiated in the Eurocurrency market to suit borrowers' needs.

Eurobond Market When long-term funds are needed, borrowing in the Eurobond market is a viable alternative for leading multinational corporations. The **Eurobond** issues are sold simultaneously in several national capital markets, but denominated in a currency different from that of the nation in which the bonds are issued. The most widely used currency in the Eurobond market is the U.S. dollar. The next currency in importance is the deutsche mark. Eurobond issues are underwritten by an international syndicate of banks and securities firms. Eurobonds of longer than seven years in maturity generally have a sinking-fund provision.

Disclosure requirements in the Eurobond market are much less stringent than those required by the Securities and Exchange Commission (SEC) in the

United States. Furthermore the registration costs in the Eurobond market are lower than those charged in the United States. In addition the Eurobond market offers tax flexibility for borrowers and investors alike. All these advantages of Eurobonds enable the borrowers to raise funds at a lower cost. Nevertheless a caveat may be in order with respect to the effective cost of borrowing in the Eurobond market. When a multinational firm borrows by issuing a foreign currency denominated debt issue on a long-term basis, it creates transaction exposure, a kind of foreign exchange risk. If the foreign currency appreciates in value during the bond's life, the cost of servicing the debt could be prohibitively high. Many U.S. multinational firms borrowed at an approximately 7 percent coupon interest by selling Eurobonds denominated in deutsche marks and Swiss francs in the late 1960s and early 1970s. Nevertheless these U.S. firms experienced an average debt service cost of approximately 13 percent, which is almost twice as much as the coupon rate. This increased cost occurred because the U.S. dollar fell with respect to these currencies. Therefore currency selection for denominating Eurobond issues must be made with extreme care and foresight. To lessen the impact of foreign exchange risk, some recently issued Eurobond issues were denominated in multicurrency units.

International Equity Markets   The entire amount of equity capital comes from the parent company for a *wholly owned* foreign subsidiary, but a majority of foreign affiliates are not owned completely by their parent corporations. In Malaysia, majority ownership of a foreign affiliate must be held by the local citizens. In some other countries, the parent corporations are allowed to own their affiliates completely in the initial stages, but they are required to relinquish partial ownership to local citizens after five or seven years. To avoid nationalistic reactions to wholly owned foreign subsidiaries, such multinational firms as Unilever Ltd., Schlumberger, General Motors, Ford Motor Company, and IBM sell shares to worldwide stockholders. It is also believed that widespread foreign ownership of the firm's common stock encourages the loyalty of foreign stockholders and employees toward the firm. Thus selling common stock to residents of foreign countries is not only an important financing strategy, but it is also a risk-minimizing strategy for many multinational corporations.

As you have learned in Chapter 14, a well-functioning secondary market is essential to entice investors into owning shares. To attract investors from all over the world, reputable multinational firms list their shares on major stock exchanges around the world. About 40 foreign companies are listed on the New York Stock Exchange, and the American Stock Exchange lists more than 70 foreign firms. Several hundred foreign issues are traded in the over-the-counter market. Even more foreign firms would sell stock issues in the United States and list on the NYSE and AMEX were it not for the tough and costly disclosure rules in effect in this country and enforced by the Securities and Exchange Commission. Many foreign corporations, such as Hoechst, Honda, Hitachi, Sony, Magnet Metals Ltd., DeBeers, and the like, accommodate

American investors by issuing **American Depository Receipts (ADRs).** All the American-owned shares of a foreign company are placed in trust in a New York bank. The bank, in turn, will issue its depository receipts to the American stockholders and will maintain a stockholder ledger on these receipts, thus enabling the holders of ADRs to sell or otherwise transfer them as easily as they transfer any American company shares. ADR prices tend to move parallel with the prices of the underlying securities in their home markets.

Looking elsewhere around the world, approximately 70 U.S. firms have listed their shares on the Toronto Stock Exchange and some 50 on the Montreal Exchange. Similarly more than 100 U.S. firms have listed their shares on the London Stock Exchange. Approximately 160 foreign issues are listed on the Bourse de Paris, including 37 U.S. stocks. In addition a number of foreign securities are traded on the French hors cote (OTC) market. Fully half the stocks listed on the Amsterdam stock exchange are foreign. To obtain exposure in an international financial community, listing securities on world stock exchanges is a step in the right direction for a multinational firm. This international exposure also brings an additional responsibility for the MNC to understand the preferences and needs of heterogeneous groups of investors of various nationalities. The MNC may have to print and circulate its annual financial statements in many languages. Some foreign investors are more risk-averse than their counterparts in the United States and prefer dividend income over less-certain capital gains. Common stock ownership among individuals in countries like Japan and Norway is relatively insignificant, with financial institutions holding substantial amounts of common stock issues. Institutional practices around the globe also vary significantly when it comes to issuing new securities. Unlike the United States, European commercial banks play a dominant role in the securities business. They underwrite stock issues, manage portfolios, vote the stock they hold in trust accounts, and hold directorships on company boards. In Germany the banks also run an over-the-counter market in many stocks.

The International Finance Corporation   Whenever a multinational company has difficulty raising equity capital due to lack of adequate private risk capital in a foreign country, the firm may explore the possibility of selling partial ownership to the **International Finance Corporation (IFC).** This is a unit of the World Bank Group. The International Finance Corporation was established in 1956, and it is owned by 119 member countries of the World Bank. Its objective is to further economic development by promoting private enterprises in these countries. The profitability of a project and its potential benefit to the host country's economy are the two criteria the IFC uses to decide whether to assist a venture. The IFC participates in private enterprise through buying equity shares of a business, providing long-term loans, or a combination of the two for up to 25 percent of the total capital. The IFC expects the other partners to assume managerial responsibility, and it does not exercise its voting rights as a stockholder. The IFC helps finance new ventures as well as the expansion of existing ones in a variety of industries. Once the venture is well established, the IFC sells its investment position to private investors to free up its capital.

Some Unsettled Issues in International Finance

As firms become multinational in scope, the nature of their financial decisions also becomes more complex. A multinational firm has access to more sources of funds than a purely domestic corporation. Interest rates and market conditions vary between the alternate sources of funds, and corporate financial practices may differ significantly between countries. For example the debt ratios in many foreign countries are higher than those used by U.S. firms. A foreign affiliate of an American firm faces a dilemma in its financing decision: Should it follow the parent firm's norm or that of the host country? Who must decide this? Will it be decided at the corporate headquarters in the United States or by the foreign affiliate? This is a matter of control over financial decisions. Dividend policy is another area of debate. Should the parent company dictate the dividends the foreign affiliate must distribute or should it be left completely to the discretion of the foreign affiliate? Foreign government regulations may also influence the decision. Questions like these do not have clear-cut answers. The complex environment in which the MNCs operate does not permit simple and clear-cut solutions. Obviously, each situation has to be evaluated individually, and specific guidelines for decision making must be established. Such coordination, it is to be hoped, will result in cohesive policies in the areas of working capital management, capital structure, and dividend decisions throughout the MNC network.

Summary

When a domestic business firm crosses its national borders to do business in other countries, it enters a riskier and more complex environment. A multinational firm is exposed to foreign exchange risk and political risk in addition to the usual business and financial risks. In general international business operations have been more profitable than domestic operations, and this higher profitability is one factor that motivates business firms to go overseas. International operations account for a significant proportion of the earnings for many American firms. U.S. multinational firms have played a major role in promoting economic development and international trade for several decades, and now foreign firms have started to invest huge amounts of capital in the United States.

International business transactions are denominated in foreign currencies. The rate at which one currency unit is converted into another is called the exchange rate. In today's global monetary system, the exchange rates of major currencies are fluctuating rather freely. These "freely" floating exchange rates expose multinational business firms to foreign exchange risk. To deal with this foreign currency exposure effectively, the financial executive of an MNC must understand foreign exchange rates and how they are determined. Foreign exchange rates are influenced by differences in inflation rates among countries, by differences in interest rates, by governmental policies, and by the expectations of the participants in the foreign exchange markets. The international financial manager can reduce the firm's foreign currency exposure by hedging in the forward exchange market, in the money markets, and in the currency futures market.

Multinational companies have made billions of dollars worth of direct investments in foreign countries over the years. Lower production costs overseas, tax deferral provisions, less foreign competition, and benefits of international diversification are some of the motivational factors behind the flow of direct investment between nations. Foreign direct investments are usually quite large in size and many of them are exposed to enormous political risk. Although discounted cash flow analysis is applied to screen the projects in the initial stages, strategic considerations and political risk are often the overriding factors in reaching the final decision. One of the most important differences between domestic and international investments is that the information on foreign investments is generally less complete and often less accurate. Therefore analyzing a foreign investment proposal is more difficult than analyzing a domestic investment project.

Financing international trade and investment is another important area of international finance that one must understand to raise funds at the lowest cost possible. The multinational firm has access to both the domestic and foreign capital markets. The Export-Import Bank finances American exports to foreign countries. Borrowing in the Eurobond market may appear less expensive at times, but the effect of foreign exchange risk on debt servicing cost must be weighed carefully before borrowing in these markets. Floating common stock in foreign capital markets is also a viable financing alternative for many multinational companies. The International Finance Corporation, which is a subsidiary of the World Bank, also provides debt capital and equity capital to qualified firms. These alternative sources of financing may significantly differ with respect to cost, terms, and conditions. Therefore, the financial executive must carefully locate and use the proper means to finance international business operations.

List of Terms

Discussion Questions

1. What risks does a foreign affiliate of a multinational firm face in today's business world?
2. What allegations are sometimes made against foreign affiliates of multinational firms and against the multinational firms themselves?
3. List the factors that affect the value of a currency in foreign exchange markets.
4. Explain how exports and imports tend to influence the value of a currency.
5. Differentiate between the spot exchange rate and the forward exchange rate.
6. What is meant by translation exposure in terms of foreign exchange risk?
7. What factors influence a U.S. business firm to go overseas?
8. What procedure(s) would you recommend for a multinational company in studying exposure to political risk? What actual strategies can be used to guard against such risk?
9. What factors beyond the normal domestic analysis go into a financial feasibility study for a multinational firm?
10. What is a letter of credit?
11. Explain the functions of the following agencies:
   Overseas Private Investment Corporation (OPIC).
   Export-Import Bank (Eximbank).
   Foreign Credit Insurance Association (FCIA).
   International Finance Corporation (IFC).
12. What are the differences between a parallel loan and a fronting loan?
13. What is LIBOR? How does it compare to the U.S. prime rate?
14. What is the danger or concern in floating a Eurobond issue?
15. What are ADRs?
16. Comment on any dilemmas that multinational firms and their foreign affiliates may face in regard to debt ratio limits and dividend payouts.

1. Using the foreign exchange rates for January 1, 1993, in Table 21–2, determine the number of U.S. dollars required to buy the following amounts of foreign currencies.

   a. 5,000 guilders.

   b. 2,000 rand.

   c. 10,000 deutsche marks.

   d. 100,000 yen.

   e. 60,000 rupees.

   Exchange rates

2. Obtain a recent copy of *The Wall Street Journal* and recalculate the currency exchanges of problem 1. How do these figures compare to those obtained in the above problem? Has the dollar strengthened or weakened against these currencies?

   Exchange rates

3. *The Wall Street Journal* reported the following spot and forward rates for the Swiss franc ($/SF) as of January 1, 1993:

   Spot and forward rates

Spot	$0.6780
30-day forward	$0.6752
90-day forward	$0.6715
180-day forward . . .	$0.6681

   a. Was the Swiss franc selling at a discount or premium in the forward market on January 1, 1993?

   b. What was the 30-day forward premium (or discount) in percent?

   c. What was the 90-day forward premium (or discount) in percent?

   d. Suppose you executed a 90-day forward contract to exchange 100,000 Swiss francs into U.S. dollars. How many dollars would you get 90 days hence?

   e. Assume a Swiss bank entered into a 180-day forward contract with Citicorp to buy $100,000. How many francs will the Swiss bank deliver in six months to get the U.S. dollars?

4. Suppose an Austrian shilling is selling for $0.0868 and an Irish punt is selling for $1.6164. What is the exchange rate (cross rate) of the Austrian shilling to the Irish punt? That is, how many Austrian shillings are equal to an Irish punt?

   Cross rates

5. Suppose a French franc is selling for $0.1801 and a Maltese lira is selling for $2.4531. What is the exchange rate (cross rate) of the French franc to the Maltese lira? That is, how many French francs are equal to a Maltese lira?

   Cross rates

6. From the base price level of 100 in 1966, German and U.S. price levels in 1993 stood at 200 and 410, respectively. If the 1966 $/DM exchange rate was $0.30/DM, what should the exchange rate be in 1993? Suggestion: Using the purchasing power parity theory, adjust the

   Purchasing power theory

exchange rate to compensate for inflation. That is, determine the relative rate of inflation between the United States and Germany and multiply this times $/DM of 0.30.

Continuation of
purchasing power theory

7. In problem 6, if the United States had somehow managed no inflation since 1966, what should the exchange rate be in 1993, using the purchasing power parity theory?

Adjusting returns for
exchange rates

8. An investor in the United States bought a one-year New Zealand security valued at 195,000 New Zealand dollars. The U.S. dollar equivalent was $100,000. The New Zealand security earned 16 percent during the year, but the New Zealand dollar depreciated 5 cents against the U.S. dollar during the time period ($0.51/NZD to $0.46/NZD). After transferring the funds back to the United States, what was the investor's return on her $100,000? Determine the total ending value of the New Zealand investment in New Zealand dollars and then translate this value to U.S. dollars. Then compute the return on the $100,000.

Adjusting returns for
exchange rates

9. A French investor buys 100 shares of Ford Motor Co. for $4,000 ($40 per share). Over the course of a year, Ford goes up by 6 points.

   a. If there is a 10 percent gain in the value of the dollar versus the French franc, what will be the total percentage return to the French investor? First determine the new dollar value of the investment and multiply this figure by 1.10. Divide this answer by $4,000 and get a percentage value, and then subtract 100 percent to get the percentage return.

   b. Now assume the stock increases by 8 points, but the dollar decreases by 10 percent versus the French franc. What will be the total percentage return to the French investor? Use 0.90 in place of 1.10 in this case.

Hedging exchange rate
risk

10. You are the vice-president of finance for International Resources, Inc., headquartered in Denver, Colorado. In January 1993 your firm's Canadian subsidiary obtained a six-month loan of 100,000 Canadian dollars from a bank in Denver to finance the acquisition of a titanium mine in Quebec province. The loan will also be repaid in Canadian dollars. At the time of the loan, the spot exchange rate was U.S. $0.7798/Canadian dollar and the Canadian currency was selling at a discount in the forward market. The June 1993 futures contract (Face value = $100,000 per contract) was quoted at U.S. $0.7763.

   a. Explain how the Denver bank could lose on this transaction if it does not hedge.

   b. If the bank does hedge, what is the maximum amount it can lose?

Selected References

Aggarwal, Raj. "International Differences in Capital Structure Norms." *Management International Review* 21, no. 1 (1981), pp. 75–88.

Black, Fisher, and Robert Litterman. "Global Portfolio Optimization." *Financial Analysts Journal* 48 (September–October 1992), pp. 28–43.

Choi, Frederick D. S., and Richard M. Levitz. "International Accounting Diversity: Does It Affect Market Participants?" *Financial Analysts Journal* 47 (July–August 1991), pp. 73–82.

Doukas, John, and Nickolaos G. Travlos. "The Effect of Corporate Multinationalism on Shareholders' Wealth: Evidence from International Acquisitions." *Journal of Finance* 43 (December 1988), pp. 1161–75.

Flood, Eugene, Jr., and Donald R. Lessard. "On the Measurement of Operating Exposure to Exchange Rates: A Conceptual Approach." *Financial Management* 15 (Spring 1986), pp. 25–36.

Gentry, James A., D. R. Metha, S. K. Bhattacharya, R. Cobbaut, and J. Scaringella. "An International Study of Management Perceptions of the Working Capital Process." *Journal of International Business Studies* 6 (Spring–Summer 1979), pp. 28–38.

Hodder, James E. "Evaluation of Manufacturing Investments: A Comparison of U.S. and Japanese Practices." *Financial Management* 15 (Spring 1986), pp. 17–24.

Jorion, Philippe. "The Exchange-Rate Exposure of U.S. Multinationals." *Journal of Business* 63 (July 1990), pp. 331–45.

Kester, W. Carl. "Capital and Ownership Structure: A Comparison of United States and Japanese Manufacturing Corporations." *Financial Management* 15 (Spring 1986), pp. 5–16.

Koveos, Peter, and Bruce Seifert. "Purchasing Power Parity and Black Markets." *Financial Management* 14 (Autumn 1985), pp. 40–46.

Lessard, Donald R. "World, National, and Industrial Factors in Equity Returns." *Journal of Finance* 29 (May 1974), pp. 379–91.

Marr, Wayne M., John L. Trimble, and Raj Varma. "On the Integration of International Capital Markets: Evidence from Eurocurrency Offerings." *Financial Management* 20 (Winter 1991), pp. 11–21.

Misawa, Mitsura. "Financing Japanese Investments in the United States: Case Studies of a Large and Medium-Sized Firm." *Financial Management* 14 (Winter 1985), pp. 5–12.

Naidu, G. N. "How to Reduce Transaction Exposure in International Lending." *Journal of Commercial Bank Lending* 63 (June 1981), pp. 39–46.

APPENDIX 21A   **Cash Flow Analysis and the Foreign Investment Decision**

Direct foreign investments are often relatively large. As we mentioned in the chapter, these investments are exposed to some extraordinary risks, such as foreign exchange fluctuations and political interference, which are nonexistent for domestic investments. Therefore the final decision is often made at the board of directors level after considering the financial feasibility and the strategic importance of the proposed investment. Financial feasibility analysis for foreign investments is basically conducted in the same manner as it is for domestic capital budgets. Certain important differences exist, however, in the treatment of foreign tax credits, foreign exchange risk, and remittance of cash flows. To see how these are handled in foreign investment analysis, let us consider a hypothetical illustration.

Tex Systems, Inc., a Texas-based manufacturer of computer equipment, is considering the establishment of a manufacturing plant in Salaysia, a country in Southeast Asia. The Salaysian plant will be a wholly owned subsidiary of Tex Systems, and its estimated cost is 90 million ringgits (2 ringgits = $1). Based on the exchange rate between ringgits and dollars, the cost in dollars is $45 million. In addition to selling in the local Salaysian market, the proposed subsidiary is expected to export its computers to the neighboring markets in Singapore, Hong Kong, and Thailand. Expected revenues and operating costs are as shown in Table 21A–1. The country's investment climate, which reflects the foreign exchange and political risks, is rated BBB (considered fairly

TABLE 21A-1   **Cash flow analysis of a foreign investment**

	Projected Cash Flows (million ringgits unless otherwise stated)					
	Year 1	**Year 2**	**Year 3**	**Year 4**	**Year 5**	**Year 6**
Revenues	45.00	50.00	55.00	60.00	65.00	70.00
− Operating expenses	28.00	30.00	30.00	32.00	35.00	35.00
− Depreciation	10.00	10.00	10.00	10.00	10.00	10.00
Earnings before Salaysian taxes.	7.00	10.00	15.00	18.00	20.00	25.00
− Salaysian income tax (25%)	1.75	2.50	3.75	4.50	5.00	6.25
Earnings after foreign income taxes.	5.25	7.50	11.25	13.50	15.00	18.75
= Dividends repatriated	5.25	7.50	11.25	13.50	15.00	18.75
Gross U.S. taxes (30% of foreign earnings before taxes) . . .	2.10	3.00	4.50	5.40	6.00	7.50
− Foreign tax credit	1.75	2.50	3.75	4.50	5.00	6.25
Net U.S. taxes payable	0.35	0.50	0.75	0.90	1.00	1.25
Aftertax dividend received by Tex Systems	4.90	7.00	10.50	12.60	14.00	17.50
Exchange rate (ringgits/$)	2.00	2.04	2.08	2.12	2.16	2.21
Aftertax dividend (U.S. $).	2.45	3.43	5.05	5.94	6.48	7.92
PV$_{IF}$ (at 20%)	0.833	0.694	0.579	0.482	0.402	0.335
PV of dividends ($)	2.04 +	2.38 +	2.92 +	2.86 +	2.60 +	2.65 = $15.45

safe) by a leading Asian business journal. After considering the investment climate and the nature of the industry, Tex Systems has set a target rate of return of 20 percent for this foreign investment. Salaysia has a 25 percent corporate income tax rate and has waived the withholding tax on dividends repatriated (forwarded) to the parent company. A dividend payout ratio of 100 percent is assumed for the foreign subsidiary. Tex Systems' marginal tax rate is 30 percent. It was agreed by Tex Systems and the Salaysian government that the subsidiary will be sold to a Salaysian entrepreneur after six years for an estimated 30 million ringgits. The plant will be depreciated over a period of six years using the straight-line method. The cash flows generated through depreciation cannot be remitted to the parent company until the subsidiary is sold to the local private entrepreneur six years from now. The Salaysian government requires the subsidiary to invest the depreciation-generated cash flows in local government bonds yielding an aftertax rate of 15 percent. The depreciation cash flows thus compounded and accumulated can be returned to Tex Systems when the project is terminated. Although the value of ringgits in the foreign exchange market has remained fairly stable for the past three years, the projected budget deficits and trade deficits of Salaysia may result in a gradual devaluation of ringgits against the U.S. dollar at the rate of 2 percent per year for the next six years.

Note: The analysis in Table 21A–1 is primarily done in terms of ringgits. Expenses (operating, depreciation, and Salaysian income taxes) are subtracted from revenues to arrive at earnings after foreign income taxes. These earnings are then repatriated (forwarded) to Tex Systems in the form of dividends. Dividends repatriated thus begin at 5.25 ringgits (in millions) in Year 1 and increase to 18.75 ringgits in Year 6. The next item, gross U.S. taxes, refers to the unadjusted U.S. tax obligation. As specified, this is equal to 30 percent of foreign earnings before taxes (earnings before Salaysian taxes).[1] For example, gross U.S. taxes in the first year are equal to:

Earnings before Salaysian taxes	7.00
30% of foreign earnings before taxes	30%
Gross U.S. taxes	2.10

From gross U.S. taxes, Tex Systems may take a foreign tax credit equal to the amount of Salaysian income tax paid. Gross U.S. taxes minus this foreign tax credit are equal to net U.S. taxes payable. Aftertax dividends received by Tex Systems are equal to dividends repatriated minus U.S. taxes payable. In the first year, the values are:

Dividends repatriated	5.25
Net U.S. taxes payable	−0.35
Aftertax dividends received by Tex Systems	4.90

The figures for aftertax dividends received by Tex Systems are all stated in ringgits (the analysis up to this point has been in ringgits). These ringgits will now be converted into dollars. The initial exchange rate is 2.00 ringgits per dollar, and this will go up by 2 percent per year.[2] For the first year, 4.90 ringgits will be translated into 2.45 dollars. Since values are stated in millions, this will represent $2.45 million. Aftertax dividends in U.S. dollars grow from $2.45 million in year 1 to $7.92 million in year 6. The last two rows of Table 21A–1 show the present value of these dividends at a 20 percent discount rate. The *total* present value of aftertax dividends received by Tex Systems adds up to $15.45 million. Repatriated dividends will be just one part of the cash flow. The second part consists of depreciation-generated cash

---

[1] If foreign earnings had not been repatriated, this tax obligation would not be due.

[2] The 2 percent appreciation means the dollar is equal to an increasing amount of ringgits each year. The dollar is appreciating relative to ringgits, and ringgits are depreciating relative to the dollar. Since Tex Systems earnings are in ringgits, they are being converted at a less desirable rate each year. Big Tex may eventually decide to hedge its foreign exchange risk exposure.

flow accumulated and reinvested in Salaysian government bonds at a 15 percent rate per year. The compound value of reinvested depreciation cash flows (10 million ringgits per year) is:

10 million ringgits $\times$ 8.754* = 87.54 million ringgits after six years

*Future value at 15 percent for six years (Appendix C at end of book).

These 87.54 million ringgits must now be translated into dollars and then discounted back to the present. Since the exchange rate is 2.21 ringgits per dollar in the 6th year (fourth line from the bottom in Table 21A–1), the dollar equivalent of 87.54 million ringgits is:

87.54 million ringgits $\div$ 2.21 = \$39.61 million

The \$39.61 million can now be discounted back to the present, by using the present value factor for six years at 20 percent (Appendix B).

$$
\begin{array}{r}
\$39.61 \quad \text{million} \\
\times \quad 0.335 \ \text{PV}_{\text{IF}} \\
\hline
\$13.27 \quad \text{million}
\end{array}
$$

The final benefit to be received is the 30 million ringgits when the plant is sold six years from now.[3] We first convert this to dollars and then take the present value.

30 million ringgits $\div$ 2.21 = \$13.57 million

The present value of \$13.57 million after six years at 20 percent is:

$$
\begin{array}{r}
\$13.57 \quad \text{million} \\
\times \quad 0.335 \ \text{PV}_{\text{IF}} \\
\hline
\$ \ 4.55 \quad \text{million}
\end{array}
$$

The present value of all cash inflows in dollars is equal to:

Present value of dividends	\$15.45 million
Present value of repatriated accumulated depreciation	13.27
Present value of sales price for plant	4.55
Total present value of inflows	\$33.27 million

The cost of the project was initially specified as 90 million ringgits, or \$45 million. Thus we see the total present value of inflows in dollars is less than the cost, and the project has a negative net present value.

Total present value of inflows	\$33.27 million
Cost	45.00
Net present value	(\$11.73 million)

---

[3]Capital gains taxes are not a necessary consideration in foreign transactions of this nature.

21A–1. The Office Automation Corporation is considering a foreign investment. The initial cash outlay will be $10 million. The current foreign exchange rate is 2 francs = $1. Thus the investment in foreign currency will be 20 million francs. The assets have a useful life of five years and no expected salvage value. The firm uses a straight-line method of depreciation. Sales are expected to be 20 million francs and operating cash expenses 10 million francs every year for five years. The foreign income tax rate is 25 percent. The foreign subsidiary will repatriate all aftertax profits to Office Automation in the form of dividends. Furthermore the depreciation cash flows (equal to each year's depreciation) will be repatriated during the same year they accrue to the foreign subsidiary. The applicable cost of capital that reflects the riskiness of the cash flows is 16 percent. The U.S. tax rate is 40 percent of foreign earnings before taxes.

a. Should the Office Automation Corporation undertake the investment, if the foreign exchange rate is expected to remain constant during the five-year period?

b. Should Office Automation undertake the investment if the foreign exchange rate is expected to be as follows:

Cash flow analysis with a foreign investment

Year 0	$1 = 2.0 francs
Year 1	$1 = 2.2 francs
Year 2	$1 = 2.4 francs
Year 3	$1 = 2.7 francs
Year 4	$1 = 2.9 francs
Year 5	$1 = 3.2 francs

Appendixes

APPENDIX A   Future value of $1, FV_{IF} $FV = PV(1 + i)^n$

Percent

Period	1%	2%	3%	4%	5%	6%	7%	8%	9%	10%	11%
1	1.010	1.020	1.030	1.040	1.050	1.060	1.070	1.080	1.090	1.100	1.110
2	1.020	1.040	1.061	1.082	1.103	1.124	1.145	1.166	1.188	1.210	1.232
3	1.030	1.061	1.093	1.125	1.158	1.191	1.225	1.260	1.295	1.331	1.368
4	1.041	1.082	1.126	1.170	1.216	1.262	1.311	1.360	1.412	1.464	1.518
5	1.051	1.104	1.159	1.217	1.276	1.338	1.403	1.469	1.539	1.611	1.685
6	1.062	1.126	1.194	1.265	1.340	1.419	1.501	1.587	1.677	1.772	1.870
7	1.072	1.149	1.230	1.316	1.407	1.504	1.606	1.714	1.828	1.949	2.076
8	1.083	1.172	1.267	1.369	1.477	1.594	1.718	1.851	1.993	2.144	2.305
9	1.094	1.195	1.305	1.423	1.551	1.689	1.838	1.999	2.172	2.358	2.558
10	1.105	1.219	1.344	1.480	1.629	1.791	1.967	2.159	2.367	2.594	2.839
11	1.116	1.243	1.384	1.539	1.710	1.898	2.105	2.332	2.580	2.853	3.152
12	1.127	1.268	1.426	1.601	1.796	2.012	2.252	2.518	2.813	3.138	3.498
13	1.138	1.294	1.469	1.665	1.886	2.133	2.410	2.720	3.066	3.452	3.883
14	1.149	1.319	1.513	1.732	1.980	2.261	2.579	2.937	3.342	3.797	4.310
15	1.161	1.346	1.558	1.801	2.079	2.397	2.759	3.172	3.642	4.177	4.785
16	1.173	1.373	1.605	1.873	2.183	2.540	2.952	3.426	3.970	4.595	5.311
17	1.184	1.400	1.653	1.948	2.292	2.693	3.159	3.700	4.328	5.054	5.895
18	1.196	1.428	1.702	2.026	2.407	2.854	3.380	3.996	4.717	5.560	6.544
19	1.208	1.457	1.754	2.107	2.527	3.026	3.617	4.316	5.142	6.116	7.263
20	1.220	1.486	1.806	2.191	2.653	3.207	3.870	4.661	5.604	6.727	8.062
25	1.282	1.641	2.094	2.666	3.386	4.292	5.427	6.848	8.623	10.835	13.585
30	1.348	1.811	2.427	3.243	4.322	5.743	7.612	10.063	13.268	17.449	22.892
40	1.489	2.208	3.262	4.801	7.040	10.286	14.974	21.725	31.409	45.259	65.001
50	1.645	2.692	4.384	7.107	11.467	18.420	29.457	46.902	74.358	117.39	184.57

APPENDIX A (concluded)   Future value of $1

Percent

Period	12%	13%	14%	15%	16%	17%	18%	19%	20%	25%	30%
1. . . .	1.120	1.130	1.140	1.150	1.160	1.170	1.180	1.190	1.200	1.250	1.300
2. . . .	1.254	1.277	1.300	1.323	1.346	1.369	1.392	1.416	1.440	1.563	1.690
3. . . .	1.405	1.443	1.482	1.521	1.561	1.602	1.643	1.685	1.728	1.953	2.197
4. . . .	1.574	1.630	1.689	1.749	1.811	1.874	1.939	2.005	2.074	2.441	2.856
5. . . .	1.762	1.842	1.925	2.011	2.100	2.192	2.288	2.386	2.488	3.052	3.713
6. . . .	1.974	2.082	2.195	2.313	2.436	2.565	2.700	2.840	2.986	3.815	4.827
7. . . .	2.211	2.353	2.502	2.660	2.826	3.001	3.185	3.379	3.583	4.768	6.276
8. . . .	2.476	2.658	2.853	3.059	3.278	3.511	3.759	4.021	4.300	5.960	8.157
9. . . .	2.773	3.004	3.252	3.518	3.803	4.108	4.435	4.785	5.160	7.451	10.604
10. . . .	3.106	3.395	3.707	4.046	4.411	4.807	5.234	5.696	6.192	9.313	13.786
11. . . .	3.479	3.836	4.226	4.652	5.117	5.624	6.176	6.777	7.430	11.642	17.922
12. . . .	3.896	4.335	4.818	5.350	5.936	6.580	7.288	8.064	8.916	14.552	23.298
13. . . .	4.363	4.898	5.492	6.153	6.886	7.699	8.599	9.596	10.699	18.190	30.288
14. . . .	4.887	5.535	6.261	7.076	7.988	9.007	10.147	11.420	12.839	22.737	39.374
15. . . .	5.474	6.254	7.138	8.137	9.266	10.539	11.974	13.590	15.407	28.422	51.186
16. . . .	6.130	7.067	8.137	9.358	10.748	12.330	14.129	16.172	18.488	35.527	66.542
17. . . .	6.866	7.986	9.276	10.761	12.468	14.426	16.672	19.244	22.186	44.409	86.504
18. . . .	7.690	9.024	10.575	12.375	14.463	16.879	19.673	22.091	26.623	55.511	112.46
19. . . .	8.613	10.197	12.056	14.232	16.777	19.748	23.214	27.252	31.948	69.389	146.19
20. . . .	9.646	11.523	13.743	16.367	19.461	23.106	27.393	32.429	38.338	86.736	190.05
25. . . .	17.000	21.231	26.462	32.919	40.874	50.658	62.669	77.388	95.396	264.70	705.64
30. . . .	29.960	39.116	50.950	66.212	85.850	111.07	143.37	184.68	237.38	807.79	2,620.0
40. . . .	93.051	132.78	188.88	267.86	378.72	533.87	750.38	1,051.7	1,469.8	7,523.2	36,119.
50. . . .	289.00	450.74	700.23	1,083.7	1,670.7	2,566.2	3,927.4	5,988.9	9,100.4	70,065.	497,929.

APPENDIX B   Present value of $1, PV_{IF} $PV = FV\left[\dfrac{1}{(1+i)^n}\right]$

Percent

Period	1%	2%	3%	4%	5%	6%	7%	8%	9%	10%	11%	12%
1	0.990	0.980	0.971	0.962	0.952	0.943	0.935	0.926	0.917	0.909	0.901	0.893
2	0.980	0.961	0.943	0.925	0.907	0.890	0.873	0.857	0.842	0.826	0.812	0.797
3	0.971	0.942	0.915	0.889	0.864	0.840	0.816	0.794	0.772	0.751	0.731	0.712
4	0.961	0.924	0.885	0.855	0.823	0.792	0.763	0.735	0.708	0.683	0.659	0.636
5	0.951	0.906	0.863	0.822	0.784	0.747	0.713	0.681	0.650	0.621	0.593	0.567
6	0.942	0.888	0.837	0.790	0.746	0.705	0.666	0.630	0.596	0.564	0.535	0.507
7	0.933	0.871	0.813	0.760	0.711	0.665	0.623	0.583	0.547	0.513	0.482	0.452
8	0.923	0.853	0.789	0.731	0.677	0.627	0.582	0.540	0.502	0.467	0.434	0.404
9	0.914	0.837	0.766	0.703	0.645	0.592	0.544	0.500	0.460	0.424	0.391	0.361
10	0.905	0.820	0.744	0.676	0.614	0.558	0.508	0.463	0.422	0.386	0.352	0.322
11	0.896	0.804	0.722	0.650	0.585	0.527	0.475	0.429	0.388	0.350	0.317	0.287
12	0.887	0.788	0.701	0.625	0.557	0.497	0.444	0.397	0.356	0.319	0.286	0.257
13	0.879	0.773	0.681	0.601	0.530	0.469	0.415	0.368	0.326	0.290	0.258	0.229
14	0.870	0.758	0.661	0.577	0.505	0.442	0.388	0.340	0.299	0.263	0.232	0.205
15	0.861	0.743	0.642	0.555	0.481	0.417	0.362	0.315	0.275	0.239	0.209	0.183
16	0.853	0.728	0.623	0.534	0.458	0.394	0.339	0.292	0.252	0.218	0.188	0.163
17	0.844	0.714	0.605	0.513	0.436	0.371	0.317	0.270	0.231	0.198	0.170	0.146
18	0.836	0.700	0.587	0.494	0.416	0.350	0.296	0.250	0.212	0.180	0.153	0.130
19	0.828	0.686	0.570	0.475	0.396	0.331	0.277	0.232	0.194	0.164	0.138	0.116
20	0.820	0.673	0.554	0.456	0.377	0.312	0.258	0.215	0.178	0.149	0.124	0.104
25	0.780	0.610	0.478	0.375	0.295	0.233	0.184	0.146	0.116	0.092	0.074	0.059
30	0.742	0.552	0.412	0.308	0.231	0.174	0.131	0.099	0.075	0.057	0.044	0.033
40	0.672	0.453	0.307	0.208	0.142	0.097	0.067	0.046	0.032	0.022	0.015	0.011
50	0.608	0.372	0.228	0.141	0.087	0.054	0.034	0.021	0.013	0.009	0.005	0.003

Percent

Period	13%	14%	15%	16%	17%	18%	19%	20%	25%	30%	35%	40%	50%
1	0.885	0.877	0.870	0.862	0.855	0.847	0.840	0.833	0.800	0.769	0.741	0.714	0.667
2	0.783	0.769	0.756	0.743	0.731	0.718	0.706	0.694	0.640	0.592	0.549	0.510	0.444
3	0.693	0.675	0.658	0.641	0.624	0.609	0.593	0.579	0.512	0.455	0.406	0.364	0.296
4	0.613	0.592	0.572	0.552	0.534	0.515	0.499	0.482	0.410	0.350	0.301	0.260	0.198
5	0.543	0.519	0.497	0.476	0.456	0.437	0.419	0.402	0.328	0.269	0.223	0.186	0.132
6	0.480	0.456	0.432	0.410	0.390	0.370	0.352	0.335	0.262	0.207	0.165	0.133	0.088
7	0.425	0.400	0.376	0.354	0.333	0.314	0.296	0.279	0.210	0.159	0.122	0.095	0.059
8	0.376	0.351	0.327	0.305	0.285	0.266	0.249	0.233	0.168	0.123	0.091	0.068	0.039
9	0.333	0.300	0.284	0.263	0.243	0.225	0.209	0.194	0.134	0.094	0.067	0.048	0.026
10	0.295	0.270	0.247	0.227	0.208	0.191	0.176	0.162	0.107	0.073	0.050	0.035	0.017
11	0.261	0.237	0.215	0.195	0.178	0.162	0.148	0.135	0.086	0.056	0.037	0.025	0.012
12	0.231	0.208	0.187	0.168	0.152	0.137	0.124	0.112	0.069	0.043	0.027	0.018	0.008
13	0.204	0.182	0.163	0.145	0.130	0.116	0.104	0.093	0.055	0.033	0.020	0.013	0.005
14	0.181	0.160	0.141	0.125	0.111	0.099	0.088	0.078	0.044	0.025	0.015	0.009	0.003
15	0.160	0.140	0.123	0.108	0.095	0.084	0.074	0.065	0.035	0.020	0.011	0.006	0.002
16	0.141	0.123	0.107	0.093	0.081	0.071	0.062	0.054	0.028	0.015	0.008	0.005	0.002
17	0.125	0.108	0.093	0.080	0.069	0.060	0.052	0.045	0.023	0.012	0.006	0.003	0.001
18	0.111	0.095	0.081	0.069	0.059	0.051	0.044	0.038	0.018	0.009	0.005	0.002	0.001
19	0.098	0.083	0.070	0.060	0.051	0.043	0.037	0.031	0.014	0.007	0.003	0.002	0
20	0.087	0.073	0.061	0.051	0.043	0.037	0.031	0.026	0.012	0.005	0.002	0.001	0
25	0.047	0.038	0.030	0.024	0.020	0.016	0.013	0.010	0.004	0.001	0.001	0	0
30	0.026	0.020	0.015	0.012	0.009	0.007	0.005	0.004	0.001	0	0	0	0
40	0.008	0.005	0.004	0.003	0.002	0.001	0.001	0.001	0	0	0	0	0
50	0.002	0.001	0.001	0.001	0	0	0	0	0	0	0	0	0

APPENDIX C Future value of an annuity of $1, FV_{IFA} $FV_A = A\left[\dfrac{(1+i)^n - 1}{i}\right]$

Period	1%	2%	3%	4%	5%	6%	7%	8%	9%	10%	11%
1	1.000	1.000	1.000	1.000	1.000	1.000	1.000	1.000	1.000	1.000	1.000
2	2.010	2.020	2.030	2.040	2.050	2.060	2.070	2.080	2.090	2.100	2.110
3	3.030	3.060	3.091	3.122	3.153	3.184	3.215	3.246	3.278	3.310	3.342
4	4.060	4.122	4.184	4.246	4.310	4.375	4.440	4.506	4.573	4.641	4.710
5	5.101	5.204	5.309	5.416	5.526	5.637	5.751	5.867	5.985	6.105	6.228
6	6.152	6.308	6.468	6.633	6.802	6.975	7.153	7.336	7.523	7.716	7.913
7	7.214	7.434	7.662	7.898	8.142	8.394	8.654	8.923	9.200	9.487	9.783
8	8.286	8.583	8.892	9.214	9.549	9.897	10.260	10.637	11.028	11.436	11.859
9	9.369	9.755	10.159	10.583	11.027	11.491	11.978	12.488	13.021	13.579	14.164
10	10.462	10.950	11.464	12.006	12.578	13.181	13.816	14.487	15.193	15.937	16.722
11	11.567	12.169	12.808	13.486	14.207	14.972	15.784	16.645	17.560	18.531	19.561
12	12.683	13.412	14.192	15.026	15.917	16.870	17.888	18.977	20.141	21.384	22.713
13	13.809	14.680	15.618	16.627	17.713	18.882	20.141	21.495	22.953	24.523	26.212
14	14.947	15.974	17.086	18.292	19.599	21.015	22.550	24.215	26.019	27.975	30.095
15	16.097	17.293	18.599	20.024	21.579	23.276	25.129	27.152	29.361	31.772	34.405
16	17.258	18.639	20.157	21.825	23.657	25.673	27.888	30.324	33.003	35.950	39.190
17	18.430	20.012	21.762	23.698	25.840	28.213	30.840	33.750	36.974	40.545	44.501
18	19.615	21.412	23.414	25.645	28.132	30.906	33.999	37.450	41.301	45.599	50.396
19	20.811	22.841	25.117	27.671	30.539	33.760	37.379	41.446	46.018	51.159	56.939
20	22.019	24.297	26.870	29.778	33.066	36.786	40.995	45.762	51.160	57.275	64.203
25	28.243	32.030	36.459	41.646	47.727	54.865	63.249	73.106	84.701	98.347	114.41
30	34.785	40.588	47.575	56.085	66.439	79.058	94.461	113.28	136.31	164.49	199.02
40	48.886	60.402	75.401	95.026	120.80	154.76	199.64	259.06	337.89	442.59	581.83
50	64.463	84.579	112.80	152.67	209.35	290.34	406.53	573.77	815.08	1,163.9	1,668.8

Percent

APPENDIX C (concluded)   Future value of an annuity of $1

Percent

Period	12%	13%	14%	15%	16%	17%	18%	19%	20%	25%	30%
1. . .	1.000	1.000	1.000	1.000	1.000	1.000	1.000	1.000	1.000	1.000	1.000
2. . .	2.120	2.130	2.140	2.150	2.160	2.170	2.180	2.190	2.200	2.250	2.300
3. . .	3.374	3.407	3.440	3.473	3.506	3.539	3.572	3.606	3.640	3.813	3.990
4. . .	4.779	4.850	4.921	4.993	5.066	5.141	5.215	5.291	5.368	5.766	6.187
5. . .	6.353	6.480	6.610	6.742	6.877	7.014	7.154	7.297	7.442	8.207	9.043
6. . .	8.115	8.323	8.536	8.754	8.977	9.207	9.442	9.683	9.930	11.259	12.756
7. . .	10.089	10.405	10.730	11.067	11.414	11.772	12.142	12.523	12.916	15.073	17.583
8. . .	12.300	12.757	13.233	13.727	14.240	14.773	15.327	15.902	16.499	19.842	23.858
9. . .	14.776	15.416	16.085	16.786	17.519	18.285	19.086	19.923	20.799	25.802	32.015
10. . .	17.549	18.420	19.337	20.304	21.321	22.393	23.521	24.701	25.959	33.253	42.619
11. . .	20.655	21.814	23.045	24.349	25.733	27.200	28.755	30.404	32.150	42.566	56.405
12. . .	24.133	25.650	27.271	29.002	30.850	32.824	34.931	37.180	39.581	54.208	74.327
13. . .	28.029	29.985	32.089	34.352	36.786	39.404	42.219	45.244	48.497	68.760	97.625
14. . .	32.393	34.883	37.581	40.505	43.672	47.103	50.818	54.841	59.196	86.949	127.91
15. . .	37.280	40.417	43.842	47.580	51.660	56.110	60.965	66.261	72.035	109.69	167.29
16. . .	42.753	46.672	50.980	55.717	60.925	66.649	72.939	79.850	87.442	138.11	218.47
17. . .	48.884	53.739	59.118	65.075	71.673	78.979	87.068	96.022	105.93	173.64	285.01
18. . .	55.750	61.725	68.394	75.836	84.141	93.406	103.74	115.27	128.12	218.05	371.52
19. . .	63.440	70.749	78.969	88.212	98.603	110.29	123.41	138.17	154.74	273.56	483.97
20. . .	72.052	80.947	91.025	102.44	115.38	130.03	146.63	165.42	186.69	342.95	630.17
25. . .	133.33	155.62	181.87	212.79	249.21	292.11	342.60	402.04	471.98	1,054.8	2,348.80
30. . .	241.33	293.20	356.79	434.75	530.31	647.44	790.95	966.7	1,181.9	3,227.2	8,730.0
40. . .	767.09	1,013.7	1,342.0	1,779.1	2,360.8	3,134.5	4,163.21	5,529.8	7,343.9	30,089.	120,393.0
50. . .	2,400.0	3,459.5	4,994.5	7,217.7	10,436.	15,090.	21,813.	31,515.	45,497.	280,256.	1,659,760.

639

APPENDIX D Present value of an annuity of $1, PV_{IFA} $PV_A = A\left[\dfrac{1 - \dfrac{1}{(1 + i)^n}}{i}\right]$

Percent

Period	1%	2%	3%	4%	5%	6%	7%	8%	9%	10%	11%	12%
1.....	0.990	0.980	0.971	0.962	0.952	0.943	0.935	0.926	0.917	0.909	0.901	0.893
2.....	1.970	1.942	1.913	1.886	1.859	1.833	1.808	1.783	1.759	1.736	1.713	1.690
3.....	2.941	2.884	2.829	2.775	2.723	2.673	2.624	2.577	2.531	2.487	2.444	2.402
4.....	3.902	3.808	3.717	3.630	3.546	3.465	3.387	3.312	3.240	3.170	3.102	3.037
5.....	4.853	4.713	4.580	4.452	4.329	4.212	4.100	3.993	3.890	3.791	3.696	3.605
6.....	5.795	5.601	5.417	5.242	5.076	4.917	4.767	4.623	4.486	4.355	4.231	4.111
7.....	6.728	6.472	6.230	6.002	5.786	5.582	5.389	5.206	5.033	4.868	4.712	4.564
8.....	7.652	7.325	7.020	6.733	6.463	6.210	5.971	5.747	5.535	5.335	5.146	4.968
9.....	8.566	8.162	7.786	7.435	7.108	6.802	6.515	6.247	5.995	5.759	5.537	5.328
10....	9.471	8.983	8.530	8.111	7.722	7.360	7.024	6.710	6.418	6.145	5.889	5.650
11....	10.368	9.787	9.253	8.760	8.306	7.887	7.499	7.139	6.805	6.495	6.207	5.938
12....	11.255	10.575	9.954	9.385	8.863	8.384	7.943	7.536	7.161	6.814	6.492	6.194
13....	12.134	11.348	10.635	9.986	9.394	8.853	8.358	7.904	7.487	7.103	6.750	6.424
14....	13.004	12.106	11.296	10.563	9.899	9.295	8.745	8.244	7.786	7.367	6.982	6.628
15....	13.865	12.849	11.939	11.118	10.380	9.712	9.108	8.559	8.061	7.606	7.191	6.811
16....	14.718	13.578	12.561	11.652	10.838	10.106	9.447	8.851	8.313	7.824	7.379	6.974
17....	15.562	14.292	13.166	12.166	11.274	10.477	9.763	9.122	8.544	8.022	7.549	7.102
18....	16.398	14.992	13.754	12.659	11.690	10.828	10.059	9.372	8.756	8.201	7.702	7.250
19....	17.226	15.678	14.324	13.134	12.085	11.158	10.336	9.604	8.950	8.365	7.839	7.366
20....	18.046	16.351	14.877	13.590	12.462	11.470	10.594	9.818	9.129	8.514	7.963	7.469
25....	22.023	19.523	17.413	15.622	14.094	12.783	11.654	10.675	9.823	9.077	8.422	7.843
30....	25.808	22.396	19.600	17.292	15.372	13.765	12.409	11.258	10.274	9.427	8.694	8.055
40....	32.835	27.355	23.115	19.793	17.159	15.046	13.332	11.925	10.757	9.779	8.951	8.244
50....	39.196	31.424	25.730	21.482	18.256	15.762	13.801	12.233	10.962	9.915	9.042	8.304

APPENDIX D (concluded)   Present value of an annuity of $1

Percent

Period	13%	14%	15%	16%	17%	18%	19%	20%	25%	30%	35%	40%	50%
1	0.885	0.877	0.870	0.862	0.855	0.847	0.840	0.833	0.800	0.769	0.741	0.714	0.667
2	1.668	1.647	1.626	1.605	1.585	1.566	1.547	1.528	1.440	1.361	1.289	1.224	1.111
3	2.361	2.322	2.283	2.246	2.210	2.174	2.140	2.106	1.952	1.816	1.696	1.589	1.407
4	2.974	2.914	2.855	2.798	2.743	2.690	2.639	2.589	2.362	2.166	1.997	1.849	1.605
5	3.517	3.433	3.352	3.274	3.199	3.127	3.058	2.991	2.689	2.436	2.220	2.035	1.737
6	3.998	3.889	3.784	3.685	3.589	3.498	3.410	3.326	2.951	2.643	2.385	2.168	1.824
7	4.423	4.288	4.160	4.039	3.922	3.812	3.706	3.605	3.161	2.802	2.508	2.263	1.883
8	4.799	4.639	4.487	4.344	4.207	4.078	3.954	3.837	3.329	2.925	2.598	2.331	1.922
9	5.132	4.946	4.772	4.607	4.451	4.303	4.163	4.031	3.463	3.019	2.665	2.379	1.948
10	5.426	5.216	5.019	4.833	4.659	4.494	4.339	4.192	3.571	3.092	2.715	2.414	1.965
11	5.687	5.453	5.234	5.029	4.836	4.656	4.486	4.327	3.656	3.147	2.752	2.438	1.977
12	5.918	5.660	5.421	5.197	4.988	4.793	4.611	4.439	3.725	3.190	2.779	2.456	1.985
13	6.122	5.842	5.583	5.342	5.118	4.910	4.715	4.533	3.780	3.223	2.799	2.469	1.990
14	6.302	6.002	5.724	5.468	5.229	5.008	4.802	4.611	3.824	3.249	2.814	2.478	1.993
15	6.462	6.142	5.847	5.575	5.324	5.092	4.876	4.675	3.859	3.268	2.825	2.484	1.995
16	6.604	6.265	5.954	5.668	5.405	5.162	4.938	4.730	3.887	3.283	2.834	2.489	1.997
17	6.729	6.373	6.047	5.749	5.475	5.222	4.988	4.775	3.910	3.295	2.840	2.492	1.998
18	6.840	6.467	6.128	5.818	5.534	5.273	5.033	4.812	3.928	3.304	2.844	2.494	1.999
19	6.938	6.550	6.198	5.877	5.584	5.316	5.070	4.843	3.942	3.311	2.848	2.496	1.999
20	7.025	6.623	6.259	5.929	5.628	5.353	5.101	4.870	3.954	3.316	2.850	2.497	1.999
25	7.330	6.873	6.464	6.097	5.766	5.467	5.195	4.948	3.985	3.329	2.856	2.499	2.000
30	7.496	7.003	6.566	6.177	5.829	5.517	5.235	4.979	3.995	3.332	2.857	2.500	2.000
40	7.634	7.105	6.642	6.233	5.871	5.548	5.258	4.997	3.999	3.333	2.857	2.500	2.000
50	7.675	7.133	6.661	6.246	5.880	5.554	5.262	4.999	4.000	3.333	2.857	2.500	2.000

APPENDIX E   **Using Calculators for Financial Analysis**

This appendix is designed to help you use either an algebraic calculator (Texas Instruments BA-35 Student Business Analyst) or the Hewlett-Packard 12C financial calculator. We realize that most calculators come with comprehensive instructions, and this appendix is meant only to provide basic instructions for commonly used financial calculations.

There are always two things to do before starting your calculations as indicated in the first table: clear the calculator and set the decimal point. If you do not want to lose data stored in memory, do not perform steps 2 and 3 in the first box below.

Each step is listed vertically as a number followed by a decimal point. After each step you will find either a number or a calculator function denoted by a box ☐ . Entering the number on your calculator is one step and entering the function is another. Notice that the HP 12C is color coded. When two boxes are found one after another, you may have an ☐f☐ or a ☐g☐ in the first box. An ☐f☐ is orange coded and refers to the orange functions above the keys. After typing the ☐f☐ function, you will automatically look for an orange coded key to punch. For example, after ☐f☐ in the first Hewlett-Packard box (right-hand panel), you will punch in the orange color coded ☐REG☐ . If the ☐f☐ function is not followed by another box, you merely type in ☐f☐ and the value indicated.

	Texas Instruments BA-35	**Hewlett-Packard 12C**
First clear the calculator	1. ☐ON/C☐ ☐ON/C☐ 2. 0 3. ☐STO☐ Clears Memory	1. ☐CLX☐ Clears screen 2. ☐f☐ 3. ☐REG☐ Clears Memory
Set the decimal point The TI BA-35 has two choices: 2 decimal points or variable decimal points. The screen will indicate Dec 2 or the decimal will be variable. The HP 12C allows you to choose the number of decimal points. If you are uncertain, just provide the indicated input exactly as shown on the right.	1. ☐2nd☐ 2. ☐STO☐	1. ☐f☐ 2. 4 (# of decimals)

The ☐g☐ is coded blue and refers to the functions on the bottom of the function keys. After the ☐g☐ function key, you will automatically look for blue coded keys. This first occurs on page 647 of the appendix.

Familiarize yourself with the keyboard before you start. In the more complicated calculations, keystrokes will be combined into one step.

In the first four calculations on pages 643 and 644 we simply instruct you on how to get the interest factors for Appendixes A, B, C, and D. We have chosen to use examples as our method of instruction.

		Texas Instruments BA-35	**Hewlett-Packard 12C**
A.	Appendix A Future Value of $1 i = 9% or .09; n = 5 years $FV_{IF} = (1 + i)^n$ Future Value = Present Value $\times FV_{IF}$ $FV = PV \times FV_{IF}$ Check the answer against the number in Appendix A. Numbers in the appendix are rounded. Try different rates and years.	To Find Interest Factor 1. 1 2. + 3. .09 (interest rate) 4. $\boxed{=}$ 5. $\boxed{y^x}$ 6. 5 (# of periods) 7. = answer 1.538624	To Find Interest Factor 1. 1 2. $\boxed{\text{enter}}$ 3. .09 (interest rate) 4. + 5. 5 (# of periods) 6. $\boxed{y^x}$ answer 1.5386

		Texas Instruments BA-35	**Hewlett-Packard 12C**
B.	Appendix B Present Value of $1 i = 9% or .09; n = 5 years $PV_{IF} = 1/(1 + i)^n$ Present Value = Future Value $\times PV_{IF}$ $PV = FV \times PV_{IF}$ Check the answer against the number in Appendix B. Numbers in the appendix are rounded.	To Find Interest Factor Repeat steps 1 through 7 above. Continue with step 8. 8. $\boxed{1/x}$ answer .6499314	To Find Interest Factor Repeat steps 1 through 6 above. Continue with step 7. 7. $\boxed{1/x}$ answer .6499

		Texas Instruments BA-35	**Hewlett-Packard 12C**
C.	Appendix C Future Value of an Annuity of $1 i = 9% or .09; n = 5 years $FV_{IFA} = \dfrac{(1 + i)^n - 1}{i}$ Future Value = Annuity $\times FV_{IFA}$ $FV_A = A \times FV_{IFA}$ Check your answer with Appendix C. Repeat example using different numbers and check your results with the number in Appendix C. Numbers in appendix are rounded.	To Find Interest Factor Repeat steps 1 through 7 in part A of this section. Continue with step 8. 8. $\boxed{-}$ 9. 1 10. $\boxed{=}$ 11. $\boxed{\div}$ 12. .09 13. $\boxed{=}$ answer 5.9847106	To Find Interest Factor Repeat steps 1 through 6 in part A of this section. Continue with step 7. 7. 1 8. $\boxed{-}$ 9. .09 10. $\boxed{\div}$ answer 5.9847

		Texas Instruments BA-35	Hewlett-Packard 12C
D.	Appendix D Present Value of an Annuity of $1 i = 9% or .09; n = 5 years $PV_{IFA} = \dfrac{1 - [1/(1 + i)^n]}{i}$ Present Value = Annuity × PV_{IFA} $PV_A = A \times PV_{IFA}$ Check your answer with Appendix D. Repeat example using different numbers and check your results with the number in Appendix D. Numbers in appendix are rounded.	To Find Interest Factor Repeat steps 1 through 8 in parts A & B. Continue with step 9. 9. $\boxed{-}$ 10. 1 11. $\boxed{=}$ 12. $\boxed{+/-}$ 13. $\boxed{\div}$ 14. .09 15. $\boxed{=}$ answer 3.8896513	To Find Interest Factor Repeat steps 1 through 7 in parts A & B. Continue with step 8. 8. 1 9. $\boxed{-}$ 10. $\boxed{CHS}$ 11. .09 12. $\boxed{\div}$ answer 3.8897

On the following pages, you can determine bond valuation, yield to maturity, net present value of an annuity, net present value of an uneven cash flow, internal rate of return for an annuity, and internal rate of return for an uneven cash flow.

Bond Valuation Using both the TI BA-35 and the HP 12C

Solve for P_b = Price of the bond

Given:

I_t = \$80 annual coupon payments or 8% coupon (\$40 semiannually)

P_n = \$1,000 principal (par value)

n = 10 years to maturity (20 periods semiannually)

Y = 9.0% yield to maturity or required rate of return (4.5% semiannually)

You may choose to refer to Chapter 10 for a complete discussion of bond valuation.

	Texas Instruments BA-35	Hewlett-Packard 12C
BOND VALUATION All steps begin with number 1. Numbers following each step are keystrokes followed by a box ☐ . Each box represents a keystroke and indicates which calculator function is performed. The Texas Instrument calculator requires that data be adjusted for semiannual compounding, otherwise it assumes annual compounding. The Hewlett-Packard 12C internally assumes that semiannual compounding is used and requires annual data to be entered. The HP 12C is more detailed in that it requires the actual day month and year. If you want an answer for a problem that requires a given number of years (e.g., 10 years), simply start on a date of your choice and end on the same date 10 years later, as in the example.	Set Finance Mode ☐2nd☐ ☐FIN☐ Set decimal to 2 places Decimal ☐2nd☐ ☐STO☐ 1. 40 (semiannual coupon) 2. ☐PMT☐ 3. 4.5 (yield to maturity) semiannual basis 4. ☐% i☐ 5. 1000 (principal) 6. ☐FV☐ 7. 20 (semiannual periods to maturity) 8. ☐N☐ 9. ☐CPT☐ 10. ☐PV☐ answer 934.96 Answer is given in dollars, rather than % of par value.	Clear memory ☐f☐ ☐REG☐ Set decimal to 3 places ☐f☐ 3 1. 9.0 (yield to maturity) 2. ☐i☐ 3. 8.0 (coupon in percent) 4. ☐PMT☐ 5. 1.091994 (today's date month−day−year)* 6. ☐enter☐ 7. 1.092004 (maturity date month−day−year)* 8. ☐f☐ 9. ☐Price☐ Answer 93.496 Answer is given as % of par value and equals \$934.96. If Error message occurs, clear memory and start over. *See instructions in the third paragraph of the first column.

Yield to Maturity on both the TI BA-35 and HP 12C

Solve for Y = yield to maturity

Given:

P_b = $895.50 price of bond
I_t = $80 annual coupon payments or 8% coupon ($40 semiannually)
P_n = $1,000 principal (par value)
n = 10 years to maturity (20 periods semiannually)

You may choose to refer to Chapters 10 and 11 for a complete discussion of yield to maturity.

	Texas Instruments BA-35	Hewlett-Packard 12C
YIELD TO MATURITY All steps are numbered. All numbers following each step are keystrokes followed by a box ⬚ . Each box represents a keystroke and indicates which calculator function is performed. The Texas Instruments BA-35 does not internally compute a semiannual rate, so the data must be adjusted to reflect semiannual payments and periods. The answer received in step 10 is a semiannual rate, which must be multiplied by 2 to reflect an annual yield. The Hewlett-Packard 12C internally assumes that semiannual payments are made and, therefore, the answer in step 9 is the annual yield to maturity based on semiannual coupons. If you want an answer on the HP for a given number of years (e.g., 10 years), simply start on a date of your choice and end on the same date 10 years later, as in the example.	Set Finance Mode ⬚2nd ⬚FIN Set decimal to 2 places Decimal ⬚2nd ⬚STO 1. 20 (semiannual periods) 2. ⬚N 3. 1000 (par value) 4. ⬚FV 5. 40 (semiannual coupon) 6. ⬚PMT 7. 895.50 (bond price) 8. ⬚PV 9. ⬚CPT 10. ⬚% i answer 4.83% 11. ⬚× 12. 2 13. ⬚= answer 9.65% (annual rate)	Clear memory ⬚f ⬚REG Set decimal ⬚f 2 1. 89.55 (bond price as a percent of par) 2. ⬚PV 3. 8.0 (annual coupon in %) 4. ⬚PMT 5. 1.091994 (today's date month–day–year)* 6. ⬚enter 7. 1.092004 (maturity date month–day–year)* 8. ⬚f 9. ⬚YTM answer 9.65% In case you receive an Error message, you have probably made a keystroke error. Clear the memory ⬚f ⬚REG and start over. ――――――― *See instructions in the third paragraph of the first column.

Net Present Value of an Annuity on both the TI BA-35 and the HP 12C

Solve for PV = present value of annuity

n = 10 years (number of years cash flow will continue)

PMT = $5,000 per year (amount of the annuity)

i = 12% (cost of capital K_a)

Cost = $20,000

You may choose to refer to Chapter 12 for a complete discussion of net present value.

	Texas Instruments BA-35	**Hewlett-Packard 12C**
NET PRESENT VALUE OF AN ANNUITY All steps are numbered and some steps include several keystrokes. All numbers following each step are keystrokes followed by a box [ ]. Each box represents a keystroke and indicates which calculator function is performed on that number. The calculation for the present value of an annuity on the TI BA-35 requires that the project cost be subtracted from the present value of the cash inflows. The HP 12C could solve the problem exactly with the same keystrokes as the TI. However, since the HP uses a similar method to solve uneven cash flows, we elected to use the method that requires more keystrokes but includes a negative cash outflow for the cost of the capital budgeting project. To conserve space, several keystrokes have been put into one step.	Set Finance Mode [2nd] [FIN] Set decimal to 2 places Decimal [2nd] [STO] 1. 10 (years of cash flow) 2. [N] 3. 5000 (annual payments) 4. [PMT] 5. 12 (cost of capital) 6. [% i] 7. [CPT] 8. [PV] 9. [−] 10. 20,000 11. [=] answer $8,251.12	Set decimal to 2 places [f] 2 [f] [REG] clears memory 1. 20000 (cash outflow) 2. [CHS] changes sign 3. [g] 4. [CFo] 5. 5000 (annual payments) 6. [g] [CFj] 7. 10 [g] [Nj] (years) 8. 12 [i] (cost of capital) 9. [f] [NPV] answer $8,251.12 If an Error message appears, start over by clearing the memory with [f] [REG].

Net Present Value of an Uneven Cash Flow on both the TI BA-35 and the HP 12C

Solve for NPV = net present value

$n = 5$ years (number of years cash flow will continue)

PMT = \$5,000 (yr. 1); 6,000 (yr. 2); 7,000 (yr. 3); 8,000 (yr. 4); 9,000 (yr. 5)

$i = 12\%$ (cost of capital K_a)

Cost = \$25,000

You may choose to refer to Chapter 12 for a complete discussion of net present value concepts.

	Texas Instruments BA-35	Hewlett-Packard 12C
NET PRESENT VALUE OF AN UNEVEN CASH FLOW All steps are numbered and some steps include several keystrokes. All numbers following each step are keystrokes followed by a box ☐ . Each box represents a keystroke and indicates which calculator function is performed on that number. Because we are dealing with uneven cash flows, each number must be entered. The TI BA-35 requires that you make sure of the memory. In step 2, you enter the future cash inflow in year 1 and, in step 3, you determine its present value, which is stored in memory. After the first 1-year calculation, following year present values are calculated in the same way and added to the stored value using the ☐SUM☐ key. Finally, the recall key ☐RCL☐ is used to recall the present value of the total cash inflows. The HP 12C requires each cash flow to be entered in order. The ☐CFo☐ key represents the cash flow in time period 0. The ☐CFj☐ key automatically counts the year of the cash flow in the order entered and so no years need be entered. Finally, the cost of capital of 12% is entered and the ☐f☐ key and ☐NPV☐ key are used to complete the problem.	Clear memory ☐ON/C☐ 0 ☐STO☐ Set decimal 2 places Decimal ☐2nd☐ ☐STO☐ Set finance mode ☐2nd☐ ☐FIN☐ 1. 12 ☐% i☐ 2. 5000 ☐FV☐ 3. 1 ☐N☐ ☐CPT☐ ☐PV☐ ☐SUM☐ 4. 6000 ☐FV☐ 5. 2 ☐N☐ ☐CPT☐ ☐PV☐ ☐SUM☐ 6. 7000 ☐FV☐ 7. 3 ☐N☐ ☐CPT☐ ☐PV☐ ☐SUM☐ 8. 8000 ☐FV☐ 9. 4 ☐N☐ ☐CPT☐ ☐PV☐ ☐SUM☐ 10. 9000 ☐FV☐ 11. 5 ☐N☐ ☐CPT☐ ☐PV☐ ☐SUM☐ 12. ☐RCL☐ (answer 24420.90) 13. ☐−☐ 14. 25000 (cash outflow) 15. ☐=☐ answer −\$579.10 Negative Net Present Value	Set decimal to 2 places ☐f☐ 2 ☐f☐ ☐REG☐ clears memory 1. 25000 (cash outflow) 2. ☐CHS☐ changes sign 3. ☐g☐ ☐CFo☐ 4. 5000 ☐g☐ ☐CFj☐ 5. 6000 ☐g☐ ☐CFj☐ 6. 7000 ☐g☐ ☐CFj☐ 7. 8000 ☐g☐ ☐CFj☐ 8. 9000 ☐g☐ ☐CFj☐ 9. 12 ☐i☐ 10. ☐f☐ ☐NPV☐ answer −\$579.10 Negative Net Present Value If you receive an Error message, you have probably made a keystroke error. Clear memory with ☐f☐ ☐REG☐ and start over with step 1.

Internal Rate of Return for an Annuity on both the TI BA-35 and the HP 12C

Solve for IRR = internal rate of return

n = 10 years (number of years cash flow will continue)
PMT = $10,000 per year (amount of the annuity)
Cost = $50,000 (this is the present value of the annuity)

You may choose to refer to Chapter 12 for a complete discussion of internal rate of return.

	Texas Instruments BA-35	Hewlett-Packard 12C
INTERNAL RATE OF RETURN ON AN ANNUITY All steps are numbered and some steps include several keystrokes. All numbers following each step are keystrokes followed by a box ☐. Each box represents a keystroke and indicates which calculator function is performed on that number. The calculation for the internal rate of return on an annuity on the TI BA-35 requires relatively few keystrokes. The HP 12C requires more keystrokes than the TI BA-35, because it needs to use the function keys ☐ f and ☐ g to enter data into the internal programs. The HP method requires that the cash outflow be expressed as a negative, while the TI BA-35 uses a positive number for the cash outflow. To conserve space, several keystrokes have been put into one step.	Clear memory ON/C 0 STO Set Finance Mode 2nd FIN Set decimal to 2 places Decimal 2nd STO 1. 10 (years of cash flow) 2. N 3. 10000 (annual payments) 4. PMT 5. 50000 (present value) 6. PV 7. CPT 8. % i answer is 15.10% At an internal rate of return of 15.10%, the present value of the $50,000 outflow is equal to the present value of $10,000 cash inflows over the next 10 years.	Set decimal to 2 places f 2 f REG clears memory 1. 50000 (cash outflow) 2. CHS changes sign 3. g 4. CFo 5. 10000 (annual payments) 6. g CFj 7. 10 g Nj (years) 8. f IRR answer is 15.10% If an Error message appears, start over by clearing the memory with f REG .

Internal Rate of Return with an Uneven Cash Flow on both the TI BA-35 and the HP 12C

Solve for IRR = internal rate of return (return which causes present
value of outflows to equal present value of the inflows).

n = 5 years (number of years cash flow will continue)

PMT = $5,000 (yr. 1); 6,000 (yr. 2); 7,000 (yr. 3); 8,000 (yr. 4); 9,000 (yr. 5)

Cost = $25,000

You may choose to refer to Chapter 12 for a complete discussion of internal rate of return.

	Texas Instruments BA-35	**Hewlett-Packard 12C**
INTERNAL RATE OF RETURN ON UNEVEN CASH FLOW	Clear memory ON/C 0 STO	Set decimal to 2 places
All steps are numbered and some steps include several keystrokes. All numbers following each step are keystrokes followed by a box ⬜. Each box represents a keystroke and indicates which calculator function is performed on that number.	Set decimal 2 places Decimal 2nd STO Set finance mode 2nd FIN	f 2 f REG clears memory 1. 25000 (cash outflow) 2. CHS changes sign 3. g CFo
Because we are dealing with uneven cash flows, the mathematics of solving this problem with the TI BA-35 is not possible. A more advanced algebraic calculator would be required.	1. 12 % i (your IRR est.) 2. 5000 FV 3. 1 N CPT PV STO 4. 6000 FV	4. 5000 g CFj 5. 6000 g CFj 6. 7000 g CFj 7. 8000 g CFj
However, for the student willing to use trial and error, the student can use the NPV method and try different discount rates until the NPV equals zero. Check Chapter 12 on methods for approximating the IRR. This will provide a start.	5. 2 N CPT PV SUM 6. 7000 FV 7. 3 N CPT PV SUM 8. 8000 FV 9. 4 N CPT PV SUM	8. 9000 g CFj 9. f IRR answer 11.15% If you receive an Error message, you have probably made a keystroke error. Clear memory with
The HP 12C requires each cash flow to be entered in order. The CFo key represents the cash flow in time period 0. The CFj key automatically counts the year of the cash flow in the order entered and so no years need be entered. To find the internal rate of return, use the f IRR keys and complete the problem.	10. 9000 FV 11. 5 N CPT PV SUM 12. RCL (answer 24,420.90) 13. − 14. 25000 (cash outflow) 15. = Answer −$579.10. Negative NPV. Start over with a lower discount rate (try 11.15). Answer is 24999.75. With a cash outflow of $25,000, the IRR would be 11.15%.	f REG and start over with step 1.

Glossary

accelerated cost recovery system (ACRS) A system that specifies the allowable depreciation recovery period for different types of assets. The normal recovery period is generally shorter than the physical life of the asset.

after-acquired property clause A requirement in a bond issue stipulating that any new equipment purchased after the issue be placed under the original mortgage.

aftermarket The market for a new security offering immediately after it is sold to the public.

agency theory This theory examines the relationship between the owners of the firm and the managers of the firm. While management has the responsibility for acting as the agent for the stockholders in pursuing their best interests, the key question considered is: How well does management perform this role?

agent One who sells or "places" an asset for another party. An agent works on a commission or fee basis. Investment bankers sometimes act as agents for their clients.

aging of accounts receivable Analyzing accounts by the amount of time they have been on the books.

American Depository Receipts (ADR) These receipts represent the ownership interest in a foreign company's common stock. The shares of the foreign company are put in trust in a New York bank. The bank, in turn, issues its depository receipts to the American stockholders of the foreign firm. Many ADRs are listed on the NYSE and many more are traded in the over-the-counter market.

American Stock Exchange (AMEX) The second largest national organized security exchange in the United States.

annual percentage rate (APR) A measure of the *effective* rate on a loan. One uses the actuarial method of compound interest when calculating the APR.

annuity A series of consecutive payments or receipts of equal amount.

ARBs (arbitrageurs) Specialists in merger investments who attempt to capitalize on the difference between the value offered and the current market price of the acquisition candidate.

articles of incorporation A document that establishes a corporation and specifies the rights and limitations of the business entity.

articles of partnership An agreement between the partners in a business that specifies the ownership interest of each, the methods of distributing profits, and the means for withdrawing from the partnership.

asset-backed securities Public offerings backed by receivables as collateral. Essentially, a firm factors (sells) its receivables in the securities markets.

asset depreciation range This represents the expected physical life of an asset. Generally, the midpoint of the ADR is utilized to determine what class an asset falls into for depreciation purposes.

asset utilization ratios A group of ratios that measures the speed at which the firm is turning over or utilizing its assets. We measure inventory turnover, fixed asset turnover, total asset turnover, and the average time it takes to collect accounts receivable.

assignment The liquidation of assets without going through formal court procedures. In order to affect an assignment, creditors must agree on liquidation values and the relative priority of claims.

automated clearinghouse (ACH) An ACH transfers information between one financial institution and another and from account to account via computer tape. There are approximately 30 regional clearinghouses throughout the United States that claim the membership of over 10,000 financial institutions.

average collection period The average amount of time accounts receivable have been on the books. It may be computed by dividing accounts receivable by average daily credit sales.

B

balance of payments The term refers to a system of government accounts that catalogs the flow of economic transactions between countries.

balance sheet A financial statement that indicates what assets the firm owns and how those assets are financed in the form of liabilities or ownership interest.

bank holding company A legal entity in which one key bank owns a number of affiliate banks as well as other nonbanking subsidiaries engaged in closely related activities.

banker's acceptance Short-term securities that frequently arise from foreign trade. The acceptance is a draft that is drawn on a bank for approval for future payment and is subsequently presented to the payer.

bankruptcy The market value of a firm's assets are less than its liabilities, and the firm has a negative net worth. The term is also used to describe in-court procedures associated with the reorganization or liquidation of a firm.

bear market A falling or lethargic stock market. The opposite of a bull market.

best efforts A distribution in which the investment banker agrees to work for a commission rather than actually underwriting (buying) the issue for resale. It is a procedure that is often used by smaller investment bankers with relatively unknown companies. The investment banker is not directly taking the risk for distribution.

beta A measure of the volatility of returns on an individual stock relative to the market. Stocks with a beta of 1.0 are said to have risk equal to that of the market (equal volatility). Stocks with betas greater than 1.0 have more risk than the market, while those with betas of less than 1.0 have less risk than the market.

blanket inventory liens A secured borrowing arrangement in which the lender has a general claim against the inventory of the borrower.

bond ratings Bonds are rated according to risk by Standard & Poor's and Moody's Investor Service. A bond that is rated Aaa by Moody's has the lowest risk, while a bond with a C rating has the highest risk. Coupon rates are greatly influenced by a corporation's bond rating.

book-entry transactions A transaction in which no actual paper or certificate is created. All transactions simply take place on the books via computer entries.

book value (See net worth.)

brokers Members of organized stock exchanges who have the ability to buy and sell securities on the floor of their respective exchanges. Brokers act as agents between buyers and sellers.

bull market A rising stock market. There are many complicated interpretations of this term, usually centering on the length of time that the market should be rising in order to meet the criteria for classification as a bull market. For our purposes, a bull market exists when stock prices are strong and rising and investors are optimistic about future market performance.

business risk The risk related to the inability of the firm to hold its competitive position and maintain stability and growth in earnings.

C

call premium The premium paid by a corporation to call in a bond issue before the maturity date.

call provision Used for bonds and some preferred stock. A call allows the corporation to retire securities before maturity by forcing the bondholders to sell bonds back to it at a set price. The call provisions are included in the bond indenture.

capital Sources of long-term financing that are available to the business firm.

capital asset pricing model A model that relates the risk-return trade-offs of individual assets to market returns. A security is presumed to receive a risk-free rate of return plus a premium for risk.

capital lease A long-term, noncancelable lease that has many of the characteristics of debt. Under FASB Statement 13, the lease obligation must be shown directly on the balance sheet.

capital markets Competitive markets for equity securities or debt securities with maturities of more than one year. The best examples of capital market securities are common stock, bonds, and preferred stock.

capital rationing Occurs when a corporation has more dollars of capital budgeting projects with positive net present values than it has money to invest in them. Therefore, some projects that should be accepted are excluded because financial capital is rationed.

capital structure theory A theory that addresses the relative importance of debt and equity in the overall financing of the firm.

carrying costs The cost to hold an asset, usually inventory. For inventory, carrying costs include such items as interest, warehousing costs, insurance, and material-handling expenses.

cash budget A series of monthly or quarterly budgets that indicate cash receipts, cash payments, and the borrowing requirements for meeting financial requirements. It is constructed from the pro forma income statement and other supportive schedules.

cash discount A reduction in the invoice price if payment is made within a specified time period. An example would be 2/10, net 30.

cash flow A value equal to income after taxes plus noncash expenses. In capital budgeting decisions, the usual noncash expense is depreciation.

cash flow cycle The pattern in which cash moves in and out of the firm. The primary consideration in managing the cash flow cycle is to ensure that inflows and outflows of cash are properly synchronized for transaction purposes.

cash flows from financing activities Cash flow that is generated (or reduced) from the sale or repurchase of securities or the payment of cash dividends. It is the third section presented in the statement of cash flows.

cash flows from investing activities Cash flow that is generated (or reduced) from the sale or purchase of long-term securities or plant and equipment. It is the second section presented in the statement of cash flows.

cash flows from operating activities Cash flow information that is determined by adjusting net income for such items as depreciation expense, changes in current assets and liabilities, and other items. It is the first section presented in the statement of cash flows.

certificates of deposit A certificate offered by banks, savings and loans, and other financial institutions for the deposit of funds at a given interest rate over a specified time period.

clientele effect The effect of investor preferences for dividends or capital gains. Investors tend to purchase securities that meet their needs.

coefficient of correlation The degree of associated movement between two or more variables. Variables that move in the same direction are said to be positively correlated, while negatively correlated variables move in opposite directions.

coefficient of variation A measure of risk determination that is computed by dividing the standard deviation for a series of numbers by the expected value. Generally, the larger the coefficient of variation, the greater the risk.

combined leverage The total or combined impact of operating and financial leverage.

commercial paper An unsecured promissory note that large corporations issue to investors. The minimum amount is usually $25,000.

common equity The common stock or ownership capital of the firm. Common equity may be supplied through retained earnings or the sale of new common stock.

common stock Represents the ownership interest of the firm. Common stockholders have the ultimate right to control the business.

common stock equity The ownership interest in the firm. It may be represented by new shares or retained earnings. The same as net worth.

common stock equivalent Warrants, options, and any convertible securities that pay less than two thirds of the average Aa bond yield at the time of issue.

compensating balances A bank requirement that business customers maintain a minimum average balance. The required amount is usually computed as a percentage of customer loans outstanding or as a percentage of the future loans to which the bank has committed itself.

composition An out-of-court settlement in which creditors agree to accept a fractional settlement on their original claim.

compounded semiannually A compounding period of every six months. For example, a five-year investment in which interest is compounded semiannually would indicate an n value equal to 10 and an i value at one half the annual rate.

conglomerate A corporation that is made up of many diverse, often unrelated divisions. This form of organization is thought to reduce risk, but may create problems of coordination.

consolidation The combination of two or more firms, generally of equal size and market power, to form an entirely new entity.

contribution margin The contribution to fixed costs from each unit of sales. The margin may be computed as price minus variable cost per unit.

conversion premium The market price of a convertible bond or preferred stock minus the security's conversion value.

conversion price The conversion ratio divided into the par value. The price of the common stock at which the security is convertible. An investor would usually not convert the security into common stock unless the market price were greater than the conversion price.

conversion ratio The number of shares of common stock an investor will receive if he or she exchanges a convertible bond or convertible preferred stock for common stock.

conversion value The conversion ratio multiplied by the market price per share of common stock.

convertible Eurobonds Convertible Eurobonds are dollar-denominated and sold primarily in Western European countries. They have the safety of a bond but the chance to grow with U.S. stock prices since they are convertible into a U.S. firm's stock.

convertible exchangeable preferred A form of preferred stock that allows the company to force conversion from convertible preferred stock into convertible debt. This can be used to allow the company to take advantage of falling interest rates or to allow the company to change aftertax preferred dividends into tax-deductible interest payments.

convertible security A security that may be traded into the company for a different form or type of security. Convertible securities are usually bonds or preferred stock that may be exchanged for common stock.

corporate stock repurchase A corporation may repurchase its shares in the market as an alternative to paying a cash dividend. Earnings per share will go up, and, if the price-earnings ratio remains the same, the stockholder will receive the same dollar benefit as through a cash dividend. A corporation may also justify the repurchase of its stock because it is at a very low price or to maintain constant demand for the shares. Reacquired shares may be used for employee options or as part of a tender offer in a merger or acquisition. Firms may also reacquire part of their shares as a protective device against being taken over as a merger candidate.

corporation A form of ownership in which a separate legal entity is created. A corporation may sue or be sued, engage in contracts, and acquire property. It has a continual life and is not dependent on any one stockholder for maintaining its legal existence. A corporation is owned by stockholders who enjoy the privilege of limited liability. There is, however, the potential for double taxation in the corporate form of organization: the first time at the corporate level in the form of profits, and again at the stockholder level in the form of dividends.

cost-benefit analysis A study of the incremental costs and benefits that can be derived from a given course of action.

cost of capital The cost of alternative sources of financing to the firm. (Also see weighted average cost of capital.)

cost of goods sold The cost specifically associated with units sold during the time period under study.

cost of ordering The cost component in the inventory decision model that represents the expenditure for acquiring new inventory.

coupon rate The actual interest rate on the bond, usually payable in semiannual installments. The coupon rate normally stays constant during the life of the bond and indicates what the bondholder's annual dollar income will be.

credit terms The repayment provisions that are part of a credit arrangement. An example would be a 2/10, net 30 arrangement in which the customer may deduct 2 percent from the invoice price if payment takes place in the first 10 days. Otherwise, the full amount is due.

creditor committee A committee set up to run the business while an out-of-court settlement is reached.

cross rates The relationship between two foreign currencies expressed in terms of a third currency (the dollar).

cumulative preferred stock If dividends from one period are not paid to the preferred stockholders, they are said to be in arrears and are then added to the next period's dividends. When dividends on preferred stock are in arrears, no dividends can legally be paid to the common stockholders. The cumulative dividend feature is very beneficial to preferred stockholders since it assures them that they will receive all dividends due before common stockholders can get any dividends.

cumulative voting Allows shareholders more than one vote per share. They are allowed to multiply their total shares by the number of directors being elected to determine their total number of votes. This system enables minority shareholders to elect directors even though they do not have 51 percent of the vote.

currency futures contract A futures contract that may be used for hedging or speculation in foreign exchange.

current cost accounting One of two methods of inflation-adjusted accounting approved by the Financial Accounting Standards Board in 1979. Financial statements are adjusted to the present, using current cost data, rather than an index. This optional information may be shown in the firm's annual report.

current yield The yearly dollar interest or dividend payment divided by the current market price.

D

dealer paper A form of commercial paper that is distributed to lenders through an intermediate dealer network. It is normally sold by industrial companies, utility firms, or financial companies too small to have their own selling network.

dealers Participants in the market who transact security trades over the counter from their own inventory of stocks and bonds. They are often referred to as market makers, since they stand ready to buy and sell their securities at quoted prices.

debenture A long-term unsecured corporate bond. Debentures are usually issued by large firms having excellent credit ratings in the financial community.

debt utilization ratios A group of ratios that indicates to what extent debt is being used and the prudence with which it is being managed. Calculations include debt to total assets, times interest earned, and fixed charge coverage.

decision tree A tabular or graphical analysis that lays out the sequence of decisions that are to be made and highlights the differences between choices. The presentation resembles branches on a tree.

deferred annuity An annuity that will not begin until some time period in the future.

degree of combined leverage (DCL) A measure of the total combined effect of operating and financial leverage on earnings per share. The percentage change in earnings per share is divided by the percentage change in sales at a given level of operation. Other algebraic statements are also used, such as Formula 5–7 and footnote 3 in Chapter 5.

degree of financial leverage (DFL) A measure of the impact of debt on the earnings capability of the firm. The percentage change in earnings per share is divided by the percentage change in earnings before interest and taxes at a given level of operation. Other algebraic statements are also used, such as Formula 5–5.

degree of operating leverage (DOL) A measure of the impact of fixed costs on the operating earnings of the firm. The percentage change in operating income is divided by the percentage change in volume at a given level of operation. Other algebraic statements are also used, such as Formula 5–3 and footnote 2 in Chapter 5.

depreciation The allocation of the initial cost of an asset over its useful life. The annual expense of plant and equipment is matched against the revenues that are being produced.

depreciation base The initial cost of an asset that is multiplied by the appropriate annual depreciation percentage in Table 12–9 to determine the dollar depreciation.

dilution of earnings This occurs when additional shares of stock are sold without creating an immediate increase in income. The result is a decline in earnings per share until earnings can be generated from the funds raised.

direct paper A form of commercial paper that is sold directly by the lender to the finance company. It is also referred to as finance paper.

discount rate The rate at which future sums or annuities are discounted back to the present.

discounted loan A loan in which the calculated interest payment is subtracted or discounted in advance. Because this lowers the amount of available funds, the effective interest rate is increased.

disinflation A leveling off or slowdown of price increases.

dividend payment date The day on which a stockholder of record will receive his or her dividend.

dividend payout The percentage of dividends to earnings after taxes. It can be computed by dividing dividends per share by earnings per share.

dividend reinvestment plans Plans that provide the investor with an opportunity to buy additional shares of stock with the cash dividends paid by the company.

dividend valuation model A model for determining the value of a share of stock by taking the present value of an expected stream of future dividends.

dividend yield Dividends per share divided by market price per share. Dividend yield indicates the percentage return that a stockholder will receive on dividends alone.

dual trading Exists when one security, such as General Motors common stock, is traded on more than one stock exchange. This practice is quite common between NYSE-listed companies and regional exchanges.

Dun & Bradstreet A credit-rating agency that publishes information on over 3 million business establishments through its *Reference Book*.

Du Pont system of analysis An analysis of profitability that breaks down return on assets between the profit margin and asset turnover. The second, or modified, version shows how return on assets is translated into return on equity through the amount of debt that the firm has. Actually return on assets is divided by $(1 - \text{debt/assets})$ to arrive at return on equity.

Dutch auction preferred stock A preferred stock security that matures every seven weeks and is sold (reauctioned) at a subsequent bidding. The concept of Dutch auction means the stock is issued to the bidder willing to accept the lowest yield and then to the next lowest bidder and so on until all the preferred stock is sold.

E

earnings per share The earnings available to common stockholders divided by the number of common stock shares outstanding.

economic ordering quantity (EOQ) The most efficient ordering quantity for the firm. The EOQ will allow the firm to minimize the total ordering and carrying costs associated with inventory.

efficient frontier A line drawn through the optimum point selections in a risk-return trade-off diagram. Each point represents the best possible trade-off between risk and return (the highest return at a given risk level or the lowest risk at a given return level).

efficient market hypothesis Hypothesis that suggests markets adjust very quickly to new information and it is very difficult for investors to select portfolios of securities that outperform the market. The efficient market hypothesis may be stated in many different forms, as indicated in Chapter 14.

electronic funds transfer A system in which funds are moved between computer terminals without the use of written checks.

Eurobonds Bonds payable or denominated in the borrower's currency, but sold outside the country of the borrower, usually by an international syndicate. This market is dominated by bonds stated in U.S. dollars.

Eurodollar certificate of deposit A certificate of deposit based on U.S. dollars held on deposit by foreign banks.

Eurodollar loans Loans made by foreign banks denominated in U.S. dollars.

Eurodollars U.S. dollars held on deposit by foreign banks and loaned out by those banks to anyone seeking dollars.

European Community (EC) 92 The development of a strong economic bond between 12 European countries. EC 92 calls for elimination of border controls, common standards for trade and commerce, integrated financial markets, and other similar measures.

exchange rate The relationship between the value of two or more currencies. For example, the exchange rate between U.S. dollars and French francs is stated as dollars per francs or francs per dollar.

ex-dividend date Four business days before the holder-of-record date. On the ex-dividend date the purchase of the stock no longer carries with it the right to receive the dividend previously declared.

exercise price The price at which a warrant (or other similar security) allows the investor to purchase common stock.

expectations hypothesis The hypothesis maintains that the yields on long-term securities are a function of short-term rates. The result of the hypothesis is that, when long-term rates are much higher than short-term rates, the market is saying that it expects short-term rates to rise. Conversely, when long-term rates are lower than short-term rates, the market is expecting short-term rates to fall.

expected value A representative value from a probability distribution arrived at by multiplying each outcome by the associated probability and summing up the values.

Eximbank (Export-Import Bank) An agency of the U.S. government that facilitates the financing of U.S. exports through its miscellaneous programs. In its direct loan program, the Eximbank lends money to foreign purchasers of U.S. products—such as aircraft, electrical equipment, heavy machinery, computers, and the like. The Eximbank also purchases eligible medium-term obligations of foreign buyers of U.S. goods at a discount from face value. In this discount program, private banks and other lenders are able to rediscount (sell at a lower price) promissory notes and drafts acquired from foreign customers of U.S. firms.

expropriate The action of a country in taking away or modifying the property rights of a corporation or individual.

ex-rights The situation in which the purchase of common stock during a rights offering no longer includes rights to purchase additional shares of common stock.

extension An out-of-court settlement in which creditors agree to allow the firm more time to meet its financial obligations. A new repayment schedule will be developed, subject to the acceptance of creditors.

external corporate funds Corporate financing raised through sources outside of the firm. Bonds, common stock, and preferred stock fall in this category.

external reorganization A reorganization under the formal bankruptcy laws, in which a merger partner is found for the distressed firm. Ideally, the distressed firm should be merged with a strong firm in its own industry, although this is not always possible.

F

factoring Selling accounts receivable to a finance company or a bank.

federal deficit Government expenditures are greater than government tax revenues, and the government must borrow to balance revenues and expenditures. These deficits act as an economic stimulus.

federally sponsored credit agencies Federal agencies, such as the Federal Home Loan Banks and the Federal Land Bank, that issue securities.

federal surplus Government tax receipts are greater than government expenditures. Surpluses have a dampening effect on the economy.

Federal National Mortgage Association (Fannie Mae) A former government agency that provides a secondary market in mortgages. It is now private.

Federal Reserve discount rate The rate of interest that the Fed charges on loans to the banking system. A monetary tool for management of the money supply.

field warehousing An inventory financing arrangement in which collateralized inventory is stored on the premises of the borrower but is controlled by an independent warehousing company.

FIFO A system of writing off inventory into cost of goods sold, in which the items purchased first are written off first. Referred to as first-in, first-out.

finance paper A form of commercial paper that is sold directly to the lender by the finance company. It is also referred to as direct paper.

Financial Accounting Standards Board A privately supported rule-making body for the accounting profession.

financial capital Common stock, preferred stock, bonds, and retained earnings. Financial capital appears on the corporate balance sheet under long-term liabilities and equity.

financial disclosure Presentation of financial information to the investment community.

financial futures market A market that allows for the trading of financial instruments related to a future point in time. A purchase or sale occurs in the present, with a reversal necessitated in the future to close out the position. If a purchase (sale) occurs initially, then a sale (purchase) will be necessary in the future. The market provides for futures contracts in Treasury bonds, Treasury bills, certificates of deposits, GNMA certificates, and many other instruments. Financial futures contracts may be executed on the Chicago Board of Trade, the Chicago Mercantile Exchange, the New York Futures Exchange, and other exchanges.

financial intermediary A financial institution, such as a bank or a life insurance company, that directs other people's money into such investments as government and corporate securities.

financial lease A long-term, noncancelable lease. The financial lease has all the characteristics of long-term debt.

financial leverage A measure of the amount of debt used in the capital structure of the firm.

financial risk The risk related to the inability of the firm to meet its debt obligations as they come due.

financial sweetener Usually refers to equity options, such as warrants or conversion privileges, attached to a debt security. The sweetener lowers the interest cost to the corporation.

fiscal policy The tax policies of the federal government and the spending associated with its tax revenues.

fixed costs Costs that remain relatively constant regardless of the volume of operations. Examples are rent, depreciation, property taxes, and executive salaries.

float The difference between the corporation's recorded cash balance on its books and the amount credited to the corporation by the bank.

floating rate bond A bond in which the interest payment changes with market conditions.

floating rate preferred stock The quarterly dividend on the preferred stock changes with market rates. The market price is considerably less volatile than it is with regular preferred stock.

floor value Usually equal to the pure bond value. A convertible bond will not sell at less than its floor value even when its conversion value is below the pure bond value.

flotation cost The distribution cost of selling securities to the public. The cost includes the underwriter's spread and any associated fees.

forced conversion Occurs when a company calls a convertible security that has a conversion value greater than the call price. Investors will take the higher of the two values and convert the security to common stock, rather than take a lower cash call price.

Foreign Credit Insurance Association (FCIA) An agency established by a group of 60 U.S. insurance companies. It sells credit export insurance to interested exporters. The FCIA promises to pay for the exported merchandise if the foreign importer defaults on payment.

foreign exchange risk A form of risk that refers to the possibility of experiencing a drop in revenue or an increase in cost in an international transaction due to a change in foreign exchange rates. Importers, exporters, investors, and multinational firms alike are exposed to this risk.

foreign trade deficit A deficit that occurs because Americans buy more foreign goods than American companies sell to foreigners.

forward rate A rate that reflects the future value of a currency based on expectations. Forward rates may be greater than the current spot rate (premium) or less than the current spot rate (discount).

founders' shares Stock owned by the original founders of a company. It often carries special voting rights that allow the founders to maintain voting privileges in excess of their proportionate ownership.

free cash flow Cash flow from operating activities, minus expenditures required to maintain the productive capacity of the firm, minus dividend payouts.

fronting loan A parent company's loan to a foreign subsidiary is channeled through a financial intermediary, usually a large international bank. The bank fronts for the parent in extending the loan to the foreign affiliate.

fully diluted earnings per share Equals adjusted earnings after taxes divided by shares outstanding, plus common stock equivalents, plus all convertible securities.

future value The value that a current amount grows to at a given interest rate over a given time period.

future value of an annuity The sum of the future value of a series of consecutive equal payments.

futures contract A contract to buy or sell a commodity at some specified price in the future.

G

going private The process by which all publicly owned shares of common stock are repurchased or retired, thereby eliminating listing fees, annual reports, and other expenses involved with publicly owned companies.

golden parachute Highly attractive termination payments made to current management in the event of a takeover of the company.

goodwill An intangible asset that reflects value above that generally recognized in the tangible assets of the firm.

H

hedging To engage in a transaction that partially or fully reduces a prior risk exposure by taking a position that is the opposite of your initial position. As an example, you own some copper now but also engage in a contract to sell copper in the future at a set price.

historical cost accounting The traditional method of accounting, in which financial statements are developed based on original cost minus depreciation.

holder-of-record date Stockholders owning the stock on the holder-of-record date are entitled to receive a dividend. In order to be listed as an owner on the corporate books, the investor must have bought the stock before it went ex-dividend.

holding company A company that has voting control of one or more other companies. It often has less than a 50 percent interest in each of these other companies.

homemade leverage The use of leverage directly by investors in place of corporate leverage. It allows investors to bring into balance the value of unlevered and levered firms by providing the "missing leverage" themselves. Homemade leverage is part of the initial Modigliani and Miller approach.

horizontal integration The acquisition of a competitor.

humped yield curve A yield curve in which intermediate rates are higher than both short- and long-term rates.

hurdle rate The minimum acceptable rate of return in a capital budgeting decision.

I

income statement A financial statement that measures the profitability of the firm over a time period. All expenses are subtracted from sales to arrive at net income.

incremental depreciation The depreciation on a new asset minus the depreciation on an old asset. Incremental depreciation is multiplied times the tax rate to determine its tax shield benefit.

indenture A legal contract between the borrower and the lender that covers every detail regarding a bond issue.

indexing An adjustment for inflation incorporated into the operation of an economy. Indexing may be used to revalue assets on the balance sheet and to automatically adjust wages, tax deductions, interest payments, and a wide variety of other categories to account for inflation.

inflation The phenomenon of prices increasing with the passage of time.

inflation premium A premium to compensate the investor for the eroding effect of inflation on the value of the dollar.

information content of dividends This theory of dividends assumes that dividends provide information about the financial health and economic expectations of the company. If this is true, corporations must actively manage their dividends to provide the market with information.

insider trading This occurs when someone has information that is not available to the public and then uses this information to profit from trading in a company's common stock.

installment loan A borrowing arrangement in which a series of equal payments are used to pay off the loan.

interest factor The tabular value to insert into the various present value and future value formulas. It is based on the number of periods (n) and the interest rate (i).

interest rate parity theory A theory based on the interplay between interest rate differentials and exchange rates. If one country has a higher interest rate than another country after adjustments for inflation, interest rates and foreign exchange rates will adjust until the foreign exchange rates and money market rates reach equilibrium (are properly balanced between the two countries).

internally generated funds Funds generated through the operations of the firm. The principal sources are retained earnings and cash flow added back from depreciation and other noncash deductions.

internal rate of return (IRR) A discounted cash flow method for evaluating capital budgeting projects. The IRR is a discount rate that makes the present value of the cash inflows equal to the present value of the cash outflows.

internal reorganization A reorganization under the formal bankruptcy laws. New management may be brought in and a redesign of the capital structure may be implemented.

international diversification Achieving diversification through many different foreign investments that are influenced by a variety of factors.

International Finance Corporation (IFC) An affiliate of the World Bank established with the sole purpose of providing partial seed capital for private ventures around the world. Whenever a multinational company has difficulty raising equity capital due to lack of adequate private risk capital, the firm may explore the possibility of selling equity or debt (totaling up to 25 percent) to the International Finance Corporation.

intrinsic value As applied to a warrant, this represents the market value of common stock minus the exercise price. The difference is then multiplied by the number of shares each warrant entitles the holder to purchase.

inventory profits Profits generated as a result of an inflationary economy, in which old inventory is sold at large profits because of increasing prices. This is particularly prevalent under FIFO accounting.

inverted yield curve A downward-sloping yield curve. Short-term rates are higher than long-term rates.

investment banker A financial organization that specializes in selling primary offerings of securities. Investment bankers can also perform other financial functions, such as advising clients, negotiating mergers and takeovers, and selling secondary offerings.

investment tax credit (ITC) A percentage of the purchase price of an asset that may be directly deducted from the tax obligation of the firm. It tends to be temporary in nature as the government continually extends and then withdraws ITCs. The typical level for ITCs over the decades has been 7 percent of the purchase price.

J

just-in-time inventory management (JIT) A system of inventory management that stresses taking possession of inventory just before the time it is needed for production or sale. It greatly reduces the cost of carrying inventory.

L

lease A contractual arrangement between the owner of equipment (lessor) and the user of equipment (lessee), which calls for the lessee to pay the lessor an established lease payment. There are two kinds of leases: financial leases and operating leases.

letter of credit A credit letter normally issued by the importer's bank, in which the bank promises to pay out the money for the merchandise when delivered.

level production Equal monthly production used to smooth out production schedules and employ manpower and equipment more efficiently and at a lower cost.

leverage The use of fixed-charge items with the intent of magnifying the potential returns to the firm.

leveraged buyout Existing management or an outsider makes an offer to "go private" by retiring all the shares of the company. The buying group borrows the necessary money, using the assets of the acquired firm as collateral. The buying group then repurchases all the shares and expects to retire the debt over time with the cash flow from operations or the sale of corporate assets.

LIBOR (See London Interbank Offered Rate.)

life cycle A curve illustrating the growth phases of a firm. The dividend policy most likely to be employed during each phase is often illustrated.

LIFO A system of writing off inventory into cost of goods sold in which the items purchased last are written off first. Referred to as last-in, first-out.

limited partnership A special form of partnership to limit liability for most of the partners. Under this arrangement, one or more partners are designated as general partners and have unlimited liability for the debts of the firm, while the other partners are designated as limited partners and are only liable for their initial contribution.

liquidation A procedure that may be carried out under the formal bankruptcy laws when an internal or external reorganization does not appear to be feasible, and it appears that the assets are worth more in liquidation than through a reorganization. Priority of claims becomes extremely important in a liquidation because it is unlikely that all parties will be fully satisfied in their demands.

liquidity The relative convertibility of short-term assets to cash. Thus, marketable securities are highly liquid assets, while inventory may not be.

liquidity premium theory This theory indicates that long-term rates should be higher than short-term rates. The premium of long-term rates over short-term rates exists because short-term securities have greater liquidity, and, therefore, higher rates have to be offered to potential long-term bond buyers to entice them to hold these less liquid and more price sensitive securities.

liquidity ratios A group of ratios that allows one to measure the firm's ability to pay off short-term obligations as they come due. Primary attention is directed to the current ratio and the quick ratio.

listing requirements Financial standards that corporations must meet before their common stock can be traded on a stock exchange. Listing requirements are not standard, but are set by each exchange. The requirements for the NYSE are the most stringent.

lockbox system A procedure used to expedite cash inflows to a business. Customers are requested to forward their checks to a post office box in their geographic region, and a local bank picks up the checks and processes them for rapid collection. Funds are then wired to the corporate home office for immediate use.

London Interbank Offered Rate (LIBOR) An interbank rate applicable for large deposits in the London market. It is a benchmark rate, just like the prime interest rate in the United States. Interest rates on Eurodollar loans are determined by adding premiums to this basic rate. Most often, LIBOR is lower than the U.S. prime rate.

M

majority voting All directors must be elected by a vote of more than 50 percent. Minority shareholders are unable to achieve any representation on the board of directors.

managing investment banker An investment banker who is responsible for the pricing, prospectus development, and legal work involved in the sale of a new issue of securities.

margin requirement A rule that specifies the amount of cash or equity that must be deposited with a brokerage firm or bank, with the balance of funds eligible for borrowing. Margin is set by the Board of Governors of the Federal Reserve Board.

marginal corporate tax rate The rate that applies to each new dollar of taxable income. For a corporation, the maximum rate is in the mid-30 percent range. The marginal rate is lower for smaller corporations.

marginal cost of capital The cost of the last dollar of funds raised. It is assumed that each dollar is financed in proportion to the firm's optimum capital structure.

marginal principle of retained earnings The corporation must be able to earn a higher return on its retained earnings than a stockholder would receive after paying taxes on the distributed dividends.

market efficiency Markets are considered to be efficient when (1) prices adjust rapidly to new information; (2) there is a continuous market, in which each successive trade is made at a price close to the previous price (the faster the price responds to new information and the smaller the differences in price changes, the more efficient the market); and (3) the market can absorb large dollar amounts of securities without destabilizing the prices.

market risk premium A premium over and above the risk-free rate. It is represented by the difference between the market return (K_m) and the risk-free rate (R_f), and it may be multiplied by the beta coefficient to determine the additional risk-adjusted return on a security.

market stabilization Intervention in the secondary markets by an investment banker to stabilize the price of a new security offering during the offering period. The purpose of market stabilization is to provide an orderly market for the distribution of the new issue.

market value maximization The concept of maximizing the wealth of shareholders. This calls for a recognition not only of earnings per share but also how they will be valued in the marketplace.

maturity date The date on which the bond is retired and the principal (par value) is repaid to the lender.

merger The combination of two or more companies, in which the resulting firms maintain the identity of the acquiring company.

merger premium The part of a buyout or exchange offer that represents a value over and above the market value of the acquired firm.

monetary policy Management by the Federal Reserve Board of the money supply and the resultant interest rates.

money market accounts Accounts at banks, savings and loans, and credit unions in which the depositor receives competitive money market rates on a typical minimum deposit of $1,000. These accounts may generally have three deposits and three withdrawals per month and are not meant to be transaction accounts, but a place to keep minimum and excess cash balances. These accounts are insured by various appropriate governmental agencies up to $100,000.

money market funds A fund in which investors may purchase shares for as little as $500 or $1,000. The fund then reinvests the proceeds in high-yielding $100,000 bank CDs, $25,000–$100,000 commercial paper, and other large-denomination, high-yielding securities. Investors receive their pro rata portion of the interest proceeds daily as a credit to their shares.

money markets Competitive markets for securities with maturities of one year or less. The best examples of money market instruments would be Treasury bills, commercial paper, and negotiable certificates of deposit.

mortgage agreement A loan that requires real property (plant and equipment) as collateral.

multinational corporation A firm doing business across its national borders is considered a multinational enterprise. Some definitions require a minimum percentage (often 30 percent or more) of a firm's business activities to be carried on outside its national borders.

municipal securities Securities issued by state and local government units. The income from these securities is exempt from federal income taxes.

mutually exclusive The selection of one choice precludes the selection of any other competitive choice. For example, several machines can do an identical job in capital budgeting. If one machine is selected, the other machines will not be used.

N

NASDAQ National Market The segment of the over-the-counter market with the largest companies.

NASDAQ Small-Cap Market The list includes companies centered in one city or state with little national ownership or small development companies, with stock priced as low as 25 cents per share, or companies that are closely held by the founders, with very few shares available for trading.

National Association of Security Dealers (NASD) An industry association that supervises the over-the-counter market.

National Market List The list of the best-known and most widely traded securities in the over-the-counter market.

net income (NI) approach Under the net income approach, it is assumed the firm can raise all the funds it desires at a constant cost of debt and equity. Since debt tends to have a lower cost than equity, the more debt utilized the lower the overall cost of capital and the higher the valuation of the firm.

net operating income (NOI) approach Under this approach, the cost of capital and valuation do not change with the increased utilization of debt. Under this proposition, the low cost of debt is assumed to remain constant with greater debt utilization, but the cost of equity increases to such an extent that the cost of capital remains unchanged.

net present value (NPV) The NPV equals the present value of the cash inflows minus the present value of the cash outflows with the cost of capital used as a discount rate. This method is used to evaluate capital budgeting projects. If the NPV is positive, a project should be accepted.

net present value profile A graphic presentation of the potential net present values of a project at different discount rates. It is very helpful in comparing the characteristics of two or more investments.

net trade credit A measure of the relationship between the firm's accounts receivable and accounts payable. If accounts receivable exceed accounts payable, the firm is a net provider of trade credit; otherwise, it is a net user.

net worth, or book value Stockholders' equity minus preferred stock ownership. Basically, net worth is the common stockholders' interest as represented by common stock par value, capital paid in excess of par, and retained earnings. If you take all the assets of the firm and subtract its liabilities and preferred stock, you arrive at net worth.

New York Stock Exchange (NYSE) The largest organized security exchange in the United States. It also has the most stringent listing requirements.

nominal GDP GDP (gross domestic product) in current dollars without any adjustments for inflation.

nominal yield A return equal to the coupon rate on a bond.

nonfinancial corporation A firm not in the banking or financial services industry. The term would primarily apply to manufacturing, wholesaling, and retail firms.

nonlinear break-even analysis Break-even analysis based on the assumption that cost and revenue relationships to quantity may vary at different levels of operation. Most of our analysis is based on *linear* break-even analysis.

normal yield curve An upward-sloping yield curve. Long-term interest rates are higher than short-term rates.

O

open-market operations The purchase and sale of government securities in the open market by the Federal Reserve Board for its own account. The most common method for managing the money supply.

operating lease A short-term, nonbinding obligation that is easily cancelable.

operating leverage A reflection of the extent to which fixed assets and fixed costs are utilized in the business firm.

optimum capital structure A capital structure that has the best possible mix of debt, preferred stock, and common equity. The optimum mix should provide the lowest possible cost of capital to the firm.

Overseas Private Investment Corporation (OPIC) A government agency that sells insurance policies to qualified firms. This agency insures against losses due to inconvertibility into dollars of amounts invested in a foreign country. Policies are also available from OPIC to insure against expropriation and against losses due to war or revolution.

over-the-counter markets Markets for securities (both bonds and stock) in which market makers, or dealers, transact purchases and sales of securities by trading from their own inventory of securities.

P

par value Sometimes referred to as the face value or the principal value of the bond. Most bond issues have a par value of $1,000 per bond. Common and preferred stock may also have an assigned par value.

parallel loan A U.S. firm that wishes to lend funds to a foreign affiliate (such as a Dutch affiliate) locates a foreign parent firm (such as a Dutch parent firm) that wishes to loan money to a U.S. affiliate. Avoiding the foreign exchange markets entirely, the U.S. parent lends dollars to the Dutch affiliate in the United States, while the Dutch parent lends guilders to the American affiliate in the Netherlands. At maturity, the two loans would each be repaid to the original lender. Notice that neither loan carries any foreign exchange risk in this arrangement.

participating preferred stock A small number of preferred stock issues are participating with regard to corporate earnings. For such issues, once the common stock dividend equals the preferred stock dividend, the two classes of securities may share equally in additional dividend payments.

partnership A form of ownership in which two or more partners are involved. Like the sole proprietorship, a partnership arrangement carries unlimited liability for the owners. However, there is only single taxation for the partners, an advantage over the corporate form of ownership.

passbook savings account A savings account in which a passbook is used to record transactions. It is normally the lowest yielding investment at a financial institution.

payback A value that indicates the time period required to recoup an initial investment. The payback does not include the time-value-of-money concept.

percent-of-sales method A method of determining future financial needs that is an alternative to the development of pro forma financial statements. We first determine the percentage relationship of various asset and liability accounts to sales, and then we show how that relationship changes as our volume of sales changes.

permanent current assets Current assets that will not be reduced or converted to cash within the normal operating cycle of the firm. Though from a strict accounting standpoint the assets should be removed from the current assets category, they generally are not.

perpetuity An investment without a maturity date.

planning horizon The length of time it takes to conceive, develop, and complete a project and to recover the cost of the project on a discounted cash flow basis.

pledging accounts receivables Using accounts receivable as collateral for a loan. The firm usually may borrow 60 to 80 percent of the value of acceptable collateral.

point-of-sales terminals Computer terminals in retail stores that either allow digital input or use optical scanners. The terminals may be used for inventory control or other purposes.

poison pill A strategy that makes a firm unattractive as a potential takeover candidate. For example, when a potential unwanted buyer accumulates a given percentage of a firm's common stock, such as 25 percent, the other shareholders receive rights to purchase additional shares at very low prices. This makes the firm more difficult to acquire. Poison pills may take many different forms.

pooling of interests A method of financial recording for mergers, in which the financial statements of the firms are combined, subject to minor adjustments, and goodwill is *not* created.

portfolio effect The impact of a given investment on the overall risk-return composition of the firm. A firm must consider not only the individual investment characteristics of a project but also how the project relates to the entire portfolio of undertakings.

precautionary balances Cash balances held for emergency purposes. Precautionary cash balances are more likely to be important in seasonal or cyclical industries where cash inflows are more uncertain.

preemptive right The right of current common stockholders to maintain their ownership percentage on new issues of common stock.

preferred stock A hybrid security combining some of the characteristics of common stock and debt. The dividends paid are not tax-deductible expenses of the corporation, as is true of the interest paid on debt.

present value The current or discounted value of a future sum or annuity. The value is discounted back at a given interest rate for a specified time period.

present value of an annuity The sum of the present value of a series of consecutive equal payments.

price-earnings ratio The multiplier applied to earnings per share to determine current value. The P/E ratio is influenced by the earnings and sales growth of the firm, the risk or volatility of its performance, the debt-equity structure, and other factors.

primary earnings per share Adjusted earnings after taxes divided by shares outstanding plus common stock equivalents.

prime rate The rate that a bank charges its most creditworthy customers.

private placement The sale of securities directly to a financial institution by a corporation. This eliminates the middleman and reduces the cost of issue to the corporation.

profitability ratios A group of ratios that indicates the return on sales, total assets, and invested capital. Specifically, we compute the profit margin (net income to sales), return on assets, and return on equity.

pro forma balance sheet A projection of future asset, liability, and stockholders' equity levels. Notes payable or cash is used as a plug or balancing figure for the statement.

pro forma financial statements A series of projected financial statements. Of major importance are the pro forma income statement, the pro forma balance sheet, and the cash budget.

pro forma income statement A projection of anticipated sales, expenses, and income.

program trading Computer-based trigger points in the market are established for unusually big orders to buy or sell securities by institutional investors.

prospectus A document that includes the important information that has been filed with the Securities and Exchange Commission through the registration statement. It contains the list of officers and directors, financial reports, potential uses of funds, and the like.

proxy This represents the assignment of the voting right to management or a group of outsiders.

public placement The sale of securities to the public through the investment banker–underwriter process. Public placements must be registered with the Securities and Exchange Commission.

public warehousing An inventory financing arrangement in which inventory, used as collateral, is stored with and controlled by an independent warehousing company.

purchase of assets A method of financial recording for mergers, in which the difference between the purchase price and the adjusted book value is recognized as goodwill and amortized over a maximum time period of 40 years.

purchasing power parity theory A theory based on the interplay between inflation and exchange rates. A parity between the purchasing powers of two countries establishes the rate of exchange between the two currencies. Currency exchange rates, therefore, tend to vary inversely with their respective purchasing powers in order to provide the same or similar purchasing power.

pure bond value The value of the convertible bond if its present value is computed at a discount rate equal to interest rates on straight bonds of equal risk, without conversion privileges.

R

real capital Long-term productive assets (plant and equipment).

real GDP (gross domestic product) In current dollars adjusted for inflation.

real rate of return The rate of return that an investor demands for giving up the current use of his or her funds on a noninflation-adjusted basis. It is payment for forgoing current consumption. Historically, the real rate of return demanded by investors has been of the magnitude of 2 to 3 percent.

refunding The process of retiring an old bond issue before maturity and replacing it with a new issue. Refunding will occur when interest rates have fallen and new bonds may be sold at lower interest rates.

regional stock exchanges Organized exchanges outside of New York that list securities.

reinvestment assumption An assumption must be made concerning the rate of return that can be earned on the cash flows generated by capital budgeting projects. The NPV method assumes the rate of reinvestment to be the cost of capital, while the IRR method assumes the rate to be the actual internal rate of return.

repatriation of earnings Earnings returned to the multinational parent company in the form of dividends.

replacement cost The cost of replacing the existing asset base at current prices as opposed to original cost.

replacement cost accounting Financial statements based on the present cost of replacing assets.

replacement decision The capital budgeting decision on whether to replace an old asset with a new one. An advance in technology is often involved.

required rate of return That rate of return that investors demand from an investment to compensate them for the amount of risk involved.

reserve requirements The amount of funds that commercial banks must hold in reserve for each dollar of deposits. Reserve requirements are set by the Federal Reserve Board and are different for savings and checking accounts. Low reserve requirements are stimulating; high reserve requirements are restrictive.

residual claim to income The basic claim that common stockholders have to income that is not paid out to creditors or preferred stockholders. This is true regardless of whether these residual funds are paid out in dividends or retained in the corporation.

residual theory of dividends This theory of dividend payout states that a corporation will retain as much earnings as it may profitably invest. If any income is left after investments, the firm will pay dividends. This theory assumes that dividends are a passive decision variable.

restructuring Redeploying the asset and liability structure of the firm. This can be accomplished through repurchasing shares with cash or borrowed funds, acquiring other firms, or selling off unprofitable or unwanted divisions.

reverse LBO A leveraged buyout taking a

company private, followed by a return to the public markets with a new issue of stock.

rights offering A sale of new common stock through a preemptive rights offering. Usually one right will be issued for every share held. A certain number of rights may be used to buy shares of common stock from the company at a set price that is lower than the market price.

rights-on The situation in which the purchase of a share of common stock includes a right attached to the stock.

risk A measure of uncertainty about the outcome from a given event. The greater the variability of possible outcomes, on both the high side and the low side, the greater the risk.

risk-adjusted discount rate A discount rate used in the capital budgeting process that has been adjusted upward or downward from the basic cost of capital to reflect the risk dimension of a given project.

risk-averse An aversion or dislike for risk. In order to induce most people to take larger risks, there must be increased potential for return.

risk-free rate of return Rate of return on an asset that carries no risk. U.S. Treasury bills are often used to represent this measure, although longer-term government securities have also proved appropriate in some studies.

risk premium A premium associated with the special risks of an investment. Of primary interest are two types of risk, business risk and financial risk. Business risk relates to the inability of the firm to maintain its competitive position and sustain stability and growth in earnings. Financial risk relates to the inability of the firm to meet its debt obligations as they come due. The risk premium will also differ (be greater or less) for different types of investments (bonds, stocks, and the like).

S

safety stock of inventory Inventory that is held in addition to regular needs to protect against being out of an item.

Saturday night special A merger tender offer that is made just before the market closes for the weekend and takes the target company's officers by surprise.

secondary offering The sale of a large block of stock in a publicly traded company, usually by estates, foundations, or large individual stockholders. Secondary offerings must be registered with the SEC and will usually be distributed by investment bankers.

secondary trading The buying and selling of publicly owned securities in secondary markets, such as the New York Stock Exchange and the over-the-counter markets.

secured debt A general category of debt, which indicates that the loan was obtained by pledging assets as collateral. Secured debt has many forms and usually offers some protective features to a given class of bondholders.

Securities Act of 1933 An act that is sometimes referred to as the truth in securities act, because it requires detailed financial disclosures before securities may be sold to the public.

Securities Acts Amendments of 1975 The major feature of this act was to mandate a national securities market.

Securities and Exchange Commission (SEC) The primary regulatory body for security offerings in the United States.

Securities Exchange Act of 1934 Legislation that established the Securities and Exchange Commission (SEC) to supervise and regulate the securities markets.

securitization of assets The issuance of a security that is specifically backed by the pledge of an asset.

security market line A line or equation that depicts the risk-related return of a security based on a risk-free rate plus a market premium related to the beta coefficient of the security.

segmentation theory A theory that Treasury securities are divided into market segments by various financial institutions investing in the market. The changing needs, desires, and strategies of these investors tend to strongly influence the nature and relationship of short-term and long-term interest rates.

self-liquidating assets Assets that are converted to cash within the normal operating cycle of the firm. An example is the purchase and sale of seasonal inventory.

self-liquidating loan A loan in which the use of funds will ensure a built-in or automatic repayment scheme.

semivariable costs Costs that are partially fixed but still change somewhat as volume changes. Examples are utilities and "repairs and maintenance."

serial payment Bonds with serial payment provisions are paid off in installments over the life of the issue. Each bond has its own predetermined date of maturity and receives interest only to that point.

shareholder wealth maximization Maximizing the wealth of the firm's shareholders through achieving the highest possible value for the firm in the marketplace. It is the overriding objective of the firm and should influence all decisions.

shelf registration A process that permits large companies to file one comprehensive registration statement (under SEC Rule 415), which outlines the firm's financing plans for up to the next two years. Then, when market conditions appear to be appropriate, the firm can issue the securities without further SEC approval.

simulation A method of dealing with uncertainty, in which future outcomes are anticipated. The model may use random variables for inputs. By programming the computer to randomly select inputs from probability distributions, the outcomes generated by a simulation are distributed about a mean, and, instead of generating one return or net present value, a range of outcomes with standard deviations is provided.

sinking fund A method for retiring bonds in an orderly process over the life of a bond. Each year or semiannually, a corporation sets aside a sum of money equal to a certain percentage of the total issue. These funds are then used by a trustee to purchase the bonds in the open market and retire them. This method will prevent the corporation from being forced to raise a large amount of capital at maturity to retire the total bond issue.

sole proprietorship A form of organization that represents single-person ownership and offers the advantages of simplicity of decision making and low organizational and operating costs.

speculative premium The market price of the warrant minus the warrant's intrinsic value is an example of a speculative premium.

spontaneous sources of funds Funds arising through the normal course of business, such as accounts payable generated from the purchase of goods for resale.

spot rate The rate at which the currency is traded for immediate delivery. It is the existing cash price.

standard deviation A measure of the spread or dispersion of a series of numbers around the expected value. The standard deviation tells us how well the expected value represents a series of values.

statement of cash flows Formally established by the Financial Accounting Standards Board in 1987, the purpose of the statement of cash flows is to emphasize the critical nature of cash flow to the operations of the firm. The statement translates accrual-based net income into actual cash dollars.

step-up in the conversion price A feature that is sometimes written into the contract, which allows the conversion ratio to decline in steps over time. This feature encourages early conversion when the conversion value is greater than the call price.

stock dividend A dividend paid in stock, rather than cash. A book transfer equal to the market value of the stock dividend is made from retained earnings to the capital stock and paid-in-capital accounts. The stock dividend may be symbolic of corporate growth, but it does not increase the total value of the stockholders' wealth.

stock split A division of shares by a ratio set by the board of directors—2 for 1, 3 for 1, 3 for 2, and so on. Stock splits usually indicate the company's stock has risen in price to a level that the directors feel limits the trading appeal of the stock. The par value is divided by the ratio set, and the new shares are issued to the current stockholders of record to increase their shares to the stated level. For example, a two-for-one split would increase your holdings from one share to two shares.

stockholders' equity The total ownership position of preferred and common stockholders.

straight-line depreciation A method of depreciation, which takes the depreciable cost of an asset and divides it by the asset's useful life to determine the annual depreciation expense. Straight-line depreciation creates uniform depreciation expenses for each of the years in which an asset is depreciated.

Subchapter S corporation A special corporate form of ownership, in which profit is taxed as direct income to the stockholders and thus is only taxed once, as would be true of a partnership. The stockholders still receive all the organizational benefits of a corporation, including limited liability. The Subchapter S designation can apply only to corporations with up to 35 stockholders.

subordinated debenture An unsecured bond, in which payment to the holder will occur only after designated senior debenture holders are satisfied.

supernormal growth Superior growth a firm may achieve during its early years, before leveling off to more normal growth. Supernormal growth is often achieved by firms in emerging industries.

synergy The recognition that the whole may be equal to more than the sum of the parts. The "2 + 2 = 5" effect.

T

takeover tender offer An unfriendly offer that is not initially negotiated with the management of the target firm. The offer is usually made directly to the stockholders of the target firm.

tax loss carry-forward A loss that can be carried forward for a number of years to offset future taxable income and perhaps be utilized by another firm in a merger or an acquisition.

Tax Reform Act of 1986 Tax legislation that eliminated many of the abuses in the tax code and, at the same time, lowered the overall tax rates.

technical insolvency When a firm is unable to pay its bills as they come due.

temporary current assets Current assets that will be reduced or converted to cash within the normal operating cycle of the firm.

term loan An intermediate-length loan, in which credit is generally extended from one to seven years. The loan is usually repaid in monthly or quarterly installments over its life, rather than with one single payment.

term structure of interest rates The term structure shows the relative level of short-term and long-term interest rates at a point in time.

terms of exchange The buyout ratio or terms of trade in a merger or an acquisition.

three-sector economy The economy consists of three sectors—business, government, and households. Typically, households have been major suppliers of funds, while business and government have been users of funds.

tight money A term to indicate time periods in which financing may be difficult to find and interest rates may be quite high by normal standards.

trade credit Credit provided by sellers or suppliers in the normal course of business.

traditional approach to cost of capital Under the traditional approach, the cost of capital initially declines with the increased use of low-cost debt, but it eventually goes up due to the greater risk associated with increasing debt.

transaction exposure Foreign exchange gains and losses resulting from *actual* international transactions. These may be hedged through the foreign exchange market, the money market, or the currency futures market.

transactions balances Cash balances held to pay for planned corporate expenditures such as supplies, payrolls, and taxes, as well as the infrequent acquisitions of long-term fixed assets.

translation exposure The foreign-located assets and liabilities of a multinational corporation, which are denominated in foreign currency units, and are exposed to losses and gains due to changing exchange rates. This is called accounting or translation exposure.

Treasury bills Short-term obligations of the federal government with maturities of up to one year.

Treasury notes Intermediate-term obligations of the federal government with maturities from three to five years.

treasury stock Corporate stock that has been reacquired by the corporation.

trend analysis An analysis of performance that is made over a number of years in order to ascertain significant patterns.

trust receipt An instrument acknowledging that the borrower holds the inventory and proceeds for sale in trust for the lender.

two-step buyout An acquisition plan in which the acquiring company attempts to gain control by offering a very high cash price for 51 percent of the shares of the target company. At the same time the acquiring company announces a second lower price that will be paid, either in cash, stocks, or bonds, at a subsequent point in time.

U

underpricing When new or additional shares of stock are to be sold, investment bankers will generally set the price at slightly below the current market value to ensure a receptive market for the securities.

underwriting The process of selling securities and, at the same time, assuring the seller a specified price. Underwriting is done by investment bankers and represents a form of risk taking.

underwriting spread The difference between the price that a selling corporation receives for an issue of securities and the price at which the issue is sold to the public. The spread is the fee that investment bankers and others receive for selling securities.

underwriting syndicate A group of investment bankers that is formed to share the risk of a security offering and also to facilitate the distribution of the securities.

U.S. government securities Securities directly issued by the United States Treasury.

V

variable costs Costs that move directly with a change in volume. Examples are raw materials, factory labor, and sales commissions.

vertical integration The acquisition of customers or suppliers by the company.

W

warrant An option to buy securities at a set price for a given time period. Warrants commonly have a life of one to five years or longer and a few are perpetual.

weighted average cost of capital The computed cost of capital determined by multiplying the cost of each item in the optimal capital structure by its weighted representation in the overall capital structure and summing up the results.

white knight A firm that management calls on to help it avoid an unwanted takeover offer. It is an invited suitor.

working capital management The financing and management of the current assets of the firm. The financial manager determines the mix between temporary and permanent "current assets" and the nature of the financing arrangement.

Y

yield The interest rate that equates a future value or an annuity to a given present value.

yield curve A curve that shows interest rates at a specific point in time for all securities having equal risk but different maturity dates. Usually, government securities are used to construct such curves. The yield curve is also referred to as the term structure of interest rates.

yield to maturity The required rate of return on a bond issue. It is the discount rate used in present-valuing future interest payments and the principal payment at maturity. The term is used interchangeably with market rate of interest.

Z

zero-coupon rate bond A bond that is initially sold at a deep discount from face value. The return to the investor is the difference between the investor's cost and the face value received at the end of the life of the bond.

Index

USE OF COLOR IN THE SEVENTH EDITION . . .

Throughout the seventh edition, Block and Hirt make color an integral part of the presentation of finance concepts. Below we highlight several specific areas in the text where you will find color applied consistently across several illustrations in order to enhance your learning experience. We hope that the addition of color in this edition assists your understanding and your ability to retain the concepts discussed.

In Chapter 3 . . .
In this chapter, the colors red and green are used to demonstrate the composition of financial ratios. Beginning with Table 3–1 *on page 55*, red is used to signify the income statement portion and green is used to signify the balance sheet section of a financial statement for the hypothetical Saxton Company. This color scheme then continues to be used throughout Chapter 3 as the four categories of ratios are presented. The use of red and green immediately alerts you to the portion of the financial statement from which the numerator and denominator in each ratio have been derived.

For example, see the profitability ratios *on page 54*. Note that in ratio #3, return on equity, color is used to show that **net income** comes from the income statement and **stockholders' equity** comes from the balance sheet.

In Chapter 4 . . .
In Chapter 4, the key color is green. Green is used in Chapter 4 in Tables 4–7, 4–13, and 4–15 to identify calculations that contribute to the pro forma balance sheet (Table 4–17). *See pages 93–95* for the pro forma balance sheet and its detailed explanation.

In Chapter 5 . . .
In this chapter, red numbers indicate operating income **losses**; green numbers indicate operating income **profits**; and a white background indicates breakeven. This color scheme applies to Tables 5–2, 5–3, and 5–4, as well as to Figures 5–1 and 5–2. *See pages 112–115*.

In Chapter 6 . . .
Figures 6–5, 6–6, 6–7, and 6–8 are color related in Chapter 6. Red represents **short-term financing** and green represents **long-term financing**. *See pages 150–153*.